UNDERSTAND

SURVIVAL GUIDE

KARWIN K / SHUTTERSTOCK ©

CAMELS OUTSIDE
JAISALMER P132

SPECIAL FEATURES

Welcome to Rajasthan, Delhi & Agra

Here is India's quintessential land of maharajas and medieval forts, palaces and tigers, and kaleidoscopic festivals. Rajasthan really is the jewel in India's crown.

The Golden Triangle

The Golden Triangle is a traveller's survey of Indian icons. It usually kicks off at the daunting mega-metropolis of Delhi, with its majestic Mughal heritage. It then angles to Agra, where one of the world's most famous tombs, the Taj Mahal, defines the city with its exquisite proportions. The triangle is completed at Jaipur – a city painted pink with some of the most colourful bazaars in India. Jaipur is the capital and gateway to Rajasthan, and once you've slept in a palace, explored a medieval fort or swayed on a camel, you'll want to experience more.

Fortified Opulence

Rajasthan's big-ticket attractions are its magnificent forts and palaces. Powerful forts with battle-scarred ramparts loom from mountain tops. Spiked doors that once held war elephants at bay open onto the twisting approaches to the palaces within. Austere and practical give way to opulence once safely inside. Carved marble and stone, fountains and coloured glass decorate the halls of business and rooms of pleasure. All across Rajasthan there are numerous forgotten forts and lovingly restored palaces, including Jaisalmer's fairy-tale desert outpost, Amber's honey-hued fort-palace and Jodhpur's imposing Mehrangarh to name just a few.

Land of Kings

Rajasthan is literally the Land of the Kings. It is home to the chivalrous Rajputs, and its heritage is ingrained with pride and tradition. The upper echelons of this medieval society built magnificent palaces and forts, many of which are now sumptuous hotels and impressive museums. In addition, stunning handicrafts and fine arts were developed through patronage by the maharajas. Village life remains steeped in tradition but, just like the rest of India, the pace of change is accelerating. Turbaned men still barter for decorated camels – they just relay the successful deal home via a smartphone.

Celebration of Colour

The intensity and spectrum of colour in Rajasthan is impossible to ignore. The rainbow of fire-engine red turbans and emerald green and canary yellow saris is simply dazzling. Little wonder so many fashion designers find their inspiration and raw materials in this state. The lucky visitor might even see a flash of orange while tiger-spotting in Ranthambhore National Park. Easier to catch on a camera are the bright hues of Rajasthan's many festivals: from garishly decorated camels in Pushkar, or painted elephants in Jaipur, to the rainbow explosions of Diwali and Holi, celebrated across the region.

Why I Love Rajasthan

By Lindsay Brown, Writer

India's largest state is also one of its most connected, with a network of railways between all the major cities. Train travel is the ideal way to step out of the tourist bubble and immerse yourself in the world of everyday Rajasthan. Here new technologies race ahead but old technologies linger. Camel carts still thread the chaotic streets now dominated by combustion engines. Wandering the old alleys and bazaars, you still come across tea and spice dealers, with ancient weighing scales being the only obvious technology in sight. (Oh sure, there's a smartphone tucked away somewhere.)

For more about our writers, see p312

Above: Gadi Sagar (p131), Jaisalmer

Rajasthan, Delhi & Agra

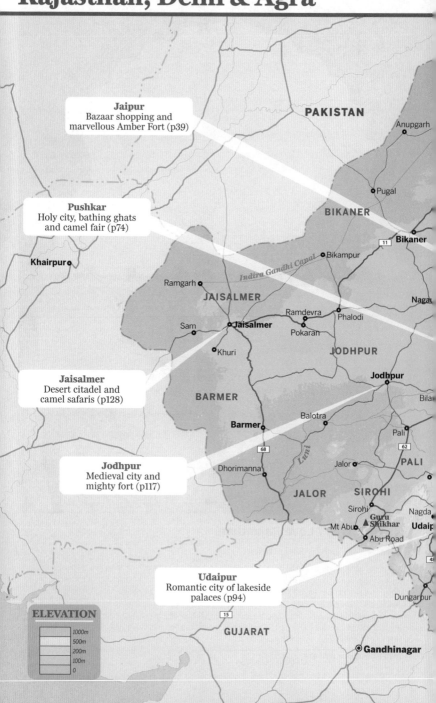

Jaipur
Bazaar shopping and marvellous Amber Fort (p39)

Pushkar
Holy city, bathing ghats and camel fair (p74)

Jaisalmer
Desert citadel and camel safaris (p128)

Jodhpur
Medieval city and mighty fort (p117)

Udaipur
Romantic city of lakeside palaces (p94)

PAKISTAN

Anupgarh

Pugal

BIKANER

Bikaner

11

Khairpur

Bikampur

Indira Gandhi Canal

Ramgarh

JAISALMER

Nagau

Sam

Jaisalmer

Ramdevra

Pokaran

Phalodi

Khuri

JODHPUR

Jodhpur

Bila

BARMER

Balotra

Pali

Barmer

62

68

Luni

Jalor

PALI

Dhorimanna

JALOR

SIROHI

Sirohi

Nagda

Mt Abu

Guru Shikhar

Udaip

Abu Road

Dungarpur

ELEVATION

	1000m
	500m
	200m
	100m
	0

15

GUJARAT

Gandhinagar

Shekhawati
Magical mural-adorned *havelis* (p111)

Delhi
Mega-city with monuments aplenty (p148)

Taj Mahal, Agra
Marble monument to love (p199)

Ranthambhore National Park
Tigers in the jungle (p79)

Bundi
Fairy-tale palace and exquisite step-wells (p83)

Chittorgarh
Immense mountain-top fort (p89)

0   200 km
0   100 miles

INDIA

HARYANA

UTTAR PRADESH

MADHYA PRADESH

Rajasthan, Delhi & Agra's
Top 12

1

Taj Mahal, Agra

1 Perhaps the single most famous building on the planet, the Taj Mahal (p199) is as much a monument to love as it is to death. The Mughal emperor Shah Jahan constructed this magnificent mausoleum to honour his beloved third wife, Mumtaz Mahal, who died tragically in childbirth. Clad in pearlescent white marble, and intricately inlaid with calligraphy, semiprecious stones and intricate floral designs representing the eternal paradise, the Taj is the pinnacle of Mughal creativity, and one of the most perfectly proportioned buildings ever constructed, anywhere, ever.

Jaipur

2 The capital of Rajasthan is a city of mystery and romance, of desert fortresses and palaces where ladies of court moved behind hidden screens. In the Pink City of Jaipur (p39), you can dip into the extravagant lifestyle of the Rajput maharajas, while the surrounding bazaars teem with the comings and goings of ordinary citizens. No visit to Rajasthan would be complete without a stop in this fabulous and frenetic city to explore the wealth of architecture, sample the restaurants, and peruse the craft and jewellery shops. Below: Nahargarh (p47)

OLENA TUR / SHUTTERSTOCK ©

UMANG SHRESTHA / SHUTTERSTOCK ©

Historic Delhi

3 India's captivating capital (p148) bears the scars of a string of former empires, from tombs and fortresses left behind by sultans and warlords to the broad streets laid out by British colonials. Delhi may be chaotic today, but it rewards visitors with an abundance of riches: fabulous food and culture; Mughal relics and maze-like markets; New Delhi, with its political monuments and museums; the ancient forts of Tughlaqabad and Purana Qila; and ruined wonders at the Qutab Minar (pictured below) and Mehrauli. Come and be mesmerised by 3000 years of history.

Jaisalmer Fort

4 The 12th-century Jaisalmer Fort (p129) defiantly rises from the flat desert lands, a vision from childhood memories of tales such as 'Ali Baba and the Forty Thieves'. The reality is no less romantic. Castellated golden-stone bastions and elephant-size doors protect a warren of narrow bazaars and Jain and Hindu temples, all bustling with life and commerce – almost a quarter of the city's population lives inside the fort. Overseeing the bazaars is the former maharaja's seven-storey palace, now a fascinating museum.

NILA NEWSOM / SHUTTERSTOCK ©

DMITRY RUKHLENKO / SHUTTERSTOCK ©

Amber Fort, Jaipur

5 Before moving to Jaipur, the fort palace of Amber (p61) was the capital of the Kachwaha clan. The honey-coloured citadel rises gradually along a sloping ridge surrounded by even higher ridges capped with other battlements and watchtowers. From the beautiful geometric gardens and Maota Lake, you can roam up to the main square, Jaleb Chowk. From here, wander freely through the palace grounds, halls of audience, the magnificent three-storey Ganesh Pol, the once-taboo *zenana* (women's quarters) and the still-glittering Jai Mandir.

Jodhpur

6 The ancient capital of the kingdom of the Marwar, Jodhpur (p117) rewards the traveller with Rajasthan's most spectacular fort and, from its ramparts, one of India's iconic views. Mehrangarh seems to emerge organically from its rocky pedestal to protect the Blue City. From this elevated fortress, the old city of Jodhpur, a sea of blue-block houses, hums and jostles like a seething ocean. Beyond the teeming city, jeep safaris explore the home of the desert-dwelling Bishnoi, a people who have been protecting the natural environment for aeons.

Riding Camels in the Thar Desert

7 For a quintessential Rajasthani experience, hop aboard a ship of the desert for an extended safari (p132) or simple overnight jaunt into the windswept dunes of the Great Thar Desert. From a camel's back, you can see herds of gazelles and meet desert-dwelling villagers. At the end of the day, you can make chapatis over an open fire, witness a cultural performance and fall blissfully asleep under a Persian carpet of glittering stars. You can organise a camel safari in Jaisalmer, as well as Bikaner and Osian.

WANPHEN CHAWARUNG / SHUTTERSTOCK ©

Ranthambhore National Park

8 There are only a handful of places left where you can see the magnificent tiger in the wild. Ranthambhore National Park (p79) is one such place and your chances of spotting a tiger are very good. This former hunting reserve is a majestic setting for a tiger safari. There are lush ravines, crocodile-infested lakes and a crumbling fort straight out of *The Jungle Book*. Spotted deer graze in the dappled light of an open wood, their eyes, nostrils and ears twitching for the sight, smell or sound of a striped predator.

Bundi

9 Bundi (p83) is a delight. A town where you can experience most facets of Rajasthani culture and heritage, yet tourism remains low key. The picturesque, slowly decaying Bundi Palace (pictured top right) tumbles down a rock-strewn slope beneath the ramparts of the even more ancient fort of Taragarh. Inside the once-luxurious palace are fading memories – gold and turquoise murals evoking a glorious past. Below the palace, a bazaar bustles with colour and commerce around spectacular *baoris*, or stepwells, magnificently carved portals to once-precious water reserves.

Pushkar Camel Fair

10 Some come for the camels, some come to bathe away their sins, some come just for the fun. Pushkar's extraordinary camel fair (p76) is Rajasthan's signature event, combining Hindu spiritualism, camel commerce and cultural celebration. The camels, cattle and Mawari steeds arrive early so that the livestock purchasing and selling can be completed before the frivolity of the *mela* (fair) takes over and before the full-moon ceremony of Kartik Purnima, when pilgrims bathe and set candles afloat in a holy lake.

Havelis of Shekhawati

11 In the arid plains of northern Rajasthan, the district known as Shekhawati (p111) boasts a crumbling treasure of once-lavish *havelis*. The walls of these grand homes, built by wealthy traders, can't speak, but they certainly tell a damn good story with their colourful and often whimsical murals. Shekhawati's dusty towns, including Nawalgarh, Fatehpur and Mandawa (pictured below), offer a lot more than the celebrated *havelis,* however. Travellers who take time out to be immersed in village life will discover a rich and deeply conservative culture.

Udaipur

12 Following the fall of Chittorgarh, Maharana Udai Singh II moved the Mewar capital to Udaipur (p94) in 1568. The city is dominated by the sprawling City Palace, which commands the eastern shoreline of Udaipur's centrepiece, Lake Pichola. The enormous palace complex houses a museum, a couple of swish heritage hotels and the erstwhile royal family. The mirror-surfaced lake, in turn, hosts one of Rajasthan's most renowned palaces, the wedding-cake Lake Palace (pictured bottom), now also an exclusive five-star hotel and occasional movie set.

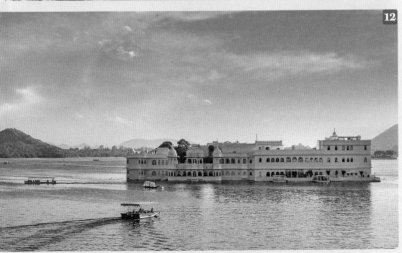

Need to Know

For more information, see Survival Guide (p261)

Currency
Indian rupee (₹)

Language
Hindi, Rajasthani (five regional dialects), English

Visas
Apart from citizens of Nepal, Bhutan and the Maldives, everyone needs to apply for a visa before arriving in India.

Money
Most urban centres have ATMS accepting Visa, MasterCard, Cirrus, Maestro and Plus cards. Carry cash as backup. MasterCard and Visa are the most widely accepted credit cards.

Mobile Phones
Roaming connections are excellent in urban areas; poorer in the countryside. Local prepaid SIMs are widely available; the paperwork is fairly straightforward but you may have to wait two to four hours for activation.

Time
India Standard Time (GMT/UTC plus 5½ hours)

When to Go

Warm to hot summers, mild winters
Tropical climate, wet & dry seasons
Dry climate
Desert, dry climate

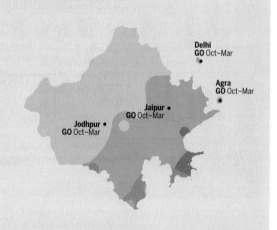

Delhi
GO Oct–Mar

Agra
GO Oct–Mar

Jaipur •
GO Oct–Mar

Jodhpur •
GO Oct–Mar

High Season
(Dec–Feb)

➡ Pleasant daytime temperatures, but can get cold at night.

➡ Peak tourists, peak prices – prebook all flights and accommodation.

➡ Domestic flights can be delayed owing to fog.

Shoulder Season
(Sep–Nov, Mar)

➡ Warm nights suit many visitors fleeing colder climes.

➡ Ranthambhore National Park opens in October as the migratory birds arrive at Keoladeo National Park.

Low Season
(Apr–Aug)

➡ By April it's warming up and June is very hot awaiting the monsoon, which brings the rain in July and August.

➡ Ranthambhore National Park closes at the end of June.

Useful Websites

Incredible India (www.incredibleindia.org) Official India tourism site.

IndiaMike (www.indiamike.com) Popular travellers' forum.

Lonely Planet (www.lonelyplanet.com/india) Destination information, hotel bookings, traveller forum and more.

Rajasthan Tourism Development Corporation (www.rtdc.tourism.rajasthan.gov.in) Rajasthan government tourism site.

Festivals of India (www.festivalsofindia.in) All about Indian festivals.

Important Numbers

To dial numbers from outside India, dial your international access code, India's country code then the number (minus the '0' used for dialling domestically).

Country code	☏91
International access code (in India)	☏00
Emergency (Ambulance/Fire/Police)	☏112

Exchange Rates

Australia	A$1	₹51.58
Bangladesh	Tk100	₹85.46
Canada	C$1	₹53.65
Euro zone	€1	₹81.47
Japan	¥100	₹63.20
New Zealand	NZ$1	₹48.80
UK	£1	₹90.57
US	US$1	₹71.73

For current exchange rates, see www.xe.com.

Daily Costs

**Budget:
Less than ₹2500**

➡ Dorm bed: ₹200–400

➡ Double room in budget hotel: ₹600–1500

➡ Thali or pizza: ₹200–350

➡ Bus or train ticket: ₹30–350

**Midrange:
₹2500–10,000**

➡ Double room in a hotel: ₹1500–5000

➡ Lunch or dinner in a local restaurant: ₹300–1000

➡ Admission to forts and museums: ₹500-600

➡ Taxi for a short sightseeing jaunt: ₹500–3000

**Top End:
More than ₹10,000**

➡ Double room in a hotel: ₹5000+

➡ Lunch or dinner in a hotel: ₹1000–3000

➡ Cocktails and wine: ₹1500–3000

➡ Hire car and driver: ₹900–1500

Opening Hours

Official business hours are 9.30am to 5.30pm Monday to Friday, with many offices closing for a lunch hour around 1pm. Many sights are open from dawn to dusk.

Banks 10am–2pm or 4pm Monday to Friday, to noon or 1pm Saturday

Post Offices 10am–4pm Monday to Friday, to noon Saturday

Restaurants 8am–10pm or lunch; noon–2.30pm or 3pm; 7–10pm or 11pm

Shops 9am–9pm, some closed Sunday

Arriving in Delhi & Jaipur

Indira Gandhi International Airport (Delhi) This is the closest major international airport. There is a prepaid taxi booth where you can book a taxi for a fixed price (including luggage), thus avoiding commission scams. Many hotels will arrange airport pick-ups with advance notice – these are often complimentary at top-end hotels but for a fee at others. Because of the late-night arrival of many international flights, a hotel-room booking and airport pick-up is advised.

Jaipur International Airport Jaipur's airport receives a limited number of flights from the Middle East and Thailand. Check for the latest information as other destinations are planned. The airport has a prepaid taxi booth and many Jaipur hotels can organise airport pick-ups.

Getting Around

Transport in India is reasonably priced, quick and efficient (if not always comfortable).

Train Extensive coverage of the country, inexpensive and heavily used; advance booking is recommended.

Car Hiring a car with a driver doesn't cost a fortune, and is recommended over driving yourself.

Bus Cheaper and slower than trains, but a useful and practical alternative. Overnight sleeper buses are best avoided due to accidents, theft and harassment.

For much more on **getting around**, see p277

PLAN YOUR TRIP NEED TO KNOW

First Time Rajasthan, Delhi & Agra

For more information, see Survival Guide (p261)

Checklist

➡ Make sure your passport is valid for at least six months beyond your arrival date.

➡ Get appropriate vaccinations.

➡ Make copies of your passport information page and visa; carry hard copies and email digital copies to yourself.

➡ Check airline baggage restrictions.

➡ Inform your debit-/credit-card company you're heading away.

➡ Arrange appropriate travel insurance.

What to Pack

➡ Sunscreen, sunglasses, hat and mosquito repellent

➡ Small torch (flashlight) for poorly lit streets and/or power cuts

➡ Earplugs – the noise can be a nuisance

➡ Sleeping-bag sheet (to cover hotel linen and for those overnight train journeys)

Top Tips for Your Trip

➡ Take advantage of composite sightseeing tickets, especially in Jaipur; it saves a bundle, though you have to 'do it all' in two consecutive days.

➡ Book accommodation and transport well ahead if travelling around Diwali. This is when much of India is on the move and on holiday.

➡ Even if you never eat yoghurt, breakfast on the daily fresh offerings of curd in Rajasthan – and do try a lassi. You and your gut will be ever grateful.

➡ Procure an Indian SIM or set up an internet call service on your device to make calling home an inexpensive exercise.

➡ Don't attempt to cover too many towns too quickly: travel between centres can be slow and tedious.

Sleeping

Accommodation in Rajasthan ranges from grungy back-packer hostels with concrete floors, plywood walls and cold 'bucket' showers to opulent palaces fit for a modern-era maharaja.

Palaces & Heritage Hotels

Rajasthan is famous for its wonderful heritage hotels created from palaces, forts and *havelis* (traditional, ornately decorated residences). There are hundreds and it often doesn't cost a fortune to stay in one: some are the height of luxury and priced accordingly, but many are simpler, packed with character and set in stunning locations.

What to Wear

Rajasthan is still conservative and traditional and so non-revealing clothes, for both women and men, will help reduce unwanted attention and avoid offence. Steer clear of sleeveless tops and tiny shorts. Wearing Indian-style clothes is viewed favourably by the locals and is appropriate for the climate. Slip-on shoes make visiting shrines and temples a breeze, and women should wear or carry a scarf to cover the head in some places of worship.

Bargaining

Unless shopping in fixed-price shops (such as government emporiums and fair-trade cooperatives), bargaining is the norm.

Tipping

Restaurants A service fee is often already included your bill and tipping is optional. Elsewhere, a tip is appreciated.

Hotel Bellboys appreciate anything from around ₹20 to ₹100.

Train/airport Porters appreciate anything from around ₹20 to ₹100.

Taxi/rickshaw drivers A tip is not mandatory/expected.

Hire car with driver A tip is recommended (around ₹100 per day) for more than a couple of days of good service.

Jaisalmer Fort (p129)

Etiquette

Dress modestly Avoid stares by not wearing tight, sheer or skimpy clothes.

Have head cover handy For women (and sometimes men) visiting some places of worship – especially gurdwaras (Sikh temples).

Shoes It's polite to remove shoes before entering homes and places of worship.

Photos Best to ask before photographing people, ceremonies or sacred sites.

Namaste Saying *namaste* with hands together in a prayer gesture is a respectful Hindu greeting.

Shake, don't hug Shaking hands is fine but hugs between strangers is not the norm.

Handy hint The right hand is for eating and shaking hands; the left hand is the 'toilet' hand.

Eating

Rajasthan has a home-grown cuisine, both veg and non-veg, reflecting its desert surroundings and local produce. Nevertheless, you're more likely to find pizza or butter chicken than *govind ghatta* on a tourist hotel's menu. Most restaurants in tourist destinations attempt to cover all the options with popular North Indian curries, pizza and pasta and a few Chinese dishes. It's worth seeking out restaurants that specialise in Rajasthani cuisine.

If You Like...

Palatial Pampering

The phenomenal wealth of the feudal kings and princes was as exclusive as it was vast. At that time, only by luck of birth or special invitation could one have experienced the splendid interiors. But now the erstwhile royals rely on tourism and the palaces have become luxury hotels where you can sleep like a maharaja.

Jaipur Regional nobles built palaces around this city, so you'll find an embarrassment of palatial digs. (p50)

Udaipur Ticks all the boxes for the most romantic setting with the picture-perfect Taj Lake Palace. (p101)

Jodhpur Boasts one of the last palaces to be built before the royals lost their gravy trains – the Umaid Bhawan Palace. (p120)

Jhalawar Be a guest of the erstwhile royals and enjoy their sumptuous digs. (p89)

Wildlife

If you are fascinated by India's incredible wildlife – particularly its legendary tigers and amazing birdlife – then Rajasthan should be high on your list of Indian states to visit. The national parks of Rajasthan started out as hunting reserves for the maharajas. The habitats and animal populations were fiercely protected until the maharajas and their guests went on a shooting spree. In later years, with modern weapons, this turned into wholesale slaughter and led to a conservation ethos and the establishment of national parks.

Ranthambhore National Park Amazing scenery and one of the best places to spot a wild tiger in India, or the world. (p79)

Keoladeo National Park An internationally recognised wetland attracting scores of seasonal migrants – a bird-watcher's paradise. (p63)

Sariska Tiger Reserve & National Park Tigers were reintroduced here after the reserve controversially lost its own population to poaching. (p69)

Jhalana Leopard Reserve On the outskirts of Jaipur and one of your best chances to see these elusive cats. (p49)

Kumbhalgarh Wildlife Sanctuary No tigers, but a leopard hotspot and great birdwatching. (p106)

Bazaar Shopping

Rajasthan really is one of the easiest places to spend money, with its bustling bazaars, traditional art, colourful crafts, gorgeous fabrics, miniature paintings, blue pottery, magic carpets and much more. The cardinal rule here is to bargain and bargain hard.

Old Delhi Mughal-era bazaars transport shoppers back centuries, with stalls selling everything from kites to car jacks, plus excellent street food. (p187)

Jodhpur Antiques (faux-old and old), homewares, bric-a-brac and pungent spices – it's all here. (p124)

Jaipur Arts and crafts, as well as amazing jewellery and gems, abound in the bazaars of the Old City. (p57)

Pushkar Explore cluttered Sadar Bazaar, chock-a-block full with embroidered textiles and hippie paraphernalia. (p78)

Udaipur Among the bounty of art and crafts, the ancient art of miniature painting stands tall here. (p103)

Fabulous Festivals

Rich in religion and tradition, Rajasthan has scores of vibrant festivals. Most festivals follow either the Indian lunar calendar (a complex system determined by astrologers) or the Islamic calendar (which falls about 11 days earlier each year; 12 days earlier in leap years) and therefore change annually relative to the Gregorian calendar.

Diwali Celebrated on the 15th day of Kartika (October/November), featuring crazy amounts of fireworks. (p23)

Holi People celebrate the beginning of spring (February/March) by spraying coloured water and *gulal* (powder) at one another. (p21)

Pushkar Camel Fair Rajasthan's biggest event – part agricultural show, part cultural festival and part Hindu pilgrimage. (p76)

Dussehra Mela Kota (and elsewhere) fills with the smell of fireworks as enormous firecracker-stuffed effigies are burnt to mark the victory of Rama over the demon Ravana. (p50)

Deserts & Camels

Rajasthan's great Thar Desert is criss-crossed by ancient trade routes and dotted with traditional villages where life continues in a fashion very similar to more romantic times. Slow loping camels remain an important method of transport even in this frantic era and they remain integral to traditional desert culture.

Jaisalmer Evocative overnight camel safaris – sweeping sand

PLAN YOUR TRIP IF YOU LIKE...

Top: Holi celebrations (p21)

Bottom: Market shop, Delhi (p187)

Chittorgarh (p89

dunes, traditional dances and a charpoy under the stars. (p128)

Jodhpur The centre for exploring the desert homelands of the Bishnoi, a people who hold all animals sacred. (p117)

Bikaner Travel in a traditional camel cart through the arid scrubland while visiting villages and sleeping on dunes. (p140)

Osian For a most authentic experience, staying in village huts or under the stars and eating simple fare. (p126)

Mighty Forts

The feudal past of Rajasthan has left a sturdy architectural legacy of defensive fortresses. These massive buildings evoke the past and are quite rightly the focus of tourists and would-be time travellers.

Delhi This historically strategic city has imperial forts like other places have traffic islands. (p152)

Agra Agra's red sandstone fort was started by Akbar and become the prison of his grandson Shah Jahan. (p202)

Chittorgarh A massive citadel capping a mountain plateau – its battle-scarred bastions embrace palaces, temples and towers. (p89)

Jodhpur A blue city spread beneath the ramparts of the hulk of Mehrangarh, Rajasthan's most commanding fort. (p118)

Jaisalmer A golden sandstone castle that drifts in the desert and is still inhabited. (p129)

Junagarh Another hulk of over-engineering encompassing a delicately carved peaceful interior. (p141)

Month by Month

January

Midwinter cool lingers throughout the north and it's downright cold in the desert night air. Pleasant daytime weather and several festivals make it a popular time to travel, so book ahead.

✿ Sankranti

Sankranti, the Hindu festival marking the sun's passage across the Tropic of Capricorn, is celebrated in many ways throughout India. In Jaipur it's the mass kite-flying that steals the show. Held on 14 or 15 January.

✿ Jaipur Literature Festival

The Jaipur Literature Festival has grown into the world's biggest free literature festival, attracting local and international authors and poets. Readings, debates, music and even the odd controversy keep it energised.

February

The weather remains comfortable in Rajasthan, with very little rain and plenty of festivals. The days are getting marginally warmer but it's still ideal travelling weather.

✿ Shivaratri

Held in February or March, Shivaratri, a day of Hindu fasting, recalls the *tandava* (cosmic victory dance) of Lord Shiva. Temple processions are followed by the chanting of mantras and the anointing of linga (phallic images of Shiva). Upcoming dates: 21 February 2020, 11 March 2021.

✿ Jaisalmer Desert Festival

Three-day celebration of desert culture, with many events in the Sam Sand dunes. Camel races, turban-tying contests, traditional puppetry and the famous Mr Desert competition are part of the fun. (p136)

✿ Vasant Panchami

Hindus dress in yellow and place books, musical instruments and other educational objects in front of idols of Saraswati, the goddess of learning, to receive her blessing. The holiday may fall in January.

March

The end of the main travel season, March sees the last of the cool days of winter as daytime temperatures creep above 30°C.

✿ Holi

One of North India's most exuberant festivals; Hindus celebrate the beginning of spring, in either February or March, by throwing coloured water and *gulal* (powder) at anyone within range. On the night before Holi, bonfires symbolise the demise of the demoness Holika. Upcoming dates: 9 March 2020, 28 March 2021.

✿ Jaipur Elephant Festival

Taking place on the day before Holi (so it can fall in February), the Jaipur Elephant Festival celebrates the pachyderm's place in Indian culture. There are elephant dress parades and competitions such as polo and tug-of-war, but animal welfare groups have criticised the treatment of elephants taking part in these events.

🏃 Wildlife-Watching

As the weather warms up and water sources dry out, animals tend to congregate at the few remaining water sources. This can improve your chances of spotting tigers and leopards.

April

✨ Rama's Birthday

During Ramanavami (one to nine days) in March or April, Hindus celebrate Rama's birth with processions, music, fasting and feasting, enactments of the Ramayana, and ceremonial weddings of Rama and Sita idols. Upcoming dates: 2 April 2020, 21 April 2021.

✨ Ramadan (Ramazan)

Thirty days of dawn-to-dusk fasting mark the ninth month of the Islamic calendar. Muslims traditionally turn their attention to God, with a focus on prayer and purification. Ramadan begins around 24 April 2020 and 13 April 2021.

May

The region heats up with daytime temperatures over 40°C. Life slows down as the humidity builds up in anticipation of the monsoon.

✨ Eid al-Fitr

Muslims celebrate the end of Ramadan with three

days of festivities, starting 30 days after the start of the fast. Upcoming dates: 24 May 2020, 13 May 2021.

✨ Summer Festival

Rajasthan's hill station, delightful Mt Abu, celebrates summer (or perhaps the town's climatological defiance of summer) with a three-day carnival. There are boat races on Nakki Lake, fireworks and traditional music and dances.

✕ Mango Madness

Mangoes are indigenous to India, which might be why they're so ridiculously good here. The season starts in March, but in May the fruit is sweet, juicy and everywhere. A hundred varieties grow here, but the Alphonso is known as 'king'.

June & July

Life retreats indoors during the hot June days when temperatures still soar over 40°C. Monsoon storms increase in energy, bringing much-needed respite, though nights remain hot and humid. Come July it's really raining, with many a dusty road becoming an impassable quagmire. You may be tempted by the reduced accommodation rates and smaller crowds.

August

It's very much monsoon season and the relief is palpable. In a good season there's copious, but not constant, rainfall and temperatures are noticeably lower (but still steamy).

✨ Brothers and Sisters

On Raksha Bandhan (Narial Purnima), girls fix amulets known as *rakhis* to the wrists of brothers and close male friends to protect them in the coming year. Brothers reciprocate with gifts and promises to take care of their sisters.

✨ Independence Day

This public holiday on 15 August marks the anniversary of India's independence from Britain in 1947. Celebrations are a countrywide expression of patriotism, with flag-hoisting ceremonies (the biggest one is in Delhi), parades and patriotic cultural programs.

✨ Janmastami

Held in August or September, Krishna's birthday celebrations are marked by fasting, *puja* (prayers), offering sweets, and other rituals. Upcoming dates: 11 August 2020, 30 August 2021.

✨ Ganesh Chaturthi

Hindus celebrate Ganesh Chaturthi, the birth of the elephant-headed god, with verve in August or September, particularly in Ranthambhore Fort. Thousands gather at the abandoned fort and clay idols of Ganesh are paraded. Upcoming dates: 22 August 2020 and 10 September 2021.

✨ Teej

The festival of Teej in July or August celebrates the arrival of the monsoon and the marriage of Parvati to Shiva. Three-day celebrations across Rajasthan, particularly Jaipur, culminate in a street procession of the Teej idol. (p50)

September

The rain begins to ease, though temperatures are still high. By the end of September, Rajasthan and Delhi are all but finished with the monsoon.

October

Occasional heavy showers aside, this is when North India starts to get its travel mojo on. October brings festivals, national park openings and more comfortable temperatures, with post-monsoon lushness.

Navratri

Held in September or October, the Hindu 'Festival of Nine Nights' leading up to Dussehra celebrates the goddess Durga in all her incarnations. Special dances are performed and the goddesses Lakshmi and Saraswati are also venerated. Most areas will celebrate around 17 October 2020 and 7 October 2021.

Dussehra

In September or October, colourful Dussehra celebrates the victory of the Hindu god Rama over the demon-king Ravana and the triumph of good over evil. Dussehra is big in Kota, where effigies of Ravana are ritually burned. Upcoming dates: 8 October 2019, 25 October 2020, 14 October 2021.

 Gandhi's Birthday

The national holiday of Gandhi Jayanti is a solemn celebration of Mohandas Gandhi's birth, on 2 October, with prayer meetings at his cremation site at Raj Ghat (p161) in Delhi. Schools and businesses close for the day.

Diwali

In the lunar month of Kartika, in October or November, Hindus celebrate Diwali for five days, giving gifts, lighting fireworks and burning lamps to lead Lord Rama home. This is India's main holiday time and it is hard to get transport or hotel rooms. Upcoming dates: 27 October 2019, 14 November 2020, 4 November 2021.

November

The climate is blissful, with warm days and cooler nights. The peak season is getting into full swing. Lower temperatures mean higher prices and more tourist buses.

Pushkar Camel Fair

Rajasthan's premier cultural event takes place in the Hindu lunar month of Kartika (October or November). As well as camel trading, there is horse and cattle trading and an amazing fairground atmosphere. It culminates with ritual bathing in Pushkar's holy lake. (p76)

Eid-Milad-un-Nabi

The Islamic festival of Eid-Milad-un-Nabi celebrates the birth of the Prophet Mohammed with prayers and processions. It falls in the third month of the Islamic calendar. Upcoming dates: around 10 November 2019, 29 October 2020, 19 October 2021.

December

December is peak tourist season for a reason: the daytime weather is glorious, the humidity is low and the nights are cool. The mood is festive and it seems everyone is getting married.

⊙ Weddings!

Marriage season peaks in December and you may see a *baraat* (bridegroom's procession), replete with white horse and brass band, on your travels. Across Rajasthan, loud music and spectacular parties are the way they roll, with brides in *mehndi* (ornate henna designs) and pure gold.

Birdwatching

Many of India's spectacular winter migrants complete their travels and set up nesting colonies. Keoladeo National Park is an internationally renowned wetland and birdwatching destination. (p63)

Camel Treks in Rajasthan

The cool winter (November to February) is the time to mount a camel and ride through the Rajasthan sands. See the Thar Desert from a whole new perspective: observe gazelles, make dinner over an open fire and camp out in the dunes.

Itineraries

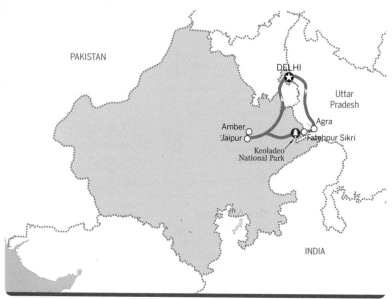

PAKISTAN

DELHI

Uttar
Pradesh

Amber
Jaipur

Agra
Fatehpur Sikri

Keoladeo
National Park

INDIA

The Golden Triangle

One route is so well loved it even has a name: the Golden Triangle. This classic Delhi–Agra–Jaipur trip can be squeezed into a single week and gives a tantalising taste of the splendours of Rajasthan.

Spend a day or two in **Delhi** finding your feet and seeing the big-draw sights, such as the magnificent Mughal Red Fort and Jama Masjid, India's largest mosque. Then catch a fast train to **Agra** to spend a day being awed by the Taj Mahal and the mighty Agra Fort. Only an hour away is **Fatehpur Sikri**, a beautiful Mughal city dating from the apogee of Mughal power. It can be visited on the way to Bharatpur, in Rajasthan, where you can enjoy a natural respite from the cities at **Keoladeo National Park**, one of the world's foremost bird reserves. Having relaxed and recharged with nature, you can now take a train to **Jaipur**. Spend a couple of days in and around Rajasthan's hectic, dusky-pink capital, seeing the City Palace and **Amber Fort** and stocking up on blue pottery, dazzling jewellery and Rajasthani puppets before heading back to Delhi.

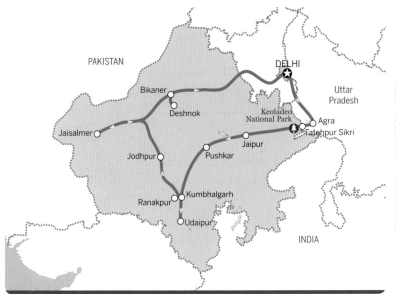

 Royal Rajasthan

With a fortnight to spare, you can forget triangles and go all out for a multifaceted loop taking in Rajasthan's most spectacular cities, all erstwhile capitals of former princely states, boasting fairy-tale palaces and formidable fortresses.

You will most likely start from the nation's capital of **Delhi** to see the Mughal monuments, such as the massive Red Fort. No trip to India is complete without a visit to the Taj Mahal at **Agra**. Spend two days here viewing the Taj during the day, at night and from the maze-like Agra Fort. Spend a day exploring the ghost city of **Fatehpur Sikri**, before heading to **Keoladeo National Park** for birdwatching. Next stop is the pink city of **Jaipur**, where you will want to spend two or three days exploring the palaces of Jaipur and Amber and the shopping bazaars of the Old City.

From Jaipur, head to the sacred lake of **Pushkar**, where you can release your inner hippie or attend the camel fair. Move on to the romantic lake-town of **Udaipur**, visiting the rambling City Palace and the impressive Jagdish Temple as well as doing some shopping, relaxing on rooftops, and peering at the lake and its famous floating palace. From Udaipur, head towards the extraordinary, bustling, blue city of Jodhpur. Take time to stop at the milk-white Jain temple complex of **Ranakpur** and the isolated, dramatic fortifications of **Kumbhalgarh** – as they are fairly close together, you can visit them en route to Jodhpur within a day. In **Jodhpur**, visit the spectacular Mehrangarh, a fort that towers protectively over the city like a storybook fortress.

Next take an overnight train to the Golden City, **Jaisalmer**, a giant sandcastle in the desert, with its beautiful Jain temples and exquisite merchants' *havelis* (traditional, ornately decorated mansions). Take a short camel safari through the bewitching landscape of sweeping dunes and sleep under the stars. If you have the time on your way back to Delhi, break your journey with a stop in the desert city of **Bikaner**, home of the impregnable Junagarh Fort and nearest city to the famous rat temple of **Deshnok**. From Bikaner catch one of several trains back to Delhi.

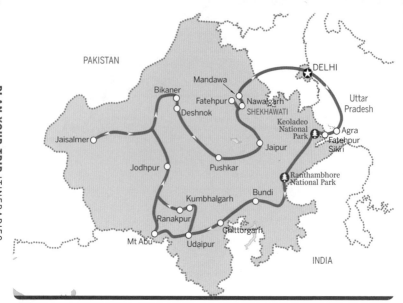

A Month-Long Sojourn

4 WEEKS

A month will allow you to explore Delhi, Agra and Rajasthan to their fullest extent, with plenty of time to linger along the way whenever a particular destination takes your fancy.

After arriving in **Delhi** and exploring the city sights, take the train down to **Agra** to gaze at the picture-perfect Taj Mahal, explore Agra Fort and have a day trip out to the abandoned Mughal city of **Fatehpur Sikri**. To experience Rajasthan's wild side, head to the World Heritage–listed birdwatching paradise of **Keoladeo National Park**, where the sheer numbers of nesting birdlife will astound you. This can be followed by a tiger safari at **Ranthambhore National Park**, one of your best bets in all India for spotting a tiger.

Take a Kota-bound train southwest for a stop at the charming settlement of **Bundi** to explore the crumbling palace and its magical art. From here it is a short train ride to **Chittorgarh** where one of Rajasthan's most impressive fortresses occupies a mountain plateau. Next stop is **Udaipur**, where you can relax after your travels with a few easy days of sightseeing, elegant dining and souvenir shopping.

From Udaipur it's worth side-tripping to **Mt Abu** to see the extraordinary Delwara Temples before going north to Jodhpur. Alternatively, head north to Jodhpur, stopping on the way to see the magnificent fort at **Kumbhalgarh** and the Jain temples of **Ranakpur**. From **Jodhpur** it's an easy train or bus ride to **Jaisalmer**, the desert town with a romantic, picturesque fort rising from the golden sands. Here you can spend a few days exploring *havelis* and temples, before taking an overnight camel trek into the desert. After Jaisalmer, head east across the desert to **Bikaner**.

Travel south from Bikaner, stopping at the fascinating rat temple of **Deshnok** before coming to rest at the sacred pilgrimage town of **Pushkar**. At Pushkar you may be in time for the famous camel festival; otherwise, just put your feet up for a few days and soak up the serenity.

From Pushkar, it's a short hop to **Jaipur**, with its fabulous citadel at Amber and great shopping. Head north to **Shekhawati** for a few days, inspecting *havelis* at **Mandawa**, **Nawalgarh** and **Fatehpur**, before returning to Delhi.

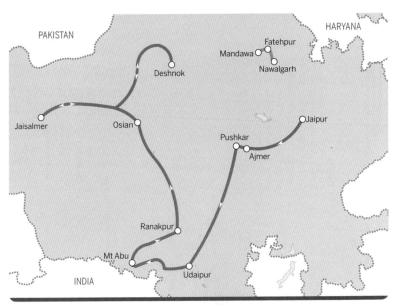

 Sacred Rajasthan

3 WEEKS

Temples abound in Rajasthan. These include Hindu and Jain edifices, plus mosques, gurdwaras and a scattering of churches. Here are some of the more noteworthy.

Starting in **Jaipur**, there's the popular Ganesh Temple that sees scores of worshippers every Wednesday. Other temples in Jaipur include the Govind Devji (Krishna) Temple inside the city palace, and Galta the 'monkey temple', swarming with monkeys.

Ajmer boasts one of the most important Sufi shrines in the world, the Dargah of Khwaja Muin-ud-din Chishti, and the fascinating Soniji Ki Nasiyan (Red) Temple; its unremarkable exterior hides a fantastical golden diorama depicting the Jain concept of the ancient world. **Pushkar** has one of the very few temples devoted to Brahma.

At **Udaipur**, the Hindu Jagdish Temple is always a riot of colour and fervent worshipping, while up at **Mt Abu**, the intricately carved Delwara Temples are Jain masterpieces. The Chaumukha Mandir in **Ranakpur** and Mahavira Temple in **Osian** can be visited on the way to **Jaisalmer**, whose fort shelters several finely carved Jain temples. Last on the list is Karni Mata, the rat temple of **Deshnok**, south of Bikaner.

 Painted Shekhawati

4 DAYS

The fabulous frescoes of Shekhawati can be scouted out in three or four days by moving between three or four of the region's towns. A bonus is the chance to stay in restored *havelis* once inhabited by prosperous traders, and to explore the backstreets on foot.

Nawalgarh is only a couple of hours' drive from Jaipur and offers accommodation ranging from thatch-roofed rural huts to grand and luxurious *havelis*. There's even a palace. Base yourself here to visit restored *havelis* and museums; don't forget to wander around and discover the fading gems on lesser-known, crumbling *havelis*.

From Nawalgarh head north to **Mandawa**. Mandawa can lay claim to the most accommodation options suited for travellers, including a grand castle, and it also has several *havelis* worth a look for their whimsical murals of 18th-century life.

West of Mandawa, is the dusty hamlet of **Fatehpur**, a town now famed for its restored Le Prince Haveli, where French artist Nadine Le Prince rejuvenated the frescoes and hosted visiting artists. It is now an inviting boutique hotel amid a town of deteriorating yet tantalising treasures.

Off the Beaten Track – Rajasthan

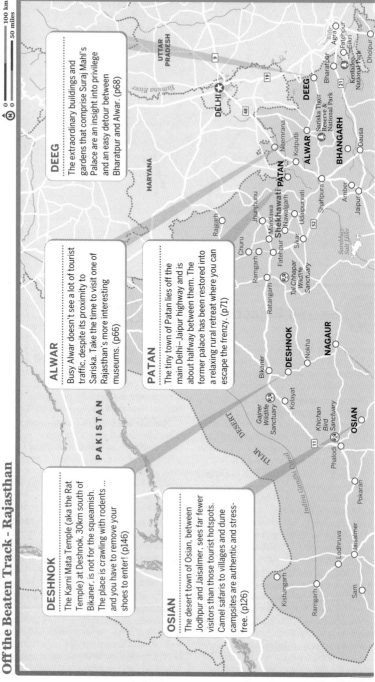

DEEG
The extraordinary buildings and gardens that comprise Suraj Mahl's Palace are an insight into privilege and an easy detour between Bharatpur and Alwar. (p68)

ALWAR
Busy Alwar doesn't see a lot of tourist traffic, despite its proximity to Sariska. Take the time to visit one of Rajasthan's more interesting museums. (p66)

PATAN
The tiny town of Patan lies off the main Delhi–Jaipur highway and is about halfway between them. The former palace has been restored into a relaxing rural retreat where you can escape the frenzy. (p71)

DESHNOK
The Karni Mata Temple (aka the Rat Temple) at Deshnok, 30km south of Bikaner, is not for the squeamish. The place is crawling with rodents ... and you have to remove your shoes to enter! (p146)

OSIAN
The desert town of Osian, between Jodhpur and Jaisalmer, sees far fewer visitors than those tourist hotspots. Camel safaris to villages and dune campsites are authentic and stress-free. (p126)

0 — 100 km
0 — 50 miles

UTTAR PRADESH

Yamuna River

DELHI

HARYANA

PAKISTAN

THAR DESERT

Indira Gandhi Canal

Rajgarh

Churu

Ramgarh

Ratangarh

Bikaner

Nokha

Gajner Wildlife Sanctuary

Kolayat

Khichan Bird Sanctuary

Phalodi

Pokaran

Sam

Lodhruva

Jaisalmer

Ramgarh

Kishangarh

Jhunjhunu

Mandawa

Nawalgarh

Fatehpur

Sikar

Udaipurvati

Shekhawati

PATAN

Shahpura

Amber

Jaipur

Sambhar Salt Lake

Tal Chhapar Wildlife Sanctuary

DESHNOK

NAGAUR

OSIAN

Neemrana

Kotputli

Sariska Tiger Reserve & National Park

ALWAR

BHANGARH

Dausa

DEEG

Bharatpur

Keoladeo National Park

Agra

Fatehpur Sikri

Dholpur

KARAULI

Offers the chance to stay with former royalty in a comfortable Raj-era bungalow, visit an old city palace, and tour a nature reserve, all far from crowds of tourists. (p82)

JHALAWAR

The immense, forgotten fort at Gagron rests at the confluence of two rivers reached by narrow village roads; and you can stay in royal splendor at Jhalawar's Prithvi Vilas. (p88)

NAGAUR

Off the tourist trail, yet with a camel and cattle festival to rival Pushkar's, Nagaur provides an authentic taste of Rajasthan and the chance to stay in an upmarket hotel in a fort. (p128)

BHANGARH

The intriguing ghost city of Bhangarh was deserted three centuries ago, but is strangely well preserved and infamously haunted. (p69)

Travel with Children

Fascinating, frustrating, thrilling and fulfilling – India is as much of an adventure for children as it is for parents. Though the sensory overload may be, at times, overwhelming for younger kids, the colours, scents, sights and sounds of India more than compensate by setting young imaginations ablaze.

Best Regions for Kids

Keoladeo National Park

Here, the kids can let go of your hand and jump on a bike. Let them ride along the car-free road and tick off as many feathered species as they can.

Jodhpur

Let imaginations run wild at mighty Mehrangarh; older kids can let fly on the exhilarating Flying Fox.

Ranthambhore National Park

What kid won't be thrilled to see a wild tiger? And there's a mesmerising jungle fortress straight out of Kipling's *Jungle Book* to explore.

Amber

Climbing up to Amber Fort and learning about the splendid, if tyrannical, lives of the ruling classes is sure to inspire.

Sam Sand Dunes

Riding a gentle and dignified camel across the shifting sand dunes is a delight for young and old.

Rajasthan for Kids

Being a family-oriented society, Rajasthan is a very child-friendly destination. That doesn't necessarily translate into a travel-with-children-friendly destination, however. Smaller children, in particular, will be constantly coddled, offered treats and smiles and warm welcomes. And while all this is fabulous for outgoing children, it may prove tiring, or even disconcerting or frightening, for those of a more retiring disposition. Remember, though, that the attention your children will inevitably receive is almost always good natured; kids are the centre of life in many Indian households and your own will be treated – usually for better rather than worse – just the same.

Eating

Feeding your brood is fairly easy in the well-touristed parts of Rajasthan and you'll find Western and Chinese dishes with a bit of searching. Look out for multi-cuisine restaurants, should your little one be saying 'not curry again'.

Adventurous eaters will delight in experimenting with a vast range of tastes and textures: paneer (unfermented cheese) dishes, simple dhal (a curried lentil dish), creamy korma (curry-like braised dish), buttered naan (tandoor-baked bread), pilau (rice) and *momos* (steamed or fried dumplings) are all firm favourites. Few children, no matter how culinarily unadventurous, can resist the finger-food fun of a vast South Indian dosa (rice pancake).

Sleeping

Rajasthan offers such an array of accommodation – from budget boxes to former palaces of the maharajas – that you're bound to be able to find something that will appeal to the whole family. Hotels will almost always come up with an extra bed or two for a nominal charge. Most places won't mind fitting one, or maybe two, children into a regular-sized double room along with their parents. Any more is pushing your luck – look for two rooms that have an adjoining door.

On the Road

Travel in Rajasthan can be arduous for the whole family. Plan fun, easy days to follow longer car, bus or train rides, and pack plenty of diversions. An iPod, tablet or laptop with a stock of movies downloaded makes an invaluable travel companion, as do books, light toys and games. The golden rule is to expect your best-laid plans to take a hit every now and then.

Travelling on the road with kids anywhere in India requires constant vigilance. Be especially cautious of road traffic – pedestrians are at the bottom of the feeding chain and road rules are routinely ignored.

Health

Health care of a decent standard, even in the most traveller-frequented parts of Rajasthan, is not as easily available as you might be used to. The recommended way to track down a doctor at short notice is through your hotel. In general, the most common concerns for on-the-road parents include heat rash, skin complaints such as impetigo, insect bites or stings and diarrhoea. If your child takes special medication, bring along an adequate stock in case it's not easily found locally.

Children's Highlights
Fortress Splendours

Jaipur (p61) Live out legends in the majestic citadel of Amber.

Jaisalmer (p129) Recreate the *Arabian Nights* in Jaisalmer's desert fortress.

Jodhpur (p118) Amaze their imaginations with the storybook fort and palace.

Bundi (p83) Spooky abandoned palace with colourful art and smelly bats.

Wildlife Wonders

Ranthambhore National Park (p79) Tigers, jungles, jeep safaris and an abandoned mountaintop fort.

Keoladeo National Park (p63) The chance to go cycling on car-free roads to spot wildlife.

Sariska Tiger Reserve & National Park (p69) Numerous deer, monkeys and other wildlife, and just maybe a tiger.

Kichan (p127) Beautiful demoiselle cranes in astounding numbers fostered by villagers.

Jhalana Leopard Safari (p49) Spot spotted cats on the edge of Jaipur.

Planning
Before you Go

Remember to visit your doctor to discuss vaccinations, health advisories and other health-related issues involving your children well in advance of travel. For helpful hints, see Lonely Planet's *Travel with Children,* and the 'Kids to Go' section of Lonely Planet's Thorn Tree forum (www.lonelyplanet.com/thorntree).

What to Pack

If you're travelling with a baby or toddler, there are several items worth packing in quantity: nappies, nappy-rash cream, extra bottles, wet wipes, infant formula and jars or dehydrated packets of favourite foods. You can get these items in many parts of Rajasthan, too, but brands may be unfamiliar. Another good idea is a baby backpack/carrier; a pusher or pram is superfluous, since there are few places with pavements wide enough to use one. For older children, make sure you bring sturdy footwear, a hat, child-friendly insect repellent and sun lotion.

Plan Your Trip
Wildlife Watching

Rajasthan is a magnet for wildlife watchers, not least because much of the wildlife has been squeezed into the tiny remnants of forests that have been protected in national parks and tiger reserves. With few exceptions these habitats, and their highly prized inhabitants, were once protected hunting reserves for the exclusive use of the rich and powerful. However, there is also a proud tradition of certain rural Rajasthani tribes living with and nurturing wildlife, and this, too, has left a rich legacy for today's wildlife watchers.

Wildlife Highlights

Best for Birds

In addition to the rightly celebrated treasure that is Keoladeo National Park, there is another avian highlight. One of Rajasthan's quirkiest and spectacular displays occurs when thousands of demoiselle cranes descend on the tiny pond at Kichan on winter mornings and evenings to receive a feed of donated grain.

Best for Tigers

The successful protection of tigers at Ranthambhore National Park makes it one of the best places in India to see these undisputed kings and queens of the jungle.

Best Times

Migratory birds start arriving in numbers in October and start leaving for colder climes in March. The cooler weather from October to March also makes jungle safaris more comfortable for tiger spotters.

Keoladeo National Park

Keoladeo National Park (p63) is a world-famous destination for birdwatchers. Its artificial wetlands have been in existence long enough to ensure a steady population of resident birds plus an amazing seasonal boom of migratory species in winter. Species include painted storks (in abundance), sarus cranes, spoonbills, ibis, kingfishers, egrets and another 390-odd other species! Access is easy, cycling and walking tracks thread through the park, expert guides are on hand, and you can even sit back in a rickshaw and be pedalled to the best spots.

Ranthambhore National Park

Featuring a high density of Bengal tigers, the 1334-sq-km Ranthambhore National Park (p79) is the highlight destination for wildlife-watchers in Rajasthan. However it does suffer from its popularity, feeling

Top: Purple sunbird, Keoladeo National Park (p63)

Bottom: Tigers, Ranthambhore National Park (p79)

ARCHNA SINGH / SHUTTERSTOCK ©

Deer in Sariska Tiger Reserve & National Park (p6

somewhat like an open-range zoo crawling with trucks and 4WDs packed with noisy tourists, rather than a wilderness experience. That said, the scenery is stunning and the wildlife, including mugger crocodiles, leopards, monkeys and deer, is plentiful. Best time to visit is October to April.

Sariska Tiger Reserve & National Park

Covering 866 sq km of the Aravali Range, Sariska Tiger Reserve and National Park (p69) is famous for losing all its tiger population to poaching in the early 2000s. Since then tigers have been relocated here from Ranthambhore and have successfully bred. Tiger tourism has resumed and sightings, though on the rise, are still rare. Sariska is also home to leopards, sambar deer, nilgai, chital, wild boars and jackals; the best time to visit is November to June.

Jhalana Forest Reserve

The Jhalana Forest Reserve is right on the edge of the frantic city of Jaipur, and yet it is one of the best places in India to spot the usually shy and elusive leopard. Jhalana Leopard Safari (p49) is the sole operator of safaris in this 21-sq-km reserve and organises hotel pickup and drop-off in Jaipur. The reserve is also home to hyenas, monkeys, deer and nilgai, and is a prime birdwatching destination, especially in summer.

Regions at a Glance

Rajasthan is India in microcosm. Its long and often turbulent history is witnessed in the monumental architecture of the forts and palaces of the Rajput maharajas down to the tiny mud-and-thatch villages. Rajasthan is not an empty desert landscape of endless sweeping dunes. Instead, it is a timeless, surprisingly well-populated, arid region. Cleverly cultivated and with monsoonal blessings, ancient groundwater and a canal bringing Himalayan water, this desert supports scores of villages and is even abundant with wildlife. In an already colourful country, Rajasthan might be the most dazzling of India's regions – there are festivals galore, tigers to spot, desert vistas and cool jungles to explore, and enough fine arts and crafts to make you wish you had a greater luggage allowance.

Rajasthan

Forts & Palaces
Animal Encounters
Festivals

Rajput Grand Designs

The splendid palaces and mighty forts of Rajasthan demonstrate the wealth and power of the Rajputs who once dominated the area. The region is replete with magnificent architecture, from Jaipur's graceful Hawa Mahal to the marvellous fort of Jodhpur.

On Safari

Rajasthan is a great place to get closer to nature: whether it's tracking tigers in Ranthambhore National Park, spotting colourful birds in Keoladeo National Park or exploring the desert on a camel safari out of Jaisalmer or Bikaner.

Holidays & Celebrations

Heading the list is the celebrated camel fair in the Hindu pilgrimage town of Pushkar. Other showstoppers include Jaipur's famous literature and elephant festivals and Jaisalmer's Desert Festival. As with the rest of India, Diwali and Holi are celebrated with exuberance.

p38

Delhi

....

Food
Shopping
Ruins

....

From Street Food to Modern Indian

Delhi serves up a stunning calvacade of flavour; sample fabulous Indian fine dining or munch on fresh-from-the-fire *Dilli-ka-Chaat* (Delhi's delectable street food).

Bazaars & Boutiques

Delhi is a wonderland of bazaars, boutiques and emporiums. Leave space in your luggage for intricately wrought handicrafts, Indian clothing, exotic homewares, prints and paintings, musical instruments and all manner of religious paraphernalia.

Historic Sites

The ruins of seven imperial cities are scattered throughout Delhi, and its Mughal relics rank among India's finest: wander in and out of centuries of history at the Red Fort, Humayun's tomb, Hauz Khas, Qutb Minar, Mehrauli, Purana Qila and time-scarred Tughlaqabad.

p148

Agra & the Taj Mahal

....

Architecture
Tombs
Forts

....

Mughal Splendours

Agra has India's finest Mughal remains – not just the Taj Mahal but also a trump hand of fortresses, mosques and mausoleums, and even a vast, ruined city at eroded Fatehpur Sikri, Akbar's abandoned capital.

World's Finest Mausoleums

The Taj Mahal, built for Shah Jahan's lamented wife, is the pinnacle of Mughal architectural achievement, but don't miss Akbar's mausoleum, another decorative masterpiece, or the dainty Itimad-ud-Daulah.

Agra Fort

Robust and resilient, Agra Fort is surrounded by 2.5km of towering sandstone walls, providing protection for a string of beautiful palaces and mosques that hint at the complex, structured lives of its Mughal inhabitants.

p197

On the Road

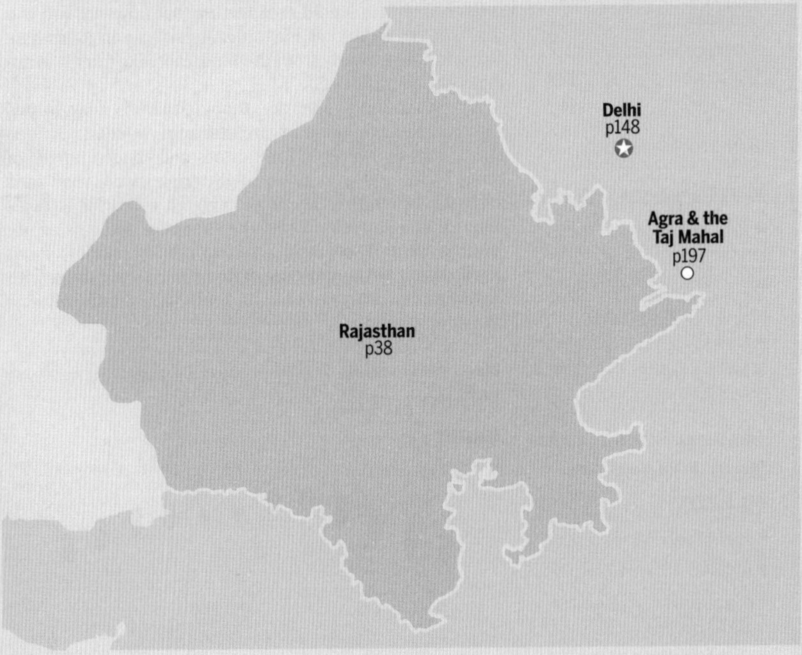

Delhi
p148
★

Agra & the
Taj Mahal
p197
○

Rajasthan
p38

Rajasthan

POP 77.1 MILLION

Best Places to Eat

➡ Peacock Rooftop Restaurant (p55)

➡ Jagat Niwas Palace Hotel (p102)

➡ Niro's (p55)

➡ Ambrai (p102)

➡ Shri Mishrilal Hotel (p124)

Best Places to Stay

➡ Hotel Pearl Palace (p50)

➡ Inn Seventh Heaven (p77)

➡ Jagat Niwas Palace Hotel (p100)

➡ Hotel Ranthambhore Regency (p81)

➡ Haveli Braj Bhushanjee (p85)

➡ Narendra Bhawan (p144)

Why Go?

It is said there is more history in Rajasthan than in the rest of India put together. Welcome to the Land of the Kings – a realm of maharajas, majestic forts and lavish palaces. India is littered with splendid architecture, but nowhere will you find fortresses quite as magnificent as those in Rajasthan, rising up imperiously from the landscape like fairy-tale mirages or epic movie sets.

As enchanting as they are, though, there is more to this spectacular state than its architectural wonders. This is also a land of sweeping sand dunes and shaded jungle, of camel trains and wild tigers, of glittering jewels, vivid saris and vibrant culture. There are enough colourful festivals here to fill a calendar, while the shopping and cuisine are nothing short of spectacular. In truth, Rajasthan just about has it all – it is the must-see state of India, brimming with startling, thought-provoking and, ultimately, unforgettable attractions.

When to Go
Jaipur

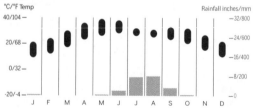

Dec–Feb Pleasant daytime temperatures, but can get cold at night; peak tourists, peak prices.

Sep–Nov, Feb & Mar Warm nights suit many visitors fleeing colder climes.

Apr–Aug April and June are very hot awaiting the monsoon, which brings the rain in July and August.

History

Rajasthan is the ancestral home of the Rajputs, warrior clans who claim to originate from the sun, moon and fire, and who have controlled this part of India for more than 1000 years. While they forged marriages of convenience and temporary alliances, pride and independence were always paramount, and this lack of unity led to the Rajputs becoming vassals of the Mughal empire.

Mughal rule of Rajasthan was marked by rebellion, uprisings and tragedy, as whole cities committed *jauhar* (ritual mass suicide) rather than submit to the Mughals. As the Mughal empire declined, the Rajputs clawed back their independence and signed treaties with the British allowing individual Rajput kingdoms to operate as independent princely states under the umbrella of British rule.

At Independence, Rajasthan's many maharajas were allowed to keep their titles and property holdings and were paid an annual stipend commensurate with their status to secure their participation in the union. However, this favourable arrangement lapsed in the 1970s and Rajasthan submitted fully to central control.

EASTERN RAJASTHAN

The cities and sites of eastern Rajasthan are easily accessible from Jaipur, as well as Agra and Delhi (all stops on the Golden Triangle). For immersion in history, see Alwar and Deeg's evocative palaces, plus the magnificent forts at Bharatpur and Ranthambhore.

Wildlife enthusiasts will relish the opportunities available at Ranthambhore, Sariska Tiger Reserve and Keoladeo. Tiger-spotting is unsurpassed at Ranthambhore, which has provided the tigers to repopulate Sariska, while Keoladeo, India's premier bird sanctuary, hosts an astonishing population of resident and migratory birds in a picturesque wetland setting.

Travellers of all descriptions are drawn to Pushkar, a pastel blue town that hosts an extravagant, internationally renowned camel fair. Pushkar is also a Hindu pilgrimage site and legendary travellers' halt to chill and shop, while nearby Ajmer hosts the extraordinary dargah (shrine or place of burial of a Muslim saint) of Khwaja Muin-ud-din Chishti, India's most important Muslim pilgrimage site.

Jaipur

📍 0141 / POP 3.1 MILLION

Enthralling, historical Jaipur, Rajasthan's capital, is the gateway to India's most flamboyant state. The city's colourful, chaotic streets ebb and flow with a heady brew of old and new. Careering buses dodge dawdling camels, leisurely cycle-rickshaws frustrate swarms of motorbikes, and everywhere buzzing autorickshaws watch for easy prey. In the middle of this cacophony and mayhem, the splendours of Jaipur's majestic past are islands of relative calm evoking a different pace and another world.

At the city's heart, the City Palace continues to house the former royal family; the Jantar Mantar, the royal observatory, maintains a heavenly aspect; and the honeycomb Hawa Mahal gazes on the bazaar below. And just out of sight, in the arid hill country surrounding the city, is the fairy-tale grandeur of Amber Fort, Jaipur's star attraction.

History

Jaipur is named after its founder, the great warrior-astronomer Jai Singh II (1688–1743), who came to power at age 11 after the death of his father, Maharaja Bishan Singh. Jai Singh could trace his lineage back to the Rajput clan of Kachhwahas, who consolidated their power in the 12th century. Their capital was at Amber (pronounced 'amer'), about 11km northeast of present-day Jaipur, where they built the impressive Amber Fort.

The kingdom grew wealthier and wealthier, and this, plus the need to accommodate the burgeoning population and a paucity of water at the old capital at Amber, prompted the maharaja in 1727 to commence work on a new city – Jaipur.

Northern India's first planned city, it was a collaborative effort using Singh's vision and the impressive expertise of his chief architect, Vidyadhar Bhattacharya. Jai Singh's grounding in the sciences is reflected in the precise symmetry of the new city. The paucity of good facing stone and rapidity of the build led to the rendering of the city walls, followed by orange-pink paint to mimic the stone fortresses of Delhi and Agra.

In 1876 Maharaja Ram Singh had the entire Old City freshly painted pink (traditionally the colour of hospitality) to welcome the Prince of Wales (later King Edward VII), reinforcing the city's tone. Today all residents of the Old City are compelled by law to preserve the salmon-pink facade.

RAJASTHAN JAIPUR

Rajasthan Highlights

❶ Jaisalmer (p128)
Visiting the 12-century sandstone fort and riding a camel over sand dunes.

❷ Udaipur (p94)
Kicking back at a lakeside restaurant in Rajasthan's most romantic city.

❸ Pushkar (p74)
Attending Pushkar's extraordinary camel fair, which combines Hindu spiritualism, camel commerce and cultural celebration.

❹ Jodhpur (p117)
Viewing the Blue City from the ramparts of Rajasthan's most spectacular fort, Mehrangarh.

❺ Ranthambhore National Park (p79)
Exploring this former hunting reserve where your chances of spotting a tiger are excellent.

❻ Jaipur (p39)
Wandering the colourful bazaars of the Pink City and exploring Amber Fort.

❼ Bundi (p83)
Experiencing Rajasthani culture and heritage in a town where tourism remains low key.

❽ Shekhawati (p111) Discovering the whimsical murals decorating a crumbling treasure trove of once-lavish *havelis*.

❾ Chittorgarh (p89) Immersing oneself in the romanticism of Rajput myth and legend at this enormous, sprawling and tragic fortress.

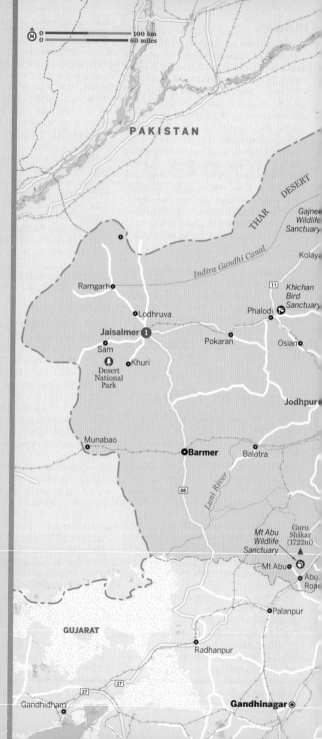

◉ Sights

◉ Old City

The Old City (often referred to as the Pink City) is both a marvel of 18th-century town planning and a place you could spend days exploring – it's the beating heart of Jaipur.

Avenues divide the Pink City into neat rectangles, each specialising in certain crafts, as ordained in the Shilpa-Shastra (an ancient Hindu treatise on architecture). The main bazaars in the Old City include Johari Bazaar, Tripolia Bazaar, Bapu Bazaar and Chandpol Bazaar.

The whole is partially encircled by a crenellated wall punctuated at intervals by grand gateways. The major gates are Chandpol (*pol* means 'gate'), Ajmer Gate and Sanganeri Gate.

★ **City Palace**   PALACE
(☑ 0141-4088888; www.royaljaipur.in; Indian/foreigner incl camera ₹130/500, guide from ₹300, audio guide ₹200, Royal Grandeur tour Indian/foreigner ₹2500/3000; ⊙ 9.30am-5pm) A complex of courtyards, gardens and buildings, the impressive City Palace is right in the centre of the Old City. The outer wall was built by Jai Singh II, but within it the palace has been enlarged and adapted over the centuries. There are palace buildings from different eras, some dating from the early 20th century. It is a striking blend of Rajasthani and Mughal architecture.

The price of admission includes entry to Royal Gaitor (p47) and the Cenotaphs of the Maharanis (p47), as well as to Jaigarh, a long climb above Amber Fort (p61). This composite ticket is valid for two days and costs Indi-

---

ⓘ COMPOSITE TICKETS

Consider buying a composite ticket (Indian/foreigner ₹300/1000), which gives you entry to Amber Fort, Central Museum, Jantar Mantar, Hawa Mahal, Isarlat and Narhargarh and is valid for two days from the time of purchase. It can be bought from any of the listed sites. A separate ticket (Indian/foreigner ₹190/500; two days) includes entry to the City Palace, Royal Gaitor, Cenotaphs of the Maharanis and Jaigarh; for foreigners this ticket is included with entry to the City Palace.

---

ans an extra ₹60 on top of City Palace entry (no extra cost for foreigners).

➡ **Mubarak Mahal**

Entering through Virendra Pol, you'll see the Mubarak Mahal (Welcome Palace), built in the late 19th century for Maharaja Madho Singh II as a reception centre for visiting dignitaries. Its multiarched and colonnaded construction was cooked up in an Islamic, Rajput and European stylistic stew by the architect Sir Swinton Jacob. It now forms part of the **Maharaja Sawai Mansingh II Museum**, containing a collection of royal costumes and superb shawls, including Kashmiri pashmina. One remarkable exhibit is Sawai Madho Singh I's capacious clothing; it's said he was a cuddly 2m tall, 1.2m wide and 250kg.

➡ **The Armoury**

The Anand Mahal Sileg Khana – the Maharani's Palace – houses the Armoury, which has one of the best collections of weapons in the country. Many of the ceremonial items are elegantly engraved and inlaid, belying their grisly purpose.

➡ **Diwan-i-Khas (Sarvatobhadra)**

Set between the Armoury and the Diwan-i-Am art gallery is an open courtyard known in Sanskrit as Sarvatobhadra. At its centre is a pink-and-white, marble-paved gallery that was used as the Diwan-i-Khas (Hall of Private Audience), where the maharajas would consult their ministers. Here you can see two enormous silver vessels, each 1.6m tall and reputedly the largest silver objects in the world.

➡ **Diwan-i-Am Art Gallery**

Within the lavish Diwan-i-Am (Hall of Public Audience) is this art gallery. Exhibits include a copy of the entire Bhagavad Gita handwritten in tiny script, and miniature copies of other holy Hindu scriptures, which were small enough to be easily hidden in the event that zealot Mughal armies tried to destroy the sacred texts.

➡ **Pitam Niwas Chowk & Chandra Mahal**

Located towards the palace's inner courtyard is Pitam Niwas Chowk. Here four glorious gates represent the seasons – the **Peacock Gate** depicts autumn, the **Lotus Gate** signifies summer, the **Green Gate** represents spring, and finally the **Rose Gate** embodies winter.

Beyond this *chowk* (square) is the private palace, the Chandra Mahal, which is still the residence of the descendants of the royal family; you can take a 45-minute Royal Grandeur guided tour of select areas.

★ **Jantar Mantar** HISTORIC SITE
(Indian/foreigner ₹50/200, guide ₹200, audio guide ₹100; ⊘9am-4.30pm) Adjacent to the City Palace is Jantar Mantar, an observatory begun by Jai Singh II in 1728 that resembles a collection of bizarre giant sculptures. Built for measuring the heavens, the name is derived from the Sanskrit *yanta mantr,* meaning 'instrument of calculation', and in 2010 it was added to India's list of Unesco World Heritage Sites. Paying for a local guide is highly recommended if you wish to learn how each fascinating instrument works.

Jai Singh liked astronomy even more than he liked war and town planning. Before constructing the observatory he sent scholars abroad to study foreign constructs. He built five observatories in total, and this is the largest and best preserved (it was restored in 1901). Others are in Delhi, Varanasi and Ujjain. No traces of the fifth, the Mathura observatory, remain.

A valid composite ticket will also gain you entry.

★ **Hawa Mahal** HISTORIC BUILDING
(Palace of Breeze; Sireh Deori Bazaar; Indian/foreigner incl camera ₹50/200, guide ₹200, audio guide ₹177; ⊘9am-5.30pm) Jaipur's most distinctive landmark, the Hawa Mahal is an extraordinary pink-painted, delicately honeycombed hive that rises a dizzying five storeys. It was constructed in 1799 by Maharaja Sawai Pratap Singh to enable ladies of the royal household to watch the life and processions of the city. The top offers stunning views over Jantar Mantar and the City Palace in one direction and over Sireh Deori Bazaar in the other.

There's a small museum (⊘Sat-Thu), with miniature paintings and some rich relics, such as ceremonial armour, which help evoke the royal past.

Claustrophobes should be aware that the narrow corridors can sometimes get extremely cramped and crowded inside the Hawa Mahal.

Entrance is from the back of the complex. To get here, return to the intersection on your left as you face the Hawa Mahal, turn right and then take the first right again through an archway. Shopkeepers can show you another way – past their shops!

A valid composite ticket will also gain you entry.

DON'T MISS

HEAVEN-PIERCING MINARET
....
Piercing the skyline near the City Palace is the unusual Isarlat (Iswari Minar Swarga Sal or Heaven-Piercing Minaret; Indian/foreigner ₹50/200; ⊘9am-4.30pm), erected in the 1740s by Jai Singh II's son and successor Iswari. The entrance is around the back of the row of shops fronting Chandpol Bazaar – take the alley 50m west of the minaret along the bazaar or go via the Atishpol entrance to the City Palace compound, 150m east of the minaret. You can spiral to the top of the 43m minaret for excellent views.

Iswari ignominiously killed himself by snakebite (in the Chandra Mahal) rather than face the advancing Maratha army – his 21 wives and concubines then did the necessary noble thing and committed *jauhar* (ritual mass suicide by immolation) on his funeral pyre.

A valid composite ticket will also gain you entry.

◉ **New City**

By the mid-19th century it became obvious that the well-planned city was bulging at the seams. During the reign of Maharaja Ram Singh (1835–80) the seams ruptured and the city burst out beyond its walls. Civic facilities, such as a postal system and piped water, were introduced. This period gave rise to a part of town very different from the bazaars of the Old City, with wide boulevards, landscaped grounds and grand European-influenced buildings. All of this is rather hard to appreciate in today's fuming, beeping, traffic-clogged thoroughfares.

Central Museum MUSEUM
(Albert Hall; J Nehru Marg; Indian/foreigner ₹40/300, audio guide Hindi/English ₹118/177; ⊘9.30am-5pm Tue-Sun) This museum is housed in the spectacularly florid Albert Hall, south of the Old City. The building was designed by Sir Swinton Jacob, and combines elements of English and North Indian architecture, as well as huge friezes celebrating the world's great cultures. It was known as the pride of the new Jaipur when it opened in 1887. The grand old building hosts an eclectic array of tribal dress, dioramas, sculptures, miniature paintings, carpets, musical instruments and even an Egyptian mummy.

Royal Gaitor (p47) **2.** Rambagh Palace (p53)
Sisodia Rani Palace Garden

Jaipur Lazy Days

Jaipur is crowded, clogged with traffic, and severely polluted. There's no denying it. And so here's a few suggestions on where to go in and around this major metropolis to escape the clamour and de-jangle nerves.

Palatial Pampering

Look no further than Jaipur's palaces of both major and minor former royals to find the sort of pampering and luxury accoutrements that pleasured the princes of yore. Head to the **Rambagh Palace** (p53) for fine dining, top-end spa treatments, or just the chance to while away time in grand surroundings. Nearby the more down-to-earth **Narain Niwas Palace Hotel** (p53) has a splendid pool and shady lawns.

Parks & Gardens

Jaipur is blessed with parks and gardens that provide a welcome oasis of green. However, to get away from the traffic beeps, head out to the peaceful **Sisodia Rani Palace Garden** (Indian/foreigner ₹50/200; ⏰8am-5pm) or **Royal Gaitor** (p47), featuring the cenotaphs of past royals and a serene ambience. And if you're up for a game of golf, there's the **Rambagh Golf Club** (www.rambaghgolfclub.com) near the Rambagh Palace.

Body, Mind & Soul

Massage and yoga are available in and around Jaipur. Call for ayurvedic massage from **Kerala Ayurveda Kendra** (p49), or organise a relaxing yoga regime at the **Madhavanand Girls College** (p49) at sunrise.

Jaipur

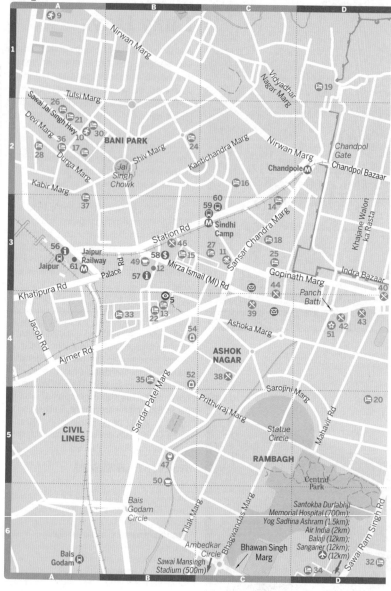

Ram Niwas Bagh

PARK

(₹20; ⏰8am-8pm) Adjacent to, but a world away from, busy MI Rd is this oasis where you can wander through geometric gardens of roses, palms and ferns. Alternatively, find yourself a shady patch of grass to sit and read a book or take to the jogging track.

⊙ City Edge

Surrounding the city are several historic sites including forts, temples, palaces and gardens. Some of these can be visited on the way to Amber Fort.

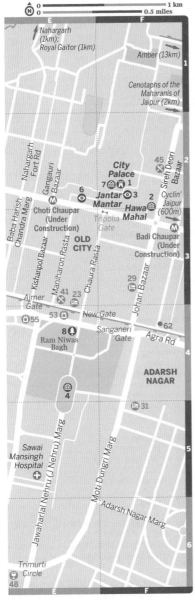

Nahargarh
(1km);
Royal Gaitor (1km)

Amber (13km)

Cenotaphs of the
Maharanis of
Jaipur (2km)

**City
Palace**
45

7 1
6 Jantar 3
Mantar Hawa
Hawa Mahal
Choti Chaupar
(Under
Construction)
OLD
CITY

Nahargarh
Fort Rd
Gangauri
Bazaar
Sireh Deori
Bazaar
Cyclin'
Jaipur
(600m)
Tripolia
Gate
Baba Harish
Chandra Marg
Kishanpol Bazaar
Maniharon Rasta
Chaura Rasta
Johari Bazaar

Badi Chaupar
(Under
Construction)

29
41 23
Ajmer
Gate
53 New Gate
55
8
Ram Niwas
Bagh
Sanganeri
Gate
62
Agra Rd

**ADARSH
NAGAR**

4
31

Sawai
Mansingh
Hospital

Moti Dungri Marg
Jawaharlal Nehru (J Nehru) Marg
Adarsh Nagar Marg

Trimurti
Circle
48

construction. Whatever was built in the day crumbled in the night. The prince agreed to leave on condition that the fort was named for him. The views are glorious and there's a restaurant that's perfect for a cold beer.

One way to visit is to climb the steep, winding 2km path to the top, starting from the end of Nahargarh Fort Rd. To drive, you have to detour via the Amber area in a circuitous 8km round trip.

A valid composite ticket (p42) will also gain you entry.

Royal Gaitor   HISTORIC SITE
(Gatore ki Chhatriyan; Indian/foreigner ₹20/30; ☉9am-5pm) The royal cenotaphs, just outside the city walls, beneath Nahargarh, feel remarkably undiscovered and are an appropriately restful place to visit. The stone monuments are beautifully and intricately carved. Maharajas Pratap Singh, Madho Singh II and Jai Singh II, among others, are honoured here. Jai Singh II has the most impressive marble cenotaph, with a dome supported by 20 carved pillars.

Jal Mahal   HISTORIC BUILDING
(Water Palace; ☉closed to the public) Near the cenotaphs of the maharanis of Jaipur, and beautifully situated in the watery expanse of Man Sagar, is this dreamlike palace. Its origins are uncertain, but it was believed to have been extensively restored if not built by Jai Singh II (1734). It's currently undergoing restoration under the auspices of the Jal Tarang (www.jaltarang.in) project.

**Cenotaphs of the
Maharanis of Jaipur**   HISTORIC SITE
(Maharani ki Chhatri; Amber Rd; Indian/foreigner ₹20/30; ☉9am-5pm) About 5km from the centre, along the road to Amber, the cenotaphs of the maharanis of Jaipur are worth a visit for a tranquil stroll.

Galta   HINDU TEMPLE
Squeezed between cliffs in a rocky valley, Galta is a desolate, if evocative, place. The temple houses a number of sacred tanks, into which some daring souls jump from the adjacent cliffs. The water is claimed to be several elephants deep and fed from a spring that falls through the mouth of a sculpted cow.

There are some original frescos in reasonable condition in a chamber at the end of the bottom pool, including those depicting athletic feats, the maharaja playing polo,

Nahargarh   FORT
(Tiger Fort; Indian/foreigner ₹50/200; ☉10am-5pm) Built in 1734 and extended in 1868, this sturdy fort overlooks the city from a sheer ridge to the north. The story goes that the fort was named after Nahar Singh, a dead prince whose restless spirit was disrupting

Jaipur

and the exploits of Krishna and the *gopis* (milkmaids).

It is also known as the Monkey Temple and you will find hundreds of monkeys living here – bold and aggressive macaques and more graceful and tolerable langurs. You can purchase peanuts at the gate to feed to them, but be prepared to be mobbed by teeth-baring primates.

Although only a few kilometres east of the City Palace, Galta is about 10km by road from central Jaipur. An autorickshaw should charge around ₹500 return with waiting time; a taxi will charge at least ₹800.

On the ridge above Galta is the Surya Mandir (Temple of the Sun God), which rises 100m above Jaipur and can be seen from the eastern side of the city. A 2.5km-long walking trail climbs up to the temple from Suraj Pol, or you can walk up from the Galta side. There are hazy views over the humming city.

Activities

A few hotels will let you use their pool for a daily fee; try those at Narain Niwas Palace Hotel (p53) and **Mansingh Hotel** (Sansar Chandra Marg; nonguests ₹350; ⊙7am-8pm).

Kerala Ayurveda Kendra AYURVEDA
(☑0141-4022446; www.keralaayurvedakendra. com; 32 Indra Colony, Bani Park; ⊙9am-9pm) Is Jaipur making your nerves jangle? Get help through ayurvedic massage and therapy. Treatments include *sirodhara* (₹1750/2800 for 50/90 minutes), where medicated oil is steadily streamed over your forehead to reduce stress, tone the brain and help with sleep disorders. Massages (male therapist for male clients and female for female clients) cost from ₹900 for 50 minutes.

It offers free transport to/from your hotel.

Jhalana Leopard Safari SAFARI
(☑9929400009; https://jhalanaleopard.business. site; Jhalana Forest Reserve; Indian per 6-seat 4WD ₹4500, foreigner per person ₹2500; ⊙6.45-9.30am & 3-5.50pm winter, 5.45-8.50am & 3.45-6.15pm summer) Jhalana Leopard Safari has the sole contract for running safaris in this city-edge forest reserve. The reserve is only 21 sq km, surrounded by human settlement, and the habitat for more than 20 leopards. The 2¾-hour safaris don't necessarily venture very far from the front gate but we can confirm that leopards can be spotted less than 100m from this gate – and effortlessly jumping over the 2m-high fences!

The reserve is also home to hyenas, monkeys, deer and nilgai (blue bull), and is a prime birdwatching destination, especially in summer.

The price for foreigners includes hotel transfer to and from Jaipur and a seat in a shared 4WD.

Yog Sadhna Ashram YOGA
(☑9314011884; Bapu Nagar; ⊙closed Tue) Free classes take place among trees off University Rd (near Rajasthan University) and incorporate breathing exercises, yoga asanas (postures) and exercise. Most of the classes are in Hindi, but some English is spoken in the 7.30am to 9.30am class. You can visit for individual classes, or register for longer courses.

Madhavanand Girls College YOGA
(C19 Behari Marg, Bani Park; ⊙6-7am) This college runs free casual yoga classes every day in both Hindi and English. Very convenient if you happen to be lodging in Bani Park – the college is next door to Madhuban hotel.

Courses

Jaipur Cooking Classes COOKING
(☑9928097288; www.jaipurcookingclasses.com; 33 Gyan Vihar, Nirman Nagar; class veg/nonveg from ₹2100/3800) Popular cooking classes with chef Lokesh Mathur, who has more than 25 years' experience working in the restaurant and hotel business. Classes cover both classic dishes and Rajasthani menus and can be veg or nonveg. After a three-hour lesson, you sit down for a lunch or dinner of what you've prepared. Lokesh's kitchen is outside the western outskirts of Jaipur, near Ajmer Rd.

Call ahead for exact directions for your driver.

Dhamma Thali Vipassana Meditation Centre HEALTH & WELLBEING
(☑0141-2680220; www.thali.dhamma.org; courses by donation) This serene *vipassana* meditation centre is tucked away in the hilly countryside near Galta, a 12km drive east of the city centre. It runs courses in meditation for both beginners and more advanced students throughout the year. Courses are usually for 10 days, during which you must observe noble silence – no communication with others.

Tours

Cyclin' Jaipur CYCLING
(☑7728060956; www.cyclinjaipur.com; 3hr tour ₹2000; ⊙tour 6.45-9.45am) Get up early to beat the traffic for a tour of the Pink City by bike, exploring the hidden lanes, temples, markets and food stalls of Jaipur. It's a fun way to learn about the workings and culture of the Old City before the gridlock and fumes set in. Breakfast (street food) and refreshments during the tour are included, and helmets are provided on demand.

Tours start at Karnot Mahal, on Ramganj Chaupar in the Old City. Tailor-made walking and food tours are also available.

Vintage Jeep Tour TOURS
(☑0141-2373700, 9829404055; www.pearlpalace heritage.com/exclusive-vintage-jeep-tour-jaipur; Lane 2, 54 Gopal Bari; per person ₹2500; ⊙9am-5.30pm) A fun way to explore Jaipur's major sights (including Amber and the City Palace)

TOP STATE FESTIVALS

Jaisalmer Desert Festival (p136) A chance for moustache twirlers to compete in the Mr Desert contest.

Gangaur (☉Mar/Apr) A festival honouring Shiva and Parvati's love, celebrated statewide but with fervour in Jaipur.

Mewar Festival (☉Mar/Apr) Udaipur's version of Gangaur, with free cultural events and a colourful procession down to the lake.

Teej (☉Jul/Aug) Jaipur and Bundi honour the arrival of the monsoon and Shiva and Parvati's marriage.

Dussehra Mela (Kota; ☉Oct/Nov) Commemorates Rama's victory over Ravana (the demon king of Lanka). It's a spectacular time to visit Kota – the huge fair features 22m-tall firecracker-stuffed effigies.

Marwar Festival (p121) Celebrates Rajasthani heroes through music and dance; one day is held in Jodhpur, the other in Osian.

Pushkar Camel Fair (p76) The most famous festival in the state; it's a massive congregation of camels, horses and cattle, pilgrims and tourists.

is by jeep – a genuine US Army 1942 Ford Jeep. With a dedicated driver and a guide on board, you are guaranteed to be part of a small tour group (maximum three guests), giving great flexibility. Admission prices and lunch costs are not included.

RTDC Transport Unit TOURS
(☑0141-2371641; www.rtdctourism.rajasthan.gov.in; RTDC Hotel Gangaur, Sanjay Marg; half-/full-day tour ₹400/500; ☉8am-6.30pm Mon-Sat) Full-day tours take in all the major sights of Jaipur (including Amber Fort), with a lunch break at Nahargarh. The lunch break can be as late as 3pm, so have a big breakfast. Rushed half-day tours (8am to 1pm, 11.30am to 4.30pm, and 1.30pm to 6.30pm) still squeeze in Amber. The tour price doesn't include admission charges.

Departing at 6.30pm, the **Pink City by Night tour** (₹700) explores several well-known sights (outside viewing only) and includes dinner at Nahargarh.

Tours depart from Jaipur train station; the company also picks up and takes bookings from the RTDC Hotel Teej, RTDC Hotel Gangaur and the tourist information office at the Jaipur Railway Station.

🛏 Sleeping

Jaipur accommodation pretty much covers all bases, and travellers are spoiled for choice in all budget categories. From May to September, most midrange and top-end hotels offer bargain rates, dropping prices by 25% to 50%.

🛏 Around MI Road

⭐**Hotel Pearl Palace** HOTEL **$**
(☑0141-2373700, 9414236323; www.hotelpearlpalace.com; Hari Kishan Somani Marg, Hathroi Fort; r ₹1310-1240; ❈🛜) The legendary Pearl Palace continues to exceed guests' expectations with excellent rooms that defy their tariffs. There's quite a range of rooms to choose from, and all are spotless and stylish, with modern amenities and bathrooms. Services include money changing, city tours and travel arrangements, and the hotel features the excellent Peacock Rooftop Restaurant (p55). Advance booking is recommended.

Karni Niwas GUESTHOUSE **$**
(☑0141-2365433, 9929777488; www.hotelkarniniwas.com; C5 Motilal Atal Marg; r ₹850-1000, with AC ₹1650; ❈@🛜) This friendly hotel has clean, cool and comfortable rooms, though mattresses may be a bit thin. There's no restaurant, but there is a kitchen and relaxing plant-decked terraces to enjoy room service on. And being so central, restaurants aren't far away. The owner shuns commissions for rickshaw drivers; free pickup from the train or bus station is available.

Jaipur Janta HOSTEL **$**
(☑9829040897; www.jaipurjanta.com; 3 Jalupura Scheme, Gopinath Marg; dm ₹350-600; ❈🛜) This sparkling, spacious and relaxing hostel comes from the folks at Arya Niwas, and is adjacent to another of their concerns: Jai Niwas. There's a kitchen for guest use, and courses, such as cooking, are available. It

has a shoes-off policy inside, but there are lockers – and shoe covers if you want to stay shod. Book direct for a discount.

Roadhouse Hostel Jaipur   HOSTEL **$**
(☑ 7313301301; www.roadhousehostels.com; D-76 Prithviraj Rd; dm/s/d ₹300/1000/1200; ❄ 🛜) This bright and friendly hostel is in a quiet residential part of town, but it's not too far from all the restaurants on MI Rd. Six- and eight-bed dorms are spotless and have air-con, and there are a couple of private rooms. There is a free-use kitchen and games room, and management will help with transport tickets.

There's a handy rickshaw stand at the end of the road.

★ **Atithi Guest House**   GUESTHOUSE **$$**
(☑ 0141-2378679; www.atithijaipur.com; 1 Park House Scheme Rd; s/d ₹1344/1456, with AC ₹1680/1904; ❄ @ 🛜) This nicely presented modern guesthouse, well situated between MI and Station Rds, offers strikingly clean, simple rooms dotted around a quiet courtyard. It's central but peaceful, and the service is friendly and helpful. Vegetarian meals are available (the quality coffee, tea, bakery offerings and thali are particularly recommended), and you can have a drink on the very pleasant rooftop terrace.

★ **Hotel Arya Niwas**   HOTEL **$$**
(☑ 0141-2372456; www.aryaniwas.com; Sansar Chandra Marg; s/d incl breakfast from ₹1700/2350; ❄ @ 🛜) Just off Sansar Chandra Marg, this very popular travellers' haunt has a travel desk, book and gift shop, and a range of in-house activities, from block printing and cooking to yoga lessons. The spotless rooms vary in layout and size so check out a few. Outside, there's an extensive verandah facing a soothing expanse of lawn to loll about on.

For a hotel of 125 rooms it is very well run with several eco-initiatives, including reducing plastic wherever possible and providing clean drinking water on every floor and a re-usable bottle in every room. The vegetarian restaurant also has espresso coffee.

Pearl Palace Heritage   HOTEL **$$**
(☑ 9772558855, 0141-4106599; www.pearlpalace heritage.com; Lane 2, 54 Gopal Bari; r ₹4720-5900; ❄ 🛜) The second hotel for the successful Pearl Palace team is an upper-midrange property, featuring a lift, five-star hotel linen and some extraordinary decor. Stone carvings adorn the corridors and each spacious room vibrantly recreates an individual Indian theme, such as a village hut, a Rajput fort, or a mirror-lined palace boudoir. Modern facilities have been carefully integrated into the appealing traditional designs.

The air-conditioned, top-floor restaurant specialises in Indian regional cuisines, but also has some Continental comfort food.

All Seasons Homestay   HOMESTAY **$$**
(☑ 9460387055, 0141-2369443; www.allseasons homestayjaipur.com; 63 Hathroi Fort; s/d from ₹2128/2240; ❄ 🛜) Ranjana and her husband Dinesh run this welcoming homestay in their lovely bungalow on a quiet backstreet behind Hathroi Fort. There are 10 pristine guest rooms, two of which have small kitchens for longer stays. There's a pleasant lawn, home-cooked meals and cooking lessons. Advance booking is recommended.

Nana-ki-Haveli   HERITAGE HOTEL **$$**
(☑ 0141-2615502; www.nanakihaveli.com; Fateh Tiba; r ₹1800-3000; ❄ 🛜) Tucked away off Moti Dungri Marg is this tranquil place with comfortable, simple rooms decorated with a few traditional flourishes. It's hosted by a lovely family, feels more like a homestay than a hotel, and is a good choice for solo female travellers. It's fronted by a relaxing lawn and offers home-style cooking and discounted rooms in summer.

Alsisar Haveli   HERITAGE HOTEL **$$$**
(☑ 0141-2368290; www.alsisar.com; Sansar Chandra Marg; s/d incl breakfast from ₹7605/10,530; ❄ @ 🛜 🏊) This heritage hotel housed in a gracious 19th-century mansion is set in beautiful green gardens, and has a lovely swimming pool and grand dining room. It's a veritable oasis. Its bedrooms don't disappoint either, with elegant Rajput arches and antique furnishings. Perhaps a little impersonal because it hosts many tour groups; occasional discounts can be found by booking directly online.

Hotel Diggi Palace   HERITAGE HOTEL **$$$**
(☑ 0141-2373091; www.hoteldiggipalace.com; off Sawai Ram Singh Rd; s/d/ste incl breakfast from ₹6490/7080/8790; ❄ 🛜 🏊) About 1km south of Ajmer Gate, this former residence of the *thakur* (nobleman) of Diggi is surrounded by vast, tree-shaded lawns and is refreshingly peaceful. All rooms are spacious with large bathrooms – you don't get significantly more luxury or room size for choosing a more expensive suite. It's a bit faded and well worn but genuinely friendly.

Organic produce from the hotel's own gardens and farms are used in the restaurant. It is also the venue for the Jaipur Literature Festival (www.jaipurliteraturefestival.org; ⊙ Jan).

🛏 Bani Park

The Bani Park area is relatively peaceful, away from main roads, but only about 2km west of the Old City (northwest of MI Rd).

Vinayak Guest House   HOTEL $
(☑ 9829867297, 0141-2205260; vinayakguesthouse@yahoo.co.in; 4 Kabir Marg, Bani Park; dm ₹299, r ₹500-1100; ❄🛜) This welcoming guesthouse is in a small, quiet street behind busy Kabir Marg, very convenient to the train station. The air-con dorm features big lockers and a hot shower. There is a variety of different rooms and tariffs; those with air-con also have great renovated bathrooms and are your best option. The vegetarian restaurant on the rooftop gets good reports.

Krishna Palace   HOTEL $
(☑ 0141-2201395; www.krishnapalace.com; E26 Durga Marg, Bani Park; r ₹1400, with AC from ₹2240; ❄🛜) Krishna Palace is conveniently located near the train and bus stations (and free pickup is on offer). Rooms are generally spacious, well maintained and comfortable, and there are some quiet corners and a relaxing lawn to retreat to with a book. There is also a splendid rooftop restaurant and a helpful travel desk.

⭐ Madhuban   HOTEL $$
(☑ 0141-2200033; www.madhuban.net; D237 Behari Marg; s/d/ste incl breakfast from ₹2460/2800/4250; ❄@🛜🏊) Madhuban has bright, antique-furnished, spotlessly clean rooms, plus a private enclosed garden for alfresco meals. The vibrantly frescoed restaurant serves Rajasthani specialities in addition to continental and North Indian dishes, and sits beside the courtyard plunge pool. The relatively peaceful locale of Bani Park makes this place a comfortable stay. Bus and train station pickup available.

Dera Rawatsar   HOTEL $$
(☑ 0141-2200770; www.derarawatsar.com; D194 Vijay Path, Bani Park; r incl breakfast ₹4500-5500, ste ₹8000; ❄@🛜🏊) Situated in a quiet suburban street and yet close to the bus station, this hotel is managed by three generations of women of a Bikaner noble family. The hotel has a range of lovely decorated rooms,

sunny courtyards, and offers home-style Indian meals. It is a relaxing and gracious option for all travellers, and a particularly good choice for families and female travellers.

Hotel Anuraag Villa   HOTEL $$
(☑ 0141-2201679; www.anuraagvilla.com; D249 Devi Marg; r ₹1344, with AC from ₹2352; ❄🛜) This quiet and comfortable option has no-fuss, spacious rooms and an extensive lawn where you can find some quiet respite from the hassles of sightseeing. It has a highly commended vegetarian restaurant with its kitchen on view, and efficient, helpful staff.

Jaipur Inn   HOTEL $$
(☑ 0141-2201121, 9829013660; www.jaipurinn.com; B17 Shiv Marg, Bani Park; r from ₹1250, with AC from ₹1500; ❄🛜) A long-time budget travellers' favourite offering an assortment of eclectic and individual rooms. Inspect a few before settling in. Plus points include the helpful manager and several common areas where travellers can make a coffee, use the wi-fi, or grab a meal. Yoga and Bollywood dance lessons can be had on the rooftop.

Hotel Meghniwas   GUESTHOUSE $$$
(☑ 0141-4060100; www.meghniwas.com; C9 Sawai Jai Singh Hwy; r/ste ₹5900/7670; ❄🛜🏊) In a building erected by Brigadier Singh in 1950 and run by his gracious descendants, this very welcoming hotel has comfortable and spotless rooms, with traditional carved-wood furniture and leafy outlooks. The standard rooms are spacious, and although it's on a major road it is set well back behind a leafy garden. There's a first-rate restaurant and an inviting pool.

Jas Vilas   GUESTHOUSE $$$
(☑ 0141-2204902; www.jasvilas.com; C9 Sawai Jai Singh Hwy; s/d incl breakfast from ₹6730/7670; ❄🛜🏊) This small but impressive hotel was built in 1950 and is still run by the same charming family. It offers spacious rooms, most of which face the large sparkling pool set in a romantic courtyard. Three garden-facing rooms are wheelchair accessible. In addition to the relaxing courtyard and garden, there is a cosy dining room and helpful management.

Shahpura House   HERITAGE HOTEL $$$
(☑ 0141-4089100; www.shahpura.com; D257 Devi Marg; r/ste from ₹11,520/14,800; ❄🛜🏊) Elaborately built and decorated in traditional style, this heritage hotel offers immaculate rooms, some with balconies, featuring

murals, coloured-glass lamps, flatscreen TVs, and even ceilings covered in small mirrors (in the suites). This rambling palace has a durbar (royal court) hall with a huge chandelier, and a cosy cocktail bar.

There's also an inviting swimming pool and an elegant rooftop terrace restaurant that stages cultural shows.

🛏 Old City

Hotel Sweet Dream   HOTEL $
(☎0141-2314409; www.hotelsweetdreamjaipur.in; Nehru Bazaar; s/d ₹1000/1455, with AC from ₹1900/2240; ﹡🛜) Probably the best option right inside the Old City, and one of Jaipur's better budget hotels. Many of the rooms have been renovated and enlarged, so inspect more than one room. There are increasing amenities the higher up the price scale (or the rickety elevator) you go. There's a bar plus an excellent rooftop terrace restaurant.

Hotel Bissau Palace   HERITAGE HOTEL $$
(☎0141-2304391; www.bissaupalace.com; outside Chandpol; r ₹3540-7080; ﹡🛜🏊) This is a worthy choice if you want to stay in a palace. It's located just outside the city walls, less than 10 minutes' walk from Chandpol (a gateway to the Old City). There's a swimming pool, a handsome wood-panelled library and three restaurants. The hotel has oodles of heritage atmosphere, with antique furnishings and mementos.

🛏 Rambagh Environs

Rambagh Palace   HERITAGE HOTEL $$$
(☎0141-2385700; www.tajhotels.com; Bhawani Singh Marg; r from ₹57,220; ﹡@🛜🏊) This splendid palace was once the Jaipur pad of Maharaja Man Singh II and his glamorous wife Gayatri Devi. Veiled in hectares of manicured gardens, the hotel – run by the luxury Taj Group brand – has fantastic views across the immaculate lawns. More expensive rooms are naturally the most sumptuous.

Nonguests can join in the magnificence by dining in the lavish restaurants or drinking tea on the gracious verandah. At least treat yourself to a drink at the spiffing Polo Bar (p56).

Narain Niwas Palace Hotel   HERITAGE HOTEL $$$
(☎0141-2561291; www.hotelnarainniwas.com; Narain Singh Rd; s/d incl breakfast from ₹8500/8800; P﹡@🛜🏊) In Kanota Bagh, just south of the city, this genuine heritage ho-

tel has genuine heritage splendour. There's a lavish dining room with liveried staff, an old-fashioned verandah on which to drink tea, and antiques galore. The standard rooms are in a garden wing and aren't as spacious as the high-ceilinged deluxe rooms (₹14,720), which vary in atmosphere and amenities.

A new wing of deluxe rooms features a lift and modern rooms with a few tasteful traditional flourishes. Out back you'll find a large secluded pool (nonguests ₹300 for two hours between 8am and 4pm – guests only after 4pm), a heavenly spa, and sprawling lawns and tree-shaded gardens adorned with strutting peacocks.

🍴 Eating

🍴 Around MI Road

Indian Coffee House   CAFE $
(MI Rd; coffee ₹27-46, snacks & mains ₹25-60; ⊙6am-9pm) Set back from the street, down an easily missed alley, this traditional coffee house (a venerable co-op institution) offers a pleasant cup of filtered coffee in very relaxed surroundings. Aficionados of Indian Coffee Houses will not be disappointed by the fan-cooled, spare, pale-yellow ambience. Inexpensive *pakoras* (deep-fried battered vegetables) and dosas grace the menu.

Old Takeaway the Kebab Shop   KEBAB $
(242 MI Rd; kebabs ₹90-180; ⊙6-11pm) One of several similarly named roadside kebab shops on this stretch of MI Rd, this one (next to the mosque) is the original (so we're told) and the best (we agree). It knocks up outstanding tandoori kebabs, including paneer, mutton and tandoori chicken. Like the sign says: a house of delicious nonveg corner.

Jal Mahal   ICE CREAM $
(MI Rd; cups & cones ₹30-120; ⊙10am-11pm) This great little ice-cream parlour has been going since 1952. There are around 50 flavours to choose from, but if it's hot outside, it's hard to beat mango. There are also plenty of other ice-cream concoctions, including sundaes and banana splits, many with fanciful names.

Rawat Kachori   SWEETS $
(Station Rd; kachori ₹30, lassi ₹50, sweets per kg ₹350-850; ⊙6am-10pm) Head to this popular takeaway with an attached restaurant for delicious Indian sweets and famous kachori (potato masala in a fried pastry case), a

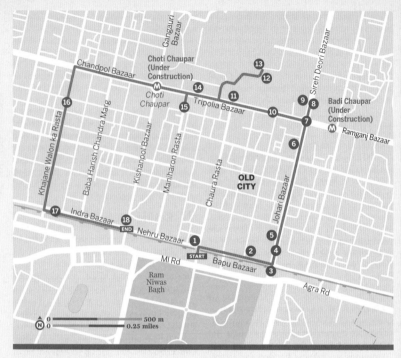

City Walk
Pink City

START NEW GATE
END AJMER GATE
LENGTH 4.5KM; THREE TO FIVE HOURS

Entering the old city from **1 New Gate**, turn right into **2 Bapu Bazaar**, inside the city wall. Brightly coloured bolts of fabric, jootis and aromatic perfumes make the street a favourite destination for Jaipur's women. At the end of Bapu Bazaar you'll come to **3 Sanganeri Gate**. Turn left into **4 Johari Bazaar**, the jewellery market, where you will find jewellers, goldsmiths and artisans doing highly glazed meenakari (enamelwork), a speciality of Jaipur.

Continuing north you'll pass the famous **5 LMB Hotel** (check out the sweets counter), the **6 Jama Masjid** with its tall minarets, and the bustling **7 Badi Chaupar** public square. Be careful crossing the road here; works for the underground metro have added to the usual mayhem. To the north is **8 Sireh Deori Bazaar**, also known as Hawa Mahal Bazaar. The name is derived from the spectacular **9 Hawa Mahal** (p43), a short distance

north. Turning left on **10 Tripolia Bazaar**, you will see a lane leading to the entrance to the Hawa Mahal. A few hundred metres west is the **11 Tripolia Gate**. This is the main entrance to the **12 Jantar Mantar** (p43) and **13 City Palace** (p42), but only the maharaja's family may enter here. The public entrance is via the less ostentatious Atishpol (Stable Gate), a little further along.

Head back to Tripolia Bazaar and resume your walk west past **14 Isarlat** (p43), which is well worth the climb for the view. Cross the bazaar (when safe) at the minaret and head west. The next lane on the left is **15 Maniharon Rasta**, the best place to buy colourful lac (resin) bangles.

Back on Tripolia Bazaar, continue west to cross Choti Chaupar to Chandpol Bazaar until you reach a traffic light. Turn left into **16 Khajane Walon ka Rasta**, where you'll find marble and stoneware carvers at work. Continue south until you reach a broad road just inside the city wall, **17 Indra Bazaar**. Follow the road east towards **18 Ajmer Gate**, which marks the end of the tour.

scrumptious savoury snack. A salty or sweet lassi should fill you up for the afternoon.

★**Peacock Rooftop Restaurant** MULTICUISINE **$$**

(☑0141-2373700; Hotel Pearl Palace, Hari Kishan Somani Marg; mains ₹150-390; ⊙7am-11pm) This multilevel rooftop restaurant at the Hotel Pearl Palace gets rave reviews for its excellent yet inexpensive cuisine (Indian, Chinese and continental) and fun ambience. The attentive service, whimsical furnishings and romantic view towards Hathroi Fort make it a first-rate restaurant. In addition to the dinner menu, there are healthy breakfasts and great-value burgers, pizzas and thalis for lunch. It's wise to make a booking for dinner.

Four Seasons MULTICUISINE **$$**

(☑0141-2375450; D43A Subhash Marg; mains ₹230-300; ⊙11am-10.45pm; 📶🅿) Four Seasons is one of Jaipur's best vegetarian restaurants. It's a popular place with dining on two levels and a glass wall to the busy kitchens. There's a great range of dishes on offer, including tasty Rajasthani specialities, South Indian dosas, Chinese fare, and a selection of thalis and pizzas. Note that the Italian menu starts at 1pm. No alcohol.

Anokhi Café INTERNATIONAL **$$**

(☑0141-4007245; 2nd fl, KK Sq, C-11 Prithviraj Marg; mains ₹250-350; ⊙10am-7.30pm; 📶🅿) This serene and cool cafe with a fashionable organic vibe is the perfect place to come if you're craving a crunchy, well-dressed salad, a quiche or a thickly filled sandwich – or just a respite from the hustle with a latte or an iced tea. Whole fresh loaves of organic bread can be also purchased.

Handi Restaurant NORTH INDIAN **$$**

(☑0141-4917115; MI Rd; mains ₹240-440; ⊙noon-11pm) Handi has been satisfying customers since 1967, with scrumptious tandoori and barbecue dishes and rich Mughlai curries. In the evenings it sets up a smoky kebab stall at the entrance to the restaurant. Good vegetarian items are also available. The rooftop section (6pm to 11pm) has a bar.

It's opposite the main post office, tucked at the back of the Maya Mansions.

Surya Mahal SOUTH INDIAN **$$**

(☑0141-2362811; MI Rd; mains ₹150-320, thali ₹240-350; ⊙8am-11pm; 📶🅿) This popular option near Panch Batti specialises in South Indian vegetarian food; try the tasty *dhal makhani* (black lentils and red kidney beans). There are also Chinese and Italian dishes, and good ice creams, sundaes and cool drinks. No alcohol.

Natraj INDIAN **$$**

(☑0141-2375804; MI Rd; mains ₹180-250, thali ₹270-550; ⊙8.30am-10.45pm; 📶🅿) Not far from Panch Batti is this classy vegetarian place, which has an extensive menu featuring North Indian, Continental and Chinese cuisine and booth seats. Diners are blown away by the potato-encased 'vegetable bomb' curry. There's a good selection of thalis and South Indian food as well as a great array of Indian sweets.

★**Niro's** INDIAN **$$$**

(☑0141-2374493; www.nirosindia.com; MI Rd; mains ₹400-580; ⊙10am-11pm; 📶) Established in 1949, Niro's is a long-standing favourite on MI Rd that, like a good wine, only improves with age. Escape the chaos of the street by ducking into its cool, clean, mirror-ceilinged sanctum to savour veg and nonveg Indian cuisine with professional service. Classic Chinese and Continental food are available, but the Indian menu is definitely the pick.

Even locals rave about the butter chicken and rogan josh. Beer and wine are served.

Handi Fusion MULTICUISINE **$$$**

(☑0141-4096969; Maya Mansions, MI Rd; mains ₹285-510, thali veg/nonveg ₹560/715; ⊙noon-11pm; 📶) Handi Fusion is casual, verging on elegant, and welcoming, with an army of attentive waiters and a bar serving cold beer and wine. It offers generous helpings of excellent veg and nonveg Indian cuisine, including aromatic Rajasthani specials such as the Jaisalmeri *laal maas* (mutton curry). Continental and Chinese food is also on offer, but the curry-and-beer combo is hard to beat.

Jaipur Modern Kitchen MEDITERRANEAN **$$$**

(☑0141-4113000; www.jaipurmodern.com; 51 Sardar Patel Marg, C-Scheme; mains ₹350-600; ⊙11am-10.30pm; 📶🅿) Within the eponymous homewares and fashion showroom (p58) is this super Mediterranean cafe showcasing organic ingredients and supporting local sustainable agriculture. The tasty pizzas, pasta and wraps are all made in-house, and gluten-free dishes are available. There's a special emphasis on locally grown quinoa; the Q menu features soups, appetisers, mains and desserts, all containing the versatile seed.

Little Italy ITALIAN $$$
(☎0141-4022444; 3rd fl, KK Sq, Prithviraj Marg; mains ₹320-500; ⏰noon-10pm; ❄) The best Italian restaurant in Jaipur, Little Italy is part of a national chain that offers excellent vegetarian pasta, risotto and wood-fired pizzas in contemporary surroundings. The menu is extensive and includes some Mexican items, plus first-rate Italian desserts. It's licensed and there's an attached sister concern, Little India, with an Indian and Chinese menu.

Old City

Pandit Kulfi ICE CREAM $
(10-111 Sireh Dion Mahal (Hawa Mahal Rd), Old City; cone plain/flavoured ₹20/30; ⏰11am-11.30pm) Despite the crusty exterior this tiny shop has a delightfully creamy centre. Pandit gets rave reviews for its conical *kulfi* (firm-textured ice cream) on a stick. Flavours include pistachio, chocolate, custard apple, mango and *paan* (betel nut). If you are here around 4pm you can see the *kulfi* being poured into the conical moulds and set in a box of salted ice.

Mohan INDIAN $
(144-5 Nehru Bazaar; mains ₹30-150, thali ₹85; ⏰9am-10.30pm; ✍) Tiny Mohan is easy to miss: it's a few steps down from the footpath on the corner of the street. It's basic, cheap and a bit grubby, but the vegetarian thalis, curries (half-plate and full plate available) and snacks are freshly cooked and very popular.

LMB INDIAN $$
(☎0141-2565844; Johari Bazaar; mains ₹230-390; ⏰8am-11pm; ❄✍) Laxmi Misthan Bhandar, LMB to you and me, is a vegetarian restaurant in the Old City that's been going strong since 1954. A welcoming air-conditioned refuge from frenzied Johari Bazaar, LMB is also an institution with its singular decor, attentive waiters and extensive sweet counter. Now it is no longer sattvik (pure vegetarian), you can order meals with onion and garlic.

Hotel Sweet Dream MULTICUISINE $$
(☎0141-2314409; www.hotelsweetdreamjaipur.in; Nehru Bazaar; mains ₹135-290; ❄) This hotel in the Old City has a splendid restaurant on the roof with views down to bustling Nehru Bazaar. It's a great place to break the shopping spree and grab a light lunch or a refreshing *makhania* lassi (a filling, saffron-flavoured lassi). The menu includes pizza and Chinese, but the Indian is best.

Drinking & Nightlife

Many bars around town tend to be oppressive, smoke-filled, all-male affairs; however, most upper-end hotel bars are good for casual drinking.

★**Lassiwala** CAFE
(MI Rd; lassi small/large ₹30/60; ⏰from 7.30am) This famous, much-imitated institution is a simple place that whips up fabulous, creamy lassis in clay cups. They close when sold out – so get here early to avoid disappointment! Will the real Lassiwala please stand up? It's the one that says 'Shop 312' and 'Since 1944', directly next to the alleyway. Imitators spread to the right as you face it.

★**Curious Life** CAFE
(☎0141-2229877; www.facebook.com/curiouslifecoffeeroasters; P25 Yudhisthira Marg, C-Scheme; coffees from ₹150; ⏰9am-10pm; 📶) The latest coffee trends brew away in this showcase of Indian hipsterhood. Single-origin, espresso, French press, AeroPress, V60 pour over – you name it, you'll find it brewing here among the predominantly 20-something crowd. There are also smoothies, shakes, pancakes and muffins. The coffee chemistry going on behind the counter borders on the obsessive – just how the customers like it.

★**Bar Palladio** BAR
(☎0141-2565556; www.bar-palladio.com; Narain Niwas Palace Hotel, Narain Singh Rd; cocktails from ₹600; ⏰6-11pm) This cool bar-restaurant has an extensive drinks list and an Italian food menu (mains ₹360 to ₹420). The vivid blue theme of the romantic Orientalist interior flows through to candlelit outdoor seating, making this a very relaxing place to sip a drink, snack on bruschetta and enjoy a conversation. **Il Teatro** is an occasional live-music event at the bar – see the website for dates.

Polo Bar BAR
(Rambagh Palace Hotel, Bhawan Singh Marg; ⏰noon-midnight) This spiffing watering hole adorned with polo memorabilia boasts arched, scalloped windows framing the neatly clipped lawns. A bottle of beer costs from ₹400, a glass of wine from ₹600, and cocktails from ₹650. Delicious snacks are also available throughout the day.

100% Rock BAR
(Hotel Shikha, Yudhishthir Marg, C-Scheme; pint of beer/cocktails from ₹220/380; ⏰11am-12.30am; 📶) Attached to, but separate from, Hotel

Shikha, this is the closest thing there is to a beer garden in Jaipur, with plenty of outdoor seating as well as an overly dim air-conditioned room with a small dance floor. Two-for-one beer and cocktail offers last from opening to 10.30pm, understandably making this place popular.

Café Coffee Day CAFE
(Radisson Hotel, MI Rd; coffees ₹80-150; ⊙10am-10pm) The India-wide franchise that successfully delivers espresso, plus the occasional creamy concoction and muffin, has several branches in Jaipur. In addition to this one, sniff out the brews at Paris Point on Sawai Jai Singh Hwy (aka Collectorate Rd), at the Central Museum, and near the exit point at Amber Fort.

☆ Entertainment

Jaipur isn't a big late-night party town, though many of its hotels put on some sort of evening music, dance or puppet show. English-language films are occasionally screened – check the cinemas and local press for details.

Cricket has a huge and passionate following in India. If you want to see what all the fuss is about, you can watch the local team, the Rajasthan Royals, batting and bowling in the Indian Premier League at their home ground, the **Sawai Mansingh Stadium** (SMS Stadium; Bhawan Singh Marg).

★Raj Mandir Cinema CINEMA
(☑0141-2379372; www.therajmandir.com; Baghwandas Marg; tickets ₹150-400; ⊙reservations 10am-6pm, screenings 12.30pm, 3pm, 6.30pm & 10pm) Just off MI Rd, Raj Mandir is *the* place to go to see a Hindi film in India. This opulent cinema looks like a huge pink cream cake, with a meringue auditorium and a circular foyer somewhere between a temple and Disneyland. Bookings can be made one hour to seven days in advance at window 11.

Chokhi Dhani LIVE PERFORMANCE
(☑0141-5165000; www.chokhidhani.com; Tonk Rd; adult/child incl thali from ₹700/400; ⊙6-11pm) Chokhi Dhani, meaning 'special village', is a mock Rajasthani village 20km south of Jaipur, and is a fun place to take kids. There are open-air restaurants where you can enjoy a tasty Rajasthani thali, plus a bevy of traditional entertainment – dancers, acrobats, snack stalls – and adventure-park-like activities for kids to swing on, slide down and hide in.

🛍 Shopping

Jaipur is a shopper's paradise. Commercial buyers come here from all over the world to stock up on the amazing range of jewellery, gems, textiles and crafts that come from all over Rajasthan. You'll have to bargain hard, particularly around major tourist sights.

Many shops can send your parcels home for you – often for less than if you do it yourself.

The city is still loosely divided into traditional artisans' quarters. **Bapu Bazaar** is lined with saris and fabrics, and is a good place to buy trinkets. **Johari Bazaar** and **Sireh Deori Bazaar** are where many jewellery shops are concentrated, selling gold, silver and highly glazed enamelwork known as meenakari, a Jaipur speciality. You may also find better deals for fabrics with the cotton merchants of Johari Bazaar.

Kishanpol Bazaar is famous for textiles, particularly *bandhani* (tie-dye). **Nehru Bazaar** also sells fabric, as well as jootis (traditional, often pointy-toed, slip-on shoes), trinkets and perfume. The best place for bangles is Maniharon Rasta.

Plenty of factories and showrooms are strung along the length of the road to Amber, between Zorawar Singh Gate and the Park Regis Hotel, to catch the tourist

SHOPPING FOR GEMS

Jaipur is famous for precious and semi-precious stones. There are many shops offering bargain prices, but you do need to know your gems. The main area for gem-dealing is around the Muslim area of Pahar Ganj, in the southeast of the Old City. Here you can see stones being cut and polished in workshops tucked off narrow backstreets.

One of the oldest scams in India is the gem scam, where tourists are fooled into thinking they can buy gems to sell at a profit elsewhere. To receive an authenticity certificate, you can deposit your gems at the **gem-testing laboratory** (☑0141-2568221; www.gtljaipur.info; Rajasthan Chamber Bhawan, MI Rd; ⊙10am-4pm Mon-Sat) between 10am and 4pm, then return the following day between 4pm and 5pm to pick up the certificate. The service costs ₹1050 per stone, or ₹1650 for same-day service, if deposited before 1pm.

traffic. Here you'll find huge emporiums selling block prints, blue pottery, carpets and antiques. Note that these shops are used to busloads of tourists swinging in to blow their cash, so you'll need to wear your bargaining hat.

Rickshaw-wallahs, hotels and travel agents will be getting a hefty cut from any shop they steer you towards. Many unwary visitors get talked into buying things for resale at inflated prices, especially gems. Beware of these get-rich-quick scams.

Rajasthali   ARTS & CRAFTS
(MI Rd; ⊙11am-7.30pm Mon-Sat) This state-government-run emporium, opposite Ajmer Gate, is packed with quality Rajasthani artefacts and crafts, including enamelwork, embroidery, pottery, woodwork, jewellery, puppets, block-printed sheets, miniatures, brassware, mirrorwork and more. Scout out prices here before launching into the bazaar; items can be cheaper at the markets, but the quality is often higher at the state emporium for not much more money.

Jaipur Modern   FASHION & ACCESSORIES
(☑0141-4112000; www.jaipurmodern.com; 51 Sardar Patel Marg, C-Scheme; ⊙11am-9pm) This contemporary showroom offers local arts and crafts, clothing, homewares, stationery and fashion accessories. The staff are relaxed (no hard sell here) and if you are not in the mood to shop, there's a great cafe serving organic South Indian coffee and Mediterranean snacks.

Inde Rooh   CLOTHING
(☑9829404055, 9929442022; www.inderooh.com; Hotel Pearl Palace, Hari Kishan Somani Marg; ⊙10.30am-10.30pm) This tiny outlet in the Hotel Pearl Palace highlights the talents of Jaipur's traditional block printers blended with contemporary design. Handmade and stitched, the quality and value of the women's and men's clothing compares well with Jaipur's more famous fashion houses. Homewares are also available.

Anokhi   CLOTHING, TEXTILES
(www.anokhi.com; 2nd fl, KK Sq, C-11 Prithviraj Marg; ⊙10am-8pm) Anokhi is a classy, up-market boutique selling stunning high-quality textiles such as block-printed fabrics, tablecloths, bed covers, cosmetic bags and scarves, as well as a range of well-designed, beautifully made clothing that combines Indian and Western influences. There's a wonderful organic cafe on the premises and a decent bookshop in the same building.

Silver Shop   JEWELLERY
(Hotel Pearl Palace, Hari Kishan Somani Marg; ⊙6-10pm) A trusted jewellery shop backed by the Hotel Pearl Palace, which hosts the store. A money-back guarantee is offered on all items. Find it under the peacock canopy in the hotel's Peacock Rooftop Restaurant.

ⓘ Information

MEDICAL SERVICES
Most hotels can arrange a doctor on-site.
Santokba Durlabhji Memorial Hospital (SDMH; ☑0141-2566251; www.sdmh.in; Bhawan Singh Marg) Private hospital, with 24-hour emergency department, helpful staff and clear bilingual signage. Consultancy fee ₹400.
Sawai Mansingh Hospital (SMS Hospital; ☑0141-2518597, 0141-2518222; Sawai Ram Singh Rd) State-run, but part of Soni Hospitals Group (www.sonihospitals.com). Before 3pm, outpatients go to the CT & MRI Centre; after 3pm, go to the adjacent Emergency Department.

MONEY
There are plenty of places to change money, including numerous hotels, and masses of ATMs, most of which accept foreign cards.
Thomas Cook (☑0141-2360940; Jaipur Towers, MI Rd; ⊙9.30am-6pm) Changes cash and travellers cheques.

POST
DHL Express (☑0141-2361159; www.dhl.co.in; G8, Geeta Enclave, Vinobha Marg; ⊙10am-8pm) Look for the branch on MI Rd then walk down the lane beside it to find DHL Express. For parcels, the first kilogram is expensive, but each 500g thereafter is cheap. All packaging is included in the price. Credit cards and cash accepted.
Main Post Office (☑0141-2368740; MI Rd; ⊙8am-7.45pm Mon-Fri, 10am-5.45pm Sat) A cost-effective and efficient institution, though the back-and-forth can infuriate. The parcel-packing-wallahs outside the post office must first pack, stitch and wax seal your parcel for a small fee before sending.

TOURIST INFORMATION
Jaipur Vision and *Jaipur City Guide* are two useful, inexpensive booklets available at bookshops and some hotel lobbies (where they are free). They feature up-to-date listings, maps, local adverts and features.
RTDC Tourist Office (☑0141-5110598; www.rajasthantourism.gov.in; Paryatan Bhavan,

Sanjay Marg; ⊙ 9.30am-6pm Mon-Sat) Has maps and brochures on Jaipur and Rajasthan. Additional branches at the **airport** (☑ 0141-2725708; ⊙ 9am-5pm Mon-Fri) and the **train station** (☑ 0141-2315714; Platform 1; ⊙ 24hr).

❶ Getting There & Away

AIR

Jaipur International Airport (☑ 0141-2550623; www.jaipurairport.com) is located 12km southeast of the city.

It's possible to arrange flights to Jaipur from Europe, the US and other places, via Delhi. A few direct flights run to/from Bangkok and the Gulf.

Air India (www.airindia.com) Daily flights to/from Delhi and Mumbai.

Alliance Air (www.airindia.in/alliance-air.htm) Weekly flights to/from Agra.

IndiGo (www.goindigo.in) Flights to/from Ahmedabad, Bengaluru (Bangalore), Chennai, Delhi, Hyderabad, Kolkata, Mumbai and Pune.

Jet Airways (www.jetairways.com) Flights to Delhi and Mumbai.

SpiceJet (www.spicejet.com) Daily flights to/from Delhi.

Thai Smile (www.thaismileair.com) Three weekly flights to/from Bangkok.

BUS

Rajasthan State Road Transport Corporation (RSRTC, aka Rajasthan Roadways; www.rsrtc.rajasthan.gov.in) buses all leave from the **main bus station** (Station Rd), picking up passengers at Narain Singh Circle (where you can also buy tickets). There's a left-luggage office (per bag

per 24hr ₹20) at the main bus station, as well as a prepaid autorickshaw stand.

Ordinary buses are known as 'express' buses, but there are also 'deluxe' and 'super deluxe' buses (coaches), which vary a lot but are generally more expensive and comfortable (usually with air-con) than ordinary express buses. Deluxe buses leave from Platform 3, tucked away in the right-hand corner of the bus station. Unlike ordinary express buses, seats can be booked in advance from the **reservation office** (☑ 0141-5116032; ⊙ 8am-6pm).

With the exception of those going to Delhi (half-hourly), deluxe buses are much less frequent than ordinary buses.

There are numerous private bus companies servicing Jaipur from outside the main bus station. A useful service for Pushkar is **Jai Ambay Travelling Agency** (☑ 0141-2205177; www.jaiambaytravellingagency.com; 2 D Villa Station Rd; ₹350), which has a direct, daily, air-con coach (₹350) leaving for Pushkar at 9am arriving at 12.30pm.

CAR & MOTORCYCLE

Most hotels and the RTDC tourist office can arrange a car and driver. Depending on the vehicle, costs are ₹9 to ₹12 per kilometre, with a minimum rental rate equivalent to 250km per day. Also expect to pay a ₹200 overnight charge, and note that you will have to pay for the driver to return to Jaipur even if you are not returning.

You can hire, buy or fix a Royal Enfield Bullet (and lesser motorbikes) at **Rajasthan Auto Centre** (☑ 9829188064, 0141-2568074; www.royalenfieldsalim.com; Sanganeri Gate, Sanjay Bazaar; ⊙ 10am-8pm Mon-Sat, to 2pm Sun), the

MAIN BUSES FROM JAIPUR

DESTINATION	FARE (₹)	TIME (HR)	FREQUENCY
Agra	265, AC 563	5½	hourly
Ajmer	150, AC 302	2½	at least hourly
Bharatpur	195, AC 410	4½	at least hourly
Bikaner	361, AC 716	5½-7	hourly
Bundi	240	5	hourly
Chittorgarh	339, AC 574	7	hourly
Delhi	274, AC 900	5½	at least hourly
Jaisalmer	593	14	2 daily
Jhunjhunu	181, AC 320	3½-5	half-hourly
Jodhpur	331, AC 713	5½-7	hourly
Kota	252	5	hourly
Mt Abu	AC 919	10½-13	1 daily
Nawalgarh	145, AC 258	2½-4	hourly
Pushkar	160	3	3 daily
Udaipur	420, AC 767	10	at least hourly

cleanest little motorcycle workshop in India. To hire a 350cc Bullet costs ₹600 per day (including two helmets) within Jaipur.

TRAIN

The **reservation office** (☑ enquiries 131, reservations 135; ⊙ 8am-2pm & 3-8pm) is to your left as you enter Jaipur train station. It's open for advance reservations only (more than five hours before departure). Join the queue for 'Freedom Fighters and Foreign Tourists' (counter 769).

For same-day travel, buy your ticket at the northern end of the train station at Platform 1, window 10 (closed 6am to 6.30am, 2pm to 2.30pm and 10pm to 10.30pm).

Station facilities on Platform 1 include an RTDC tourist office, Tourism Assistance Force (police), a cloakroom for left luggage (₹20 per bag per 24 hours), retiring rooms, restaurants and air-conditioned waiting rooms for those with 1st-class and 2AC train tickets.

There's a prepaid autorickshaw stand and local taxis at the road entrance to the train station.

Services include the following:

Agra sleeper ₹205, 3½ to 4½ hours, nine daily

Ahmedabad sleeper from ₹370, nine to 13 hours, seven daily (12.30am, 2.20am, 4.25am, 5.35am, 8.40am, 2.20pm and 8.35pm)

Ajmer (for Pushkar) sleeper from ₹100, two hours, 21 daily

Bikaner sleeper ₹275, 6½ to 7½ hours, four daily (12.05am, 5am, 4.15pm and 9.45pm)

Delhi sleeper ₹135, 4½ to six hours, at least nine daily (1am, 2.50am, 4.40am, 5am, 6am, 2.35pm, 4.25pm, 5.50pm and 11.15pm), more on selected days

Jaisalmer sleeper ₹350, 12 hours, three daily (11.10am, 4.15pm and 11.45pm)

Jodhpur sleeper from ₹250, 4½ to six hours, 10 daily (12.45am, 2.45am, 6am, 9.25am, 11.10am, 11.25am, 12.20pm, 5pm, 10.40pm and 11.45pm)

Ranthambhore NP (Sawai Madhopur) sleeper ₹180, two to three hours, at least nine daily (12.30am, 5.40am, 6.40am, 11.05am, 2pm, 4.50pm, 5.35pm, 7.35pm and 8.25pm), more on selected days

Udaipur sleeper ₹270, seven to eight hours, three daily (6.15am, 2pm and 11pm)

❶ Getting Around

If you have the apps, both Uber and Ola operate in Jaipur and both offer cheaper services than autorickshaws, without the need to haggle the price down from an unreasonable starting point.

TO/FROM THE AIRPORT

There are no bus services from the airport. An autorickshaw/taxi costs at least ₹350/450. There's a prepaid taxi booth inside the terminal.

AUTORICKSHAW

Autorickshaw drivers at the bus and train stations might just be the pushiest in Rajasthan. If they are open use the fixed-rate prepaid autorickshaw stands instead. Keep hold of your docket to give to the driver at the end of the journey. In other cases be prepared to bargain

MAJOR TRAINS FROM JAIPUR

DESTINATION	TRAIN	DEPARTURE	ARRIVAL	FARE (₹)
Agra (Cantonment)	19666 Udaipur–Kurj Exp	6.15am	11am	205/540 (A)
Agra (Fort)	22987 All–AF Superfast	8.10am	12.20pm	122/430 (C)
Ahmedabad	12958 Adi Sj Rajdhani	12.30am	9.40am	1230/1680 (B)
Ajmer (for Pushkar)	12195 Ajmer–AF Intercity	9.40am	11.50am	110/345 (C)
Bikaner	12307 Howrah–Jodhpur Exp	12.45am	8.15am	275/705 (A)
Delhi (New Delhi)	12016 Ajmer Shatabdi	5.50pm	10.40pm	750/1395 (D)
Delhi (Sarai Rohilla)	12985 Dee Double Decker	6am	10.30am	505/1205 (D)
Jaisalmer	14659 Delhi–JSM Exp	11.45pm	11.45am	350/935 (A)
Jodhpur	22478 Jaipur–Jodhpur SF Exp	6am	11am	515/625 (E)
Sawai Madhopur	12466 Intercity Exp	11.05am	1.15pm	180/325/560 (F)
Udaipur	19665 Jaipur–Udaipur Exp	11pm	6.35am	270/715 (A)

Fares: (A) sleeper/3AC, (B) 3AC/2AC, (C) 2nd-class seat/AC chair, (D) AC chair/1AC, (E) AC chair/3AC, (F) sleeper/AC chair/3AC

hard – expect to pay at least ₹100 from either station to the Old City.

CYCLE-RICKSHAW

You could do your bit for the environment (but not the poor fellow's lungs) by flagging down a lean-limbed cycle-rickshaw rider. Though it can be uncomfortable watching someone pedalling hard to transport you, this *is* how they make a living. A short trip costs about ₹50.

PUBLIC TRANSPORT

Jaipur Metro (🖳 0141-2385790; www.jaipur metrorail.in; fare ₹6-17, 1-day tour card ₹50) currently operates about 10km of track, known as the Pink Line, and nine stations. The track starts southwest of the Pink City in Mansarovar, travels through Civil Lines, and currently terminates at Chandpol. At the time of writing, the continuation of this track through the Pink City from Chandpol to Badi Chaupar was under construction. Fares are between ₹6 (one to two stations) and ₹17 (six to eight stations).

TAXI

There are unmetered taxis available, which will require negotiating a fare.

Metro Cabs (🖳 0414-4244444; www.metro cabs.in; flagfall incl 2km ₹50, then per km ₹10-12, plus per min ₹1, 10pm-6am 25% surcharge; ⏰24hr) Taxis can be hired for sightseeing from ₹999.

Around Jaipur

Jaipur's environs have some fascinating historical sites and interesting towns and villages that make great day trips. A comprehensive network of local buses and the ease of finding a taxi or autorickshaw make getting to these regions simple (if not always comfortable). It's also possible to join a (rather rushed) tour run by the RTDC that includes a commentary on the various places visited.

Amber

The magnificent, formidable, honey-hued fort of Amber (pronounced 'amer'), an ethereal example of Rajput architecture, rises from a rocky mountainside about 11km northeast of Jaipur, and is the city's must-see sight.

Amber was the former capital of Jaipur state. It was built by the Kachhwaha Rajputs, who hailed from Gwalior, in present-day Madhya Pradesh, where they reigned for over 800 years. The construction of the fort, which was begun in 1592 by Maharaja Man Singh, the Rajput commander of Akbar's army, was financed with war booty. It was later extended and completed by the Jai Singhs before they moved to Jaipur on the plains below.

The town of Amber, below the fort, is also worth visiting, especially the Anokhi Museum of Hand Printing. From the museum you can walk around the ancient town to the restored Panna Meena Baori (step-well) and Jagat Siromani Temple (known locally as the Meera Temple).

◉ Sights

★ Amber Fort   FORT

(Indian/foreigner ₹100/500, night entry ₹100, guide ₹200, audio guide ₹200-250; ⏰8am-6pm, night entry 7-9pm) This magnificent fort comprises an extensive palace complex, built from pale yellow and pink sandstone, and white marble, and is divided into four main sections, each with its own courtyard. It is possible to visit the fortress on elephant-back, but animal welfare groups have criticised the keeping of elephants at Amber because of reports of abuse, and because carrying passengers can cause lasting injuries to the animals.

As an alternative, you can trudge up to the fort from the road in about 10 minutes, or take a 4WD to the top and back for ₹450 (good for up to five passengers), including a one-hour wait time. For night entry, admission for foreigners drops to the Indian price.

However you arrive, you will enter Amber Fort through the Suraj Pol (Sun Gate), which leads to the Jaleb Chowk (Main Courtyard), where returning armies would display their war booty to the populace – women could view this area from the veiled windows of the palace. The ticket office is directly across the courtyard from the Suraj Pol. If you arrive by car you will enter through the Chand Pol (Moon Gate) on the opposite side of Jaleb Chowk. Hiring a guide or grabbing an audio guide is highly recommended, as there are very few signs and many blind alleys.

From Jaleb Chowk, an imposing stairway leads up to the main palace, but first it's worth taking the steps just to the right, which lead to the small Siladevi Temple, with its gorgeous silver doors featuring repoussé (raised relief) work.

Heading back to the main stairway will take you up to the second courtyard and the Diwan-i-Am (Hall of Public Audience), which has a double row of columns, each

WORTH A TRIP

ABHANERI

The tiny village of Abhaneri, about 95km east of Jaipur, is home to one of Rajasthan's most unusual and spectacular sights. With around 11 visible levels (depending on groundwater level) of zigzagging steps, the 10th-century Chand Baori (⊙ dawn-dusk) FREE is an engineering and geometric wonder. Flanking this cavernous step-well is a small crumbling palace, where royals used to picnic and bathe in private rooms (water was brought up by ox-power).

A three-day festival held in September features local folk musicians, street performances and arts and crafts. The venue is, of course, the magnificent step-well. Abhaneri village is about 10km north off National Hwy 21, the main Agra–Jaipur highway. From Jaipur catch a bus to Sikandra (₹78, 1½ hours), from where you can hop in a crowded share taxi (₹10) for the 5km trip to Gular. From Gular catch a share taxi or minibus to Abhaneri (another 5km and ₹10). For those with their own transport, Abhaneri and its step-well is a worthwhile stop between Jaipur and Agra/Bharatpur.

topped by a capital in the shape of an elephant, and latticed galleries above.

The maharaja's apartments are located around the third courtyard – you enter through the fabulous Ganesh Pol, decorated with beautiful frescoed arches. The Jai Mandir (Hall of Victory) is noted for its inlaid panels and multimirrored ceiling. Carved marble relief panels around the hall are fascinatingly delicate and quirky, depicting cartoon-like insects and sinuous flowers. Opposite the Jai Mandir is the Sukh Niwas (Hall of Pleasure), with an ivory-inlaid sandalwood door and a channel that once carried cooling water right through the room. From the Jai Mandir you can enjoy fine views from the palace ramparts over picturesque Maota Lake below.

The zenana (secluded women's quarters) surrounds the fourth courtyard. The rooms were designed so that the maharaja could embark on his nocturnal visits to his wives' and concubines' respective chambers without the others knowing, as the chambers are independent but open onto a common corridor.

The Amber sound-and-light show (☑ 0141-2530844; Kesar Kiyari complex; Indian/foreigner ₹100/200; ⊙ English 7.30pm, Hindi 8.30pm) takes place below the fort in the complex near Maota Lake.

Jaigarh
FORT

(Indian/foreigner ₹50/100, car ₹50, Hindi/English guide ₹200/300; ⊙ 9am-5pm) A scrubby green hill rises above Amber and is topped by the imposing Jaigarh, built in 1726 by Jai Singh. The stern fort, punctuated by whimsical-hatted lookout towers, was never captured and has survived intact through the centuries. It's an uphill walk (about 1km) from Amber and offers great views from the Diwa Burj watchtower. The fort has reservoirs, residential areas, a puppet theatre and the world's largest wheeled cannon, Jaya Vana.

During the Mughal empire, Jaipur produced many weapons for the Mughal and Rajput rulers. The cannon, a most spectacular example, was made in the fort foundry, which was constructed in Mughal times. The huge weapon dates from 1720, has a barrel around 6m long, is made from a mix of eight different metals and weighs 50 tonnes. To fire it requires 100kg of gunpowder, and it has a range of 30km. It's debatable how many times this great device was used.

A sophisticated network of drainage channels feeds three large tanks that used to provide water for all the soldiers, residents and livestock living in the fort. The largest tank has a capacity for 22.8 million litres of water. The fort served as the treasury of the Kachhwahas, and for a long time people were convinced that at least part of the royal treasure was still secreted in this large water tank. The Indian government even searched it to check, but found nothing.

Within the fort is an armoury and museum, with the essential deadly weapons collection and some royal knick-knacks, including interesting photographs, maps of Jaigarh, spittoons, and circular 18th-century playing cards. The structure also contains various open halls, including the Shubhat Niwas (Meeting Hall of Warriors), which has some weather-beaten sedan chairs and drums lying about.

Admission is free with a valid ticket from the Jaipur City Palace (p42) that is less than two days old.

Anokhi Museum of Hand Printing   MUSEUM

(☑ 0141-2530226; Anokhi Haveli, Kheri Gate; adult/child ₹80/25; ⊙ 10.30am-4.30pm Tue-Sat, from 11am Sun, closed May–mid-Jul) This interesting museum in a restored *haveli* (traditional, ornately decorated residence) documents the art of hand-block printing, from old traditions to contemporary design. You can watch masters carve unbelievably intricate wooden printing blocks and even have a go at printing your own scarf or T-shirt. There's a cafe and gift shop, too.

🛏 Sleeping

★ Mosaics Guesthouse   GUESTHOUSE $$

(☑ 0141-2530031,   9950457218;   www.mosaics guesthouse.com; Siyaram Ki Doongri; s/d incl breakfast ₹3400/4000; ❄ 🛜) Get away from it all at this gorgeous arty place (the French owner is a mosaic artist and will show off his workshop) with four lovely rooms, courtyard garden, and a rooftop terrace with beautiful fort views. Set-price Franco-Indian meals cost ₹800/1000 for veg/nonveg. It's about 1km past the fort near Kunda Village – head for Siyaram Ki Doongri, where you'll find signs. There are discounts in summer.

❶ Getting There & Away

Frequent buses to Amber depart from near the Hawa Mahal in Jaipur (non-AC/AC ₹14/25, every 15 minutes), which will drop you opposite where you start your climb up to the entrance of Amber Fort.

Elephant rides and 4WDs start 100m further down the hill from the bus drop-off, but many visitors avoid the elephant rides because of the potential harm that this can cause to elephants.

An autorickshaw/taxi will cost at least ₹400/700 for the return trip from Jaipur. The Vintage Jeep Tour (p49) and RTDC city tours (p50) include Amber Fort.

Bharatpur

☑ 05644 / POP 254,860

Bharatpur is famous for its wonderful Unesco-listed Keoladeo National Park, a wetland and significant bird sanctuary. Apart from the park, Bharatpur also has a few historic vestiges and a good museum worth visiting, though it wouldn't be worth making the journey here for these sights alone. The old town is busy, noisy and not

particularly visitor-friendly. Bharatpur hosts the boisterous and colourful Brij Festival just prior to Holi celebrations.

◉ Sights

Lohagarh   FORT

FREE The still-inhabited, 18th-century Lohagarh, or Iron Fort, was so named because of its sturdy defences. Despite being somewhat forlorn and derelict, it is still impressive, and sits at the centre of town, surrounded by a moat. There's a northern entrance, at Austdhatu (Eight-Metal) Gate – apparently the spikes on the gate are made of eight different metals – and a southern entrance, at Lohiya Gate.

Maharaja Suraj Mahl, constructor of the fort and founder of Bharatpur, built two towers, the Jawahar Burj and the Fateh Burj, within the ramparts to commemorate his victories over the Mughals and the British. The fort also contains three old palaces within its precincts, one of which contains a museum.

★ Museum   MUSEUM

(Lohargarh; Indian/foreigner ₹20/100; ⊙ noon-8pm Tue-Sun) One of the Lohagarh palaces, centred on a tranquil courtyard, houses this museum, which has royal artefacts, including weaponry, miniature paintings, metalwork and pottery. There are two sculpture galleries flanking the impressive Durbar Hall, which includes some beautiful 7th- to 10th-century pieces. Don't miss the palace's original *hammam* (Turkish bath), which retains some fine carvings and frescoes.

◉ Keoladeo National Park

This tremendous bird sanctuary and national park (Indian/foreigner ₹75/500, video ₹600/900, guide per hr ₹250, bike/mountain-bike/binoculars rental per day ₹50/60/100, bicycle rickshaw per hr ₹150; ⊙ 6am-6pm Apr-Sep, 6.30am-5.30pm Oct-Mar) has long been recognised as one of the world's most important bird breeding and feeding grounds. In a good monsoon season over one-third of the park can be submerged, hosting more than 360 species within its 29 sq km. The marshland patchwork is a wintering area for aquatic birds, including visitors from Afghanistan, Turkmenistan, China and Siberia. The park is also home to deer, nilgai (antelope) and boar, which can be readily spotted.

Keoladeo originated as a royal hunting reserve in the 1850s. It continued to supply the tables of the maharajas with fresh game until as late as 1965. In 1982 Keoladeo was declared a national park and it was listed as a World Heritage Site in 1985.

By far the best time to visit this park is October to February, when you should see many migratory birds. At other times it can be dry and relatively bird-free.

Visiting the Park

The best times to visit the park are in the morning and evening, but note that park admission entitles you to only one entrance per day. One narrow road (no motorised vehicles are permitted past checkpoint 2) runs through the park, and a number of tracks and pathways fan out from it and thread their way between the shallow wetlands.

Generally speaking, the further away from the main gate you go, the more interesting the scenery, and the more varied the wildlife becomes.

Only the government-authorised cycle-rickshaws (recognisable by their yellow licence plate) are allowed beyond checkpoint 2, and they can only travel along the park's larger tracks. You don't pay an admission fee for the drivers, but they charge ₹150 per hour; some are very knowledgeable.

An excellent way to see the park is by hiring a bicycle at the park entrance. Having a bike is a wonderfully quiet way to travel, and allows you to avoid bottlenecks and take in the serenity on your own. However, we recommend that lone female travellers who wish to cycle do so with a guide (who

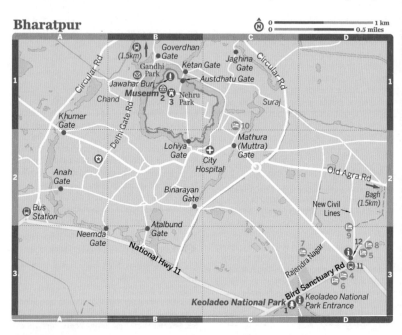

Bharatpur

Bharatpur

will cycle alongside you), as we've had more than one report of lone women being harassed by young men inside the park in recent years.

You should get a small map with your entrance ticket, though the park isn't big, so it's difficult to get lost.

🛏 Sleeping & Eating

There are numerous options a short walk northeast of the park entrance. These traveller-friendly hotels can usually organise guides and binocular hire.

The hotels that cater for visitors to the park all have restaurants that are of a good standard and which cater to a broad range of tastes.

Falcon Guest House　　　GUESTHOUSE **$**
(📞8619965315, 05644-223815; falconguesthouse@hotmail.com; Gori Shankur Colony; s/d from ₹600/800, r with AC ₹1200-2000; 🌐@🗑) The Falcon may well be the pick of a bunch of hotels all in a row and all owned by the same extended family. It's a well-kept, snug place to stay, run by the affable Mrs Rajni Singh. There is a range of comfortable, good-sized rooms at different prices, including a family room. The best rooms have balconies.

Husband Tej Singh is an ornithologist and is happy to answer any bird-related questions. Flavoursome home-cooked food is served in the garden restaurant.

Kiran Guest House　　　GUESTHOUSE **$**
(📞9828269930, 9460912641; www.kiranguesthouse.com; 364 Rajendra Nagar; r ₹400-800, with AC ₹1100; 🌐🗑) Managed by eager-to-please brothers, this guesthouse delivers great value, with seven simple, clean and spacious rooms and a pleasant rooftop where you can eat tasty home cooking. It's on a quiet road not far from Keoladeo park. Nature guiding and free pickup from the Bharatpur train and bus stations are offered.

New Spoonbill Guesthouse　　　HOTEL **$**
(📞05644-223571, 7597412553; www.hotelspoonbill.com; Gori Shankur Colony; s/d ₹700/800, with AC ₹1000/1100; 🌐@🗑) Owned and run by the same family as the original Spoonbill Hotel down the road, this place has simple but smart rooms, each with a small terrace. The larger rooms are great, with lots of windows. The dining room looks onto the garden, and delicious home-cooked meals, plus milk from the home cow, are available.

Royal Guest House　　　HOTEL **$**
(📞9414315457; www.royalguesthousebharatpur.com; B-15 New Civil Lines, near Saras Circle; r ₹600-800, with AC ₹1000; 🌐@🗑) Rooms at the Royal are all clean and fresh, and the rooftop restaurant is cosy, making the whole place feel more like a homestay than a guesthouse. The ultrakeen management, who live on the premises, do money changing and run a sister operation, Royal Farm, 3.5km from here.

Shagun Guest House　　　GUESTHOUSE **$**
(📞9828687488; rajeevshagun@hotmail.com; d ₹150, without bathroom ₹120; 🗑) This unusual tree-shaded courtyard guesthouse, in a quiet corner of the old town, is extremely basic, and has only four rooms, but it comes with bags of character. It's run by the affable Rajeev, a keen environmental campaigner who is knowledgeable about the bird sanctuary and the old fort.

⭐**Hotel Sunbird**　　　HOTEL **$$**
(📞05644-225701, 8764943438; www.hotelsunbird.com; Bird Sanctuary Rd; s/d incl breakfast from ₹1950/2260; 🌐🗑) This popular, well-run place close to the Keoladeo park entrance may look modest from the road, but out back there's a lovely garden (with bar) and spacious rooms with balconies. Rooms are clean and comfortable and the restaurant dishes up a good range of tasty veg and non-veg dishes. Packed lunches and guided tours for the park are available.

⭐**Birder's Inn**　　　HOTEL **$$**
(📞7297991613, 05644-227346; www.birdersinn.com; Bird Sanctuary Rd; s/d incl breakfast from ₹3500/3900; 🌐@🗑🍴) The Birder's Inn is a popular, long-standing base for exploring Keoladeo National Park. There is a multi-cuisine restaurant and a small pool to cool off in. The rooms are airy, spacious and nicely decorated, and are set far back from the road in well-tended gardens. Guides from the hotel are available for Keoladeo.

Royal Farm　　　GUESTHOUSE **$$**
(📞9414315457; www.royalfarmbharatpur.com; Agra Rd; r ₹1400, with AC ₹1600; 🌐🗑) There are just six spacious rooms in this quaint farmhouse set back from the busy Agra Rd. The rooms have marble floors, solar hot water, good mattresses and flatscreen TVs. This farmhouse has an organic farm and a milking cow and a buffalo to help supply the ingredients for the vegetarian kitchen.

RAJASTHAN BHARATPUR

The Bagh   HOTEL $$$

(☑9982935555, 05644-225415; www.thebagh. com; Old Agra Rd; r/ste from ₹6300/8300; ❋@❀☀) A picturesque hotel 2km from town, the Bagh has 38 elegant rooms spread out in separate pavilions and nestled in a former royal orchard. All rooms boast cool marble floors, antique furnishings and wonderful bathrooms. Decor is traditional, but the cool, clean lines have a contemporary feel. The mature 4-hectare garden here has masses of birds if you want to keep twitching.

❶ Information

Main Post Office (☉10am-1pm & 2-5pm Mon-Sat) Near Gandhi Park.

Tourist Office (☑05644-222542; Saras Circle; ☉9.30am-6pm) On the crossroads about 700m from the national park entrance; has a free map of Bharatpur and Keoladeo National Park.

❶ Getting There & Away

BUS

Buses running between Agra and Jaipur will drop you at Saras Circle by the tourist office or outside the Keoladeo park entrance if you ask.

Services from Bharatpur bus station and Saras Circle include the following:

Agra with/without AC ₹164/72, 1½ hours, half-hourly around the clock from Saras Circle

Alwar ₹136, four hours, hourly until 5.30pm from main bus station

Deeg ₹39, one hour, hourly until 8pm from main bus station

Delhi ₹201, five hours, four buses daily, 4.30am, 6.11am, 6.30am, 9.30am from main bus station

Fatehpur Sikri ₹29, 30 minutes, half-hourly around the clock from Saras Circle

Jaipur ₹195, 4½ hours, half-hourly around the clock from main bus station

TRAIN

The train station is about 4km from Keoladeo and the main hotel area; a rickshaw should cost around ₹70. There is a **railway booking office** (Saras Circle; ☉8am-2pm Mon-Sat) in the same building as the tourist office.

Agra 2nd-class seat/sleeper/3AC ₹60/145/500, 1½ to two hours, nine daily between 4.45am and 8.10pm

Delhi 2nd-class seat/sleeper/3AC ₹110/170/540, three to four hours, 12 trains daily, plus three other services on selected days

Jaipur 2nd-class seat/sleeper/3AC ₹110/150/510, three to four hours, nine daily between 2am and 10pm

Ranthambhore NP (Sawai Madhopur) 2nd-class seat/sleeper/3AC ₹135/170/540, two to three hours, 10 daily between 1am and 9.40pm. These trains all continue to Kota (four hours) from where you can catch buses to Bundi.

❶ Getting Around

A cycle- or autorickshaw from the bus station to the main hotel area should cost around ₹40 (add an extra ₹40 from the train station).

Alwar

☑0144 / POP 341,430

Alwar is perhaps the oldest of the Rajasthani kingdoms, forming part of the Matsya territories of Viratnagar in 1500 BC. It became known again in the 18th century under Pratap Singh, who pushed back the rulers of Jaipur to the south and the Jats of Bharatpur to the east, and who successfully resisted the Marathas. It was one of the first Rajput states to ally itself with the fledgling British empire, although British interference in Alwar's internal affairs meant this partnership was not always amicable.

Alwar is the nearest town to Sariska Tiger Reserve & National Park and has a fascinating museum and interesting fort, but it sees relatively few tourists.

MAJOR TRAINS FROM BHARATPUR

DESTINATION	TRAIN	DEPARTURE	ARRIVAL	FARE (₹)
Agra (Cantonment)	19666 Udz–Kurj Exp	9.46am	10.55am	145/500 (A)
Delhi (Hazrat Nizamuddin)	12059 Kota–Jan Shatabdi	9.25am	12.30pm	110/410 (B)
Jaipur	19665 Kurj–Udaipur Exp	6.55pm	10.50pm	150/510 (A)
Sawai Madhopur	12904 Golden Temple Mail	10.30am	12.55pm	170/540 (C)

Fares: (A) sleeper/3AC, (B) 2nd-class/AC chair, (C) 2nd class/3AC

◉ Sights

City Palace
HISTORIC BUILDING

(Vinay Vilas Mahal) Under the gaze of Bala Quila fort sprawls the colourful and convoluted City Palace complex, with massive gates and a tank reflecting a symmetrical series of ghats and pavilions. Today most of the complex is occupied by government offices, overflowing with piles of dusty papers and soiled by pigeons and splatters of *paan* (a mixture of betel nut and leaves for chewing).

Hidden within the City Palace is the excellent Alwar Museum.

★ Alwar Museum
MUSEUM

(Government Museum; Indian/foreigner ₹50/100; ⊘ 9.45am-5.15pm Tue-Sun) Hidden within the City Palace is the excellent Alwar Museum. Its eclectic exhibits evoke the extravagance of the lifestyle of the maharajas: stunning weapons, stuffed Scottish pheasants, royal ivory slippers, miniature paintings, royal vestments, a solid silver table, and stone sculptures, such as an 11th-century carving of Vishnu.

Somewhat difficult to find in the Kafkaesque tangle of government offices, it's on the top floor of the palace, up a ramp from the main courtyard. There should be plenty of people around to point you in the right direction and from there you can follow the signs.

Cenotaph of Maharaja Bakhtawar Singh
HISTORIC BUILDING

(Chhatri of Moosi Rani; City Palace) This double-storey edifice, resting on a platform of sandstone, was built in 1815 by Maharaja Vinay Singh, in memory of his father. To gain access to the cenotaph, take the steps to the far left when facing the palace. The cenotaph is also known as the Chhatri of Moosi Rani, after one of the mistresses of Bakhtawar Singh who performed self-immolation on his funeral pyre – after this act she was promoted to wifely status.

Bala Quila
FORT

(Indian/foreigner ₹10/200, car ₹50, safari gypsy ₹1350; ⊘ 6am-6pm) This imposing fort stands 300m above Alwar, its fortifications hugging the steep hills that line the eastern edge of the city. Predating the time of Pratap Singh, it's one of the few forts in Rajasthan built before the rise of the Mughals, who used it as a base for attacking Ranthambhore. Mughal emperors Babur and Akbar have stayed overnight here, and Prince Salim (later Emperor Jehangir) was exiled in Salim Mahal for three years.

Now in ruins, the fort houses a radio transmitter station and parts are off limits. The surrounding hills are under the auspices of Sariska Tiger Reserve & National Park and subsequently reserve entry fees apply (and heavy fines if you aren't out before sunset). You can walk the very steep couple of kilometres up to the fort entrance or take the road. The ticket office is at the bottom of the hill west of the city palace.

🛏 Sleeping & Eating

RTDC Hotel Meenal
HOTEL $

(☏ 0144-2347352; meenal@rtdc.in; Topsingh Circle; s/d ₹900/1100, with AC ₹1100/1300; ※) A respectable option with tidy yet bland and tired rooms typical of the chain. It's located about 1km south of town on the way to Sariska, so it's quiet and leafy, though a long way from the action.

★ Hotel Aravali
HOTEL $$

(☏ 0144-2332883; reservations.alwar@gmail.com; Nehru Rd; r incl breakfast from ₹2950, ste ₹7080; ※ ⊚ ◈) One of the town's best choices, this conveniently located hotel has been partly refurbished. Cheaper rooms are a little worn and weary but rooms are large and well furnished and have big bathrooms. The multi-cuisine Bridge Restaurant is one of the best in town, and there's a bar. Turn left out of the train station and it's about 300m down the road.

Prem Pavitra Bhojnalaya
INDIAN $

(near Hope Circle; mains ₹80-120; ⊘ 10.30am-4pm & 6.30-10pm; ☑) Alwar's renowned restaurant has been going since 1957. In the heart of the old town, it serves fresh, tasty pure-veg food – try the delicious dhal fry with Desai ghee and *palak paneer* (unfermented cheese chunks in a pureed spinach gravy). The servings are big; half-serves are available. Finish off with its famous 'special *kheer*' (creamy rice pudding).

Bridge Restaurant
MULTICUISINE $$

(☏ 0144-23322316; Hotel Aravali, Nehru Rd; mains ₹250-500; ⊘ 7am-11pm; ※) The plush restaurant in the Hotel Aravali is possibly the best in town, especially for tandoor and nonveg. The curries are generous and delicious plus there is a small range of Chinese and Continental dishes, including fish and chips, Greek salad and stir-fried rice.

Drinking & Nightlife

Gigil Cafe CAFE

(Moti Dungri Rd; ⊙ 7am-11pm; 🛜) Breezy Gigil Cafe has introduced espresso coffee to Alwar. There's also bakery items and a multi-cuisine veg restaurant kicks of at 10am. The baristas are not yet proficient, but they are keen and by the time you read this the coffees should be great. You can sit under a shady pergola streetside or inside to cool off under the AC.

 Information

State Bank of India (SBI; Company Bagh Rd; ⊙ 9.30am-4pm Mon-Fri, to 12.30pm Sat) Changes major currencies and has an ATM. Near the bus station.

Tourist Office (📞 0144-2347348; Nehru Rd; ⊙ 9.30am-6pm Mon-Fri) Can only offer a map of Alwar (if it is open when it should be). Near the train station.

🛈 Getting There & Around

A cycle-rickshaw between the bus and train stations costs around ₹40. Look out for the shared taxis (₹10 to ₹15) that ply fixed routes around town. They come in the form of white minivans and have the word 'Vahini' printed on their side doors. One handy route goes past Hotel Aravali, the tourist office and the train station before continuing on to the bus station and terminating a short walk from the City Palace complex.

A return taxi to Sariska Tiger Reserve & National Park will cost you around ₹1500.

BUS

The Alwar **bus station** (Old Bus Stand Rd) is near Manu Marg. Services include the following:

Bharatpur ₹128, four hours, hourly from 7am to 8.30pm

WORTH A TRIP

SURAJ MAHL'S PALACE

At the centre of Deeg – a small, rarely visited, dusty tumult of a town about 35km north of Bharatpur – stands the incongruously glorious **Suraj Mahl's Palace** (Indian/foreigner ₹25/300; ⊙ 9am-5pm Sat-Thu), edged by stately formal gardens. It's one of India's most beautiful and carefully proportioned palace complexes. Pick up a map and brochure at the entrance; photography is not permitted in some of the bhavans (buildings).

Built in a mixture of Rajput and Mughal architectural styles, the 18th-century **Gopal Bhavan** is fronted by imposing arches to take full advantage of the early-morning light. Downstairs is a lower storey that becomes submerged during the monsoon as the water level of the adjacent tank, **Gopal Sagar**, rises. It was used by the maharajas until the early 1950s, and contains many original furnishings, including faded sofas, huge punkas (cloth fans) that are more than 200 years old, chaise longues, a stuffed tiger, elephant-foot stands, and fine porcelain from China and France.

In an upstairs room at the rear of the palace is an Indian-style marble dining table – a stretched, oval-shaped affair raised just 20cm off the ground. Guests sat around the edge, and the centre was the serving area. In the maharaja's bedroom is an enormous 3.6m by 2.4m wooden bed with silver legs.

Two large tanks lie alongside the palace, the aforementioned Gopal Sagar to the east and **Rup Sagar** to the west. The well-maintained gardens and flowerbeds, watered by the tanks, continue the extravagant theme with more than 2000 fountains. Many of these fountains are in working order and coloured waters pour forth during the monsoon festival in August.

The **Keshav Bhavan** (Summer or Monsoon Pavilion) is a single-storey edifice with five arches along each side. Tiny jets spray water from the archways and metal balls rumble around in a water channel imitating monsoon thunder. Deeg's massive walls (which are up to 28m high) and 12 vast bastions, some with their cannons still in place, are also worth exploring. You can walk up to the top of the walls from the palace.

Other bhavans (in various states of renovation) include the marble **Suraj Bhavan**, reputedly taken from Delhi and reassembled here, the **Kishan Bhavan** and, along the northern side of the palace grounds, the **Nand Bhavan**.

Deeg is an easy day trip (and there's nowhere good to stay) from Bharatpur or Alwar by car. All the roads to Deeg are rough and the buses crowded. Frequent buses run to and from Alwar (₹60, 2½ hours) and Bharatpur (₹28, one hour).

Deeg ₹87, 2½ hours, eight services from 5am to 8.30pm

Delhi ₹177, four hours, every 20 minutes from 5am to 9pm

Jaipur ₹160, four hours, half-hourly from 5am to 5.10pm

Sariska ₹40, one hour, several daily until 10.30pm.

TRAIN

The **train station** (Nehru Rd) is fairly central. Around a dozen daily trains leave for Delhi (sleeper/3AC ₹140/500, three to four hours) throughout the day.

It's also three to four hours to Jaipur (sleeper/3AC ₹170/540) from here. Sixteen trains depart daily and prices are almost identical to those for Delhi.

Sariska Tiger Reserve & National Park

☑ 0144

Enclosed within the dramatic, shadowy folds of the Aravalli Hills, the **Sariska Tiger Reserve & National Park** (☑ 0144-2841333; www.rajasthanwildlife.in; Indian/foreigner ₹105/570, safari vehicle ₹1250, temple-bound vehicle ₹250; ☉ safaris 7-10.30am & 2-5.30pm Nov-Feb, 6.30-10am & 2.30-6pm Mar-Jun & Oct) is a tangle of remnant semideciduous jungle and craggy canyons sheltering streams and lush greenery. It covers 866 sq km (including a core area of 498 sq km), and is home to peacocks, monkeys, majestic sambars, nilgai, chital, wild boars and jackals.

In 2018 there were 17 tigers roaming the reserve, including five newborn cubs. Poaching, however, by local villagers is an ongoing problem. Although you may not spot a tiger in Sariska, it is still a fascinating wildlife-filled sanctuary. The best time to see wildlife is November to March, and you'll see most activity in the evening. The park is closed to safaris from 1 July to 30 September, though still open for temple pilgrimages.

⊙ Sights

Besides wildlife, Sariska has some fantastic sights within the reserve and around its periphery, which are well worth seeking out. If you take a longer tour, you can ask to visit one or more of these. Some are also accessible by public bus.

Hanuman Temple   HINDU TEMPLE
(☉ Tue & Sat 6am-6pm) This small Hanuman temple, deep in the park, has a recumbent idol, adapted from a rock, which is painted orange and shaded by silver parasols. People give offerings of incense and receive tiny parcels of holy ash. From the temple there is a pleasant walk, for more than 1km, to Pandu pol, a gaping natural arch.

Kankwari Fort   FORT
Deep inside the sanctuary, this imposing small jungle fort, 22km from Sariska, offers amazing views over the plains of the national park, dotted with red mud-brick villages. A four- to five-hour 4WD safari (one to five passengers plus mandatory guide) to Kankwari Fort from the Forest Reception Office near the reserve entrance costs ₹5100 with two foreign passengers.

This fort is the inaccessible place that Aurangzeb chose to imprison his brother, Dara Shikoh, Shah Jahan's chosen heir to the Mughal throne, for several years before he was beheaded.

Bhangarh   HISTORIC SITE
Around 55km south from Sariska, beyond the inner park sanctuary and out in open countryside, is this deserted, well-preserved and notoriously haunted city. Founded in 1631 by Madho Singh, it had 10,000 dwellings, but was suddenly and mysteriously deserted about 300 years ago. It's best reached by car (parking ₹50) or taxi but can be reached by a twice-daily bus (₹39) that runs through the sanctuary to nearby Golaka village. Check what time the bus returns, otherwise you risk getting stranded.

🏃 Activities

Private cars, including taxis, are limited to sealed roads heading to the Hanuman temple and are allowed only on Tuesday and Saturday. The best way to visit the park is by gypsy (open-topped, six-passenger 4WD), which can explore off the main tracks. Gypsy safaris start at the park entrance, and vehicle with driver is ₹3350 (hire and entry) for a three-hour safari; the vehicles can take up to five people (including guide). Guides are mandatory (₹400 for three hours) and you also have to factor in personal entry fees and GST.

Bookings can be made at the **Forest Reception Office** (Safari Booking Office; ☑ 0144-2841333; www.rajasthanwildlife.in; Jaipur Rd; ☉ 6.55-7.30am & 1-3pm Nov-Jan, 6.25-7am & 12.30-2.30pm Mar-Jun & Oct), where buses will drop you.

SARISKA'S TIGER TALE

Sariska Tiger Reserve took centre stage in one of India's most publicised wildlife dramas. In 2005 an Indian journalist broke the news that the tiger population here had been eliminated in 2004, a report that was later confirmed officially after an emergency census was carried out.

An inquiry into the crisis recommended fundamental management changes before tigers be reintroduced to the reserve. Extra funding was proposed to cover relocation of villages within the park as well as increasing the protection force. But action on the recommendations has been slow and incomplete despite extensive media coverage and a high level of concern in India. At present, there are 29 villages in the core area and another 140 villages in close proximity.

Nevertheless, a pair of tigers from Ranthambhore National Park were moved by helicopter to Sariska in 2008. By 2010, five tigers had been transferred. However, in November 2010 the male of the original pair was found dead, having been poisoned by local villagers, who are not supportive of the reintroduction. The underlying problem: the inevitable battle between India's poorest and ever-expanding village populace with the rare and phenomenally valuable wildlife on their doorstep. Plans to relocate and reimburse villagers inside the park have largely failed to come to fruition, and illegal marble mining and clashes between cattle farmers and park staff continue to be a problem.

In early 2012 the first cubs were sighted. At the time of writing Sariska's tiger population was thought to be 17.

Only time will tell if the reintroduction of tigers into Sariska is successful – inbreeding in the small population is an understandably high concern. Poachers are another. Despite much vaunted successes for Project Tiger (http://projecttiger.nic.in) at a national level, Sariska remains a sad indictment of tiger conservation in India, from the top government officials down to the underpaid forest guards.

Sleeping & Eating

RTDC Hotel Tiger Den HOTEL $$
(0144-2841342; tigerden@rtdc.in; r incl 2 meals ₹2724, with AC from ₹3396; ❄☎) Hotel Tiger Den isn't fancy – a cement block fronted by a lawn and backed by a rambling garden. Its best feature is that it is very close to the reserve entrance. On the plus side the management is friendly, there is a bar, and the rooms have balconies with a pleasant outlook. Bring a mosquito net or repellent.

Hotel Sariska Palace HERITAGE HOTEL $$$
(7340186019; www.thesariskapalace.in; r ₹10,750, ste from ₹13,500; ❄☎☀) Near the reserve entrance is this imposing former hunting lodge of the maharajas of Alwar. There's a driveway leading from opposite the Forest Reception Office. Rooms have soaring ceilings and soft mattresses, and those in the annex by the swimming pool have good views. The Fusion Restaurant here serves expensive Indian and Continental dishes.

Sariska Tiger Heaven HOTEL $$$
(9251016312; www.sariskatigerheaven.com; Thanagazi; r incl all meals from ₹7500; ❄☀) This isolated place about 3km west of the bus stop at Thanagazi village will pick you up from the village's bus stop (₹200). Rooms are set in stone-and-tile cottages and have big beds and windowed alcoves. It's a tranquil, if overpriced, place to stay. Staff can arrange 4WDs and safaris and guides to the reserve.

Information

Interpretation Centre (⊙8am-7pm) Near the reserve's booking office. Gives an honest and sobering appraisal of Sariska's past, present and ongoing threats. It's worth a look, and there's a small souvenir shop attached.

Getting There & Away

Sariska is 35km from Alwar, a convenient town from which to approach the reserve. There are crowded buses from Alwar (₹35, one to 1½ hours, hourly) and on to Jaipur (₹129, four hours). Buses stop in front of the Forest Reception Office.

A return taxi from Alwar to Sariska Tiger Reserve & National Park will cost you around ₹1500.

Patan

☑ 01574

The small village of Patan is a wonderful place to stay with a fascinating story to tell. Patan's place in history was sealed when one of Rajasthan's epic battles took place here in 1790. On one side were the Rajputs, loosely affiliated with the Mughal armies, and on the other side were the well-trained Maratha armies, who enjoyed the services of French mercenary General Benoît de Boigne. The French general won the day and the Rajputs lost more than men and pride; Patan itself was looted for three days, and to this day the old town is still largely abandoned within its crumbling walls.

Patan remains the homeland of the Tanwar Rajputs, and the palace, which was built after the battle, has been beautifully restored into peaceful and luxurious accommodation by the descendants of the royal family.

Patan Mahal　　　　　HERITAGE HOTEL **$$$**
(☑ 01574-282311, Jaipur 0141-2200033; www.patanmahal.com; s/d incl breakfast from ₹7320/7550; ❄@🛜🛏) The suite-sized rooms at Patan Mahal have all been painstakingly restored and furnished in plush and comfortable style. This is a relaxing retreat where you won't be distracted by TV. You can laze instead in a luxurious marble pool or find a sunny nook to read a book. The extensive grounds also include organic gardens that supply the kitchen and excellent restaurant.

❶ Getting There & Away

Patan is a 23km detour off the Delhi–Jaipur National Hwy 48 at Kotputli, which is 110km from Jaipur and 160km from Delhi. A seat on the bus from Kotputli to Patan costs ₹30. Contact Patan Mahal to arrange a taxi from Jaipur (₹4000). A taxi from Delhi will cost ₹6000.

Ajmer

☑ 0145 / POP 542,320

Ajmer is a bustling, chaotic city, 130km southwest of Jaipur and just 13km from the Hindu pilgrimage town of Pushkar. It surrounds the expansive lake of Ana Sagar, and is itself ringed by the rugged Aravalli Hills. Ajmer is Rajasthan's most important site in terms of Islamic history and heritage. It contains one of India's most important Muslim pilgrimage centres, the shrine of Khwaja Muin-ud-din Chishti, who founded the Chishtiya order, the prime Sufi order

in India. As well as some superb examples of early Muslim architecture, Ajmer is also a significant centre for the Jain religion, possessing an amazing golden Jain temple. However, with Ajmer's combination of high-voltage crowds and traffic, especially during Ramadan and the anniversary of the saint's death, most travellers choose to use Ajmer as a stepping stone to laid-back Pushkar.

◉ Sights

Dargah of Khwaja
Muin-ud-din Chishti　　　ISLAMIC SHRINE
(www.dargahajmer.com; ⏰4am-9pm) This is the tomb of Sufi saint Khwaja Muin-ud-din Chishti, who came to Ajmer from Persia in 1192 and died here in 1236. The tomb gained its significance during the time of the Mughals – many emperors added to the buildings here. Construction of the shrine was completed by Humayun, and the gate was added by the Nizam of Hyderabad. Mughal emperor Akbar used to make the pilgrimage to this dargah from Agra every year.

You have to cover your head in certain parts of the shrine, so remember to take a scarf or cap – there are plenty for sale at the colourful bazaar leading to the dargah, along with floral offerings and delicious toffees.

The main entrance is through Nizam Gate (1915). Inside, the green and white mosque, Akbari Masjid, was constructed in 1571 and is now an Arabic and Persian school for religious education. The next gate is called the Shahjahani Gate, as it was erected by Shah Jahan, although it is also known as 'Nakkarkhana', because of the two large *nakkharas* (drums) fixed above it.

A third gate, Buland Darwaza (16th century), leads into the dargah courtyard. Flanking the entrance of the courtyard are the *degs* (large iron cauldrons), one donated by Akbar in 1567, the other by Jehangir in 1631, for offerings for the poor.

Inside this courtyard, the saint's domed tomb is surrounded by a silver platform. Pilgrims believe that the saint's spirit will intercede on their behalf in matters of illness, business or personal problems, so the notes and holy string attached to the railings around are thanks or requests.

Pilgrims and Sufis come from all over the world on the anniversary of the saint's death, the Urs, in the seventh month of the

Ajmer

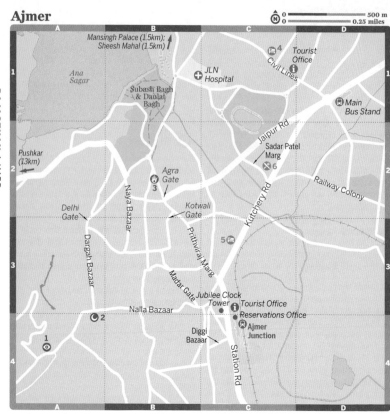

N 0 ___ 500 m
0 ___ 0.25 miles

Ajmer

◎ **Sights**
1 Adhai-din-ka-Jhonpra..........................A4
2 Dargah of Khwaja Muin-ud-din
    Chishti...A4
3 Soniji Ki Nasiyan (Red) Temple..........B2

🛏 **Sleeping**
4 Badnor House.......................................C1
5 Haveli Heritage Inn.............................C3

🍽 **Eating**
6 Mango Curry/Mango Masala C2

Islamic lunar calendar. The crowds can be
suffocating.

Bags must be left in the cloakroom (₹10
each, with camera ₹20) outside the main
entrance.

Soniji Ki Nasiyan (Red) Temple   JAIN TEMPLE
(Golden Temple; Prithviraj Marg; ₹10; ☉8.30am-
5.30pm) This marvellous Jain temple, built

in 1865, is also known as the Golden Temple,
due to its amazing golden diorama in the
double-storey temple hall. The intricate diorama depicts the Jain concept of the ancient
world, with 13 continents and oceans, the
golden city of Ayodhya, flying peacock and
elephant gondolas, and gilded elephants
with many tusks. The hall is also decorated
with gold, silver and precious stones. It's
unlike any other temple in Rajasthan and is
well worth a visit.

Adhai-din-ka-Jhonpra   HISTORIC SITE
(Two-and-a-Half-Day Building; ☉dawn-dusk) Beyond the Dargah of Khwaja Muin-ud-din
Chishti, on the outskirts of town, are the
extraordinary ruins of the Adhai-din-ka-
Jhonpra mosque. According to legend, construction in 1153 took only 2½ days. Others
say it was named after a festival lasting 2½
days. It was originally built as a Sanskrit college, but in 1198 Mohammed of Ghori seized
Ajmer and converted the building into a

mosque by adding a seven-arched wall covered with Islamic calligraphy in front of the pillared hall.

🛏 Sleeping & Eating

Haveli Heritage Inn
HOTEL $$

(☏ 0145-2621607; www.haveliheritageinn.com; Kutchery Rd; r ₹1340-3000; ❋ @ 🛜) Set in a 140-year-old *haveli*, this welcoming city-centre oasis is arguably Ajmer's best mid-range choice. The high-ceilinged rooms are spacious (some are almost suites), simply decorated, air-cooled and set well back from the busy road. There's a pleasant, paved courtyard and the hotel is infused with a family atmosphere, complete with home-cooked meals.

Badnor House
GUESTHOUSE $$

(☏ 0145-2627579; www.badnorhouse.com; Savitri Girls' College Rd, Civil Lines; s/d incl breakfast ₹2600/3000; ❋ 🛜) This guesthouse provides an excellent opportunity to stay with a delightful family and receive down-to-earth hospitality. There are five heritage-style doubles with period furnishings and TVs, which are separated from the family's large bungalow.

Mansingh Palace
HOTEL $$$

(☏ 0145-2425702; www.mansinghhotels.com; Circular Rd, Vaishali Nagar; r from ₹4200, ste ₹7000; ❋ @ 🛜 🛝) This modern and comfortable option, on the shores of Ana Sagar about 3km from the centre, is rather out of the way. However, the attractive and spacious rooms, some with views and balconies, make this one of Ajmer's best choices. The hotel has a shady garden, a bar and a seriously good restaurant, the Sheesh Mahal.

⭐ Sheesh Mahal
MULTICUISINE $$

(☏ 0145-2425702; Circular Rd, Vaishali Nagar; mains ₹180-480; ⊗ noon-3pm & 7-10.30pm) This upmarket restaurant, located in Ajmer's top hotel, the Mansingh Palace, offers excellent Indian, Continental and Chinese dishes, as well as a buffet when the tour groups pass through. The service is slick, the AC and beer are on the chilly side, and the food is very good; it also has a bar.

Mango Curry/ Mango Masala
MULTICUISINE $$

(☏ 0145-2422100; Sadar Patel Marg; mains ₹160-320; ⊗ 9am-11pm; ❋) With dim, bar-like lighting and American diner decor, this is a popular Ajmer hang-out. It's divided in two: Mango Masala is no alcohol and vegetarian, while Mango Curry has plenty of good non-veg options. Pizzas, Chinese, and North and South Indian dishes are available throughout, plus there's cakes and ice cream, and a bakery/deli for takeaways.

ℹ Information

ATMs are easy to come by, especially in the area around the train station.

Tourist office (Ajmer Junction Train Station; ⊗ 9am-5pm)

Tourist office (☏ 0145-2627426; RTDC Hotel Khadim; ⊗ 9am-5pm Mon-Fri)

ℹ Getting There & Away

For those pushing on to Pushkar, haggle hard for a private taxi – ₹350 to ₹400 is a good rate.

BUS

Government-run buses leave from the **main bus stand** (Jaipur Rd) in Ajmer, from where buses to Pushkar (₹20, 30 minutes) also leave throughout the day. In addition to these buses, there are less-frequent 'deluxe' coach services running

MAJOR TRAINS FROM AJMER

DESTINATION	TRAIN	DEPARTURE	ARRIVAL	FARE (₹)
Agra (Agra Fort Station)	12988 Ajmer–SDAH Exp	12.45pm	6.50pm	265/675 (A)
Delhi (New Delhi)	12016 Ajmer Shatabdi	2.05pm	10pm	905/1725 (B)
Jaipur	12991 Udaipur–Jaipur Exp	11.30am	1.30pm	85/325/495 (C)
Jodhpur	15014 Ranighat Express	1.35pm	5.35pm	170/510 (A)
Udaipur	09721 Jaipur–Udaipur SF SPL	8.25am	1.15pm	140/590/995 (C)

Fares: (A) sleeper/3AC, (B) AC chair/1AC, (C) 2nd-class seat/AC chair/3AC to major destinations such as Delhi and Jaipur. There is a 24-hour cloakroom at the bus stand (₹20 per bag per day).

DESTINATION	FARE (₹)	DURATION (HR)
Agra	392	10
Ahmedabad	556	13
Bharatpur	330	7
Bikaner	267	7
Bundi	184	5
Chittorgarh	195, AC 348	5
Delhi	400, AC 1182	8½
Jaipur	148, AC 300	2½
Jaisalmer	464	11
Jodhpur	205, AC 441	6
Udaipur	301, AC 537	9

TRAIN

Ajmer is a busy train junction. To book tickets, go to booth 5 at the train station's **reservations office** (Station Rd; ⊙ 8am-8pm Mon-Sat, to 2pm Sun). Services include the following:

Agra (Agra Fort Station) sleeper/AC chair ₹265/570, 6½ hours, at least seven daily (1.35am, 2.10am, 3.40am, 6am, 12.50pm, 2.55pm and 11.55pm)

Chittorgarh sleeper/3AC ₹180/560, three hours, at least six daily (1.25am, 2.15am, 1pm, 4.10pm, 8.30pm and 9pm)

Delhi (mostly to Old Delhi or New Delhi stations) 2nd-class seat/sleeper ₹175/290, eight hours, at least 11 daily around the clock

Jaipur 2nd-class seat/sleeper/AC chair ₹100/150/325, two hours, at least 24 throughout the day

Jodhpur sleeper/3AC ₹170/510, four to five hours, two direct daily (1.35pm and 2.25pm)

Mt Abu (Abu Road) sleeper/3AC ₹245/550, five hours, 12 daily

Mumbai sleeper/3AC ₹500/1320, around 19 hours, at least three daily (11.10am, 4.40pm and 7.20pm)

Udaipur sleeper ₹235, five hours, four daily (1.25am, 2.15am, 8.25am and 4.10pm)

Pushkar

📞 0145 / POP 21,630

Pushkar has a magnetism all of its own – it's quite unlike anywhere else in Rajasthan. It is world famous for its spectacular Camel Fair, which takes place in the Hindu month of Kartika (October/November). If you are anywhere nearby at the time you would be crazy to miss it.

For the rest of the year Pushkar remains a prominent Hindu pilgrimage town, humming with *puja* (prayers), bells, drums and devotional songs. The town wraps itself around a holy lake featuring 52 bathing ghats and 400 milky-blue temples, including one of the world's few Brahma temples. The main street is one long bazaar, selling anything to tickle a traveller's fancy, from hippy-chic tie-dye to didgeridoos. The result is a muddle of religious and tourist scenes. Yet, despite the commercialism, the town remains enchantingly mystic and relaxed.

Pushkar is only 11km from Ajmer, separated from it by rugged Nag Pahar (Snake Mountain).

⊙ Sights

Fifty-two bathing ghats surround the lake, where pilgrims bathe in the sacred waters. If you wish to join them, do so with respect. Remember, this is a holy place: remove your shoes and don't smoke, kid around or take photographs.

Some ghats have particular importance: Vishnu appeared at Varah Ghat in the form of a boar, Brahma bathed at Brahma Ghat, and Gandhi's ashes were sprinkled at Gandhi Ghat, formerly Gau Ghat.

Pushkar has hundreds of temples, though few are particularly ancient, as they were mostly desecrated by Aurangzeb and subsequently rebuilt.

Old Rangji Temple   HINDU TEMPLE

Old Rangji Temple (c 1844) is close to the bazaar and is alternatively empty and peaceful or alive with chanting worshippers.

Savitri Mata Temple   HINDU TEMPLE

(Saraswati Temple) The ropeway (9.30am to 7.30pm, return trip ₹119) makes the ascent to the hilltop Saraswati Temple a breeze. The temple overlooks the lake and the views are fantastic at any time of day. Alternatively, you could take the one-hour trek up before dawn to beat the heat and capture the best light.

Brahma Temple   HINDU TEMPLE

Pushkar's most famous temple is the Brahma Temple, said to be one of the few such temples in the world as a result of a curse by Brahma's consort, Saraswati. The temple is marked by a red spire, and over the entrance gateway is the *hans* (goose symbol) of Brahma. Inside, the floor and walls are engraved with dedications to the dead.

Pap Mochani (Gayatri) Temple HINDU TEMPLE
The sunrise views over town from Pap Mochani (Gayatri) Temple, reached by a track behind the Marwar bus stand, are well worth the 30-minute climb.

🏯 Courses

Cooking Bahar COOKING
(☑ 0145-2773124; www.cookingbahar.com; Mainon ka Chowk; class ₹1200) Part of the Saraswati Music School family, Deepa conducts cooking classes that cover three vegetarian courses.

Saraswati Music & Dance School MUSIC
(☑ 9829333548, 9828297784; www.hemantdevaradance.com; Mainon ka Chowk; dance classes per hour from ₹500, music-class prices on application) Birju teaches tabla (drums), flute, harmonium and singing; brother Hemant teaches dance, including *kathak* (classical dance), Rajasthani folk and Bollywood dance. Birju

RAJASTHAN PUSHKAR

Pushkar

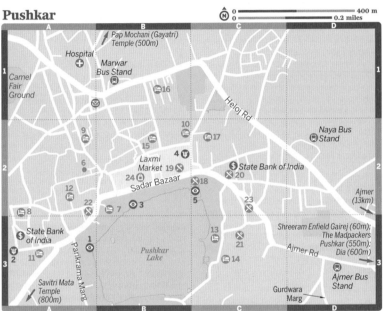

Pushkar

PUSHKAR CAMEL FAIR

Come the month of Kartika, the eighth lunar month of the Hindu calendar and one of the holiest, Thar camel drivers spruce up their ships of the desert and start the long walk to Pushkar in time for Kartik Purnima (Full Moon). Each year around 200,000 people converge on the **Pushkar Camel Fair** (⊙ Oct/Nov), bringing with them some 50,000 camels, horses and cattle.

The place becomes an extraordinary swirl of colour, sound and movement, thronged with musicians, mystics, tourists, traders, animals, devotees and camera crews.

Trading begins a week before the official fair (a good time to arrive to see the serious business), but by the time the RTDC mela (fair) starts, business takes a back seat and the bizarre sidelines (snake charmers, children balancing on poles etc) jostle onto centre stage. Even the cultural program seems peculiar, with contests for the best moustache, and most beautifully decorated camel. Visitors are encouraged to take part. See if you fancy taking part in the costumed wedding parade, or join a Visitors versus Locals sports contest such as traditional Rajasthani wrestling.

It's hard to believe, but this seething mass is all just a sideshow. Kartik Purnima is when Hindu pilgrims come to bathe in Pushkar's sacred waters. The religious event builds in tandem with the camel fair in a wild, magical crescendo of incense, chanting and processions to dousing day, the last night of the fair, when thousands of devotees wash away their sins and set candles afloat on the holy lake.

Although fantastical, mystical and a one-off, it must be said that it's also crowded, noisy (light sleepers should bring earplugs) and occasionally tacky. Those affected by dust and/or animal hair should bring appropriate medication. However, it's a grand epic, and not to be missed if you're anywhere within camel-spitting distance.

The fair usually takes place in November, but dates change according to the lunar calendar.

---

often conducts evening performances (7pm to 8pm), and also sells instruments.

🛏 Sleeping

Owing to Pushkar's star status among backpackers, there are far more budget options than midrange, though many budget properties have a selection of midrange-priced rooms. At the time of the camel fair, prices multiply up to three-fold or more, and it's essential to book several weeks ahead.

★ Hotel Everest   HOTEL $
(☑ 0145-2773417, 9414666958; www.pushkarhotel everest.com; off Sadar Bazaar; r ₹300-850, with AC ₹1120-1288; ❄@🛜) This welcoming budget hotel is nestled in the quiet laneways north of Sadar Bazaar. It's run by a friendly father-and-son team who can't do too much for their appreciative guests. The rooms are variable in size, colourful and spotless, and the beds are comfortable. The rooftop is a pleasant retreat for meals or just relaxing with a book.

Ask here about private excursions into Pushkar's hinterland to see temples and the famous Aloo Baba, a potato-eating sadhu.

Hotel Tulsi Palace   HOTEL $
(☑ 8947074663; www.hoteltulsipalacepushkar. co.in; VIP Rd, Holika Chowk; r ₹500-700, with AC ₹1000-1500; 🛜) Tulsi Palace is a great budget choice with a variety of bright and airy rooms around a central courtyard. The attached Little Prince Cafe on the 2nd-floor verandah serves Continental breakfasts and Indian lunch and dinner, and has prime street-life views. The friendly staff will help with your transport needs.

Hotel Kanhaia Haveli   HOTEL $
(☑ 0145-2772146; www.pushkarhotelkanhaia.com; Choti Basti; r ₹400-600, with AC ₹1500-2000; ❄🛜) With a vast range of rooms, from budget digs to suites, you are sure to find a room and price that suits. Rooms get bigger and lighter, with more windows, the more you spend (though all are scrupulously clean). Some rooms have balconies, while all have cable TV. There is a multicuisine restaurant with views on the rooftop.

Look out for the new venture Jashoda Mystic Haveli, another renovated *haveli*, only 40m away and due to open in 2019.

The Madpackers Pushkar HOSTEL $
(☑ 0145-2773444; pushkar@themadpackers.in; Panch Kund Marg; dm/d incl breakfast from ₹550/2900; ❄ 🛜) This welcoming, brightly coloured hostel, boasts abundant potted plants and a range of well-appointed rooms and dorms. It is out along Panch Kund Rd, a short walk southeast of the lake. The blue-domed rooftop terrace is very communal, with guests mingling, munching and watching the satellite TV.

Hotel White House GUESTHOUSE $
(☑ 0145-2772147; www.pushkarwhitehouse.com; off Heloj Rd; r ₹350-950, with AC ₹1000-1500; ❄ @ 🛜) This family run place is indeed white, with spotless rooms. Some are decidedly on the small side, but the nicest are generous and have balconies. It's efficiently run and there is good organic traveller fare and views from the plant-filled rooftop restaurant. Yoga is offered, as is a welcome brew of mango tea for every guest.

Hotel Akash HOTEL $
(☑ 0145-2772498; filterboy21@yahoo.com; Badi Basti; d ₹600, s/d without bathroom ₹300/500; 🛜) A simple budget place with keen young management and a large neem tree sprouting up from the courtyard to shade the rooftop terrace. Rooms are basic fan-cooled affairs that open out to a balcony restaurant good for spying on the street below.

Bharatpur Palace HOTEL $
(☑ 0145-2772320; www.hotelbharatpurpalace.com; Sadar Bazaar; d ₹1680, without bathroom ₹1344; ❄ 🛜) This rambling building occupies one of the best spots in Pushkar, on the upper levels adjacent to Gandhi Ghat. It features aesthetic blue-washed simplicity: bare-bones rooms with unsurpassed views of the holy lake. The rooftop terrace (with restaurant) has sublime vistas, but respect for bathing pilgrims is paramount for intended guests.

Hotel Paramount Palace HOTEL $
(☑ 0145-2772428; www.pushkarparamount.com; r ₹400-1500, with AC ₹2000; ❄ 🛜) Perched on the highest point in Pushkar overlooking an old temple, this welcoming hotel has excellent views of the town and lake (and lots of stairs). The rooms vary widely; the best have lovely balconies, stained-glass windows and are good value. There's a dizzyingly magical rooftop terrace and a small garden with hammocks.

Hotel Navaratan Palace HOTEL $
(☑ 0145-2772145; www.navratanpalace.com; near Brahma Temple; s/d incl breakfast ₹800/900, with AC ₹1000/1200; ❄ 🛜 🛁) This hotel has a lovely enclosed garden with a fabulous pool (nonguests ₹100), children's playground and pet tortoises. The rooms, crammed with carved wooden furniture, are clean and comfortable but small.

★**Inn Seventh Heaven** HERITAGE HOTEL $$
(☑ 0145-5105455; www.inn-seventh-heaven.com; Choti Basti; r ₹1350-3750; ❄ @ 🛜) Enter this lovingly converted *haveli* through heavy wooden doors into an incense-perfumed courtyard, with a marble fountain in the centre and surrounded by tumbling vines. There are a dozen individually decorated rooms on three levels, all with traditionally crafted furniture and comfortable beds. Rooms vary in size, from the downstairs budget rooms to the spacious Asana suite.

On the roof you'll find the excellent Sixth Sense restaurant (p78), as well as sofas and swing chairs for relaxing with a book. Early booking (two-night minimum, no credit cards) is recommended.

Hotel Sunset HOTEL $$
(☑ 0145-2772725; Parikrama marg; r ₹1200-1600) Behind the popular Sunset Cafe is a garden and a double-storey row of rooms all with TVs, AC and comfortable beds. The quiet location and access to a good atmospheric restaurant make this a good choice.

Dia B&B $$
(☑ 0145-5105455; www.diahomestay.com; Panch Kund Marg; r incl breakfast ₹3550-4950; ❄ @ 🛜) This beautifully designed B&B by the folks at Inn Seventh Heaven has five very private doubles a short walk from town. The rooms are straight out of a design magazine and will have you swooning (and extending your booking). You can dine here at the cosy rooftop restaurant or head to the Sixth Sense restaurant at Inn Seventh Heaven.

Hotel Pushkar Palace HERITAGE HOTEL $$$
(☑ 0145-2772001; www.hotelpushkarpalace.com; s/d/ste incl breakfast ₹8260/8730/19,200; ❄ @ 🛜) Once belonging to the maharaja of Kishangarh, the top-end Hotel Pushkar Palace has a romantic lakeside setting. The rooms have carved wooden furniture and beds, and all rooms above the ground floor, and all the suites, look directly out onto the lake: no hotel in Pushkar has better views.

A pleasant outdoor dining area overlooks the lake.

Eating

Pushkar has plenty of atmospheric eateries with lake views, and menus reflecting backpacker tastes and preferences. Strict vegetarianism, forbidding even eggs, is the order of the day.

Pushkar is a holy town: alcohol is banned (which doesn't mean it isn't available) and restaurants tend to close early.

Naryan Café   CAFE $
(Mahadev Chowk, Sadar Bazaar; breakfast from ₹90; ⊙6am-10pm) Busy any time of day, this is particularly popular as a breakfast stop: watch the world go by with a fresh coffee (from ₹40) or juice (from ₹50) and an enormous bowl of homemade muesli, topped with a mountain of fruit.

Shri Vankatesh   INDIAN $
(Choti Basti; mains ₹60-170; ⊙9am-10pm) Head to this no-nonsense local favourite and tuck into some dhal, paneer or kofta, before mopping up the sauce with freshly baked chapatis and washing it all down with some good old-fashioned chai. The thalis (₹100 to ₹150) are excellent value, too. Watch your food being cooked or head upstairs to watch people go by on the street below.

Falafel & Laffa Wrap Stalls   MIDDLE EASTERN $
(Sadar Bazaar; wraps ₹100-200; ⊙7.30am-10.30pm) Perfect for quelling a sudden attack of the munchies, and a big hit with Israeli travellers, these adjacent roadside joints knock up a choice selection of filling falafel-and-hummus wraps. Eat them while sitting on stools on the road or devour them on the hoof.

Out of the Blue   MULTICUISINE $$
(Sadar Bazaar; mains ₹160-300; ⊙8am-11pm; 🕿) Distinctly a deeper shade of blue in this sky-blue town, Out of the Blue is a reliable restaurant. The menu ranges from noodles and *momos* (Tibetan dumplings) to pizza, pasta, falafel and pancakes. A nice touch for those averse to stairs is the street-level espresso coffee bar (coffees ₹70 to ₹120) and German bakery.

Honey & Spice   MULTICUISINE $$
(Laxmi Market, off Sadar Bazaar; mains ₹90-250; ⊙8.15am-6pm; ✐) 🖉 Run by a friendly family, this tiny wholefood breakfast and lunch place has delicious South Indian coffee and

homemade cakes. Even better are the salad bowls and hearty vegetable combo stews served with brown rice – delicious, wholesome and a welcome change from frequently oil-rich Indian food.

Sixth Sense   MULTICUISINE $$
(Inn Seventh Heaven, Choti Basti; mains ₹120-300; ⊙8am-2.30pm & 6-10.30pm; 🕿) This chilled rooftop restaurant is a great place to head to even if you didn't score a room in the popular hotel. The pizza and the Indian seasonal vegetables and rice are all very good, as is the filter coffee and fresh juice. Its ambience is immediately relaxing and the pulley apparatus that delivers food from the ground-floor kitchen is a delight.

Sunset Café   MULTICUISINE $$
(✐0145-2772725; mains ₹170-390; ⊙7.30am-midnight; 🕿) Right on the eastern ghats, this cafe has sublime lake views from its front porch and rooftop. It offers the usual traveller menu, including curries, pizza and pasta, plus there's a German bakery serving reasonable cakes. The lakeside setting is perfect at sunset and gathers a crowd.

Om Shiva
Garden Restaurant   MULTICUISINE $$
(✐0145-2772305; www.omshivagardenrestaurant.com; mains ₹150-290; ⊙8am-11pm; 🕿) This traveller stalwart near Naya Rangji Temple continues to satisfy, with wood-fired pizzas and espresso coffee featuring on its predominately Italian and North Indian menu. It's hard to pass on the pizzas, but there are also some Mexican and Chinese dishes and 'German bakery' items to try.

Shopping

Sadar Bazaar   MARKET
Pushkar's Sadar Bazaar is lined with enchanting little shops and is a good place for picking up gifts. Many of the vibrant Rajasthani textiles originate from Barmer, south of Jaisalmer, or Gujarat. There's plenty of silver and beaded jewellery catering both to local and foreign tastes, including some heavy tribal pieces. Expect to haggle.

Information

The nearest government tourist office is in Ajmer. Your hotel hosts are almost always up to speed with the latest tourist information.

Post office (off Heloj Rd; ⊙9.30am-5pm Mon-Fri) Near the Marwar bus stand.

State Bank of India (SBI; Sadar Bazaar; ⊙10am-4pm Mon-Fri, to 12.30pm Sat) Changes cash. The ATM accepts international cards.

State Bank of India (SBI) Near Brahma Temple.

Beware of anyone giving you flowers to offer a *puja* (prayer): before you know it you'll be whisked to the ghats in a well-oiled hustle and asked for a personal donation of up to ₹1000. Other priests here do genuinely live off the donations of others and this is a tradition that goes back centuries – but walk away if you feel bullied and always agree on a price before taking a red ribbon (a 'Pushkar passport') or flowers.

During the camel fair, Pushkar is besieged by pickpockets working the crowded bazaars. You can avoid the razor gang by not using thin-walled day packs and by carrying your pack in front of you. At any time of year, watch out for rampaging motorbikes ridden by inconsiderate youths in the bazaar.

🛈 Getting There & Away

Pushkar's tiny train station is so badly connected it's not worth bothering with. Use Ajmer junction train station instead.

A private taxi to Ajmer costs ₹300 to ₹400 (note that it's almost always more expensive in the opposite direction). To enter Pushkar by car there is a toll of ₹20.

BUS

Frequent buses to/from Ajmer (₹20, 30 minutes) depart from the Naya Bus Stand, and also from the Ajmer Bus Stand on the road heading eastwards out of town. Most other buses leave from the Naya Bus Stand, though some may still use the old Marwar Bus Stand (but not RSRTC buses).

Local travel agencies sell tickets for private buses – you should shop around. These buses often leave from Ajmer, but the agencies should provide you with free connecting transport. Check whether your bus is direct, as many services from Pushkar aren't. And note, even if they are direct buses they may well stop for some time in Ajmer.

A useful service for getting to Pushkar from Jaipur is Jai Ambay Travelling Agency (p59), which has a direct, daily, air-con coach (₹350) leaving for Pushkar at 9am and arriving at 12.30pm. The return journey waits for some time in Ajmer and is not so useful.

🛈 Getting Around

There are no autorickshaws in central Pushkar, but it's a breeze to get around on foot. If you want to explore the surrounding countryside, you could try hiring a motorbike (₹300 per day) from one of the many places around town. For something more substantial, try **Shreeram Enfield Gairej** (Ajmer Rd; per day ₹800), which hires and sells Enfield Bullets.

Ranthambhore National Park

🗗 07462

This famous **national park** (www.rajasthanwildlife.in; ⊙Oct-Jun) is the best place to spot wild tigers in Rajasthan. It comprises 1334 sq km of wild jungle scrub hemmed in by rocky ridges, and at its centre is the 10th-century Ranthambhore Fort. Scattered around the fort are ancient temples and mosques, hunting pavilions, crocodile-filled lakes and vine-covered *chhatris* (cenotaphs). The park was a maharajas' hunting ground until 1970, a curious 15 years after it had become a sanctuary.

Seeing a tiger (around 60 to 67 in 2018) is partly a matter of luck; leave time for two or three safaris to improve your chances. But remember there's plenty of other wildlife to see, including more than 300 species of birds.

It's 10km from Sawai Madhopur (the gateway town for Ranthambhore) to the first gate of the park, and another 3km to the main gate and Ranthambhore Fort.

BUSES FROM PUSHKAR (NAYA BUS STAND)

DESTINATION	FARE (₹)	TIME (HR)	FREQUENCY
Bikaner	253	6	hourly
Bundi	200	6	daily (6am)
Jaipur	160	4	9 daily (5.15am, 6.45am, 7.15am, 7.45am, 8.30am, 9am, 10am, 12.46pm, 2.11pm)
Jodhpur	185	5	3 daily (7.10am, 5.50pm)

◉ Sights

Ranthambhore Fort   FORT

(⊙ 6am-6pm) **FREE** From a distance, the magical 10th-century Ranthambhore Fort is almost indiscernible on its hilltop perch – as you get closer, it seems almost as if it is growing out of the rock. It covers an area of 4.5 sq km, and affords peerless views from the disintegrating walls of the Badal Mahal (Palace of the Clouds), on its northern side. The ramparts stretch for more than 7km, and seven enormous gateways are still intact. To visit on the cheap, join the locals who go to the fort to visit the temple dedicated to Ganesh. Shared 4WDs (₹40 per person) go from the train station to

the park entrance – say 'national park' and they'll know what you want. From there, other shared 4WDs (₹20 per person) shuttle to and from the fort, which is inside the park. Alternatively you can hire your own gypsy (and driver) through your hotel for about ₹1500 for three hours.

🏃 Activities

Safaris take place in the early morning and late afternoon, starting between 6am and 7am or between 2pm and 3.30pm, depending on the time of year. Each safari lasts for around three hours. The mornings can be exceptionally chilly in the open vehicles, so bring warm clothes.

Ranthambhore National Park

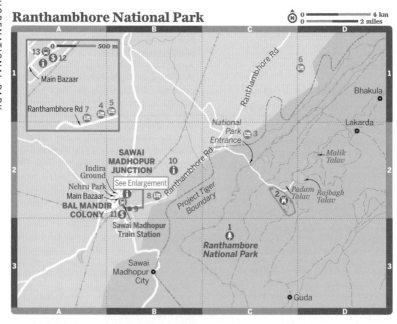

Ranthambhore National Park

The best option is to travel by gypsy (six-person, open-topped 4WD; Indian/ foreigner ₹974/1714). You still have a chance of seeing a tiger from a canter (20-seat, open-topped truck; ₹617/1357), but other passengers can be very rowdy.

Be aware that the rules for booking safaris (and prices) are prone to change. You can book online through the park's official website (www.rajasthanwildlife.in), or go in person to the safari booking office. And to be sure of bagging a seat in a vehicle, start queuing at least an hour (if not two) before the safaris are due to begin – meaning a very early start for morning safaris! Booking with agencies and hotels is much simpler, but be aware that they add a commission (₹100 to ₹800 per person per safari) to the official rates.

🛏 Sleeping & Eating

Many visitors are on packages that include all meals. In any case, it is usually most convenient to eat in your own hotel.

Hotel Aditya Resort   HOTEL $

(☑9414728468; www.hoteladityaresort.com; Ranthambhore Rd; r ₹400-700, with AC ₹900; 🕸@🛜) This friendly place is one of the better of the few in the budget category along Ranthambhore Rd. There are just six simple, unadorned rooms (four have air-con); try to get one with an outside window. The rooftop restaurant is a simple affair but the food consistently gets good reports.

The staff will help with safari bookings, but be sure to ask how much they are charging for the service.

Vatika Resort   BOUTIQUE HOTEL $$

(☑07462-222457; www.ranthambhorevatikaresort. com; Ranthambhore Rd; s/d incl breakfast ₹1800/ 2250, incl all meals ₹2800/3250; 🕸@🛜) A lovely little hotel with simple but immaculate rooms, each with terrace seating overlooking a beautifully tended, flower-filled garden. It's about 1km beyond the main strip of accommodation on Ranthambhore Rd (although still 5km before the park's main gate), so much quieter than elsewhere. It's 3km from Hammir Circle roundabout.

Tiger Safari Resort   HOTEL $$

(☑07462-221137; www.tigersafariresort.com; Ranthambhore Rd; r incl breakfast ₹2590; 🕸@🛜🏊) A reasonable midrange option, with spacious doubles and 'cottages' (larger rooms with bigger bathrooms) facing a garden and small pool. The management is adept at organising safaris and wake-up calls before the morning safari. As per all the other hotels, a commission is added for this service, so ask for a breakdown of the costs.

⭐ Hotel Ranthambhore Regency   HOTEL $$$

(☑07462-221176; www.ranthambhor.com; Ranthambhore Rd; s/d incl all meals from ₹7670/873022; 🕸@🛜🏊) A very professional place that caters to tour groups but can still provide great service to independent travellers. It has immaculate, well-appointed rooms (marble floors, flatscreen TVs etc), which would rate as suites in many hotels. The central garden with an inviting pool is a virtual oasis, and there's a plush bar, an efficient restaurant and a pampering spa.

⭐ Khem Villas   BOUTIQUE HOTEL $$$

(☑07462-252099; www.khemvillas.com; Khem Villas Rd; s/d incl all meals ₹14,000/16,000, tents ₹21,500/27,000, cottages ₹24,500/29,500; 🕸@🛜) Set in 9 hectares of organic farmland and reforested jungle, this splendid ecolodge was created by the Singh Rathore family, the driving force behind the conservation of tigers at Ranthambhore. The accommodation ranges from colonial-style bungalow rooms to luxury tents and sumptuous stone cottages. Privacy is guaranteed – you can even bathe under the stars.

Aangan   BOUTIQUE HOTEL $$$

(s/d incl breakfast ₹7080/8260; 🕸🛜) This boutique hotel has just five guest rooms and is set in an orchard metres from the park boundary. Rooms are spacious with air-con and personalised service. Guests are invited to participate and learn cooking skills with the chef and there's yoga on the rooftop with views to the wild hills and jungle.

ℹ Information

There's a **State Bank of India** (SBI; ⊙10am-2pm or 4pm Mon-Fri, to 1pm Sat), including an ATM, just by Hammir Circle, and an SBI ATM outside the train station.

Ranthambore Adventure Tours (☑9414214460; www.ranthambhore adventuretours.com; Ranthambhore Rd; ⊙4am-8.30pm) Reputable safari booking agency.

Safari booking office (off Ranthambhore Rd, Shilpgram; ⊙5-6am & 1-2.30pm) Seats in gypsies and canters can be reserved on the website, though a single gypsy (with a premium price) and five canters are also kept for direct booking at the Forest Office. It's located in the Shilpgram campus out along Ranthambhore Rd.

Tourist office (☑ 07462-220808; Train Station; ⊙ 9.30am-6pm Mon-Fri, 10am-4pm Sat & Sun) Has maps of Sawai Madhopur.

ⓘ Getting There & Away

There are very few direct buses to anywhere of interest, so it's always preferable to take the train.

TRAIN

Sawai Madhopur junction station is near Hammir Circle, which leads to Ranthambhore Rd.

Agra (Agra Fort Station) sleeper ₹200, six hours, three daily (11.35am, 4.10pm, 11pm)

Delhi 2nd-class/sleeper/3AC ₹140/260/660, 5½ to eight hours, 13 daily

Jaipur 2nd-class seat/sleeper/3AC ₹95/180/560, two hours, 11 to 13 daily

Keoladeo NP (Bharatpur) 2nd-class/sleeper/3AC ₹85/170/540, 2½ hours, 10 to 13 daily

Kota (from where you can catch buses to Bundi) 2nd-class/sleeper/3AC ₹90/170/550, one to two hours, hourly

ⓘ Getting Around

Bicycle hire (around ₹40 per day) is available in the main bazaar. Autorickshaws are available at the train station; it's ₹60 to ₹120 for an autorickshaw from the train station to Ranthambhore Rd, depending on where you get off. Many hotels will pick you up from the train station for free if you call ahead.

If you want to walk, turn left out of the train station and follow the road up to the overpass (200m). Turn left and cross the bridge over the railway line to reach a roundabout (200m), known as Hammir Circle. Turn left here on to Ranthambhore Rd to find accommodation.

Karauli

☑ 07464 / POP 82,960

Founded in 1348, Karauli is the home of Shri Madan Mohanji, an incarnation of Krishna, and has some important Krishna temples attracting many pilgrims. Around 23km from Karauli is the massively popular temple of **Kaila Devi** – thousands of devotees flood the town en route to the temple during the Navratri celebrations in March/April and September/October.

Completely off the tourist trail, the area is also famous for its red-sandstone quarries

and for its lac (resin) bangles. Twenty-five kilometres away from Karauli is the rugged **Kaila Devi Game Sanctuary**, which adjoins the buffer zone of Ranthambhore National Park.

Around 40km from town, along a potholed road, is a tragically ruined fort, **Timangarh**. Built around 1100 and reconstructed in 1244, this once-mighty fort overlooks a lake filled with water lilies. It was deserted 300 years ago, and has been destroyed by looters over the past 50 years. You'll need to hire a taxi to get here, and one that can manage the track.

⊙ Sights

Old City Palace PALACE
(Indian/foreigner ₹40/300; ⊙ 6am-8.30pm) The mainly 17th-century old city palace was constructed over different periods; the oldest part has existed for 600 years. Occupied by the Karauli royal family until around the 1940s, the palace is rundown and worn, but there are ongoing restorations and it's very atmospheric. It's worth tipping the guard to get them to guide you. There's a **Krishna temple** (⊙ 5-11.30am & 4-8pm) in the compound.

🛏 Sleeping

Bhanwar Vilas Palace HERITAGE HOTEL $$$
(☑ 9929773744; www.karauli.com; Bagh Khana; r ₹5900, ste ₹8260; ❋🔊🏊) Bhanwar Vilas Palace, owned and run by Maharaja Krishna Chandra Pal, is closer to a large country manor than a palace. A back-in-time place, it features a billiard room, shady verandahs, rambling grounds, classic cars in the garages, Marwari horses in the stables, and comfortable period rooms. Excursions to nearby points of interest, including the old city palace, can be organised.

The hotel is in Baghi Khana, on the southern outskirts of Karauli.

ⓘ Getting There & Away

Karauli is 180km southeast of Jaipur, and buses run half-hourly between the two cities (₹204, five hours).

The nearest train stations are Gangapur (31km) and Hindaun (30km), both on the main Delhi–Mumbai line.

UDAIPUR & SOUTHERN RAJASTHAN

Bundi

📞 0747 / POP 103,290

Bundi is a captivating town of narrow lanes of Brahmin-blue houses with a temple at every turn. There are fascinating step-wells, reflective lakes, and colourful bazaars. Dominating Bundi is a fantastical palace of faded parchment cupolas and loggias rising from the hills behind the town. Though an increasingly popular traveller hang-out, Bundi attracts nothing like the tourist crowds of places such as Jaipur or Udaipur. Few places in Rajasthan retain so much of the magical atmosphere of centuries past.

Bundi came into its own in the 12th century when a group of Chauhan nobles from Ajmer was pushed south by Mohammed of Ghori. They wrested the Bundi area from the Mina and Bhil tribes and made Bundi the capital of their kingdom, known as Hadoti. Bundi was generally loyal to the Mughals from the late 16th century on, but it maintained its independent status until incorporated into the state of Rajasthan after 1947.

⊙ Sights

Bundi has around 60 beautiful *baoris* (step-wells), some right in the town centre. The majesty of many of them is unfortunately diminished by their lack of water today – a result of declining groundwater levels – and by the rubbish that collects in them which no one bothers to clean up. The most impressive, Raniji-ki-Baori (Queen's Step-Well; Indian/foreigner ₹50/200; ⊙9.30am-5pm), is 46m deep and decorated with sinuous carvings, including the avatars of Lord Vishnu. The Nagar Sagar Kund is a pair of matching step-wells just outside the old city's Chogan Gate.

Three sights around town, the Raniji-ki-Baori, 84-Pillared Cenotaph (Indian/foreigner ₹50/200; ⊙9.30am-5pm) and Sukh Mahal, can be visited using a composite ticket (Indian/foreigner ₹75/350) – a great saving if you plan to visit two or more of these sights.

Bundi Palace
PALACE

(Garh Palace; Indian palace/fort/camera ₹80/100/50, foreigner palace, fort & camera ₹500; ⊙8am-6pm) This extraordinary, partly decaying edifice – described by Rudyard Kipling

as 'the work of goblins rather than of men' – almost seems to grow out of the rock of the hillside it stands on. Though large sections are still closed up and left to the bats, the rooms that are open hold a series of fabulous, fading turquoise-and-gold murals that are the palace's chief treasure. The palace is best explored with a local guide (₹700 half-day plus ₹100 for guide entry).

The palace was constructed during the reign of Rao Raja Ratan Singh (r 1607-31) and added to by his successors. Part of it remained occupied by the Bundi royals until 1948.

If you are going up to Taragarh as well as the palace, get tickets for both at the palace entrance. Once inside the palace's Hathi Pol (Elephant Gate), climb the stairs to the Ratan Daulat or Diwan-i-Am (Hall of Public Audience), with a white marble coronation throne. You then pass into the Chhatra Mahal, added by Rao Raja Chhatra Shabji in 1644, with some fine but rather weathered murals. Stairs lead up to the Phool Mahal (1607), the murals of which include an immense royal procession, and then the Badal Mahal (Cloud Palace; also 1607), with Bundi's very best murals, including a wonderful Chinese-inspired ceiling, divided into petal shapes and decorated with peacocks and Krishnas.

★ Chitrasala
PALACE

(Umaid Mahal; ⊙8am-6pm) Within the Bundi Palace complex is the Chitrasala, a small 18th-century palace built by Rao Ummed Singh. To find it, exit through the palace's Hathi Pol (Elephant Gate) and walk around the corner uphill. Above the palace's garden courtyard are several rooms covered in beautiful paintings. There are some great Krishna images, including a detail of him sitting up a tree playing the flute after stealing the clothes of the *gopis* (milkmaids).

The back room to the right is the Sheesh Mahal, badly damaged but still featuring some beautiful inlaid glass, while back in the front room there's an image of 18th-century Bundi itself.

Taragarh
FORT

(Star Fort; ₹100, camera/video ₹50/100; ⊙8am-5pm) This ramshackle, partly overgrown 14th-century fort, on the hilltop above Bundi Palace, is a wonderful place to ramble around – but take a stick to battle the overgrown vegetation, help the knees on the steep climb and provide confidence when surrounded by testosterone-charged macaques. To reach it, just continue on the path up behind the Chitrasala.

Jait Sagar LAKE
Round the far side of Taragarh, about 2km north from the centre of town, this pictur-

esque, 1.5km-long lake is flanked by hills and strewn with pretty lotus flowers during the monsoon and winter months. At its near end, the **Sukh Mahal** (Indian/foreigner ₹50/200; ⊙9.30am-5pm Tue-Sun) is a small summer palace surrounded by terraced gar-

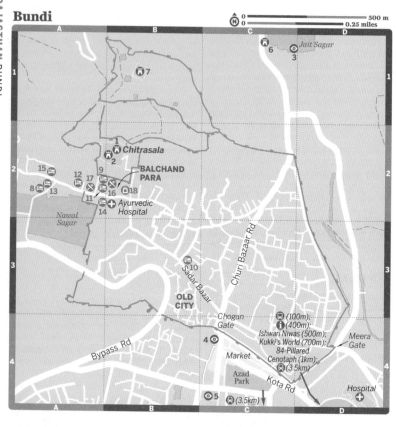

Bundi

dens where Rudyard Kipling once stayed and wrote part of *Kim*.

Tours

Keshav Bhati　　　　　　　　TOURS
(☏9414394241; bharat_bhati@yahoo.com) Keshav Bhati is a retired Indian Air Force officer with a passion for Bundi. He is also an official tour guide with an encyclopaedic knowledge of the region and is highly recommended. Tour prices are negotiable.

Kukki's World　　　　　　　　TOURS
(☏9828404527; www.kukkisworld.com; 43 New Colony; half-/full-day tour for 2 people US$58/67) OP 'Kukki' Sharma is a passionate amateur archaeologist who has discovered around 70 prehistoric rock-painting sites around Bundi. His trips get you out into the villages and countryside, which he knows like the back of his hand. You can visit his collection of finds and select sites from his laptop at his house (near the main police station) beforehand.

Sleeping

Shivam Tourist Guest House　GUESTHOUSE $
(☏9460300272, 0747-2447892; Balchand Para; s/d ₹550/700, r with AC ₹1000-1200) This guesthouse is run by two energetic young couples who are keen to help travellers get the most from their stay in Bundi. Rooms are simple but comfortable, brightly painted and spotless; the better rooms are upstairs. There is an all-veg rooftop restaurant with great sunset and palace views.

Cooking and henna-design classes are offered, plus ayurvedic massage and they can help with booking transport.

Annpurna Haveli　　　　　GUESTHOUSE $
(☏0747-2447055, 9602605455; www.annpurna havelibundi.com; Balchand Para; r ₹800, with AC incl breakfast ₹1200; ❋ 🛜) Annpurna is a very peaceful family-run guesthouse of just six rooms opposite Nawal Sagar. The simple and clean rooms are a great budget choice, and the best rooms have lake views. Home-cooked meals are enjoyed either in the dining room or on the roof in fine weather.

★ **Haveli Braj Bhushanjee**　HERITAGE HOTEL $$
(☏0747-2442322, 9783355866; www.kiplingsbun di.com; Balchand Para; r ₹1500-6000; ❋ 🛜) This rambling 200-year-old *haveli* is run by the very helpful and knowledgeable Braj Bhushanjee family, descendants of the former prime ministers of Bundi. It's Bundi's first

guesthouse and an enchanting place with original stone interiors, a private garden, splendid rooftop views, beautiful, well-preserved murals, and all sorts of other historic and valuable artefacts.

The terrific range of accommodation includes some lovely, modernised rooms that are still in traditional style. It's a fascinating living museum where you can really get a feel for Bundi's heritage. The *haveli* serves delicious vegetarian meals with rice, wheat flour and vegetables sourced from its own farm.

Hotel Bundi Haveli　　　　　HOTEL $$
(☏9929291552, 0747-2446716; www.hotelbundi haveli.com; Balchand Para; r ₹1300-4750; ❋ 🛜) The exquisitely renovated Bundi Haveli blends contemporary style and sophistication with heritage architecture. Spacious rooms, white walls, stone floors, colour highlights and framed artefacts are coupled with modern plumbing and electricity. Yes, it's very comfortable and relaxed and there's a lovely rooftop dining area with palace views and an extensive, mainly Indian menu (mains ₹150 to ₹280).

Dev Niwas　　　　　HERITAGE HOTEL $$
(☏8233345394, 0747-2442928; www.jagatcol lection.com; Maaji Sahib-ki-Haveli, Sadar Bazaar; r ₹950, with AC ₹3920, ste ₹5040; ❋ 🛜) Dev Niwas is a fine *haveli*, just off the busy Sadar Bazaar. Inside is a peaceful oasis with courtyards and open-sided pavilions. Rooms are very different, yet they are all comfortably furnished and fitted with modern bathrooms. The open-sided restaurant has cushion seating and there are great views of the fort.

Ummaiud Bagh Resort　　　TENTED CAMP $$
(☏0747-2442397; www.ummaidbaghresort.com; Baanganga Rd, Jait Sagar; tent incl breakfast ₹3500; ❋ 🛜) This delightfully peaceful and tree-shaded bagh (garden) on the shores of Jait Sagar belongs to the Maharaja of Dugari, one of the Bundi royals. Accommodation is in luxury tents with attached bathrooms. There is a tented pavilion for dining, winter bonfires and a bar. Birdwatchers have a viewing tower and over 150 species of migratory and resident birdlife to tick off.

Ishwari Niwas　　　　　HERITAGE HOTEL $$
(☏0747-2442414; www.ishwariniwas.com; 1 Civil Lines; r ₹3400-4500; ❋ 🛜) This graceful colonial-era hotel is run by a family with Bundi royal ancestry. Rooms are arranged

around a peaceful courtyard garden; those in the old wing are variable and atmospheric, and those in the new wing are spacious and modern. All are comfortable and well appointed. The dining hall sports stuffed beasts and a very interesting old map of Bundi.

Kasera Heritage View GUESTHOUSE $$
(0747-2444679, 9983790314; www.kaseraherit
ageview.com; s/d from ₹1200/1500, with AC from ₹1800/2200; ❄@⊗) A revamped *haveli*, Kasera has an incongruously modern lobby, but offers a range of slightly more authentic rooms. The welcome is friendly, it's all cheerfully decorated, the rooftop restaurant has great views, and discounts of 20% to 30% are offered in summer.

The owners' sister *haveli*, Kasera Paradise, just below the palace, has the same contact details and rates.

Haveli Katkoun GUESTHOUSE $$
(0747-2444311, 9414539146; www.katkounhaveli
bundi.com; s/d ₹700/1200, r with AC ₹1800-2200; ❄⊗) Just outside the town's western gate, Katkoun is a completely revamped *haveli* with friendly family management who live downstairs. It has large, spotless rooms offering superb views on both sides, to either the lake or palace, and has an open-sided rooftop restaurant (mains ₹100 to ₹250), known for its Indian nonveg dishes.

Bundi Vilas HERITAGE HOTEL $$$
(0747-2444614, 9214803556; www.bundivilas.
com; r incl breakfast from ₹6000; ❄@⊗) This 300-year-old *haveli* up a side alley has been tastefully renovated with golden Jaisalmer sandstone, earth-toned walls and deft interior design. The five deluxe and two suite rooms exude period character yet have excellent bathrooms. Set in the lee of the palace walls, this guesthouse has commanding views of the town below and palace above from the rooftop terrace restaurant.

✖ Eating

★ Bundi Vilas INDIAN $$
(0747-2444614; www.bundivilas.com; Balchand Para; set dinner ₹800; ⊗7-10pm; ⊗☑) The most romantic restaurant in Bundi welcomes visitors from other hotels. Dine in the sheltered yet open-sided terrace, or on the rooftop with uninterrupted views of the fort. It's wise to book as spots are limited for the candlelit dinner experience beneath the floodlit palace. The set dinner offers several

courses of exquisite food, and beer and wine are available.

Morgan's Place MULTICUISINE $$
(7833863447; Kasera Paradise Hotel; mains ₹250-400; ⊗9am-10pm; ⊗) Morgan's Place is a relaxed (possibly overly relaxed) rooftop restaurant. If you're in the mood for caffeine (it serves espresso coffee), don't mind climbing lots of stairs, and aren't in a hurry, then it delivers. It also serves fresh juice, respectable wood-fired, thin-crust pizza, pasta, chicken schnitzel and falafel.

Rainbow Cafe MULTICUISINE $$
(9887210334; mains ₹120-300, thalis ₹250-500; ⊗7am-11pm; ⊗) Bohemian ambience with chill-out tunes, floor-cushion seating, good snacks and 'special' lassis. You need to be patient, but food eventually emerges from the tiny kitchen. Located on the rooftop of the town's western gate and caged off from marauding macaques with a bamboo trellis.

🔒 Shopping

★ Yug Art ART
(www.yugartbundi.com; near Surang Gate; portrait postcard ₹1000-2000, comics from ₹3000; ⊗10am-7.30pm) Many art shops will offer you Rajasthani miniatures, but Yug Art offers to put you into one. Provide a photo and you can be pictured on elephant-back or in any number of classical scenes. Alternatively, Yug will record your India trip in a unique travel comic – you help with the script and he'll provide the artwork.

ℹ Information

Head to Sadar Bazar to find ATMs.

Ayurvedic Hospital (0747-2443708; Balchand Para; ⊗9am-1pm & 4-6pm Mon-Sat, 9-11am Sun) This charitable hospital prescribes natural plant-based remedies. There are medicines for all sorts of ailments, from upset tummies to arthritis, and many of them are free.

Tourist office (0747-2443697; Kota Rd; ⊗8.30am-6pm) Offers bus and train schedules and free maps.

ℹ Getting There & Away

Shivam Tourist Guest House (p85) is a licensed bus agency that charges smaller commissions than many of the travel agents in the bazaar. They can also book train tickets and exchange currency.

THE MINI MASTERPIECES OF BUNDI & KOTA

Some of Rajasthan's finest miniature and mural painting was produced around Bundi and Kota, the ruling Hada Rajputs being keen artistic patrons. The style combined the dominant features of folk painting – intense colour and bold forms – with the Mughals' concern with naturalism.

The Bundi and Kota schools were initially similar, but developed markedly different styles, though both usually have a background of thick foliage, cloudy skies and scenes lit by the setting sun. When architecture appears it is depicted in loving detail. The willowy women sport round faces, large petal-shaped eyes and small noses – forerunners of Bollywood pin-ups.

The Bundi school is notable for its blue hues, with a palette of turquoise and azure unlike anything seen elsewhere. Bundi Palace in particular hosts some wonderful examples.

In Kota you'll notice a penchant for hunting scenes with fauna and dense foliage – vivid, detailed portrayals of hunting expeditions in Kota's once thickly wooded surrounds. Kota's City Palace has some of the best-preserved wall paintings in the state.

RAJASTHAN KOTA

BUS

For Ranthambhore, it's quicker to catch the train or a bus to Kota, then hop on a train to Sawai Madhopur. Direct services from **Bundi bus stand** (Kota Rd) include the following:

Ajmer ₹186, four hours, hourly

Chittorgarh 163, 4½ hours, two daily

Jaipur ₹236, five hours, hourly

Jodhpur ₹370, eight hours, five daily

Kota ₹39, 40 minutes, every 15 minutes

Pushkar ₹200, 4½ hours, one daily

Sawai Madhoper ₹120, five hours, three daily

TRAIN

Bundi station is 4km south of the old city. There are no daily trains to Jaipur, Ajmer or Jodhpur. It's better to take a bus, or to catch a train from Kota or Chittorgarh.

Agra (Agra Fort Station) sleeper ₹160, 12½ hours, daily (5.30pm)

Chittorgarh sleeper/3AC ₹180/540, 2½ to 3½ hours, three to five daily (2.10am, 2.25am, 7.05am, 9.17am and 11pm)

Delhi (Hazrat Nizamuddin) sleeper ₹315, eight to 12 hours, two daily (5.45pm and 10.38pm)

Sawai Madhopur sleeper ₹180, 2½ to five hours, three daily (5.30pm, 5.45pm and 10.28pm; the last train is the fastest)

Udaipur sleeper/3AC ₹220/540, five hours, daily (12963 Mewar Express; 2.10am)

Varanasi 3AC ₹1325, 23½ hours, Wednesday only (19669 Humsafar; 4.55pm)

❶ Getting Around

An autorickshaw from town to the train station costs ₹80 by day and ₹120 at night.

Kota

📞 0744 / POP 1 MILLION

An easy day trip from Bundi, Kota is a gritty industrial and commercial city on the Chambal, Rajasthan's only permanent river. You can take boat trips on the river here, for bird- and crocodile-watching, or explore the city's old palace.

Historically a city of strategic importance, Kota still has an army base. It also has a spectacular palace with an excellent museum.

◉ Sights

City Palace   PALACE, MUSEUM

(Kotah Garh; www.kotahfort.com; Indian/foreigner ₹100/300; ⊙10am-4.30pm) The City Palace, and the fort that surrounds it, make up one of the largest such complexes in Rajasthan. This was the royal residence and centre of power, housing the Kota princedom's treasury, courts, arsenal, armed forces and state offices. The palace, entered through a gateway topped by rampant elephants, contains the offbeat **Rao Madho Singh Museum**, where you'll find everything for a respectable Raj existence, from silver furniture to weaponry, as well as perhaps India's most depressingly moth-eaten stuffed trophy animals.

🏃 Activities

Boat Trips   BOATING

(per person 5min/1hr ₹60/1300; ⊙10.30am-dusk) Take a hiatus from the city on a Chambal River boat trip. The river upstream of Kota is part of the **Darrah National Park** and it's beautiful, with lush vegetation and craggy cliffs on either side. Boats start from **Chambal Gardens** (Indian/foreigner ₹2/5), 1.5km south of the fort on the river's east bank. Maximum of six people per boat. Trips provide the opportunity to spot a host of birds, as well as gharials (thin-snouted, fish-eating crocodiles) and muggers (keep-your-limbs-inside-the-boat crocodiles).

Sleeping

Palkiya Haveli   HERITAGE HOTEL **$$**
(☑0744-2387844; www.palkiyahaveli.com; Mokha Para; s/d ₹2580/3300; ❄️🛜) This exquisite *haveli* has been in the same family for 200 years. Set in a deliciously peaceful corner of the old city, about 800m east of the City Palace, it's a lovely, relaxing place to stay, with welcoming hosts, a high-walled garden and a courtyard with a graceful neem tree. There are impressive murals and appealing heritage rooms, and the food is top-notch.

ℹ️ Information

Tourist Office (☑0744-2327695; RTDC Hotel Chambal; ⊙9.30am-6pm Mon-Sat) Has free maps of Kota.

ℹ️ Getting There & Away

BUS

Services from the main bus stand (on Bundi Rd, east of the bridge over the Chambal River) include the following:

Ajmer (for Pushkar) ₹230, four to five hours, at least 10 daily

Bundi ₹39, 40 minutes, every 15 minutes throughout the day

Chittorgarh ₹216, four hours, half-hourly from 6am

Jaipur ₹252, five hours, hourly from 5am
Udaipur ₹320 to ₹380, six to seven hours, at least 10 daily

TRAIN

Kota is on the main Mumbai–Delhi train route via Sawai Madhopur, so there are plenty of trains to choose from, though departure times aren't always convenient.

Agra (Fort) sleeper ₹225, five to nine hours, at least four daily (7.30am, 9.50am, 2.40pm and 9pm)

Chittorgarh sleeper ₹170, three to four hours, three to four daily (1.10am, 1.25am, 6.05am and 8.45am)

Delhi (New Delhi or Hazrat Nizamuddin) sleeper ₹315, five to eight hours, almost hourly

Jaipur sleeper ₹225, four hours, six daily (2.55am, 7.40am, 8.55am, 12.35pm, 5.35pm and 11.50pm), plus other trains on selected days

Mumbai sleeper ₹490, 14 hours, five daily fast trains (7.45am, 2.25pm, 5.30pm, 9.05pm and 11.45pm)

Sawai Madhopur 2nd-class seat/sleeper ₹125/180, one to two hours, more than 24 daily

Udaipur sleeper ₹245, six hours, one or two daily (1.10am and 1.30am)

ℹ️ Getting Around

Minibuses and shared autorickshaws link the train station and main bus stand (₹10 per person). A private autorickshaw costs ₹50 to ₹100.

Jhalawar

☑07432 / POP 66,920
Jhalawar is a sprawling town 84km south of Kota that sees few travellers, but has some interesting sights in the surrounding area,

MAJOR TRAINS FROM KOTA

DESTINATION	TRAIN	DEPARTURE	ARRIVAL	FARE (₹)
Agra	19037/19039 Avadh Exp	2.40pm	9.50pm	225/600/850 (A)
Chittorgarh	29020 Dehradun Exp	8.45am	11.35am	170/635/1180 (B)
Delhi (Hazrat Nizamuddin)	12903 Golden Temple Mail	11.05am	6.45pm	315/805/1115/1855 (D)
Jaipur	12955 Mumbai–Jaipur Exp	8.55am	12.40pm	225/580/780/1275 (D)
Mumbai	12904 Golden Temple Mail	2.25pm	5.20pm	490/1275/1805/3035 (D)
Sawai Madhopur	12059 Shatabdi	5.55am	7.03am	125/370 (C)
Udaipur	12963 Mewar Exp	1.30am	7.15am	245/580/780/1275 (D)

Fares: (A) sleeper/3AC/2AC, (B) sleeper/2AC/1AC, (C) 2nd class/AC chair, (D) sleeper/3AC/2AC/1AC

part of their appeal being that they are so seldom visited.

Jhalawar was once the capital of a small princely state created in 1838 by Zalim Singh, the charismatic regent of Kota. Singh signed a treaty with the British on behalf of the young Kota prince, and in return received Jhalawar for his descendants to rule in their own right – his fort and palace still dominate the centre of Jhalawar.

The town is situated at the centre of an opium-producing region, evidence of which you'll see during winter, when the fields are carpeted with picturesque pink and white poppies.

◉ Sights

Gagron Fort   FORT
(◷ dawn-dusk) Don't miss a trip to this spectacular fort, 7km north of Jhalawar. Almost 1km long, it's set high above the confluence of the Kalisindh and Ahu rivers. The rivers surround the building on three sides, while on the fourth is a deep moat. Though not as famous as those at Chittorgarh, Jodhpur and Jaisalmer, the huge fort occupies a prominent place in the annals of Rajput chivalry and has been fought over for centuries.

Ghar Palace   MUSEUM
(Government Museum of Jhalawar; Indian/foreigner ₹20/100; ◷ 9.45am-5.15pm Tue-Sun) Inside the walled fort in the town centre, this sprawling cream-and-terracotta palace was built by Maharaja Madan Singh in 1838. It houses the Government Museum of Jhalawar on the 1st floor. There are galleries of fine sculptures including temple ruins from the surrounding district, excellent miniature paintings and some gruesome weapons. The palace itself features several well-preserved Ramayana and Krishna murals and paintings of poets.

🛏 Sleeping

★ Prithvi Vilas   HERITAGE HOTEL $$$
(☎ 9891349555, 07432-231099; www.visitjhalawar.com; s/d incl all meals from ₹7480/6890; ❋ 🛜 🛖) The former hunting lodge of the rulers of Jhalawar sits proudly in acres of peaceful gardens and farmland and is now a family home as well as a very special homestay. There are just four guest rooms in the main palace, plus another four in an annexe. The rooms are large and eclectic.

❶ Information

Tourist Office (☎ 07432-230081; Hospital Rd (NH 52); ◷ 9.30am-6pm Mon-Fri) An office that may be able to rustle up a brochure with a town map. Inside the grounds of the now defunct RTDC Motel Jhalawar Chandrawati.

❶ Getting There & Away

The road from Kota to Jhalawar continues to be 'under construction' but is reasonable for the most part. Buses to Kota (₹90, 2½ hours, half-hourly) leave from the bus stand, 1km southeast of the fort.

Jhalawar Rd station has a train connection with Kota (2nd-class seat ₹60, 1¼ hours) twice a day.

Chittorgarh (Chittor)

☑ 01472 / POP 184,000
Chittorgarh is the largest fort complex in India, nearly 6km long and 500m across, and is a fascinating place to explore. It sits atop a hill that rises abruptly from the plains, its defensive walls augmented on all sides by 150m-plus cliffs.

Chittorgarh's history epitomises Rajput romanticism, chivalry and tragedy, and it holds a special place in the hearts of many Rajputs. Three times (in 1303, 1535 and 1568) Chittorgarh was under attack from a more powerful enemy; each time, its people chose death before dishonour. The men donned saffron martyrs' robes and rode out from the fort to certain death, while the women and children immolated themselves on huge funeral pyres. After the last of the three sackings, Rana Udai Singh II fled to Udaipur, where he established a new capital. In 1616, Jehangir returned Chittor to the Rajputs. There was no attempt at resettlement, though it was restored in 1905.

◉ Sights

★ Chittorgarh   FORT
(Indian/foreigner ₹40/600; ◷ dawn-dusk) A zig-zag ascent of more than 1km starts at **Padal Pol** and leads through six gateways to the main gate on the western side, the **Ram Pol** (the former back entrance). Inside Ram Pol is a still-occupied village; turn right here for the **ticket office** (◷ dawn-dusk). The rest of the plateau is deserted except for the wonderful palaces, towers and temples that survive from the fort's heyday, along with a few recent temples. A loop road runs around the plateau.

IGOR PLOTNIKOV / SHUTTERSTOCK ©

1. Gateway, Amber Fort (p61) 2. Jodhpur from Mehrangarh (p118)
3. Chittorgarh (p89) 4. Kumbhalgarh (p105)

PHOTOFF / SHUTTERSTOCK ©

Forts of Rajasthan

Emblematic and evocative, the medieval forts of Rajasthan capture the eye and the imagination of travellers and locals alike. These massive fortifications have stood the test of time, resisting enemy attacks and withstanding weather extremes. No longer representing political power, they remain a focal point for many of Rajasthan's cities and towns.

➜ Nestled in the rugged Aravalli Range, just 11km from Jaipur, **Amber Fort** (p61) encompasses peaceful courtyards and palaces protected by formidable yellow-stone battlements.

➜ **Mehrangarh** (p118), literally Majestic Fort, is just that. Rising abruptly from a sheer rocky ridge in the middle of Jodhpur, it casts its stony glare across the city to the deserts beyond.

➜ **Jaisalmer Fort** (Golden Fort; p129) rises out of the Great Thar Desert like a movie set. The fort's 99 bastions and inclined walls encompass a bustling town with palaces, temples and shops.

➜ The fort at **Chittorgarh** (p89) is the largest fort in India and one of the most historically significant in Rajasthan. It perches atop a 180m rocky rise with cliffs dropping from all sides to the surrounding plains.

➜ **Junagarh** (p141) presides over Bikaner not from a lofty hilltop, but through its powerful architecture boasting 37 bastions, 12m-high walls and a 7m-deep moat.

➜ The mighty walls of **Kumbhalgarh** (p105) stretch some 36km along an 1100m-high ridge in the Aravalli Range and are second only to the Great Wall of China in length.

➜ Clad in jungle vines and populated with langur monkeys, **Ranthambhore Fort** (p80) emerges both from the forested ravines and your wildest imaginings to bring Kipling's stories to life.

➜ At the confluence of the Kalisindh and Ahu rivers, 10km from Jhalawar, the large and impressive **Gagron Fort** (p89) is off the tourist trail and well worth the trip.

A typical vehicular exploration of the fort takes two to three hours. Licensed guides charging around ₹400 for up to four hours are available for either walking or autorickshaw tours, usually at the ticket office. There's a sound-and-light show at dusk (Hindi/English ₹100/200); the English show is on Fridays.

➤ **Meera & Kumbha Shyam Temples**

Both of these temples southeast of the **Rana Kumbha Palace** were built by Rana Kumbha in the ornate Indo-Aryan style, with classic, tall *sikharas* (spires). The **Meera Temple**, the smaller of the two, is now associated with the mystic-poetess Meerabai, a 16th-century Mewar royal who was poi-

Chittorgarh (Chittor)

Chittorgarh (Chittor)

◎ **Top Sights**

◎ **Sights**

🛏 **Sleeping**

🍽 **Eating**

soned by her brother-in-law but survived due to the blessings of Krishna. The **Kumbha Shyam Temple** (Temple of Varah) is dedicated to Vishnu and its carved panels illustrate 15th-century Mewar life.

➡ **Tower of Victory**

The glorious **Tower of Victory** (Jaya Stambha), symbol of Chittorgarh, was erected by Rana Kumbha in the 1440s, probably to commemorate a victory over Mahmud Khilji of Malwa. Dedicated to Vishnu, it rises 37m in nine exquisitely carved storeys, and you can climb the 157 narrow stairs (the interior is also carved) to the 8th floor, from where there's a good view of the area.

Below the tower, to the southwest, is the **Mahasati** area, where there are many *sati* (ritual suicide of widow on husband's funeral pyre) stones – this was the royal cremation ground and was also where 13,000 women committed *jauhar* (ritual mass suicide by immolation) in 1535. The **Samidheshwar Temple**, built in the 6th century and restored in 1427, is nearby. Notable among its intricate carving is a Trimurti (three-faced) figure of Shiva.

➡ **Gaumukh Reservoir**

Walk down beyond the Samidheshwar Temple and at the edge of the cliff is a deep tank, the Gaumukh Reservoir, where you can feed the fish. The reservoir takes its name from a spring that feeds the tank from a *gaumukh* (cow's mouth) carved into the cliffside.

➡ **Padmini's Palace**

Continuing south, you reach the **Kalika Mata Temple**, an 8th-century sun temple damaged during the first sacking of Chittorgarh and then converted to a temple for the goddess Kali in the 14th century. **Padmini's Palace** stands about 250m further south, beside a small lake with a central pavilion. The bronze gates to this pavilion were carried off by Akbar and can now be seen in Agra Fort.

➡ **Suraj Pol & Tower of Fame**

Suraj Pol, on the fort's east side, was the main gate and offers fantastic views across the cultivated plains. Opposite is the **Neelkanth Mahadev Jain Temple**. A little further north, the 24m-high **Tower of Fame** (Kirtti Stambha), dating from 1301, is smaller than the Tower of Victory. Built by a Jain merchant, the tower is dedicated to Adinath, the first Jain *tirthankar* (one of the 24 revered Jain teachers) and is decorated with naked figures of various other *tirthankars*,

indicating that it is a monument of the Digambara (sky-clad) order. A narrow stairway leads up the seven storeys to the top. Next door is a 14th-century Jain temple.

🛏 Sleeping & Eating

Chittorgarh Fort Haveli   HOTEL **$**
(☏ 9829170190; www.chittorgarhforthaveli.com; Ram Pol, Chittorgarh Fort; r from ₹1200; 🛜) The newest accommodation inside the fort, this refurbished *haveli* provides clean and comfortable rooms at a budget price. Rooms are furnished simply, but in traditional Rajput style, and some have great views. A small range of meals, including breakfast, is available on the pleasant rooftop terrace.

★ **Padmini Haveli**   HERITAGE HOTEL **$$**
(☏ 9414734497, 9414110090; www.thepadmini haveli.com; Annapoorna Temple Rd, Shah Chowk, Village, Chittorgarh Fort; r/ste incl breakfast ₹4200/5200; 🌀 @ 🛜) This fabulous guesthouse with charming, enthusiastic and well-informed hosts is the best accommodation within the fort. Stylish rooms have granite bathrooms and traditional decoration, and open onto the communal courtyard of the *haveli*. The hosts are official Chittorgarh guides and they live on-site, providing Italian coffee and delicious homemade meals and jams.

There are only six rooms, four standard and two suites, so booking is advised. This white-washed *haveli* with a large black door can be hard to find in the labyrinthine laneways of the village, so call first.

Hotel Pratap Palace   HOTEL **$$**
(☏ 01472-240099; www.hotelpratappalacechittaur garh.com; off Maharana Pratap Setu Marg; s/d from ₹2650/3140; 🌀 @ 🛜) This hotel has a range of rooms, though its business as a lunch stop for bus groups takes precedence over its accommodation enterprise. Even the more expensive rooms can suffer from poor maintenance, and cleanliness standards could be higher. There's a large multicuisine restaurant that produces buffets for tour groups. Try to order à la carte if you can.

The owners also run village tours, horse rides and the upmarket Hotel Castle Bijaipur out of town.

Hotel Castle Bijaipur   HERITAGE HOTEL **$$$**
(☏ 01472-276351; www.castlebijaipur.co.in; Bijaipur; s/d from ₹4500/5000, ste ₹10000; 🌀 🛜 ♨) This fantastically set 16th-century palace is an ideal rural retreat 41km by road east of

Chittorgarh. It's a great place to settle down with a good book, compose a fairy-tale fantasy or just laze around. Rooms are romantic and luxurious, and there's a pleasant garden courtyard and an airy restaurant serving Rajasthani food. It's popular with tour groups.

Reservations should be made through the website or through Chittor's Hotel Pratap Palace. The owners can arrange transfer from Chittor as well as horse and 4WD safaris, birdwatching, cooking classes, massage and yoga.

Chokhi Dhani Garden Family Restaurant INDIAN $
(☑9413716593; Bundi Rd; mains ₹80-150, thalis ₹120-290; ⊙9am-10.30pm; ※☑) This fan-cooled roadside *dhaba* (a casual eatery, serving snacks and basic meals) has extra seating in the back. It does a good-value selection of vegetarian dishes, including filling thalis and a variety of North and South Indian dishes.

ℹ Information

Main post office (Bhilwara Rd; ⊙10am-4pm Mon-Fri, to noon Sat)

State Bank of India (SBI; Bundi Rd)

Tourist office (☑01472-241089; Station Rd; ⊙10am-1.30pm & 2-5pm Mon-Sat) Friendly and helpful, with a town map and brochure.

ℹ Getting There & Away

BUS

Services from the Chittorgarh **bus stand** (Bundi Rd) include the following:

Ajmer (for Pushkar) ₹197, AC ₹347, four hours, hourly until midafternoon

Bundi ₹163, four hours, three daily

Jaipur ₹339, AC ₹660, seven hours, around every 1½ hours

Kota ₹198, four hours, hourly

Udaipur ₹120, AC ₹255, 2½ hours, half-hourly

TRAIN

Ajmer (for Pushkar) sleeper ₹135, three hours, five to seven daily (12.30am, 2.50am, 8.20am, 11.20am, 1.55pm, 5.15pm and 10.30pm)

Bundi sleeper ₹200, two to 3½ hours, three daily (2.50pm, 3.35pm and 8.45pm)

Delhi (Delhi Sarai Rohilla or Hazrat Nizamuddin) sleeper ₹530, 10 hours, two fast trains daily (7.30pm and 8.45pm)

Jaipur sleeper ₹195, 5½ hours, four to five daily (12.30am, 2.50am, 8.20am, 8.35am and 4.15pm)

Sawai Madhopur sleeper ₹275, four to nine hours, three daily (2.50pm, 3.45pm and 8.45pm; the latest is the quickest)

Udaipur sleeper ₹200, two hours, six to seven daily (4.25am, 5.05am, 5.35am, 1.55pm, 2.25pm, 4.50pm and 7.25pm)

ℹ Getting Around

A full tour of the fort by autorickshaw should cost around ₹400 to ₹500 return. You can arrange this yourself in town.

Udaipur

☑0294 / POP 451,100

Udaipur has a romance of setting unmatched in Rajasthan and arguably in all India – snuggling beside tranquil Lake Pichola, with the purple ridges of the Aravalli Range stretching away in every direction. Fantastical palaces, temples, *havelis* and countless narrow, crooked, timeless streets

MAJOR TRAINS FROM CHITTORGARH

DESTINATION	TRAIN	DEPARTURE	ARRIVAL	FARE (₹)
Ajmer (for Pushkar)	12991 Udaipur–Jaipur Exp	8.20am	11.25am	135/515/765/715 (A)
Bundi	29019 MDS–Kota Exp	3.35pm	5.45pm	200/1020/1715 (B)
Delhi (Hazrat Nizamuddin)	12964 Mewar Exp	8.45pm	6.35am	530/1425/2030/3430 (C)
Jaipur	12991 Udaipur–Jaipur Exp	8.20am	1.30pm	195/720/885 (D)
Sawai Madhopur	29019 MDS–Kota Exp	3.35pm	9.25pm	275/1020/1715 (B)
Udaipur	19329 Udaipur City Exp	4.50pm	7.15pm	200/720/1020/1715 (C)

Fares: (A) 2nd-class seat/AC chair/3AC/1st-class seat, (B) sleeper/2AC/1AC, (C) sleeper/3AC/2AC/1AC, (D) 2nd-class seat/AC chair/3AC

add the human counterpoint to the city's natural charms. For the visitor there's the serenity of boat rides on the lakes, the bustle and colour of bazaars, a lively arts scene, the quaint old-world feel of its heritage hotels, tempting shops and some lovely countryside to explore on wheels, feet or horseback.

Udaipur's tag of 'the most romantic spot on the continent of India' was first applied in 1829 by Colonel James Tod, the East India Company's first political agent in the region. Today the romance is wearing slightly thin as ever-taller hotels compete for the best view and traffic clogs ancient thoroughfares.

History

Udaipur was founded in 1568 by Maharana Udai Singh II following the final sacking of Chittorgarh by the Mughal emperor Akbar. This new capital of Mewar had a much less vulnerable location than Chittorgarh. Mewar still had to contend with repeated invasions by the Mughals and, later, the Marathas, until British intervention in the early 19th century. This resulted in a treaty that protected Udaipur from invaders while allowing Mewar's rulers to remain effectively all-powerful in internal affairs. The ex-royal family remains influential and in recent decades has been the driving force behind the rise of Udaipur as a tourist destination.

◎ Sights

★ City Palace   PALACE
(www.eternalmewar.in; adult/child ₹30/15; ☺9am-11pm) Surmounted by balconies, towers and cupolas towering over the lake, the imposing City Palace is Rajasthan's largest palace, with a facade 244m long and 30.4m high. Construction was begun in 1599 by Maharana Udai Singh II, the city's founder, and it later became a conglomeration of structures (including 11 separate smaller palaces) built and extended by various maharanas, though it still manages to retain a surprising uniformity of design.

You can enter the complex through Badi Pol (Great Gate; City Palace Rd) at the northern end, or the Sheetla Mata Gate to the south. Tickets for the City Palace Museum are sold at both entrances. Note: you must pay the ₹30 City Palace entrance ticket in order to pass south through Chandra Chowk Gate, en route to the Crystal Gallery or Rameshwar Ghat for the Lake Pichola boat rides, even if you have a City Palace Museum ticket.

Inside Badi Pol, eight arches on the left commemorate the eight times maharanas were weighed here and their weight in gold or silver distributed to the lucky locals. You then pass through the three-arched Tripolia Gate into a large courtyard, Manek Chowk. Spot the large tiger-catching cage, which worked rather like an oversized mousetrap, and the smaller one for leopards.

★ City Palace Museum   MUSEUM
(City Palace; adult/child ₹300/100, guide per hr ₹250, audio guide ₹200; ☺9.30am-5.30pm, last entry 4.30pm) The main part of the City Palace is open as the City Palace Museum, with rooms extravagantly decorated with mirrors, tiles and paintings, and housing a large and varied collection of artefacts. It's entered from Ganesh Chowk, which you reach from Manek Chowk.

The City Palace Museum begins with the Rai Angan (Royal Courtyard), the very spot where Udai Singh met the sage who told him to build a city here. Rooms along one side contain historical paintings, including several of the Battle of Haldighati (1576), in which Mewar forces under Maharana Pratap, one of the great Rajput heroes, gallantly fought the army of Mughal emperor Akbar to a stalemate.

As you move through the palace, highlights include the Baadi Mahal (1699), where a pretty central garden gives fine views over the city. Kishan (Krishna) Vilas has a remarkable collection of miniatures from the time of Maharana Bhim Singh (r 1778–1828). The story goes that Bhim Singh's daughter Krishna Kumari drank a fatal cup of poison here to solve the dilemma of rival princely suitors from Jaipur and Jodhpur who were both threatening to invade Mewar if she didn't marry them. The Surya Choupad features a huge, ornamental sun – the symbol of the sun-descended Mewar dynasty – and opens into Mor Chowk (Peacock Courtyard) with its lovely mosaics of peacocks, the favourite Rajasthani bird.

The southern end of the museum comprises the Zenana Mahal, the royal ladies' quarters, built in the 17th century. It now contains a long picture gallery with lots of royal hunting scenes (note the comic strip-style of the action in each painting). The Zenana Mahal's central courtyard, Laxmi Chowk, contains a beautiful white pavilion and a stable of howdahs (seat for carrying people on an elephant's back), palanquins and other people-carriers.

RAJASTHAN UDAIPUR

Crystal Gallery
GALLERY

(City Palace; adult/child incl audio guide ₹700/450; ⊙9am-7pm) Houses rare crystal that Maharana Sajjan Singh (r 1874–84) ordered from F&C Osler & Co in England in 1877. The maharana died before it arrived, and all the items stayed forgotten and packed up in boxes for 110 years. The extraordinary, extravagant collection includes crystal chairs, sofas, tables and even beds. The rather hefty admission fee also includes entry to the grand Durbar Hall (City Palace). Tickets are available at the City Palace gates or the Crystal Gallery entrance. Photography is prohibited.

Government Museum
MUSEUM

(Indian/foreigner ₹20/100; ⊙10am-5pm Tue-Sun) Entered from Ganesh Chowk, this museum has a splendid collection of jewel-like miniature paintings of the Mewar school and a turban that belonged to Shah Jahan, creator of the Taj Mahal. Stranger exhibits include a stuffed monkey holding a lamp. There are also regal maharana portraits in profile, documenting Mewar's rulers along with the changing fashions of the moustache.

★ Lake Pichola
LAKE

Limpid and large, Lake Pichola reflects the grey-blue mountains on its mirror-like surface. It was enlarged by Maharana Udai Singh II, following his foundation of the city, by flooding Picholi village, which gave the lake its name. The lake is now 4km long and 3km wide, but remains shallow and dries up completely during severe droughts. The City Palace complex, including the gardens at its southern end, extends nearly 1km along the lake's eastern shore.

Boat trips (Rameshwar Ghat; adult/child 10am-2pm ₹400/200, 3-5pm ₹700/400; ⊙10am-5pm) leave roughly hourly from Rameshwar Ghat, within the City Palace complex (note, you have to pay ₹30 to enter). The trips make a stop at Jagmandir Island, where you

Udaipur

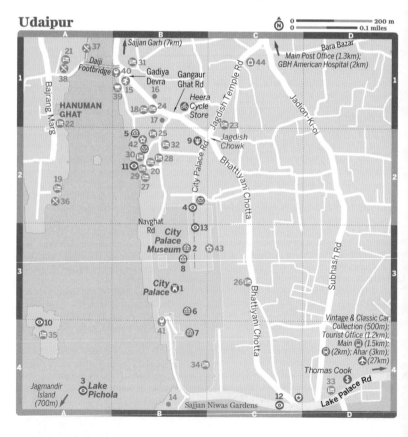

can stay for as long as you like before taking any boat back. Take your own drinks and snacks, though, as those sold on the island are extortionately expensive. You can also take 25-minute boat rides from **Lal Ghat** (Lal Ghat Rd; ₹250 per person) throughout the day without the need to enter the City Palace complex: it's worth checking in advance what time the popular sunset departure casts off.

Jagmandir Island ISLAND
The palace on Jagmandir Island, about 800m south of Jagniwas, was built by Maharana Karan Singh II in 1620, added to by his successor Maharana Jagat Singh, and then changed very little until the last few years when it was partly converted into another (smaller) hotel. When lit up at night it has more romantic sparkle to it than the Lake Palace. As well as the seven hotel rooms, the island has a restaurant, bar and spa, which are open to visitors.

With its entrance flanked by a row of enormous stone elephants, the island has an ornate 17th-century tower, the **Gol Mahal**, carved from bluestone and containing a small exhibit on Jagmandir's history, plus a garden and lovely views across the lake.

Jagdish Temple HINDU TEMPLE
(⊙5.30am-2pm & 4-10pm) Reached by a steep, elephant-flanked flight of steps, 150m north of the City Palace's Badi Pol, the busy Indo-Aryan Jagdish Temple was built by Maharana Jagat Singh in 1651. The wonderfully carved main structure enshrines a black stone image of Vishnu as Jagannath, Lord of the Universe. There's also a brass image of the Garuda (Vishnu's man-bird vehicle) in a shrine facing the main structure.

Udaipur

Bagore-ki-Haveli   MUSEUM
(Gangaur Ghat; Indian/foreigner ₹50/100, camera ₹50; ⊙9.30am-5.30pm) This gracious 18th-century *haveli*, set on the water's edge at Gangaur Ghat, was built by a Mewar prime minister and has since been carefully restored. There are 138 rooms set around courtyards, some arranged to evoke the period during which the house was inhabited, while others house cultural displays, including – intriguingly enough – the world's biggest turban.

The *haveli* also houses a gallery featuring a fascinating collection of period photos of Udaipur and a bizarre collection of world-famous monuments carved out of polystyrene.

Sajjan Garh   PALACE
(Monsoon Palace) Perched on top of a distant hill like a fairy-tale castle, this melancholy, neglected late-19th-century palace was constructed by Maharana Sajjan Singh. Originally an astronomical centre, it became a monsoon palace and hunting lodge. Now government owned, it's in a sadly dilapidated state, but visitors stream up here for the marvellous views, particularly at sunset. It's 5km west of the old city as the crow flies, about 9km by the winding road.

At the foot of the hill you enter the 5-sq-km **Sajjan Garh Wildlife Sanctuary** (Indian/foreigner ₹50/300, car ₹200). A good way to visit is with the daily sunset excursion in a minivan driven by an enterprising taxi driver who picks up tourists at the entrance to Bagore-ki-Haveli at Gangaur Ghat every day at 5pm. The round trip costs ₹350 per person, including waiting time (but not the sanctuary fees). His minivan has 'Monsoon Palace–Sajjangarh Fort' written across the front of it. Alternatively, autorickshaws charge ₹200 one way to the sanctuary gate, which they are not allowed to pass. Share taxis ferry people the final 4km up to the palace for ₹200 per person.

Vintage & Classic Car Collection   MUSEUM
(Garden Hotel, Lake Palace Rd; adult/child ₹350/200; ⊙9am-9pm) The maharanas' car collection makes a fascinating diversion, for what it tells about their elite lifestyle and for the vintage vehicles themselves. Housed within the former state garage are 22 splendid vehicles, including the beautiful 1934 Rolls-Royce Phantom used in the Bond film *Octopussy,* and the Cadillac convertible that whisked Queen Elizabeth II to the airport in 1961. The museum is a 10-minute walk east along Lake Palace Rd.

🏃 Activities

Krishna Ranch   HORSE RIDING
(☑9828059505; www.krishnaranch.com; full day incl lunch ₹3700) Experienced owner-guide Dinesh Jain leads most trips himself, riding local Marwari horses. The ranch is situated in beautiful countryside near Hawala village, 7km northwest of Udaipur. There are also attractive cottages (p101) at the ranch.

Prakash Yoga   YOGA
(☑0294-2524872; inside Chandpol; by donation; ⊙classes 8am & 7pm) A friendly hatha yoga centre with hour-long classes. The teacher has more than 20 years' experience. It's tucked inside Chandpol, near the footbridge, but well signed.

🍳 Courses

Shashi Cooking Classes   COOKING
(☑9929303511; www.shashicookingclasses.blogspot.com; Sunrise Restaurant, 18 Gangaur Ghat Rd; 4hr class ₹1500; ⊙classes 10.30am & 5.30pm) Readers rave about Shashi's high-spirited classes, where you can learn to cook many fundamental Indian dishes. Classes go for 3½ to four hours and include a free recipe booklet.

Sushma's Cooking Classes   COOKING
(☑7665852163; www.cookingclassesinudaipur.com; Hotel Krishna Niwas, 35 Lal Ghat; 2hr class ₹1500) A highly recommended cooking class run by the enthusiastic Sushma. Classes

---

ANIMAL AID UNLIMITED

The spacious refuge of **Animal Aid Unlimited** (☑9784005989, 9829843726; www.animalaidunlimited.org; Badi Village) treats around 200 street animals a day (mainly dogs, donkeys and cows) and answers more than 3000 emergency rescue calls a year. The refuge welcomes volunteers and visitors: you can visit between 9am and noon without needing to call first. The refuge is in Badi village, 7km northwest of Udaipur.

A round trip by autorickshaw, including waiting time, costs around ₹500. Call Animal Aid Unlimited if you see an injured or ill street animal in Udaipur.

offer up anything from traditional Rajasthani dishes and learning how to make spice mixes, through bread-making to the all-important method of making the perfect cup of chai.

Prem Musical Instruments MUSIC
(✆9414343583; 28 Gadiya Devra; per hr ₹700; ⊙9am-8.30pm) Rajesh Prajapati (Bablu) is a successful local musician who gives sitar, tabla and flute lessons. From his tiny shop established in 1997 he also sells and repairs instruments and can arrange performances.

Ashoka Arts ARTS & CRAFTS
(Hotel Gangaur Palace, Ashoka Haveli, Gangaur Ghat Rd; per hr from ₹200) Learn the basics of classic miniature painting from a local master.

Tours

Art of Bicycle Trips CYCLING
(✆8769822745; www.artofbicycletrips.com; 27 Gadiya Devra, inside Chandpol; half-day tour ₹2000) This well-run outfit offers a great way to get out of the city. The Lakecity Loop is a 30km half-day tour that quickly leaves Udaipur behind to have you wheeling through villages, farmland and along the shores of Fateh Sagar and Badi Lakes. Other options include a vehicle-supported trip further afield to Kumbhalgarh and Ranakpur. Bikes are well maintained and all come with helmets.

Millets of Mewar WALKING
(✆8890419048; www.milletsofmewar.org; Hanuman Ghat; per person ₹2000) Health-food specialists Millets of Mewar (p102) organises two-hour city tours (minimum two people) on which you can meet local artisans who live and work in Udaipur. Tours should be booked a day in advance; they leave from the restaurant at 10am.

Sleeping

Many budget and midrange lodgings cluster close to the lake, especially on its eastern side in Lal Ghat. This area is a tangle of streets and lanes close to the City Palace. It's Udaipur's tourist epicentre and has numerous eateries and shops. Directly across the water from Lal Ghat, Hanuman Ghat has a slightly more local vibe and often better views, though you're certainly not out of the tourist zone.

Lal Ghat

Lal Ghat Guest House GUESTHOUSE $
(✆0294-2525301, 9414812491; www.lalghat.com; 33 Lal Ghat; dm ₹250, r ₹750, with AC ₹2000; ❋@🖥) This mellow guesthouse by the lake was one of the first to open in Udaipur, and it's still a sound choice, with an amazing variety of older and newer rooms. Accommodation ranges from a spruce, nonsmoking dorm (with curtained-off beds and lockers under the mattresses) to the best room, which sports a stone wall, a big bed, a big mirror and air-con.

Bunkyard Hostel HOSTEL $
(✆9166656366; Lal Ghat; dm ₹550, r from ₹1700; ❋🖥) Bright and cheerful, Bunkyard has colourful rooms, helpful staff and a rooftop restaurant with lake views. There's free chai on the roof at sunset. Note that the dorm is air-conditioned.

Nukkad Guest House GUESTHOUSE $
(✆0294-2411403; nukkad_raju@yahoo.com; 56 Ganesh Ghati; s without bathroom ₹200, r ₹550-800; 🖥) Nukkad has clean and simple fan-cooled rooms radiating off a vertigo-inspiring central atrium. On the roof there's a sociable restaurant were you can access the hotel's wi-fi. Join afternoon cooking classes and morning yoga sessions (by donation) without stepping outside the door – just don't stay out past curfew or get caught washing your clothes in your bathroom.

Akshara Guest House HOTEL $
(✆9414233571; akshara.guesthouse@gmail.com; 73 Gangaur Ghat Rd; r fan only ₹1200, with AC ₹3000; ❋🖥) This small hotel of just six rooms, two with air-con and views, is found above Cafe Edelweiss (p101) and is run by the same management. Rooms are clean and comfortable and, of course, located in the heart of the tourist district.

Jaiwana Haveli HOTEL $$
(✆9829005859, 0294-2411103; www.jaiwanahaveli.com; 14 Lal Ghat; r incl breakfast ₹5000; ❋@🖥) Professionally run by two helpful brothers and efficient staff, this smart place has spotless, unfussy rooms with good beds, TVs and attractive block-printed fabrics. Book a corner room for views. The rooftop restaurant has great lake views and Indian food (mains ₹250 to ₹595), plus there's a mod cafe (p102) on the ground floor.

RAJASTHAN UDAIPUR

New Section

Hotel Baba Palace
HOTEL **$$**

(☎ 0294-2427126; www.hotelbabapalace.com; Jagdish Chowk; r incl breakfast from ₹2000; ❄ 🛜) This central hotel has sparkling rooms with decent beds behind solid doors and there's an elevator. It's eye to eye with the Jagdish Temple, so many of the rooms have interesting views; all have air-conditioning and TVs, some have delightfully canopied beds. On top there's the popular Mayur Rooftop Cafe. Free airport pickups available.

Hotel Krishna Niwas
HOTEL **$$**

(☎ 0294-2420163, 9414167341; www.hotelkrishna niwas.com; 35 Lal Ghat; d ₹1750-2499; ❄ @ 🛜) Run by an artist family, Krishna Niwas has smart, clean, air-conditioned rooms; those with views are smaller, and some come with balconies. There are splendid vistas from the rooftop, and a decent restaurant. You can also try your own cooking or paint your own miniature after taking an in-house cooking lesson (p98) or painting course (₹1200 for three hours).

Pratap Bhawan
HOTEL **$$**

(☎ 0294-2560566; www.pratapbhawanudaipur. com; 12 Lal Ghat; r ₹1650-2500; ❄ 🛜) A curving marble staircase leads up from the wide lobby to large rooms with big bathrooms and, in many cases, cushioned window seats. A deservedly popular place, with the excellent rooftop Charcoal restaurant.

Poonam Haveli
HOTEL **$$**

(☎ 0294-2410303; www.hotelpoonamhaveli.com; 39 Lal Ghat; r incl breakfast ₹3480; ❄ @ 🛜) A modern place decked out in traditional style, friendly Poonam has 16 spacious, spotlessly clean rooms with marble floors, big beds, TVs and spare but tasteful decor, plus pleasant sitting areas. None of the rooms enjoy lake views, but the rooftop Winter garden restaurant does, and it also makes wood-fired pizzas among the usual Indian and traveller fare. There is an elevator.

Hotel Gangaur Palace
HERITAGE HOTEL **$$**

(☎ 0294-2422303; www.ashokahaveli.com; Ashoka Haveli, 339 Gangaur Ghat Rd; s ₹800, d ₹1500-3000; ❄ @ 🛜) This elaborate, faded *haveli* is set around a stone-pillared courtyard, with a wide assortment of rooms on several floors. It's gradually moving upmarket with an elevator and with bright rooms featuring lake views, wall paintings and window seats.

The hotel also has an in-house palm reader, a fixed-price art shop, art school (p99), and a rooftop cafe and restaurant.

★ Jagat Niwas
Palace Hotel
HERITAGE HOTEL **$$$**

(☎ 0294-2420133, 7073000378; www.jagatniwas palace.com; 23-25 Lal Ghat; r incl breakfast from ₹5096; ❄ 🛜 ⛵) This leading hotel set in two converted lakeside *havelis* takes the location cake, and staff are efficient and always courteous. The lake-view rooms are charming, with carved wooden furniture, cushioned window seats and pretty prints. Rooms without a lake view are as comfortable and attractive, and considerably cheaper, than those with the view.

Kankarwa Haveli
HERITAGE HOTEL **$$$**

(☎ 0294-2411457; www.kankarwahaveli.com; 26 Lal Ghat; r/ste incl breakfast from ₹3200/7450; ❄ 🛜) This is one of Udaipur's few hotels that are genuine old *havelis*, as opposed to new buildings made to look like old *havelis*. It's right by the lake, and the whitewashed and pastel-hued rooms, set around a courtyard, have a lovely simplicity with splashes of colour. Rooms vary in size and outlook, and there's a rooftop vegetarian restaurant.

Hanuman Ghat

Dream Heaven
GUESTHOUSE **$**

(☎ 9928258222, 0294-2431038; www.dreamheav en.co.in; r ₹400-1200; ❄ @ 🛜) This higgledy-piggledy building boasts clean rooms with wall hangings and paintings. Bathrooms are smallish, though some rooms have a decent balcony and/or views. The food at the rooftop restaurant (dishes ₹120 to ₹200), which overlooks the lake, is fresh and tasty; it's the perfect place to chill out on a pile of cushions.

goStops Udaipur
HOSTEL **$**

(☎ 1133138155; www.gostops.com; dm incl breakfast ₹425-500; r incl breakfast ₹2130, with AC ₹2660; ❄ 🛜) The attractions of this buzzing place include the rooftop space to chill out, the colourful decor and the sheer number of activities, including walks, yoga, bike rides and painting courses, that are scheduled regularly. It is relatively peaceful, too.

Amet Haveli
HERITAGE HOTEL **$$**

(☎ 0294-2431085; www.amethaveliudaipur.com; s/d from ₹3750/4130; ❄ @ 🛜 ⛵) A 350-year-old heritage building on the lakeshore, with delightful rooms featuring cushioned window seats, coloured glass and little shutters. They're set around a pretty courtyard and pond. Splurge on one with a balcony or giant bathtub. One of Udaipur's most romantic restaurants, Ambrai (p102), is part of the hotel.

City Palace

Hotel Raj Palace HERITAGE HOTEL $$
(www.hotelrajpalaceudaipur.com; 103 Bhatiyani Chauhatta; r from ₹1680; ❋🏶🛏) This 300-year-old *haveli* snuggling up to the back wall of the city palace, is a little rough and worn around the edges. But there's plenty of character, a delightful swimming pool (with waterfall) and a couple of shady courtyards. Rooms are, for the most part, renovated with modern bathrooms and traditional touches. There's a restaurant on-site.

Shiv Niwas Palace Hotel HERITAGE HOTEL $$$
(📞0294-2528016; www.hrhhotels.com; City Palace Complex; r ₹14,000-72,000; ❋🏶🛏) This hotel, in the former palace guest quarters, has opulent common areas such as its pool courtyard, bar and lawn garden. Some of the suites are truly palatial, filled with fountains and silver, but the standard rooms are poorer value. Go for a suite, or just for a drink, meal or massage. Rates drop dramatically from April to September.

Taj Lake Palace HERITAGE HOTEL $$$
(📞0294-2428800; www.tajhotels.com; r from ₹35,000; ❋@🏶🛏) The icon of Udaipur, this romantic white-marble palace seemingly floating on the lake is extraordinary, with open-air courtyards, lotus ponds and a small, mango-tree-shaded pool. Rooms are hung with breezy silks and filled with carved furniture. Some of the cheapest overlook the lily pond rather than the lake; the mural-decked suites will make you truly feel like a maharaja.

Other Areas

Rangniwas Palace Hotel HERITAGE HOTEL $$
(📞0294-2523890; www.rangniwaspalace.com; Lake Palace Rd; s/d from ₹1460/1760, ste ₹5900; ❋🏶🛏) This 19th-century palace has plenty of heritage character, though some rooms are rather old-fashioned. There's a central garden with a small pool shaded by mature palms. The quaint rooms in the older section are the most appealing, while the suites – featuring terraces with swing seats or balcony window seats overlooking the garden – are a delight.

Krishna Ranch COTTAGE $$
(📞9828059506, 9828059505; www.krishnaranch. com; s/d incl breakfast from ₹2200/2500; ❋🏶) 🌿 This delightful countryside retreat has five cottages set around the grounds of a small farm. Each comes with attached bathroom (with solar-heated shower), tasteful decor and farm views. Meals are prepared using organic produce grown on the farm. The ranch is 7km from town, near Badi village, but there's free pickup from Udaipur.

It's an ideal base for the hikes and horse treks (p98) that the management – a Dutch-Indian couple – organise from here, though you don't have to sign up for the treks to stay here.

Eating

Udaipur has scores of sun-kissed rooftop restaurants, many with mesmerising lake views. The fare is not always that inspiring or varied, but competition keeps most places striving for improvement.

Lal Ghat

Cafe Edelweiss CAFE $
(73 Gangaur Ghat Rd; sandwiches from ₹180; ⊙8am-8pm; 🏶) This itsy cafe serves tasty baked goods and real coffee. Offerings include sticky cinnamon rolls, chocolate cake and apple crumble. There's muesli or eggs for breakfast, and various sandwiches available all day.

Charcoal MULTICUISINE $$
(📞9414235252; www.charcoalpb.com; Pratap Bhawan, 12 Lal Ghat; mains ₹180-550; ⊙8am-11pm; 🏶) As the name implies, barbecue, satay and tandoor specials feature at this innovative rooftop restaurant. There are plenty of vegetarian and juicy meat dishes on offer and the homemade soft corn tacos with a variety of fillings are deservedly popular.

Mayur Rooftop Cafe MULTICUISINE $$
(Hotel Baba Palace, Jagdish Chowk; mains ₹210-380; ⊙7am-10pm; ❋🏶) This delightful rooftop restaurant has a great view of the multihued light show on the Jagdish Temple. Choose between the air-con room or the breezy open section. The usual multicuisine themes fill out the menu, and the quality is top-notch. The Rajasthani thali is a great way to introduce yourself to Rajasthani

cuisine – quite different from the standard North Indian cuisine.

Vegetarians will love the choice of nine paneer dishes.

★ **Jagat Niwas Palace Hotel**   INDIAN $$$
(☑ 0294-2420133; 23-25 Lal Ghat; mains ₹250-500; ☺ 7-10am, noon-3pm & 6-10pm) A wonderful, classy, rooftop restaurant with superb views towards the city palace, Lake Pichola and Hanuman Ghat. Choose from an extensive selection of mouthwatering curries (tempered for Western tastes) – mutton, chicken, fish, veg – as well as the tandoori classics. There's a tempting cocktail menu, Indian wine and icy-cold beer. Book ahead for dinner.

Savage Garden   MEDITERRANEAN $$$
(☑ 8890627181; 73 Gangaur Ghat Rd; mains ₹280-520; ☺ 11am-11pm) Savage Garden does a winning line in soups, chicken, and homemade pasta dishes. Try ravioli with goat ragu, and the signature sweet-savoury chicken breast stuffed with cashew nuts and paneer cheese and served with carrot rice. The splendid rooftop setting (up a narrow set of stairs) is above Cafe Edelweiss (and run by the same management).

✖ Hanuman Ghat

Millets of Mewar   INDIAN $
(☑ 8769348440; www.milletsofmewar.org; mains ₹130-250, thali ₹250; ☺ 8.30am-10.30pm; 🛜) 🍃 Local millet is used where possible instead of wheat and rice at this environmentally aware, slow-food restaurant. There are vegan options, gluten-free dishes, fresh salads, and juices and herbal teas. Also on the menu are multigrain sandwiches and millet pizzas, plus regular curries, Indian snacks, pasta and pancakes.

Little Prince   MULTICUISINE $$
(Daiji Footbridge; mains ₹180-290, veg thali ₹350; ☺ 8.30am-11pm) This lovely open-air eatery looking towards the quaint Daiji Footbridge dishes up delicious veg and nonveg meals. There are plenty of Indian options, along with pizzas, pastas and some original variations on the usual multicuisine theme, including Korean and Israeli dishes. The ambience is super relaxed and the service friendly.

★ **Ambrai**   NORTH INDIAN $$$
(☑ 0294-2431085; www.amethaveliudaipur.com; Amet Haveli; mains ₹320-690; ☺ 12.30-3pm &

7.30-10.30pm) Set at lakeshore level, looking across the water to the floodlit City Palace in one direction and Jagniwas in the other, this is one highly romantic restaurant at night with candlelit, white-linen tables beneath spreading rayan trees. And the service and cuisine do justice to its fabulous position, with terrific tandoor and curries and a bar to complement the dining.

🍷 Drinking & Nightlife

Paps Juices   JUICE BAR
(inside Chandpol; ☺ 9am-8pm) This bright-red spot is tiny but very welcoming, and a great place to refuel during the day with a shot of Vitamin C from a wide range of delicious juice mixes. If you want something more substantial, the various muesli mixes are pretty good, too.

Jaiwana Bistro Lounge   CAFE
(☑ 9829005859; Jaiwana Haveli, 14 Lal Ghat; ☺ 7am-10.30pm; 🛜) This modern, cool and clean cafe has espresso coffee and fresh healthy juices to help wash down the tasty bakery items and other main meals.

Jheel's Ginger Coffee Bar & Bakery   CAFE
(Jheel Palace Guest House, 56 Gangaur Ghat Rd; ☺ 8am-8pm; 🛜) This small but slick cafe by the water's edge is on the ground floor of Jheel Palace Guest House. Large windows and a waterside sit-out afford good lake views, and the coffee is excellent. It also does a range of cakes and snacks. Note, you can take your coffee up to the open-air rooftop restaurant if you like.

Sunset Terrace   BAR
(Fateh Prakash Palace Hotel; ☺ 7am-10.30pm) On a terrace overlooking Lake Pichola, this bar is perfect for a sunset gin and tonic. It's also a restaurant (mains ₹800 to ₹1500), with live music performed every night.

☆ Entertainment

Dharohar   DANCE
(☑ 0294-2523858; Bagore-ki-Haveli; Indian/foreigner ₹90/150, camera ₹150; ☺ ticket sales 6.15pm, show 7pm) The beautiful Bagore-ki-Haveli (p98) hosts the best (and most convenient) opportunity to see Rajasthani folk dancing, with nightly shows of colourful, energetic Marwari, Bhil and western Rajasthani dances, as well as traditional Rajasthani puppetry.

Mewar Sound & Light Show
LIVE PERFORMANCE

(Manek Chowk, City Palace; adult/child from ₹250/150; ⊙7pm Sep-Apr, 8pm May-Aug) Fifteen centuries of intriguing Mewar history are squeezed into one atmospheric hour of commentary and light switching – in English from September to April, in Hindi other months. Seating is either on a raised platform (Hathnal ki Chandni) or at ground level (Manmek Chowk).

Shopping

Tourist-oriented shops – selling miniature paintings, woodcarvings, silver jewellery, bangles, spices, camel-bone boxes, and a large variety of textiles – line the streets radiating out from Jagdish Chowk. Udaipur is known for its local crafts, particularly miniature painting in the Rajput-Mughal style, as well as some interesting contemporary art.

The local market area extends east from the old clock tower at the northern end of Jagdish Temple Rd, and buzzes loudest in the evening. It's fascinating as much for browsing and soaking up local atmosphere as it is for buying. Bara Bazar, immediately east of the old clock tower, sells silver and gold, while its narrow side street, Maldas St, specialises in saris and fabric. A little further east, traditional shoes are sold on Mochiwada.

Foodstuffs and spices are mainly found around the new clock tower at the east end of the bazaar area, and Mandi Market, 200m north of the tower.

Sadhna
CLOTHING

(⊡0294-2454655; www.sadhna.org; Jagdish Temple Rd; ⊙10.30am-7pm) 🖉 This is the crafts outlet for Seva Mandir, a long-established NGO working with rural and tribal people. The small, hard-to-see shop sells attractive fixed-price textiles; profits go to the artisans and towards community development work.

ⓘ Information

EMERGENCY
Police (⊡0294-2414600, emergency 100; Bhattiyani Chotta, Sheetla Mata Gate) The tourism police office. There are also police posts at Suraj Pol, Hati Pol and Delhi Gate, three of the gates in the old-city wall.

MEDICAL SERVICES
GBH American Hospital (⊡emergency 9352304050, enquiries 0294-2426000; www. gbhamericanhospital.com; Meera Girls College Rd, 101 Kothi Bagh, Bhatt Ji Ki Bari) Modern private hospital with 24-hour emergency service, about 2km northeast of the old city.

MONEY
There are ATMs along Gangaur Ghat Rd, City Palace Rd, near the bus stand and outside the train station.

Thomas Cook (Lake Palace Rd; ⊙9.30am-6.30pm Mon-Sat) Changes cash and travellers cheques.

POST
DHL (1 Town Hall Rd; ⊙10am-7pm Mon-Sat) Has a free collection service within Udaipur.

DHL Express (⊡0294-2525301, 9414812491; Lal Ghat Guest House, Lal Ghat) Conveniently situated inside Lal Ghat Guest Huse.

Main post office (Chetak Circle; ⊙10am-1pm & 1.30-6pm Mon-Sat) North of the old city.

Post office (City Palace Rd; ⊙10am-4pm Mon-Sat) Tiny post office that sends parcels (including packaging them up), and there are virtually no queues. Beside the City Palace's Badi Pol ticket office.

RSRTC BUSES FROM UDAIPUR

DESTINATION	FARE (₹)	TIME (HR)	FREQUENCY
Ahmedabad	235, AC 580	5	6 daily from 5.30am
Ajmer (for Pushkar)	296	7-10	hourly from 5am
Bundi	328	6	daily (7.45am)
Chittorgarh	120, AC 210	2½	half-hourly from 5.15am
Delhi	672, AC 1766	15	2 or 4 daily
Jaipur	424, AC 767	9	hourly
Jodhpur	273, AC 599	6-8	hourly
Kota	321	7	hourly
Mt Abu (Abu Road)	198	4	daily (8.45am)

TOURIST INFORMATION

The official **tourist office** (📞 0294-2411535; Fateh Memorial Bldg, Airport Rd; ⏰10am-5pm Mon-Fri) is situated near Suraj Pol and is of little use apart from supplying a map. Small tourist offices operate erratically at the train station and airport.

ⓘ Getting There & Away

AIR

Udaipur's airport, 25km east of town, is served by flights from Delhi, Mumbai and other hubs. A prepaid taxi from the airport to the Lal Ghat area costs ₹450.

Air India (📞1860-2331407, 011-24667473; www.airindia.com) Flies daily to Mumbai and Delhi.

IndiGo (📞 011-43513200; www.goindigo.in) Two direct flights daily to Delhi and one direct flight daily to Mumbai and Jaipur.

Jet Airways (📞91-39893333; www.jetairways.com) Flies twice daily to Delhi and daily to Mumbai.

SpiceJet (📞0987-1803333; www.spicejet.com) Flies daily to Delhi and Mumbai.

BUS

RSRTC and private buses run from the main bus stand, 1.5km east of the City Palace. Turn left at the end of Lake Palace Rd, take the first right then cross the main road at the end, just after passing through the crumbling old Suraj Pol. It's around ₹50 in an autorickshaw.

If arriving by bus, turn left out of the bus stand, cross the main road, walk through Suraj Pol then turn left at the end of the road before taking the first right into Lake Palace Rd.

Private bus tickets can also be bought at any one of the many travel agencies lining the road leading from Jagdish Temple to Daiji Footbridge.

TRAIN

The train station is about 2.5km southeast of the City Palace, and 1km directly south of the main

bus stand. An autorickshaw between the train station and Jagdish Chowk should cost around ₹100 to ₹150.

There are no direct trains to Abu Road, Jodhpur or Jaisalmer.

Agra sleeper ₹530, 13 hours, daily (10.20pm)

Ajmer (for Pushkar) seat/sleeper ₹195/325, five hours, four daily (6am, 3.05pm, 5.15pm and 10.20pm), via Chittorgarh (seat/sleeper ₹115/230, two hours)

Bundi sleeper ₹220, 4½ hours, daily (6.15pm)

Delhi sleeper ₹560, 12 hours, two daily (5.15pm and 6.15pm)

Jaipur seat/sleeper ₹240/375, around seven hours, three daily (6am, 3.05pm and 10.20pm)

ⓘ Getting Around

Most hotels, guesthouses and travel agencies (many of which are on the road leading down to the lake from Jagdish Temple) can organise a car and driver to just about anywhere you want. As an example, a return day trip to Ranakpur and Kumbhalgarh will cost you around ₹3000 per vehicle.

AUTORICKSHAW

These are unmetered, so you should agree on a fare before setting off – the normal fare anywhere in town is around ₹50 to ₹100. You will usually have to go through the rigmarole of haggling, walking away etc to get this fare. Some drivers ask tourists for ₹150 or more. It costs around ₹400 to ₹500 to hire an autorickshaw for a day of local sightseeing.

The commission system is in place, so you'll need to tenaciously pursue your first choice of accommodation.

BICYCLE & MOTORCYCLE

A cheap and environmentally friendly way to buzz around is by bicycle (around ₹200 per day), although motorcycle traffic and pollution make it very tiresome if not dangerous. Scooters and motorbikes, meanwhile, are great for exploring the surrounding countryside.

MAJOR TRAINS FROM UDAIPUR

DESTINATION	TRAIN	DEPARTURE	ARRIVAL	FARE (₹)
Agra (Cantonment)	19666 Udaipur–Kurj Exp	10.20pm	11am	530/1450 (A)
Ajmer (for Pushkar)	09722 Udaipur–Jaipur SF SPL	3.05pm	8pm	195/840 (B)
Bundi	12964 Mewar Exp	6.15pm	10.35pm	285/765 (A)
Chittorgarh	12982 Chetak Exp	5.15pm	7.10pm	230/765 (A)
Delhi (Hazrat Nizamuddin)	12964 Mewar Exp	5.15pm	5.05am	560/1500 (A)
Jaipur	12991 Udaipur–Jaipur Exp	6am	1.35pm	240/1075 (B)

Fares: (A) sleeper/3AC, (B) 2nd-class seat/AC chair

Heera Cycle Store (📞 9950611973; off Gangaur Ghat Rd; ⏱ 7.30am-8pm) hires out bicycles/scooters/Bullets for ₹200/500/800 per day (with a deposit of US$200/400/500); you must show your passport and driver's licence. There are numerous other hire companies in and around Lal Ghat.

Around Udaipur

Kumbhalgarh

📞 02954

About 80km north of Udaipur is Kumbhalgarh, a remote historical fort, outwardly fulfilling expectations of the chivalrous and warlike Rajput era. Its associated battlements are said to be second only to the Great Wall of China in extent. However, the poor condition and barren rooms of the palace complex do nothing to evoke the splendour of the past let alone justify the inflated admission price for foreigners.

The rugged Kumbhalgarh Wildlife Sanctuary (p106) can also be visited from Kumbhalgarh.

◎ Sights

Kumbhalgarh   FORT
(Indian/foreigner ₹40/600; ⏱ 9am-6pm) One of the many forts built by Rana Kumbha (r 1433–68), under whom Mewar reached its greatest extents, this isolated fort with a derelict palace is perched 1100m above sea level, with hazy views melting into the distance. The journey to the fort, along twisting roads through the Aravalli Hills, is a highlight in itself, while the crumbling empty palace complex within the fort hardly justifies the foreigner entry price.

Kumbhalgarh was the most important Mewar fort after Chittorgarh, and the rulers, sensibly, used to retreat here in times of danger. Not surprisingly, Kumbhalgarh was only taken once in its entire history. Even then, it took the combined armies of Amber, Marwar and Mughal emperor Akbar to breach its strong defences, and they only managed to hang on to it for two days.

The fort's thick walls stretch about 36km; they're wide enough in some places for eight horses to ride abreast and it's possible to walk right round the circuit (allow two days). They enclose around 360 intact and ruined temples, some of which date back to the Mauryan period in the 2nd century BC,

as well as palaces, gardens, step-wells and 700 cannon bunkers.

If you're staying here and want to make an early start on your hike around the wall, you may still get into the fort before 9am, although no one will be around to sell you a ticket.

There's a sound and light show (in Hindi) at the fort at 6.30pm (Indian/foreigner ₹118/236).

⏹ Sleeping & Eating

Kumbhal Castle   HOTEL $$
(📞 9116616217; www.thekumbhalcastle.com; Fort Rd; r from ₹3130; ❋ 🛜 ✖) The Kumbhal Castle, 2km from the fort, has old-fashioned but pleasant rooms featuring bright bedspreads and window seats, shared balconies and good views. The superdeluxe rooms are considerably bigger and worth considering for the few hundred extra rupees. There's an in-house restaurant.

Aodhi   HOTEL $$$
(📞 8003722333; www.hrhhotels.com; r from ₹8160; ❋ @ 🛜 ✖) Just under 2km from the fort is this luxurious and blissfully tranquil hotel with an inviting pool, rambling shady gardens and winter bonfires. The spacious rooms, in different styles of stone cottages, have private terraces, balconies or pavilions, and are decorated with wildlife and botanical art.

Nonguests can dine in the restaurant, where good North Indian fare is the pick of the options on offer, or have a drink in the cosy Chopal Bar. Room rates plummet from April to September.

❶ Getting There & Away

A day-long round trip in a private car from Udaipur to Kumbhalgarh and Ranakpur will cost around ₹3000 per car. This is by far the best way to tackle these sights.

You can get there by bus, but will need to be happy to be sardined into a battered bus and prepared for cancellations leaving you potentially stranded (don't say we didn't warn you). From Udaipur's main bus stand, catch a Ranakpur-bound bus as far as Saira (₹81, 2¼ hours, hourly), a tiny crossroads town where you can change for a bus to Kumbhalgarh (₹43, one hour, hourly). That bus, which will be bound for Kelwara, will drop you at the start of the approach road to the fort, leaving you with a 1.5km uphill walk to the entrance gate.

The last bus back to Saira swings by at 5.30pm (and is always absolutely jam packed). The last

WORTH A TRIP

KUMBHALGARH WILDLIFE SANCTUARY

Ranakpur is a great base for exploring the hilly, densely forested **Kumbhalgarh Wildlife Sanctuary** (Indian/foreigner ₹50/300, 4WD or car ₹200; ⊙ safaris 6-9am & 3-4.30pm), which extends over some 600 sq km. It's known for its leopards and deer, although the chances of spotting antelopes, gazelles, deer and possibly sloth bears are higher, especially from March to June. You will certainly see some of the sanctuary's 200-plus bird species.

Beside the park office, near the Ranakpur Jain temples, is the recommended tour company **Evergreen Safari** (☑ 7568830064; 4WD 2½hr ₹2500). There are also several safari outfits on the road leading up to Kumbhalgarh Fort, including **A-one Tour & Safari** (☑ 8003854293; Pratap Circle; 4WD 2½hr ₹3500; ⊙ safaris 6-9am & 3-4.30pm). Most hotels will use these or similar outfits to organise your safari.

There's a ticket office for the sanctuary right beside where the bus drops you off for the Jain temples, but the nearest of the sanctuary's four entrances is 2km beyond here.

bus from Saira back to Udaipur leaves at around 8pm. To get to Ranakpur from Kumbhalgarh, head first to Saira then change for Ranakpur (₹23, 40 minutes, at least hourly).

Ranakpur

On the western slopes of the Aravalli Hills, 75km northwest of Udaipur, and 12km west of Kumbhalgarh as the crow flies (but 50km by road, via Saira), the village of Ranakpur hosts one of India's biggest and most important Jain temple complexes.

The village also makes a great base for exploring the impressive Kumbhalgarh Wildlife Sanctuary or for taking a day trip to visit the fort at Kumbhalgarh (p105).

◉ Sights

Chaumukha Mandir   JAIN TEMPLE
(Ranakpur Jain Temple; Indian/foreigner free/₹200, camera or cell phone ₹100; ⊙ Jains 6am-7pm, non-Jains noon-5pm) Built in the 15th century in milk-white marble, the main temple of Ranakpur, Chaumukha Mandir (Four-Faced Temple), is dedicated to Adinath, the first *tirthankar* (great Jain teacher), depicted in the many Buddha-like images in the temple. An incredible feat of Jain devotion, the temple is a complicated series of 29 halls, 80 domes and 1444 individually engraved pillars. The interior is completely covered in knotted, lovingly wrought carving, and has a marvellously calming sense of space and harmony. Entry includes audio guide.

Shoes, cigarettes, food and all leather articles must be left at the entrance (there are lockers, ₹10); women who are menstruating are asked not to enter.

Also exquisitely carved and well worth inspecting are two other Jain temples, dedicated to Neminath (the 22nd *tirthankar*) and Parasnath (the 23rd *tirthankar*), both within the complex, and a nearby Sun Temple. About 1km from the main complex is the Amba Mata Temple.

🛏 Sleeping & Eating

⭐ **Aranyawas**   HOTEL $$$
(☑ 02956-293029; www.aranyawas.com; r from ₹6500; ❄ @ ☒) In secluded, tree-shaded grounds off Hwy 32, 12km south of the temple, Aranyawas has 20 attractive rooms in two-storey stone cottages. They aren't fancy, but are spacious, neat and tasteful, with pine furnishings and, in most cases, balconies overlooking a river and jungle-clad hills. There's a large pool inspired by *baori* (stepwells), surrounded by trees, and a bonfire for evening drinks in winter.

The restaurant (mains ₹250 to ₹350, buffet lunch or dinner ₹550) is a lovely place to stop for a meal and is open to nonguests as well.

Ranakpur Hill Resort   HOTEL $$$
(☑ 9829157303; www.ranakpurhillresort.com; Ranakpur Rd; s/d from ₹5900/6490; ❄ @ 🛜 ☒) This is a well-run hotel with a decent pool and shady gardens, around which are arranged the attractive cottages sporting marble floors, stained glass, floral wall paintings and touches of mirrorwork. There is also a multicuisine restaurant, and horse-riding packages can be arranged. Check for discounts on the website. It's 3.5km north of the temple complex, along Hwy 32.

ⓘ Getting There & Away

A day-long round trip in a taxi or hired car from Udaipur to Ranakpur and Kumbhalgarh costs around ₹3000.

It's uncomfortable and incredibly time-consuming, and therefore not recommended, to travel by local bus. Nevertheless, here are the details. Direct buses to Ranakpur leave roughly hourly from the main bus stands in both Udaipur (₹98, three hours) and Jodhpur (₹197, four to five hours). You'll be dropped outside the temple complex unless you state otherwise. Return buses stop running around 7pm. Buses departing for Udaipur can drop you at Saira (₹23, 40 minutes, hourly), about 25km south of Ranakpur, to connect with a bus to Kumbhalgarh (₹43, one hour, hourly).

Mt Abu

☏ 02974 / POP 22,940 / ELEV 1200M

Rajasthan's only hill station nestles among green forests on the state's highest mountain at the southwestern end of the Aravalli Hills and close to the Gujarat border. Quite unlike anywhere else in Rajasthan, Mt Abu provides Rajasthanis, Gujaratis and a small number of foreign tourists with respite from scorching temperatures and arid terrain elsewhere. It's a particular hit with honeymooners and middle-class families from Gujarat.

Mt Abu town sits towards the southwestern end of the plateau-like mountain, which stretches about 19km from end to end and 6km from east to west. The town is surrounded by the 289-sq-km Mt Abu Wildlife Sanctuary, which extends over most of the mountain.

The mountain is of great spiritual importance for both Hindus and Jains and has more than 80 temples and shrines, most notably the exquisite Jain temples at Delwara, built between 400 and 1000 years ago.

◉ Sights

The white-clad people you'll see around town are members of the **Brahma Kumaris World Spiritual University** (www.bkwsu.com), a worldwide organisation that has its headquarters here in Mt Abu. The university's **Universal Peace Hall** (Om Shanti Bhawan; ⊘8am-6pm), just north of Nakki Lake, has free 30-minute tours that include an introduction to the Brahma Kumaris philosophy (be prepared for a bit of proselytising). The organisation also runs the **World Renewal Spiritual Museum** (⊘8am-8pm) FREE in the town centre.

Nakki Lake LAKE
Scenic Nakki Lake, the town's focus, is one of Mt Abu's biggest attractions. It's so named because, according to legend, it was scooped out by a god using his *nakh* (nails). Some Hindus thus consider it a holy lake. It's a pleasant 45-minute stroll around the perimeter – the lake is surrounded by hills, parks and strange rock formations. The best known, **Toad Rock**, looks like a toad about to hop into the lake.

The 14th-century **Raghunath Temple** (⊘dawn-dusk) stands near the lake's southern shore. **Boating** (pedalo per person ₹200, shikara ₹1100) here is popular.

Sunset Point VIEWPOINT
(Indian/foreigner ₹50/300) Sunset Point is a popular place to watch the brilliant setting sun. Hordes stroll out here every evening to catch the end of the day, the food stalls and all the usual jolly hill-station entertainment. To get there, follow Sunset Point road west of the polo ground out of town.

Mt Abu Wildlife Sanctuary WILDLIFE RESERVE
(Indian/foreigner ₹50/300, vehicle ₹200; ⊘8am-5pm) This 289-sq-km sanctuary covers much of the mountain plateau and surrounds the town of Mt Abu. It is home to leopards, deer,

TREKKING & TWITCHING IN MT ABU

Getting off the well-worn tourist trail and out into the forests and hills of Mt Abu is a revelation. This is a world of isolated shrines and lakes, weird rock formations, fantastic panoramas, nomadic villagers, orchids, wild fruits, plants used in ayurvedic medicine, sloth bears (which are fairly common), wild boars, langurs, and even the occasional leopard. There are more than 150 bird species recorded including the prized green avadavat and red spurfowl.

A warning from the locals before you set out: it's very unsafe to wander unguided in these hills. Travellers have been mauled by bears and, even more disturbing, have been mugged (and worse) by other people.

foxes and bears. Contact Mt Abu Treks to arrange an overnight stay.

☞ Tours

★ Mt Abu Treks   TREKKING
(☏9414154854; www.mount-abu-treks.blogspot.com; Hotel Lake Palace; 3-4hr trek per person ₹700, full day incl lunch ₹1500) Mahendra 'Charles' Dan arranges tailor-made treks ranging from gentle village visits to longer, wilder expeditions into Mt Abu Wildlife Sanctuary.

He's passionate and knowledgeable about the local flora and fauna. Short treks are available as well as an overnight village trek including all meals (₹3500). Transport to/from trailheads and the sanctuary entrance fee (Indian/foreigner ₹50/300) is extra.

Shri Ganesh Hotel   TREKKING
(☏02974-237292; http://shri-ganesh.hotels-rajasthan.com; per person 2hr ₹300, 4hr ₹1000) This hotel organises good short hikes, starting at 7am and 4pm.

Mt Abu

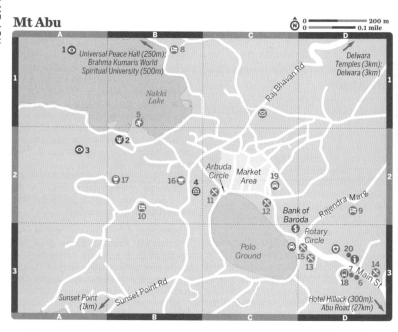

Mt Abu

DELWARA TEMPLES

The remarkable Jain **Delwara Temples** (donations welcome; ☉ Jains 6am-6pm, non-Jains noon-6pm) are Mt Abu's most remarkable attraction and feature some of India's finest temple decoration. They predate the town of Mt Abu by many centuries and were built when this site was just a remote mountain wilderness. It's said that the artisans were paid according to the amount of dust they collected, encouraging them to carve ever more intricately. Whatever their inducement, there are two temples here in which the marble work is dizzyingly intense.

The older of the two is the **Vimal Vasahi**, on which work began in 1031 and was financed by a Gujarati chief minister named Vimal. Dedicated to the first *tirthankar* (great Jain teacher), Adinath, it took 1500 masons and 1200 labourers 14 years to build, and allegedly cost ₹185.3 million. Outside the entrance is the **House of Elephants**, featuring a procession of stone elephants marching to the temple, some of which were damaged long ago by marauding Mughals. Inside, a forest of beautifully carved pillars surrounds the central shrine, which holds an image of Adinath himself.

The **Luna Vasahi Temple** is dedicated to Neminath, the 22nd *tirthankar*, and was built in 1230 by the brothers Tejpal and Vastupal for a mere ₹125.3 million. Like Vimal, the brothers were both Gujarati government ministers. The marble carving here took 2500 workers 15 years to create, and its most notable feature is its intricacy and delicacy, which is so fine that, in places, the marble becomes almost transparent. The many-layered lotus flower that dangles from the centre of the dome is a particularly astonishing piece of work.

As at other Jain temples, leather articles (including belts and shoes), cameras and phones must be left at the entrance, and menstruating women are asked not to enter.

Delwara is about 3km north of Mt Abu town centre: you can walk there in less than an hour, or hop aboard a shared taxi (₹10 per person) from up the street opposite Chacha Cafe. A taxi all to yourself should be ₹200 round trip, with one hour of waiting time.

RSRTC TOURS
(half-/full-day tours ₹50/110; ☉ full day 9.30am, half-day 1pm) The RSRTC runs bus tours of Mt Abu's main sights, leaving from the bus stand where reservations can be made. Both tours visit Achalgarh, Guru Shikhar and the Delwara temples and end at Sunset Point. The full-day tour also includes Adhar Devi, the Brahma Kumaris Peace Hall and Honeymoon Point. Admission and camera fees and the ₹20 guide fee are extra.

🛏 Sleeping

Room rates can double, or treble, during the peak seasons – mid-May to mid-June, Diwali and Christmas/New Year – but generous discounts are often available at other times close to midrange and top-end places. If you intend to come here during Diwali, you'll need to book way ahead and you won't be able to move for the crowds. Many hotels have an ungenerous 9am checkout time.

⭐ **Shri Ganesh Hotel** HOTEL $
(☎ 02974-237292; http://shri-ganesh.hotels-rajasthan.com; dm ₹350, s/d without bathroom ₹500/600, r with bathroom ₹700-1500; ❄ @ ☎)

A fairly central and popular budget spot, Shri Ganesh is well set up for travellers, with an inexpensive cafe-restaurant and plenty of helpful travel information. Rooms are very well kept; clean and tidy. Daily forest walks and cooking lessons are on offer.

Hotel Lake Palace HOTEL $$
(☎ 02974-237154; www.savshantihotels.com; r from ₹3580; ❄ ☎) The Lake Palace has an excellent location right beside the lake and away from the crowds. There are a couple of terraces overlooking the lake and promenade. Rooms are simple, uncluttered and clean. All have air-conditioning and some have semiprivate lake-view balconies. There is a rooftop multicuisine restaurant, too.

Kishangarh House HERITAGE HOTEL $$$
(☎ 02974-238092; Rajendra Marg; cottages ₹5500, r from ₹6500, all incl breakfast; ❄ ☎) The former summer residence of the maharaja of Kishangarh is now an interesting though faded and forlorn heritage hotel. The deluxe rooms in the main building are big, with extravagantly high ceilings. The cottage rooms at the back are smaller and cosier. There's a

delightful sun-filled drawing room and lovely terraced gardens.

Hotel Hillock HOTEL $$$
(☑ 02974-238463; www.hotelhillock.com; Raj Bhavan Rd; r ₹11,800; ✳ ☎ ☀) Plush and contemporary but with Rajasthani colours and designs, Hillock's rooms are some of the most comfortable in Mt Abu. Add to that the fine Mayur restaurant, the On The Rocks bar, and delightful gardens sporting a cool pool and you have one of the hill station's top options.

 ## Eating

Arbuda INDIAN $
(Arbuda Circle; mains ₹110-250, thali ₹170; ☺ 8am-10.30pm; ☑) This big restaurant is set on a sweeping open terrace filled with chrome chairs. It's very popular for its vegetarian Gujarati, Punjabi and South Indian food, and does fine Continental breakfasts and fresh juices.

Chacha Cafe MULTICUISINE $$
(Main St; mains ₹180-450; ☺ 11am-11pm; ✳ ☎) A very neat, bright pure-veg eatery with excellent service and cold beer. Downstairs there's booths and welcome air-con, upstairs is outside and ideal in the cool evenings. The presentable fare ranges from dosas and biryanis to pizzas, vegetarian burgers and cashew curry.

Kanak Dining Hall INDIAN $$
(Lake Rd; thali Gujarati/Punjabi ₹180/250; ☺ 8.30am-3.30pm & 7.30-10.30pm) The excellent all-you-can-eat thalis are contenders for Mt Abu's best meals. There's seating indoors in the busy dining hall or outside under a canopy. It's conveniently located near the bus stand for the lunch break during the all-day RSRTC tour.

Tandoori Bites BARBECUE $$
(Main St; mains ₹130-370; ☺ 12.30-11.30pm) This bright eatery near the taxi stand sets up a barbecue out the front to entice customers with the delicious smoky smells. It does a good range of vegetarian curries and veg barbecue, though there's no doubt this is an excellent choice for carnivores on a budget.

Mulberry Tree Restaurant MULTICUISINE $$$
(Hilltone Hotel, Main St; mains ₹250-460; ✳) Mt Abu's Gujarati tourists make veg thalis the order of the day in the town, so if you're craving a bit of nonveg, the smart Mulberry Tree Restaurant is a good upmarket place to go. There are plenty of meaty Indian options on the menu and alcohol is available to wash it down.

Drinking & Nightlife

Café Coffee Day CAFE
(coffee from ₹116; ☺ 9am-11pm) A branch of the popular caffeine-supply chain. The tea and cakes aren't bad either.

Polo Bar BAR
(☑ 02974-235176; Jaipur House; beer & cocktails ₹240; ☺ 11.30am-3.30pm & 7.30-11pm) The terrace at the Jaipur House, formerly the maharaja of Jaipur's summer palace, is a dreamy place for an evening tipple, with divine views over the hills, lake and the town's twinkling lights.

Information

There are ATMs on Raj Bhavan Rd, including one outside the tourist office, as well as on Lake Rd.

Bank of Baroda (Main St; ☺ 10am-3pm Mon-Fri, to 12.30pm Sat) Changes currency and travellers cheques, and does credit-card advances. Has ATM.

Main post office (Raj Bhavan Rd; ☺ 9am-5pm Mon-Sat)

MAJOR TRAINS FROM ABU ROAD

DESTINATION	TRAIN	DEPARTURE	ARRIVAL	FARE (₹)
Ahmedabad	19224 JAT ADI Exp	10.50am	3pm	140/495/700(A)
Delhi (New Delhi)	12957 Swarna J Raj Exp	8.50pm	7.30am	1845/2725/3155 (B)
Jaipur	19707 Aravali Exp	9.40am	7pm	260/700/1000 (A)
Jodhpur	19223 Ahmedabad–Jammu Tawi Exp	3.30pm	8.05pm	185/495/700 (A)
Mumbai	19708 Aravali Exp	4.50pm	6.35am	355/970/ 1400(A)

Fares: (A) sleeper/3AC/2AC, (B) 3AC/2AC/1AC

Tourist office (Main St; ☉9am-5.30pm Mon-Fri) Opposite the main bus stand, this centre distributes free maps of town.

❶ Getting There & Away

Access to Mt Abu is by a dramatic 28km-long road that winds its way up thickly forested hillsides from the town of Abu Road, where the nearest train station is located. Many buses from other cities go all the way up to Mt Abu, some only go as far as Abu Road. Buses (₹35, one hour) run between Abu Road and Mt Abu half-hourly from about 6am to 7pm. Share taxis cost ₹30. A private taxi from Abu Road to Mt Abu is ₹700 by day or ₹1000 by night. Vehicles are charged when entering Mt Abu (small/large car ₹100/200).

BUS

There are government and private (usually more comfortable and more expensive) bus services to various points. **Rajasthan Travels** (www.rajasthanbus.com; Main St; per person ₹100; ☉9.30am-5pm) runs buses to Ahmedabad (seat/sleeper ₹460/650), Jaipur (₹500/600, one daily 7pm) and Udaipur (₹260, 8.30am), among others destinations. It has several booths around town including one near the main bus stand. Services from Mt Abu's main bus stand include the following:

Ahmedabad seat/sleeper ₹460/650, six hours, several daily

Jaipur seat/sleeper/AC ₹500/600/916, 11 hours, several daily

Jodhpur ₹306, seven hours, three daily (6.30am, 8.45am, 12.30pm)

Udaipur ₹260, 4½ hours, several daily

TRAIN

Abu Road station is on the line between Delhi and Mumbai via Ahmedabad. An autorickshaw from Abu Road train station to Abu Road bus stand costs ₹20. Mt Abu has a train **reservations office** (Main St; ☉8am-2pm Mon-Sat), above the tourist office, with quotas on most of the express trains.

❶ Getting Around

There are no autorickshaws in Mt Abu, but it is easy to get around on foot. Motorcycles and scooters are not hired to foreigners in Mt Abu, forcing foreigners to hire a taxi or walk to the outlying sights.

To hire a jeep or taxi for sightseeing costs about ₹700/1500 per half-day/day. There's a taxi stand down by the polo ground on Main St. Shared taxis to Delwara leave from a separate stand beside the market. Alternatively, many hotels can arrange a vehicle with driver.

NORTHERN RAJASTHAN (SHEKHAWATI)

Far less visited than other parts of Rajasthan, the Shekhawati region is renowned for its extraordinary painted *havelis* (traditional, ornately decorated residences), highlighted with dazzling, often whimsical, murals. These works of art are found in tiny towns connected by single-track roads that run through desolate countryside north of Jaipur. Today it seems curious that such attention and money were lavished on these out-of-the-way houses, but these were once the homelands of wealthy traders and merchants.

From the 14th century onwards, Shekhawati's towns were important trading posts on caravan routes from Gujarati ports to the fertile and booming cities of the Ganges plain. The expansion of the British port cities of Calcutta (now Kolkata) and Bombay (Mumbai) in the 19th century could have been the death knell for Shekhawati, but the merchants moved to these cities, prospered, and sent funds home to construct and decorate their extraordinary abodes.

Nawalgarh

📞01594 / POP 95,350

Nawalgarh is a small town almost at the very centre of the Shekhawati region. With some excellent accommodation options, it makes a great base for exploring the region. It boasts several fine *havelis* and a colourful and mostly pedestrian-friendly bazaar.

◉ Sights

Dr Ramnath A Podar Haveli Museum   MUSEUM

(www.podarhavelimuseum.org; Indian/foreigner ₹80/100, camera ₹30; ☉8.30am-6.30pm) Built in 1902 on the eastern side of town, and known locally as 'Podar Haveli', this is one of the region's few buildings to have been thoroughly restored. The paintings of this *haveli* are the most vivid murals in town, although purists point to the fact that they have been simply repainted rather than restored.

On the ground floor are galleries on Rajasthani culture, including costumes, turbans, musical instruments and models of Rajasthan's forts.

Morarka Haveli Museum   MUSEUM

(₹70; ☉8am-7pm) This museum has well-presented original paintings, preserved for

Shekhawati

decades behind doorways blocked with cement, plus there is ongoing restoration. The inner courtyard hosts some gorgeous Ramayana scenes; look out for the slightly incongruous image of Jesus on the top storey, beneath the eaves in the courtyard's southeast corner.

Bhagton ki Choti Haveli   HISTORIC BUILDING
(Bhagat Haveli; ₹50; ⊙8am-6pm) Under the eaves on the external western wall of Bhagton ki Choti Haveli is a locomotive and a steamship. Above them, elephant-bodied *gopis* (milkmaids) dance. Adjacent to this, women dance during the Holi festival. Inside you'll find a host of other murals, including one strange picture (in a room on the western side) of a European man with a cane and pipe, and a small dog on his shoulder. Next to him, an apparently melancholy English woman plays an accordian.

🏃 Activities

Roop Niwas Kothi   HORSE RIDING
(☑01594-223388; www.royalridingholidays.com; Kothi Rd) Roop Niwas Kothi specialises in high-end fully catered horse excursions (US$200 to US$260 per day) into the rolling Shekhawati countryside. Short rides are available as well as elaborate excursions that last from overnight to a week and include

accommodation in luxury tents. Its stables primarily offer handsome, high-spirited, Marwari horses, local to Rajasthan.

👉 Tours

Ramesh Jangid's Tourist Pension   TOURS
(☑01594-224060; www.touristpension.com) Ramesh Jangid organises guided hiking trips (two to three days per person from ₹2250), guided camel-cart rides (half-day for two people ₹2400) to outlying villages, and guided bicycle tours (half-day for two people ₹3500) of Nawalgarh. Lessons in cooking, woodcarving and local crafts such as *bandhani* (tie-dyeing) can also be arranged.

🛏 Sleeping

Nawalgarh Homestay   HOMESTAY $
(☑9414491281, 7665711416; Chiraniya Mill, off Kothi Rd; 🛜) This homestay under the recommended New Bungli Restaurant is run by the same small group of families. Rooms are simple, spacious, cool and clean and you have the benefits of the excellent homestyle food prepared for the restaurant, plus the advantage of having in-house guides to show you the town's *havelis*.

DS Bungalow   HOMESTAY $
(☑9983168916, 9828828116; s/d ₹500/800; 🛜) Run by a friendly, down-to-earth couple, this

simple place with clean, air-cooled rooms is a little out of town on the way to Roop Niwas Kothi. It's backed by a garden with a pleasant outdoor mud-walled restaurant serving delicious home cooking. The more energetic can arrange camel tours here.

Apani Dhani GUESTHOUSE $$
(☑ 01594-222239; www.apanidhani.com; s/d from ₹990/1670, r with AC from ₹2790; ❈ 🛜) 🏊 This award-winning ecotourism venture is a relaxing place on the edge of town. Rooms with comfortable beds are in cosy mud-hut, thatched-roof bungalows set around a bougainvillea-shaded courtyard. The adjoining organic farm supplies food, and there are solar lights, water heaters and compost toilets. Tours around the area, via bicycle, car, camel cart or on foot, can be arranged. Note that there is a 'no alcohol' policy here.

**Ramesh Jangid's
Tourist Pension** GUESTHOUSE $$
(☑ 01594-224060; www.touristpension.com; s/d from ₹950/1290; @ 🛜) 🏊 This guesthouse, run by genial Rajesh, son of Ramesh at Apani Dhani, offers homey, clean accommodation in spacious, cool rooms with big beds. Some rooms have furniture carved by Rajesh's grandfather, and the more expensive rooms also have murals created by visiting artists. Pure-veg meals (breakfast ₹200, lunch ₹250, dinner ₹300) made with organic ingredients are available, and include a delectable thali. The family also arranges all sorts of tours around Shekhawati.

On the western edge of town, near the Maur Hospital, this pension is well known, so if you get lost, just ask a local to point you in the right direction.

Grand Haveli & Resort HERITAGE HOTEL $$
(☑ 9460780212, 01594-225301; www.grandhaveli. com; Baori Gate; r incl breakfast from ₹4000; ❈ 🛜 🏊) The rooms at this beautifully renovated *haveli* are individual, spacious and very atmospheric, with heritage furnishings. The two-tiered, multicuisine restaurant, Jharoka, overlooks a timeless scene of *chhatris* (cenotaphs) through a large window. The hotel has developed more rooms across the road. These are more standard and less atmospheric, but large and comfortable.

Roop Niwas Kothi HERITAGE HOTEL $$$
(☑ 01594-222008; www.roopniwaskothi.com; Kothi Rd; r from ₹5600; ❈ 🛜 🏊) About 4km

east of town is a converted palace partitioned into two hotels. Roop Niwas Kothi is one sibling and has a back-to-the-Raj feel, lovely grounds and old-fashioned but well-maintained rooms with good bathrooms. Horse-riding tours can be arranged here, and the excellent restaurant is open to nonguests for lunch and dinner (bookings required).

✖️ Eating

⭐ **New Bungli Restaurant** NORTH INDIAN $$
(☑ 9414491281; Chiraniya Mill, off Kothi Rd; mains ₹175-370; ⊙ 8am-10pm; 🛜) Under billowing sails this breezy, rooftop restaurant delivers high-quality food. The veg and nonveg curries, including rich *laal maas* (mutton curry), creamy *palak paneer* (unfermented cheese chunks in a pureed spinach gravy) and a lovely dish using small local eggplants, are all professionally prepared and served. You can even get a free cooking class by watching your meal being prepared.

ℹ️ Information

State Bank of India (SBI; Bala Qila Fort; ⊙ 10am-4pm Mon-Fri, to noon Sat) Changes currency and travellers cheques; there's also an SBI ATM near Baori Gate.

ℹ️ Getting There & Away

BUS

The **main bus stand** (State Hwy 8) is little more than a dusty car park accessed through a large yellow double-arched gateway. Services run roughly every hour to Jaipur (₹145 to ₹258, 3½ hours), Jhunjhunu (₹40, one hour) and Mandawa (₹35, 45 minutes).

TRAIN

Nawalgarh is on the route of the Sikar Dee Express. The train departs Dehli Sarai Rohilla station at 6.50am (on Wednesday and Friday) and at 11.25pm (on Tuesday, Thursday and Saturday). It arrives at Nawalgarh station at 12.15pm and 5am (the following day) respectively. The fare is sleeper/3AC ₹195/510; other classes are available. The trains continue to Sikar (arriving 1.10pm and 5.45am) on broad gauge, but beyond Sikar to Jaipur work is ongoing to convert the old metre-gauge track.

In the opposite direction, the trains depart Nawalgarh at 2.46pm (on Wednesday and Friday) and 11.43pm (Wednesday, Friday and Sunday) arriving at Delhi at 8.45pm and 5.40am respectively.

Jhunjhunu

 01592 / POP 118,500

Shekhawati's most important commercial centre has a different atmosphere from the region's smaller towns, with lots of traffic and concrete, and the hustle and bustle that befits the district capital. On the other hand, it does have a few appealing *havelis* and a colourful bazaar.

◉ Sights

Mohanlal Ishwardas
Modi Haveli   HISTORIC BUILDING
(Nehru Bazaar; ₹50; ⊘ 8am-6pm) On the northern side of Nehru Bazaar is Mohanlal Ishwardas Modi Haveli (1896). A train runs merrily across the front facade. Above the entrance to the outer courtyard are scenes from the life of Krishna. On a smaller, adjacent arch are British imperial figures, including monarchs and robed judges. Facing them are Indian rulers, including maharajas and nawabs.

Around the archway, between the inner and outer courtyards, there are some glass-covered portrait miniatures, along with some fine mirror-and-glass tilework.

Modi Havelis   HISTORIC BUILDING
(Nehru Bazaar; ₹50; ⊘ 8am-6pm) The Modi Havelis face each other and house some of Jhunjhunu's best murals and woodcarving. The *haveli* on the eastern side has a painting of a woman in a blue sari sitting before a gramophone; a frieze depicts a train, alongside which soldiers race on horses. The spaces between the brackets above show the Krishna legends. The *haveli* on the western side has some comical pictures, featuring some remarkable facial expressions and moustaches.

Khetri Mahal   HISTORIC BUILDING
(₹50; ⊘ dawn-dusk) A series of small laneways at the western end of Nehru Bazaar (a short rickshaw drive north of the bus station) leads to the imposing Khetri Mahal, a small palace dating from around 1770 and once one of Shekhawati's most sophisticated and beautiful buildings. It's believed to have been built by Bhopal Singh, Sardul Singh's grandson, who founded Khetri. Unfortunately, it now has a desolate, forlorn atmosphere, but the architecture remains a superb open-sided collection of intricate arches and columns.

⌸ Sleeping

Hotel Jamuna Resort   HOTEL $$
(⧉ 01592-232871, 8955976348; www.hoteljamunaresort.in; Mahavir Path, near Nath Ka Tilla; r incl breakfast ₹750, deluxe ₹2200-2600; ☒ ☎ ☒) Hotel Jamuna Resort has everything the traveller needs for a bargain price. The rooms in the older wing are either vibrantly painted with murals or decorated with traditional mirrorwork, while the rooms in the newer wing are modern and airy. There's an inviting pool (₹100 for nonguests) set in the garden, plus purpose-built kitchens set up for in-house cooking courses.

The friendly family owning and managing the hotel have a wealth of knowledge on the villages of Shekhawati and tours can be organised here. Free pickup from the train or bus stations can be arranged.

ℹ Getting There & Away

BUS
There are two bus stands: the **main bus stand** (Paramveer Path) and the **private bus stand** (Khem Shakti Rd). Both have similar services and prices, but the government-run buses from the main bus stand run much more frequently. Shared autorickshaws run between the two (₹10 per person).

Services from the main bus stand include the following:

Bikaner ₹226, five to six hours, hourly

Delhi ₹250, five to six hours, hourly

Fatehpur ₹60, one hour, half-hourly

Jaipur ₹190, four hours, half-hourly

Mandawa ₹25, one hour, half-hourly

Nawalgarh ₹40, one hour, half-hourly

TRAIN
Jhunjhunu is on the route of the Sikar Dee Express. The train departs Delhi Sarai Rohilla station at 6.50am (on Wednesday and Friday) and at 11.25pm (on Tuesday, Thursday and Saturday). It arrives at Jhunjhunu station at 11.30am and 4.12am (the following day) respectively. The fare is sleeper/3AC ₹180/510 (other classes available). The trains continue to Sikar (arriving 1.10pm and 5.45am) on broad gauge, but beyond Sikar to Jaipur work is ongoing to convert the old metre-gauge track.

In the opposite direction, the train departs Jhunjhunu at 3.20pm (on Wednesday and Friday) and 11.27pm (Wednesday, Friday and Sunday) arriving at Delhi at 8.45pm and 5.40am respectively. There's also a train to Sikar via Nawalgarh (2nd class ₹55).

Fatehpur

📞 01571 / POP 92,600

Established in 1451 as a capital for nawabs (Muslim ruling princes), Fatehpur was their stronghold for centuries before it was taken over by the Shekhawati Rajputs in the 18th century. The wealth of the merchant community, which included the Poddar, Choudhari and Ganeriwala families, is illustrated by the town's grandiose *havelis*, *chhatris* (cenotaphs), wells and temples. It's a busy little town and many of the *havelis* are in a sad state of disrepair, with a few notable exceptions.

◉ Sights

Apart from the magnificent Le Prince Haveli, other sights include the nearby Chauhan Well; Jagannath Singhania Haveli; the Mahavir Prasad Goenka Haveli, which is often locked but has superb paintings; the Geori Shankar Haveli, with mirrored mosaics on the antechamber ceiling; and south of the private bus stand, Vishnunath Keria Haveli, and Harikrishnan Das Saraogi Haveli, with a colourful facade and iron lacework.

Le Prince Haveli   HISTORIC BUILDING

(📞 01571-233024; www.leprincehaveli.com; incl guided tour ₹250; ⊙ 9am-5pm) This 1802 *haveli* has been stunningly restored by French artist Nadine Le Prince and is one of the most exquisite *havelis* in Shekhawati. Visiting students of art history conduct the detailed guided tours (45 minutes, French or English) on the fresco technique and the history of the *havelis* and the merchants who built them. There's a small gallery and a garden bar in which to relax with a post-tour refreshment. Rooms have been converted into beautifully decorated guest rooms (p116).

SHEKHAWATI'S OUTDOOR GALLERIES

In the 18th and 19th centuries, shrewd Marwari merchants lived frugally and far from home while earning money in India's new commercial centres. They sent the bulk of their vast fortunes back to their families in Shekhawati to construct grand *havelis* (traditional, ornately decorated residences) to show their neighbours how well they were doing and to compensate their families for their long absences. Merchants competed with one another to build ever grander edifices – homes, temples, step-wells – which were richly decorated, both inside and out, with painted murals.

The artists responsible for these acres of decoration largely belonged to the caste of *kumhars* (potters) and were both the builders and painters of the *havelis*. Known as *chajeras* (masons), many were commissioned from beyond Shekhawati – particularly from Jaipur, where they had been employed decorating the new capital's palaces – and others flooded in from further afield to offer their skills. Soon, there was a cross-pollination of ideas and techniques, with local artists learning from the new arrivals.

The early paintings are strongly influenced by Mughal decoration, with floral arabesques and geometric designs. The Rajput royal courts were the next major influence; scenes from Hindu mythology are prevalent, with Krishna particularly popular.

With the arrival of Europeans, walls were embellished with paintings of the new technological marvels to which the Shekhawati merchants had been exposed in centres such as Calcutta (now Kolkata). Pictures of trains, planes, telephones, gramophones and bicycles featured, often painted from the artist's imagination. Krishna and Radha are seen in flying motorcars, while the British are invariably depicted as soldiers, with dogs or holding bottles of booze.

These days most of the *havelis* are still owned by descendants of the original families, but not inhabited by their owners, for whom small-town Rajasthan has lost its charm. Many are occupied just by a single *chowkidar* (caretaker), while others may be home to a local family. Though they are pale reflections of the time when they accommodated the large households of the Marwari merchant families, they remain a fascinating testament to the changing times in which they were created. Only a few *havelis* have been restored; many more lie derelict, slowly crumbling away.

For a full rundown on the history, people, towns and buildings of the area, track down a copy of the excellent *The Painted Towns of Shekhawati* by Ilay Cooper, which can be picked up at bookshops in the region or in Jaipur.

The *haveli* is around 2km north of the two main bus stands, down a lane off the main road. Turn right out of the bus stands, and the turnoff will eventually be on your right, or hop into an autorickshaw.

🛏 Sleeping

⭐ **Le Prince Haveli**   BOUTIQUE HOTEL **$$**
(☑ 8094880977, 01571-233024; www.leprincehav eli.com; near Chauhan Well; r from ₹990, with bathroom/AC from ₹2800/5310; ⊙ mid-Jul–mid-Apr; ❋ 🛜 ➷) The beautifully restored Le Prince Haveli has 14 highly variable, authentically decorated rooms overlooking a tranquil central courtyard. Run as a European homestay, buffet meals (Indian and French cuisine; breakfast ₹200, lunch ₹400, dinner ₹600) are served on the terrace at fixed times. The alfresco bar and pool area make a great oasis and a perfect place to unwind.

There's a 10% discount for two nights, a 20% discount for three nights or more and an additional 20% discount in mid-July to September. Ask about its stable of classic Royal Enfield Bullets for a unique guided tour around the relatively traffic-free roads of Shekhawati.

ℹ Getting There & Away

At the private bus stand and Churu Bus Stand on the Churu–Sikar road, and the central Mandawa Bus Stand, private buses leave for the following Shekhawati destinations throughout the day, departing as they fill with passengers:

Churu ₹39, one hour

Jhunjhunu ₹45, one hour

Mandawa ₹25, one hour

Nawalgarh ₹50, two hours

Ramgarh ₹25, 45 minutes

From the RSRTC bus stand, further south down the same road, buses leave for the following destinations:

Bikaner ₹195, 3½ hours, hourly

Delhi ₹290, seven hours, five daily

Jaipur ₹165, 3½ hours, two daily

Mandawa

☑ 01592 / POP 23,340

Of all the towns in the Shekhawati region, Mandawa is the one best set up for tourists, with plenty of places to stay and some decent restaurants. Expect a few touts and begging children, but this small 18th-century settlement is still a pleasant base for your *haveli* explorations.

There is only one main drag, with narrow lanes fanning off it. The easy-to-find Hotel Mandawa Haveli is halfway along this street and makes a handy point of reference. Most buses drop passengers off on the main street as well as by the bus stand.

◉ Sights

Binsidhar Newatia Haveli   HISTORIC BUILDING
This 1920s *haveli* on the northern side of the Fatehpur–Jhunjhunu road houses the State Bank of India. There are fantastically entertaining paintings on the external eastern wall, including a European woman in a chauffeur-driven car, the Wright brothers in flight watched by women in saris, a strongman hauling a car, and a bird-man flying in a winged device.

Murmuria Haveli   HISTORIC BUILDING
(₹200; ⊙ 8am-6pm) The Murmuria Haveli dates back to the 1930s. From the sandy courtyard out front, you can get a good view of the southern external wall of the adjacent double *haveli*: it features a long frieze depicting a train and a railway crossing. Nehru is depicted on horseback holding the Indian flag. Above the arches on the southern side of the courtyard are two paintings of gondolas on the canals of Venice.

Entry fee also includes access to **Goenka Double Haveli** (⊙ 8am-6pm) and **Seth Dayaram Dedraj Goenka Haveli** (Hanuman Prasad Goenka Haveli; ⊙ 8am-6pm).

🛏 Sleeping & Eating

Hotel Shekhawati   HOTEL **$**
(☑ 9314698079, 01592-223036; www.hotelshekha wati.com; r ₹400-2800; ❋ 🛜) Near Mukundgarh Rd, the only real budget choice in town is run by a registered tourist guide. Bright, comically bawdy murals painted by artistic former guests give the rooms a splash of colour. Tasty meals are served on the peaceful rooftop. Competitively priced camel, horse and 4WD tours can also be arranged here, reinforcing it as a good budget option.

Hotel Mandawa Haveli   HERITAGE HOTEL **$$**
(☑ 8890841088, 01592-223088; www.hotelman dawahaveli.com; r/ste from ₹3480/7080; ❋ 🛜) Close to Sonathia Gate, on the main road, this hotel is set in a glorious, restored 1890s *haveli* with rooms surrounding a painted courtyard. The cheapest rooms are small, so it's worth splashing out on a suite, filled with arches, window seats and countless small windows.

There's a rooftop restaurant serving delicious food; it's especially romantic at dinner time, when the lights of the town twinkle below. A set dinner costs ₹600.

Hotel Radhika
Haveli Mandawa
HERITAGE HOTEL $$
(☑ 01592-223045, 9784673645; www.hotelradh ikahavelimandawa.com; s/d/ste incl breakfast ₹2790/2800/4250; ❄️🛜) This lovely restored *haveli* sits in a quiet part of town with a small lawn and has comfortable and tasteful rooms that are traditional but without garish murals. There's a good vegetarian restaurant in-house, and it's very close to Monica Rooftop Restaurant should you crave a chicken dish.

Hotel Heritage Mandawa
HERITAGE HOTEL $$
(☑ 01592-223742, 9414647922; www.hotelheritage mandawa.com; r/ste incl breakfast from ₹1800/ 4500; ❄️🛜) This gracious old *haveli* has traditionally decorated rooms. The eclectic suites have small mezzanine levels either for the bed or the bathroom. Rooms are highly variable, so check a few. Music performances and puppet shows are held in the small garden.

Monica Rooftop Restaurant
INDIAN $$
(☑ 01592-224178, 9928207523; mains ₹120-400; ⏰8am-10pm; 🛜) This delightful rooftop restaurant, between the fort gate and main bazaar, serves tasty Indian and Chinese meals and cold beer. It's in a converted *haveli* but only the facade, rather than the restaurant itself, has frescoes.

ℹ Information

State Bank of India (SBI; Main Bazaar; ⏰10am-4pm Mon-Fri, to 1pm Sat) In Binsidhar Newatia Haveli; changes cash only. There's an SBI ATM across the road.

ℹ Getting There & Away

The main bus stand, sometimes called Bikaner bus stand, has frequent services (roughly half-hourly), including those listed below. The main bus stand is at one end of the main street, on your left as the road bears right. Note, there is also a separate Nawalgarh bus stand, just off the main drag, with services to Nawalgarh only.

Both bus stands are so small they are unrecognisable as bus stands unless a bus is waiting at them. Look for the chai stalls that cluster beside them and you should have the right spot.

Bikaner ₹233, five hours
Fatehpur ₹35, one hour
Jhunjhunu ₹25, one hour
Nawalgarh ₹35, 45 minutes

JAISALMER, JODHPUR & WESTERN RAJASTHAN

Jodhpur
☎ 0291 / POP 1,033,800

Mighty Mehrangarh, the muscular fort that towers over the Blue City of Jodhpur, is a magnificent spectacle and an architectural masterpiece. Around Mehrangarh's base, the old city, a jumble of Brahmin-blue cubes, stretches out to the 10km-long, 16th-century city wall. The Blue City really is blue! Inside is a tangle of winding, glittering, medieval streets, which never seem to lead where you expect them to, scented by incense, roses and sewers, with shops and bazaars selling everything from trumpets and temple decorations to snuff and saris.

Modern Jodhpur stretches well beyond the city walls, but it's the immediacy and buzz of the old Blue City and the larger-than-life fort that capture travellers' imaginations. This crowded, hectic zone is also Jodhpur's main tourist area. Areas of the old city further west, such as Navchokiya, are just as atmospheric, with far less hustling.

History

Driven from their homeland of Kannauj, east of Agra, by Afghans serving Mohammed of Ghori, the Rathore Rajputs fled west around AD 1200 to the region around Pali, 70km southeast of Jodhpur. They prospered to such a degree that in 1381 they managed to oust the Pratiharas of Mandore, 9km north of present-day Jodhpur. In 1459 the Rathore leader Rao Jodha chose a nearby rocky ridge as the site for a new fortress of staggering proportions, Mehrangarh, around which grew Jodha's city: Jodhpur.

Jodhpur lay on the vital trade route between Delhi and Gujarat. The Rathore kingdom grew on the profits of sandalwood, opium, dates and copper, and controlled a large area, which became cheerily known as Marwar (the Land of Death) due to its harsh topography and climate. It stretched as far west as what's now the India–Pakistan border area, and bordered with Mewar (Udaipur) in the south, Jaisalmer in the northwest,

Jodhpur

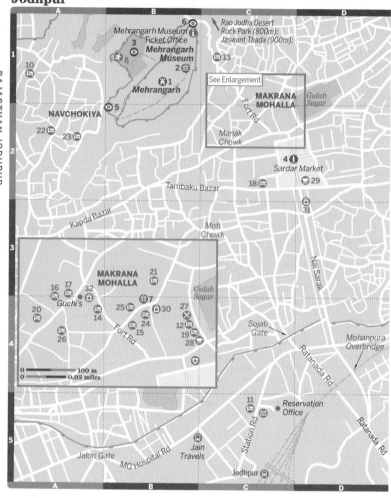

Bikaner in the north, and Jaipur and Ajmer in the east.

◎ Sights

★ Mehrangarh
FORT

(www.mehrangarh.org) **FREE** Rising perpendicular and impregnable from a rocky hill that itself stands 120m above Jodhpur's skyline, Mehrangarh is one of the most magnificent forts in India. The battlements are 6m to 36m high, and as the building materials were chiselled from the rock on which the fort stands, the structure merges with its base. Still run by the Jodhpur royal fami-

ly, Mehrangarh is packed with history and legend.

Mehrangarh's main entrance is at the northeast gate, **Jai Pol**. It's about a 300m walk up from the old city to the entrance, or you can take a winding 5km autorickshaw ride (around ₹120).

Jai Pol was built by Maharaja Man Singh in 1808 following his defeat of invading forces from Jaipur. Past the **museum ticket office** (⊙9am-5pm) and a small cafe, the 16th-century **Dodh Kangra Pol** was an external gate before Jai Pol was built, and still bears the scars of 1808 cannonball hits.

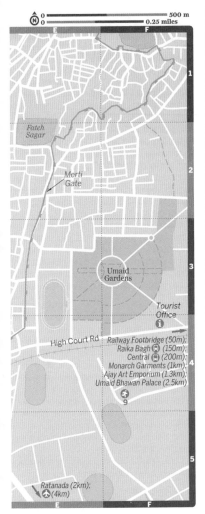

0 ____ 500 m
0 ____ 0.25 miles

Jodhpur

Through here, the main route heads up to the left through the 16th-century **Imritia Pol** and then **Loha Pol**, the fort's original entrance, with iron spikes to deter enemy elephants. Just inside the gate are two sets of small hand prints, the *sati* (ritual suicide of widow on husband's funeral pyre) marks of royal widows – the last to commit *sati* were Maharaja Man Singh's widows in 1843.

Past Loha Pol you'll find a restaurant and **Suraj Pol**, which gives access to the museum (p120). Once you've visited the museum, continue on from here to the panoramic **ramparts**, which are lined with impressive

antique artillery. The ramparts were fenced off in 2016 after a fatal selfie accident – hopefully a temporary measure, as the views are spectacular.

Also worth exploring is the right turn from Jai Pol, where a path winds down to the **Chokelao Bagh**, a restored and gorgeously planted 18th-century Rajput garden (you could lose an afternoon here lolling under shady trees reading a book), and the **Fateh Pol** (Victory Gate). You can exit here into the old city quarter of Navchokiya.

You don't need a ticket to enter the fort itself, only the museum section. However, the museum guards may not let you walk past the museum entrance, so it's better to enter from Fateh Pol if you wish to just wander about the grounds.

★ **Mehrangarh Museum**   MUSEUM
(www.mehrangarh.org; Indian/foreigner incl audio guide ₹100/600, camera/video ₹100/200, guide ₹400; ⊙9am-5pm) The fort's museum encompasses its former palace, and is a superb example of Rajput architecture. The network of courtyards and halls features stone-lattice work so finely carved that it often looks more like sandalwood than sandstone. The galleries around **Shringar Chowk** (Anointment Courtyard) display India's best collection of howdahs (seat for carrying people on an elephant's back) and Jodhpur's royal palanquin collection. The superb audio guide is included with your ticket, but bring ID or a credit card as deposit.

One of the two galleries off **Daulat Khana Chowk** displays textiles, paintings, manuscripts, headgear and the curved sword of the Mughal emperor Akbar; the other gallery is the armoury. Upstairs is a fabulous **gallery of miniature paintings** from the sophisticated Marwar school and the beautiful 18th-century **Phul Mahal** (Flower Palace), with 19th-century wall paintings depicting the 36 moods of classical ragas as well as royal portraits; the artist took 10 years to create them using a curious concoction of gold leaf, glue and cow's urine.

Takhat Vilas was the bedchamber of Maharaja Takhat Singh (r 1843–73), who had just 30 maharanis and numerous concubines. Its beautiful ceiling is covered with Christmas baubles. You then enter the extensive *zenana* (area in an upper-class home where women are secluded), the lovely latticed windows of which are said to feature more than 250 different designs (and through which the women could watch the goings-on in the courtyards). Here you'll find the **Cradle Gallery**, exhibiting the elaborate cradles of infant princes, and the 17th-century **Moti Mahal** (Pearl Palace), which was the palace's main durbar hall (royal reception hall) for official meetings and receptions, with gorgeously colourful stained glass.

Note that the museum can be suffocatingly crowded in the holiday period following Diwali.

Rao Jodha Desert Rock Park   PARK
(☑9571271000; www.raojodhapark.com; Mehrangarh; ₹100, guide ₹200; ⊙7am-6.30pm Apr-Sep, 8am-5.30pm Oct-Mar) This 72-hectare park – and model of ecotourism – sits in the lee of Mehrangarh. It has been lovingly restored and planted with native species to show the natural diversity of the region. The park is criss-crossed with walking trails that take you up to the city walls, around Devkund lake, spotting local and migratory birds, butterflies and reptiles. For an extra insight into the area's native flora and fauna, take along one of the excellent local guides.

Walks here are the perfect restorative if the Indian hustle has left you in need of breathing space. Visit in the early morning or late afternoon for the most pleasant temperatures. The visitors centre is thoughtfully put together, and there's a small cafe, too.

Jaswant Thada   HISTORIC BUILDING
(Indian/foreigner ₹30/50, camera/video ₹50, guide ₹100; ⊙9am-5pm) This milky-white marble memorial to Maharaja Jaswant Singh II, sitting above a small lake 1km northeast of Mehrangarh, is an array of whimsical domes. It's a welcome, peaceful spot after the hubbub of the city, and the views across to the fort and over the city are superb. Built in 1899, the cenotaph has some beautiful *jalis* (carved-marble lattice screens) and is hung with portraits of Rathore rulers going back to the 13th century.

Look out for the memorial to a peacock that flew into a funeral pyre.

Umaid Bhawan Palace   PALACE
(Umaid Bhawan Rd) Gaj Singh II still lives in part of this hilltop palace, built in 1929 for Maharaja Umaid Singh. It was designed by the British architect Henry Lanchester and took more than 3000 workers 15 years to complete its 365 rooms, at a cost of around ₹11 million.

The **museum** (Indian/foreigner ₹50/100; ⊙9am-5pm), which includes photos of the elegant art-deco interior plus an eccentric collection of elaborate clocks, is the only part open to casual visitors.

The building is mortarless, and incorporates 100 wagon loads of Makrana marble and Burmese teak in the interior. Apparently its construction began as a royal job-creation program during a time of severe drought. Much of the building has been turned into a suitably grand hotel. Casual visitors are not welcome at either the royal residence or the hotel.

Don't miss the maharaja's highly polished classic cars, displayed in front of the museum, by the entrance gate.

It's 3km southeast of the old city; take an autorickshaw.

Toorji Ka Jhalra HISTORIC BUILDING
(Step-well; Stepwell Sq, Makrana Mohalla) FREE
This geometrically handsome step-well (also known as a *baori* or *wav*) has been rejuvenated after decades as a rubbish dump. Its clean lines and clear, fish-filled water will leave you mesmerised. It's a great place to just sit and watch, and the attached cafe (p124) adds further incentive for a visit.

Clock Tower MONUMENT
The century-old clock tower is a city landmark surrounded by the vibrant sounds, sights and smells of Sardar Market. The market is bordered by triple-arched gateways at its northern and southern ends. The narrow, winding lanes of the old city spread out in all directions from here. Westward, you plunge into the old city's commercial heart, with crowded alleys and bazaars selling vegetables, spices, sweets, silver and handicrafts.

🏃 Activities

Flying Fox ADVENTURE SPORTS
(www.flyingfox.asia; adult/child ₹1999/1600; ⏰9am-5pm) This circuit of six zip lines flies back and forth over walls, bastions and lakes on the northern side of Mehrangarh. A brief training session is given before you start and safety standards are good: 'awesome' is the verdict of most who dare. Flying Fox has a desk near the main ticket office and its starting point is in the Chokelao Bagh. Tours last up to 1½ hours, depending on the group size. Book online for a discount on the walk-up price.

⭐ Festivals & Events

**Rajasthan International
Folk Festival** MUSIC
(www.jodhpurriff.org; ⏰Sep/Oct) The excellent Rajasthan International Folk Festival, with five days of music concerts by Indian and international artists, is held at Mehrangarh.

Marwar Festival PERFORMING ARTS
(⏰Sep/Oct) The colourful Marwar Festival includes polo and a camel tattoo.

Jodhpur Flamenco & Gypsy Festival MUSIC
(www.jfgfestival.com; Mehrangarh; ⏰Apr) Mehrangarh, this most spectacular of music venues, hosts this festival.

World Sacred Spirit Festival MUSIC
(www.worldsacredspiritfestival.org; Mehrangarh; ⏰Feb) Jodhpur hosts the World Sacred Spirit Festival, featuring international musicians playing in various settings within Mehrangarh.

🛏 Sleeping

The old city has more than 100 hotels and guesthouses, most of which scramble for your custom as soon as you get within breathing distance of Sardar Market.

If you call ahead, many lodgings can organise a pickup from the train station or bus stops, even at night. Otherwise, for most places in the old city you can avoid nonsense by getting dropped at the clock tower and walking from there.

🛏 Old City (Makrana Mohalla & Sadar Market)

HosteLavie HOSTEL $
(☑0291-2611001; www.hostelavie.com; Killi Khana, Fort Rd; dm ₹400-500, r ₹1500-1800; ❄🛜) A European-style hostel with clean air-con dorms, where each bed sports a lockable locker and mobile charging point. The dorms are four- and six-bed and each one has its own bathroom. There are also double rooms, making this a good budget option between the fort and the clock tower.

It has an excellent rooftop terrace restaurant with espresso coffee, Indian veg, and authentic Korean veg and nonveg.

Yogi Guest House GUESTHOUSE $
(☑0291-2643436; www.yogiguesthouse.com; dm ₹400, r ₹800, with AC ₹2200; ❄🛜) Yogi's is a venerable travellers' hang-out, with a clean dorm and budget rooms in a 500-year-old blue-washed *haveli* just below the fort walls. It's a friendly place with well-kept, clean rooms. There's also a lovely rooftop restaurant with great views.

Hill View Guest House GUESTHOUSE $
(☑0291-2441763, 9829153196; hill_view2004@yahoo.com; Makrana Mohalla; dm ₹150, r ₹300-700,

with AC ₹1500; ❄ 🛜) Perched above town and just below the fort walls, this hotel is run by a friendly, enthusiastic Muslim family who'll make you feel right at home. Rooms are basic, clean and simple, all with bathrooms (but not all with decent windows), and the terrace has a great view over the city. Good, home-cooked veg and nonveg food is on offer. Village and camel tours can be arranged here.

Kesar Heritage Hotel   GUESTHOUSE $
(☑ 9983216625; www.kesarheritage.com; Makrana Mohalla; r ₹900-2200; ❄ 🛜) A popular budget choice, Kesar plays a good hand with large airy rooms (a few have balconies, air-con and flatscreen TVs) and friendly, helpful management. The side-alley location puts noisily sputtering rickshaws out of earshot of light sleepers. The vegetarian rooftop restaurant gets rave reviews for its delicious food and views to Mehrangarh.

Pushp Guest House   GUESTHOUSE $
(☑ 0291-2648494; www.pushpguesthouse.com; Pipli-ki-Gali, Naya Bass, Manak Chowk; r ₹400-600, with AC ₹1000; ❄ 🛜) A small family-run guesthouse with five clean, colourful rooms with windows. It's tucked down the narrowest of alleys, but you get an up-close view of Mehrangarh from the rooftop restaurant, where owner Nikhil rustles up great vegetarian fare. Nikhil will send a rickshaw to the railway station to pick you up for ₹100.

★ Krishna Prakash
Heritage Haveli   HERITAGE HOTEL $$
(☑ 0291-2633448; www.kpheritage.com; Nayabas; r incl breakfast ₹2015-4720; ❄ @ 🛜 ✉) This multilevel heritage hotel right under the fort walls is great value and a peaceful choice. It has decorated carved furniture and colourful murals, and rooms are well proportioned; the deluxe ones are a bit more spruced up, generally bigger, and set on the upper floors, so airier. There's a shaded swimming pool and a relaxing terrace restaurant.

Free bus and train station pickups are offered and there are facilities for drivers.

Haveli Inn Pal   HERITAGE HOTEL $$
(☑ 0291-2612519; www.haveliinnpal.com; Gulab Sagar; r incl breakfast ₹3850-5150; ❄ @ 🛜) This smaller sibling of Pal Haveli is accessed through the same grand entrance, but is located around to the right in one wing of the residence. It's a simpler heritage experience, with comfortable rooms, and lake or fort views from the more expensive ones. It

has its own very good rooftop restaurant, Panorama 360°.

Free pickups from Jodhpur transport terminals are offered, and discounts are often available for single occupancy.

Jhankar Choti Haveli   HERITAGE HOTEL $$
(☑ 0291-2621390; www.jhankarhaveli.com; Makrana Mohalla; r incl breakfast ₹2500-4500; ❄ 🛜) Above the restaurant of the same name are nine delightful and spacious rooms carved out of a beautiful *haveli*. Rooms feature raw red stone walls and shiny marble floors. Antique furniture decorates the rooms, which aren't cluttered at all. And bathrooms are modern and have baths.

The Arch   HERITAGE HOTEL $$
(☑ 7014343978;   thearchboutique@gmail.com; Stepwell Sq, Makrana Mohalla; r standard/superior ₹4130/5900; ❄ 🛜) This 200-year-old stone *haveli* has been well renovated, keeping many features while opening up walls to increase room size. The decorations are stylish and the beds comfortable. On the roof is a multicuisine veg restaurant with great views of the step-well and the fort.

Look out for the new Cafe Studio on the ground floor.

Stepwell House   HOTEL $$
(☑ 0291-2614615; www.stepwellhouse.com; Stepwell Sq, Makrana Mohalla; r incl breakfast standard/superior ₹2960/4130; ❄ @ 🛜) This 250-year-old building inside the walled city is a popular, efficient and friendly place. Rooms vary greatly and are individually decorated with colour themes and paintings; many have semibalconies and fort views. The rooftop restaurant, Jharokha 360° (mains ₹270-380; ⏱ 8am-11pm), has excellent food and views. It's opposite the restored and beautiful Toorji Ka Jhalra step-well (p121).

Guests can take advantage of the swimming pool and spa at the neighbouring (and associated) Raas for an extra payment.

★ Pal Haveli   HERITAGE HOTEL $$$
(☑ 0291-3293328; www.palhaveli.com; Gulab Sagar; r incl breakfast ₹5500-10,500; ❄ @ 🛜) This stunning *haveli*, one of the best and most attractive in the old city, was built by the Thakur of Pal in 1847. There are 21 charming, spacious rooms, mostly large and elaborately decorated in traditional heritage style, surrounding a central courtyard. The family retains a small museum here. The rooftop restaurant, Indique (p124), is one of the city's finest and has incredible views.

Raas
BOUTIQUE HOTEL $$$

(☑0291-2636455; www.raasjodhpur.com; Toorji ka Jhalara; r incl breakfast from ₹26,880; ❋🖤❊) Developed from a 19th-century city mansion, Jodhpur's first contemporary-style boutique hotel is a splendid oasis of clean, uncluttered style, hidden behind castle-like gates. The red-sandstone-and-terrazzo rooms come with plenty of luxury touches. Most have balconies with great Mehrangarh views – also to be enjoyed from the lovely pool in the garden courtyard. There are two restaurants and a highly indulgent spa.

🛏 Old City (Navchokiya)

Cosy Guest House
GUESTHOUSE $

(☑9829023390, 0291-2612066; www.cosyguesthouse.com; Chuna Ki Choki, Navchokiya; r ₹400-1000, without bathroom ₹350; ❋🖤) A friendly place in an enchanting location, this 500-year-old glowing blue house has several levels of higgledy-piggledy rooftops and a mix of rooms, some monastic, others comfortable with air-con and views. There's also a relaxing rooftop restaurant.

Ask the rickshaw driver for Navchokiya Rd, from where the guesthouse is signposted, or call the genial owner Mr Joshi.

★ Singhvi's Haveli
GUESTHOUSE $$

(☑9826258920, 0291-2624293; www.singhvihaveli.com; Ramdevji-ka-Chowk, Navchokiya; r ₹900-3800; ❋🖤) This 500-odd-year-old, family-run, red-sandstone *haveli* is an understated gem. Run by two friendly brothers, Singhvi's has 13 individual rooms, ranging from simple places to lay your head to the magnificent Maharani Suite, with its 10 windows and fort view.

There's two relaxing vegetarian restaurants, one decorated with saris and floor cushions, the other a romantic rooftop with fort views.

Raj Mandir
HERITAGE HOTEL $$

(☑9829023390; www.rajmandir.info; Old Fort Rd, Navachokiya; r ₹1850-2950; ❋🖤) This beautifully renovated *haveli* boasts raw stone interiors, antique furnishings and modern bathrooms. The vegetarian rooftop restaurant has great views.

🛏 Train Station Area

Govind Hotel
HOTEL, HOSTEL $

(☑0291-2622758; www.govindhotel.com; Station Rd; dm ₹250, s/d from ₹850/950, with AC from ₹1400/1600; ❋🖤) Well set up for travellers, with helpful management and a location very convenient to the Jodhpur train station. All rooms are clean and tiled, with smart bathrooms. There's a rooftop restaurant and a coffee shop with excellent espresso and cakes.

🍴 Eating

Panorama 360°
INDIAN $$

(☑9414005479; Haveli Inn Pal, Gulab Sagar; mains ₹300-450; ⊙8am-10pm) This cosy restaurant on the rooftop of Haveli Inn Pal features great food, attentive staff and a spectacular view of the fort. It dishes up delicious breakfasts comprising (real) coffee, eggs and pancakes, and it welcomes guests from other hotels. There's great tandoori food and North Indian curries, nonveg and veg, and beer and wine are served.

Nirvana
INDIAN $$

(☑0291-2631262; 1st fl, Tija Mata ka Mandir, Tambaku Bazar; mains ₹270-350, thali ₹400-450; ⊙9am-10pm) Sharing premises with a Rama temple and a hotel, Nirvana has both an indoor cafe, covered in ancient Ramayana wall paintings, and a rooftop eating area with panoramic views. The Indian vegetarian food is among the most delicious you'll find in Rajasthan. The special thali is enormous and easily enough for two. Continental and Indian breakfasts are served in the cafe.

KP's Restaurant
MULTICUISINE $$

(☑9829241547; Killi Khana; mains ₹140-400, thali ₹260-360; ⊙7.30am-10.30pm) The rooftop restaurant at Krishna Prakash Heritage Haveli welcomes all to sample its delicious food and fort views. There are Chinese and Continental dishes, but the North Indian, including *kaju dakh* (cashew and raisin curry) and the veg or nonveg thali, are delicious. For carnivores who like it spicy, the *laal maas* (mutton curry), is the go-to dish.

Favourites such as butter chicken, dhal makhani and *palak paneer* also feature.

Jhankar Choti Haveli
MULTICUISINE $$

(☑9828031291; Makrana Mohalla; mains ₹230-300; ⊙8am-10pm; ❋🖤✍) Stone walls and big cane chairs in a leafy courtyard, along with prettily painted woodwork and whirring fans, set the scene at this semi-open-air travellers' favourite. It serves up good Indian vegetarian dishes, plus pizzas, burgers and baked-cheese dishes. There's an air-con section, a Café Coffee Day franchise and a rooftop for meals with a view.

★ **Indique** INDIAN $$$

(☑ 0291-3293328; Pal Haveli Hotel; mains ₹350-600; ☺ noon-10.30pm) This candlelit rooftop restaurant at the Pal Haveli hotel (p122) is the perfect place for a romantic dinner, with superb views to the fort, clock tower and Umaid Bhawan. The food covers traditional tandoori, biryanis and North Indian curries, but the Rajasthani *laal maas* (mutton curry) is a delight. Ask the bartender to knock you up a gin and tonic before dinner.

🍸 Drinking & Nightlife

★ **Shri Mishrilal Hotel** CAFE

(Sardar Market; ☺ 8.30am-10pm) Just inside the southern gate of Sardar Market, this place is nothing fancy, but whips up the most superb creamy *makhania* lassis (filling, saffron-flavoured lassis). These are the best in town, probably in all of Rajasthan, possibly in all of India.

★ **Cafe Sheesh Mahal** CAFE

(Pal Haveli Hotel; ☺ 9.30am-9pm) Coffee drinkers will enjoy the precious beans and the care that is bestowed on them at the deliciously air-conditioned Cafe Sheesh Mahal. The beans are of South Indian origin, roasted by Lavazza. And the pancakes (₹150) here deserve their legendary status.

Stepwell Cafe CAFE

(☑ 0291-2636455; Toorji ka Jhalra; ☺ 7.30am-10.30pm; ☎) This delightful modern cafe with espresso coffee, cakes and Italian dishes, as well as wine, spirits and beer, sits to one side of the wonderfully restored stepwell, Toorji ka Jhalra. It's a great place to relax and contemplate the time when stepwells such as these kept the city alive. Or you can just watch the kids jump into the water with an impressive booming splash.

🛍 Shopping

Plenty of Rajasthani handicrafts are available in Jodhpur, with shops selling textiles and other wares clustered around Sardar Market and along Nai Sarak. You'll need to bargain hard. The town is known for antiques.

MV Spices FOOD

(www.mvspices.com; 107 Nai Sarak; ☺ 9am-9pm) The most famous spice shop in Jodhpur (and believe us, there are lots of pretenders), MV Spices has five small branches around town, including one at Sadar Market, Me-

herangarh, that are run by the seven daughters of the founder of the original stall. It will cost around ₹100 to ₹500 for 100g bags of spices, and the owners will email you recipes so you can use your spices correctly when you get home.

Sambhali Boutique FASHION & ACCESSORIES

(Killi Khana; ☺ 10am-7pm) 🖉 This small but interesting shop sells goods made by women who have learned craft skills with the Sambhali Trust, which works to empower disadvantaged women and girls. Items include cute stuffed silk or cloth elephants and horses, bracelets made from pottery beads, silk bags, and block-printed muslin curtains and scarves.

Laxmi Niwas FASHION & ACCESSORIES

(Stepwell Sq; ☺ 9am-9pm) Several trendy and quality boutique stores with exquisite block-printed clothes, gifts and tableware can be found in this building opposite the Toorji ka Jhalra (p121) step-well. There's also a bakery and coffee shop and access to the rooftop restaurant Jharokha 360° (p122).

ⓘ Information

There are some foreign-card-friendly ATMs dotted around the city, though fewer are in the old city.

Guchi's (☑ 8233002003; Killikhana, Naya Bass, Makrana Mohalla; ☺ 8am-10pm) This travel agency exchanges currency. As well as all forms of ticketing and vehicle hire, Guchi's has fast broadband internet and a wealth of knowledge on what to do and where to go, including how to do an excursion to Osian.

Main post office (Station Rd; ☺ 9am-4pm Mon-Fri, to 3pm Sat, stamp sales only 10am-3pm Sun)

Tourist office (☑ 0291-2545083; High Court Rd; ☺ 9am-6pm Mon-Fri) Offers a free map.

ⓘ Getting There & Away

AIR

The airport is 5km south of the city centre, about ₹500 by taxi.

Jet Airways (www.jetairways.com), Air India (www.airindia.in) and SpiceJet (www.spicejet.com) fly daily to/from Delhi, Ahmedabad, Indore and Mumbai.

BUS

Government-run buses leave from the **central bus stand** (Raika Bagh), directly opposite Raika Bagh train station. Walk east along High Court

Rd, then turn right under the small tunnel. Services include the following:

Ajmer (for Pushkar) ₹227, AC ₹443, five hours, hourly until 6.30pm

Bikaner ₹266, 5½ hours, frequent from 5am to 6pm

Jaipur ₹331, AC ₹713, seven hours, frequent from 4.45am to midnight

Jaisalmer ₹272, 5½ hours, 10 daily

Mt Abu (Abu Road) ₹306, 7½ hours, nine daily until 9.30pm

Osian ₹69, 1½ hours, half-hourly until 10pm

Rohet ₹47, one hour, every 15 minutes

Udaipur ₹273, AC ₹604, seven hours, 10 daily until 6.30pm

For private buses, you can book through your hotel or an agency such as Guchi's Although it's marginally cheaper to deal directly with the bus operators on the road in front of Jodhpur train station, they have no commercial interest in you and you may find yourself on a bad bus and dropped by the roadside far from your intended destination. **Jain Travels** (☑0291-2643832; www.jaintravels.com; MG Hospital Rd; ☺7am-11pm) appears to be reliable.

Buses leave from bus stands out of town, but the operator should provide you with free transport (usually a shared autorickshaw) from their ticket office. Destinations include the following:

Ajmer (for Pushkar) ₹180, five hours, at least six daily

Bikaner seat/sleeper ₹220/320, five hours, at least five daily

Jaipur seat/sleeper ₹260/380, 7½ hours, five daily

Jaisalmer ₹300, 5½ hours, hourly

Mt Abu (direct) seat/sleeper ₹315/550, 7½ hours, daily

TAXI

You can organise taxis for intercity trips, or longer, through most accommodation places or travel agents such as Guchi's (p124); otherwise, you can deal directly with drivers. There's a taxi stand outside Jodhpur train station. A reasonable price is ₹10 per kilometre, with a minimum of 300km per day. If it is not already in the agreed price, the driver will charge an extra ₹200 for overnight stops and will also charge for his return journey. Guchi's organises one-way fares by coordinating with numerous drivers.

TRAIN

The computerised **reservation office** (Station Rd; ☺8am-8pm Mon-Sat, to 1.45pm Sun) is 300m northeast of Jodhpur train station. Window 786 sells the tourist quota. Services include the following:

Ajmer (for Pushkar) sleeper/3AC ₹185/510, 5½ hours, two daily (6.20am and 7.10am)

Bikaner sleeper/3AC ₹210/530, 5½ to seven hours, five to eight daily (7.25am, 7.45am, 9.50am, 10.25am, 10.55am, 2.25pm, 2pm and 8.25pm)

Delhi sleeper/3AC ₹380/986, 11 to 14 hours, four daily (6.20am, 11.15am, 7.45pm and 9.25pm)

Jaipur sleeper/3AC ₹250/625, five to six hours, six to 12 daily from 1.45am to 11.25pm

Jaisalmer sleeper/3AC ₹215/565, five to seven hours, three or four daily (5.30am, 7.25am, 6pm and 11.40pm)

Mumbai sleeper/3AC ₹485/1270, 16 to 19 hours, two to six daily (3.20am, 5.10am, 5.30am, 2.30pm, 6.30pm, 6.45pm); all go via Abu Rd for Mt Abu (4½ hours)

Udaipur There are no direct trains; change at Marwar Junction.

✪ Getting Around

Despite the absurd claims of some autorickshaw drivers, the fare between the clock tower area and the train stations or central bus stand should be around ₹70 to ₹80.

MAJOR TRAINS FROM JODHPUR

DESTINATION	TRAIN	DEPARTURE	ARRIVAL	FARE (₹)
Ajmer (for Pushkar)	54801 Jodhpur–Ajmer Fast Passenger	7.10am	12.35pm	185/510
Bikaner	14708 Ranakpur Exp	9.50am	3.30pm	210/530
Delhi	12462 Mandor Exp	7.45pm	6.40pm	380/986
Jaipur	14854 Marudhar Exp	9.30am	3.30pm	250/625
Jaisalmer	14810 Jodhpur–Jaisalmer Exp	11.40pm	6.10am	215/565
Mumbai	14707 Ranakpur Exp	2.30pm	9.40am	485/1270

Fares: sleeper/3AC

ⓘ CROSSING TO PAKISTAN: JODHPUR TO KARACHI

For Karachi (Pakistan), the 14889 Thar Express, alias the Jodhpur–Munabao Link Express, leaves Bhagat Ki Kothi station, 4km south of the Jodhpur train station, at 1am on Saturday only. You need to arrive at the station six hours before departure – the same time it takes to reach Munabao (about 7am) on the border. There you undergo lengthy border procedures before continuing to Karachi (assuming you have a Pakistan visa) in a Pakistani train, arriving about 2am on Sunday. Accommodation is sleeper only, with a total sleeper fare of around ₹800 from Jodhpur to Karachi. In the other direction the Pakistani train leaves Karachi at about 11pm on Friday, and the Indian train 14890 leaves Munabao at 7pm on Saturday, reaching Jodhpur at 11.50pm. It is currently not possible to book this train online; you will need to go to the station.

Border Hours

Visas are not available at the border, which is open only when the trains (from Jodhpur and Karachi) are arriving/departing.

Foreign Exchange

There are no official money changers at the border. However, changing money at the border and on the trains with unofficial money changers is possible.

Onward Transport

The Pakistani train takes you into Karachi Cantonment Railway Station, where taxis are available.

Around Jodhpur

Southern Villages

A number of largely traditional villages are strung along and off the Pali road southeast of Jodhpur. Most hotels and guesthouses in Jodhpur offer tours to these villages, often called Bishnoi village safaris. The Bishnoi are a Hindu sect who follow the 500-year-old teachings of Guru Jambheshwar, who emphasised the importance of protecting the environment. Many visitors are surprised by the density – and fearlessness – of wildlife such as blackbuck, nilgai (antelope), chinkara (gazelle) and desert fox around the Bishnoi villages.

The 1730 sacrifice of 363 villagers to protect khejri trees is commemorated in September at Khejadali village, where there is a memorial to the victims fronted by a small grove of khejri trees.

At Guda Bishnoi, the locals are traditionally engaged in animal husbandry. There's a small lake (Indian/foreigner ₹20/80) – full only after a good monsoon – where migratory birds, such as demoiselle cranes, and mammals, such as blackbucks and chinkaras, can be seen, particularly at dusk when they come to drink.

The village of Salawas is a centre for weaving beautiful *dhurries* (rugs), a craft also practised in many other villages. A co-operative of 42 families here runs the Roopraj Dhurry Udyog (☑9982400416; www.rooprajdurry.com; ☉dawn-dusk), through which all profits go to the artisans. A 1m by 1.5m *dhurrie* costs a minimum of ₹5000, including shipping. Other families are involved in block-printing.

Other Muslim villages, such as Singhasini, comprise potter families. Using hand-turned (and powered) wheels they produce big earthenware pots known as *matka*, used for storing and cooling water.

Bishnoi village tours tend to last four hours in total and cost around ₹800 per person. Those run by Deepak Dhanraj of Bishnoi Village Safari (☑9829126398; www.bishnoivillagesafari.com; half-day tour per person ₹800) get good feedback, but many other places do them.

Osian

☑02922 / POP 12,550

The ancient Thar Desert town of Osian, 65km north of Jodhpur, was an important trading centre between the 8th and 12th centuries. Known as Upkeshpur, it was dominated by the Jains, whose wealth left a legacy of exquisitely sculpted, well-preserved temples. The **Mahavira Temple** (⊙6am-8.30pm) surrounds an image of the 24th *tirthankar* (great Jain teacher), formed from sand and milk. **Sachiya Mata Temple** (⊙6am-7.15pm) is an impressive walled complex where both Hindus and Jains worship.

Osian, along with Jodhpur, co-hosts the Marwar Festival (p121), a colourful display of Rajasthani folk music, dance and costume held every September/October.

🗗 Tours

Gemar Singh   SAFARI
(📞9460585154; www.hacra.org; per person per day around ₹3150) A native of Bhikamkor village, northwest of Osian, Gemar Singh arranges popular camel safaris, homestays, camping, desert walks and 4WD trips in the deserts around Osian and its Rajput and Bishnoi villages. The emphasis here is on channelling the benefits of tourism to local people. Pickup from Osian bus station, or from Jodhpur, can be arranged. Minimum two people per trip.

🛏 Sleeping

Guesthouse   GUESTHOUSE $
(📞9414440479; bhanusharma.osian@gmail.com; s/d without bathroom ₹400/600) Raju Bhanu Sharma, a personable Brahmin priest, has an echoing guesthouse geared towards pilgrims near the Mahavira Temple. Rooms are simple, with shared bathroom and bucket hot water.

ℹ Getting There & Away

Frequent buses depart from Jodhpur to Osian (₹69, 1½ hours). Buses also run from Phalodi (₹90, two hours). Trains between Jodhpur and Jaisalmer also stop here. A return taxi from Jodhpur costs about ₹2000.

Kichan & Phalodi

📞02925
Mornings and afternoons in the winter months see huge flocks of graceful demoiselle cranes flock to the tiny village of Kichan. The village is 5km east of Phalodi, a town at the junction of roads from Jodhpur, Jaisalmer, Bikaner and Nagaur.

Phalodi surrounds a crumbling 15th-century fort. The town rose to prominence during the 18th century when Jain business families trading in salt built impressive *havelis* and colourful, extravagant Jain temples, including the domed **Shri Parashnath temple** (camera ₹20), which glistens with gold and Belgian glass. The most prominent *haveli*, **Dadha Haveli**, now houses the Lal

---

WORTH A TRIP

THE DEMOISELLE CRANES OF KICHAN

From late August or early September to the end of March, you can witness the extraordinary sight of hundreds of demoiselle cranes (*Anthropoides virgo*) wintering near Kichan. Numbers may reach several thousand by midwinter. Around sunrise and in the late afternoon, the birds circle overhead, then make a dramatic descent for the grain that villagers spread for them at the **Birds Feeding Home** on the western side of the village (turn left as you enter Kichan from Phalodi). It was the 18th-century French queen Marie Antoinette who dubbed the cranes 'demoiselle', for their grace, when some were taken to France from the Russian steppes. Here they are known as *kurja*.

Brown-grey birds with a black chest and throat, demoiselle cranes stand about 75cm tall, and have a long neck and a short beak. In traditional Marwari songs, women beseech the cranes to bring back messages from their loved ones when they return from distant lands. The flock consumes a phenomenal 600kg of grain each day, which is funded by (very welcome) donations.

The feeding of the cranes dates back some 150 years. The sight of these wonderful birds in such large numbers descending on the feeding ground is truly awe-inspiring, and the noise of the assembly is amazing. It's an experience that shouldn't be missed if you're in the area. During the day, many of the cranes can be found around a small lake on the east side of Kichan.

The demoiselle cranes also winter in Pakistan and Africa. To migrate they must cross the Himalaya from their breeding range, which extends over a wide belt spanning eastern Europe, Central Asia and eastern China.

Niwas hotel and the small Dadha Heritage Museum (Indian/foreigner ₹20/100; ⊙9am-5pm), which contains coins and Jain and Hindu manuscripts, paintings, and silver, bronze and copper sculptures from many parts of India.

🛌 Sleeping

Lal Niwas GUESTHOUSE $$
(☑02925-223813; www.lalniwas.com; Dadha Haveli, Dadha Mohalla, Phalodi; s/d from ₹3540/4130; ❉🛜🖥) This splendidly carved deep terracotta *haveli* in the old part of Phalodi boasts balconies, courtyards and a tangle of passages. Each rooms is different, decorated in the traditional style with heavy wooden furniture. The hotel has a multicuisine restaurant and bar, and management acts as the de facto information office for the region and can organise visits to Kichan.

ⓘ Getting There & Away

Several RSRTC buses depart each day from Phalodi to Jodhpur (₹147, 2½ hours, via Osian), Jaisalmer (₹163, 3½ hours) and Bikaner (₹171, 3½ hours).

Phalodi has rail connections with Jodhpur (sleeper/3AC ₹150/510, 2½ hours, three daily), Jaisalmer (₹180/560, 2½ to 3½ hours, five daily) and Bikaner (₹180/560, 2¾ hours, daily).

A return autorickshaw from Phalodi to Kichan costs about ₹190 including an hour's wait.

Nagaur

☑01582 / POP 110,800
The busy town of Nagaur is built around the massive 12th-century Ahhichatragarh, and is a good stop between Jodhpur and Bikaner. In medieval times Nagaur was hotly contested between rival regional powers. It was finally acquired by Jodhpur in the early 18th century.

◉ Sights

Ahhichatragarh FORT
(Fort of the Hooded Cobra; Indian/foreigner ₹50/200, camera ₹50, English-speaking guide ₹100; ⊙9am-1pm & 2-5pm) Nagaur's massive 12th-century Ahhichatragarh underwent a two-decade, Unesco-award-winning restoration program under the auspices of Jodhpur's Mehrangarh Museum Trust. Inside the vast walls, the focal point is the central Rajput-Mughal palace group, built around beautiful pools. You can admire the very ingenious system of channels and ducts that brought water to the fountains and bathhouse of the Abha Mahal, palace of the Nagaur Maharaja Amar Singh (r 1634–44), from a well near the ramparts.

🎉 Festivals & Events

Nagaur Fair FAIR
(⊙Jan/Feb) The colourful Nagaur Fair is a smaller but even more camel- and cattle-focused version of the Pushkar Camel Fair (p76), and worth diverting for.

🛌 Sleeping & Eating

Ranvas HERITAGE HOTEL $$$
(☑01582-241277; www.ranvasnagaur.com; r incl breakfast ₹15,000-18,000; ❉🛜🖥) A luxury hotel within the fort, beautifully set within the former quarters of the 16 wives of the 18th-century Maharaja Bakht Singh. The 27 rooms occupy what were 10 separate *havelis*, each of which has its own courtyard. Elegant, modern soft furnishings contrast with the ancient, raw stone walls for a luxurious yet traditional ambience. There are two restaurants.

ⓘ Getting There & Away

Half-hourly RSRTC buses between Jodhpur and Bikaner stop at Nagaur (₹135, 2½ to three hours from either place).

Trains between Jodhpur and Bikaner also stop here:
Bikaner sleeper/3AC ₹140/540, three hours, five to eight daily
Jodhpur sleeper/3AC ₹160/540, 3½ hours, six to eight daily

Jaisalmer

☑02992 / POP 65,470
The fort of Jaisalmer is a breathtaking sight: a massive sandcastle rising from the sandy plains like a mirage from a bygone era. No place better evokes exotic camel-train trade routes and desert mystery. Ninety-nine bastions encircle the fort's still-inhabited twisting lanes. Inside are shops swaddled in bright embroideries, a royal palace and numerous businesses looking for your tourist rupee. Despite the rampant commercialism, it's hard not to be enchanted by this desert citadel. Beneath the ramparts, particularly to the north, the narrow streets of the old city conceal magnificent *havelis*, all carved from the same golden-honey sandstone as the fort – hence Jaisalmer's designation as the Golden City.

A city that has come back almost from the dead in the past half-century, Jaisalmer may be remote, but it's certainly not forgotten – indeed it's one of Rajasthan's biggest tourist destinations.

History

Jaisalmer was founded way back in 1156 by a leader of the Bhati Rajput clan named Jaisal. The Bhatis, who trace their lineage back to Krishna, ruled right through to Independence in 1947.

The city's early centuries were tempestuous, partly because its rulers relied on looting for want of other income, but by the 16th century Jaisalmer was prospering from its strategic position on the camel-train routes between India and Central Asia. It eventually established cordial relations with the Mughal empire. In the mid-17th century, Maharawal Sabal Singh expanded the Jaisalmer princedom to its greatest extents by annexing areas that now fall within the administrative districts of Bikaner and Jodhpur.

Under British rule the rise of sea trade (especially through Mumbai) and railways saw Jaisalmer's importance and population decline. Partition in 1947, with the cutting of trade routes to Pakistan, seemingly sealed the city's fate. But the 1965 and 1971 wars between India and Pakistan gave Jaisalmer new strategic importance, and since the 1960s, the Indira Gandhi Canal to the north has brought revitalising water to the surrounding desert.

Today, tourism, wind-power generation, solar-power generation and the area's many military installations are the pillars of the city's economy.

◉ Sights

★ Jaisalmer Fort   FORT

(Golden Fort) Jaisalmer's fort is a living urban centre, with about 3000 people residing within its walls. It is honeycombed with narrow winding lanes, lined with houses and temples – along with a large number of handicraft shops, guesthouses and restaurants. You enter the fort from the east, near Gopa Chowk, and pass through four massive gates on the zigzagging route to the upper section. The final gate opens into the square that forms the fort's centre, Dashera Chowk.

Founded in 1156 by the Rajput ruler Jaisal and reinforced by subsequent rulers, Jaisalmer Fort was the focus of a number of battles between the Bhatis, the Mughals of Delhi and the Rathores of Jodhpur. In re-

cent years, the fabric of the fort has faced increasing conservation problems due to unrestricted water use caused, in the most part, by high tourist numbers.

★ Fort Palace Museum   PALACE

(Indian/foreigner incl audio guide ₹100/500, camera ₹100; ⊙ 8am-6pm, from 9am Nov-Mar) Towering over the fort's main square, and partly built on top of the Hawa Pol (the fourth fort gate), is the former rulers' elegant seven-storey palace. Highlights of the tour include the mirrored and painted Rang Mahal (the bedroom of the 18th-century ruler Mulraj II), a gallery of finely wrought 15th-century sculptures donated to the rulers by the builders of the fort's temples, and the spectacular 360-degree views from the rooftop.

One room contains an intriguing display of stamps from the former Rajput states. On the eastern wall of the palace is a sculpted pavilion-style balcony. Here drummers raised the alarm when the fort was under siege. You can also see numerous round rocks piled on top of the battlements, ready to be rolled onto advancing enemies. Much of the palace is open to the public – floor upon floor of small rooms provide a fascinating sense of how such buildings were designed for spying on the outside world. The doorways connecting the rooms of the palace are quite low. This isn't a reflection on the stature of the Rajputs, but was a means of forcing people to adopt a humble, stooped position in case the room they were entering contained the maharawal.

The last part of the tour moves from the king's palace (Raja-ka-Mahal) into the queen's palace (Rani-ka-Mahal), which contains an interesting section on Jaisalmer's annual Gangaur processions in spring. The worthwhile 1½-hour audio-guide tour (available in six languages) is included with the entry fee, but you must leave a ₹2000 deposit, or your passport, driver's licence or credit card.

Jain Temples   JAIN TEMPLE

(Indian/foreigner ₹50/200; ⊙ Chandraprabhu, Rikhabdev & Gyan Bhandar 8am-noon, other temples 11am-noon) Within the fort walls is a maze-like, interconnecting treasure trove of seven beautiful yellow sandstone Jain temples, dating from the 15th and 16th centuries. Opening times have a habit of changing, so check with the caretakers. The intricate carving rivals that of the marble Jain temples in Ranakpur and Mt Abu, and has an extraordinary quality because of the soft, warm stone.

RAJASTHAN JAISALMER

Jaisalmer

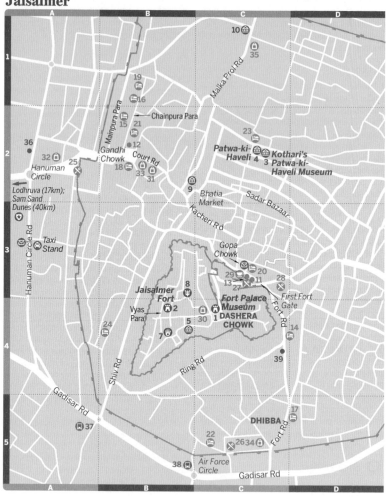

Shoes and all leather items must be removed before entering the temples.

Chandraprabhu is the first temple you come to, and you'll find the ticket stand here. Dedicated to the eighth *tirthankar* (great Jain teacher), whose symbol is the moon, it was built in 1509 and features fine sculpture in the *mandapa* (temple forechamber), the intensely sculpted pillars of which form a series of *toranas* (architraves). To the right of Chandraprabhu is the tranquil Rikhabdev temple, with fine sculptures around the walls, protected by glass cabinets, and pillars beautifully sculpted with *apsaras* (celestial nymphs) and gods.

Behind Chandraprabhu is Parasnath, which you enter through a beautifully carved *torana* culminating in an image of the Jain *tirthankar* at its apex. A door to the south leads to small Shitalnath, dedicated to the 10th *tirthankar*, whose image is composed of eight precious metals. A door in the northern wall leads to the enchanting, dim chamber of Sambhavanth – in the front courtyard, Jain priests grind sandalwood in mortars for devotional use. Steps lead down to the Gyan Bhandar, a fascinating tiny underground library founded in 1500, which houses priceless ancient illustrated manuscripts. The remaining two temples, Shantinath and

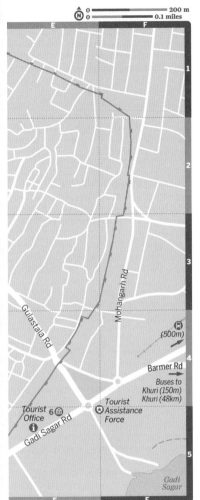

Kunthunath, were built in 1536 and feature plenty of sensual carving. Note, the restrictive visiting times are for non-Jains. The temples are open all day for worshippers.

Gadi Sagar   LAKE

This stately tank, southeast of the city walls, was Jaisalmer's vital water supply until 1965, and because of its importance it is surrounded by small temples and shrines. The tank was built in 1367 by Maharawal Gadsi Singh, taking advantage of a natural declivity that already retained some water. It's a waterfowl favourite in winter, but can almost dry up before the monsoon.

Laxmi Narayan Temple   HINDU TEMPLE

The Hindu Laxmi Narayan Temple, in the centre of the fort, is simpler than the Jain

JAISALMER CAMEL SAFARIS

Trekking around by camel is the most evocative and fun way to sample Thar Desert life. Don't expect dune seas, however – the Thar is mostly arid scrubland sprinkled with villages and wind turbines, with occasional dune areas popping out here and there. You will often come across fields of millet, and children herding flocks of sheep or goats, the neck bells of which tinkle in the desert silence.

Most trips now include 4WD rides to get you to less frequented areas. The camel riding is then done in two two-hour batches, one before lunch, one after. It's hardly camel *trekking*, but it's a lot of fun nevertheless. A cheaper alternative to arranging things in Jaisalmer is to base yourself in the small village of Khuri (p140), 48km southwest, where similar camel rides are available, but you're already in the desert when you start.

Before You Go

Competition between safari organisers is cutthroat and standards vary. Most hotels and guesthouses are very happy to organise a camel safari for you. While many provide a good service, some may cut corners and take you for the kind of ride you didn't have in mind. A few low-budget hotels in particular exert considerable pressure on guests to take 'their' safari. Others specifically claim 'no safari hassle'.

You can also organise a safari directly with one of the several reputable specialist agencies in Jaisalmer. Since these agencies depend exclusively on safari business it's particularly in their interest to satisfy their clients. It's a good idea to talk to other travellers and ask two or three operators what they're offering.

A one-night safari, leaving Jaisalmer in the afternoon and returning the next morning, with a night on some dunes, is a minimum to get a feel for the experience: you'll probably get 1½ to two hours of riding each day. You can trek for several days or weeks if you wish. The longer you ride, the more understanding you'll gain of the desert's villages, oases, wildlife and people.

The best-known dunes, at Sam (p134), 40km west of Jaisalmer, are always crowded in the evening and are more of a carnival than a back-to-nature experience. The dunes near Khuri are also quite busy at sunset, but quiet the rest of the time. Operators all sell trips now to 'nontouristy' and 'off-the-beaten-track' areas. Ironically, this has made Khuri quieter again, although Sam still hums with day-tripper activity.

With 4WD transfers included, typical rates are between ₹1200 and ₹2500 per person for a one-day, one-night trip (leaving one morning and returning the next). This should include meals, mineral water, blankets and sometimes a thin mattress. Check that there will be one camel for each rider. You can pay for greater levels of comfort (eg tents, better food), but *always* get it all down in writing.

You should get a cheaper rate (₹1100 to ₹1600 per person) if you leave Jaisalmer in the afternoon and return the following morning. A quick sunset ride in the dunes at Sam costs around ₹800 per person, including 4WD transfer. At the other end of the scale, you can arrange for a 20-day trek to Bikaner. Expect to pay between ₹1200 and ₹2000 per person per day for long, multiday trips, depending on the level of support facilities (4WDs, camel carts etc).

temples here and has a brightly decorated dome. Devotees offer grain, which is distributed before the temple. The inner sanctum has a repoussé silver architrave around its entrance, and a heavily garlanded image enshrined within.

Baa Ri Haveli MUSEUM
(☑02992-252907; Fort; ₹50) This 450-year-old *haveli*, once belonging to Brahmin priests that advised the maharajah, now houses an interesting museum on its several levels. Artefacts from all aspects of fort life from cooking to clothing are on display.

★**Patwa-ki-Haveli** HISTORIC BUILDING
(Indian/foreigner ₹50/200; ⊙9am-6pm) The biggest fish in the *haveli* pond is Patwa-ki-Haveli, which towers over a narrow lane, its intricate stonework like honey-coloured lace. Divided into five sections, it was built between 1800 and 1860 by five Jain broth-

What to Take

A wide-brimmed hat (or Lawrence of Arabia turban), long trousers, a long-sleeved shirt, insect repellent, toilet paper, a torch (flashlight), sunscreen, a water bottle (with a strap), and some cash (for a tip to the camel men, if nothing else) are recommended. Women should consider wearing a sports bra, as a trotting camel is a bumpy ride. It can get cold at night, so if you have a sleeping bag bring it along, even if you're told that lots of blankets will be supplied. During summer, rain is not unheard of, so come prepared.

Which Safari?

Recommendations shouldn't be a substitute for doing your own research. Whichever agency you go for, insist that all rubbish is carried back to Jaisalmer.

Thar Desert Tours (☑9414365333; www.tharcamelsafarijaisalmer.com; Gandhi Chowk; ◷8.30am-7.30pm) This well-run operator charges ₹1300 per person per day including water and meals, adjusting prices depending on trip times. It limits tours to five people maximum, and we receive good feedback about them. Customers pay 80% upfront.

Sahara Travels (☑02992-252609, 9414319921; www.saharatravelsjaisalmer.com; Gopa Chowk; ◷6am-8pm) Run by the son of the late LN Bissa (aka Mr Desert), this place is very professional and transparent. Prices for an overnight trip (9am to 11am the following day) are ₹2100 per person, all inclusive. A cheaper overnight alternative that avoids the midday sun starts at 2pm and finishes at 11am for ₹1650.

Trotters (☑9828929974; www.trottersjaisalmer.net; Gopa Chowk; ◷5.30am-9.00pm) This company is transparently run with a clear price list showing everything on offer, including trips to 'off-the-beaten-track' areas as well as cheaper jaunts to Sam or Khuri. Prices for an overnight trip (6.30am to 11am/5.30pm the following day) are ₹2250 to ₹2450 per person, all inclusive.

In the Desert

Camping out at night, huddling around a tiny fire beneath the stars and listening to the camel drivers' songs, is magical.

There's always a long lunch stop during the hottest part of the day. At resting points the camels are unsaddled and hobbled; they'll often have a roll in the sand before limping away to browse on nearby shrubs, while the camel drivers brew chai or prepare food. The whole crew rests in the shade of thorn trees.

Take care of your possessions, particularly on the return journey. Any complaints you do have should be reported, either to the **Superintendent of Police** (☑02992-252233), the tourist office (p139) or the intermittently staffed **Tourist Assistance Force** (Gadi Sagar Rd) posts inside the First Fort Gate and on the Gadi Sagar access road.

The camel drivers will expect a tip (up to ₹100 per day is welcomed) at the end of the trip; don't neglect to give them one.

ers who made their fortunes in brocade and jewellery. It's all very impressive from the outside; however, the first of the five sections, the privately owned **Kothari's Patwa-ki-Haveli Museum** (Indian/foreigner ₹100/250; ◷9am-6pm), richly evokes 19th-century life and is the only one worth paying entry for.

Other sections include two largely empty government-owned 'museums' and two private sections containing shops.

Nathmal-ki-Haveli HISTORIC BUILDING
(◷8am-7pm) This late-19th-century *haveli*, once the prime minister's house, is still partly inhabited. It has an extraordinary exterior, dripping with carvings, and the 1st floor has paintings using gold leaf. The left and right wings were the work of brothers, whose competitive spirits apparently produced this virtuoso work; the two sides are similar, but not identical. Sandstone elephants guard the entrance to what is effectively a shop.

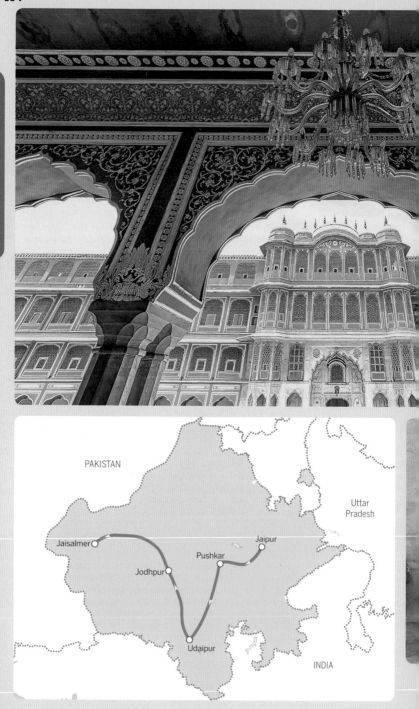

PAKISTAN

Uttar
Pradesh

Jaisalmer

Jaipur

Pushkar

Jodhpur

Udaipur

INDIA

MANJIK / SHUTTERSTOCK ©

Rajasthan's Coloured Cities

2 WEEKS

Pink, blue, white and gold: either through design or serendipity, these are the singular and defining colours of Rajasthan's epic cities: Jaipur, Jodhpur, Udaipur and Jaisalmer. With a fortnight to spare you can plunge into this palette, capture all the grandeur, and scope out all the possibilities of these colour-coded cities.

The pink city of **Jaipur** (p39), in particular the bustling Old City within the salmon-pink walls and city gates, deserves exploring on foot. Iconic buildings, such as the Hawa Mahal, and even small shops receive a new coat of pink paint on a regular basis; the colour is meant to give the rendered walls a solid-stone impression. The Old City's bazaars are laid out in a grid adhering to an ancient Hindu treatise. Bangle makers, silver- and goldsmiths, gemstone dealers, marble carvers and silk merchants: each lay claim to a street where competitors and compatriots are held close.

Head southwest to the Brahmin-blue town of **Pushkar** (p74). The 52 ghats that surround the lake are shades of pale blue fading to pure white. Pushkar attracts pilgrims and poseurs in equal proportion, and the population quadruples during its famous Camel Fair. Continuing southwest the road leads to the romantic lakeside city of **Udaipur** (p94), a city for rest and relaxation, where you can sip on a chai while gazing at the brilliant white Lake Place floating in the centre of Lake Pichola. This idyllic palace reflected in dark still waters has earned many admirers and a few imitators, giving the city its White City sobriquet.

North of Udaipur is the true blue city of **Jodhpur** (p117). Beneath a towering island of rock, capped by the fort of Mehrangarh, is a sea of indigo-washed cubes: blocky *havelis*, jumbled cheek by jowl in the medieval Old City. For whatever reason – Brahmin tradition, indigo's insecticide properties or the cool imparted by blue hue – blue is the colour of Jodhpur and its ageless alleys.

If Jodhpur is the gateway to the Great Thar Desert, the golden city of **Jaisalmer** (p128) is its capital. A convergence point for ancient trade routes, this fortified oasis is constructed solely of Jaisalmer's honey-coloured sandstone. The great castle, a glowing sunset apparition, shelters around 500 families, carved stone temples, shops, restaurants and businesses.

ARUN SAMBHU MISHRA / SHUTTERSTOCK ©

Top: City Palace (p42), Jaipur
Bottom: Street market, Jodhpur (p117)

Desert Cultural Centre & Museum

MUSEUM

(☏02992-253723; Gadi Sagar Rd; museum ₹50, camera ₹50, combined museum & puppet show ₹100; ⏱9am-6pm, puppet shows 6.30-8.30pm) This interesting little museum tells the history of Rajasthan's princely states and has exhibits on traditional Rajasthani culture. Features include Rajasthani music (with video), textiles, a *kavad* (a brightly painted mobile story box/shrine made of wood), and a *phad* (scroll painting) depicting the story of the Rajasthani folk hero Pabuji, used by travelling singers as they recite Pabuji's epic exploits. It also hosts nightly half-hour **puppet shows** with English commentary. The ticket includes admission to the Jaisalmer Folklore Museum.

Thar Heritage Museum

MUSEUM

(☏9414150762; Main Rd, Artists Colony; ₹100; ⏱10am-8pm) This private museum has an intriguing assortment of Jaisalmer artefacts, from turbans, musical instruments, fossils and kitchen equipment, to displays on birth, marriage, death and opium customs. It's brought alive by the guided tour you'll get from its founder, local historian and folklorist LN Khatri. Look for the snakes and ladders game that acts as a teaching guide to Hinduism's spiritual journey. If the door is locked you'll find Mr Khatri at his shop, Desert Handicrafts Emporium (p139), on Court Rd.

Tours

The tourist office (p139) runs sunset tours to the Sam Sand Dunes though these are invariably disappointing because of the crowds, litter and harassment. Other tours visit Amar Sagar, Lodhruva and Bada Bagh by car. Your best bet is to find a camel safari operator who can take you away from the noisy crowds.

Festivals & Events

Jaisalmer Desert Festival

CULTURAL

(⏱Jan/Feb) Jaisalmer celebrates its desert culture with the action-packed Desert Festival, featuring camel races, camel polo, folk music, snake charmers, turban-tying contests, and the famous Mr Desert competition. Many events take place at the Sam Sand Dunes.

Sleeping

While staying in the fort might appear to be Jaisalmer's most atmospheric choice, habitation inside the fort – driven in no small part by tourism – is causing irreparable damage to the monument. As a result, we don't recommend staying inside. Fortunately, there's a wide choice of good places to stay outside the fort. You'll get massive discounts between April and August, when Jaisalmer is hellishly hot.

Arya Haveli

GUESTHOUSE $

(☏9782585337; www.aryahaveli.com; Mainpura Para; dm incl breakfast ₹275, r fan only ₹350-650, r with AC incl breakfast ₹1500; ✴🛜) Helpful staff add to a stay at this spruced-up guesthouse. Rooms are well appointed and looked after; the cheaper ones face an internal courtyard, the best have their own balcony. The top-floor Blues Cafe is a nice place to relax to some good music and tasty food.

Hostel Renuka

HOTEL $

(Renuka Camel Safari; ☏02992-252757, 9414150291; www.renukacamelsafari.com; Chainpura Para; dm ₹150, r ₹350-750; ✴🛜) Spread over three floors, Hostel Renuka has squeaky-clean rooms – the best have balconies, bathrooms and air-conditioning. It's been warmly accommodating guests since 1988, so management knows its stuff. The roof terrace has great fort views and a good restaurant, and the hotel offers free pickup from the bus and train stations.

Hotel Tokyo Palace

HOTEL $

(☏9414721282, 02992-255483; www.tokyopalace.net; Dhibba Para; dm ₹200, r incl breakfast ₹1500-3000; ✴🛜🛋) Well run by honest, traveller-friendly management, this hotel has clean midrange rooms, some with lovely window seats, as well as plenty of budget options, including separate basement dorms for men and women (bathrooms are the next level up). A big bonus is the pool and relaxing rooftop restaurant.

Hotel Gorakh Haveli

HOTEL $

(☏02992-252978, 9680020049; www.hotelgorakhhaveli.com; Dhibba Para; r from ₹900, with AC incl breakfast ₹1250-2500; ✴🛜) A pleasantly low-key spot south of the fort, Gorakh Haveli is a modern place built with traditional sandstone and some attractive carving. Rooms are comfy and spacious, staff are amiable, and there's a reasonable all-veg, multicuisine rooftop restaurant (mains ₹30 to ₹150), with fort views, of course. A 30% discount on rooms is offered in summer.

Shahi Palace
HOTEL $

(✆ 9660014495, 02992-255920; www.shahipalacehotel.com; off Shiv Rd; r ₹550-2550; ❅ 🛜) Shahi Palace is a deservedly popular option. It's a modern building in the traditional style with carved sandstone. It has attractive rooms with raw sandstone walls, colourful embroidery, and carved stone or wooden beds. The cheaper rooms are mostly in two annexes along the street, Star Haveli and Oasis Haveli. The rooftop restaurant (mains ₹100 to ₹220) is excellent. Camel safaris can be organised.

Indian veg and nonveg dishes are available, plus some European fare, cold beer and a superb evening fort view. Free pickup from the train and bus station.

Hotel Swastika
HOTEL $

(✆ 02992-252483; swastikahotel@yahoo.com; Chainpura Para; dm ₹100, s/d/tr ₹200/300/400, r with AC ₹600; ❅ 🛜) In this long-running place, the only thing you'll be hassled about is to relax. Rooms are plain, quiet, clean and very good for the price; some have little balconies. There are plenty of restaurants nearby.

★ Hotel Nachana Haveli
HERITAGE HOTEL $$

(✆ 02992-252110; www.nachanahaveli.com; Goverdhan Chowk; s/d/ste incl breakfast ₹4250/4750/5750; ❅ 🛜) This 280-year-old royal *haveli*, set around three courtyards – one with a tinkling fountain – is a fascinating hotel with a highly regarded restaurant (p138). The raw sandstone rooms have arched stone ceilings and the ambience of a medieval castle. They are sumptuously and romantically decorated. The common areas come with all the Rajput trimmings, including swing chairs and antiques.

Although centrally located, the hotel is set back from the road and the stone walls ensure a peaceful sleep.

Hotel Shanti Home
BOUTIQUE HOTEL $$

(✆ 02992-251474, 9928738269; shantihomejsm@gmail.com; Dhibba Para; r incl breakfast ₹1200-2500; ❅ 🛜) Near the fort gate this unassuming small hotel has just seven delightful, bright, spacious and stylish rooms, all well appointed with comfortable beds. There's a great rooftop restaurant, Flavours, enjoying fort views. And there's a handy ATM on the premises.

Hotel Pleasant Haveli
HOTEL $$

(✆ 02992-253253; www.pleasanthaveli.com; Chainpura Para; r from ₹2300; ❅ 🛜) This welcoming place has lots of lovely carved stone, a beautiful rooftop (with nonveg restaurant) and just a handful of spacious and attractive colour-themed rooms, all with modern, well-equipped bathrooms, minifridge and air-con; at least one has an over-bed mirror and dual showers. Complimentary water bottles and free pickups from transport terminals are available.

Killa Bhawan Lodge
HOTEL $$

(✆ 02992-253833; www.killabhawan.com; Patwa-ki-haveli Chowk; r incl breakfast ₹3480-4130; ❅ 🛜) Near Patwa-ki-Haveli, this small hotel is a delight. There are only a handful of big and beautifully decorated rooms, a pleasant rooftop restaurant, KB Cafe, that looks up to the fort, and free water bottles, tea and coffee all day.

★ 1st Gate Home Fusion
BOUTIQUE HOTEL $$$

(✆ 02992-254462, 9462554462; www.1stgate.in; First Fort Gate; r incl breakfast from ₹8790; ❅ 🛜) Italian-designed and superslick, this is Jaisalmer's most sophisticated hotel and it's beautiful throughout, with a desert-meets-contemporary-boutique vibe. The location lends it one of the finest fort views in town, especially from its split-level, open-air restaurant-cafe area. Rooms are immaculate with complimentary minibar (soft drinks), fruit basket and bottled water replenished daily.

Breakfast includes espresso coffee, and there is a plunge pool, gym and spa.

★ Suryagarh
HOTEL $$$

(✆ 02992-269269; www.suryagarh.com; Kahala Fata, Sam Rd; r/ste incl breakfast from ₹21,760/26,880; ❅ @ 🛜 ❅) The undisputed king in this category, Suryagarh rises like a fortress beside the Sam road, 14km west of town. It's a relatively new building in traditional Jaisalmer style centred on a huge palace-like courtyard with beautiful carved stonework. Features include a fabulous indoor pool and a multicuisine restaurant, Nosh (mains ₹650 to ₹800; nonguests welcome). Rooms follow the traditional/contemporary theme.

It's a spectacular place, but it doesn't stop there. A great range of activities and excursions are on offer plus nightly entertainment.

✕ Eating & Drinking

Chandan Shree Restaurant INDIAN $
(near Hanuman Circle; mains ₹100-200; ⊙7am-11pm; 🖉) An always busy (and rightfully so) vegetarian dining hall serving up a huge range of tasty, spicy South Indian, Gujarati, Rajasthani, Punjabi and Bengali dishes.

★Saffron MULTICUISINE $$
(Hotel Nachana Haveli, Goverdhan Chowk; mains ₹245-385, thali veg/nonveg ₹385/545; ⊙7am-11pm) On the spacious roof terrace of Hotel Nachana Haveli, the veg and nonveg food here is excellent. It's a particularly atmospheric place in the evening, with private and communal lounges and more formal seating arrangements. The Indian food is hard to beat, though the Italian isn't too bad either. Alcohol is served and the thali is generous.

Monica Restaurant MULTICUISINE $$
(☑9414149496; Amar Sagar Pol; mains ₹100-300, veg/nonveg thali ₹225/400; ⊙8.30am-3pm & 6.30-10pm) The airy open-air dining room at Monica just about squeezes in a fort view, but if you end up at a table with no view, console yourself with the excellent veg and nonveg options. Meat from the tandoor is particularly well flavoured and succulent, the thalis varied, and the salads fresh and tasty.

Jaisal Italy ITALIAN $$
(☑02992-253504; www.jaisalitaly.com; First Fort Gate; mains ₹130-330, thali ₹220-350; ⊙7.30am-11pm; ❋🖥) Just inside First Fort Gate, Jaisal Italy has decent vegetarian Italian and Indian dishes, including bruschetta, antipasti, pasta, pizza, salad and desserts, plus Spanish omelettes. All this is served up in an exotically decorated indoor restaurant (cosy in winter, deliciously air-conditioned in summer) or on a delightful terrace atop the lower fort walls, with cinematic views. Alcohol is served.

Desert Boy's Dhani INDIAN $$
(Dhibba Para; mains ₹120-350, thali ₹350-450; ⊙11am-4pm & 7-11pm; ❋🖥🖉) A walled-garden restaurant where tables are spread around a large, stone-paved courtyard shaded by a spreading tree. There's also traditional cushion seating undercover and in an air-conditioned room. Rajasthani music and dance are performed from 8pm to 10pm nightly, and it's a very pleasant place to eat

excellent, good-value Rajasthani and other Indian veg dishes.

★1st Gate Home Fusion ITALIAN, INDIAN $$$
(☑02992-254462, 9462554462; First Fort Gate; mains ₹360-500; ⊙7.30am-10.30pm; 🖥🖉) Sitting atop the boutique hotel of the same name, this split-level, open-air terrace has dramatic fort views and a mouthwatering menu of authentic vegetarian Italian and Indian dishes. Also on offer are excellent wood-fired pizzas, delicious desserts, and good strong Italian coffee. Wine (by the bottle or glass), beer and cocktails are also available.

Bhang Shop CAFE
(Gopa Chowk; lassi from ₹150) Jaisalmer's licensed Bhang Shop is a simple, unpretentious place. The magic ingredient is bhang: cannabis buds and leaves mixed into a paste with milk, ghee and spices. As well as lassi, it also does a range of bhang-laced cookies and cakes – choose either medium or strong. Bhang is legal, but it doesn't agree with everyone, so go easy.

🔒 Shopping

Jaisalmer is famous for its stunning embroidery, bedspreads, mirrorwork wall hangings, oil lamps, stonework and antiques. Watch out when purchasing silver items: the metal is sometimes adulterated with bronze.

There are several good *khadi* (homespun cloth) shops where you can find fixed-price tablecloths, rugs and clothes, with a variety of patterning techniques including tie-dye, block printing and embroidery. Try Zila Khadi Gramodan Parishad (Malka Prol Rd; ⊙10am-6pm Mon-Sat), Khadi Gramodyog Bhavan (Dhibba; ⊙10am-6pm Mon-Sat) or Gandhi Darshan Emporium (near Hanuman Circle; ⊙11am-7pm Fri-Wed).

Bellissima ARTS & CRAFTS
(Dashera Chowk; ⊙8am-9pm) This small shop near the fort's main square sells beautiful patchworks, embroidery, paintings, bags, rugs, cushion covers and all types of Rajasthani art. Proceeds assist underprivileged women from surrounding villages, including those who have divorced or been widowed.

Jaisalmer Handloom ARTS & CRAFTS
(www.jaisalmerhandloom.com; Court Rd; ⊙9am-10pm) This place has a big array of bedspreads, tapestries, clothing (ready-made and custom-made, including silk) and oth-

er textiles, made by its own workers and others. If you need an embroidered camel-saddle-cloth (and who doesn't?), try for one here.

Desert Handicrafts Emporium ARTS & CRAFTS
(Court Rd; ⊙9.30am-9.30pm) With some unusual jewellery, paintings and all sorts of textiles, this is one of the most original of numerous craft shops around town.

❶ Information

There are ATMs near the fort gate, near Hanuman Circle, on Shiv Rd, and outside the train station. Lots of licensed money changers are in and around Gandhi Chowk, east of Hanuman Circle.

Main post office (Hanuman Circle Rd; ⊙10am-5pm Mon-Sat) West of the fort.

Post office (Gopa Chowk; ⊙10am-5pm Mon-Fri, to 1pm Sat) Just outside the fort gate; sells stamps and you can send postcards.

Tourist office (✆02992-252406; Gadi Sagar Rd; ⊙9.30am-6pm) Has a free town map.

❶ Getting There & Away

AIR

Jaisalmer's new airport, 5km south of town, had been lying mothballed for a few years, but in 2018 SpiceJet (www.spicejet.com) commenced daily flights to/from Ahmedabad, Jaipur, Delhi and Mumbai.

BUS

RSRTC buses leave from the **main bus stand** (Shiv Rd). There are services to Ajmer (₹466, 9½ hours) and Jodhpur (₹272, 5½ hours) throughout the day. Buses to Khuri (₹39, one hour) depart from a stand just off Gadi Sagar Rd on Barmer Rd.

A number of private bus companies have ticket offices at Hanuman Circle. **Hanuman Travels** (✆9413362367) and **Swagat Travels** (✆02992-252557) are typical. The buses themselves leave from the **private bus stand** (Air Force Circle). Typical services include the following:

Ajmer (for Pushkar) seat/sleeper ₹310/480, nine hours, two or three daily

Bikaner ₹215/430, 5½ hours, three to four daily

Jaipur ₹420/550, 11 hours, two or three daily

Jodhpur ₹210/420, five hours, half-hourly from 6am to 10pm

Udaipur ₹370/480, 12 hours, one or two daily

TAXI

One-way taxis (you pay for the empty return trip) cost about ₹5000 to Jodhpur, ₹5500 to Bikaner or ₹9000 to Udaipur. There's a taxi stand on Hanuman Circle Rd.

TRAIN

The **train station** (⊙ticket office 8am-8pm Mon-Sat, to 1.45pm Sun) is on the eastern edge of town, just off the Jodhpur road. There's a reserved ticket booth for foreigners.

Bikaner sleeper/3AC ₹250/625, around six hours, two or three daily (11.25am, 10.10am and 11.55pm)

Delhi ₹450/1205, 18 hours, two or three daily (1am, 1.25am and 4.45pm) via Jaipur (12 hours)

Jaipur ₹350/935, 12 hours, three daily (1am, 4.45pm and 11.55pm)

Jodhpur ₹215/565, five to six hours, three daily (1am, 7am and 4.45pm)

❶ Getting Around

AUTORICKSHAW

It costs around ₹50 from the train station to Gandhi Chowk, north of the fort.

CAR & MOTORCYCLE

It's possible to hire taxis or 4WDs from the stand on Hanuman Circle Rd. To Khuri, the Sam Sand Dunes or Lodhruva, expect to pay from ₹1200 return including a wait of about an hour or so.

Shiva Bikes (✆9461113600; First Fort Gate; motorbike per day ₹500-2000; ⊙8am-9pm) A licensed hire place with motorbikes (including Royal Enfield Bullets) and scooters for exploring town and nearby sights. Helmets and area maps are included.

MAJOR TRAINS FROM JAISALMER

DESTINATION	TRAIN	DEPARTURE	ARRIVAL	FARE (₹)
Bikaner	12467 Leelan Exp	11.55pm	5.20am	250/625
Delhi	14660 Jaisalmer–Delhi Exp	4.45pm	11.15am	450/1205
Jaipur	14660 Jaisalmer–Delhi Exp	4.45pm	4.50am	350/935
Jodhpur	14809 Jaisalmer–Jodhpur Exp	7am	1pm	215/565

Fares: sleeper/3AC

Around Jaisalmer

Sam Sand Dunes

The silky **Sam dunes** (vehicle/camel ₹50/80), 41km west of Jaisalmer along a good sealed road, are one of the most popular excursions from the city. About 2km long, the dunes are undeniably among the most picturesque in the region. Some camel safaris camp here, but many more people just roll in for sunset, to be chased across the sands by tenacious camel owners offering short rides. Plenty more people stay overnight in one of the several tent resorts near the dunes.

The place acquires something of a carnival atmosphere from late in the afternoon until the next morning, making it somewhere to avoid if you're after a solitary desert experience.

If you're organising your own camel ride on the spot, expect to pay ₹300 for a one-hour sunset ride, but beware tricks from camel men such as demanding more money en route.

Khuri

☑ 03014

The village of Khuri, 48km southwest of Jaisalmer, has quite extensive dune areas attracting their share of sunset visitors, and a lot of mostly smallish 'resorts' offering overnight camel safari packages. It also has a number of low-key guesthouses where you can stay in tranquillity in a traditional-style hut with clay-and-dung walls and thatched roof, and venture out on interesting camel trips in the relatively remote and empty surrounding area.

Khuri is within the **Desert National Park**, which stretches over 3162 sq km southwest of Jaisalmer to protect part of the Thar ecosystem, including wildlife such as the desert fox, desert cat, chinkara (gazelle), nilgai (antelope), and some unusual birdlife including the endangered great Indian bustard.

Be aware that the commission system is entrenched in Khuri's larger accommodation options. If you just want a quick camel ride on the sand dunes, expect to pay around ₹150 per person.

🛏 Sleeping

⭐ **Badal House** HOMESTAY $
(☑ 8107339097; napsakhuri@gmail.com; r/hut per person incl full board ₹400/300) Here you can stay in a family compound in the centre of the village with a few spotlessly clean, mud-walled, thatch-roofed huts and equally spotless rooms (a couple have their own cold shower and squat toilet), and enjoy good home cooking. Former camel driver Badal Singh is a charming, gentle man who charges ₹650 for a camel safari with a night on the dunes.

He doesn't pay commission so don't let touts warn you away.

The Mama's Resort & Camp TENTED CAMP $$
(☑ 9414205970, 03014-274042; www.themamas jaisalmer.com; cottage/tent ₹7500/8500) This is a well-regarded tent camp, with gorgeous en-suite luxury tents tricked out with Jaisalmer fabrics, as well as small mud-brick cottages with simpler but still comfortable rooms. There's sunset camel safaris, delicious meals and Rajasthani music and dancing in the evening, and it is all included in the package.

ℹ Getting There & Away

You can catch local buses from Jaisalmer to Khuri (₹39, one hour) from a road just off Gadi Sagar Rd. Walking from Jaisalmer Fort towards the train station, take the second right after the tourist office, then wait by the tree on the left, with the small shrine beside it. Buses pass here at around 10am, 1.30pm, 3pm and 4pm.

Return buses from Khuri to Jaisalmer leave at roughly 8am, 10am, 11.30am and 3pm.

A taxi from Jaisalmer will cost at least ₹1500. Even if you are staying here you will be paying for the return trip.

Bikaner

☑ 0151 / POP 644,400

Bikaner is a vibrant, dust-swirling desert town with a fabulous fort and an energising outpost feel. It's less dominated by tourism than many other Rajasthan cities, though it has plenty of hotels and a busy camel-safari scene, which attracts plenty of travellers looking to avoid the crowding that occasionally occurs around Jaisalmer-based safaris.

The city was founded in 1488 by Rao Bika, a son of Rao Jodha, Jodhpur's founder, though the two Rathore ruling houses later had a serious falling out over who had the right to keep the family heirlooms. Bikaner grew quickly as a staging post on the great caravan trade routes from the late 16th century onwards, and flourished under a friendly relationship with the Mughals, but declined as the Mughals did in the 18th century. By the 19th century the area was markedly backward, but managed to turn its fortunes around by hiring out camels to the British during the First Anglo-Afghan War. In 1886 it was the first desert princely state to install electricity.

⊙ Sights

★ Junagarh FORT
(Indian/foreigner ₹50/300, video ₹150, audio guide ₹50, personal guide ₹350; ⊙10am-5.30pm, last entry 4.30pm) This most impressive fort was constructed between 1589 and 1593 by Raja Rai Singh, ruler of Bikaner and a general in the army of the Mughal emperor Akbar. You enter through the Karan Prole (Court Rd) gate on the east side and pass through three more gates before the ticket office for the palace museum. An audio guide (requiring an identity document as a deposit) is available in English, French, German and Hindi, and is very informative.

The beautifully decorated Karan Mahal was the palace's Diwan-i-Am (Hall of Public Audience), built in the 17th and 18th centuries. Anup Mahal Chowk has lovely carved *jarokhas* (balcony windows) and *jali* (carved lattice screens), and was commissioned in the late 17th century by Maharaja Anup Mahal. Rooms off here include the sumptuous Anup Mahal, a hall of private audience with walls lacquered in red and gold, and the Badal Mahal (Cloud Palace), the walls of which are beautifully painted with blue cloud motifs and red and gold lightning.

The Gaj Mandir, the suite of Maharaja Gaj Singh (r 1745–87) and his two top wives, is a fantastic symphony of gold paint, colourful murals, sandalwood, ivory, mirrors, niches and stained glass. From here you head up to the palace roof to enjoy the views and then down eventually to the superb Ganga Durbar Hall of 1896, with its pink stone walls covered in fascinating relief carvings. You then move into Maharaja Ganga Singh's office and finally into the Vikram Vilas Durbar Hall, where pride of place goes to a WWI De Havilland DH-9 biplane bomber: General Maharaja Sir Ganga

Singh commanded the Bikaner Camel Corps during WWI and was the only non-white member of Britain's Imperial War Cabinet during the conflict.

Prachina Cultural Centre & Museum MUSEUM
(Junagarh; Indian/foreigner ₹30/100; ⊙9am-6pm) Across the fort's main courtyard from the palace entrance, this museum is fascinating and well labelled. It focuses on the Western influence on the Bikaner royals before Independence, including crockery from England and France and menu cards from 1936, as well as some exquisite costumes, jewellery and textiles, and exhibits on contemporary Bikaner crafts.

Old City AREA
Still with a faint medieval feel despite the fume-belching motorbikes and autorickshaws, this labyrinth of narrow, winding streets conceals a number of fine *havelis*, and a couple of notable Jain temples just inside the southern wall, 1.5km southwest of Bikaner Junction train station. It makes for an interesting wander – we guarantee you'll get lost at least once. It's encircled by a 7km-long, 18th-century wall with five entrance gates, the main entrance being the triple-arched Kothe Gate.

★ Bhandasar Temple JAIN TEMPLE
(⊙5am-1pm & 5.30-11.30pm) Of Bikaner's two Jain temples, Bhandasar is particularly beautiful, with yellow-stone carving and vibrant paintings. The interior of the temple is stunning. The pillars bear floral arabesques and depictions of the lives of the 24 *tirthankars* (great Jain teachers). It's said that 40,000kg of ghee was used instead of water in the mortar, which locals insist seeps through the floor on hot days. The priest may ask for a donation for entry, although a trust pays for the temple upkeep.

☞ Tours

Camel Man TOURS
(☑0151-2231244, 9829217331, 9799911117; www.camelman.com; Vijay Guest House, Jaipur Rd; half-/full-/multiday trip per person per day from ₹1000/1400/1800) The standout Bikaner safari operator in terms of quality, reliability and transparency of what's on offer is Vijay Singh Rathore, aka Camel Man, who operates from Vijay Guest House (p143).

Bikaner

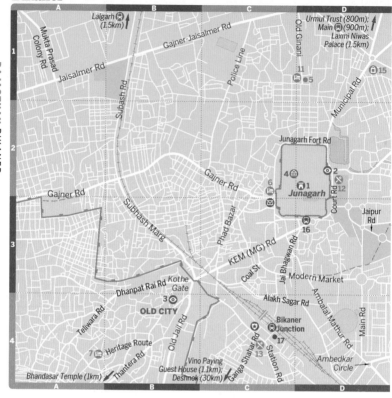

Laigarh (1.5km)
Mukta Prasad Colony Rd
Gajner-Jaisalmer Rd
Police Line
Old Ginani
Urmul Trust (800m);
Main (900m);
Laxmi Niwas
Palace (1.5km)
Jaisalmer Rd
Subash Rd
11
5
15
Junagarh Fort Rd
Municipal Rd
Gajner Rd
4
6
2
Gajner Rd
Junagarh
1
12
Subhash Marg
Phad Bazar
Court Rd
Jaipur Rd
16
KEM (MG) Rd
Jai Bhagwan Rd
Dhanpat Rai Rd
Kothe Gate
Coal St
Modern Market
3
OLD CITY
Alakh Sagar Rd
Ambalai Mathur Rd
Teliwara Rd
Old Jail Rd
Bikaner Junction
Main Rd
7
Heritage Route
Thantera Rd
Vino Paying
Guest House (1.1km);
Deshnok (30km)
Ganga Shahar Rd
13
17
Station Rd
Ambedkar Circle
Bhandasar Temple (1km)

Vino Desert Safari   TOURS
(☑ 9414139245, 0151-2270445; www.vinodesert
safari.com; Vino Paying Guest House; overnight per
person ₹2500, multiday trek per person per day
₹1500-2000) A popular and long-established
outfit, Vino Desert Safari is run by Vinod
Bhojak, of Vino Paying Guest House .

Vinayak Desert Safari   TOURS
(☑ 9414430948, 0151-2202634; www.vinayakdes
ertsafari.com; Vinayak Guest House, Old Ginani; per
person from ₹900) Vinayak Desert Safari runs
4WD safaris with zoologist Jitu Solanki. This
safari focuses on desert animals and birds
including the impressive cinereous vulture,
with its 3m wingspan, which visits the area
in numbers from November to March. Jitu
can organise botanical and birdwatching
tours to Bikaner, Tal Chhapar Sanctuary, Gajner Wildlife Sanctuary, Kichan and Desert
National Park.

Bikaner by Cycle   CYCLING
(☑ 9799911117; www.bikanerbycycle.com; Vijay
Guest House, Jaipur Rd; incl breakfast ₹1500) Hite-
shwar Singh Rathore, son of the Camel Man,
and also based at Vijay Guest House, runs
morning bicycle tours of the Old City that
include a local breakfast. Quality bikes and
helmets are supplied.

🎊 Festivals & Events

Bikaner Camel Festival   CULTURAL
(Karni Singh Stadium; ☉Jan) Bikaner celebrates its two-day Camel Festival on the
second Saturday and Sunday of January It
features parades of decorated camels, camel races, camel milking, camel beauty contests, as well as traditional folk dancing and
singing.

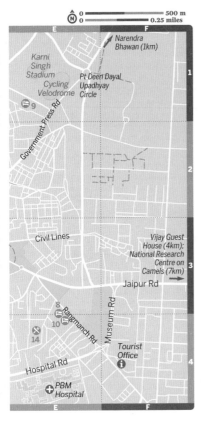

0 — 500 m
0 — 0.25 miles

Narendra
Bhawan (1km)

Karni
Singh
Stadium
Cycling
Velodrome

Pt Deen Dayal
Upadhyay
Circle

Government Press Rd

Civil Lines

Vijay Guest
House (4km);
National Research
Centre on
Camels (7km)

Jaipur Rd

Rangmanch Rd

Museum Rd

Tourist
Office

Hospital Rd

PBM
Hospital

Bikaner

◉ Top Sights
1 Junagarh D2

◉ Sights
2 Karan Prole D2
3 Old City B4
4 Prachina Cultural Centre &
    Museum.................................. C2

Activities, Courses & Tours
5 Vinayak Desert Safari................ D1

Sleeping
6 Bhairon Vilas............................. C2
7 Bhanwar Niwas......................... A4
8 Chandra Niwas Guest House..............E3
9 Hotel Harasar Haveli.................E1
10 Udai Niwas E4
11 Vinayak Guest House D1

Eating
    Café Indra................................(see 10)
12 Gallops..................................... D2
13 Heeralal's.................................. C4
14 Road Runner Cafe..................... E4
    Shakti Dining.........................(see 14)

Drinking & Nightlife
    Ganesha Coffee Lounge...............(see 6)

Shopping
15 Bikaner Miniature Arts D1

Transport
16 Private Bus Stand D3
17 Reservations Office................... C4

🛏 Sleeping

⭐ **Vijay Guest House**   GUESTHOUSE $
(📞9799911117, 9829217331; www.camelman.com; Jaipur Rd; dm ₹150, r ₹600-1000, with AC ₹1200-1500, ste ₹1800; 🌬🛜) About 4km east of the centre, this is a home away from home, with spacious, light-filled rooms, a warm welcome and good home-cooked meals. Owner Vijay is a camel expert and a recommended safari operator. Free pickup and drop-off from the train station.

As well as camel trips, 4WD outings to sights around Bikaner, cooking classes and tours to the owner's house in the village of Thelasar, Shekhawati, are offered.

Vinayak Guest House   GUESTHOUSE $
(📞9414410948, 0151-2202634; vinayakguestouse@gmail.com; Old Ginani; r ₹400-800, with AC ₹1000; 🌬🛜) This place offers eight varied and clean rooms in a quiet family house

with a little garden (hot water by bucket only in budget rooms). On offer are a free pick-up service, good home-cooked food, cooking lessons, bicycles (₹50 per day), and camel safaris and wildlife trips with Vinayak Desert Safari. It's about half a kilometre north of Junagarh.

Vino Paying Guest House   GUESTHOUSE $
(📞9414139245, 0151-2270445; www.vinodesertsafari.com; Ganga Shahar; s/d ₹350/500; 🛜) This guesthouse, in a family home 3km south of the main train station, is a cosy choice and the base of a good camel-safari operator. It has six rooms in the house and seven around the garden; all are fan-cooled. Home-cooked food is served and cooking classes are on offer. It's opposite Gopeshwar Temple; free pickup from train and bus stations are offered.

BIKANER CAMEL SAFARIS

Bikaner is an excellent alternative to the Jaisalmer camel-safari scene. There are fewer people running safaris here, so the hassle factor is quite low. Camel trips tend to be in the areas east and south of the city and focus on the isolated desert villages of the Jat, Bishnoi, Meghwal and Rajput peoples. Interesting wildlife can be spotted here, such as nilgais (antelope), chinkaras (gazelle), desert foxes, spiny-tailed lizards and plenty of birds including, from September to March, the demoiselle crane.

Three days and two nights is a common camel-safari duration, but half-day, one-day and short overnight trips are all possible. If you're after a serious trip, Kichan is a seven-day trek. The best months to head into the desert are October to February. Avoid mid-April to July, when it's searingly hot.

Typical costs are ₹1800 to ₹2500 per person per day including overnight camping, with tents, mattresses, blankets, meals, mineral water, one camel per person, a camel cart to carry gear (and sometimes tired riders), and a guide in addition to the camel men.

Many trips start at Raisar, about 8km east of Bikaner.

Chandra Niwas Guest House HOTEL $

(☏0151-2200796, 9413659711; chandraniwas@ yahoo.in; Rangmanch Rd, Civil Lines; r ₹500, with AC ₹800-2000; ❄🛜) This small, tidy and welcoming guesthouse is in a relatively quiet location, though still handy to Bikaner's sights. The rooms are very clean and comfortable, and there is a lovely terrace restaurant where you can get a veg/nonveg thali for ₹180/250, plus a downstairs restaurant and a coffee shop next door.

★Bhairon Vilas HERITAGE HOTEL $$

(☏9928312283, 0151-2544751; www.bhaironvilas. com; s/d from ₹2240/2800; ❄🛜🍽) This hotel on the western side of Junagarh is run by a former Bikaner prime minister's great-grandson. Rooms are mostly large and are eclectically and elaborately decorated with antiques, gold-threaded curtains and old family photographs. There's a bar straight out of the *Addams Family*, a garden restaurant, a coffee shop, and a boutique that specialises in beautiful, original wedding saris.

Camel safaris and local guides can be arranged here.

Udai Niwas HOMESTAY $$

(☏0151-2223447, 9971795447; Rangmanch Rd, Civil Lines; s/d ₹2240/2800; ❄) This friendly and relaxed homestay is set behind its cheerful associated Café Indra. The six guest rooms are large, spotless and comfortable, and you can choose to eat the delicious home-cooked meals with the family in the dining room or not. There's even a laundry to do your own washing.

Hotel Harasar Haveli HOTEL $$

(☏0151-2209891; www.harasar.com; r ₹1344-3300; ❄🛜) At this modern hotel with the frontage of an old sandstone *haveli* you'll find unexpectedly grand accommodation divided into four price points. The decor is stylish: that's not fancy blue and gold wallpaper in your room, but exquisitely hand-painted floral patterns. Old dark-wood furniture continues the classy character. Service is excellent, and the in-house restaurant on the terrace serves alcohol.

Located opposite Karni Singh Stadium, about 1km northeast of Junagarh.

Narendra Bhawan HOTEL $$$

(☏7827151151; www.narendrabhawan.com; Karni Nagar, Gandhi Colony; r from ₹7670; ❄🛜🍽) This former residence of the former Maharaja of Bikaner Narendra Singh has been renovated into a fine hotel that pays respect to its previous owner in its tasteful and sometimes eclectic decoration. It is a stately building, yet there is a welcoming, relaxed vibe from the staff. The high-quality food and rooftop pool add to the luxe feel.

Bhanwar Niwas HERITAGE HOTEL $$$

(☏0151-2529323; www.bhanwarniwas.com; Rampuria St; r from ₹6000; ❄@🛜) This superb hotel has been developed out of the beautiful Rampuria Haveli – a gem in the old city, 300m southwest of the City Kotwali police station. It has 26 spacious and delightfully decorated rooms, featuring stencil-painted wallpaper, marble or mosaic floors and antique furnishings. Comfortable common rooms drip with antiques and are arranged around a large courtyard.

 Eating & Drinking

★Gallops   MULTICUISINE $$
(☑0151-3200833; www.gallopsbikaner.com; Court Rd; mains ₹225-600; ☺10am-10pm; ❄☎) This contemporary cafe and restaurant close to the Junagarh entrance is known as 'Glops' to rickshaw-wallahs. There are snacks such as pizzas, wraps and sandwiches, and a good range of Indian and Chinese veg and non-veg dishes. You can sit outside or curl up in an armchair in the air-conditioned interior with a cold beer or an espresso coffee.

Café Indra   CAFE $$
(☑8287895446; Rangmanch Rd, Civil Lines; mains ₹130-380; ☺11.30am-10.30pm; ❄☎) This bright and clean cafe is a great place to relax with an espresso coffee or a cool drink, and equally good as a place for veg and non-veg lunch or dinner, with an array (and two sizes) of wood-fired pizzas, burgers and wraps.

Shakti Dining   INDIAN $$
(☑9928900422; Prithvi Niwas, Civil Lines; mains ₹150-260; ☺11am-11pm; ❄☎) Central and modern, Shakti Dining serves good Indian classics in a garden setting or inside in air-conditoned comfort. No alcohol. Also here is the funky Road Runner Cafe (mains ₹150-260; ☺11am-11pm; ❄☎) for a more casual dining experience.

Heeralal's   MULTICUISINE $$
(☑0151-2205551; Station Rd; mains ₹150-210, thali ₹175-270; ☺7.30am-10.30pm; ❄✎) This bright and hugely popular 1st-floor restaurant serves up pretty good veg Indian dishes, plus a few Chinese mains and pizzas (but unfortunately no beer), amid large banks of plastic flowers. It's a good place to sit and relax if waiting for a train. The ground-floor

fast-food section is less appealing, but it does have a good sweets counter.

Ganesha Coffee Lounge   CAFE
(coffee ₹80-120; ☺10am-9pm; ☎) With cool tunes and magical atmosphere inside the compound of Bhairon Vilas, Ganesha has good coffee, organic tea, cold drinks and cakes.

🛍 Shopping

Bikaner Miniature Arts   ART
(☑9829291431; www.bikanerminiturearts.com; Municipal Rd; ☺9am-8pm) The Swami family has been painting miniatures in Bikaner for four generations, and now runs this art school and gallery. The quality of work is astounding, and cheaper than you'll find in some of the bigger tourist centres. Art classes can be arranged.

ℹ Information

Main post office (☺9am-4pm Mon-Fri, to 2pm Sat) Near Bhairon Vilas hotel.

PBM Hospital (☑0151-2525312; Hospital Rd) One of Rajasthan's best government hospitals, with 24-hour emergency service.

Tourist office (☑0151-2226701; ☺9.30am-6pm Mon-Fri) This friendly office (near Pooran Singh Circle) can answer most tourism-related questions and provide transport schedules and maps.

ℹ Getting There & Away

AIR

Alliance Air (www.airindia.in/alliance-air.htm), a subsidiary of Air India, flies to/from Delhi and Jaipur daily.

BUS

There's a private bus stand outside the southern wall of Junagarh with similar services (albeit slightly more expensive and less frequent) to the government-run services from the main bus stand, which is 2km directly north of the fort

MAJOR TRAINS FROM BIKANER JUNCTION

DESTINATION	TRAIN	DEPARTURE	ARRIVAL	FARE (₹)
Delhi (Sarai Rohilla)	22471 Dee Intercity SF Exp	9.30am	5.25pm	300/780
Jaipur	12467 Leelan Exp	6am	12.35pm	275/705
Jaisalmer	12468 Leelan Exp	11.05pm	5.45am	250/625
Jodhpur	14887 KLK-BME Exp	11am	4.06pm	170/510

Fares: sleeper/3AC

(autorickshaw ₹20). In addition to those leaving from the main bus stand, there are buses to Deshnok that leave from a stand on National Hwy 89, 3km south of Bikaner Junction railway station.

Services from the main bus stand include the following:

Ajmer (for Pushkar) ₹269, six hours, half-hourly until 6pm

Delhi ₹445, 11 hours, at least four daily

Deshnok ₹35, one hour, half-hourly until 4.30pm

Jaipur ₹334, with AC ₹716, seven hours, hourly until 5.45pm

Jaisalmer ₹309, 7½ hours, noon daily

Jhunjhunu ₹226, five hours, four daily (7.30am, 8.30am, 12.20pm and 6.30pm)

Jodhpur ₹243, five hours, half-hourly until 6.30pm

Pokaran ₹211, five hours, hourly until 12.45pm

For Jaisalmer, it's sometimes faster to head to Pokaran (which has more departures) and change there.

TRAIN

The main train station is Bikaner Junction, with a computerised **reservations office** (⊙8am-10pm Mon-Sat, to 2pm Sun) in a separate building just east of the main station building. The foreigners' window is 2931. A couple of other useful services go from Lalgarh station in the north of the city (autorickshaw ₹60).

Delhi (Delhi Sarai Rohilla) sleeper/3AC ₹300/780, eight to 14 hours, three to six daily (6.30am, 9.30am, 4.45pm, 5.05pm, 7.50pm and 11.30pm)

Jaipur ₹275/705, 6½ hours, five or six daily (12.10am, 6am, 10am, 6.45pm, 11.10pm and 11.55pm)

Jaisalmer ₹250/625, 5½ hours, two or three daily (7am, 6.30pm and 11.05pm)

Jodhpur ₹170/510, five hours, six to seven daily (12.45am, 6.30am, 7.10am, 11am, 1.40pm, 9.40pm and 10.10pm)

No direct trains go to Ajmer for Pushkar.

❶ Getting Around

An autorickshaw from the train station to Juna-garh palace should cost less than ₹50, but you'll probably be asked for more.

Around Bikaner

There are some very interesting temples and old cenotaphs dotted around Bikaner, and you can also make a half-day trip to the fascinating National Research Centre on Camels. To experience a safari-style desert night in a luxury tent, look at the packages available at Raisar Camp (☐9829063446; www.raisarcamp.com; off National Hwy 11, Raisar Village; per person incl dinner, breakfast & camel safari ₹2900).

WORTH A TRIP

THE TEMPLE OF RATS

The extraordinary Karni Mata Temple (Deshnok; camera/video ₹30/50; ⊙4am-10pm) at Deshnok, 30km south of Bikaner, is one of India's weirder attractions. Its resident mass of holy rodents is not for the squeamish, but most visitors to Bikaner brave the potential for ankle-nipping and put a half-day trip here on their itinerary. Frequent buses leave from Bikaner's main bus stand but also from a bus stop south of town on the road to Deshnok and Nagaur. A return autorickshaw/taxi from Bikaner with a one-hour wait costs around ₹600/800.

Karni Mata lived in the 14th century and performed many miracles during her lifetime. When her youngest son, Lakhan, drowned, she ordered Yama (the god of death) to bring him back to life. Yama said he was unable to do so, but that Karni Mata, as an incarnation of Durga, could restore Lakhan's life. This she did, decreeing that members of her family would no longer die but would be reincarnated as *kabas* (rats). Around 600 families in Deshnok claim to be descendants of Karni Mata and that they will be reincarnated as *kabas*.

The temple isn't, in fact, swarming with rats, but there are a lot of them here, especially in nooks and crannies and in areas where priests and pilgrims leave food for them. And yes, you do have to take your shoes off to enter the temple: it's considered highly auspicious to have a *kaba* run across your feet – you may be graced in this manner whether you want it or not.

You can find food and drinks for yourself at the numerous snack stalls outside.

◉ Sights

National Research Centre on Camels
AGRICULTURAL CENTER

(☑ 0151-2230183; www.nrccamel.res.in; Indian/ foreigner ₹50/200, camera ₹100, rides ₹100; ⊘ noon-6pm) The National Research Centre on Camels is 8km southeast of central Bikaner, beside the Jodhpur–Jaipur Bypass. While here you can visit baby camels, go for a short ride and look around the small museum. There are about 400 camels, of four different breeds. The British Army had a camel corps drawn from Bikaner during WWI. Guides are available from ₹50. The on-site Camel Milk Parlour offers samples to try including *kulfi* (flavoured firm-textured ice cream) and lassi.

The round trip from Bikaner, including a half-hour wait at the camel farm, is around ₹300/₹600 for an autorickshaw/taxi. Don't rely on the fact that there may be an available autorickshaw waiting outside: always organise a round trip.

Delhi

011 / POP 29 MILLION / ELEV 250M

Best Places to Eat

➡ Karim's (p177)

➡ Darbar (p179)

➡ Andhra Pradesh Bhawan Canteen (p181)

➡ Naivedyam (p183)

➡ Potbelly (p183)

➡ Rajdhani (p182)

Best Places to Stay

➡ Diya Bed & Breakfast (p173)

➡ Madpackers Hostel (p177)

➡ Haveli Dharampura (p172)

➡ Lutyens Bungalow (p176)

➡ Imperial (p175)

Why Go?

You need patience to love Delhi. At first it slaps you in the face – whack! – and you're left to pick yourself up, unsure quite what hit you. It's hectic, noisy, polluted and unfeasibly overcrowded, but give it some time and you soon realise that the chaos that knocked you flying is the very thing that makes this wonderful city tick.

Hugely historic, and in parts intensely spiritual, Delhi bursts with life like few other places on Earth, and is forced by the sheer weight of humanity to dance to its own unique, unpredictable rhythm. Learn to skip to its beat, though, and you'll soon find its charms become irresistible.

Ride a cycle-rickshaw through mesmerising Old Delhi, with its frenetic bazaars and sizzling street food; take an autorickshaw to the suburbs for tumbledown ruins, leafy parks and Raj-era monuments; or hop on the sky train to glitzy Gurgaon (Gurugram) for a peek at the India of the future.

When to Go
Delhi

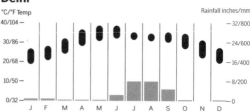

Oct–Mar Delhi at its best: chilly mornings, but warm days. Smog can spoil November.	**May–Aug** The months to avoid – hot, humid and uncomfortable.	**Jun–Sep** Monsoon season sees still-high temperatures and frequent downpours.

History

One of the world's oldest continually inhabited major settlements, Delhi is a city of layers; built, destroyed and rebuilt several times. It has had numerous incarnations, some easier to distinguish than others, but it is commonly agreed that there are eight historical cities of Delhi, most of which have left their indelible mark in the city's fascinating array of archaeological remains.

The first city for which clear archaeological evidence remains was Lal Kot, or Qila Rai Pithora, founded by the Hindu king Prithvi Raj Chauhan in the 12th century. The city fell to Afghan invaders in 1191, and for the next 600 years Delhi was ruled by a succession of Muslim sultans and emperors. The first, Qutub-ud-din Aibak, razed the Hindu city and used its stones to construct Mehrauli and the towering Qutab Minar.

Qutub-ud-din Aibak's 'Mamluk' (Slave) dynasty was quickly replaced by the Khilji dynasty, following a coup. The Khiljis constructed a new capital at Siri, northeast of Mehrauli, supplied with water from the royal tank at Hauz Khas. Following another coup, the Tughlaq sultans seized the reins, creating a new fortified capital at Tughlaqabad, and two more cities – Jahanpanah and Firozabad – for good measure.

The Tughlaq dynasty fell after Tamerlane stormed through town in 1398, opening the door for the Sayyid and Lodi dynasties, the last of the Delhi sultanates, whose tombs are scattered around the Lodi Garden. The scene was set for the arrival of the Mughals.

Babur, the first Mughal emperor, seized Delhi in 1526, and a new capital rose at Shergarh (the present-day Purana Qila), presided over by his son, Humayun.

Frantic city building continued throughout the Mughal period. Shah Jahan gained the Peacock Throne in 1627 and raised a new city, Shahjahanabad, centred on the Red Fort. The Mughal city fell in 1739 to the Persian Nadir Shah, and the dynasty went into steep decline. The last Mughal emperor, Bahadur Shah Zafar, was exiled to Burma (Myanmar) by the British for his role in the 1857 First War of Independence; there were some new rulers in town.

Initially Calcutta had been declared the capital of British India but at the Delhi Durbar of 1911, held at the Coronation Park, King George V announced the shifting of the capital back to Delhi. It was time for another bout of construction.

The architect Edwin Lutyens drew up plans for a new city of wide boulevards and stately administrative buildings to accommodate the colonial government – New Delhi was born. Its centrepiece was Rajpath, a vast boulevard leading from Rashtrapati Bhavan (the President's Palace) all the way to India Gate, Delhi's iconic 42m-tall war-memorial arch.

Partition – the devastating division of British India in 1947 that eventually led to the creation of the three independent dominions of Bangladesh, India and Pakistan – saw Delhi ripped apart as hundreds of thousands of Muslim inhabitants fled north while Sikh and Hindu refugees flooded inwards, a trauma from which some say the city has never recovered. The modern metropolis certainly faces other challenges, too – traffic, pollution, overpopulation, crime and the deepening chasm between rich and poor. However, the city continues to flourish, with its new, modern satellite cities spreading Delhi further and further outwards.

DELHI HISTORY

TOP DELHI FESTIVALS

Check online to confirm exact dates, or contact India Tourism Delhi (p192).

Republic Day (⊘ 26 Jan, Rajpath) A spectacular military parade.

Beating of the Retreat (⊘ 29 Jan, Rashtrapati Bhavan) More military pageantry in Rajpath.

Independence Day (⊘ 15 Aug, Red Fort) India celebrates its independence from Britain.

Dussehra (⊘ Sep/Oct) Hindu celebration of good over evil with parades of colourful effigies.

Qutab Festival (⊘ Oct/Nov, Qutab Minar Complex) Sufi singing and classical music and dance at the Qutab Minar complex.

Diwali (⊘ Oct/Nov) Fireworks across the city for the Festival of Light.

Delhi International Arts Festival (⊘ Nov/Dec) Exhibitions, performing arts, film, literature and culinary events.

Delhi Highlights

1 Red Fort (p152)
Exploring this Mughal masterpiece, imagining its former traumas and splendours.

2 Qutab Minar Complex (p168)
Visiting Delhi's first Islamic city at sunrise, and gasping at its majestic centrepiece tower, the world's tallest brick minaret.

3 Old Delhi's Bazaars (p187) Losing yourself in the street-market mayhem of Old Delhi's lost-in-time alleyways around Chandni Chowk.

4 Humayun's Tomb (p164) Enjoying the architectural virtuosity and mirror-image gardens of Delhi's most spectacular resting place.

5 Purana Qila (p164) Exploring the tumbledown ruins of Delhi's 'Old Fort'

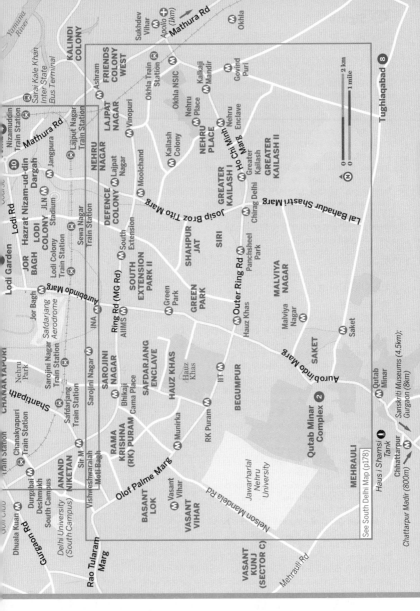

before picnicking in the gardens.

6 Lodi Garden (p165) Joining local families as you roam around the lawns, bamboo groves, and tree-shaded pathways of Delhi's loveliest park.

7 Street food (p177) Sampling Old Delhi's flavour-packed street food from hole-in-the-wall eateries in and around Chandni Chowk.

8 Tughlaqabad (p169) Marvelling at the immense 14th-century ruined fort that briefly ruled Delhi in its third incarnation.

9 Jama Masjid (p153) Experiencing the serenity of the 'Friday Mosque', with its wide open courtyard.

10 Hazrat Nizam-ud-din Dargah (p165) Drinking in the mystical, magical atmosphere and hearing qawwali (Islamic devotional singing) at this hallowed Sufi shrine.

◉ Sights

Most sights in Delhi are easily accessible by metro, though to reach some you'll have to take a rickshaw or taxi (or endure a fair walk) from the station, even if it bears the same or a similar name to the sight, eg Qutab Minar and Tughlaqabad. Old Delhi's sights are nicely concentrated so are best visited on foot; it's fascinating to walk the bustling lanes in any case. And if you get tired, just hail a passing cycle-rickshaw. Taking a walking tour is a great way to get accustomed to Old Delhi's frenetic streets. New Delhi's wide, tree-lined avenues are pleasant to walk along, but distances can be vast, so you'll often want to make use of passing autorickshaws. Sights in Delhi's more southerly districts are much more spread out so they're difficult to visit in one hit; plan accordingly.

Note that many tourist sights are closed on Mondays.

◉ Old Delhi

★ Red Fort   FORT

(Map p156; Indian/foreigner ₹50/600, with card payment ₹35/550, video ₹25, audio guide in Hindi/English or Korean ₹69/118; ⊘ dawn-dusk Tue-Sun; Ⓜ Chandni Chowk) Founded by Emperor Shah Jahan and surrounded by a magnificent 18m-high wall, this fort took 10 years to construct (1638–48) and is rumoured to have had the decapitated bodies of prisoners built into the foundations for luck. It once overlooked the Yamuna River, which has now shrunk to some distance away. A tree-lined waterway, known as *nahr-i-bihisht* (river of paradise), once ran out of the fort and along Chandni Chowk, fed by the Yamuna.

Shah Jahan never took up full residence here, after his disloyal son, Aurangzeb, imprisoned him in Agra Fort.

The last Mughal emperor of Delhi, Bahadur Shah Zafar, was flushed from the Red Fort in 1857 and exiled to Burma (Myanmar) for his role in the First War of Independence. The British destroyed buildings and gardens inside the fortress walls and replaced them with barrack blocks for the colonial army.

The audio guide tour, by acclaimed company Narrowcasters, is worthwhile as it brings the site to life.

Controversially, in 2018 the government leased out the job of maintaining the fort to a private firm, the Dalmia Bharat Group, prompting accusations from conservationists that it had sold the country's heritage. Dalmia soon began wholesale renovations, including

laying new red-sandstone pathways over some of the existing quartzite stone paths.

At the time of writing, all the Red Fort's museums were closed for renovations. With the exception of the arcades at Chatta Chowk and Diwan-i-Am, it was not possible to enter the interiors of the buildings inside the fort, but the main structures are expected to reopen once renovations are complete. The fort's sound-and-light show was also suspended as part of the revamp.

➡ **Lahore Gate**

The main entrance to the Red Fort is hidden by a defensive bastion built in front by Shah Jahan's son Aurangzeb. During the struggle for independence, nationalists promised to raise the Indian flag over the gate, an ambition that became a reality on 15 August 1947. The Prime Minister makes a speech here every Independence Day.

➡ **Chatta Chowk**

(Covered Bazaar) This imperial bazaar used to cater to royal women and glitter with silk and jewels for sale. Today's wares are rather more mundane souvenirs.

➡ **Diwan-i-Am**

(Hall of Public Audiences) This arcade of sandstone columns was where the emperor greeted guests and dignitaries from a throne on the raised marble platform, which is backed by fine pietra dura (inlaid stone) work that features Orpheus, incongruously, and is thought to be Florentine.

➡ **Diwan-i-Khas**

(Hall of Private Audiences) This hall was used for bowing and scraping to the emperor. Above the corner arches to the north and south is inscribed in Urdu, 'If there is paradise on the earth – it is this, it is this, it is this'. Nadir Shah looted the legendary jewel-studded Peacock Throne from here in 1739. Bahadur Shah Zafar became the last Mughal emperor here in May 1857, but was exiled by the British seven months later.

➡ **Khas Mahal**

(Special Palace) South of the public area of the Diwan-i-Khas is the Khas Mahal, where the emperor lived and slept, shielded from prying eyes by lace-like carved marble screens. A cooling channel of water, the *nahr-i-bihisht* (river of paradise), once flowed through the apartments to the adjacent Rang Mahal (Palace of Colour), home to the emperor's chief wife. The exterior of the palace was once lavishly painted; inside is an elegant lotus-shaped fountain.

MAJNU-KA-TILLA: DELHI'S TIBETAN QUARTER

Majnu-ka-Tilla is an enclave that has served as a base for Tibetan refugees since around 1960, and its traffic-free alleyways are a great place to shop for Tibetan trinkets and Buddhist-based souvenirs; try Akama (☺9.30am-8.30pm) or the market (p188). There are some lovely cafes, too; Ama (H40 Tibetan Colony; dishes ₹150-300, coffee from ₹85; ☺7am-9.45pm; ☎) is the most popular, though Kham Coffee (15A Tibetan Colony, ☺8.30am-9.30pm) has a more traditional Tibetan feel. Wongdhen House (☎011-23816689; 15A New Tibetan Colony, r from ₹700, without bathroom ₹500; ✷☎) is a friendly budget guesthouse, with its 4th-floor terrace opening out onto views of the river and Delhi's new, iconic Signature Bridge (New Aruna Colony, Wazirabad).

The enclave is 2km from Vidhan Sabha metro station; turn right out of Gate 2, then right at the second set of traffic lights, and cross the busy main road at the end (there's a footbridge). It's ₹30 to ₹40 in an autorickshaw.

DELHI SIGHTS

➡ Shahi Burj

(Emperor's Tower) This three-storey octagonal tower that was Shah Jahan's favoured workplace. From here he planned the running of his empire. In front of the tower is what remains of an elegant formal garden, centred on the Zafar Mahal, a sandstone pavilion surrounded by a deep, empty water tank. At the time of research, the Shahi Burj could only be viewed from outside.

➡ Salimgarh

(☺10am-5pm Tue-Sun) Across a bridge from the Red Fort, but part of the same complex, this fort was established by Salim Shah Suri in 1546, so predates its grander neighbour. Salimgarh was later used as a prison, first by Aurangzeb and later by the British; you can visit the ruined mosque and a small prison building.

★ Jama Masjid   MOSQUE
(Friday Mosque; Map p156; camera & video each ₹300, tower ₹100; ☺non-Muslims 8am-1hr before sunset, minaret 9am-5.30pm; Ⓜ Jama Masjid) A beautiful pocket of calm at the heart of Old Delhi's mayhem, the capital's largest mosque is built on a 10m elevation, towering above the surrounding hubbub. It can hold a mind-blowing 25,000 people. The red-sandstone and marble structure, known also as the 'Friday Mosque', was Shah Jahan's final architectural triumph, built between 1644 and 1658. The four watchtowers were used for security. There are two minarets standing 40m high, one of which can be climbed for amazing views. There are numerous entrance gates, but only Gate 1 (south side), Gate 2 (east), and Gate 3 (north) allow access to the mosque for visitors. The eastern gate was originally for imperial use only. Entrance is free, but you have to buy a ₹300 ticket if you

are carrying any sort of camera (including a camera phone), even if you don't intend to use it. Once inside, you can buy a separate ₹100 ticket to climb the 121 steps up the narrow southern minaret (notices say that unaccompanied women are not permitted). From the top of the minaret, you can see how architect Edwin Lutyens incorporated the mosque into his design of New Delhi – the Jama Masjid, Connaught Place and Sansad Bhavan (Parliament House) are in a direct line.

Visitors should dress conservatively and remove their shoes before entering the mosque, though you can carry your shoes with you inside if you wish to leave from a different gate, or are worried about losing them (many locals do this).

Chandni Chowk   AREA
(Map p156; Ⓜ Chandni Chowk) Old Delhi's main drag is lined by Jain, Hindu and Sikh temples, plus a church, with the Fatehpuri Masjid at one end. Tree-lined and elegant in Mughal times, the thoroughfare is now mindbendingly chaotic, with tiny little ancient bazaars tentacling off it. In the Mughal era, Chandni Chowk centred on a pool that reflected the moon, hence the name, 'moonlight place'. The main street is almost impossible to cross, full as it is of cars, hawkers, motorcycles, rickshaws and porters.

Digambara Jain Temple   JAIN TEMPLE
(Map p156; Chandni Chowk; ☺6am-noon & 6-9pm; Ⓜ Lal Qila) Opposite the Red Fort is the red sandstone Digambara Jain Temple, built in 1658. Interestingly, it houses a bird hospital (donations appreciated; ☺10am-5pm) established in 1956 to further the Jain principle of preserving all life, treating 30,000 birds a year. Remove shoes and leather items before entering the temple.

Red Fort

HIGHLIGHTS

The main entrance to the Red Fort is through **❶ Lahore Gate** – the bastion in front of it was built by Aurangzeb for increased security. You can still see bullet marks on the gate, dating from 1857, the First War of Independence, when the Indian army rose up against the British.

Walk through the Chatta Chowk (Covered Bazaar), which once sold silks and jewellery to the nobility; beyond it lies Naubat Khana, a part white-plaster, part russet-red building, which houses Hathi Pol (Elephant Gate), so called because visitors used to dismount from their elephants or horses here as a sign of respect. From here it's straight on to the **❷ Diwan-i-Am**, the Hall of Public Audiences.

Behind this are the private palaces, the **❸ Khas Mahal** and the **❹ Diwan-i-Khas**. Entry to this Hall of Private Audiences, the fort's most expensive building, was only permitted to the officials of state. The artificial stream the Nahr-i-Bihisht (Stream of Paradise) used to run a cooling channel of water through all these buildings.

Nearby is the **❺ Moti Masjid (Pearl Mosque)** and south is the Mumtaz Mahal, which before renovations housed the Museum of Archaeology, or you can head north, where the Red Fort gardens are dotted by palatial pavilions and old British barracks. Here you'll find the **❻ Baoli**, a spookily deserted water tank, though you can no longer climb down into it. Another five minutes' walk – across a road, then a railway bridge – brings you to the island fortress of Salimgarh.

(Note that many of the fort buildings were closed for renovations at the time of research, but the pavilions can be viewed from outside, and most structures are expected to reopen once the renovations are complete.)

TOP TIPS

➡ To avoid crowds, get here early or late in the day; avoid weekends and public holidays.

➡ Bring the fort to life with the excellent audio guide, available at the ticket office.

Baoli
The Red Fort step well is seldom visited and is a hauntingly deserted place, even more so when you consider its chambers were used as cells by the British from August 1942.

Salimgarh

❻

Museum on India's Struggle for Freedom (closed for renovations)

Chatta Chowk

Lahore Gate
Lahore Gate is particularly significant, as it was here that Jawaharlal Nehru raised the first tricolour flag of independent India in 1947.

❶

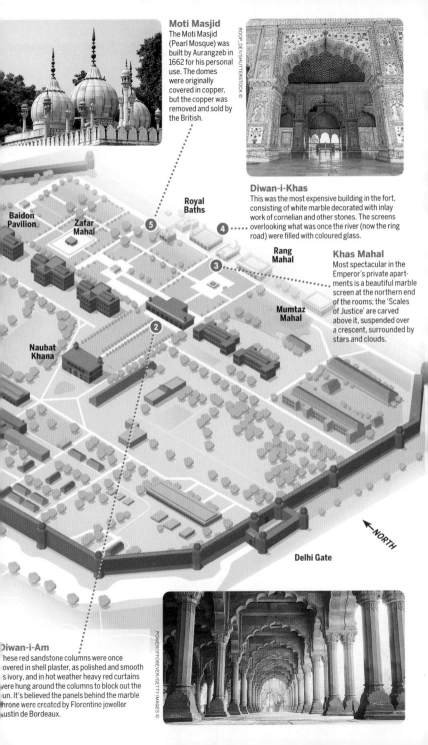

Moti Masjid
The Moti Masjid (Pearl Mosque) was built by Aurangzeb in 1662 for his personal use. The domes were originally covered in copper, but the copper was removed and sold by the British.

ROOP_DEV/SHUTTERSTOCK ©

Diwan-i-Khas
This was the most expensive building in the fort, consisting of white marble decorated with inlay work of cornelian and other stones. The screens overlooking what was once the river (now the ring road) were filled with coloured glass.

Royal Baths

Baidon Pavilion

Zafar Mahal

Rang Mahal

Khas Mahal
Most spectacular in the Emperor's private apartments is a beautiful marble screen at the northern end of the rooms; the 'Scales of Justice' are carved above it, suspended over a crescent, surrounded by stars and clouds.

Mumtaz Mahal

Naubat Khana

← NORTH

Delhi Gate

Diwan-i-Am
These red sandstone columns were once covered in shell plaster, as polished and smooth as ivory, and in hot weather heavy red curtains were hung around the columns to block out the sun. It's believed the panels behind the marble throne were created by Florentine jeweller Austin de Bordeaux.

POWEROFFOREVER/GETTY IMAGES ©

Old Delhi

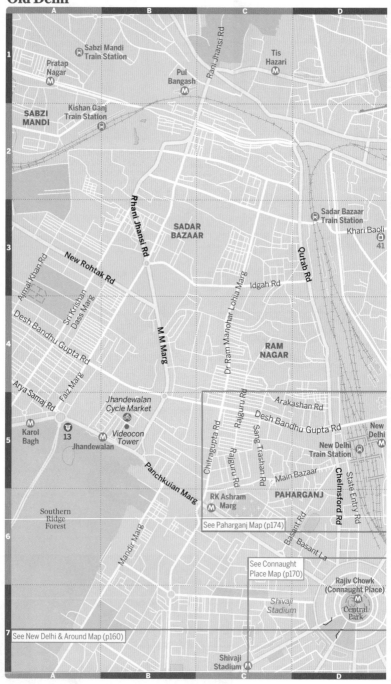

See Paharganj Map (p174)

See Connaught Place Map (p170)

See New Delhi & Around Map (p160)

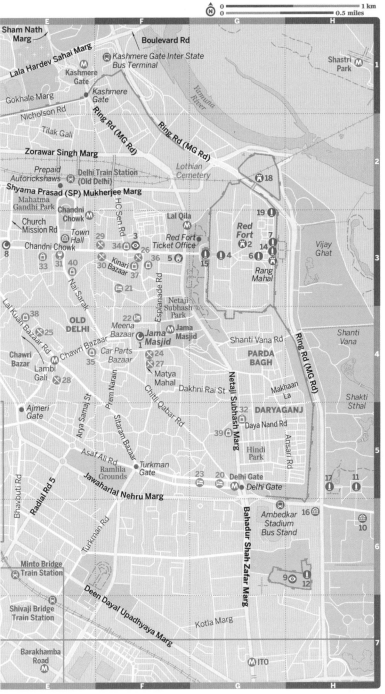

DELHI

0 1 km
0 0.5 miles

Sham Nath Marg

Lala Hardev Sahai Marg

Boulevard Rd

Kashmere Gate Inter State Bus Terminal

Shastri Park

Kashmere Gate

Kashmere Gate

Gokhale Marg

Nicholson Rd

Ring Rd (MG Rd)

Tilak Gali

Ring Rd (MG Rd)

Yamuna River

Zorawar Singh Marg

Prepaid Autorickshaws

Delhi Train Station (Old Delhi)

Lothian Cemetery

18

Shyama Prasad (SP) Mukherjee Marg

Mahatma Gandhi Park

HC Sen Rd

Lal Qila

19

Church Mission Rd

Chandni Chowk

Town Hall

Red Fort

Red Fort Ticket Office

7

14

Vijay Ghat

Chandni Chowk

29

34

3

26

36

5

6

Rang Mahal

33

31

40

30

Kinari Bazaar

37

15

4

21

Lal Kuan Bazaar Rd

38

25

OLD DELHI

22

Meena Bazaar

Jama Masjid

Jama Masjid

Shanti Vana Rd

Shanti Vana

Chawri Bazaar

Car Parts Bazaar

35

24

27

PARDA BAGH

Chawri Bazaar

Lambi Gali

28

Matya Mahal

Dakhni Rai St

Makhaan La

Shakti Sthal

Ajmeri Gate

Prem Narain

Sitaram Bazaar

Chitti Qabar Rd

Netaji Subhash Marg

32

DARYAGANJ

Daya Nand Rd

39

Hindi Park

Ansari Rd

Arya Samaj St

Asaf Ali Rd

Turkman Gate

Ramlila Grounds

Jawaharlal Nehru Marg

23

20

Delhi Gate

Delhi Gate

17

11

Bhavbuti Rd

Radial Rd 5

Turkman Rd

Bahadur Shah Zafar Marg

Ambedkar Stadium Bus Stand

16

10

Minto Bridge Train Station

Deen Dayal Upadhyaya Marg

9

12

Shivaji Bridge Train Station

Barakhamba Road

Kotla Marg

ITO

Old Delhi

Fatehpuri Masjid   MOSQUE

(Map p156; Chandni Chowk; ◎5am-9.30pm; Ⓜ Chandni Chowk) Built by Fatehpuri Begum, one of Shah Jahan's wives, this 17th-century mosque is a haven of tranquillity after the frantic streets outside. The central pool was taken from a noble house, hence the elaborate shape. After the First War of Independence, the mosque was sold to a Hindu nobleman by the British for ₹19,000 and returned to Muslim worship in exchange for four villages 20 years later.

◉ Paharganj

Ramakrishna Mission   HINDU TEMPLE

(Ramakrishna Ashram; Map p174; www.rkmdelhi. org; Ramakrishna Marg; ◎5am-noon & 4-9pm Apr-Sep, 3.30-8.30pm Oct-Mar; Ⓜ Ramakrishna Ashram Marg) Amid the chaos of Paharganj, the temple that gives the metro station here its name is a wonderfully calming escape, with a landscaped garden leading to a simple meditation hall. The morning and evening *aarti* (auspicious lighting of lamps or candles), at 5am and sunset, are atmospheric times to visit. At other times, people simply meditate in peace.

◉ New Delhi

Connaught Place   AREA

(Map p170; Ⓜ Rajiv Chowk) This confusing circular shopping district was named after George V's uncle, the Duke of Connaught, and fashioned after the Palladian colonnades of Bath. Greying, whitewashed, colonnaded streets radiate out from the central circle of Rajiv Chowk, with blocks G to N in the outer circle and A to F in the inner circle. Today they mainly harbour brash, largely interchangeable but popular, bars, and international chain stores, plus a few good hotels and restaurants. Touts are rampant.

Rajpath   AREA

(Map p160; Ⓜ Central Secretariat) Rajpath (Kingsway) is a vast parade linking India Gate to the offices of the Indian government. Built on an imperial scale between 1914 and 1931, this complex was designed by Edwin Lutyens and Herbert Baker, and underlined the ascendance of the British rulers. Yet just 16 years later, the Brits were out on their ear and Indian politicians were pacing the corridors of power. At the western end of Rajpath the official residence of the president of India, Rashtrapati Bhavan (☑011-23015321; www.rashtrapati

sachivalaya.gov.in/rbtour; ₹50; ⊙9am-4pm Fri-Sun, online reservation required), now partially open to the public via guided tour, is flanked by the mirror-image, dome-crowned North Secretariat and South Secretariat. These house government ministries and are not open to the public. The Indian parliament meets nearby at the Sansad Bhavan (Map p160), a circular, colonnaded edifice at the end of Sansad Marg, also not open to the public.

At Rajpath's eastern end is mighty India Gate. This 42m-high stone memorial arch, designed by Lutyens, pays tribute to around 90,000 Indian soldiers who died in WWI, the Northwest Frontier operations and the 1919 Anglo-Afghan War.

★ **Gurdwara Bangla Sahib** SIKH TEMPLE
(Map p160; Ashoka Rd; ⊙4am-9pm; Ⓜ Patel Chowk) This magnificent white-marble gurdwara (Sikh temple), topped by glinting golden onion domes, was constructed at the site where the eighth Sikh guru, Harkrishan Dev, stayed before his 1664 death. Despite his tender years, the six-year-old guru tended to victims of Delhi's cholera and smallpox epidemic, and the waters of the large tank are said to have healing powers. It's full of colour and life, yet tranquil, and live devotional songs waft over the compound. As at all gurdwaras, free meals are served to pilgrims daily. Just inside the entrance to the complex is a small museum, chronicling the history of Sikhism and its gurus and martyrs.

Agrasen ki Baoli MONUMENT
(Map p170; Hailey Lane; ⊙dawn-dusk; Ⓜ Janpath) This atmospheric 14th-century step-well was once set in the countryside, till the city grew up around it; 103 steps descend to the bottom, flanked by arched niches. It's a remarkable thing to discover among the office towers southeast of Connaught Place. It's garnered more attention since it was used as a shelter by Aamir Khan in the 2015 movie *PK*.

Jantar Mantar HISTORIC SITE
(Map p170; Sansad Marg; Indian/foreigner video ₹25; ⊙dawn-dusk; Ⓜ Patel Chowk) This is one of five observatories built by Maharaja Jai Singh II, ruler of Jaipur. Constructed in 1725, Jantar Mantar (derived from the Sanskrit word for 'instrument', but which has also become the Hindi word for 'abracadabra') is a quiet park containing a collection of curving geometric buildings that are carefully calibrated to monitor the movement of the stars and planets.

Jhandewalan
Hanuman Temple HINDU TEMPLE
(Map p156; Link Rd, Jhandewalan; ⊙dawn-dusk; Ⓜ Jhandewalan) This temple is not to be missed (it's actually hard to miss) if you're in Karol Bagh. Take a short detour to see the 34m-tall Hanuman statue that soars above both the roads and the raised metro line. Getting up close, there are passageways through the mouths of demons to a series of atmospheric, deity-filled chambers.

Crafts Museum MUSEUM
(Map p160; ☎011-23371641; Bhairon Marg; Indian/foreigner ₹20/200; ⊙10am-5pm Tue-Sun; Ⓜ Pragati Maidan) Much of this lovely museum is outside, including tree-shaded carvings and life-size examples of village huts from various regions of India. Displays celebrate the traditional crafts of India, with some beautiful textiles on display indoors, such as embroidery from Kashmir and cross-stitch from Punjab. Highlights include a huge wooden 18th-century temple chariot from Maharashtra. Artisans sell their products in the rear courtyard. The museum also includes the excellent Cafe Lota (p182) and a very good shop.

National Museum MUSEUM
(Map p160; ☎011-23019272; www.national museumindia.gov.in; Janpath; Indian/foreigner ₹20/650, camera ₹20/300; ⊙10am-6pm Tue-Sun, free guided tour 10.30am & 2.30pm Tue-Fri, 10.30am, 11.30am, 2.30pm & 3pm Sat & Sun; Ⓜ Udyog Bhawan) This glorious, if dusty, museum is full of treasures. Mind-bogglingly ancient, sophisticated figurines from the Harappan civilisation, almost 5000 years old, include the remarkable Dancing Girl, and there are also some fine ceramics from the even older Nal civilisation. Other items include Buddha

LOCAL KNOWLEDGE
CHANGING OF THE GUARD
Members of the public can make a rare foray into the forecourt of Rashtrapati Bhavan (p158) to witness the twice-weekly Changing of the Guard ceremony. It's held at 8am on Saturdays (10am mid-March to mid-November) and at 4.30pm on Sundays (5.30pm mid-March to mid-November) and lasts around 45 minutes. Entry is via Gate 2 or Gate 37. Numbers are limited. Bring your passport.

New Delhi & Around

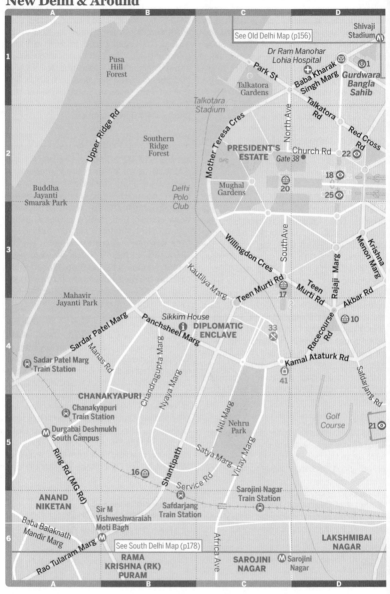

See Old Delhi Map (p156)

Shivaji Stadium

Dr Ram Manohar Lohia Hospital

Park St

Pusa Hill Forest

Talkatora Gardens

Talkatora Stadium

Baba Kharak Singh Marg

North Ave

Gurdwara Bangla Sahib

1

Talkatora Rd

Red Cross Rd

Mother Teresa Cres

PRESIDENT'S ESTATE

Church Rd

Gate 38

22

Upper Ridge Rd

Southern Ridge Forest

Delhi Polo Club

Mughal Gardens

18

20

25

Buddha Jayanti Smarak Park

Willingdon Cres

South Ave

Krishna Menon Marg

Kautilya Marg

Teen Murti Rd

Teen Murti Rd

Rajaji Marg

Akbar Rd

Mahavir Jayanti Park

Sardar Patel Marg

Panchsheel Marg

Sikkim House

DIPLOMATIC ENCLAVE

17

33

10

Racecourse Rd

Sadar Patel Marg Train Station

Manas Rd

Chandragupta Marg

Nyaya Marg

Kamal Ataturk Rd

41

Safdarjang Rd

CHANAKYAPURI

Chanakyapuri Train Station

Durgabai Deshmukh South Campus

Niti Marg

Nehru Park

Golf Course

21

Ring Rd (MG Rd)

Shantipath

Satya Marg

Vinay Marg

16

Service Rd

Sarojini Nagar Train Station

ANAND NIKETAN

Sir M Vishweshwaraiah Moti Bagh

Safdarjang Train Station

Baba Balaknath Mandir Marg

Rao Tularam Marg

See South Delhi Map (p178)

Africa Ave

LAKSHMIBAI NAGAR

RAMA KRISHNA (RK) PURAM

SAROJINI NAGAR

Sarojini Nagar

---

relics, exquisite jewellery, miniature paintings, medieval woodcarvings, textiles and musical instruments. Don't miss the immense, five-tier wooden temple chariot built in South India in the 19th century and now on display just inside the museum gates.

Gandhi Smriti   MUSEUM

(Map p160; ☑ 011-23012843; 5 Tees Jan Marg; ⊙10am-5pm Tue-Sun, closed 2nd Sat of month; Ⓜ Lok Kalyan Marg) FREE This poignant memorial to Mahatma Gandhi is in Birla House, where he was shot dead on the grounds by a

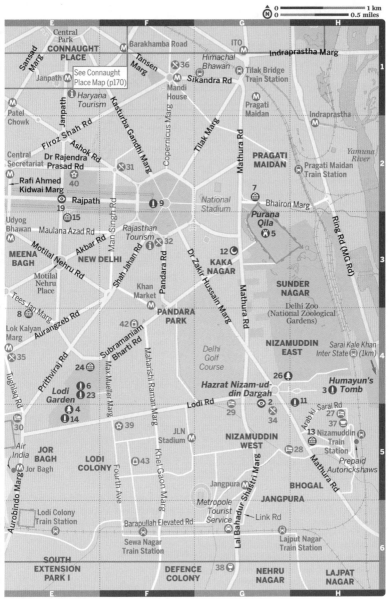

Hindu zealot on 30 January 1948, after campaigning against intercommunal violence.

The house itself is where Gandhi spent his last 144 days. The exhibits include film footage, modern art, and rooms preserved just as Gandhi left them. The small clothes shop within the grounds sells garments made from *khadi,* homespun cotton that was championed by Gandhi during the Independence movement.

Raj Ghat　　　　　MONUMENT
(Map p156; ◉10am-8pm; Ⓜ Jama Masjid) FREE
This peaceful, well maintained park contains

New Delhi & Around

a simple black-marble platform marking the spot where Mahatma Gandhi was cremated following his assassination in 1948. It's a thought-provoking spot, inscribed with what are said to have been Gandhi's final words, *Hai Ram* ('Oh, God'). Every Friday (the day he died) commemorative prayers are held here at 5pm, as well as on 2 October and 30 January, his birth and death anniversaries. Despite being perfect picnic territory, you're not allowed to bring food into the park, and there's nowhere to buy any once inside. Further north you'll find memorials commemorating where Jawaharlal Nehru, Indira Gandhi and Rajiv Gandhi were cremated. South from Raj Ghat, just across Kisan Ghat Rd, are some equally peaceful landscaped gardens containing Gandhi Darshan (Map p156; Kisan Ghat Rd; ⊙10am-5pm Mon-Sat; Mi Indraprastha) FREE, a pavilion displaying photos relating to the Mahatma.

National Gandhi
Museum   MUSEUM
(Map p156; ☑011-23310168; http://gandhi
museum.org; Raj Ghat; ⊙9.30am-5.30pm Tue-Sun; Mi Jama Masjid) FREE An interesting museum preserving some of Gandhi's personal belongings, including his spectacles and even two of his teeth. You can also listen to his voice on the other end of a telephone receiver. Movingly and somewhat macabrely, also here are the dhoti, shawl and watch he was wearing when he was assassinated, and one of the bullets that killed him.

Indira Gandhi Memorial Museum MUSEUM
(Map p160; ☑011-23010094; 1 Safdarjang Rd; ☻9.30am-4.45pm Tue-Sun; Ⓜ Lok Kalyan Marg) ▣FREE In the residence of controversial former prime minister Indira Gandhi is this interesting museum devoted to her life and her political-heavyweight family. It displays her personal effects, including the blood-stained sari she was wearing when she was assassinated in 1984; in the back garden a glass-covered pathway traces her final steps before she was shot and killed by two security guards. Many rooms in the house are preserved as they were, providing a window into the family's life.

Nehru Memorial Museum MUSEUM
(Map p160; ☑011-23016734; www.nehrumemorial.nic.in; Teen Murti Rd; ☻9am-5.30pm Tue-Sun; Ⓜ Udyog Bhawan) ▣FREE Built for the British commander-in-chief and previously called 'Flagstaff House', the stately Teen Murti Bhavan was later the official residence of Jawaharlal Nehru (India's first prime minister). It's now a museum devoted to Nehru's life and work; the bedroom, study and drawing room are preserved as if he'd just popped out.

On the grounds is a 14th-century hunting lodge, built by Feroz Shah, and a more recent planetarium (☑011-23014504; www.nehru planetarium.org; 40min show adult/child ₹80/50; ☻shows English 11.30am & 3pm, Hindi 1.30pm & 4pm), which has shows about the stars in Hindi and English.

Feroz Shah Kotla HISTORIC SITE
(Map p156; Bahadur Shah Zafar Marg; Indian/foreigner ₹25/300, with card payment ₹20/250, video ₹25; ☻dawn-dusk; Ⓜ ITO) Firozabad, the fifth city of Delhi, was built by Feroz Shah Tughlaq in 1354, the first city here to be built on the river. Only the fortress remains, with crumbling walls protecting the Jama Masjid (Friday mosque), a *baoli* (step-well), and the pyramid-like Hawa Mahal (included in Feroz Shah Kotla entry; ☻dawn-dusk), topped by a 13m-high sandstone Ashoka Pillar inscribed with 3rd-century-BC Buddhist edicts. There's an otherworldly atmosphere to the ruins.

Entrance is free after 2pm every Thursday when crowds gather at the mosque and other points of importance to light candles and incense and leave bowls of milk to appease Delhi's djinns (invisible spirits), who are said to occupy the underground chambers beneath the ruins.

Shoes should be removed when entering the mosque and Hawa Mahal.

⊙ South Delhi

★**Hauz Khas** AREA
(Map p178; ☻dawn-dusk; Ⓜ IIT) Built by Sultan Ala-ud-din Khilji in the 13th century, Hauz Khas means 'noble tank', and its reservoir once covered 28 hectares. It collected enough water during the monsoon to last Siri Fort throughout the dry season. Today it's much smaller, but still a beautiful place to be, thronged by birds and surrounded by parkland. Overlooking it are the impressive ruins of Feroz Shah's 14th-century madrasa (Map p178; Ⓜ IIT, Green Park, Hauz Khas), or religious school, and his tomb (Map p178; Ⓜ Green Park), which he had built before his death in 1388.

To reach the lake shore, either cut through the adjacent Deer Park (p189) during daylight hours, which has more ruined tombs and a well-stocked deer enclosure, or walk past all the Hauz Khas shops, beyond No 50, and enter the grounds of Feroz Shah's madrasa, from where you can look out over the lake before climbing down to the water's edge.

There are numerous Lodi-era tombs scattered along the access road to Hauz Khas Village, and in nearby Green Park.

Bahai House of Worship TEMPLE
(Lotus Temple; Map p178; ☑011-26444029; www.bahaihouseofworship.in; Kalkaji; ☻9am-7pm Tue-Sun Apr-Sep, to 5.30pm Oct-Mar; Ⓜ Okhla NSIC, Kalkaji Mandir, Nehru Place) Designed for tranquil worship, Delhi's beautiful Lotus Temple offers a rare pocket of calm in the hectic city. This architectural masterpiece was designed by Iranian-Canadian architect Fariburz Sahba in 1986. It is shaped like a lotus flower, with 27 delicate-looking white-marble petals. The temple was created to bring faiths together; visitors are invited to pray or meditate silently according to their own beliefs. The attached visitor centre tells the story of the Bahai faith. Photography is prohibited inside the temple. Bear in mind that it gets very busy at weekends, with long queues and far less tranquillity.

Siri Fort FORT
(Map p178; Ⓜ Hauz Khas, Green Park) Only some of the walls remain of this 14th-century fort, built by Ala-ud-din Khilji as the second of the seven historical cities of Delhi. They are impressive nonetheless, and it is said that the heads of 8000 Mongols were buried into the foundations! Within the boundaries of

SIRI FORT AUDITORIUM

Built within the ruined grounds of the 14th-century Siri Fort (p163), this **venue** (Map p178; https://in.bookmyshow.com; Aug Kranti Marg, Siri Fort Institutional Area, Siri Fort; Ⓜ Green Park) is one of Delhi's premier auditoriums and the headquarters of the Directorate of Film Festivals. The main auditorium has a capacity of 700 and is a great place to take in a concert, a play or a film screening. Check the website for schedules.

the walls is an auditorium, a sports complex and the village of Shahpur Jat (p189), which contains an interesting collection of boutique shops and cafes hidden amongst its tight network of alleyways.

☉ Sunder Nagar, Nizamuddin & Lodi Colony

★**Purana Qila**   FORT

(Old Fort; Map p160; ☑ 011-24353178; Mathura Rd; Indian/foreigner ₹25/300, with card ₹20/250, moat ₹20, video ₹25, sound-and-light show adult/child ₹100/50; ☉ dawn-dusk; Ⓜ Pragati Maidan) Shh, whisper it quietly: this place is better than the Red Fort. Delhi's 'Old Fort' isn't as magnificent in size and grandeur, but it's far more pleasant to explore, with tree-shaded landscaped gardens to relax in, crumbling ruins to climb over (and even under, in the case of the tunnels by the mosque) and no uptight guards with whistles telling you not to go here and there.

Ringed by a moat, part of which has been refilled with water, and accessed through the majestically imposing Bada Darwaza gateway, this 16th-century fort is where Mughal Emperor Humayun met his end in 1556, tumbling down the steps of the Sher Mandal, which he used as a library.

The fort had been built by Afghan ruler Sher Shah (1538–45), during his brief ascendancy over Humayun. It's well worth a visit, with its peaceful gardens studded with well-preserved ancient red-stone monuments, including the intricately patterned Qila-i-Kuhran Mosque (Mosque of Sher Shah), behind which are tunnels to explore and parts of the outer walls that can be climbed upon. There's also a small museum (closed on Fridays) set within the walls just inside Bada Darwaza gateway. The sound-and-light show, which is performed in the

evening beside the Humayuni Darwaza gateway, is also non-operational on Fridays.

An elongated lake has been created from the fort's former moat, and in late afternoon is well worth wandering along as the sun lights up the towering walls above it, making for fabulous sunset photos. You'll have to buy an extra ₹20 'moat ticket' along with your main ticket in order to explore it.

Across busy Mathura Rd are more relics from the city of Shergarh, including the beautiful **Khairul Manazil mosque** (Map p160; Mathura Rd; Ⓜ Pragati Maidan), still used by local Muslims and a favoured haunt of flocks of pigeons.

★**Humayun's Tomb**   MONUMENT

(Map p160; Mathura Rd; Indian/foreigner ₹40/600, with car payment ₹35/550, video ₹25; ☉ dawn-dusk; Ⓜ JLN Stadium, Hazrat Nizamuddin) Humayun's tomb is sublimely well proportioned, seeming to float above its symmetrical gardens. It's thought to have inspired the Taj Mahal, which it predates by 60 years. Constructed for the Mughal emperor in the mid-16th century by Haji Begum, Humayun's Persian-born wife, the tomb marries Persian and Mughal elements, with restrained decoration enhancing the architecture. The arched facade is inlaid with bands of white marble and red sandstone, and the building follows strict rules of Islamic geometry, with an emphasis on the number eight.

The beautiful surrounding gardens contain the tombs of the emperor's favourite barber – an entrusted position given the proximity of the razor to the imperial throat – and Haji Begum. This was where the last Mughal emperor, Bahadur Shah Zafar, took refuge before being captured and exiled by the British in 1857.

To the right as you enter the complex, **Isa Khan's tomb** is a fine example of Lodi-era architecture, constructed in the 16th century. Further south is the monumental **Khan-i-Khanan's tomb** (Rahim Khan Marg; Indian/foreigner ₹25/300, with card payment ₹20/250; ☉ dawn-dusk; Ⓜ Hazrat Nizamuddin), plundered in Mughal times to build Safdarjang's tomb.

As part of a huge ongoing restoration project, a new state-of-the-art visitor centre is being built just outside the entrance, and will have underground walkways linking the complex with neighbouring Sunder Nursery and Hazrat Nizam-ud-din Dargah across Mathura Rd.

Sunder Nursery   PARK
(Map p160; Mathura Rd; Indian/foreigner ₹35/100; ☉dawn-dusk; Ⓜ Hazrat Nizamuddin or JLN Stadium) One of Delhi's newest tourist sights, this wonderful park was an overgrown wasteland until recent renovations brought the 16th-century Mughal gardens back to something approaching their former glory. It's now a vast landscaped heritage park with clipped lawns, delicate waterways and a network of paths dotted with fruit trees, flower beds, tree-shaded benches and numerous 16th-century Mughal tombs and pavilions, some of which still lie in a charming state of ruin, some of which have been lovingly restored.

The central pathway has been created upon the line of the Mughal-era Grand Trunk Road and leads all the way from the entrance to the water gardens at the border with Delhi's zoo. Off the sides are woods to explore, a bonsai garden and more Mughal ruins. The restoration project is a work in progress, but this is already proving to be one of Delhi's standout green spaces.

⭐**Hazrat Nizam-
ud-din Dargah**   SHRINE
(Map p160; off Lodi Rd; ☉24hr; Ⓜ JLN Stadium) Visiting the marble shrine of Muslim Sufi saint Nizam-ud-din Auliya is Delhi's most mystical, magical experience. The dargah is hidden away in a tangle of bazaars selling rose petals, attars (perfumes) and offerings, and on some evenings you can hear the *qawwali* (Islamic devotional singing of the Sufis), amid crowds of devotees. The ascetic Nizam-ud-din died in 1325 at the ripe old age of 92. His doctrine of tolerance made him popular not only with Muslims, but with adherents of other faiths, too.

Later kings and nobles wanted to be buried close to Nizam-ud-din, hence the number of nearby Mughal tombs. Other tombs in the compound include the graves of Jahanara (daughter of Shah Jahan) and the renowned Urdu poet Amir Khusru. Scattered around the surrounding alleyways are more tombs and a huge *baoli* (step-well). Entry is free, but visitors may be asked to make a donation. You must remove your shoes before entering the shrine, but there's no need to do so whilst wandering the bazaars that approach it, despite pushy shoe keepers telling you otherwise; follow the lead from visiting locals.

A tour with the Hope Project (p171), which ends at the shrine, is recommended for some background.

⭐**Lodi Garden**   PARK
(Map p160; Lodi Rd; ☉6am-8pm Oct-Mar, 5am-8pm Apr-Sep; Ⓜ Khan Market, Jor Bagh) Delhi's loveliest escape was originally named after the wife of the British Resident, Lady Willingdon, who had two villages cleared in 1936 in order to landscape a park containing the Lodi-era tombs. Today, these lush, tree-shaded gardens – a favoured getaway for Delhi's elite, local joggers and courting couples – help protect more than 100 species of trees and more than 50 species of birds and butterflies as well as half a dozen or so fabulously captivating 15th-century Mughal monuments.

The twin tombs of Bada Gumbad and Sheesh Gumbad, both built 1494, the c 1450 bulbous Mohammed Shah's tomb and the 1518 fortress-like walled complex of Sikander Lodi's tomb, are the park's most notable structures, but also look for Athpula, an eight-piered bridge spanning a small lake, which dates from Emperor Akbar's reign.

MONKEYS AT THE HANUMAN TEMPLE

For some almost guaranteed monkey-watching action, head to the much-revered **Hanuman Temple** (Hanuman Mandir; Map p170; Baba Kharak Singh Rd, Connaught Place; ☉dawn-dusk; Ⓜ Rajiv Chowk) near Connaught Place. Dedicated to the Monkey God Hanuman, loyal friend of Rama in the Ramayana, this Hindu temple is always busy with devotees, but particularly so on Tuesdays and Saturdays. Though discouraged by the authorities (and sometimes fined for doing so) devotees like to offer food to the troops of monkeys who hang out in the trees outside the temple. Monkeys are thought to be reincarnations of Hanuman so having one take food from your hand is auspicious.

It's important to note that you shouldn't try to feed the monkeys yourself. Though they spend their lives in the city centre, these are wild animals, and numerous people have been attacked by them outside this temple. Take photos and videos by all means, but don't get too close, particularly if there are baby monkeys in the troop that the adults might be protecting.

SAIKO3P/SHUTTERSTOCK ©

1. Lodi Garden (p165)
Dotted with 15th century Mughal monuments the gardens are a favourite for Delhi locals.

2. Red Fort (p152)
This 380-year-old building allegedly has the decapitated bodies of prisoners built into its foundations.

3. Humayun's Tomb (p164)
Said to be the inspiration for the Taj Mahal in Agra, this tomb follows strict Islamic geometry.

4. Jama Masjid (p153)
Holding up to 25,000 people, Delhi's largest mosque still allows space for reflection.

★ **Akshardham Temple** HINDU TEMPLE
(☏ 011-43442344; www.akshardham.com; National Hwy 24, Noida turning; temple free, exhibitions & water show ₹250, water show ₹80; ⊙ temple 9.30am-6.30pm Tue-Sun, exhibitions 9.30am-5pm, water show after sunset; Ⓜ Akshardham) Delhi's largest temple, the Gujarati Hindu Swaminarayan Group's Akshardham Temple was built in 2005, and is breathtakingly lavish. Artisans used ancient techniques to carve the pale red sandstone into elaborate reliefs, including 20,000 deities, saints and mythical creatures. The centrepiece is a 3m-high gold statue of Bhagwan Shri Swaminarayan surrounded by more, fabulously intricate carvings.

The 'exhibitions' ticket includes a boat ride through 10,000 years of Indian history, with animatronics telling stories from the life of Swaminarayan.

Visiting the temple is more of a theme-park experience than a spiritual one, such are the tourist crowds and the security, but the architecture of the main buildings, and artisanship of their carvings is exceptional. A shame, then, that you cannot take photographs. Cameras, along with pretty much all other possessions apart from your wallet and passport, must be deposited in the free bag-drop by the entrance. You also cannot bring food and drink inside, but there's an outdoor food court within the complex.

The temple is in Delhi's eastern suburbs, but just 200m walk from Akshardham metro station.

Safdarjang's Tomb MONUMENT
(Map p160; Aurobindo Marg; Indian/foreigner ₹25/300, video ₹25; ⊙ dawn-dusk; Ⓜ Jor Bagh) Built by the Nawab of Avadh for his father, Safdarjang, this grandiose, highly decorative mid-18th-century tomb, set within palm-lined gardens, is an example of late-Mughal architecture. There were insufficient funds for all-over marble, so materials to cover the dome were taken from the nearby mausoleum of Khan-i-Khanan, and it was finished in red sandstone.

◉ **Greater Delhi & Gurgaon (Gurugram)**

★ **Qutab Minar Complex** HISTORIC SITE
(Map p178; ☏ 011-26643856; Indian/foreigner ₹40/600, with card payment ₹35/550; ⊙ dawn-dusk; Ⓜ Qutab Minar) If you only have time to visit one of Delhi's ancient ruins, make it this. The first monuments here were erected by the sultans of Mehrauli, and subsequent rulers expanded on their work, hiring the finest craftspeople and artisans to set in stone the triumph of Muslim rule. The complex is studded with ruined tombs and monuments, the majestic highlight of which is the Qutab Minar, a 73m-tall 12th-century tower, after which this complex is named.

Ala-ud-din's sprawling madrasa (Islamic school) and tomb stand in ruins at the rear of the complex, while Altamish is entombed in a magnificent sandstone and marble mausoleum almost completely covered in Islamic calligraphy.

The **Qutab Festival** (⊙ Nov/Dec) of Indian classical music and dance takes place here.

To reach the complex, turn right out of Qutab Minar metro station, then turn left up the first slip road (after about 500m) and you'll soon reach the entrance.

➡ **Quwwat-ul-Islam Masjid**
(Might of Islam Mosque) At the foot of the Qutab Minar stands the first mosque to be built in India. An inscription over the east gate states that it was built with materials obtained from demolishing '27 idolatrous temples'. As well as intricate carvings that show a clear fusion of Islamic and pre-Islamic styles, the walls of the mosque are studded with sun disks, *shikharas* (rising towers) and other recognisable pieces of Hindu and Jain masonry. This was Delhi's main mosque until 1360.

➡ **Iron Pillar**
In the courtyard of the Quwwat-ul-Islam Masjid is a 6.7m-high iron pillar that is much more ancient than any of the surrounding monuments. It hasn't rusted over the past 1600 years, due to both the dry atmosphere and its incredible purity. A six-line Sanskrit inscription indicates that it was initially erected outside a Vishnu temple, possibly in Bihar, in memory of Chandragupta II, who ruled from AD 375 to 413. Scientists are at a loss as to how the iron was cast using the technology of the time.

★ **Mehrauli Archaeological Park** PARK
(Map p178; ⊙ dawn-dusk; Ⓜ Qutab Minar) FREE There are extraordinary riches scattered around Mehrauli, with more than 440 monuments – from the 10th century to the British era – dotting a forest and the village itself behind the forest. In the forest, most impressive are the time-ravaged tombs of Balban and Quli Khan, his son, and the Jamali Khamali mosque, attached to the tomb of the Sufi poet Jamali. To the west is the 16th-

TEMPLE TIME

For an off-beat side-trip in Gurgaon, take time out from your shopping sprees to visit **Sai Ka Angan Temple** (www.saikaangan.com; E-Block, Sushant Lok Phase I, opposite Paras Hospital, Gurgaon; ☉ dawn-dusk; M Sector 53-54), a small, peaceful complex dedicated to the pan-religion spiritual master Sai Baba of Shirdi who is regarded by his many devotees as a saint. A particularly serene time to visit is during the Thursday evening *aarti* (auspicious lighting of lamps and candles). It's 2km from Sector 53-54 metro station.

century Rajon ki Baoli, Delhi's finest stepwell, with a monumental flight of steps.

At the northern end of Mehrauli village is Adham Khan's Mausoleum, which was once used as a British residence, then later as a police station and post office. Leading northwards from the tomb are the pre-Islamic walls of Lal Kot.

To the south of the village are the remains of the Mughal palace, the Zafar Mahal, once in the heart of the jungle. Next door to it is the Sufi shrine, the Dargah of Qutab Sahib. There is a small burial ground with one empty space that was intended for the last king of Delhi, Bahadur Shah Zafar, who died in exile in Burma (Myanmar) in 1862. South of here is a Lodi-era burial ground for *hijras* (transvestites and eunuchs), **Hijron ka Khanqah** (Map p178; Kalka das Marg). The identity of those buried here is unknown, but it's a well-kept, peaceful place, revered by Delhi's *hijra* community. A little further south are Jahaz Mahal ('ship palace', also built by the Mughals) and the Haus i Shamsi tank , off Mehrauli-Gurgaon Rd.

Wild pigs scamper about the forest, while bright-green parakeets and large black kites swoop from tree to tree. Troops of monkeys clamber across the ruins, especially at dusk. Stone pillars with the names of the main sights carved onto them guide you along the maze-like network of dusty forest pathways; don't come here too late in the day, as it can be easy to get lost.

You can reach the forested part of the park by turning right out of Qutab Minar metro station then taking the small gate on your left, just as you reach the slip road that leads up to Qutab Minar. Note, there is no obvious entrance with English signage, but you'll notice the landscaped park-like area from the road.

★ **Tughlaqabad** FORT
(Indian/foreigner ₹30/300, with card payment ₹25/250; ☉ dawn-dusk; M Govind Puri) This magnificent 14th-century ruined fort, half reclaimed by jungle and gradually being encroached on by villages, was Delhi's third incarnation, built by Ghiyas-ud-din Tughlaq. The sultan poached workers from the Sufi saint Nizam-ud-din, who issued a curse that shepherds would inhabit the fort. However, it's monkeys rather than shepherds that have taken over. There are fantastic emerald-green views. Interlinking underground rooms, which you can explore, were used as storehouses.

The sultan's well-maintained sandstone mausoleum once stood in the middle of a lake, but now is separated from his fallen city by a road. It's included in the entry ticket.

The ruins of the fort are fairly deserted, so it's best to visit them in a group; you could easily spend a couple of hours exploring, so you may not wish to visit them alone. It does get hot out here, so bring plenty of water and snacks – there's nowhere to buy anything.

To reach the fort, take an autorickshaw from the Govind Puri metro station (₹50). Shared autos (₹10) tend only to take you to the end of Guru Ravi Das Marg, leaving you to walk the final 500m to the entrance.

Champa Gali ARTS CENTRE
(Map p178; Lane 3, West End Marg, Saket; M Saket) The small arty enclave known as Champa Gali is hidden away in the lanes behind the fake Dilli Haat handicrafts market ('Delhi Haat') and is one of Greater Delhi's best-kept secrets. It's a favourite for Delhi's young fashionistas, and contains a cluster of craft boutiques and cool cafes, including standout coffee roasters Blue Tokai (p186) and tea specialists Jugmug Thela (p186). It's tough to find; turn left out of Saket metro station, take the first left, then turn left down Lane 3. You'll eventually reach the open courtyard on your right, through an inconspicuous gateway with no sign.

🏃 Activities & Courses

Saffron Palate COOKING
(Map p178; ☑ 9971389993; www.saffronpalate.com; R21 Hauz Khas Enclave; per person ₹4000; M Hauz

Connaught Place

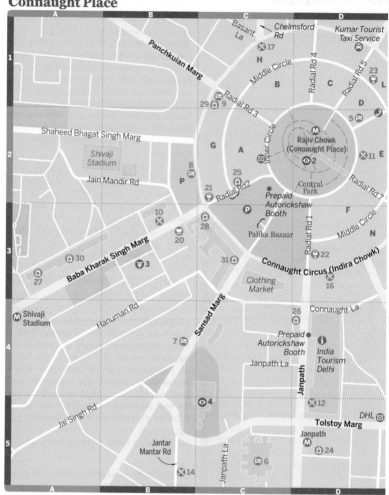

Khas) These award-winning Indian cookery classes are run by Neha Gupta in her family home and last for around three hours. The classes, which tend to start at 11am, culminate in a full-course Indian lunch.

Traveling Spoon   FOOD

(www.travelingspoon.com) Travelling Spoon connects locals with travellers wishing to experience home-made meals. Foodie travellers can choose from a clutch of hosts happy to cook, teach and serve traditional cuisine from the comfort of their homes. To find hosts, search for New Delhi on the website; prices depend on the host and meal served.

Sivananda Yoga   HEALTH & WELLBEING

(Map p178; 011-40591221; www.sivananda.org.in; A41 Kailash Colony; 3-week beginner course ₹4000; 6am-8pm Mon-Fri, 8am-12.30pm Sat, 8am-2.30pm & 5.30-7.30pm Sun; Kailash Colony) This excellent ashram offers courses and workshops for both beginners and the advanced, plus drop-in classes ranging from one to two hours. On Sunday (12.30pm to 2pm) there is a free introductory drop-in class.

Tushita Mahayana
Meditation Centre   MEDITATION

(Map p178; 011-26513400; http://tushitadelhi.com; 9 Padmini Enclave; 6.30-7.30pm Mon &

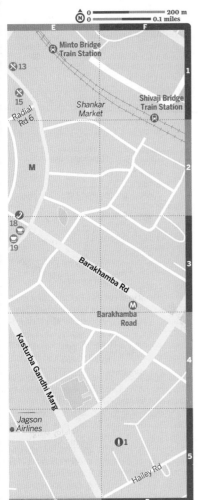

0 | 200 m
0 | 0.1 miles

Minto Bridge Train Station

13

15

Radial Rd 6

Shankar Market

Shivaji Bridge Train Station

M

18

19

Barakhamba Rd

Barakhamba Road

Kasturba Gandhi Marg

Jagson Airlines

1

Hailey Rd

Tours

★ Street Connections
WALKING

(www.streetconnections.co.uk; 3hr walk ₹750; ⊗9am-noon Mon-Sat) ⌀ This fascinating walk through Old Delhi is guided by former street children who have been helped by Salaam Baalak Trust (p171). It explores the hidden corners of Old Delhi, starting at Jama Masjid and visiting small temples and crumbling *haveli* mansions before an e-rickshaw ride takes you to the sneeze-inducing spice market then to one of SBT's shelter homes.

Salaam Baalak Trust
WALKING

(SBT; ☑ 011-23586416; www.salaambaalaktrust.com; suggested donation ₹400; ⊗10am-noon) ⌀ Founded by the mother of film director Mira Nair, following her 1988 hit film about the life of street children, *Salaam Bombay!*, this 30-year-old charity offers two-hour 'street walks' around Paharganj, guided by former street children, who tell you their own, often-shocking, stories and take you to visit a couple of the trust's 'contact points' near New Delhi train station.

Hope Project
WALKING

(☑ 011-24357081, 011-24356576; www.hopeprojectindia.org; 1½hr walk suggested donation ₹300) ⌀ The Hope Project guides interesting walks around the Muslim basti (slum) of Nizamuddin, which surrounds Hazrat Nizam-ud-din Dargah. You can specify your preferred time; one good option is to take the walk on a Friday afternoon to end for the *qawwali* (Islamic devotional singing) performed each week at the intimate shrine of Hazrat Inayat Khan. Wear modest clothing.

★ DelhiByCycle
CYCLING

(☑ 9811723720; www.delhibycycle.com; per person ₹1850; ⊗6.30-10am) Founded by a Dutch journalist, these cycle tours are the original and the best, and a thrilling way to explore Delhi. Tours focus on specific neighbourhoods – Old Delhi, New Delhi, Nizamuddin, and the banks of the Yamuna – and start early to miss the worst of the traffic. The price includes chai and breakfast. Helmets and child seats are available.

Lalli Singh Tours
OUTDOORS

(www.lallisinghadventures.com) Knowledgable and long-standing Delhi-based outfit that rents out Royal Enfield motorcycles, and at the time of research was planning to start offering tailor-made motorcycle tours, including sidecar tours of Delhi.

Thu; M Hauz Khas) FREE Twice-weekly, guided, Buddhist meditation sessions in a peaceful, temple-like meditation hall. Sessions are free. Donations are welcomed.

Kerala Ayurveda
AYURVEDA

(Map p178; ☑ 011-41754888; www.ayurvedancr.com; E-2 Green Park Extension, Green Park Market; 1hr full-body massage from ₹1700; ⊗8am-6.30pm; M Green Park) Treatments from *sarvang ksheerdhara* (massage with buttermilk) to *sirodhara* (warm oil poured on the forehead).

Connaught Place

Reality Tours & Travel　　　　TOURS
(🕿 9818227975; http://realitytoursandtravel.com; tour from ₹1000) Long-established in Mumbai, the highly professional Reality Tours is now offering tours of Delhi, including the excellent Sanjay Colony tour – a visit to a slum area of Delhi (no photographs permitted out of respect for locals' privacy). The tour guides are knowledgeable and friendly, and 80% of profits go to supporting development projects in the colony.

Other tours offered are Old Delhi Street Food, bicycle tours and a sightseeing tour.

🛌 Sleeping

Delhi hotels range from wallet-friendly dives to lavish five-stars. India was a latecomer in the hostel game, but there are now finally a decent number of hostels, offering backpacker-friendly services and good-quality dormitory accommodation in Delhi and beyond. It's wise to book ahead if you're staying in midrange or top-end accommodation, but budgeteers will have no problem getting rooms on the fly, and you'll get cheaper rates as a walk-in guest.

🛌 Old Delhi

★**GoStops**　　　　HOSTEL $
(Map p156; 🕿 011-41056226; www.gostops.com; 4/23B Asaf Ali Rd; dm ₹550-850, d ₹3300; ✳@🛜; Ⓜ Delhi Gate) This is one of the best of Delhi's new breed of hostels, in an interesting loca-

tion on the fringes of Old Delhi, with young, friendly staff, a brightly tiled kitchen, large lounge areas, and comfortable, clean dorms (with reading lamps and lockers) and smart private rooms. There are regular cookery and yoga classes and tours of the city and beyond.

Hotel Broadway　　　　HOTEL $$
(Map p156; 🕿 011-43663600; www.hotelbroadway delhi.com; 4/15 Asaf Ali Rd; s/d incl breakfast from ₹2500/3800; ✳@🛜; Ⓜ Delhi Gate) Five-storey Hotel Broadway was Delhi's first 'high-rise' when it opened in 1956, with single rooms going for ₹15. Today it's comfortable, charming, quirky, and slightly more expensive. It's worth staying here for the restaurant Chor Bizarre (p178) and Thugs bar. Some rooms have old-fashioned wood panelling, while others have been kitted out by French designer Catherine Lévy.

Hotel Aiwan-e-Shahi　　　　HOTEL $$
(Map p156; 🕿 011-47155106; www.hotelaiwan eshahi.com; 1061 Dariba, near Jama Masjid Gate 3; d ₹2400, with view ₹3000; ✳🛜; Ⓜ Jama Masjid) A new building facing Jama Masjid, this hotel has smart, comfortable rooms, some of which have great views of the mosque. The best views, though, are reserved for the 4th-floor roof-terrace restaurant and coffee shop, which nonguests are welcome to use too.

★**Haveli Dharampura**　　　　HERITAGE HOTEL $$$
(Map p156; 🕿 011-23263000; www.havelidharam pura.com; 2293 Gali Guliyan; d from ₹14,700; ✳🛜;

Ⓜ Jama Masjid) This is a beautiful restored *haveli,* full of Mughal atmosphere and centred on a courtyard. Rooms have grandiose polished-wood beds, but it's worth paying for a larger room, as the smallest are a little cramped. The excellent restaurant, Lakhori (p178), serves historic Mughal recipes, there's *kathak* dancing Friday and Sunday evenings, and high tea (4pm to 6pm) served daily on the roof terrace.

You can also watch the traditional local pursuits of *kaboötar bazi* (pigeon flying) and *patang bazi* (kite flying) from the rooftop.

🛏 Paharganj, Main Bazaar

★ Backpacker Panda HOSTEL $
(Map p174; ☑ 011-23588237; http://backpacker panda.com; 22/1 Main Bazaar; 6-/8-bed dm ₹449/429, d ₹1000; 🛜; Ⓜ Ramakrishna Ashram Marg) A great alternative to Paharganj's less-than-fancy cheap hotels, Panda offers bright, clean dorms (one is female only) with attached bathrooms, charge points, lockers, windows, clean linen and comfortable mattresses. There's a TV room, a kitchenette, and it's close to the metro.

Hotel Rak International HOTEL $
(Map p174; ☑ 011-23562478; www.hotelrakinter national.com; 820 Main Bazaar, Chowk Bawli; s/d ₹650/750, with AC ₹850/950; ❄🛜; Ⓜ Ramakrishna Ashram Marg) Hotel Rak International is off the Main Bazaar (so it's quieter) and overlooks a little square and temple. The modest rooms at this popular place are a good choice in this price range, with marble floors and bathrooms, plus, unusually, twin rooms and...windows! The pricier rooms overlook the square.

Hotel Namaskar HOTEL $
(Map p174; ☑ 011-23583456; www.namaskar hotel.com; 917 Chandiwalan, Main Bazaar; r from ₹500, with AC from ₹800; ❄🛜; Ⓜ Ramakrishna Ashram Marg) Up the narrow alley called Chandi Wali Gali, this long-running traveller cheapo is run by two amiable brothers and offers a friendly welcome. It may be humid and noisy, but the rooms get a fresh coat of powder-pink paint annually, which gives it a fresher feel than many of its peers.

Hare Rama Guest House GUESTHOUSE $
(Map p174; ☑ 011-41698544; T298, just off Main Bazaar; r from ₹700; ❄; Ⓜ Ramakrishna Ashram Marg) Opposite Ajay Guest House, down the same alley off Main Bazaar, rooms here are clean, simple, tile-floored affairs that im-

prove as you go up each floor, though few have exterior windows. The most endearing feature here, though, is the breezy rooftop restaurant.

★ Diya Bed & Breakfast B&B $$
(Map p174; ☑ 9811682348; http://stay.street connections.co.uk; top fl, 2413-2415 Tilak St, Paharganj; s/d incl breakfast ₹2000/2750; ❄🛜; Ⓜ Ramakrishna Ashram Marg) Like a serene South Delhi guesthouse, but on a Paharganj backstreet, this unique place has three lovely, well-cared-for rooms, a shared kitchen and a quiet, leafy roof terrace. It's run by the charity Street Connections (p171), and staff and management are former street kids from the Salaam Baalak Trust. It's ideal for solo women or families. Reservations essential.

Cottage Ganga Inn HOTEL $$
(Map p174; ☑ 011-23561516; www.cottageganga inn.com; 1532 Bazar Sangtrashan; r ₹1200-1500; ❄@🛜; Ⓜ Ramakrishna Ashram Marg) Quieter than most Paharganj choices, this place is tucked in a tree-shaded courtyard off the Main Bazaar, next to a nursery school. It's clean, calm, comfortable and good value. Rooms at the front have windows and cost more.

Hotel Relax HOTEL $$
(Map p174; ☑ 011-23562811; Ramdwara Rd, by Nehru Bazaar, off Main Bazaar; r ₹1200-2000; ❄🛜; Ⓜ Ramakrishna Ashram Marg) Unusually well decorated for this area and this price range, Relax is housed in an old, but attractive, property with leafy balconies and halls and corridors dotted with antique furniture. Rooms are clean and comfortable, if nothing special, but it's the common areas that make this place stand out from the crowd.

Metropolis Tourist Home HOTEL $$
(Map p174; ☑ 011-23561794; www.metropolis touristhome.com; 1634-5 Main Bazaar; r from ₹1770; ❄@🛜; Ⓜ Ramakrishna Ashram Marg) A long-standing favourite in the backpacking district, this hotel has comfortable, renovated rooms decorated in 100 shades of brown. The slightly pricey rooftop restaurant feels almost European, with its greenery, low lights and foreign clientele.

Hotel Hari Piorko HOTEL $$
(Map p174; ☑ 011-23587888; www.hotelhari piorkodelhi.com; Main Bazaar; r from ₹2500; ❄🛜; Ⓜ Ramakrishna Ashram Marg) A bit more upmarket than other places on Main Bazaar, this is definitely a hotel rather than

Paharganj

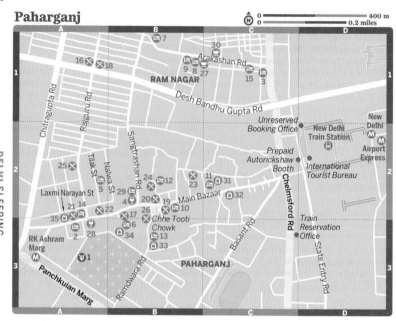

Paharganj

a guesthouse, and has well-turned-out, reasonably spacious, modern rooms. There's an OK restaurant upstairs, and a small ayurvedic spa (massage treatments from ₹800).

🛏 Paharganj, Arakashan Road

Zostel HOSTEL **$**
(Map p174; ☑ 011-23540456; www.zostel.com/zostel/Delhi; 5 Arakashan Rd; dm ₹600-650,

d ₹1680-2790; ❄ 🛈; M New Delhi) Part of the Zostel chain, this place is shabbier than some of Delhi's other backpacker hostels. However, it's got the obligatory cheerful murals, the dorms are decent (the six-bed dorm is much roomier than the eight-bed), with lockers, reading lamps and charging sockets, and it's a friendly place to meet other backpackers.

Hotel Amax Inn · HOTEL $$

(Map p174; 🖉 011-23543813; www.hotel amax.com; 8145/6 Arakashan Rd; s/d/tr from ₹950/1050/1450; ❄ @ 🛈; M Ramakrishna Ashram Marg or New Delhi) In a lane off chaotic Arakashan Rd, the Amax is a long-running traveller favourite, with clean, though occasionally stuffy, budget rooms. Staff are friendly, and clued up about traveller needs, and there's a small greenery-fringed roof terrace that connects to rooms in the slightly cheaper annex opposite. The triple (Room 403) opening onto the rooftop is worth asking for.

Hotel Godwin Deluxe · HOTEL $$

(Map p174; 🖉 011-23613797; www.godwin hotels.com; 8501 Arakashan Rd; s/d incl breakfast ₹3500/4000; ❄ @ 🛈; M Ramakrishna Ashram Marg or New Delhi) Run by the same owners as the OK, but less glitzy, Grand Godwin (Map p174; 🖉 011-23546891; 8502/41 Arakashan Rd; s/d incl breakfast ₹3000/3500; ❄ @ 🛈) next door, Godwin Deluxe offers similarly good service, and comfortable, spacious, clean rooms that are accessed either via a glass lift with street views or up a striking all-marble, spiral staircase.

Bloom Rooms @ New Delhi · HOTEL $$$

(Map p174; 🖉 011-41225666; www.staybloom. com; 8591 Arakashan Rd; s/d from ₹3500/5000; ❄ @ 🛈; M New Delhi) Bloom Rooms' white-and-yellow, pared-down designer aesthetic is unlike anything else in this 'hood, and its IKEA-like rooms surround a pleasant interior courtyard with plenty of seating. Some also have shared balconies overlooking Arakashan Rd. Pillows are soft, beds are comfortable, and there's good wi-fi plus free mineral water and tea and coffee. Check the website for discounted rates.

🛏 New Delhi

Prem Sagar Guest House · GUESTHOUSE $$

(Map p170; 🖉 011-23345263; www.premsagarguest house.com; 1st fl, 11 P-Block, Connaught Place; s/d

incl breakfast from ₹3000/4000; ❄ 🛈; M Rajiv Chowk) This old-school place, with 12 snug rooms that aren't flash but are clean. You'll get better value elsewhere, but for Connaught Place this is about as low budget as it gets. Rooms open onto a narrow, open-air atrium and there's a pot plant–filled rear terrace.

★ Imperial · HOTEL $$$

(Map p170; 🖉 011-23341234; www.theimperial india.com; Janpath; s/d from ₹20,000/22,500; ❄ @ 🛈 ▨; M Janpath) Classicism meets art deco at the Imperial, which dates from 1931 and was designed by FB Blomfield, an associate of Lutyens. Rooms have high ceilings, flowing curtains, French linen and marble baths. There's the temple-like Thai restaurant Spice Route; the 1911 bar (p185) is highly recommended; and the cafe Atrium, Imperial (p185) serves the perfect high tea.

The hallways and atriums are lined with the hotel's venerable 18th- and 19th-century art collection.

Hotel Palace Heights · HOTEL $$$

(Map p170; 🖉 011-43582610; www.hotelpalace heights.com; 26-28 D-Block, Connaught Place; s/d from ₹7080/8260; ❄ @ 🛈; M Rajiv Chowk) This small-scale boutique hotel offers some of busy Connaught Place's nicest rooms, with gleaming white linen, and caramel and amber tones. There's an excellent restaurant, Zäffrän (🖉 011-43582610; mains ₹350-650; ⏱ noon-3.30pm & 6.30-11.30pm) also.

Radisson Blu Marina · HOTEL $$$

(Map p170; 🖉 011-46909090; www.radissonblu. com; 59 G-Block, Connaught Place; s/d from ₹10,240/11,520; ❄ @ 🛈; M Rajiv Chowk) One of Connaught Place's swisher choices, the Radisson feels pleasingly luxurious, with sleek, stylish, all-mod-cons rooms, the Great Kebab Factory restaurant, and a cool bar, the Connaught, where you can sip drinks under hanging red lamps.

Park Hotel · HOTEL $$$

(Map p170; 🖉 011-23743000, reservations 1800 1027275; www.theparkhotels.com; 15 Sansad Marg; r from ₹10,000; ❄ @ 🛈 ▨; M Janpath) Conran-designed, with lots of modern flair, the Park is hip and stylish, and has all the five-star accoutrements you'd expect: a spa, smart eateries and a great poolside bar, Aqua (beers/cocktails from ₹445/845; ⏱ 11am-midnight; 🛈).

DELHI SLEEPING

🛏 South Delhi

Jugaad Hostel   HOSTEL **$**

(Map p178; ☑ 011-41077677; www.jugaadhostels.
com; F-128, 4th fl, Jhandu Mansion, Mohammad-
pur Rd, RK Puram Sector 1; dm/r from ₹700/3600;
❄ @ ⏣; M Bhikaji Cama Place) There's an urban factory feel to this excellent hostel with
wooden-crate bed frames and exposed brick
walls. Dorms and private rooms all have en
suites, and the bunk beds come with reading
lamps, charging sockets and lockers. There's
also a roof terrace with swing chairs. Staff are
friendly and helpful, and there's a women-
only dorm.

Bed & Chai   HOSTEL **$$**

(Map p178; ☑ 011-46066054; www.bedandchai.com;
R55 Hans Raj Gupta Marg; dm incl breakfast ₹850, d
from ₹2700; M Nehru Place) For a quiet stay, this
French-owned guesthouse has simple rooms,
decorated with flashes of colour and some
quirky, original design touches. There's a spa-
cious dorm and a roof terrace strewn with
Tibetan prayer flags. Rates include breakfast
that comes with excellent chai, of course.

Treetops   GUESTHOUSE **$$$**

(Map p178; ☑ 011-26854751, 9899555704; baig.
murad@gmail.com; R-8B, Hauz Khas; d from ₹5600;
❄ ⏣; M Hauz Khas) Motor-journalist-novelist-
philosopher Murad and his hobby-chef wife
Tannie have a gracious home. To stay here
feels rather like visiting some upper-crust
relatives from another era. There are two
large rooms opening onto a leafy rooftop terrace; the smaller room downstairs is cheaper
but can feel less private. Evening meals are
available.

Scarlette   GUESTHOUSE **$$$**

(Map p178; ☑ 011-41023764; www.scarlettenew
delhi.com; B2/139 Safdarjung Enclave; d from ₹6000;
❄ ⏣; M Bhikaji Cama Place) In serene, leafy
Safdarjung Enclave, and not far from Hauz
Khas Village and the Deer Park, Scarlette
is a *maison d'hôtes* (guesthouse) with four
rooms, plus an apartment, decorated with

SLEEPING PRICE RANGES

The following price ranges refer to a
double room with private bathroom and
are inclusive of tax.

$ less than ₹1000

$$ ₹1500–₹4000

$$$ more than ₹4000

---

beautiful artistic flair by the French textile-
designer owner. It's a good choice for solo
women, but note there's a minimum stay of
two days.

🛏 Sunder Nagar, Nizamuddin & Lodi Colony

⭐ **Lutyens Bungalow**   GUESTHOUSE **$$$**

(Map p160; ☑ 011-24611341; www.lutyensbungalow.
co.in; 39 Prithviraj Rd; s/d incl breakfast from
₹6500/7000; ❄ @ ⏣ ⏣; M Lok Kalyan Marg, Jorbagh) A rambling bungalow with a colonial-
era feel, surrounded by verandahs and hanging lamps, this family-run guesthouse has
a wonderful garden, with lawns, flowers
and fluttering parakeets. Rooms are pleasant, with wooden furnishings and an old-
fashioned vibe, and it's a particularly good
place to stay with kids because of the unusual amount of rambling space, and the lovely
swimming pool.

⭐ **Lodhi**   HOTEL **$$$**

(Map p160; ☑ 011-43633333; www.thelodhi.com;
Lodi Rd; r from ₹33,280, with pool ₹53,760; ❄ ⏣ ⏣;
M JLN Stadium) The Lodhi is one of Delhi's
finest luxury hotels, with huge, lovely rooms
and suites. Each room has a balcony, and the
enormous deluxe rooms are the only rooms
in Delhi with their own private plunge pools.
Attention to detail is superb. There's also a
top-notch **spa** (1hr massage from ₹3800), tennis
courts, a slimline outdoor pool, two restau-
rants and a small night club.

G-49   GUESTHOUSE **$$$**

(Bed & Breakfast; Map p160; ☑ 011-47373434; www.
bed-breakfast.asia; G-49 Nizamuddin West; r incl
breakfast from ₹5000; ❄ ⏣; M Hazrat Nizamuddin) In a green-fringed corner of Nizamuddin,
this guesthouse with leafy outlooks is owned
by local homeware designers and has stylish,
simple rooms – two with a balcony. There's
a plant-filled, fairy-lit patio and an attractive
dining room.

Bnineteen   GUESTHOUSE **$$$**

(Map p160; ☑ 011-41825500; www.bnineteen.
com; B-19 Nizamuddin East; s/d incl breakfast from
₹8000/9000; ❄ @ ⏣; M Hazrat Nizamuddin)
Architect-owned, Bnineteen is a looker. Big
contemporary rooms have large windows.
Located in posh, peaceful Nizamuddin East,
it has great views over Humayun's Tomb
from the rooftop. There's a kitchen on every
floor that comes with its own cook.

⛱ Greater Delhi & Gurgaon (Gurugram)

★**Madpackers Hostel**　　　　HOSTEL $
(Map p178; ☏ 011-41677410; S-39A 3rd fl, Panchsheel Park; dm/r from ₹650/2000; ❄ @ 🛜; Ⓜ Hauz Khas) A friendly, relaxed hostel with a bright and airy sitting room that's one of the best places in town to hang out and meet like-minded travellers. It has mixed dorms (with one female-only) and graffitied walls, and it's in a leafy area, albeit beside a superbusy highway.

Cinnamon Stays　　　　GUESTHOUSE $$
(☏ 7525952362, 011-39654545; www.cinnamon stays.in; MD 34, Eldeco Mansionz, Sector 48, Sohna Rd; r incl breakfast from ₹2500; Ⓜ Sector 55-56) There's a warm welcome at this Gurgaon homestay run by husband-and-wife team Shilpi Singh and Manish Sinha, who have gone on to start their own travel company, Unhotel (www.unhotel.in). In a peaceful detached house, rooms come with attached bathrooms, essential amenities and a scattering of kitschy wall-art featuring Bollywood personalities. Contact them for other homestay locations.

✗ Eating

While Delhiites graze all day on the city's masterful, taste-tingling *Dilli-ka-Chaat* (street-food snacks), the city's dining scene is also becoming increasingly diverse. Creative cuisine at Delhi's modern Indian restaurants now sits alongside traditional purveyors of delicate dhals and meaty Mughal delights.

Reservations are recommended for high-end restaurants.

✗ Old Delhi

★**Natraj Dahi Balle Corner**　　STREET FOOD $
(Map p156; 1396 Chandni Chowk; plates ₹50; ⏱ 10.30am-11pm; Ⓜ Chandni Chowk) This tiny place on the corner of a narrow *gali* (lane) is famous for its *dahi bhalle* (fried lentil balls served with yoghurt and garnished with chutney) and deliciously crispy *aloo tikki* (spiced potato patties), each of which costs ₹50. You'll have to elbow your way to the front of the queue to get your share, but it's worth the effort.

★**PT Gaya Prasad Shiv Charan**　　　　STREET FOOD $
(Map p156; 34 Gali Paranthe Wali; parathas ₹60-70; ⏱ 7am-10pm; Ⓜ Jama Masjid) This winding lane off Chandni Chowk has been dishing up its namesake *parathas* (traditional flat bread) fresh off the *tawa* (hotplate) for generations, originally serving pilgrims at the time of the Mughals. Walk down it from Chandni Chowk, take two turns and you'll find this, the most popular *paratha* joint of many. Stuffings include green chilli, almond, banana and more.

Bade Mia Ki Kheer　　　　STREET FOOD $
(Old Kheer Shop; Map p156; shop 2867, Lal Kuan Bazaar; kheer ₹30; ⏱ 11am-late; Ⓜ Chawri Bazaar) Established in 1880 and still run by the Siddique family, this friendly place makes nothing but superdelicious, creamy cardamom-scented *kheer* (rice pudding), usually served cold but if you're lucky and it has just made a batch, served hot.

Jalebi Wala　　　　SWEETS $
(Map p156; Dariba Corner, Chandni Chowk; jalebis ₹50, samosa ₹25; ⏱ 8am-10pm; Ⓜ Lal Qila) Century-old Jalebi Wala does Delhi's – if not India's – finest *jalebis* (deep-fried, syrupy dough), so eat up and worry about the calories tomorrow. It's ₹50 per 100g-serving (roughly one piece). It also does a mean samosa.

Kuremal Mohan Lal　　　　ICE CREAM $
(Kuremal kulfi-walla; Map p156; Kucha Pati Ram, off Sitaram Bazaar; kulfi ₹60; ⏱ noon-11pm; Ⓜ Chawri Bazaar) The Kuremal family have been making *kulfi* (traditional Indian ice cream) since 1906, and serve up delicious options including pomegranate and rose from their small shop in this alluring part of Old Delhi. Lolly-sized versions cost ₹60. Giant iced fruit balls are ₹200. Beware pretenders; the original is at shop No 526.

★**Karim's**　　　　MUGHLAI $$
(Map p156; Gali Kababyan; mains ₹120-400; ⏱ 9am-12.30am; Ⓜ Jama Masjid) Down a narrow alley off a lane leading south from Jama Masjid, Karim's has been delighting carnivores since 1913. Expect meaty Mughlai treats such as mutton *burrah* (marinated chops), delicious mutton Mughlai, and the breakfast mutton and bread combo *nahari*. There are numerous branches, including at Nizamuddin West (p183), but this no-frills, multiroomed courtyard location is the oldest and best.

Al-Jawahar　　　　MUGHLAI $$
(Map p156; Matya Mahal; dishes ₹110-400; ⏱ 7am-midnight; Ⓜ Jama Masjid) Although overshadowed by its famous neighbour, Karim's, Al-Jawahar is also fantastic, serving up tasty Mughlai cuisine at Formica tables in

DELHI EATING

South Delhi

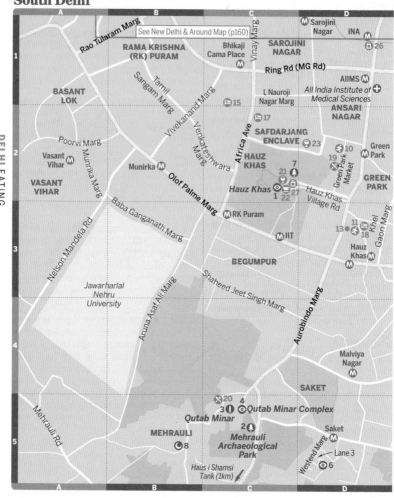

See New Delhi & Around Map (p160)

an orderly dining room, and you can watch breads being freshly made at the front. Kebabs and mutton curries dominate the menu, but it also does good butter chicken and korma.

Chor Bizarre
KASHMIRI $$$

(Map p156; ☏011-23273821; Hotel Broadway, 4/15 Asaf Ali Rd; mains ₹325-500; ⊙noon-3pm & 7.30-11pm; ⓂNew Delhi) Hotel Broadway's excellent, if quirky, restaurant has wood-panelling, traditional wooden furniture and fascinating bits of bric-a-brac, including a vintage car. More importantly it offers delicious and authentic Kashmiri cuisine, including *wazwan*, the traditional Kashmiri feast.

Lakhori
INDIAN $$$

(Map p156; ☏011-23263000; www.havelidharam pura.com; Haveli Dharampura, 2293 Gali Guliyan; tasting menus veg/nonveg ₹1800/2200; mains ₹500-900; ⊙noon-10.30pm; ☏; ⓂJama Masjid) This beautifully restored *haveli* is a labour of love by politician Vijay Goel, and it's good to see one of Old Delhi's grand *havelis* finally get some TLC. The restaurant is especially atmospheric in the evening, with tables in the courtyard and Mughlai and local recipes

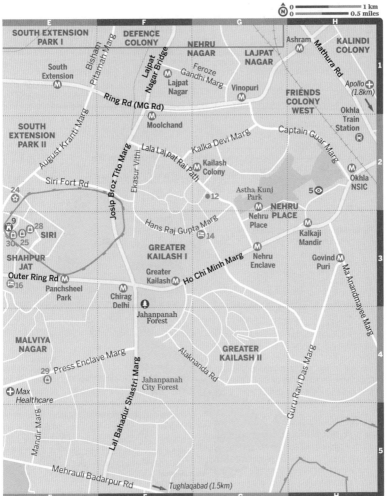

on the menu. Indian high tea (₹1100; 4pm to 6pm) is served daily on the rooftop.

On weekends there is *kathak* dancing on the balcony.

✖ Paharganj

★ Darbar
INDIAN **$**

(Map p174; Multani Dhanda, Paharganj; snacks ₹30-100, dishes ₹125-270, thalis ₹210-260; ⏱ 8.30am-11.30pm; Ⓜ Ramakrishna Ashram Marg) Considering its gritty Paharganj location and its street-food roots, the interior of this locals' favourite is strangely elegant (there's even a chandelier!). Street-food *chaat* (savoury

snacks) are served by the entrance, while the main menu focuses on rich Mughlai curries, delicate South Indian delights such as dosa and *uttapam* (savoury rice pancake), and some outstanding thalis; the 10-piece Shahi thali (₹240) is a feast.

★ Sita Ram Dewan Chand
INDIAN **$**

(Map p174; 2243 Chuna Mandi; half/full plate ₹35/60; ⏱ 8am-6pm; Ⓜ Ramakrishna Ashram Marg) A family-run hole-in-the-wall serving inexpensive portions of just one dish – *chhole bhature* (spicy chickpeas, accompanied by delicious, freshly made, puffy, fried bread with a light paneer filling). It's a traditional

South Delhi

breakfast in Delhi, but many people are partial to some at any time of day. There are no seats; instead diners stand at high tables to eat. Lassis cost ₹40.

Bikaner Sweet Corner
SWEETS $

(Map p174; Multani Dhanda, Paharganj; ⊙7.30am-11pm; Ⓜ Ramakrishna Ashram Marg) This popular local sweet shop is the place in Paharganj to come for your evening treats; try the *kaju barfi* (cashew-milk sweet wrapped in silver leaf) or the *gajar halwa* (crumbly carrot dessert served with crushed nuts). Also sells dried fruit and nuts plus other savoury snacks. Sweets are sold by weight; 100g (₹50 to ₹125) gets you six or seven pieces.

Satguru Dhaba
INDIAN $

(Map p174; 854 Mantola Mohalla, Paharganj; dishes ₹50-250, thalis ₹100; ⊙8am-midnight; Ⓜ Ramakrishna Ashram Marg) Eat like a local rather than a tourist at this popular Paharganji *dhaba* (simple roadside eatery). It's no frills, for sure, but the food is tasty, as are the prices. From Main Bazaar, walk up Chandi Wali Gali, past Hotel Namaskar. Turn left at the end and it's on your left. English menu, but no English sign.

Krishna Cafe
MULTICUISINE $

(Map p174; Chhe Tooti Chowk, Main Bazaar; dishes ₹100-250; ⊙7.30am-10.30pm; Ⓜ Ramakrishna Ashram Marg) There's a friendly welcome at this small, but popular, rooftop restaurant overlooking Main Bazaar's frenetic Tooti Chowk. The multicuisine menu includes all-day breakfasts, and the 'special tea' tastes remarkably similar to beer (nudge-nudge, wink-wink).

Madan Café
MULTICUISINE $

(Map p174; Main Bazaar; mains ₹40-120; ⊙7am-10pm; Ⓜ Ramakrishna Ashram Marg) This friendly, pint-sized, roadside eatery is probably the cheapest place to get a meal on Main Bazaar, and is great for watching the world go by with a steaming cup of chai. The multicuisine menu includes backpacker breakfasts such as pancakes, porridge and omelettes, but there's plenty of local dishes, too.

★ Tadka
INDIAN $$

(Map p174; 4986 Ramdwara Rd; mains ₹180-210; ⊙9am-10.30pm; 🖋; Ⓜ Ramakrishna Ashram Marg) Named for everyone's favourite *dhal*, Tadka's no-frills interior and relatively low prices belie its fabulously tasty menu, which includes delicious dhal (naturally), some rich, creamy paneer dishes and standout roti and naan bread. The *dum aloo* (potato skins stuffed with paneer in a tomato sauce) is divine.

⭐ **Shim Tur** KOREAN **$$**
(Map p174; 3rd fl, Navrang Guesthouse, Tooti Gali; meals ₹200-500; ⊙10.30am-11pm; M Ramakrishna Ashram Marg) The Korean food is fresh and authentic here; try the *bibimbap* (rice bowl with a mix of vegetables, egg and pickles; ₹270). But it takes determination to find this place: take the turning for the Hotel Rak International, opposite which is the grotty, unsigned Navrang Guesthouse. Follow the signs up to its rooftop and you'll find the small, bamboo-lined, softly lit terrace.

Exotic Rooftop Restaurant MULTICUISINE **$$**
(Map p174; Tooti Chowk, Main Bazaar, Paharganj; mains ₹200-400; ⊙8am-11.30pm; M Ramakrishna Ashram Marg) Currently the most popular of the numerous rooftop restaurants and cafes overlooking frenetic Tooti Chowk, Exotic is a small laid-back place with a breezy perch and a decent please-all backpacker menu (biryani, pizza, falafel, pancakes). There's no lift, so you'll have to climb up four flights of stairs, but there are cold beers (₹180) waiting for you at the top.

Brown Bread Bakery MULTICUISINE **$$**
(Map p174; ground fl, Ajay Guest House, 5084A Main Bazaar; mains ₹200-400, buffet breakfast ₹350; ⊙7.30am-10pm; ☎🖋; M Ramakrishna Ashram Marg) Transported to Delhi from its mother ship in Varanasi, this German-owned bakery-cum-cafe-cum-restaurant does standout, largely organic, health-conscious food, including Manali cheese and a fantastic range of bread, baked in a purpose-built bakery just around the corner. It's let down slightly by its gloomy, hotel-lobby location and overly nonchalant staff, but you won't find better bread anywhere in India here.

Leo's Restaurant NORTH INDIAN **$$**
(Map p174; Main Bazaar, Paharganj; dishes from ₹200; ⊙10am-11pm; ❋☎; M Ramakrishna Ashram Marg) Leo's is a good choice if you fancy a beer with your curry (you can just come for a drink if you like). It does a range of tasty North Indian dishes, plus a few Chinese offerings, and the small 'combo' meals are perfect for lunch for solo diners.

Metropolis Restaurant & Bar MULTICUISINE **$$**
(Map p174; Metropolis Tourist Home, 1634-35 Main Bazaar, Paharganj; mains ₹150-450; ⊙8am-midnight; ☎; M Ramakrishna Ashram Marg) This venerable hotel's leafy, part-shaded, rooftop restaurant offers a calming respite from the noisy streets below. There's beer (Kingfisher ₹144), wine (₹360 per glass) and a food menu consisting mostly of Indian mains (₹150 to ₹450), but also pizza, pasta and Chinese.

Malhotra NORTH INDIAN **$$**
(Map p174; 1833 Laxmi Narayan St; mains ₹170-270, thalis from ₹175; ⊙7am-11pm; ☎; M Ramakrishna Ashram Marg) One street back from the Main Bazaar chaos, Malhotra is a reliable choice, popular with locals and foreigners, and with a good menu of set breakfasts and North Indian standards, such as *mattar paneer* (pea and cottage cheese curry).

🍴 New Delhi

⭐ **Andhra Pradesh Bhawan Canteen** SOUTH INDIAN **$**
(Map p160; 1 Ashoka Rd; dishes ₹150-180, thalis ₹130, breakfast ₹75; ⊙8-10.30am, noon-3pm & 7.30-10pm; M Patel Chowk) A hallowed bargain, the canteen at the Andhra Pradesh state house serves cheap and delicious unlimited South Indian thalis to a seemingly unlimited stream of patrons. Come on Sunday for the fabled Hyderabadi chicken biryani (₹235).

⭐ **Triveni Terrace Cafe** CAFE **$**
(Map p160; 205 Tansen Marg, Mandi House; dishes ₹70-200; ⊙10am-9pm, food to 6.30pm; M Mandi House) Located in a peaceful garden-courtyard inside Triveni Art Gallery, this delightful cafe has seating on a plant-filled terrace overlooking a small, grassy amphitheatre, where dance rehearsals sometimes take place while you eat. The small menu includes tasty, good-value Indian meals and snacks (*pakora, paratha,* thali) plus toasted sandwiches and French-press coffee (₹120).

⭐ **Naturals** ICE CREAM **$**
(Map p170; 8 L-Block, Connaught Place; single scoop ₹70; ⊙11am-midnight; M Rajiv Chowk) Founder Mr Kamath's dad was a mango vendor in Mangalore, which apparently inspired his love of fruit. He went on to start Naturals, with its wonderfully creamy, fresh flavours, such as watermelon, coconut, (heavenly) mango and roasted almond.

LOCAL KNOWLEDGE

DELHI STREET FOOD

Old Delhi sizzles with the sound of *Dilli-ka-Chaat* (street-food snacks) being fried, boiled, grilled and flipped. *Chaat* to look out for include: *dahi bhalle* (fried lentil balls served with yoghurt and garnished with chutney); *aloo tikki* (spiced potato patties); *shakarkandi* (sweet potato) baked on coals on a flip-out table; and *aloo chaat* (fried pieces of parboiled potato mixed with chickpeas and chopped onions, and garnished with spices and chutney).

Aside from *Dilli-ka-Chaat*, Delhi specialities include breakfast-favourite *chole bhature* (spicy chickpeas, accompanied by puffy, fried bread with a light paneer filling); and *chole kulche*, a healthier version of *chole bhature* made with boiled chickpeas and less-greasy baked bread. *Nihari* (goat curry eaten with roti) is a popular breakfast for Delhi's Muslim population, and the only breakfast item at legendary Karim's (p177).

Kerala House Canteen   SOUTH INDIAN $
(Map p170; 3 Jantar Mantar Rd; meals ₹50; ⊙8-10am, 12.30-2.30pm & 7-9.45pm; Ⓜ Patel Chowk)
The staff canteen at Kerala House (Kerala Government HQ in Delhi) offers bargain set meals cooked with authentic Keralan spices. Lunchtimes are wildly popular with rice meals (veg, chicken, fish or buffalo) served with pappad and unlimited refills of lentil and bean side dishes. Dinner sees rice replaced with *parathas*, while *appams* (onion and coconut pancakes) are served at breakfast. Diners are sometimes asked to use the back entrance to Kerala House on Janpath Lane.

Kake-da-Hotel   MUGHLAI $
(Map p170; ☑ 9136666820; 67 Municipal Market; mains ₹90-300; ⊙noon-11.30pm; Ⓜ Rajiv Chowk)
This no-frills, always-busy *dhaba* (snack bar) is a basic hole in the wall that's hugely popular with local workers for its famous butter chicken (₹230) and other Mughlai Punjabi dishes. Staff are rushed off their feet, but the owner is welcoming to the few foreign diners who visit.

Coffee Home   INDIAN $
(Map p170; Baba Kharak Singh Marg; dishes ₹50-150; ⊙11am-8pm; Ⓜ Shivaji Stadium) Shaded under the wide reaches of an old banyan tree, the garden courtyard at Coffee Home is always busy with office workers lingering over chai and feasting on South Indian snacks such as masala dosa. It is handily located next to the government emporiums.

★ **Cafe Lota**   MODERN INDIAN $$
(Map p160; Crafts Museum; dishes ₹215-415; ⊙8am-9.30pm; Ⓜ Pragati Maidan) Bamboo slices the sunlight into flattering stripes at this outdoor restaurant offering a modern take on delicious Indian cooking from across the regions. Sample its take on fish and (sweet potato) chips, or *palak patta chaat* (crispy spinach, potatoes and chickpeas with spiced yoghurt and chutneys), as well as amazing desserts and breakfasts. It's great for kids.

★ **Hotel Saravana Bhavan**   SOUTH INDIAN $$
(Map p170; 46 Janpath; dishes ₹95-210, thalis ₹210; ⊙8am-11pm; Ⓜ Janpath) Fabulous dosas, *idlis* and other South Indian delights. With queues coming out the door, this is the biggest and the best of Delhi's Saravana Bhavan branches, and you can see dosas being made in the back. Also offers great South Indian coffee.

★ **Rajdhani**   INDIAN $$$
(Map p170; ☑ 011-43501200; 18 N-Block, Connaught Place; thalis ₹525; ⊙noon-3.30pm & 7-11pm; ☑; Ⓜ Rajiv Chowk) Thalis fit for a king. Treat yourself with food-of-the-gods vegetarian thalis that encompass a fantastic array of Gujarati and Rajasthani dishes.

Farzi Cafe   MODERN INDIAN $$$
(Map p170; ☑ 9599889700; 38 E-Block, Connaught Place; mains ₹360-560; ⊙noon-12.30am; Ⓜ Rajiv Chowk) This buzzy Connaught Place joint signifies the Delhi foodie penchant for quirkiness, with all sorts of 'molecular gastronomy' and unusual fusion dishes such as butter chicken *bao* (in a bun). It's ₹100 for Kingfisher beer, and there are *bunta* (traditional homemade fizzy pop) cocktails. There's live Sufi, Hindi and Bollywood-style pop music on Saturday nights from 9pm.

Véda   INDIAN $$$
(Map p170; ☑ 011-41513535; 27 H-Block, Connaught Place; mains ₹500-700; ⊙noon-11.30pm; Ⓜ Rajiv Chowk) Fashion designer Rohit Baal created Véda's sumptuous interior, making for Connaught Place's most dimly lit eatery,

a dark boudoir with swirling neo-Murano chandeliers and shimmering mirror mosaics. The menu proffers tasty classic Mughlai dishes (butter chicken, dhal makhani and the like) and it mixes a mean martini.

Chor Bizarre KASHMIRI $$$
(Map p160; 011-23071574; Bikaner House, Pandara Rd; mains ₹325-500; noon-3.30pm & 7-11.30pm; Khan Market) In the beautifully restored colonial-era Bikaner House, Chor Bizarre ('Thieves' Market') is a new branch of Hotel Broadway's famous restaurant on the outskirts of Old Delhi. Like the original, the interior here is also full of quirky old-fashioned charm, and the menu includes authentic, delicious dishes such as Kashmiri *haaq* (spinach with chilli).

✕ South Delhi

Evergreen CAFE $
(Map p178; S29-30 Green Park Market; dishes ₹100-200, thalis ₹165-240; 9am-9pm; Green Park) Part cafe, part sweet shop, Evergreen has been keeping punters happy since 1963 with its veg snacks, *chaat,* thalis and dosas.

★Naivedyam SOUTH INDIAN $$
(Map p178; 011-26960426; dishes ₹150-200, thalis ₹275-380; 11am-11pm; Green Park) This superb South Indian restaurant feels like a temple, with a woodcarved interior, waiters dressed as devotees, and incense burning on the exterior shrine. Diners receive a complimentary lentil soup-drink and pappadam as they browse the menu, which includes delectable dosas and to-die-for thalis.

★Potbelly NORTH INDIAN $$
(Map p178; 116C Shahpur Jat Village; dishes ₹150-450, thalis from ₹300; 12.30-11pm; Hauz Khas) It's a rare treat to find a Bihari restaurant in Delhi, and this artsy, shabby-chic place with fabulous views from its 4th-floor perch has authentic Bihari thalis and dishes such as *litti* chicken – whole-wheat balls stuffed with *sattu* (ground pulse) and served with *khada masala* chicken.

Cafe Red CAFE $$
(Map p178; 5-G Jungi House, Shahpur Jat Village, Siri Fort; mains ₹150-300; 10.30am-8.30pm; ; Hauz Khas) A fun and trendy ground-floor cafe that's hidden down an alley and serves omelettes, sandwiches, soups and pizza as well as espresso coffee and shakes. Has some patio seating, too.

Coast SOUTH INDIAN $$$
(Map p178; 011-41601717; Hauz Khas; dishes ₹360-580; noon-midnight; Green Park) A light, bright restaurant on several levels, with views over the parklands of Hauz Khas, chic Coast serves light South Indian dishes, such as *avial* (vegetable curry) with *risheri* (pumpkin with black lentils), plus tacos, burgers, salads and hit-the-spot mustard-tossed fries. Decent wine list, too.

✕ Sunder Nagar, Nizamuddin & Lodi Colony

Nagaland House INDIAN $
(Map p160; 29 Dr APJ Abdul Kalam Rd; thalis ₹120-200; 7-9am, noon-3pm & 7.30-10pm; Lok Kalyan Marg) The quiet, friendly, Nagaland canteen is a simple room overlooking a tangle of palm trees and is worth seeking out for punchy pork offerings, with dishes such as pork with bamboo shoots and a Naga-style pork thali. Veg, fish and chicken thalis are also available.

Gujarat Bhawan GUJARATI $
(Map p160; 11 Kautilya Marg, Chanakyapuri; breakfast ₹60, thalis ₹110-140; 7.30-10.30am, 12.30-3pm & 7.30-10pm; ; Lok Kalyan Marg) On a street lined with state bhavans (Bihar, Tamil Nadu, Karnataka), many of which have canteens, the Gujarat State–run canteen is typically simple, but serves up nourishing, plentiful, cheap-as-chips vegetarian home-style Gujarati thalis.

Karim's MUGHLAI $$
(Map p160; 168/2 Jha House Basti; dishes ₹120-400; 1-3pm & 6.30-11pm Tue-Sat; JLN Stadium) Hidden down the buzzing alleys that surround Hazrat Nizamuddin Dargah is this branch of historic Karim's, serving meaty Mughlai delights such as kebabs and rich curries.

★Mamagoto ASIAN $$$
(Map p160; 011-45166060; 53 Middle Lane, Khan Market; mains ₹400-800; 12.30-11.30pm; Khan Market) Fun, friendly and fabulously colourful, this laid-back east-Asian restaurant, with funky manga art and retro Chinese posters on the walls, has an eclectic menu spanning Japan, China and Southeast Asia – including noodles, dumplings and some authentically spicy hawker-style Thai food.

> ### FOOD PRICE RANGES
>
> Prices reflect the cost of a standard main meal (unless otherwise indicated). Reviews are listed by author preference within the following price categories.
>
> **$** less than ₹150
>
> **$$** ₹150–₹300
>
> **$$$** more than ₹300

Sodabottleopenerwala PARSI **$$$**

(Map p160; www.sodabottleopenerwala.in; Khan Market; mains ₹325-745; ⊙9am-midnight; Ⓜ Khan Market) The name is like a typical trade-based Parsi surname, the place emulates the Iranian cafes of Mumbai, and the food is authentic Persian, including vegetable berry pilau, mixed-berry trifle and *lagan nu custer* (Parsi wedding custard).

Perch INTERNATIONAL **$$$**

(Map p160; ☑9728603540; Khan Market; dishes ₹325-975, wine per glass ₹325-800, cocktails ₹500-650; ⊙8am-midnight; ☎; Ⓜ Khan Market) The coolification of upscale shopping enclave Khan Market continues apace with Perch, a wine bar-cafe that's all pared-down aesthetic, waiters in pencil-grey shirts, soothing music, international wines and pleasing international snacks such as Welsh rarebit and tiger prawn with soba noodles.

★**Indian Accent** INDIAN **$$$**

(Map p160; ☑011-26925151; https://indianaccent.com/newdelhi; Lodhi Hotel, Lodi Rd; dishes ₹500-1750, tasting menu veg/nonveg ₹3600/3900; ⊙noon-2.30pm & 7-10.30pm; Ⓜ JLN Stadium) Inside luxury Lodhi (p176) hotel, though privately run, Indian Accent is one of the capital's top dining experiences. Chef Manish Mehrotra works his magic using seasonal ingredients married in surprising and beautifully creative combinations. The tasting menu is astoundingly good, with wow-factor combinations such as tandoori bacon prawns or paper dosa filled with wild mushroom and water chestnuts. Dress smart. Book ahead.

✖ Greater Delhi & Gurgaon (Gurugram)

★**DLF Cyber Hub** INTERNATIONAL

(www.dlfcyberhub.com; DLF Cyber City, Phase II, NH-8; ⊙most restaurants 11am-11pm, bars to 1am; Ⓜ Cyber City) This is a food court par excel-lence, and you'll find any type of cuisine you fancy here, from Indian street food and Tibetan *momos* (dumplings) to high-end European and chic cafe bites. Tables spill out onto the large plaza; there's also an indoor 1st-floor food court with some cheaper options.

Standouts include **Burma Burma** (☑0124-4372997; www.burmaburma.in; dishes ₹300-500; ⊙noon-3pm & 7-11pm), for Southeast Asian food and fine teas; the cool **Cyber Hub Social** (dishes ₹200-500; ⊙11am-11pm) with funky terrace seating and private rooms; **Farzi Cafe** (www.farzicafe.com; dishes ₹400-600; ⊙11am-1am), for upmarket Indian street food; the People & Co (p187) for live comedy; **Yum Yum Cha** (dim sum from ₹345, sushi from ₹485; ⊙12.30-11pm) for dim sum and sushi; and Soi 7 (p187) for craft beer brewed on-site. For a cheaper, on-the-hop option, grab a samosa (₹25) and a filter coffee (₹35) from the teeny stairwell takeaway Madras Coffee House.

Olive MEDITERRANEAN **$$$**

(Map p178; ☑011-29574443; Bhulbhulaiya Rd, behind Qutab Minar, Mehrauli; pizza from ₹950, meze platters from ₹1500; ⊙noon-midnight; Ⓜ Qutab Minar) There are plenty of cafes and fast-food joints near the entrance to Qutab Minar, but if you fancy eating in style after visiting the ruins, follow the road around the back of the complex to beautiful Olive, with its *haveli* courtyard setting and award-winning Mediterranean menu.

Drinking & Nightlife

Delhi's ever-growing cafe scene has given rise to artisanal coffee, Turkish pastries and the like, while the city's bar and live-music choices are also burgeoning, though licences rarely extend later than 12.30am. For the latest places to go at night, check out Little Black Book (https://lbb.in/delhi) or Brown Paper Bag (http://brownpaperbag.in/delhi).

Old Delhi

Drinking is frowned upon in much of Muslim-dominated Old Delhi, but there are plenty of bars around the backpacker hub of Paharganj. Most are dark, seedy-looking (though really quite harmless) dive bars that are frequented almost solely by men. But there are a few OK exceptions on Main Bazaar, such as Sam's Bar (p185). Most restaurants on Main Bazaar do not have alcohol licences; some will, though, sell you a can of beer on the sly, served in a coffee mug. In such cases, be sure to drink discreetly so that you don't get them in trouble.

⭐**PT Ved Prakash Lemon Wale** JUICE BAR
(Map p156; 📞011-23920931; 5466 Ghantaghar, Chandni Chowk; lemonade ₹10; ⏰11.30am-10.30pm; Ⓜ Chandni Chowk) Quenching Chandni Chowk's thirst for over a century now, this stalwart has a menu comprising just one item: homegrown fizzy lemonade that comes from a glass bottle sealed with a marble. Summer days find this hole-in-the-wall place completely engulfed by loyal fans seeking much-needed relief from the heat.

🍷 Paharganj

Cafe Brownie CAFE
(Map p174; 41 Arakashan Rd; coffee from ₹70; ⏰7.30am-11pm; 📶; Ⓜ New Delhi Railway Station) Cute little cafe for an email catch-up, espresso in one hand, brownie or muffin in the other.

Voyage Cafe CAFE
(Map p174; 8647 Arakashan Rd; coffee from ₹50; ⏰24hr; 📶; Ⓜ New Delhi Railway Station) Cakes, shakes and very affordable Lavazza coffee, plus floor-to-ceiling windows for that full-on street-view experience.

Sam's Bar BAR
(Map p174; Main Bazaar; ⏰1pm-12.30am; Ⓜ Ramakrishna Ashram Marg) If you can nab one of the two tables by the big window overlooking Main Bazaar this is a fine place to chill with a couple of beers (from ₹115). Sam's Bar is more laid-back than most Paharganj bars, with a mixed crowd of men and women, locals and foreigners. There's a full food menu as well as drinks.

My Bar BAR
(Map p174; Main Bazaar, Paharganj; ⏰11am-12.30am; Ⓜ Ramakrishna Ashram Marg) A dark but lively bar, this place is loud and fun, with a cheery, mixed crowd of backpackers and locals, who may even start dancing... There are several other branches, in **Connaught Place** (Map p170; 49 N-Block; ⏰11am-12.30am; Ⓜ Rajiv Chowk) and Hauz Khas. Cocktails from ₹220. Beer from ₹100.

🍷 New Delhi

Chai Point CAFE
(Map p170; N-Block, Connaught Place; ⏰8am-11pm; 📶; Ⓜ Rajiv Chowk) This buzzing, split-level cafe specialises in healthy chai infusions

(masala, ginger, cardamom, lemongrass; ₹75 to ₹100) but also serves good lassis (₹119 to ₹129) and fresh coffee alongside banana cake and other sweet treats. Ask for a glass cup; otherwise you'll get your chai in a less-than-satisfying disposable paper cup.

Cha Bar CAFE
(Map p170; Oxford Bookstore, 81 N-Block, Connaught Place; tea ₹35-100, dishes ₹100-175; ⏰9.30am-9.30pm; Ⓜ Rajiv Chowk) Connaught Place's Oxford Bookstore contains the hugely popular cafe Cha Bar, with more than 150 types of tea to choose from, as well as a good-value food menu including a range of tasty biryanis (₹170). At lunchtimes it buzzes with happy, chattering, 20-something locals.

Indian Coffee House CAFE
(Map p170; 2nd fl, Mohan Singh Place, Baba Kharak Singh Marg; snacks ₹50-100, filter coffee ₹36; ⏰9am-9pm; Ⓜ Rajiv Chowk) Up on the 2nd floor of Mohan Singh Place, Indian Coffee House has faded-to-the-point-of-dilapidated charm, with the waiters' plummage-like hats and uniforms giving them a rakish swagger. You can feast on finger chips and South Indian snacks like it's 1952, and the roof terrace is a tranquil spot to linger, although watch out for marauding macaques!

⭐**Atrium, Imperial** CAFE
(Map p170; Imperial Hotel, Janpath; ⏰8am-11.30pm; Ⓜ Janpath) Is there anything more genteel than high tea at the Imperial (p175)? Sip tea from bone-china cups and pluck dainty sandwiches and cakes from tiered stands, while discussing the latest goings-on in Shimla and Dalhousie. High tea is served in the Atrium from 3pm to 6pm daily (₹1500 plus tax).

⭐**Unplugged** BAR
(Map p170; 📞011-33107701; 23 L-Block, Connaught Place; beers/cocktails from ₹145/400; ⏰noon-midnight; Ⓜ Rajiv Chowk) There's nowhere else like this in Connaught Place. You could forget you were in CP, in fact, with the big courtyard garden, wrought-iron chairs and tables, and swing seats, all under the shade of a mother of a banyan tree hung with basket-weave lanterns. There's live music on Wednesday, Friday, Saturday and Sunday evenings: anything from alt-rock to electro-fusion.

⭐**1911** BAR
(Map p170; Imperial Hotel, Janpath; ⏰11am-12.45am; Ⓜ Janpath) The Imperial, built in the 1930s, resonates with bygone splendour.

DELHI DRINKING & NIGHTLIFE

This bar is a more recent addition, but still riffs on the Raj. Here you can sip the perfect cocktail (₹1000) amid designer-clad clientele, against a backdrop of faded photos and murals of maharajas.

Lord of the Drinks BAR
(Map p170; ☑ 9999827155, 9999827144; G-72, 1st fl, Outer Circle, Connaught Place; beers/cocktails from ₹135/545, mains ₹400-800; ☺11am-1am; ⬤; Ⓜ Rajiv Chowk) A cavernous space done up in wood, leather and metal trim, with cosy corners and a huge sports TV screen. Serves trademark oversized drinks, including mugs of Kingfisher for ₹135, while everything goes on the food menu, from *bhurji* (crumbled spiced paneer) to Parmesan tart.

🍴 South Delhi

★**Hauz Khas Social** BAR
(Map p178; www.socialoffline.in/HauzKhasSocial; 12 Hauz Khas Village; ☺11am-12.30am; Ⓜ Green Park) This chilled-out restaurant-bar-club is a Hauz Khas hub, and has an urban warehouse-like interior with stone walls, high ceilings and huge plate-glass windows overlooking lush greenery and the Hauz Khas lake. There's an extensive food menu (dishes ₹200 to ₹500) plus beers, cocktails and regular live music and DJs in the evenings.

★**Piano Man Jazz Club** CLUB
(Map p178; http://thepianoman.in; B-6 Commercial Complex, Safdarjung Enclave; ☺noon-3pm & 7.30pm-12.30am; Ⓜ Green Park) The real thing, this popular, atmospheric place with proper musos is a dim-lit speakeasy with some excellent live jazz performances.

★**Ek Bar** BAR
(Map p178; D17, 1st fl, Defence Colony; ☺5pm-1am; Ⓜ Lajpat Nagar) On the upper floors of a building in the exclusive area of the Defence Colony, this place has stylish, kooky decor in deep, earth-jewel colours, serious mixology (cocktails from ₹475) showcasing Indian flavours (how about a gin and tonic with turmeric?), modern Indian bar snacks, nightly DJs, and a see-and-be-seen crowd.

Kunzum Travel Cafe CAFE
(Map p178; www.kunzum.com; T49 Hauz Khas Village; ☺11am-7.30pm Tue-Sun; ⬤; Ⓜ Green Park) 🌿 Quirky Kunzum has a pay-what-you-like policy for the French-press coffee and tea, and sells its own brand of travel guides to Delhi. There's free wi-fi, a few travel books and magazines to browse, and paints and

brushes on a table for you to produce your own artwork.

🍴 Sunder Nagar, Nizamuddin & Lodi Colony

Big Chill CAFE
(Map p160; Khan Market; ☺noon-11.30pm; Ⓜ Khan Market) Popular, film-poster-lined cafe at Khan Market, packed with chattering Delhiites. The menu is a telephone directory of Continental and Indian dishes (₹290 to ₹625). Nearby is its spin-off cakery (for cakes and pastries) and creamery (for ice cream).

Café Turtle CAFE
(Map p160; Khan Market; dishes ₹375-545; ☺8.30am-8.30pm; Ⓜ Khan Market) Allied to the Full Circle Bookstore (p190), this brightly painted boho cafe gets busy with chattering bookish types, and is ideal when you're in the mood for coffee and cake in cosy surroundings, with a leafy outdoor terrace as well. There is also a branch in **Nizamuddin East** (Map p160; 8 Nizamuddin East Market; dishes ₹375-545, coffees from ₹200; ☺8.30am-8.30pm; Ⓜ Jangpura).

🍴 Greater Delhi & Gurgaon (Gurugram)

★**Blue Tokai** CAFE
(Map p178; www.bluetokaicoffee.com; Champa Gali, Lane 3, West End Marg, Saket; coffee from ₹100, snacks ₹150-300; ☺9am-10pm; ⬤; Ⓜ Saket) Found in a magically unexpected art enclave called Champa Gali, down a lane beside the fake Dilli Haat shopping centre ('Delhi Haat'), Blue Tokai is one of a few cool cafes here, but is the one the coffee aficionados come to. They grind their own beans here and you can get serious caffeine hits such as nitrogen-infused cold brew.

★**Jugmug Thela** TEAHOUSE
(Map p178; www.jugmugthela.com; Champa Gali, Lane 3, Westend Marg, Saket; teas & coffees ₹70-100, sandwiches ₹120-280; ☺10.30am-8.30pm; ⬤; Ⓜ Saket) Another hidden surprise in Champa Gali – the mini art enclave down Lane 3 behind the fake Dilli Haat store – this tea specialist has more than 180 herbs and spices to work with. It serves delicious ayurvedic teas and other blends, plus organic coffee and fabulously unique sandwich combos (spicy potato and pomegranate; almond and banana) that shouldn't work, but do.

Soi 7 BAR

(DLF Cyber Hub; draught beer from ₹325; ⊙ 11am-1am; Ⓜ Cyber City) Up on the top floor of DLF Cyber Hub, this popular bar brews four different beers in-house (₹325 for a half-litre glass), stocks numerous single-malt whiskeys and whips up a range of cocktails. It does food, too.

☆ Entertainment

The type of entertainment common in big Western cities (theatres, concerts, sports events) is somewhat thin on the ground in Delhi, though the city does have a busy cultural scene, especially during the three-week **Delhi International Arts Festival** (DIAF; www.diaf.in; ⊙ Nov/Dec). October and March also sees annual or one-off shows and concerts (often free) happening nightly.

Kingdom of Dreams THEATRE

(☑ 0124-4528000; www.kingdomofdreams.in; Auditorium Complex, Sector 29, Gurgaon (Gurugram); shows Tue-Fri ₹1199-3199, Sat & Sun ₹1299-4199, refundable entry to Culture Gully ₹600; ⊙ 12.30pm-midnight Tue-Fri, noon-midnight Sat & Sun, showtimes vary; Ⓜ IFFCO Chowk) An entertainment extravaganza, Kingdom of Dreams offers live Bollywood-style shows that are out-and-out sensory assaults. Performances are supported by world-class techno-wizardry, as the cast swing, swoop and sing from the rafters. There's a free shuttle from the metro every 15 minutes, but it's only a 500m walk; come out of Gate 2 and take the first right.

Even if you don't fancy a show, it's worth browsing the food options on Culture Gully – a kitsch but somehow great mock-up of an Indian street that's indoors under a sky dome. The Cultural Gully entrance fee is refundable on purchase of a show ticket.

Next door is the far more modest **open-air theatre** (⊙ 7.30pm Sat; Ⓜ IFFCO Chowk) **FREE**, with free traditional-music performances every Saturday evening.

People & Co COMEDY

(www.canvaslaughclub.com; DLF Cyber Hub; ⊙ nightly; Ⓜ Cyber City) A restaurant and bar with comedy nights every evening, usually from around 7.30pm. Some nights are free. Bigger names bring a cover charge (from ₹500). Check the website for listings.

Indira Gandhi National Centre for the Arts ARTS CENTRE

(Map p160; ☑ 011-23388105; www.ignca.gov.in; 11 Mansingh Rd, near Andhra Bhavan; ⊙ 9am-5.30pm Mon-Fri; Ⓜ Janpath, Central Secretariat, Patel Chowk) A hub of cultural and artsy seminars, exhibitions and performances housed in a well-located, landscaped sprawl not far from India Gate. Frequented by culture vultures for a regular fix of classical and vocal recitals, dance performances, film screenings and literary fests. See the website for forthcoming events and activities.

Habitat World LIVE PERFORMANCE

(Map p160; ☑ 011-43663333; www.habitatworld.com; India Habitat Centre, Lodi Rd; Ⓜ Jor Bagh) This is an important Delhi cultural address, with art exhibitions, performances and concerts, mostly free. Check the website for events.

🔒 Shopping

Wares from all over India glitter in Delhi's step-back-in-time bazaars, emporiums and markets. The city is also increasingly a centre of contemporary design (especially fashion), with independent boutiques and big shiny malls.

Away from government-run emporiums and fixed-price shops, haggle hard, but with good humour. Many drivers earn a commission by taking travellers to overpriced places – don't fall for it.

🔒 Old Delhi

Chandni Chowk CLOTHING, ELECTRONICS

(Map p156; ⊙ approx 10am-7pm; Ⓜ Chandni Chowk) Old Delhi's backbone is an iconic shopping strip, dotted by temples, snarled by traffic and crammed with stores selling everything from street food to saris. Tiny bazaars lead off the main drag, so you can dive off and explore these small lanes, which glitter with jewellery, decorations, paper goods and more.

➤ Kinari Bazaar

(⊙ 11am-8pm; Ⓜ Jama Masjid) Kinari means 'hem' in Hindi, and this colour-blazing market sells all the trimmings that finish off an outfit. It's famous for *zardozi* (gold embroidery), temple trim and wedding turbans, and is extremely photogenic.

➤ Dariba Kalan

(⊙ approx 10am-8pm; Ⓜ Lal Qila) For silver (jewellery, ornaments, old coins), head for Dariba Kalan, the alley near the Sisganj Gurdwara, and with the easy-to-spot Jalebi Wala (p177) at its mouth.

➡ **Nai Sarak**

(🕙 approx 10am-8pm; Ⓜ Jama Masjid) Running south from the old Town Hall, Nai Sarak is lined with stalls selling saris, shawls, chiffon and *lehenga* (blouse and skirt combo).

➡ **Ballimaran**

(🕙 10am-8pm; Ⓜ Chandni Chowk) This area is apparently where Delhi's Yamuna boat operators once lived. Today this market street and the smaller lanes fanning off it specialise in sequined slippers and fancy, curly-toed jootis (traditional slip-on shoes).

⭐ **Spice Market**   MARKET

(Gadodia Market; Map p156; Khari Baoli; Ⓜ Chandni Chowk) It feels as if little has changed for centuries in Delhi's fabulously atmospheric, labyrinthine spice market, as labourers hustle through the narrow lanes with huge packages of herbs and spices on their heads whilst sunlight pours down through cracks in the hessian sacks hanging overhead for shade. The colours are wonderful – red chillies, yellow turmeric, green cardamons – and there's so much spice in the air, people walk around unable to suppress their sneezes.

There are eye-catching displays of everything from lentils and rice to giant jars of chutneys, pickles, nuts and tea, and you can buy small packets of items, despite it being a wholesale market.

Majnu-ka-Tilla   TIBETAN MARKET

(Tibetan Colony, Majnu-ka-Tilla; 🕙 around 10am-8pm; Ⓜ Vidhan Sabha) Delhi's Tibetan enclave, Majnu-ka-Tilla, is a fascinating tangle of tiny alleys – too narrow for vehicles – that are dotted with cheap guesthouses, Tibetan cafes, and dozens of small shops selling all manner of Tibetan trinkets and souvenirs,

---

OLD DELHI MUSICAL INSTRUMENT SHOPS

As well as the many shops and markets to explore in Old Delhi, it's worth browsing the myriad **musical instrument shops** (Map p156; 🕙 approx 10am-8pm Mon-Sat; Ⓜ Delhi Gate, Jama Masjid) along Netaji Subhash Marg for sitars, tabla sets and other beautifully crafted Indian instruments. Expect to pay upwards of ₹20,000 for a decent quality sitar, and around ₹3000 to ₹6000 for a tabla pair.

---

from prayer flags and incense sticks to free-Tibet T-shirts and Buddhist bracelets. It's 2km from Vidhan Sabha metro station (₹30 to ₹40 in an autorickshaw).

Aap Ki Pasand   DRINKS

(San-Cha Tea; Map p156; 🖅 23260373; www.aapkipasandtea.com; 15 Netaji Subhash Marg; 🕙 10am-7pm Mon-Sat; Ⓜ Jama Masjid, Delhi Gate) Specialists in the finest Indian teas, from Darjeeling and Assam to Nilgiri and Kangra. You can try before you buy, and teas come lovingly packaged in drawstring bags. There's another branch at **Santushti Shopping Complex** (San Cha; Map p160; 🖅 011-264530374; www.sanchatea.com; Santushti Shopping Complex, Racecourse Rd; 🕙 10am-7pm Mon-Sat; Ⓜ Lok Kalyan Marg).

🪧 **Paharganj**

Main Bazaar   HANDICRAFTS, CLOTHING

(Map p174; Paharganj; 🕙 10am-9pm Tue-Sun; Ⓜ Ramakrishna Ashram Marg) Backpacker Central, this crazy-busy bazaar that runs through Paharganj sells almost everything you want, and a whole lot more. It's great for buying presents, clothes, inexpensive jewellery bits and bobs, and luggage to put everything in as you're leaving India, or for hippy-dippy clothes to wear on your trip. Haggle with purpose.

Beware the street-side henna scam, where mehndi-wallahs will quote a price for a beautiful henna tattoo only later to reveal that the price was per inch.

Just south of Main Bazaar is a street-side **fruit market** (Map p174; 🕙 8am-10pm; Ⓜ Ramakrishna Ashram Marg), around the corner from which the **Vegetable & Spice Market** (Map p174; 🕙 8am-10pm; Ⓜ Ramakrishna Ashram Marg) is the best place to shop for spices in Paharganj – you should be able to get 100g bags of cumin or coriander powder for just ₹25.

Yes Helping Hands   CLOTHING

(Map p174; www.yeshelpinghands.org; Main Bazaar, Paharganj; 🕙 9am-9pm; Ⓜ Ramakrishna Ashram Marg) 🌱 With its roots in Pokhara, Nepal, this fair-trade nonprofit organisation sells quality weave and knitwear, including pashmina shawls, cashmere scarfs and hemp bags with an aim to helping provide training and employment opportunities for people with disabilities in Nepal and Ladakh.

**Delhi Foundation
of Deaf Women** ARTS & CRAFTS
(DFDW; Map p174; www.dfdw.net; 1st fl, DDA Community Hall, Mantola Mohalla, near Chandi Wali Gali, Paharganj; ⊙10am-6pm Mon-Sat; Ⓜ Ramakrishna Ashram Marg) 🔗 Beautiful handmade handicrafts (bags, purses, gift cards, bookmarks) made by members of the city's deaf foundation and sold from their community hall. Very hard to find; from Main Bazaar, walk up Chandi Wali Gali, turn right at the end, and it's soon on your right, down a tiny alley.

🏠 New Delhi

⭐**Central Cottage
Industries Emporium** ARTS & CRAFTS
(Map p170; 📞011-23326790; Janpath; ⊙10am-7pm; Ⓜ Janpath) This government-run multi-level store is a wonderful treasure trove of fixed-price, India-wide handicrafts. Prices are higher than in the state emporiums, but the selection of woodcarvings, jewellery, pottery, papier mâché, stationery, brassware, textiles (including shawls), toys, rugs, beauty products and miniature paintings makes it a glorious one-stop shop for beautiful crafts. There's the Smoothie cafe by the entrance.

⭐**Kamala** ARTS & CRAFTS
(Map p170; Baba Kharak Singh Marg; ⊙10am-7pm Mon-Sat; Ⓜ Rajiv Chowk) Crafts, curios, textiles and homewares from the Crafts Council of India, designed with flair and using traditional techniques but offering some contemporary, out-of-the-ordinary designs.

State Emporiums HANDICRAFTS, CLOTHING
(Map p170; Baba Kharak Singh Marg; ⊙11am-1.30pm & 2-6.30pm Mon-Sat; Ⓜ Shivaji Stadium) Handily in a row are these regional treasure-filled emporiums. They may have the air of torpor that often afflicts governmental enterprises, but shopping here is like travelling around India – top stops include Kashmir, for papier mâché and carpets; Rajasthan, for miniature paintings and puppets; Uttar Pradesh, for marble inlay work; Karnataka, for sandalwood sculptures; and Odisha, for stone carvings.

Khadi Gramodyog Bhawan CLOTHING
(Map p170; Regal Bldg, 24 Connaught Circus; ⊙11am-7.30pm; Ⓜ Rajiv Chowk) 🔗 Known for its excellent *khadi* (homespun cloth), including good-value shawls, *salwar kameez* and *kurta pyjama,* this three-floor shop also sells handmade paper, incense, spices, henna and lovely natural soaps.

Fabindia CLOTHING, HOMEWARES
(Map p170; www.fabindia.com; 1 A-Block, Connaught Place; ⊙10am-8.30pm; Ⓜ Rajiv Chowk) Surprisingly well-priced, high-quality, ready-made clothes in funky Indian fabrics, from elegant kurtas (long collarless shirts) and dupattas (women's scarves) to Western-style shirts, plus stylish homewares.

The Shop CLOTHING, HOMEWARES
(Map p170; 10 Regal Bldg, Sansad Marg; ⊙9.30am-7.30pm Mon-Sat, 11am-6pm Sun; Ⓜ Janpath, Rajiv Chowk) Gorgeous little boutique with a calm, no-pressure-to-buy ambience, attractive Indian clothing, and light, bright printed-cotton homewares.

Rikhi Ram MUSIC
(Map p170; 📞011-23327685; www.rikhiram.com; 8A G-Block, Connaught Place; ⊙11am-8pm Mon-Sat; Ⓜ Rajiv Chowk) A tiny, but beautiful, old shop selling professional classic and electric sitars, tablas and more. Tablas start at ₹50,000.

Janpath & Tibetan Markets ARTS & CRAFTS
(Map p170; Janpath; ⊙11.30am-7pm Mon-Sat; Ⓜ Rajiv Chowk) These twin markets, made up of small shop fronts stretching along Janpath, sell shimmering mirrorwork embroidery, colourful shawls, Tibetan bric-a-brac, brass Oms, dangly earrings and lots of clothing. There are some good finds if you rummage through the junk, and if you haggle you can get some bargains.

🏠 South Delhi

⭐**Hauz Khas Village** HANDICRAFTS, CLOTHING
(Map p178; Hauz Khas Fort Rd; ⊙11am-7pm Mon-Sat; Ⓜ IIT) This arty little enclave has narrow lanes crammed with boutiques selling designer Indian clothing, handicrafts, contemporary ceramics, handmade furniture and old Bollywood movie posters. Intriguingly, it's located beside numerous 13th- and 14th-century ruins (p163), as well as a forested deer park (⊙5am-8pm; to 7pm winter; Ⓜ IIT, Green Park) FREE and a lake. Standout eating and drinking options include Naivedyam (p183) and Hauz Khas Social (p186).

Shahpur Jat Village MARKET
(Map p178; ⊙10am-7pm Mon-Sat; Ⓜ Hauz Khas, Green Park) Located within the boundaries of the ruined walls of Siri Fort (p163; the second of Delhi's seven historic cities), this urban village contains an artsy collection of high-end clothing boutiques, health-conscious cafes and no frills eateries, many

of which are hidden amongst a network of graffiti-splattered alleyways, making this one of Delhi's more intriguing places to shop.

Standout shops include **Aum** (www. aumdelhi.com; 5G Jungi House, ⊙11am-7pm Mon-Sat; Ⓜ Hauz Khas), for fabulously colourful contemporary Indian women's clothing, and **NeedleDust** (www.needledust.com; 40B, ground fl, Shahpur Jat; ⊙10.30am-7.30pm Mon-Sat; Ⓜ Hauz Khas), for exquisite embroidered jooti (leather slippers). For food, try the excellent Bihari restaurant Potbelly (p183), or hip Cafe Red (p183).

Dilli Haat   ARTS & CRAFTS
(Map p178; Aurobindo Marg; Indian/foreigner ₹30/100; ⊙10.30am-10pm Mar-Nov, 11am-9pm Dec-Feb; Ⓜ INA) Right beside INA metro station, this popular, but somewhat stage-managed, open-air food-and-crafts market is a cavalcade of colour and sells regional handicrafts from all over India; bargain hard. At the far end are lots of regional food stands where you can sample cuisine from every corner of the country. Beware impostors; this is the only real Dilli Haat in Delhi.

🏠 Sunder Nagar, Nizamuddin & Lodi Colony

★**Khan Market**   MARKET
(Map p160; ⊙approx 10.30am-8pm Mon-Sat; Ⓜ Khan Market) 🖉 Khan Market is Delhi's most upmarket shopping enclave, the most expensive place to rent a shop in India, and is favoured by the elite and expats. Its boutiques focus on fashion, books and homewares, and it's also a good place to eat and drink.

For handmade paper, check out **Anand Stationers** (⊙10am-8pm Mon-Sat, noon-6pm Sun), or try **Mehra Bros** (⊙10am-8pm) for cool papier-mâché ornaments. Literature lovers should head to **Full Circle Bookstore** (www.fullcirclebooks.in; 23 Khan Market; ⊙8.30am-8.30pm) and **Bahrisons** (www.books atbahri.com; ⊙10.30am-7.30pm Mon-Sat, 11am-7pm Sun). For Indian clothes and homewares, hit **Fabindia** (⊙10.30am-9.30pm), **Anokhi** (www.anokhi.com; 32 Khan Market; ⊙10am-8pm), or **Good Earth** (9 ABC Khan Market; ⊙11am-8pm), and for elegantly packaged ayurvedic remedies, browse **Kama** (22A Khan Market; ⊙10.30am-8.30pm).

Meharchand Market   MARKET
(Map p160; Lodi Colony; Ⓜ JLN Stadium) Across the road from the government housing of the Lodi Colony, this is a long strip of small boutiques selling homewares and clothes. Quality clothing shops include **Play Clan** (🖉 011-24644393; www.theplayclan.com; shop 17-18; ⊙10.30am-7.30pm; 🚹; Ⓜ Jor Bagh) and **The Shop** (⊙10am-8pm Mon-Sat, 11am-7pm Sun; Ⓜ Jor Bagh), while stand-out eateries are the fully organic **Altitude Cafe & Deli** (www. thealtitudecafe.com; mains ₹340-580; ⊙8.30am-7.30pm; 🖥; Ⓜ JLN Stadium), the Middle Eastern sweets and coffee shop **Kunafa** (sweets per kg from ₹300, coffee ₹250; ⊙10am-10pm; Ⓜ JLN Stadium), and Asian-tapas restaurant **Diva Spiced** (www.divarestaurants.com; dishes ₹550-1350; ⊙11.30am-11.30pm; Ⓜ JLN Stadium).

🏠 Greater Delhi & Gurgaon (Gurugram)

Select Citywalk   MALL
(Map p178; www.selectcitywalk.com; Press Enclave Marg, Saket; ⊙10am-11pm; Ⓜ Malviya Nagar) Enormous, supermodern shopping complex containing three or four interconnected shopping malls, a handful of five-star hotels and even an art gallery. The central mall – Select Citywalk – has top-end clothing stores, plus restaurants, cafes and a couple of cinemas. Attached DLF Place contains more of the same, while quieter DLF South Court houses the stylish **Kiran Nadar Museum of Art** (Map p178; 🖉 011-49160000; www.knma.in; 145 DLF South Court Mall, Select Citywalk, Saket; ⊙10.30am-6.30pm Tue-Sun; Ⓜ Malviya Nagar) FREE.

ℹ️ Information

DANGERS & ANNOYANCES
➡ Delhi is relatively safe in terms of petty crime, though pickpocketing can be a problem in crowded areas so keep your valuables safe.

➡ Roads are notoriously congested; take extreme care when crossing them, or when walking along narrow lanes that don't have footpaths.

➡ Pollution is another real danger in Delhi. Consider wearing a properly fitting face mask.

➡ Women should never walk in lonely, deserted places, even during daylight hours.

➡ Be aware of touts at the airport, train station and around tourist areas.

➡ Beware also of fake tourist offices.

Safety & Women Travellers

Delhi has, unfortunately, a deserved reputation as being unsafe for women. Precautions include never walking around in lonely, deserted places, even during daylight hours, keeping an eye on your route so you don't get lost (download a map that you can use offline) and taking special care after dark – ensure you have a safe means of transport home with, for example, a reputable cab company or driver.

Touts

Taxi-wallahs at the airport and around tourist areas frequently act as touts for hotels, claiming that your hotel is full, poor value, dangerous, burnt down or closed, or that there are riots in Delhi. Any such story is a ruse to steer you to a hotel where they will get a commission. Insist on being taken to where you want to go – making a show of writing down the registration plate number, and phoning the autorickshaw/taxi helpline may help. Men who approach you at Connaught Place run similar scams to direct you to shops and tourist agents, often 'helpfully' informing you that wherever you're headed is closed.

Train Station Hassle

Touts at New Delhi train station endeavour to steer travellers away from the legitimate International Tourist Bureau and into private travel agencies where they earn a commission. Touts often tell people that their tickets are invalid, there's a problem with the trains, or say they're not allowed on the platform. They then 'assist' in booking expensive taxis or 3rd-class tickets passed off as something else. You're particularly vulnerable when arriving tired at night. As a rule of thumb: don't believe anyone who approaches you trying to tell you anything at the train station, even if they're wearing a uniform or have an official-looking pass.

Fake Tourist Offices

Many Delhi travel agencies claim to be tourist offices, even branding themselves with official-looking logos. There is only one India Tourism Delhi office; if you need a travel agent, ask for a list of recommended agents from them. Be wary of booking a multistop trip out of Delhi, particularly to Kashmir. Travellers are often hit for extra charges, or find out they've paid over the odds for the class of travel and accommodation.

INTERNET ACCESS

Pretty much all accommodation and most cafes, bars and restaurants offer free wi-fi access these days. There are some free wi-fi hotspots around the city, in some shopping malls, for example, and in airport buildings. Internet cafes are a thing of the past.

It's easy to gain 3G and 4G access via smartphone data packs bought for local SIM cards.

MEDIA

Newspapers The most respected English-language newspapers in terms of balanced reporting are the *Hindustan Times* (www.hindustantimes.com) and the *Indian Express* (www.indianexpress.com).

Magazines For printed listings see the long-running weekly pamphlet *Delhi Diary* (www.delhidiary.in), which is available at local bookshops. *Motherland* (www.motherlandmagazine.com) is a stylish bi-monthly cultural magazine.

What's On To check out what's on, see the ubercool Little Black Book (https://lbb.in/delhi) or Brown Paper Bag (http://brownpaperbag.in/delhi). And don't miss the Delhi Walla blog (www.thedelhiwalla.com), a wonderful window into Delhi's daily life.

MEDICAL SERVICES

Pharmacies are found on most shopping streets and in most suburban markets. Recommended hospitals include:

All India Institute of Medical Sciences (AIIMS; Map p178; 011-26589142, 011-65900669; www.aiims.edu; Ansari Nagar; AIIMS)

Apollo Hospital (011-26925858, 011-29871090; www.apollohospitals.com/locations/india/delhi; Mathura Rd, Sarita Vihar; Jasola Apollo)

Dr Ram Manohar Lohia Hospital (RML Hospital; Map p160; emergencies 011-23365525, enquiries 011-23404286; www.rmlh.nic.in; Baba Kharak Singh Marg; Patel Chowk)

Max Healthcare (Map p178; 011-26515050; www.maxhealthcare.in; Press Enclave Rd, Saket; Malviya Nagar)

MOBILE PHONES

You can use your unlocked mobile phone from home on roaming, but it's much cheaper to buy a local SIM card. You'll need your passport to register a local SIM, and the details of your accommodation in Delhi.

It's best to buy a local SIM card with a data package either from the airport when you arrive, or from a genuine branch of one of the main phone providers in the city centre; Vodafone or Airtel are the most reliable. If you go through a local shop or kiosk you may experience delays in getting connected, or be overcharged.

Airtel (Map p170; No 5 M-Block, Radial Rd 5, Connaught Place; 10am-8pm Mon-Sat; Rajiv Chowk)

Vodafone (Map p170; D27, Connaught Place; 10.30am-7.30pm Mon-Sat; Rajiv Chowk)

TOURIST INFORMATION

India Tourism Delhi (Government of India; Map p170; ☑ 011-23320008, 011-23320005; www.incredibleindia.org; 88 Janpath; ☺9am-6pm Mon-Fri, to 2pm Sat; Ⓜ Janpath) This official tourist office is a useful source of advice on Delhi, getting out of Delhi, and visiting surrounding states. But note, this is the only official tourist information centre outside the airport. Ignore touts who (falsely) claim to be associated with this office. Anyone who 'helpfully' approaches you is definitely not going to take you to the real office.

Regional tourism offices with a base in Delhi include:

Haryana Tourism (Map p160; ☑ 011-23324911; www.haryanatourism.gov.in; 36 Chander Lok Bldg, Janpath; Ⓜ Janpath)

Rajasthan Tourism (Map p160; ☑ 011-23389525, 011-23381884; www.tourism.rajasthan.gov.in; Pandara Rd, room 8, behind Bikaner House; Ⓜ Khan Market)

Sikkim House (Map p160; 011-2688302; www.sikkim.gov.in; 14 Panchsheel Marg, Chanakyapuri; Ⓜ Lok Kalyan Marg)

POST

There are post offices all over Delhi that can handle letters and parcels (most with packing services nearby, usually directly outside the entrance).

Poste restante is available at India Post's New Delhi **General Post Office** (GPO; Map p160; ☑ 011-23743602; Gole Dakhana, Baba Kharak Singh Marg; ☺10am-5pm Mon-Sat; Ⓜ Patel Chowk); it will keep parcels for up to a month before they are sent back to the sender; as well as the addressee's name, ensure mail is addressed to 'Poste Restante, c/o Postmaster, GPO, New Delhi – 110001'.

For ordinary postal services, it's quicker and easier to use smaller Branches of India Post, such as the one at **Connaught Place** (Map p170; 6 A-Block, Connaught Place; ☺8am-7.30pm Mon-Sat; Ⓜ Rajiv Chowk).

Courier services may be arranged through **DHL** (Map p170; ☑ 011-23737587; ground fl, Mercantile Bldg, Tolstoy Marg; ☺9am-9pm Mon-Sat; Ⓜ Janpath) at Connaught Place.

⊕ Getting There & Away

AIR

Indira Gandhi International Airport

(☑ 01243376000; www.newdelhiairport.in; Ⓜ IGI Airport) is about 14km southwest of the centre. International and domestic flights use Terminal 3. Ageing Terminal 1 is reserved for low-cost carriers. Free shuttle buses (present your boarding pass and onward ticket) run between the two terminals every 20 minutes,

but can take a while. Leave at least three hours between transfers to be safe.

The Arrivals hall at Terminal 3 has 24-hour foreign exchange, ATMs, prepaid taxi and car-hire counters, tourist information, a pharmacy, bookshops, cafes, a **Plaza Premium Lounge** (☑ 011-61233933; www.plazapremiumlounge.com; T3 departures hall, Indira Gandhi International Airport; s/d 3hr ₹2500/3500; Ⓜ IGI Airport) with short-stay rooms (there's another of these at Terminal 1 arrivals) and sleeping pods under the banner of **Sams Snooze at My Space** (☑ 8800444132; www.snoozeatmyspace.com; Terminal 3 International Departures, Indira Gandhi International Airport; s/tw 3hr from ₹2500/4500; ✳☎; Ⓜ IGI Airport).

You'll need to show your aeroplane ticket or boarding pass to enter the Departures building; a digital version on your phone will suffice. If you're meeting someone at the airport, you can pay ₹100 to enter the Arrivals building. Otherwise you'll have to wait outside for them.

Delhi's airport can be prone to thick fog from November to January (often disrupting airline schedules) – it's wise to allow a day between connecting flights during this period.

Airlines include:

Air India (Map p160; ☑ 011-24667100; www.airindia.com; Sri Aurobindo Marg, Safdarjung Airport Area; ☺9.30am-7pm; Ⓜ Jorbagh)

Jagson Airlines (Map p170; ☑ 011-23721593; www.jagsongroup.in; Vandana Bldg, 11 Tolstoy Marg; ☺10am-6pm Mon-Sat; Ⓜ Janpath)

SpiceJet (☑ 9871803333; www.spicejet.com; 319 Udyog Vihar, Phase-IV, Gurgaon (Gurugram); ☺9am-6pm; Ⓜ Cyber City)

BUS

Although train travel is more popular for long distances, buses are a useful option to some closer destinations, or if the trains are booked up.

Practically all state-run services leave from the large **Kashmere Gate Inter State Bus Terminal** (ISBT; Map p156; ☑ 011-23860290; Ⓜ Kashmere Gate) in Old Delhi, accessible by metro (exit gate 7). There are offices representing the states to which buses from here frequently travel to (Haryana, Punjab, Rajasthan, Himachal Pradesh, Uttar Pradesh, Uttarakhand), though they are generally useless, as tickets are instead bought from booths downstairs, beside the individual bus stands. Most destinations are served by both local buses and more comfortable, more expensive AC (air-con) buses. You can't prebook the local buses, and there's no need to anyway; just turn up and buy a ticket on the next available bus. Tickets for AC buses, which are less frequent, can be booked in advance though, either in person a day or two before, or through a travel agent or some hotels.

The **Anand Vihar Inter State Bus Terminal** (Swami Vivekanand Inter State Bus Terminal; Ⓜ Anand Vihar ISBT) has some services to Nainital and Kumaun in Uttarakhand. Some cheaper buses to destinations in Uttar Pradesh, Madhya Pradesh and Rajasthan leave from the Sarai Kale Khan Inter State Bus Terminal (ISBT) on the ring road near Nizamuddin train station. **Himachal Bhawan** (Map p160; ☎ 011-23716689; Sikandra Rd; Ⓜ Mandi House) has buses to Manali and Shimla, both in Himachal Pradesh.

There are buses to Agra, but considering the traffic at either end, you're better off taking the train.

SELECTED TRAINS FROM DELHI

DESTINATION	TRAIN NO & NAME	FARE (₹)	DURA-TION (HR)	FREQUENCY	DEPARTURES & TRAIN STATION
Agra	12280 Taj Exp	105/375 (A)	3	1 daily	6.45am NDLS
	12002 Bhopal Shatabdi	525/1020 (B)	2	1 daily	6am NDLS
Amritsar	12029 Swarna Shatabdi	905/1725 (B)	6½	1 daily	7.20am NDLS
	12013 Amritsar Shatabdi	905/1725 (B)	6	1 daily	4.30pm NDLS
Bengaluru (Bangalore)	22692 Bangalore Rajdhani	3010/4190/6795 (C)	34	4 weekly	8.45pm NZM
Chennai	12434 Chennai Rajdhani	2910/4020/6475 (C)	29	2 weekly	3.55pm NZM
	12622 Tamil Nadu Exp	780/2050/3005 (D)	33	1 daily	10.30pm NDLS
Goa (Madgaon)	12432 Trivandrum Rajdhani	2705/3780/6175 (C)	25½	3 weekly	10.55am NZM
	12780 Goa Exp	775/2040/2990 (D)	38½	1 daily	3pm NZM
Haridwar	12017 Dehradun Shatabdi	610/1200 (B)	5	1 daily	6.45am NDLS
Jaipur	12958 ADI Swama Jayanti Rajdani	825/1100/1710 (C)	4½	1 daily	7.55pm NDLS
	12916 Ashram Exp	235/595/830 (D)	5	1 daily	3.20pm DLI
	12015 Ajmer Shatabdi	655/1305 (B)	4½	1 daily	6.05am NDLS
Kalka (for Shimla)	12011 Kalka Shatabdi	615/1270 (B)	4	2 daily	7.40am NDLS
Khajuraho	12448 UP Sampark Kranti Exp	365/960/1360 (D)	10½	1 daily	8.10pm NZM
Lucknow	12004 Lucknow Swran Shatabdi	910/1865 (B)	6½	1 daily	6.10am NDLS
Mumbai	12952 Mumbai Rajdhani	2105/2925/4760 (C)	16	1 daily	4.25pm NDLS
	12954 August Kranti Rajdani	2105/2925/4760 (C)	17	1 daily	4.50pm NZM
Udaipur	12963 Mewar Exp	415/1100/1565 (D)	12½	1 daily	7pm NZM
Varanasi	12560 Shivganga Exp	415/1105//1575 (D)	12	1 daily	6.55pm NDLS

Train stations: NDLS – New Delhi; DLI – Old Delhi; NZM – Hazrat Nizamuddin
Fares: (A) 2nd class/chair car; (B) chair car/1st-class AC; (C) 3AC/2AC/1st-class AC; (D) sleeper/3AC/2AC

DELHI GETTING THERE & AWAY

Wherever you're going, it's wise to arrive at the bus station at least 30 minutes ahead of your departure time.

Note that some, more expensive, private deluxe buses leave from other locations in central Delhi – enquire at travel agencies or your hotel for details. You can also book tickets or check information on Cleartrip (www.cleartrip. com), Make My Trip (www.makemytrip.com), Goibibo (www.goibibo.com) or Red Bus (www. redbus.in).

Ambedkar Stadium Bus Stand (Map p156; ☑ 011-23318180; Ambedkar Stadium; Ⓜ Delhi Gate) has international bus services to Kathmandu in Nepal, and Lahore in Pakistan.

TRAIN

There are three main stations in Delhi: (Old) Delhi train station (aka Delhi Junction) in Old Delhi, New Delhi train station near Paharganj, and Nizamuddin train station, south of Sunder Nagar. Make sure you know which station your train is leaving from. All three have metro stations outside them.

New Delhi Railway Station (btwn Ajmeri Gate & Main Bazaar Paharganj; ⊙ 24hr; Ⓜ New Delhi) is the largest and best connected of Delhi's train stations, and the best option for foreign travellers wanting to buy train tickets, thanks to its very helpful **International Tourist Bureau** (ITB; Map p174; ☑ 011-23405156; 1st fl, New Delhi Train Station; ⊙ 6am-10pm; Ⓜ New Delhi), a ticket office reserved solely for the use of foreign travellers (you have to show a foreign passport to even be allowed inside). To find it, walk in the station's main entrance (on the Paharganj side of the train station) then, just before you reach platform 1, walk up the staircase to your right. At the 1st floor turn right and the office is along the corridor on your left. Do *not* believe anyone who tells you this ticket office has shifted, closed or burnt down – this is a scam to divert you elsewhere. Walk with confidence and ignore all 'helpful' or 'official' approaches. The ITB is a large room with about 10 or more computer terminals – don't be fooled by other 'official' offices.

Once inside, first take a queuing number. While you wait for your number, go to the information desk to one side of the room to get details of your journey. Once you know which train you wish to book, fill in one of the passenger booking slips and take it, along with your passport, to the booking desks once your number has come up. You can pay with cash or card.

There's also a public **Train Reservation Office** (Map p174; Chelmsford Rd; ⊙ 8am-8pm; Ⓜ New Delhi) a few hundred metres outside the train station, closer towards Connaught Place. Anyone, local or foreign, can buy train tickets here,

but for foreigners it makes no sense to come here where queues are longer and English-language skills less prevalent. There's also an **Unreserved Booking Office** (Map p174; New Delhi train station; ⊙ 24hr; Ⓜ New Delhi) to your right as you exit the train station (again, at the Paharganj side of the station). This is for buying same-day 'general' tickets to nearby destinations; a very cheap option, but although you'll be allowed to get on the train, you're not guaranteed a seat.

❶ Getting Around

TO/FROM THE AIRPORT

Metro The easiest and quickest way from the airport to the centre is via the metro's Airport Express line (www.delhimetrorail.com), which runs from 5.15am to 11.40pm and costs ₹60/50 from the international/domestic terminal to New Delhi Railway Station.

Bus AC buses also run from outside Terminal 3 to the centre.

Taxi Use the Delhi Traffic Police Prepaid Taxi counter outside both terminals. A trip to the centre costs ₹350 to ₹450. Many hotels can arrange a pick-up, which will be less hassle, though more expensive than arranging a taxi yourself.

AUTORICKSHAW & E-RICKSHAW

Delhi's signature green-and-yellow autorickshaws are everywhere. You never have to worry about finding one – drivers will find you! They have meters, but they are never used, so ensure you negotiate the fare clearly before you start your journey. As a guide, Paharganj to Connaught Place should cost around ₹30.

Delhi Traffic Police run a network of prepaid autorickshaw booths, where you pay a fixed fare in return for a ticket that you hand over to the driver once you reach your destination. There are 24-hour booths outside the three main train stations; **New Delhi** (Map p174; outside New Delhi Railway Station, Paharganj side; ⊙ 24hr; Ⓜ New Delhi), **Old Delhi** (Map p156; outside Old Delhi Railway Station; ⊙ 24hr; Ⓜ Chandni Chowk) and **Nizamuddin** (Map p160; outside Nizamuddin Railway Station). Other booths are outside the **India Tourism** (Map p170; 88 Janpath; ⊙ 11am-8.30pm; Ⓜ Janpath, Rajiv Chowk) Delhi office and at **Central Park** (Map p170; Central Park, Connaught Place; Ⓜ Rajiv Chowk), Connaught Place.

Fares with ordinary autos are invariably elevated for foreigners, so haggle hard, and if the fare sounds too outrageous, find another ride.

An auto ride from Connaught Place should be around ₹30 to Paharganj, ₹60 to the Red Fort, ₹70 to Humayun's Tomb and ₹100 to Hauz Khas.

TAXI APPS & AUTO APPS

Car-sharing services Uber (www.uber.com/in/en) and Ola Cabs (www.olacabs.com) have transformed travel around Delhi. Uber Autos is another option on the Uber app, and helps find you an autorickshaw rather than a taxi. They are even cheaper than the taxis.

Note that drivers will almost always call you en route, asking for directions and clarification of where you want to go (even though this information is in front of them on their phone's app), and will often not be able to speak English, so you'll sometimes have to get a bilingual local to help with communication.

Cabs also tend to take a lot longer to arrive than your app says, and they often arrive at a point that is a short walk from the agreed pick-up.

Given these issues, it's usually much quicker to hail an ordinary autorickshaw or taxi from the roadside. However, Uber and Ola do tend to work out cheaper.

However, it will be a struggle to get these prices. From 11pm to 5am there's a 25% surcharge.

To report overcharging, harassment, or other problems take the licence number and call the **Auto Complaint Line** (☏ 011-42400400, 25844444).

Delhi's ever-expanding fleet of golf-cart-lookalike e-rickshaws (electric rickshaws) offer a more environmentally friendly alternative to autorickshaws and taxis. Many of them are shared rickshaws, plying fixed routes for very cheap individual fares, but many can also be hired privately. Fares should be roughly the same as autorickshaws.

BICYCLE

Bike Rental New Delhi Municipal Council (NDMC) unveiled 250 shiny new smart bikes (www.smartbikemobility.com) in November 2018, hoping to soon expand the fleet to 500. Bikes are docked at 23 stations, mostly around central New Delhi for now, and are unlocked via a mobile app. The first 30 minutes of use is free. Foreigners need a local mobile phone number to register, but can link their account to a foreign bank card (VISA or Mastercard only). And word is, e-scooters are next!

Bike Tours DelhiByCycle (p171) offers recommended cycle tours.

Purchase To buy your own bike, head to the **Jhandewalan Cycle Market** (Map p156; ⊙11am-8pm; Ⓜ Jhandewalan), near Videocon Tower, five minutes walk from Jhandewalan metro station.

BUS

Foreign travellers rarely use Delhi's public buses, which can get crowded and are difficult to negotiate for non-Hindi-speaking passengers. But there are several useful routes, including the Airport Express bus and Bus GL-23, which connects the Kashmere Gate and Anand Vihar bus stations. Most short hops cost around ₹10.

CYCLE RICKSHAW

Cycle-rickshaws are useful (and great fun) for navigating Old Delhi and the suburbs, but they are banned from many parts of New Delhi, including Connaught Place (though they'll still drop you off there from Paharganj). Negotiate a fare before you set off – expect to pay ₹20 to ₹30 for a short trip. Tip well; it's a tough job, and many rickshaw riders are homeless and spend the nights sleeping on their rickshaws.

METRO

Delhi's **metro** (www.delhimetrorail.com; single journey ₹10-60) is fast and efficient, with signs and arrival/departure announcements in Hindi and English. Trains run from around 6am to 11pm and the first carriage in the direction of travel is reserved for women only. Trains can get insanely busy at peak commuting times (around 9am to 10am and 5pm to 6pm) – avoid travelling with luggage during rush hour if at all possible (however, the Airport Express line is much less busy and has plenty of luggage space).

Tokens (₹10 to ₹60) are sold at metro stations. A metro smart card (₹50 deposit plus ₹100 minimum initial top-up) gets you 10% off all journeys (20% outside the peak hours of 8am to noon and 5pm to 9pm). There are also tourist cards (one-day card ₹200 plus ₹50 deposit; three-day card ₹500 plus ₹50 deposit), but they're really not worth it unless you're planning on taking a lot of metro journeys, as most journeys only cost around ₹20.

Because of security concerns, all bags are X-rayed and passengers must pass through an airport-style scanner.

TAXI

Local taxis (recognisable by their black-and-yellow livery) have meters but, like the ones in autorickshaws, these are effectively ornamental as most drivers refuse to use them; ensure you negotiate a price before you start your trip.

Taxis typically charge twice the autorickshaw fare. Note that fares vary as fuel prices go up and down. From 11pm to 5am there's a 25% surcharge for autorickshaws and taxis.

Kumar Tourist Taxi Service (Map p170; ☏ 011-23415930; www.kumarindiatours.com; 14/1 K-Block, Connaught Place; ☺ 8am-9pm) A reliable company; a day of Delhi sightseeing costs from ₹3000 (an eight-hour and 80km limit applies).

Metropole Tourist Service (Map p160; ☏ 011-24310313, 9810277699; www.metrovista.co.in; 224 Defence Colony Flyover Market; ☺ 8am-6.30pm; Ⓜ Jangpura) Another reliable and long-running taxi service, and decent value, too.

Agra & the Taj Mahal

Best Places to Eat

➡ Pinch of Spice (p210)

➡ Mama Chicken (p210)

➡ Esphahan (p210)

➡ Culinary Junction (p210)

Best Places to Stay

➡ Tourists Rest House (p209)

➡ Bansi Homestay (p208)

➡ Oberoi Amarvilas (p208)

➡ Retreat (p208)

Why Go?

The Taj Mahal rises from Agra's haze as though from a dream. You've seen it in pictures, but experiencing it in person, you'll understand that it's not just a famous monument, but a love poem composed of stone. When you first glimpse it through the arched entryway, you might find yourself breathless with awe. Many hail it as the most beautiful building on the planet.

But Agra, situated along the Yamuna River in the state of Uttar Pradesh, is more than a one-sight town. For 130 years, this was the centre of India's great Mughal empire, and its legacy lives on in beautiful artwork, mouthwatering cuisine and magnificent architecture. The Taj is one of three places here that have been awarded Unesco World Heritage status, along with the immense Agra Fort and the sprawling palace complex of Fatehpur Sikri, which together make a superb trio of top-drawer sights.

When to Go

Agra

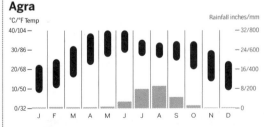

Mid-Sep–Oct The best time to visit: monsoon rains are over and summer temperatures have cooled.

Nov–Feb Daytime temperatures are comfortable but big sights are overcrowded. Evenings are nippy.

Mar Evening chill is gone but raging-hot mid-summer temperatures haven't yet materialised.

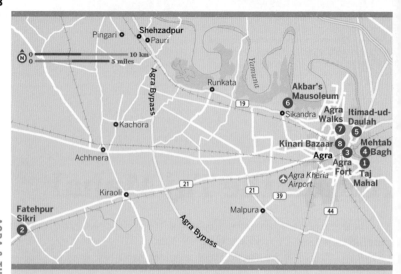

Agra & the Taj Mahal Highlights

❶ **Taj Mahal** (p199) Basking in the beauty of one of the most famous buildings in the world – a must-see!

❷ **Fatehpur Sikri** (p214) Roaming a sprawling palace complex from Mughal times, with an immense and fascinating 450-year-old mosque next door.

❸ **Agra Fort** (p202) Wandering the many rooms of one of India's most impressive ancient forts.

❹ **Mehtab Bagh** (p205) Relaxing in gardens with perfect sunset views of the Taj.

❺ **Itimad-ud-Daulah** (p205) Marvelling at the marblework of an exquisite tomb nicknamed the Baby Taj.

❻ **Akbar's Mausoleum** (p205) Visiting the impressive resting place of the greatest Mughal emperor.

❼ **Agra Walks** (p206) Strolling deeper into ancient Agra with local guides.

❽ **Kinari Bazaar** (p205) Boggling your senses in one of India's most mesmerising – and hectic – markets.

Agra

☎ 0562 / POP 1.7 MILLION

History

In 1501 Sultan Sikander Lodi established his capital here, but the city fell into Mughal hands in 1526, when Emperor Babur defeated the last Lodi sultan at Panipat, 90km north of Delhi, to found the Mughal dynasty. Agra reached the peak of its magnificence between the mid-16th and mid-17th centuries as the capital of the Mughal empire during the reigns of Akbar, Jehangir and Shah Jahan. During this period, the fort, the Taj Mahal and other major mausoleums were built. In 1638 Shah Jahan built a new city in Delhi, and his son Aurangzeb moved the capital there 10 years later.

In 1761 Agra fell to the Jats, a warrior class who looted its monuments, including the Taj Mahal. The Marathas took over in 1770, but were replaced by the British in 1803. Following the First War of Independence (Indian Uprising) in 1857, the British shifted the administration of the province to Allahabad (now Prayagraj). Deprived of its administrative role, Agra developed as a centre for heavy industry, quickly becoming famous for its chemicals industry and air pollution, before the Taj and tourism became a major source of income.

⊙ Sights

The entrance fee for Agra's five main sights – the Taj, Agra Fort, Fatehpur Sikri, Akbar's Tomb and Itimad-ud-Daulah – comprises charges from two different bodies: the Archaeological Survey of India (ASI) and the

Agra Development Association (ADA). Of the ₹1100 basic ticket for the Taj Mahal, ₹500 is a special ADA ticket, which gives you small savings on the other four sights if visited in the same day. You'll save ₹50 at Agra Fort and ₹10 each at Fatehpur Sikri, Akbar's Tomb and Itimad-ud-Daulah. You can buy this ₹500 ADA ticket at any of the five sights – just say you intend to visit the Taj later that day.

All the other sights in Agra are either free or have ASI tickets only, which aren't included in the ADA one-day offer.

Admission to all sights is free for children under 15. On Fridays, many sights offer a modest discount of ₹10 (but note that the Taj is closed on Friday).

⭐ **Taj Mahal**   HISTORIC BUILDING
(Map p207; ☎0562-2330498; www.tajmahal.gov.in; Indian/foreigner ₹50/1100, mausoleum ₹200, video ₹25; ☺dawn-dusk Sat-Thu) Poet Rabindranath Tagore described it as 'a teardrop on the cheek of eternity'; Rudyard Kipling as 'the embodiment of all things pure'; while its creator, Emperor Shah Jahan, said it made 'the sun and the moon shed tears from their eyes'. Every year, tourists numbering more than twice the population of Agra pass through its gates to catch a once-in-a-lifetime glimpse of what is widely considered the most beautiful building in the world. Few leave disappointed.

The Taj was built by Shah Jahan as a memorial for his third wife, Mumtaz Mahal, who died giving birth to their 14th child in 1631. The death of Mumtaz left the emperor so heartbroken that his hair is said to have turned grey virtually overnight. Construction of the Taj began the following year; although the main building is thought to have been built in eight years, the whole complex was not completed until 1653. Not long after it was finished, Shah Jahan was overthrown by his son Aurangzeb and imprisoned in Agra Fort, where for the rest of his days he could only gaze out at his creation through a window. Following his death in 1666, Shah Jahan was buried here alongside his beloved Mumtaz.

In total, some 20,000 people from India and Central Asia worked on the building. Specialists were brought in from as far away as Europe to produce the exquisite marble screens and pietra dura (marble inlay work) made with thousands of semiprecious stones.

The Taj was designated a World Heritage Site in 1983 and looks nearly as immacu-

DON'T MISS

TAJ MUSEUM

Within the Taj complex, on the western side of the gardens, is the small but excellent **Taj Museum** (Map p207; ☺10am-5pm Sat-Thu) FREE, housing a number of original Mughal miniature paintings, including a pair of 17th-century ivory portraits of Emperor Shah Jahan and his beloved wife Mumtaz Mahal. It also has some very well preserved gold and silver coins dating from the same period, plus architectural drawings of the Taj and some celadon plates, said to split into pieces or change colour if the food served on them contains poison.

late today as when it was first constructed – though it underwent a huge restoration project in the early 20th century.

Note: the Taj is closed every Friday to anyone not attending prayers at the mosque.

➡ **Entry & Information**
The Taj can be accessed through the west and east gates. The south gate was closed to visitors in 2018 for security concerns but can be used to exit the Taj. The east gate generally has shorter queues. There are separate queues for men and women at both gates. If you are a foreigner, once you get your ticket, you can skip ahead of the lines of Indians waiting to get in – one perk of your pricey entry fee. It's possible to buy your tickets online in advance at https://asi.payumoney.com (you'll get a ₹50 discount for your troubles), but you won't save much time as you still have to join the main security queue. A ticket that includes entrance to the mausoleum itself cost ₹200 extra.

Cameras and videos are permitted, but you can't take photographs inside the mausoleum itself. Tripods are banned.

Remember to retrieve your free 500ml bottle of water and shoe covers (included in Taj ticket price). Bags much bigger than a money pouch are not allowed inside; free bag storage is available. Any food or tobacco will be confiscated when you go through security, as will pens.

➡ **Inside the Grounds**
From both the east and west gates you first enter a monumental inner courtyard with an impressive 30m red-sandstone gateway on the south side.

continued on p202

continued on p202

Taj Mahal

TIMELINE

1631 Emperor Shah Jahan's beloved third wife, Mumtaz Mahal, dies in Buhanpur while giving birth to their 14th child. Her body is initially interred in Buhanpur itself, where Shah Jahan is fighting a military campaign, but is later moved, in a golden casket, to a small building on the banks of the Yamuna River in Agra.

1632 Construction of a permanent mausoleum for Mumtaz Mahal begins.

1633 Mumtaz Mahal is interred in her final resting place, an underground tomb beneath a marble plinth, on top of which the Taj Mahal will be built.

1640 The white-marble mausoleum is completed.

1653 The rest of the Taj Mahal complex is completed.

1658 Emperor Shah Jahan is overthrown by his son Aurangzeb and imprisoned in Agra Fort.

1666 Shah Jahan dies. His body is transported along the Yamuna River and buried underneath the Taj, alongside the tomb of his wife.

1908 Repeatedly damaged and looted after the fall of the Mughal empire, the Taj receives some long-overdue attention as part of a major restoration project ordered by British viceroy Lord Curzon.

1983 The Taj is awarded Unesco World Heritage Site status.

2002 Having been discoloured by pollution in more recent years, the Taj is spruced up with an ancient recipe known as multani mitti – a blend of soil, cereal, milk and lime once used by Indian women to beautify their skin.

Today More than three million tourists visit the Taj Mahal each year. That's more than twice the current population of Agra.

ARIS ABDULLAH/SHUTTERSTOCK ©

GO BAREFOOT

Help the environment by entering the mausoleum barefoot instead of using the free disposable shoe covers.

Pishtaqs
These huge arched recesses are set into each side of the Taj. They provide depth to the building while their central, latticed marble screens allow patterned light to illuminate the inside of the mausoleum.

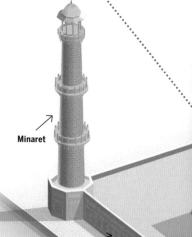

Minaret

Plinth

Entran

Marble Relief Work
Flowering plants, thought to be representations of paradise, are a common theme among the beautifully decorative panels carved onto the white marble.

FABIOLUM/GETTY IMAGES ©

LIGHT THE WAY

Use the torch on your smartphone to fully appreciate the translucency of the white marble and semi-precious stones.

Filigree Screen
This stunning screen was carved out of a single piece of marble. It surrounds both cenotaphs, allowing patterned light to fall onto them through its intricately carved *jali* (latticework).

PJHPIX/SHUTTERSTOCK ©

Central Dome
The Taj's famous central dome, topped by a brass finial, represents the vault of heaven, a stark contrast to the material world, which is represented by the square shape of the main structure.

Yamuna River

NORTH →

Cenotaphs
The cenotaphs of Mumtaz Mahal and Shah Jahan, decorated with pietra dura inlay work, are actually fake tombs. The real ones are located in an underground vault closed to the public.

COLOR CHASER/SHUTTERSTOCK ©

Calligraphy
The strips of calligraphy surrounding each of the four pishtaqs get larger as they get higher, giving the impression of uniform size when viewed from the ground. There's also calligraphy inside the mausoleum, including on Mumtaz Mahal's cenotaph.

Pietra Dura
It's believed that 35 different precious and semi-precious stones were used to create the exquisite pietra dura (marble inlay work) found on the inside and outside of the mausoleum walls. Again, floral designs are common.

FRENTUSHA/GETTY IMAGES ©

continued from p199

The ornamental gardens are set out along classical Mughal *charbagh* (formal Persian garden) lines – a square quartered by water-courses, with an ornamental marble plinth at its centre. When the fountains are not flowing, the Taj is beautifully reflected in the water.

The Taj Mahal itself stands on a raised marble platform at the northern end of the ornamental gardens, with its back to the Yamuna River. Its raised position means that the backdrop is only sky – a masterstroke of design. Purely decorative 40m-high white minarets grace each corner of the platform. After more than three centuries they are not quite perpendicular, but they may have been designed to lean slightly outwards so that in the event of an earthquake they would fall away from the precious Taj. The red-sand-stone mosque to the west is an important gathering place for Agra's Muslims. The identical building to the east, the jawab, was built for symmetry.

The central Taj structure is made of semitranslucent white marble, carved with flowers and inlaid with thousands of semi-precious stones in beautiful patterns. A perfect exercise in symmetry, the four identical faces of the Taj feature impressive vaulted arches embellished with pietra dura scroll-work and quotations from the Quran in a style of calligraphy using inlaid jasper. The whole structure is topped off by four small domes surrounding the famous bulbous central dome.

Directly below the main dome is the Cen-otaph of Mumtaz Mahal, an elaborate false tomb surrounded by an exquisite perforated marble screen inlaid with dozens of different types of semiprecious stones. Beside it, offsetting the symmetry of the Taj, is the Cenotaph of Shah Jahan, who was interred here with little ceremony by his usurping son Aurangzeb in 1666. Light is admitted into the central chamber by finely cut marble screens.

The real tombs of Mumtaz Mahal and Shah Jahan are in a basement room below the main chamber.

★ **Agra Fort** FORT
(Lal Qila; Map p203; Indian/foreigner ₹50/650, video ₹25; ☉ dawn-dusk) With the Taj Mahal overshadowing it, one can easily forget that Agra has one of the finest Mughal forts in India. Walking through courtyard after courtyard of this palatial red-sandstone and marble fortress, your amazement grows as the scale of what was built here begins to sink in.

Construction along the bank of the Yamuna River was begun by Emperor Akbar in 1565 on the site of an earlier fort. Further additions were made, particularly by his grandson Shah Jahan, using his favourite building material – white marble. The fort was built primarily as a military structure, but Shah Jahan transformed it into a palace, and later it became his gilded prison for eight years after his son Aurangzeb seized power in 1658.

The ear-shaped fort's colossal double walls rise more than 20m and measure 2.5km in circumference. The Yamuna River originally flowed along the straight eastern edge of the fort, and the emperors had their own bathing ghats here. It contains a maze of buildings, forming a city within a city, including vast underground sections, though many of the structures were destroyed over the years by Nadir Shah, the Marathas, the Jats and finally the British, who used the fort as a garrison. Even today, much of the fort is used by the military and is off-limits to the general public.

The Amar Singh Gate to the south is the sole entry point to the fort these days and where you buy your entrance ticket. Its dog-leg design was meant to confuse attackers who made it past the first line of defence – the crocodile-infested moat.

Following the plain processional way you reach a gateway and the huge red-sandstone Jehangir's Palace on the right. In front of the palace is Hauz-i-Jehangir, a huge bowl carved out of a single block of stone, which was used for bathing. The palace was probably built by Akbar for his son Jehangir. With tall stone pillars and corner brackets, it blends Indian and Central Asian architectural styles, a reminder of the Mughals' Turkestani cultural roots.

Further along the eastern edge of the fort you'll find the Khas Mahal, a beautiful marble pavilion and pool that formed the living quarters of Shah Jahan. Taj views are framed in the ornate marble grills.

The large courtyard here is Anguri Bagh, a garden that has been brought back to life in recent years. In the courtyard is an innocuous-looking entrance – now locked – that leads down a flight of stairs into a two-storey labyrinth of underground rooms and passageways where Akbar used to keep his 500-strong harem. On the northeast corner of the courtyard you can get a glimpse of the

Agra

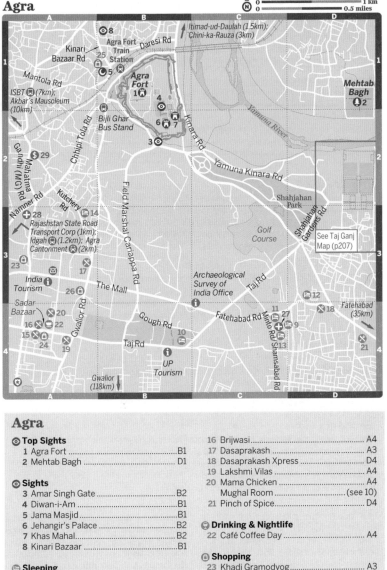

Itimad-ud-Daulah (1.5km);
Chini-ka-Rauza (3km)

See Taj Ganj
Map (p207)

Fatehabad
(35km)

UP
Tourism

Gwalior
(118km)

Agra

⊚ Top Sights
1 Agra Fort	B1
2 Mehtab Bagh	D1

⊚ Sights
3 Amar Singh Gate	B2
4 Diwan-i-Am	B1
5 Jama Masjid	B1
6 Jehangir's Palace	B2
7 Khas Mahal	B2
8 Kinari Bazaar	B1

⊜ Sleeping
9 Bansi Homestay	D4
10 Clarks Shiraz Hotel	B4
11 Hotel Amar	C4
Hotel Atithi	(see 11)
12 Howard Plaza	D3
13 N Homestay	C4
14 Tourists Rest House	A3

⊗ Eating
15 Agra Chat House	A4
16 Brijwasi	A4
17 Dasaprakash	A3
18 Dasaprakash Xpress	D4
19 Lakshmi Vilas	A4
20 Mama Chicken	A4
Mughal Room	(see 10)
21 Pinch of Spice	D4

⊜ Drinking & Nightlife
22 Café Coffee Day	A4

⊜ Shopping
23 Khadi Gramodyog	A3
24 Modern Book Depot	A4
25 Subhash Bazaar	B1
26 Subhash Emporium	A3

ⓘ Information
27 Amit Jaggi Memorial Hospital	C4
Bagpacker Travel	(see 14)
28 SR Hospital	A3
29 State Bank of India	A2

TOP TAJ VIEWS

The Taj is arguably at its most atmospheric at sunrise. This is certainly the most comfortable time to visit in summer, and although it's still popular, there are fewer crowds than later in the day. Sunset is another magical viewing time.

Inside the Grounds

You may have to pay ₹1100 for the privilege, but it's only when you're inside the grounds themselves that you can really get up close and personal with the world's most beautiful building. Don't miss inspecting the marble inlay work (pietra dura) inside the *pishtaqs* (large arched recesses) on the four outer walls. Shine the torch (flashlight) on your phone onto the pietra dura work inside the dark central chamber of the mausoleum (₹200 extra) and you'll see the translucency of both the white marble and the semiprecious stones inlaid into it.

From Mehtab Bagh

Tourists are no longer allowed to wander freely along the riverbank on the opposite side of the Yamuna River, but you can still enjoy a view of the back of the Taj from the 16th-century Mughal park Mehtab Bagh (p205), with the river flowing between you and the mausoleum. A path leading down to the river beside the park offers the same view for free, albeit from a more restricted angle. Guards stop visitors entering both spots 30 minutes before sunset.

Looking Up from the South Bank of the River

This is a great place to be for sunset. Take the path that hugs the outside of the Taj's eastern wall and walk all the way down to the small temple beside the river. You should be able to find boathands down here willing to row you out onto the water for an even more romantic view. Expect to pay around ₹150 per boat. For safety reasons, it's best not to wander down here on your own for sunset.

On a Rooftop Cafe in Taj Ganj

Perfect for sunrise shots: there are some wonderful photos to be had from the numerous rooftop cafes in Taj Ganj. We think the cafe on Saniya Palace Hotel (p206) is the pick of the bunch, with its plant-filled design and great position, but many of them are good. And all offer the bonus of being able to view the Taj with the added comfort of an early-morning cup of coffee.

From Agra Fort

With a decent zoom lens you can capture some fabulous images of the Taj from Agra Fort (p202), especially if you're willing to get up at the crack of dawn to see the sun rising up from behind it (the fort opens 30 minutes before dawn). The best places to snap from are probably the Khas Mahal or Muthamman Burj, the octagonal tower and palace where Shah Jahan was imprisoned for eight years until his death.

Shish Mahal (Mirror Palace), with walls inlaid with tiny mirrors.

Just to the north of the Khas Mahal is the Mathamman (Shah) Burj, the wonderful white-marble octagonal tower and palace where Shah Jahan was imprisoned for eight years until his death in 1666, and from where he could gaze out at the Taj Mahal, the tomb of his wife. When he died, Shah Jahan's body was taken from here by boat to the Taj. The now-closed Mina Masjid served as Shah Jahan's private mosque.

As you enter the large courtyard, along the eastern wall of the fort, is Diwan-i-Khas (Hall of Private Audiences), which was re-served for important dignitaries or foreign representatives. The hall once housed Shah Jahan's legendary Peacock Throne, which was inset with precious stones – including the famous Koh-i-noor diamond. The throne was taken to Delhi by Aurangzeb, then to Iran in 1739 by Nadir Shah and dismantled after his assassination in 1747. Overlooking the river and the distant Taj Mahal is Takhti-i-Jehangir, a huge slab of black rock with an inscription around the edge. The throne that stood here was made for Jehangir when he was Prince Salim.

Following the north side of the courtyard a side door leads to the tiny but exquisite white-marbled Nagina Masjid (Gem Mosque), built in 1635 by Shah Jahan for the ladies of the court. Down below was the Ladies' Bazaar, where the court ladies bought their goods.

A hidden doorway near the mosque exit leads down to the scallop-shaped arches of the large, open Diwan-i-Am (Hall of Public Audiences), which was used by Shah Jahan for domestic government business, and features a beautifully decorated throne room where the emperor listened to petitioners. In front of it is the small and rather incongruous grave of John Colvin, a lieutenant-governor of the northwest provinces who died of an illness while sheltering in the fort during the 1857 First War of Independence. To the north is the Moti Masjid, currently off limits to visitors. From here head back to the Amar Singh gate.

You can walk to the fort from Taj Ganj via the leafy Shah Jahan Park, or take an autorickshaw for ₹80. Food is not allowed in the fort. The fort opens 30 minutes before sunrise; the ticket office opens 15 minutes before that. Last entry is 30 minutes before sunset.

★ **Mehtab Bagh**   PARK
(Map p203; Indian/foreigner ₹25/300, video ₹25; ⊙dawn-dusk) This park, originally built by Emperor Babur as the last in a series of 11 parks on the Yamuna's east bank (long before the Taj was conceived), fell into disrepair until it was little more than a huge mound of sand. To protect the Taj from the erosive effects of the sand blown across the river, the park was reconstructed and is now one the best places from which to view the great mausoleum.

The gardens in the Taj are perfectly aligned with the ones here, and the view of the Taj from the fountain directly in front of the entrance gate is a classic. It's a popular spot at sunset; the ticket office closes 30 minutes before sunset, so don't leave it too late. An autorickshaw here from central Agra costs around ₹150.

★ **Itimad-ud-Daulah**   HISTORIC BUILDING
(Indian/foreigner ₹30/310, video ₹25; ⊙dawn-dusk) Nicknamed the Baby Taj, the exquisite tomb of Mizra Ghiyas Beg should not be missed. This Persian nobleman was Mumtaz Mahal's grandfather and Emperor Jehangir's *wazir* (chief minister). His daughter, Nur Jahan, who married Jehangir, built the tomb between 1622 and 1628, in a style similar to

the tomb she built for Jehangir near Lahore in Pakistan.

It doesn't have the same awesome beauty as the Taj, but it's arguably more delicate in appearance thanks to its particularly finely carved marble *jalis* (lattice screens). This was the first Mughal structure built completely from marble, the first to make extensive use of pietra dura and the first tomb to be built on the banks of the Yamuna, which until then had been a sequence of beautiful pleasure gardens.

You can combine a trip here with Chini-ka-Rauza (p206) and Mehtab Bagh, all on the east bank. An autorickshaw covering all three should cost about ₹500 return from the Taj, including waiting time.

★ **Akbar's Mausoleum**   HISTORIC BUILDING
(Indian/foreigner ₹30/310, video ₹25; ⊙dawn-dusk) This outstanding sandstone and marble tomb commemorates the greatest of the Mughal emperors. The huge courtyard is entered through a stunning gateway decorated with three-storey minarets at each corner and built of red sandstone strikingly inlaid with white-, yellow- and blue-marble geometric and floral patterns. The interior vestibule of the tomb is stunningly decorated with painted alabaster, creating a contrast to the plain inner tomb. The unusual upper pavillions are closed. Look for deer in the surrounding gardens.

The mausoleum is at Sikandra, 10km northwest of Agra Fort. Catch a bus (₹25, 45 minutes) headed to Mathura from Bijli Ghar (p213) bus stand; they go past the mausoleum. Or else take an autorickshaw (₹350 return) or an Ola taxi.

Kinari Bazaar   MARKET
(Map p203; ⊙11am-9pm Wed-Mon) The narrow streets behind Jama Masjid are a crazy maze

---

TOP AGRA FESTIVALS

Taj Mahotsav (www.tajmahotsav.org; ⊙Feb) A 10-day carnival of culture, cuisine and crafts – Agra's biggest party of the year.

Kailash Fair (⊙Aug/Sep) A cultural and religious fair honouring Lord Shiva.

Ram Barat (⊙Sep) An over-the-top dramatic re-creation of the royal wedding procession of Rama and Sita.

of overcrowded lanes bursting with colourful markets. There are a number of different bazaars here, each specialising in different wares, but the area is generally known as Kinari Bazaar as many of the lanes fan out from Kinari Bazaar Rd. You'll find clothing, shoes, fabrics, jewellery, spices, marblework, snack stalls and what seems like 20 million other people.

Amazingly, there is somehow room for buffaloes and even the odd working elephant to squeeze their way through the crowds. Even if you're not buying anything, just walking the streets is an experience in itself.

Chini-ka-Rauza   HISTORIC BUILDING
(⊙ dawn-dusk) **FREE** This Persian-style riverside tomb of Afzal Khan, a poet who served as Shah Jahan's chief minister, was built between 1628 and 1639. Rarely visited, it is hidden away down a shady avenue of trees on the east bank of the Yamuna but boasts a fine exterior of coloured tilework and an interior of delicate painted alabaster.

Jama Masjid   MOSQUE
(Map p203; Jama Masjid Rd; ⊙ dawn-dusk) This fine mosque, built in the Kinari Bazaar (p205) by Shah Jahan's daughter in 1648 and once connected to Agra Fort, features striking zigzag marble patterning on its domes. The entrance is on the east side.

🏃 Activities & Tours

Hotels allowing nonguests to use their swimming pools include Howard Plaza (p208), ₹1000, and Amar (Map p203; ☑ 0562-4027000; www.hotelamar.com; Fatehabad Rd), ₹650 – with slide.

Agra by Bike   CYCLING
(☑ 9368112527; www.agrabybike.com; East Gate Rd; per person US$30) John and Moses Rosario get rave reviews for their bike tours of the city and surrounding countryside, most of which end with a boat trip on the Yamuna River behind the Taj. They also offer food walks and Indian cooking classes.

Agra Walks   WALKING
(☑ 9027711144; www.agrawalks.com; ₹2500) Many folks spend but a day in Agra, taking in the Taj and Agra Fort and sailing off into the sunset. If you're interested in digging a little deeper, this excellent walking/cycle-rickshaw combo tour will show you sides of the city most tourists don't see.

Amin Tours   CULTURAL
(☑ 9837411144; www.daytourtajmahal.com) If you can't be bothered handling the logistics, look no further than this recommended agency for all-inclusive private Agra day trips from Delhi by car (from US$85 per person, depending on number in group) or express train (from US$90 per person). Caveat: if they try to take you shopping and you're not interested, politely decline.

Taj by Moonlight   TOURS
(Map p207; adult/child Indian ₹510/500, foreigner ₹750/500; ⊙ closed Fri & Ramadan) For five nights around the full moon the Taj by Moonlight is open to groups of 50 people in a series of eight 30-minute time slots between 8.30pm and 12.30am. You can only view the Taj from the entry gate viewing area and you only get 30 minutes there, making this an expensive option, but some people love it. The later time slots are best for moonlight views.

Tickets must be bought a day in advance from the Archaeological Survey of India (ASI; Map p203; ☑ 0562-2227261; www.asiagra circle.in; 22 The Mall; ⊙ 10am-6pm Mon-Fri) office; see its website for details. (Note: this office is known as the Taj Mahal Office by some rickshaw riders.) You need to go through security clearance at the Shilpgram Tourist Facilitation Centre (Taj East Gate Rd; ⊙ 9.30am-5pm Sat-Thu) first, before being taken by security on an electric bus to the eastern gate.

🛏 Sleeping

The main place for budget accommodation is the bustling area of Taj Ganj, immediately south of the Taj, while there's a high concentration of midrange hotels further south, along Fatehabad Rd. Sadar Bazaar, an area boasting good restaurants, offers another option.

🛏 Taj Ganj Area

Saniya Palace Hotel   HOTEL $
(Map p207; ☑ 8881270199; www.saniyapalace.in; Chowk Kagziyan, Taj South Gate; r with/without AC from ₹1300/600; ❋ @ 🛜) Set back from the main strip down an undesirable alleyway, this isn't the sleekest Taj Ganj option, but it tries to imbue character with marble floors and framed Mughal-style carpet wall hangings. The rooms are clean and large enough, although the bathrooms in the non-AC rooms are minuscule.

Taj Ganj

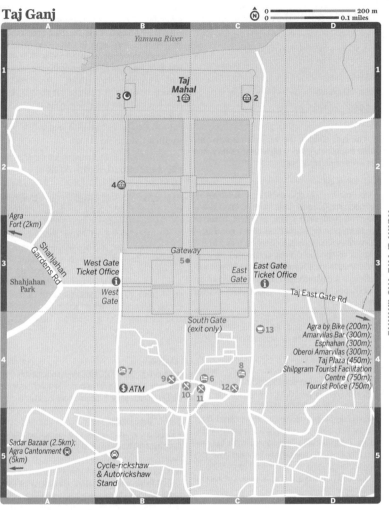

Taj Ganj

◉ Top Sights
1 Taj Mahal	B1

◉ Sights
2 Jawab	C1
3 Mosque	B1
4 Taj Museum	B2

◉ Activities, Courses & Tours
5 Taj by Moonlight	B3

◉ Sleeping
6 Hotel Kamal	C4

7 Hotel Sidhartha	B4
8 Saniya Palace Hotel	C4

◉ Eating
9 Joney's Place	B4
Saniya Palace Hotel	(see 8)
10 Shankara Vegis	B4
11 Taj Cafe	C4
12 Yash Cafe	C4

◉ Drinking & Nightlife
13 Café Coffee Day	C4

SLEEPING PRICE RANGES

Accommodation price ranges in this region are for a double room with private bathroom in high season:

$ less than ₹1500

$$ ₹1500–₹4000

$$$ more than ₹4000

The real coup is the very pleasant, plant-filled double rooftop, which trumps its rivals for optimum Taj views.

Hotel Kamal
HOTEL **$**

(Map p207; ☑ 0562-2330126; hotelkamal@hotmail.com; Taj South Gate; r with AC ₹2000, without ₹700-1400; ❄ 🛜) The smartest hotel in Taj Ganj proper, Kamal has clean, comfortable rooms with nice touches, such as framed photos of the Taj on the walls and rugs on the tiled floors. Five rooms in the newer annexe are a definite step up, with welcoming woodwork, extra space and stone-walled showers.

It has a cosy, bamboo-enclosed ground-floor restaurant and an underused rooftop restaurant with a somewhat-obscured Taj view.

Hotel Sidhartha
HOTEL **$**

(Map p207; ☑ 0562-2230901; www.hotelsidhartha.com; Taj West Gate; r with/without AC from ₹1500/950; ❄ @ 🛜) Of the 21 rooms in this West Gate staple, those on the ground floor are stylish for the price, with marble walls, cable TV and clean bathrooms with hot water. Upper-floor rooms are smaller and not as exciting. All rooms surround or overlook a small, leafy courtyard with a pleasant gazebo restaurant.

★ Oberoi Amarvilas
HOTEL **$$$**

(☑ 0562-2231515; www.oberoihotels.com; Taj East Gate Rd; d with/without balcony ₹95,000/80,500; ❄ @ 🛜 ⯐) Following Oberoi's iron-clad modus operandi of maharaja-level service, exquisite dining and properties that pack some serious wow factor, Agra's best hotel by far oozes style and luxury. Elegant interior design is suffused with Mughal themes, a composition carried over into the exterior fountain courtyard and stunning swimming pool, both of which are set in a delightful stepped water garden. All rooms (and even some bathtubs) have wonderful Taj views. Online discounts of 30% are common.

Retreat
BOUTIQUE HOTEL **$$$**

(☑ 8810022200; www.theretreat.co.in; Shilpgram Rd, Taj Nagari; r incl breakfast from ₹4500; ❄ @ 🛜 ⯐) Everything in this sleek, 51-room hotel is done up boutique-style with Indian sensibilities (lots of soothing mauve, mocha and turquoise throughout), and modern fixtures abound. It has a small pool, a sleek new bar and a multicuisine restaurant offering countrywide specialities such as Goan fish curries and Lahori kebabs. It's 2km southeast of the Taj Mahal.

🛏 Fatehabad Road Area

★ Bansi Homestay
HOMESTAY **$$**

(Map p203; ☑ 0562-2333033; www.bansihomestayagra.com; 18 Handicraft Nagar, Fatehabad Rd; s/d incl breakfast ₹3000/3500; ❄ 🛜) ⯐ A retired director of Uttar Pradesh Tourism is your host at this wonderful upscale homestay tucked away in a quiet residential neighbourhood near Fatahabad Rd. The five large rooms boast huge bathrooms with rain-style showers and flank pleasant common areas decorated with Krishna paintings. It feels more like a boutique hotel than a homestay. To find it, follow the alley past the Hotel Atithi.

N Homestay
HOMESTAY **$$**

(Map p203; ☑ 9690107860; www.nhomestay.com; 15 Ajanta Colony, Vibhav Nagar; s/d incl breakfast ₹1800/2000; ❄ 🛜) Matriarch Naghma and her helpful sons are the highlight of this wonderful homestay. Their comfortable home, tucked away in a residential neighbourhood 15 minutes' walk from the Taj's West Gate, is blissfully quiet, and two of the six rooms feature spacious balconies (₹2200).

Naghma will cook you dinner (veg/nonveg ₹400/600) and also offers cooking classes (₹1500 to ₹3500 per person). A single dorm (₹800) with four bunk beds and private bathroom offers a budget option.

Howard Plaza
HOTEL **$$$**

(The Fern; Map p203; ☑ 0562-4048600; www.howardplazaagra.com; Fatehabad Rd; s/d incl breakfast from ₹4500/5500; ❄ 🛜 ⯐) Rooms in this very welcoming hotel are decked out in elegant dark-wood furniture and stylish decorative tiling. The slightly pricier Club rooms have nicer decor and bathrooms. You won't find much to fault in either category.

The pool is starting to show its age, but there's a small, well-equipped gym and a very pleasant spa offering a whole range of ayurvedic and massage treatments, including the so-called 'erotic bath' of milk, cinnamon and honey. The breezy, open-air rooftop restaurant doubles as one of the few atmospheric bars in town at night (beer ₹325, cocktails ₹400), with distant Taj views.

Hotel Atithi   HOTEL $$$

(Map p203; ☏0562-2330880; www.hotelatithi agra.com; Fatehabad Rd; s/d from ₹3700/4500; ✴@🛜🏊) Simple but superclean and comfortable rooms here are a decent size – no reason to spring for deluxe rooms. Guests can use the murky swimming pool in the next-door garden wedding venue for free. It's set back from the road and so is quieter than most.

🛏 Sadar Bazaar Area

★Tourists Rest House   HOTEL $

(Map p203; ☏0562-2463961; www.dontworry chickencurry.com; 4/62 Kutchery Rd; s/d with AC ₹800/999, without from ₹500/650; ✴🛜) If you aren't set on sleeping under the nose of the Taj, this centrally located travellers' hub offers the best-value accommodation in Agra, if not the whole state. It's been under the watchful eye of the same family since 1965, and it's still a great choice.

If you can forgo AC, the fresh and modern cheapies are great value – and things only get better from there. All rooms come with TV, hot water and large windows, and are set around a peaceful plant-filled, palm-shaded courtyard (a real highlight) and a North Indian pure veg restaurant. The bend-over-backwards owners couldn't be more helpful and can solve most of your travel needs. Phone or email ahead for a free pickup. Damn fine masala chai too. Don't let rickshaw drivers confuse you with similarly named but inferior competition.

Clarks Shiraz Hotel   HOTEL $$$

(Map p203; ☏0562-2226121; www.hotelclarks shiraz.com; 54 Taj Rd; r incl breakfast from ₹7670; ✴@🛜🏊) Agra's original five-star hotel, opened in 1961, has done well to keep up with the hotel Joneses. The standard doubles are nothing special for this price range, but the marble-floored premium versions (₹8850) are a pleasant step up, and all bathrooms have been retiled and are spotless.

There are three good restaurants, a rooftop bar, a huge palm-fringed garden and pool area (one of Agra's best) and ayurvedic massages. Some rooms have distant Taj views.

🍴 Eating

🍴 Taj Ganj Area

Saniya Palace Hotel   MULTICUISINE $

(Map p207; Chowk Kagziyan, Taj South Gate; mains ₹100-200; ⏱6am-10pm; 🛜) With cute tablecloths, dozens of potted plants and a bamboo pergola for shade, this is the most pleasant rooftop restaurant in Taj Ganj. It also has the best rooftop view of the Taj, bar none. The kitchen is a bit rough and ready, but the Western dishes and Western-friendly Indian dishes are fine and you are really here for the views.

Taj Cafe   MULTICUISINE $

(Map p207; Chowk Kagziyan; mains ₹50-200; ⏱7am-11pm; 🛜) Up a flight of steps and overlooking Taj Ganj's busy street scene, this friendly, family-run restaurant is a nice choice if you're not fussed about Taj views. There's a good choice of breakfasts, thalis (₹90 to ₹140) and pizza (₹160 to ₹200), and the lassis here won't disappoint.

Joney's Place   MULTICUISINE $

(Map p207; Kutta Park, Taj Ganj; mains ₹70-120; ⏱5am-10.30pm) This pocket-sized institution whipped up its first creamy lassi in 1978 and continues to please despite cooking its meals in what must be Agra's smallest kitchen. The cheese and tomato 'jayfelles' (toasted sandwich), the banana lassi (with money-back guarantee) and the *malai* kofta (paneer cooked in a creamy sauce of cashews and tomato) all come recommended, but it's more about crack-of-dawn sustenance than culinary dazzle.

Shankara Vegis   VEGETARIAN $

(Map p207; Chowk Kagziyan; mains ₹90-150; ⏱8am-10.30pm; 🛜) Most restaurants in Taj Ganj ooze a distinct air of mediocrity, but Shankara Vegis is different. This cosy old-timer, with its red tablecloths and straw-lined walls, stands out for great vegetarian thalis (₹140 to ₹250) and, most pleasantly, the genuinely friendly, nonpushy ethos of its hands-on owners. Try the rooftop.

Yash Cafe   MULTICUISINE $$

(Map p207; 3/137 Chowk Kagziyan; mains ₹100-260; ⏱7am-10.30pm; 🛜) This chilled-out, 1st-floor cafe has wicker chairs, sports channels on TV, DVDs shown in the evening and a good range of meals, from good-value set breakfasts to thalis (₹90), pizza (₹90 to ₹300)

CHAAT GALLI

Fans of street food should make a beeline for the Sadaar Bazaar district . Not only will you find multiple outlets of Mama Chicken, but you can fill up in the nearby *chaat galli* (snack alley), home to a dozen excellent street-food stalls.

First port of call is Agra Chat House (Map p203; Chaat Galli, Sadar Bazaar; snacks ₹50-60; ◷1-11pm), the oldest of the street stalls, or the next-door Agarwal Chat House, to invest in a selection of aloo tikki chaat (fried potato croquettes with tamarind sauce, yoghurt, coriander and pomegranate), *dahi bada* (dumplings with yoghurt and tamarind), *chila mong dal* (lentil pancake), *bhalla* (croquette of green bean paste with yoghurt and chutney) or *galpapa* (little *puri* shells filled with flavoured sauce). At around ₹50 a dish you can afford to explore the simple menus.

For dessert, several nearby stalls sell delicious mango or *kaju pista* (cashew and pistachio) *kulfi* (firm-textured ice cream), as well as refreshing *falooda* (cold dessert of rosewater, vermicelli, jelly and milk).

As if that wasn't enough, just round the corner is Panchhi Peta, a tiny branch of Agra's most famous *peitha* shop, offering to-go boxes of Agra's famous sweet (made from pumpkin and glucose, usually flavoured with rosewater, coconut or saffron).

and Indian-style French toast (with coconut – we think they made that up). It also offers a shower and storage space (₹50 for both) to day visitors.

★ **Esphahan** NORTH INDIAN $$$
(☏0562-2231515; Taj East Gate Rd, Oberoi Amarvilas Hotel; mains ₹1550-3500; ◷dinner 6.30pm & 9pm; ✴) There are only two sittings each evening at Agra's finest restaurant, so booking ahead is essential, especially as non-hotel-guest tables are limited. The exquisite menu is chock-full of unique delicacies, with the modern fusion tasting menus and Indian thalis offering the best selection.

✕ Fatehabad Road Area

Culinary Junction INDIAN $$
(www.culinaryjunctionbyudupi.com; 1st fl Arvind Innov8, Fatehabad Rd; mains ₹200-300; ◷noon-11pm; ✐) It's worth taking a taxi out to this excellent new vegetarian restaurant in the east of town near the Trident Hotel. The tangy and tasty *paneer dhaniya adraki* (soft cheese in ginger and coriander gravy) is a treat, as is the *missi roti* (flatbread) and smoked paprika paneer tikka masala. Service is excellent and it's a modern, classy option.

Dasaprakash Xpress SOUTH INDIAN $$
(Map p203; www.dasaprakashgroup.com; 921 Heritage Villa, Fatehabad Rd; mains ₹115-250; ✴✐) The fast-food variant of the original Dasaprakash chain from Mysore offers the same great *dosas* (paper-thin lentil-flour pancakes), but in a simpler environment and at prices 40% less than the original.

★ **Pinch of Spice** MODERN INDIAN $$$
(Map p203; www.pinchofspice.in; 1076/2 Fatehabad Rd; mains ₹375-450; ◷noon-11.30pm) This modern North Indian superstar is the best spot outside five-star hotels to indulge yourself in rich curries and succulent tandoori kebabs. The *murg boti masala* (chicken tikka swimming in a rich and spicy gravy) and the *paneer lababdar* (unfermented cheese cubes in a spicy red gravy with sauteed onions) are outstanding. Portions are huge. There's also a full bar.

Located opposite the ITC Mughal Hotel. No reservations accepted.

✕ Sadar Bazaar Area

Brijwasi SWEETS $
(Map p203; Sadar Bazaar; sweets per kg from ₹320; ◷7am-11pm) Sugar-coma-inducing selection of traditional Indian sweets, nuts and biscuits on the ground floor. It's most famous for its *peda* (milk-based sweets), including excellent *rabri* (condensed milk with nuts and spices).

Lakshmi Vilas SOUTH INDIAN $
(Map p203; 50A Taj Rd; mains ₹110-130; ◷11am-10.30pm Wed-Mon; ✴✐) This no-nonsense, plainly decorated, nonsmoking restaurant is *the* place in Agra to come for affordable South Indian fare. The thali meal (₹160), served from noon to 3.30pm and 7pm to 10.30pm, is good.

★ **Mama Chicken** DHABA $$
(Map p203; Stall No 2, Sadar Bazaar; rolls ₹40-190, mains ₹230-290; ◷noon-midnight) This super-

star *dhaba* (casual eatery) is a must: duelling veg and nonveg glorified street stalls employ 24 cooks during the rush, each of whom handles outdoor tandoors, grills or pots. They whip up outrageously good 'franky' rolls (like a flatbread wrap) – including a buttery-soft chicken tikka variety – along with excellent chicken curries, superb naan breads and evening-only chicken tandoori *momos* (Tibetan dumplings).

Eat standing at outside tables or cram into the air-con dining room. Bright lights, obnoxious signage and funky Indian tunes round out the festive atmosphere – a sure-fire Agra must-try.

Dasaprakash SOUTH INDIAN **$$**
(Map p203; www.dasaprakashgroup.com; Meher Cinema Complex, Gwailor Rd; mains ₹210-360; noon-10.45pm;) Fabulously tasty and religiously clean, Dasaprakash whips up consistently great South Indian vegetarian food, including spectacular thalis (₹250 to ₹360), *dosas*, a *rasum* (South Indian soup with a tamarind base) of the day and a few token Continental dishes. The ice-cream desserts (₹100 to ₹295) are another speciality. Comfortable booth seating and wood-lattice screens make for intimate dining.

Other Dasprakash outlets in the city are no longer run by the same owners.

Mughal Room NORTH INDIAN **$$$**
(Map p203; 54 Taj Rd; mains ₹900-1500; 7.30-11pm Mon-Fri, 12.30-3pm & 7.30-11pm Sat & Sun) The best of three eating options at Clarks Shiraz Hotel, this top-floor restaurant serves up sumptuous Mughlai and regional cuisine. Come for a predinner drink (beer ₹400) at the Sunset Bar for distant views of the Taj and Agra Fort. There's live Indian classical music here every evening at 8.30pm. Book a window table.

 Drinking & Nightlife

A night out in Agra tends to revolve around sitting at a rooftop restaurant with a couple of bottles of beer (₹200). None of the restaurants in Taj Ganj are licensed, but they can find alcohol for you if you ask nicely. They also don't mind if you bring your own drinks, as long as you're discreet.

Café Coffee Day CAFE
(Map p203; www.cafecoffeeday.com; Sadar Bazaar; coffee ₹110-135; 9am-11pm) Probably the trendiest Agra outlet of India's popular café chain, this branch near Sadar Bazaar is handy when exploring the market. There's another at the **east gate** (Map p207; www.cafecoffeeday.com; 21/101 Taj East Gate; coffee ₹110-135; 6am-8pm) of the Taj.

Amarvilas Bar BAR
(Taj East Gate Rd, Oberoi Amarvilas Hotel; beer/cocktail ₹500/950; noon-midnight) For a beer or cocktail in sheer opulence, look no further than the bar at Agra's best hotel. Nonguests can wander onto the terrace with its Taj views, but staff often restrict tables to in-house guests if things are busy. Bring your best shirt.

 Shopping

Agra is well known for its marble items inlaid with coloured stones, similar to the pietra dura work on the Taj. Sadar Bazaar, the old town and the area around the Taj are full of emporiums. Cheaper versions may be made of alabaster or soapstone and are less durable.

Other popular buys include rugs, leather and gemstones, though the latter are imported from Rajasthan and are cheaper in Jaipur.

★**Subhash Emporium** ARTS & CRAFTS
(Map p203; 9410613616; www.subhashemporium.com; 18/1 Gwalior Rd; 9.30am-7pm) Some of the pieces on display at this renowned marble shop are simply stunning (ask to see the 26 masterpieces). While it's more expensive than some shops, you definitely get what you pay for: high-quality marble from Rajasthan and master craftsmanship. Items for sale include tabletops, trays, lamp bases, and candle holders that glow from the flame inside.

Prices are marked, but you can normally get a minimum 15% discount. Credit cards are accepted and shipping can be arranged.

Subhash Bazaar MARKET
(Map p203; 8am-8pm Apr-Sep, 9am-8pm Oct-Mar) Skirts the northern edge of Agra's Jama Masjid and is particularly good for silks and saris.

Modern Book Depot BOOKS
(Map p203; Sadar Bazaar; 10.45am-9.30pm Wed-Mon) Great selection of novels and books on Agra and the Mughals at this friendly, 60-year-old establishment.

Khadi Gramodyog CLOTHING
(Map p203; MG Rd; 11am-7pm Wed-Mon) Stocks simple, good-quality men's Indian clothing made from the homespun *khadi* fabric famously recommended by Mahatma Gandhi. There's no English sign – on Mahatma

THE DANCING BEAR & WORKING ELEPHANT RETIREMENT HOME

For hundreds of years, sloth bear cubs were stolen from their mothers (who were often killed) and forced through painful persuasion to become 'dancing bears', entertaining kings and crowds with their fancy footwork. In 1996 Wildlife SOS (www.wildlifesos.org) – an animal-rescue organisation that is often called around Agra to humanely remove pythons and cobras from local homes – began efforts to emancipate all of India's 1200 or so dancing bears. By 2009, nearly all were freed, and more than 200 of them live at the Agra Bear Rescue Facility (☑ 9756205080; www.wildlifesos.org; 2hr/full day ₹1500/₹5000; ☺ 9am-4pm; visiting slots 10am, noon & 3pm), inside Sur Sarovar Bird Sanctuary, 30km outside Agra on the road to Delhi.

Visitors are welcome to tour the parklike grounds and watch the bears enjoying their new, better lives. You'll have to pay the ₹500 entry fee to access the centre through the bird sanctuary.

Wildlife SOS also runs an Elephant Conservation Centre (☑ 969001182; www.wildlifesos.org; Farah; 2hr/full day ₹1500/₹5000; ☺ visiting slots 10am, noon & 3pm; ☷) ✎, closer to Mathura, which is more hands-on. You'll get to see the elephants while touring the facility and might be able to help prepare their lunch.

For both locations you should email or phone in advance to arrange one of three daily time slots (10am, noon and 3pm).

Volunteers are welcome here for a day or two weeks. Costs are US$100 per person per day, including accommodation and three meals at a volunteer house 10km away. Email volunteer@wildlifesos.org in advance.

Gandhi (MG) Rd, look for the *khadi* logo of hands clasped around a mud hut.

ℹ Information

DANGERS & ANNOYANCES

As well as the usual commission rackets and ever-present gem-import scam (p263), some specific methods to relieve Agra tourists of their hard-earned cash include the following.

Rickshaws

When taking an auto- or cycle-rickshaw to the Taj, make sure you are clear which gate you want to go to when negotiating the price. Otherwise, almost without fail, riders will take you to the roundabout at the south end of Shahjahan Gardens Rd – where expensive tongas (horse-drawn carriage) or camels wait to take tour groups to the west gate – and claim that's where they thought you meant. Only nonpolluting autos can go within a 500m radius of the Taj because of pollution rules, but they can get a lot closer than the south end of Shahjahan Gardens Rd.

Fake Marble

Lots of 'marble' souvenirs are actually alabaster, or even just soapstone. So you may be paying marble prices for lower-quality stones. The mini Taj Mahals are always alabaster because they are too intricate to carve quickly in marble.

EMERGENCY

Police Station (Map p203; Mahatma Gandhi (MG) Rd)

Tourist Police (☑ 0562-2421204; Agra Cantonment Train Station; ☺ 6.30am-9.30pm) Officers also hang around the East Gate ticket office and the UP Tourism office on Taj Rd, as well as at major sites.

MEDICAL

Amit Jaggi Memorial Hospital (Map p203; ☑ 9690107860, 0562-2230515; www.ajmh.in; off Minto Rd, Vibhav Nagar) If you're sick, Dr Jaggi, who runs this private clinic, is the man to see. He accepts most health-insurance plans from abroad; otherwise a visit runs ₹1000 (day) or ₹2000 (night). He'll even do house calls.

SR Hospital (Map p203; ☑ 0562-4025200; Laurie's Complex, Namner Rd) Agra's best private hospital.

MONEY

ATMs are everywhere, including one just south of the Hotel Sidhartha in Taj Ganj.

SBI (Map p203; Rakabganj Rd; ☺ 10am-4pm Mon-Fri, to 1pm Sat) Changes cash and travellers cheques and has an ATM.

POST

India Post (Map p203; www.indiapost.gov.in; The Mall; ☺ 10am-5pm Mon-Fri, to 4pm Sat) Agra's historic eneral Post Office (GPO) dates to 1913 and includes a handy 'facilitation office' for foreigners.

TOURIST INFORMATION

India Tourism (Map p203; ☑ 0562-2226378; www.incredibleindia.org; 191 The Mall; ☺ 9am-

5.30pm Mon-Fri) Helpful branch; has brochures on local and India-wide attractions.

UP Tourism (☑ 0562-2421204; www.up-tourism.com; Agra Cantonment Train Station; ☺ 6.30am-9.30pm) The friendly train-station branch inside the Tourist Facilitation Centre on Platform 1 offers helpful advice and is where you can book day-long bus tours of Agra. This branch doubles as the Tourist Police.

UP Tourism (Map p203; ☑ 0562-2226431; www.uptourism.gov.in; 64 Taj Rd; ☺ 10am-5pm Mon-Sat) Office on Taj Rd.

Bagpacker Travel (Map p203; ☑ 9997113228; www.bagpackertravels.com; 4/62 Kutchery Rd; ☺ 9am-9pm) An honest agency for all your travel and transport needs, including commission-free train and bus tickets, Agra day tours and multiday trips, run by the friendly Anil at Tourists Rest House. English and French spoken.

ⓘ Getting There & Away

AIR

Air India (p276) has flights from Agra's Kheria Airport three times a week to Khajuraho (and on to Varanasi), and four flights weekly to Jaipur. There are plans to upgrade the airport, though the long-planned Taj International Airport will likely now be constructed closer to Delhi than Agra, and so will be of limited use.

BUS

Luxury air-conditioned Volvo and Scania coaches use the Yamuna Expressway, making them a faster option to Delhi.

Some buses to local desinations operate from **Idgah Bus Stand** (☑ 0562-2420324; Idgah Rd):

Bharatpur ₹74, 1½ hours, every 30 minutes, 6am to 6.30pm

Delhi Non-AC ₹228, five hours, every 30 minutes, 5am to 11pm; to Delhi's Sarai Kale Khan bus station

Fatehpur Sikri ₹45, one hour, every 30 minutes, 6am to 6.30pm

Gwalior ₹131, three hours, 3pm, 6pm to 8pm

Jaipur ₹267, six hours, every 30 minutes, 5am to 11pm

Jhansi ₹215, six hours, 11am and 12.30pm

A block east of Idgah, just in front of Hotel Sakura, the tiny booth of the **Rajasthan State Road Transport Corporation** (RSRTC; ☑ 0562-2420228; www.rsrtc.rajasthan.gov.in) runs more comfortable coaches to Jaipur throughout the day. Services include non-AC (₹294, 5½ hours, 7.30am, 10am, 1pm and 11.59pm) and luxury Volvo (₹563, 4½ hours, 11.30am and 2.30pm). Women's fares are 30% less.

From the **ISBT Bus Stand** (☑ 0562-2603536):

Dehra Dun Luxury Volvo (₹1250, 10 hours, 8.30pm); AC (₹700, 4.30pm); non-AC (₹425, 7pm, 8pm, 9pm and 9.30pm).

Delhi Luxury Scania/Volvo to Sarai Kale Khan stand (₹553 to ₹582, four hours, six daily, 7am, 11am, 1pm, 3.30pm, 5.30pm, 6.30pm); AC Shatabdi to Noida (₹415, four hours, five daily).

Gorakhpur AC bus (₹1099, 16 hours, 1.45pm); non-AC (₹700, 3pm, 5pm, 9pm and 10pm).

Haridwar AC bus (₹992, 10 hours); non-AC (₹400). A few evening buses; change in Haridwar for Rishikesh.

Lucknow Luxury Scania/Volvo (₹860, 10am, 4pm, 6pm, 8.45pm); AC (₹595, 7am, 1.45pm, 6.30pm, 8pm, 8.30pm).

Prayagraj (Allahabad) Luxury Volvo (₹1215, nine hours, 7pm); non-AC (₹550, nine hours, 5pm, 7pm and 7.50pm).

Varanasi Luxury Volvo (₹1500, 11 hours, 7pm); non-AC (₹750, 13 hours, 5pm, 7pm and 7.50pm).

From the **Bijli Ghar Bus Stand** (Agra Fort Bus Stand; Map p203; ☑ 0562-2464557):

Mathura ₹76, 90 minutes, every 30 minutes, 6am to 8pm

Tundla train station ₹35, one hour, every 30 minutes, 8am to 6pm; from Tundla you can catch the 12382 Poorva Express train to Varanasi at 8.15pm if the trains from Agra are sold out.

(right margin, vertical) AGRA & THE TAJ MAHAL GETTING THERE & AWAY

....

DELHI–AGRA TRAINS FOR DAY TRIPPERS

TRIP	TRAIN NO & NAME	FARE (₹)	TIME (HR)	DEPARTURES
Delhi–Agra	12002 Shatabdi Exp	550/1010 (A)	2	6am
Agra–Delhi	12001 Shatabdi Exp	690/1050 (A)	2	9.15pm
Delhi–Agra	12280 Taj Exp	100/370 (B)	3	7am
Agra–Delhi	12279 Taj Exp	100/370 (B)	3½	6.55pm
Hazrat Nizamuddin–Agra*	12050 Gatimaan Exp	770/1505 (A)	1¾	8.10am
Agra–Hazrat Nizamuddin*	12049 Gatimaan Exp	770/1505 (A)	1¾	5.50pm

Fares: (A) AC chair/ECC, (B) 2nd-class/AC chair; * departs Saturday to Monday

MORE HANDY TRAINS FROM AGRA

DESTINATION	TRAIN NO & NAME	FARE (₹)	TIME (HR)	DEPARTURES
Gorakhpur*	19037/9 Avadh Exp	335/910/1305 (A)	15¾	10pm
Jaipur*	22988 AF All Superfast	120/430 (C)	4	2.50pm
Khajuraho	12448 UP Sampark Kranti	280/720/1010 (A)	7½	11.10pm
Kolkata (Howrah)	13008 UA Toofan Exp	555/1500 (B)	31	12.15pm
Lucknow	12180 LJN Intercity	145/515 (C)	6	5.50am
Mumbai (CST)	12138/7 Punjab Mail	580/1530/2215 (A)	23	8.35am
Varanasi*	14854/64/66 Marudhar Exp	340/930/1335 (A)	14	8.30pm

Fares: (A) sleeper/3AC/2AC, (B) sleeper/3AC only, (C) 2nd-class/AC chair;
* Leaves from Agra Fort station

Shared autos (₹10) run between Idgah and Bijli Ghar bus stands. To get to ISBT, catch an auto-rickshaw (₹200 to ₹250, depending on where your trip starts).

TRAIN

Most trains leave from Agra Cantonment (Cantt) train station, although some services to Varanasi and Jaipur go from Agra Fort station. A few trains, such as Kota PNBE Express, run as slightly different numbers on different days than those listed, but timings remain the same.

Express trains are well set up for day trippers to/from Delhi, but trains run to Delhi all day. If you can't reserve a seat, just buy a 'general ticket' for the next train (about ₹90), find a seat in sleeper class then upgrade when the ticket collector comes along. The fastest service to Delhi is the Gatimaan Express, India's fastest train, hitting speeds of 160km per hour.

For Orchha, catch one of the many daily trains to Jhansi (sleeper from ₹165, three hours), then take a shared auto to the bus stand (₹10), from where shared autos run all day to Orchha (₹20). A private autorickshaw costs ₹200 for the same route.

ⓘ Getting Around

TO/FROM THE AIRPORT

Kheria Airport is 7km east of central Agra. A taxi here costs around ₹300.

AUTORICKSHAW

Just outside Agra Cantonment train station is the **prepaid autorickshaw booth** (⏱24hr), which gives you a good guide for haggling elsewhere. Usually, trips shorter than 3km should not cost more than ₹50. Always agree on the fare before entering the rickshaw.

For a half-day (four-hour) Agra tour count on ₹400; a full-day (eight-hour) Agra tour costs from ₹600. Note: autorickshaws aren't allowed to go to Fatehpur Sikri.

CYCLE-RICKSHAW

Prices from the Taj Mahal's cycle and auto-rickshaw stand at **South Gate** (Map p207) include Agra Fort ₹40; Bijli Ghar bus stand ₹50; and Fatahabad Rd ₹30.

TAXI

Outside Agra Cantonment train station, the **prepaid taxi booth** (⏱24hr) gives a good idea of what taxis should cost. In general Ola taxis are cheapest.

A taxi to Delhi or Jaipur costs around ₹3500. A half-/full-day Agra tour costs ₹750/1000. Agree with the driver beforehand whether tolls and parking charges are included.

AROUND AGRA

Fatehpur Sikri

🔊 05613 / POP 30,000

This magnificent fortified ancient city, 40km west of Agra, was the short-lived capital of the Mughal empire between 1572 and 1585, during the reign of Emperor Akbar. Earlier, Akbar had visited the village of Sikri to consult the Sufi saint Shaikh Salim Chishti, who predicted the birth of an heir to the Mughal throne. When the prophecy came true, Akbar built his new capital here, including a stunning mosque, still in use today, and three palaces, one for each of his favourite wives – one a Hindu, one a Muslim and one a Christian (though Hindu villagers in Sikri dispute these claims).

The city was an Indo-Islamic masterpiece, but was erected in an area that supposedly suffered from water shortages and so was abandoned shortly after Akbar's death. The red-sandstone palace walls are at their most atmospheric and photogenic near sunset.

⊙ Sights

Palaces & Pavilions
PALACE

(Indian/foreigner ₹50/610, video ₹25; ☺ dawn-dusk) The main sight at Fatehpur Sikri is the stunning imperial complex of pavilions and palaces spread amid a large, abandoned 'city' peppered with Mughal masterpieces: courtyards, intricate carvings, servants quarters, vast gateways and ornamental pools. Budget half a day here.

A large courtyard dominates the northeast entrance at Diwan-i-Am (Hall of Public Audiences). Now a pristinely manicured garden, this is where Akbar presided over the courts – from the middle seat of the five equal seatings along the western wall, flanked by his advisors. It was built to utilise an echo sound system, so Akbar could hearing anything at any time from anywhere in the open space. Justice was dealt with swiftly if legends are to be believed, with public executions said to have been carried out here by elephants trampling convicted criminals to death.

The Diwan-i-Khas (Hall of Private Audiences), found at the northern end of the Pachisi Courtyard, looks nothing special from the outside, but the interior is dominated by a magnificently carved stone central column. This pillar flares to create a futuristic flat-topped plinth linked to the four corners of the room by narrow stone bridges. From this plinth Akbar is believed to have debated with scholars and ministers who stood at the ends of the four bridges.

Next to Diwan-i-Khas is the U-shaped Treasury, which houses secret stone safes in some corners (several have been left with their stone lids open for visitors to see). Elephant-headed sea monsters carved on the ceiling struts were there to protect the fabulous wealth once stored here. The so-called Astrologer's Kiosk to the left has roof supports carved in a serpentine Jain style.

Just south of the Astrologer's Kiosk is Pachisi Courtyard, named after the ancient game known in India today as ludo. The large, plus-shaped game board is visible surrounding the block in the middle of the courtyard. In the southeast corner is the most intricately carved structure in the whole complex, the tiny but elegant Rumi Sultana, which was said to be the palace built for Akbar's Turkish Muslim wife. Other theories say it was used by Akbar himself as a rest break during court sessions. Look for the defaced carved birds, animals and flowers in several marble panels.

Just west of the Pachisi Courtyard is the impressive Panch Mahal, a pavilion with five storeys that decrease in size until the top consists of only a tiny kiosk. The lower floor has 84 different columns; in total there are 176 columns.

Continuing anticlockwise will bring you to the Ornamental Pool. Here, singers and musicians would perform on the platform above the water while Akbar watched from the pavilion in his private quarters just behind, known as Daulat Khana (Abode of Fortune). At the back of the pavilion is the Khwabgah (Dream House), a sleeping area with a huge elevated stone bed platform. A water pool below the bed would have acted as a cooler in summer.

Heading west through a doorway from the Ornamental Pool reveals the Palace of Jodh Bai, and the one-time home of Akbar's Hindu wife, said to be his favourite. Set around an enormous courtyard, it blends traditional Indian columns, Islamic cupolas and turquoise-blue Persian roof tiles. Just outside, to the left of Jodh Bai's former kitchen, is the Palace of the Christian Wife. This was used by Akbar's Goan wife Mariam, who gave birth to Jehangir here in 1569. (Some believe Akbar never had a Christian wife and that Mariam was short for Mariam-Ut-Zamani, a title he gave to Jodh Bai meaning 'Beautiful like a Rose', or 'Most Beautiful Woman on Earth'.) Like many of the buildings in the palace complex, it contains elements of different religions, as befitted Akbar's tolerant religious beliefs. The domed ceiling is Islamic in style, while remnants of a wall painting of the Hindu god Shiva can also be found.

Continuing left (west) past the Maryam Garden (with a toilet) will take you west to Birbal Bhavan, ornately carved inside and out, and thought to have been the living quarters of one of Akbar's most senior ministers. The Lower Haramsara, just to the south, housed Akbar's large number of live-in female servants, though some claim it was a stables and that the circular stone loops were use to tether camels and horses.

Jama Masjid
MOSQUE

(Dargah Complex) FREE This beautiful, immense mosque was completed in 1571 and contains elements of Persian and Indian design. The main entrance, at the top of a flight of stone steps, is through the spectacular 54m-high Buland Darwaza (Victory Gate), built to commemorate Akbar's military

continued on p218

Fatehpur Sikri

A WALKING TOUR OF FATEHPUR SIKRI

You can enter this fortified ancient city from two entrances, but the northeast entrance at Diwan-i-Am (Hall of Public Audiences) offers the most logical approach to this remarkable Unesco World Heritage Site. This large courtyard (now a garden) is where Emperor Akbar presided over the trials of accused criminals.

Once through the ticket gate, you are in the northern end of the **1 Pachisi Courtyard**. The first building you see is **2 Diwan-i-Khas** (Hall of Private Audiences), the interior of which is dominated by a magnificently carved central stone column. Pitch south and enter **3 Rumi Sultana**, a small but elegant palace built for Akbar's Turkish Muslim wife.

It's hard to miss the **4 Ornamental Pool** nearby – its southwest corner provides Fatehpur Sikri's most photogenic angle, perfectly framing its most striking building, the five-storey Panch Mahal, one of the gateways to the Imperial Harem Complex, where the **5 Lower Haramsara** once housed more than 200 female servants.

Wander around the Palace of Jodh Bai and take notice of the towering ode to an elephant, the 21m-high **6 Hiran Minar**, in the distance to the northwest. Leave the palaces and pavilions area via Shahi Darwaza (King's Gate), which spills into India's second-largest mosque courtyard at **7 Jama Masjid**. Inside this immense and gorgeous mosque is the sacred **8 Tomb of Shaikh Salim Chishti**. Exit through the spectacular **9 Buland Darwaza** (Victory Gate), one of the world's most magnificent gateways.

Buland Darwaza
Most tours end with an exit through Jama Masjid's Victory Gate. Walk out and take a look behind you: Behold! The magnificent 15-storey sandstone gate, 54m high, is a menacing monolith to Akbar's reign.

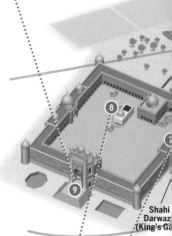

Shahi Darwaza (King's Gate)

Tomb of Shaikh Salim Chishti
Each knot in the strings tied to the 56 carved white marble designs of the interior walls of Shaikh Salim Chishti's tomb represents one wish of a maximum three.

Jama Masjid
The elaborate marble inlay work throughout the Jama Masjid complex is said to have inspired similar work 82 years later at the Taj Mahal in Agra.

ran Minar

s bizarre, seldom-visited tower off the north-
st corner of Fatehpur Sikri is decorated with
ndreds of stone representations of elephant
ks. It is said to be the place where Minar,
bar's favourite execution elephant, died.

Pachisi Courtyard
Under your feet just past Rumi Sultana is the
Pachisi Courtyard where Akbar is said to have
played the game *pachisi* (an ancient version of
ludo) using slave girls in colourful dress as pieces.

Diwan-i-Khas
Emperor Akbar modi-
fied the central stone
column inside Diwan-i-
Khas to call attention
to a new religion he
called Din-i-Ilahi (God
is One). The intricately
carved column features
a fusion of Hindu,
Muslim, Christian and
Buddhist imagery.

**Panch
Mahal**

**Diwan-i-Am
(Hall of Public
Audiences)**

Rumi Sultana
Don't miss the headless creatures carved into
Rumi Sultana's palace interiors: a lion, deer, an
eagle and a few peacocks were beheaded by
jewel thieves who swiped the precious jewels that
originally formed their heads.

Ornamental Pool
Tansen, said to be the most gifted Indian vocalist
of all time and one of Akbar's treasured nine
Navaratnas (Gems), would be showered with coins
during performances from the central platform of
the Ornamental Pool.

wer
aramsara

bar reportedly
t more than 5000
cubines, but the
) or so female
vants housed in
Lower Haramsara
e strictly business.
ots were tied to
se sandstone rings
upport partitions
ween their indi-
ual quarters.

continued from p215

victory in Gujarat. Inside is the stunning white marble tomb of Sufi saint Shaikh Salim Chishti, where women hoping to have children come to tie a thread to the *jalis* (carved lattice screens).

The saint's tomb was completed in 1581 and is entered through an original door made of ebony. Inside it are brightly coloured flower murals, while the sandlewood canopy is decorated with mother-of-pearl shell, and the marble *jalis* are among the finest in India. To the right of the tomb lie the gravestones of family members of Shaikh Salim Chishti. Just east of Shaikh Salim Chishti's tomb is the red-sandstone tomb of Islam Khan, the final resting place of Shaikh Salim Chishti's grandson and one-time governor of Bengal.

On the east wall of the courtyard is a smaller entrance to the mosque – the Shahi Darwaza (King's Gate), which leads to the palace complex.

Tours

Official Archaeological Society of India guides can be hired from the Fathehpur Sikri ticket offices at the eastern and southwestern ends of the site for ₹450 (English), but they aren't always the most knowledgeable (some are guides thanks to birthright rather than qualifications). The best guides are available in Agra, and charge ₹750. Our favourite is Pankaj Bhatnagar (☏8126995552; ₹750); he prefers to be messaged on WhatsApp.

🛏 Sleeping & Eating

Fatehpur Sikri's culinary specialty is *khataie,* the biscuits you can see piled high in the bazaar. For restaurants, head to one of the hotels.

Hotel Goverdhan   HOTEL **$**
(☏9412526585; www.hotelfatehpursikriviews. com; Agra Rd; s/d with AC ₹1400/1600, without ₹1000/1200; ❄🛜) Both the air-con and cheaper rooms at this old-time favourite are fresh and spotless, and all are set around a pleasant, well-kept garden. It has a relaxing communal balcony and terrace seating,

new beds in every room, a couple of family suites and a good restaurant (mains ₹150 to ₹220). It's a comfortable place to be based. Discounts of 25% are common.

It's right on the main road by the turn-off to the Jami Masjid.

Hotel Ajay Palace   INDIAN **$**
(☏9548801213; Agra Rd; mains ₹60-140; ⊙8am-9pm) This friendly, family-run place is a convenient lunch stop before taking the bus back to Agra. Sit on the rooftop at the large, elongated marble table and enjoy a cold beer with a view of the Jama Masjid towering above. Note that it's not 'Ajay Restaurant' inside the bus stand – it's 30m further east.

It also offers four very simple double rooms (₹500) with rock-hard mattresses, hot water by the bucket and sit-down flush toilets.

ℹ Information

DANGERS & ANNOYANCES
Take no notice of anyone who gets on the Fatehpur Sikri–Agra bus before the final stop at Idgah Bus Stand and tells you that you have arrived at the city centre or the Taj Mahal. You haven't. You're still a long autorickshaw ride away, and the man trying to tease you off the bus is – surprise surprise – an autorickshaw driver.

ℹ Getting There & Away
From the Fatehpur bus stand, buses run to Agra's Idgah Bus Stand (p213) every half-hour (₹45, one hour) until 6pm. If you miss those, walk 1km to the Mughal-style Agra Gate and another 350m to the Bypass Crossing Stop on the main road and wave down an Agra-bound bus. They pass every 30 minutes or so, day and night.

For Bharatpur (₹25, 40 minutes) or Jaipur (₹190, 4½ hours), wave down a westbound bus from the Bypass Crossing Stop.

A return taxi from Agra costs from ₹1500 for a day trip, but clarify that this includes toll and parking charges. A one-way taxi to Delhi or Jaipur costs ₹4000.

Simple passenger trains for Agra leave Fatehpur Sikri at 10.14am, 3.10pm and 3.54pm. Just buy a 'general' ticket at the station and pile in (₹20, one to two hours). The 8.16pm 19037/9 Avadh Express runs to Lucknow and Gorakhpur Junction.

Understand Rajasthan, Delhi & Agra

Rajasthan Today

Rajasthan has old bones and draws great strength from its glorious history and long-held cultural and religious traditions. Conservative forces once kept the state behind when other parts of India rapidly progressed, but lately Rajasthan has been embracing modernisation with gusto. Rajasthan is an early adopter and world leader in renewable energy, yet at the same time Rajasthanis are keen to preserve the best of the past and keep the state prospering as India's premier tourist destination.

Best on Film

Fire (1996), **Earth** (1998) and **Water** (2005) Classic trilogy of social observation by Deepa Mehta.

Gandhi (1982) The classic biopic.

Lagaan (2001) Raj-era cricketing epic by Ashutosh Gowariker.

The Darjeeling Limited (2007) Train-journey comedy filmed around Jodhpur and Udaipur.

The Best Exotic Marigold Hotel (2012) and its sequel, **The Second Best Exotic Marigold Hotel** (2015) Humour and poignancy, as elderly Westerners retire in Jaipur.

Best in Print

Desert Places (Robyn Davidson; 1996) Travels with Rabari tribespeople through the Thar Desert.

Maharanis (Lucy Moore; 2004) A delightful account of the lives and loves of three generations of Indian princesses.

A Princess Remembers: The Memoirs of the Maharani of Jaipur (Gayatri Devi and Santha Rama Rau; 1976) A life of extraordinary privilege not so much exposed as celebrated.

Rajasthan: An Oral History – Conversations with Komal Kothari (Rustom Bharucha; 2007) The living traditions and folklore of Rajasthan as told by a leading folklorist.

A Thriving Desert

Covering an area of 342,236 sq km, Rajasthan represents roughly 10% of the Indian landmass. Much of it embraces the vast Thar Desert, a surprisingly vibrant and populated desert that is liberally scattered with rural villages, ancient trade-route towns and several rapidly growing cities that were once capitals of princely states.

The desert supports life because of the monsoon rains that percolate through the sands into the water table, to be tapped throughout the year at the ubiquitous wells scattered across the country. Areas of Bikaner, Jaisalmer and Barmer have been major agricultural centres ever since the Indira Ghandi Canal brought waters from the Himalaya. In recent years Rajasthan's life-giving monsoon has become less and less predictable, however, and the scarcity of rain and rapid drop in the water table have affected livelihoods, as well as the greater environment.

Chronic droughts accelerate migration from the parched agricultural lands to the already overburdened cities. Exacerbating the day-to-day hardships, a savage dust storm heralded in the monsoon in early May 2018 left a swathe of destruction across Rajasthan and Uttar Pradesh.

Of course, a desert has two things in ample supply – sunshine and space – and so, not surprisingly, Rajasthan leads India in renewable-energy generation. In 2017 the Bhadla Solar Park, one of the largest solar parks in the world, was commissioned near Jodhpur. In 2018, Rajasthan's solar-power plants were generating more than 1300MW of electricity, and the government has committed to achieve 25GW capacity in solar-electricity generation by 2022.

The desert also plays host to wind farms; the Jaisalmer wind farm, a pioneering effort that showed great foresight, has grown to become one of the world's biggest.

The State of Tourism

Tourism is probably the most important industry in Rajasthan; it is certainly the most obvious and seems to touch nearly everyone's lives. It brings in valuable foreign revenue and provides much-needed employment. Tourism funds the conservation of Rajasthan's magnificent heritage (including its tigers) and is the life blood of the region's splendid arts and crafts industry. The eminence and durability of the tourism industry have provided many locals from all walks of life with promising career options.

A large number of Rajasthanis now earn a living by working in hotels or souvenir shops, driving taxis or sprucing up their knowledge of history to become tourist guides. In 2018 Jaisalmer finally received commercial scheduled flights at its new airport, opening up the far-flung city to short-stay visitors.

Trending Now

Living standards in Rajasthan are rising, bringing previously unaffordable luxuries within arm's reach of many of urban Rajasthan's inhabitants. To the outsider, perhaps the most obvious of these luxuries must be the motorcycle and the motor car. Cities such as Jaipur and Jodhpur have rapidly become gridlocked with commuters, the air thick with fumes and beeping horns. Rajasthan's young are on the move – and it's nearly always astride a motorcycle. Infrastructure seems to lag well behind the growing population's needs, even though flyovers, freeways and elevated metros are popping up across the state.

The economy, whether you are talking about Rajasthan or the entire country, has undeniably made giant strides in recent years; however, the challenges for today's politicians – redistribution of wealth and environmental conservation – remain unresolved and at the forefront of chai-stall or cafe conversation. In December 2018 Rajasthan went to the polls along with four other Indian states. The swing against the sitting BJP party (which had won in a landslide in 2013) followed the usual pattern of Rajasthan voting out the incumbent state government. Indian National Congress easily formed a majority with a few independents and small parties.

As in much of the world, Rajasthan continues to lose its wildlife, fertile soils and vegetation, yet environmental awareness here is high by global standards and there are admirable ongoing efforts in Rajasthan in developing renewable energy. In a land where the juxtaposition of old and new has become a hackneyed slogan, the visitor must still marvel, and take heart, at the scene of ancient cenotaphs of silk-route nobility standing shoulder to shoulder with state-of-the-art wind turbines, which are helping to address India's burgeoning energy and pollution crises.

POPULATION (RAJASTHAN): **75.6 MILLION**

POPULATION (DELHI): **29 MILLION**

GDP (PER CAPITA, RAJASTHAN): **US$1700**

NATIONAL GDP GROWTH RATE: **7%**

AREA: **342,239 SQ KM**

GDP: **US$129 BILLION**

if Rajasthan were 100 people

33 would be 14 years or younger
60 would be aged between 15 and 59 years
7 would be older than 60 years and older

belief systems
(% of population)

| 89 | 9 | 1 | 1 |
| Hindu | Muslim | Sikh | Jain |

population per sq km

DELHI   RAJASTHAN   INDIA

👤 ≈ 225 people

History

A popular Indian saying is that the state of Rajasthan alone has more history than the rest of the country put together. Given that its name literally translates as 'the land of kings', perhaps the idea holds some truth. From war-ravaged forts to elaborate palaces, Rajasthan is a landscape strewn with the legacies of human endeavour, tenacity, skill and ruthlessness.

Back Where It All Began

The 24-spoke wheel, an emblem designed by Ashoka, has been adopted as the central motif on the national flag of India, where it is rendered in blue against a white background.

The desert and arid areas of Rajasthan have been home to humans for several thousand years. Excavations in Kalibangan, near Ganganagar in northern Rajasthan, have unearthed terracotta pottery and jewellery dating back to around 3000 BC – evidence of the region's earliest known settlements. Some of these urban centres were presumably absorbed into the Harappan segment of the Indus Valley civilisation, where they flourished until the settlement was mysteriously abandoned 3700 years ago. The mass exodus, possibly triggered by flooding or a severe climatic change, rendered the region devoid of human settlement for some time, until indigenous tribes such as the Bhils and the Minas moved in to set up their own squabbling small kingdoms, thereby commencing the long history of argumentative neighbours in the region.

But even as the tribes tore away at each other, another civilisation was sprouting in the fertile plains to the east of Rajasthan, between the rivers Yamuna and Ganga (Ganges), out of the seminomadic Indo-European race known as Aryans or 'noblemen'. It was in this civilisation that Hinduism first evolved as a religious tradition and a way of life, along with a complex patriarchal social structure and the tiered caste system that the greater Indian society adheres to even today. By 1000 BC, the province had seen the establishment of at least two prominent kingdoms: the Matsya territory of Viratnagar encompassing Alwar, Bharatpur, Dholpur and Karauli; and Indraprastha, the earliest-known incarnation of Delhi, which was successively built on by several dynasties to come.

Little is known of Rajasthan's development at this time, as the mighty empires that were then strengthening their hold on the sub-

TIMELINE	10,000 BC	2600–1700 BC	c 1500 BC
	Stone Age paintings created in the Bhimbetka rock shelters, in what is now Madhya Pradesh; the art continues here for many centuries. Settlements thought to exist across the subcontinent.	The heyday of the Indus Valley civilisation; the settlement spans parts of Rajasthan, Gujarat and the Sindh province in Pakistan.	The Indo-Aryan civilisation takes root in the fertile plains of the Indo-Gangetic basin. The settlers speak an early form of Sanskrit, from which several Indian languages later evolve.

continent largely chose to pass over the state. Alexander the Great, who reached as far as Punjab on his epic campaign to conquer the 'known world', was forced to return when his troops, homesick and weary after the campaign, convinced him to retreat. The Mauryan empire (323–185 BC) had minimal impact too, largely due to its most renowned emperor, Ashoka, taking to nonviolent ways after he converted to Buddhism. In stark contrast to the atrocities he had inflicted on the eastern Indian kingdom of Kalinga, the only evidence Ashoka left of his reign in Rajasthan were Buddhist caves and stupas (Buddhist shrines) near Jhalawar, rock-cut edicts at Bairat, and an ancient Buddhist site near Sariska Tiger Reserve & National Park. Plus there's a 13m-high pillar he inscribed in Delhi.

Marauding Huns & the Advent of Kings

The insulation that Rajasthan enjoyed through its early years came to an abrupt end during the 5th century AD, when armies of fierce Hun warriors rode in from Central Asia to carry out a series of pillaging raids across North India. These raids were to alter the course of the region's history in two major ways. To begin with, they resulted in the disintegration of the Gupta dynasty, which had taken over from the Mauryas as a central power and had reigned over the country from 320 to 550. But, more importantly, they triggered a parallel invasion, as the Rajputs finally came to make Rajasthan their home and, in the absence of an overarching monarchy, grew from strength to strength to usher in the golden age of Rajasthan.

Historical evidence suggests that the Rajputs (their name meaning 'children of kings') fled their homelands in Punjab, Haryana, Gujarat and Uttar Pradesh to settle in Rajasthan, primarily to escape the wrath of the White Huns (and later the Arabs), who had begun to storm in from Pakistan and Afghanistan. Once they had arrived in Rajasthan, the Rajputs trampled over the Bhils and Minas and set up their own small fiefdoms in the face of mounting local chaos. Though they largely belonged to the lower rungs of Hindu society, volatile circumstances demanded that the Rajputs don the role of warriors, if only to fend off further advances by foreign invaders. So in spite of rigid social norms, which didn't allow for any kind of self-promotion, early Rajput clans such as the Gurjara Pratiharas crossed the caste barriers to proclaim themselves Kshatriyas, members of the warrior class, who came second only to the Brahmins (priests) in the caste hierarchy.

To facilitate their smooth transition through social ranks, and to avoid stinging criticism from the Brahmins, these early Rajput clans chose to jettison their worldly ancestry and took to trumpeting a mythological genealogy that supposedly evolved from celestial origins. From

The concepts of zero and infinity are widely believed to have been devised by eminent Indian mathematicians, such as Aryabhatta and Varahamihira, during the reign of the Guptas.

1500–1200 BC	c 1000 BC	c 540 BC	563–483 BC
The Rig-Veda, the first and longest of Hinduism's canonical texts, the Vedas, is written; three more books follow. Earliest forms of priestly Brahmanical Hinduism emerge.	Indraprastha, Delhi's first incarnation, comes into being. Archaeological excavations at the site where the Purana Qila now stands continue even today.	The writing of the Mahabharata begins. The longest epic in the world, it takes nearly 250 years to complete and mentions settlements such as Indraprastha, Pushkar and Chittorgarh.	The life of Siddhartha Gautama. The prince attains enlightenment beneath the Bodhi Tree in Bodhgaya (Bihar), thereby transforming into the Buddha (Awakened One).

the 6th century onward, some of the clans began calling themselves Suryavanshis (Descendants of the Sun), while others chose to be known as Chandravanshis (Descendants of the Moon). A third dynasty, on the other hand, traced their roots to the sacrificial fire that was lit on Mt Abu during the Mauryan era, thereby naming themselves Agnivanshis (Fire-Born).

As the Rajputs slowly consolidated their grip over Rajasthan, they earned a reputation for their chivalry, noble traditions and strict code of conduct. They gave rise to several dynasties, which established some of the most renowned princely states of Rajasthan. The largest of these kingdoms, and the third largest in India after Kashmir and Hyderabad, was Marwar. Founded by the Suryavanshi Rathores who rode in from

THE INDOMITABLE SISODIAS

In a region where invasions and political upheavals were historical norms, the Sisodias of Mewar stood out as an exception, using everything from diplomacy to sheer valour to retain an iron grip over their land. Pillage and blood baths notwithstanding, the dynasty administered its kingdom in southern Rajasthan for 1400 years. Lorded over by 76 monarchs throughout the ages, the Sisodias have one of the longest-serving dynasties in the world.

The lineage of the Sisodia kings can be traced back to a prince named Guhil, born to a Rajput queen in the 6th century AD. Orphaned soon after birth and his kingdom ransacked by Huns, at age 11 he forged an alliance with a Bhil chieftain to establish a dynasty called the Guhilots and founded the state of Mewar.

In the 12th century, the family split, resulting in a breakaway faction that relocated to the town of Sissoda and renamed themselves Sisodias. They soon took over Chittorgarh, an ancient garrison that remained under their control until it was sacked by Mughal emperor Akbar in 1568. Though it came as a major military setback, the Sisodias lost no time in retreating into the Aravalli Hills, where they put together a new capital called Udaipur. A serenely beautiful city, Udaipur was never lost to the enemy and remained the capital of Mewar until the kingdom was absorbed into the state of Rajasthan following India's independence.

The Sisodias have been credited with producing some of the most flamboyant kings ever to have reigned in Rajasthan. The family boasts names such as Rana Sanga, who died a valiant death in 1527 while fending off Mughal troops under Babur, and Maharana Pratap (1540–97), who made several daring though unsuccessful attempts to win Chittorgarh back from Akbar during his time in power. Being prolific builders, the Sisodias also gave Mewar some of its finest structures, including the Victory Tower at Chittorgarh, the grand City Palace in Udaipur, the elegant Monsoon Palace atop Sajjangarh Hill and the spectacular Lake Palace, which stands on an island amid the placid waters of Lake Pichola, also in Udaipur.

326 BC	323–185 BC	1st century AD	320–550
Alexander the Great invades India. He defeats Porus in Punjab to enter the subcontinent, but a rebellion keeps him from advancing beyond the Beas River in Himachal Pradesh.	India comes under the rule of the Maurya kings. Founded by Chandragupta Maurya, this Pan-Indian empire is ruled from Pataliputra (Patna), and briefly adopts Buddhism.	International trade booms: the region's elaborate overland trade networks connect with ports and maritime routes. Trade to Africa, the Gulf, Southeast Asia, China and Rome thrives.	The period of the Gupta dynasty, the second of India's great monarchies after the Mauryas. This era is marked by a creative surge in literature and the arts.

Uttar Pradesh, it was initially ruled from Mandore, before the seat of power was relocated to the Mehrangarh Fort in nearby Jodhpur. The Sisodias migrated from Gujarat to assemble in the folds of the Aravalli Hills to the south, where they formed the state of Mewar encompassing Chittorgarh and Udaipur. The Kachhwahas, from Gwalior in Madhya Pradesh, settled in Jaipur in eastern Rajasthan, their capital nestled in the twin fort complex of Amber and Jaigarh. Meanwhile, a fourth kingdom, called Jaisalmer, was established in the Thar Desert by the Bhattis. Obscured by the dunes, the Bhattis remained more or less entrenched in their kingdom until Jaisalmer was integrated into the state of Rajasthan after independence.

Over the years, Rajasthan saw the mushrooming of many other smaller dynasties, each of which staked a claim to its own patch of territory in the region and ruled with complete autonomy, often refusing to submit to the whims of the bigger kingdoms. The clans were so content with their tiny fiefdoms that they rarely thought of looking beyond their borders to explore and conquer newer territories.

One dynasty was the exception. The Chauhans settled in Ajmer, from where they gradually extended their rule into Haryana and Uttar Pradesh. Within Rajasthan, the Hada offshoot of the Chauhans crossed over to the Hadoti region and captured the cities of Bundi and Kota, while the Deora branch took over the nearby Sirohi area, making way for successive generations to zero in on the provinces of Ranthambhore, Kishangarh and Shekhawati. The most illustrious of the Chauhan kings, Prithviraj III, even invaded Delhi – then on one of its temporary wanes – and commissioned the building of a settlement called Qila Rai Pithora, the ramparts of which can still be seen near the Qutb Minar in Mehrauli. One of the few Hindu kings to hold fort in Delhi, Prithviraj Chauhan administered his empire from the twin capitals of Qila Rai Pithora and Ajmer, before his reign was put to an end by Islamic warriors, who galloped in by the thousands to change the face of the region forever.

The Sword of Islam

Some 400 years after the Prophet Mohammed introduced Islam into Arabia, northern India saw the arrival of Muslims. With the banner of Islam fluttering high, forces seized the province of Sindh (in Pakistan) and then moved on to occupy the formerly Buddhist city of Ghazni in neighbouring Afghanistan. At the beginning of the 11th century, Turk warriors, led by the fearsome Sultan Mahmud of Ghazni, entered India, razing hundreds of Hindu temples and plundering the region, taking away vast amounts of wealth to fill their coffers back home. The Turks made their raids into India almost an annual affair, ransacking the northern part of the country 17 times in as many years. Jolted out of their internal

---

Best Rajput Monuments

Amber Fort
(Jaipur)

Mehrangarh
(Jodhpur)

Jaisalmer Fort

Chittorgarh

Kumbhalgarh

Ranthambhore Fort

500–600	1024	1192	1206
The emergence of the Rajputs in Rajasthan. Stemming from three principal races supposedly of celestial origin, they form 36 separate clans who claim their own kingdoms across the region.	Mahmud of Ghazni raids India for the last time, ransacking on this occasion the Somnath Temple in Gujarat, where he purportedly smashes the idol with his own hands.	Prithviraj Chauhan loses Delhi to Mohammed of Ghori. The defeat effectively ends Hindu supremacy in the region, exposing Rajasthan and the subcontinent to subsequent Muslim invaders.	Ghori is murdered during a prayer session while returning to Ghazni from a campaign in Lahore. In the absence of an heir, his kingdom is usurped by his generals. The Delhi Sultanate is born.

bickering, the Rajput princes organised some hasty defence, but their army was torn to shreds even before they could retaliate. Rajasthan had been incorporated into the Islamic empire.

Delhi, located further east, was initially spared the wrath of these invaders, as the sultan largely confined his raids to Rajasthan and parts of Gujarat. Trouble, however, came by the name of Mohammed of Ghori, governor of Ghazni, who invaded India in the late 12th century, defeating Rajput king Prithviraj Chauhan in the Second Battle of Tarain. Ghori left Delhi under the governorship of Qutb-ud-din Aibak, a former Turk slave who had risen to command forces in India. With news of Ghori's death a decade and a half later, Qutb-ud-din claimed the Indian part of Ghori's empire. He declared himself sultan of the region and founded the Mamluk or Slave dynasty, giving Delhi the first of its many Islamic monarchies.

The enthronement of Qutb-ud-din Aibak began the Sultanate era of Delhi, which lasted for about 350 years. Throughout this period, Delhi was ruled by five different Islamic dynasties, before the first period of Mughal rule in 1526. The Mamluks created the city of Mehrauli, while the Khiljis seated their capital at Siri, and the Tughlaqs constructed the forts of Tughlaqabad and Firoz Shah Kotla. There was one further sultanate, founded by the rebellious governor of Bihar, Sher Shah Suri, who seized control from the Mughal emperor Humayun in 1540 and founded his brief dynasty at Shergarh before Humayun reclaimed his empire in 1555. During this period, the whole of the Gangetic basin came under the Sultanates' control, as did Rajasthan and Gujarat – the princely states there had little option but to bow down to their might.

Despite its many achievements, the Sultanate period was marked by prolonged phases of political turmoil and administrative tension. Having become the jewel of foreign eyes, Delhi was persistently being attacked from the northwest by Mongol, Persian, Turk and Afghan raiders, who all wanted to set up their own outposts in the city. Eventually, two noblemen who were disgraced by Sultan Ibrahim Lodi decided to get even by inviting Babur, prince of Kabul, to invade Delhi, paving the way for the most celebrated Islamic dynasty to roll into India.

Enter the Mughals

Babur, whose Turkic-Mongol lineage included great warriors such as Genghis Khan and Timur the Lame, marched into India through Punjab, defeating Ibrahim Lodi in the First Battle of Panipat (1526) to establish the Mughal dynasty in the country. Once he had seized Delhi, Babur focused his attention on Rajasthan, where many princely states, anticipating his moves, had already banded together to form a united front under the Sisodia king Rana Sanga. Taking advantage of the chaos in Delhi,

Rajput armies primarily consisted of cavalries. They were known to breed pedigree horses such as the Marwari and Kathiawari for use by their mounted forces.

The Great Mughals

Babur (r 1526–30)

Humayun (r 1530–56)

Akbar (r 1556–1605)

Jehangir (r 1605–27)

Shah Jahan (r 1627–58)

Aurangzeb (r 1658–1707)

1303	1321	1336	1398
Ala-ud-din Khilji sacks Chittorgarh with the intention of carrying away Sisodia queen Padmini. The queen immolates herself to escape humiliation – the first recorded instance of *sati* (ritual suicide) in Rajasthan.	The Tughlaqs come to power in Delhi. Mohammed bin Tughlaq expands his empire but becomes known for inelegant schemes, such as creating forgery-prone currency.	Foundation of the mighty Vijayanagar empire, named after its capital city, the ruins of which can be seen today in the vicinity of Hampi (in modern-day Karnataka).	Timur the Lame invades Delhi on the pretext that the Sultans of Delhi are too tolerant with their Hindu subjects. He executes more than 100,000 Hindu captives before the battle for Delhi.

the Rajputs had meanwhile clawed back into the power race, and states such as Mewar had become formidable enough to pose a considerable threat to the rulers of Delhi. Babur, however, squared everything by defeating the Rajput alliance in a blood-spattered battle where several Rajput chiefs, including Rana Sanga, fell to the enemy's wrath. The defeat, which shook the foundations of the Rajput states, also left the Mughals as the undisputed rulers of northern India.

Mughal supremacy was briefly cut back in the mid-16th century by Sher Shah Suri, who defeated Babur's successor Humayun to give Delhi its sixth and final Sultanate. Humayun reclaimed Delhi 14 years later, and upon his accidental death was succeeded by his 13-year-old son Akbar. Known as the greatest of the Mughal emperors, Akbar ruled for 49 years and, being a master diplomat, used both tact and military force to expand and consolidate the Mughal empire in India. Realising that the Rajputs could not be conquered on the battlefield alone, Akbar arranged a marriage alliance with a princess of the important Kachhwaha clan, which held Amber (and later Jaipur), and even chose Rajput warriors to head his armies. Honoured by these gestures, the Kachhwahas, unlike other Rajputs, aligned themselves with the powerful Mughals, and Akbar succeeded in winning over one of the biggest Rajput states.

Of course, when diplomacy didn't work, Akbar resorted to war; he conquered Ajmer, and later proceeded to take the mighty forts of Chittorgarh and Ranthambhore. Gradually, all the important Rajput states except Mewar had acknowledged Mughal sovereignty and become vassal states. But even as he was well on his way to becoming the supreme ruler of India, Akbar became more tolerant in many ways. He married a Hindu Rajput princess and encouraged good relations between Hindus and Muslims, giving Rajputs special privileges so that they were embraced within his empire. A monarch with great social insight, he discouraged child marriage, banned *sati* (ritual suicide of a widow on her husband's funeral pyre) and arranged special market days for women. Akbar's reign also saw an unprecedented economic boom in the country, as well as great development in art and architecture.

Known for his religious tolerance, Akbar propounded a cult called Din-i-Ilahi, which incorporated the best elements of the two principal religions of his empire: Hinduism and Islam.

The Last of the Mughal Greats

Jehangir, Akbar's son, was the next Mughal emperor (r 1605–27) and he ruled alongside his adored Persian wife, Nur Jahan, who wielded considerable power and brought Persian influences to the court. Nur Jahan also commissioned the beautiful Itimad-ud-Daulah, the first Mughal structure to be built in marble, in Agra for her parents. The Rajputs maintained cordial relationships with the Mughals through Jehangir's rule, a notable development being that Udai Singh, king of Udaipur, ended Mewar's reservations about the Muslims by befriending Jehangir.

Top History Reads

India: A History, John Keay

The Great Moghuls, Bamber Gascoigne

A History of Rajasthan, Rima Hooja

1504	1526	1540	1556
Agra is founded on the banks of the Yamuna River by Sikandar Lodi. Its glory days begin when Akbar makes it his capital and the city is briefly called Akbarabad during his reign.	Babur conquers Delhi and stuns Rajasthan by routing its confederate force, gaining a technological edge on the battlefield due to the early introduction of matchlock muskets in his army.	The Sur dynasty briefly captures Delhi from the Mughals – the loss forces the Mughals to temporarily seek help from the Rajputs.	Hemu, a Hindu general in Adil Shah Suri's army, seizes Delhi after Humayun's death. He rules for barely a month before losing to Akbar in the Second Battle of Panipat.

Best Mughal Monuments

Taj Mahal (Agra)

Fatehpur Sikri

Humayun's Tomb (Delhi)

Jama Masjid (Delhi)

Agra Fort (Agra)

Red Fort (Delhi)

Good times, however, came to an end soon after Jehangir's period in office, as his descendants' greater emphasis on Islam began to rock the relative peace in the region. Upon Jehangir's death, the prince Khurram took over, assuming the title Shah Jahan, meaning 'monarch of the world'. His reign was the pinnacle of Mughal power. Like his predecessors, Shah Jahan was a patron of the arts and some of the finest examples of Mughal art and architecture were produced during his reign, including the Taj Mahal, an extravagant work of extreme refinement and beauty. Shah Jahan also commenced work on Delhi's seventh incarnation, Shahjahanabad, constructing the Red Fort and the Jama Masjid.

Unfortunately, the emperor harboured high military ambitions and often bled the country's financial resources to meet his whims. His exhaustion of the state treasury didn't go down well with the Rajputs and towards the end of Shah Jahan's rule, the Rajputs and the Mughals had become uneasy bedfellows. Things worsened when Aurangzeb became the last great Mughal emperor in 1658, deposing his father, who died in imprisonment at the Musamman Burj in Agra eight years later. An Islamic hardliner, Aurangzeb quickly made enemies in the region. His zeal saw him devoting all his resources to extending the Mughal empire's boundaries. His government's emphasis on Islam alienated his Hindu subjects.

DELHI'S TWILIGHT YEARS

The death of Aurangzeb marked the beginning of Delhi's twilight years, a period through which the degenerating Mughal empire was laid to waste by the Marathas and the Persians. The Marathas had risen to prominence between 1646 and 1680, led by the heroic Shivaji, under whom their empire was administered by the *peshwas*, or chief ministers, who later went on to become hereditary rulers. At a time when the Mughals were struggling to hold their empire together, the Marathas supplied them with regiments from the south, gaining their own stranglehold on Delhi at the same time. The new army soon went out of control and began to take possession of the land. Contemporary Mughal rulers, who were both ineffective and cowardly, failed to curb the unruly military behaviour. The resulting confusion was capitalised on by the Persian invader Nadir Shah, who sacked Delhi in 1739 and robbed the city of much of its wealth. Seeing which way the wind was blowing, the Marathas abandoned the Mughals and joined the Persians in pillaging the capital. They soon sucked Delhi dry of all its treasures and, when there was nothing left to rob, the Marathas turned their eyes on Rajasthan. Raids and skirmishes with the Rajputs followed; cities were sacked, lives were lost and the Marathas began to win large tracts of Rajput land in the state. The absence of a central Indian authority only contributed to the mayhem, so much so that India had to wait until the early 19th century for another invasion to bring the country under a single umbrella once again.

1568	1608	1631	1674
Akbar leads his army to Chittorgarh and wrests it from the Sisodias. Udai Singh, then king of Mewar, survives the onslaught and transfers his capital to the new city of Udaipur.	After being granted trading rights by way of a royal charter, the first ships of the British East India Company sail up the Arabian Sea to drop anchor at Surat in Gujarat.	Construction of the Taj Mahal begins after Shah Jahan, devastated by the death of his wife Mumtaz Mahal, vows to build the most beautiful mausoleum in the world in her memory.	Shivaji establishes the Maratha kingdom, spanning western India and parts of the Deccan and North India. He assumes the supercilious title of Chhatrapati (Lord of the Universe).

Aurangzeb imposed punitive taxes, banned the building of new temples, destroyed many more and forbade music and ceremonies at court. Challenges to his power mounted steadily as people reacted against his dour reign. And when he claimed his rights over Jodhpur in 1678, his relations with the Rajputs turned into full-scale war. Before long, there was insurgency on all sides, which only increased when Aurangzeb died in 1707, leaving the empire in the hands of a line of inefficient successors given to bohemian excesses, who had little or no interest in running the state. The Mughal empire was on a one-way journey towards doom.

The British Drop Anchor

The British invaders came by the sea, following the Portuguese explorer Vasco da Gama, who had first discovered the sea route from Europe to India around Africa in 1498. The British East India Company, a London trading firm that wanted a slice of the Indian spice trade (having seen how well the Portuguese were doing), landed in India in the early 1600s. Granted trading rights by Jehangir, the company set up its first trading outpost in Surat in Gujarat and gradually went about extending its influence across the country, harbouring interests that went beyond mere trade. Extraordinarily enough, this commercial firm ended up nominally ruling India for 250 years.

Sooner or later, all leading European maritime nations came and pitched camp in India. Yet none managed to spread out across the country as efficiently as the British. The early English agents became well assimilated in India, learning Persian and intermarrying with local people, which gave them an edge over other European hopefuls. When the Mughal empire collapsed, they made a calculated political move, filling the power vacuum and taking over the reins of administration through a series of battles and alliances with local rulers. By the early 19th century, India was effectively under British control and the British government in London had begun to take a more direct role in supervising affairs in India, while leaving the East India Company to deal with day-to-day administrative duties.

Outside British territory, the country was in a shambles. Bandits were on the prowl in the rural areas, and towns and cities had fallen into decay. The Marathas' raids in Rajasthan continued and though the British at first ignored the feuding parties, they soon spotted an opportunity for expansion and stepped into the fray. They negotiated treaties with the leaders of the main Rajput states, offering them protection from the Marathas in return for political and military support. The trick worked. Weakened by habitual wrangling and ongoing conflicts, the rulers forfeited their independence in exchange for protection and British residents were installed in the princely states. The British ultimately

The Doctrine of Lapse, a policy formulated by Lord Dalhousie, enabled the East India Company to annex any princely state if its ruler was either found incompetent or died without a direct heir.

White Mughals by William Dalrymple tells the true story of an East India Company soldier who married an Indian Muslim princess, a tragic love story interwoven with harem politics, intrigue and espionage.

1707	1739	1747	1756
Death of Aurangzeb, the last of the Mughal greats. His demise triggers the gradual collapse of the Mughal empire as anarchy and rebellion break out across the country.	Nadir Shah plunders Delhi and carries away with him the Peacock Throne, as well as the Koh-i-noor, a magnificent diamond that eventually becomes the property of British royalty.	Afghan ruler Ahmad Shah Durrani sweeps across northern India, capturing Lahore and Kashmir, sacking Delhi and dealing another blow to the rapidly contracting Mughal empire.	The rise of the notorious Jat dynasty of Bharatpur in Rajasthan. Under the leadership of Suraj Mahl and his son Jawahar Singh, the Jats join the Marathas and Persians in looting Delhi and Agra.

eliminated the Maratha threat, but, in the process, the Rajputs were effectively reduced to puppets. Delhi's prominence as a national capital dwindled too, as the British chose to rule the country from Calcutta (now Kolkata).

The later British authorities had an elitist notion of their own superiority that was to have a lasting impact on India. The colonisers felt that it was their duty to civilise the nation, unlike the first agents of the East India Company who had seen and recognised the value in India's native culture. During the first half of the 19th century, the British brought about radical social reforms. They introduced education in the English language, which replaced Persian as the language of politics and governance. New roads and canal systems were installed, followed by the foundation of schools and universities modelled on the British system of education. In the later stages, they brought in the postal system, the

THE FIRST WAR OF INDEPENDENCE: THE INDIAN UPRISING

In 1857, half a century after having established firm control of India, the British suffered a serious setback. To this day, the causes of the Uprising (known at the time as the Indian Mutiny and subsequently labelled by nationalist historians as the War of Independence) are the subject of debate. The key factors included the influx of cheap goods, such as textiles, from Britain that destroyed many livelihoods, the dispossession of territories from many rulers and taxes imposed on landowners.

The incident that's popularly held to have sparked the Uprising, however, took place at an army barracks in Meerut in Uttar Pradesh on 10 May 1857. A rumour leaked out that a new type of bullet was greased with what Hindus claimed was cow fat, while Muslims maintained that it came from pigs; pigs are considered unclean to Muslims and cows are sacred to Hindus. Since loading a rifle involved biting the end off the waxed cartridge, these rumours provoked considerable unrest.

In Meerut, the situation was handled with a singular lack of judgement. The commanding officer lined up his soldiers and ordered them to bite off the ends of their issued bullets. Those who refused were immediately marched off to prison. The following morning, the soldiers of the garrison rebelled, shot their officers and marched to Delhi. Of the 74 Indian battalions of the Bengal army, seven (one of them Gurkhas) remained loyal, 20 were disarmed and the other 47 mutinied. The soldiers and peasants rallied around the ageing Mughal emperor in Delhi. They held Delhi for some months and besieged the British Residency in Lucknow for five months before they were finally suppressed. The incident left festering scars on both sides.

Almost immediately the East India Company was wound up and direct control of the country was assumed by the British government, which announced its support for the existing rulers of the princely states, claiming it would not interfere in local matters as long as the states remained loyal to the British.

1757	1857	1858	1869
Breaking out of its business mould, the East India Company registers its first military victory on Indian soil. Siraj-ud-Daulah, nawab of Bengal, is defeated by Robert Clive in the Battle of Plassey.	The short-lived First War of Independence breaks out across India. In the absence of a national leader, the rebels coerce the last Mughal king, Bahadur Shah Zafar, to proclaim himself emperor of India.	British government assumes control over India – with power officially transferred from the East India Company to the Crown – beginning the period known as the British Raj.	The birth of Mohandas Karamchand Gandhi in Porbandar (Gujarat) – the man who would later become popularly known as Mahatma Gandhi and affectionately dubbed 'Father of the Nation'.

telegraph and the railways, introductions that remain vital to the Indian administrative system today.

But at the same time, British bureaucracy came with controversial policies. Severe taxes were imposed on landowners and, as raw materials from India were used in British industry, cheap British-produced goods began to flood Indian markets and destroy local livelihoods. Mass anger in the country began to rise and found expression in the First War of Independence (Indian Uprising) in 1857. Soldiers and peasants took over Delhi for four months and besieged the British Residency in Lucknow for five months before they were finally suppressed by the East India Company's forces. Rajasthan also saw uprisings among the poor and middle classes, but there was little effect in the royal circles as Rajput kings continued to support the British and were rewarded for their loyalty after the British government assumed direct control of the country the following year.

> *The Proudest Day: India's Long Road to Independence* by Anthony Read and David Fisher is an engaging account of India's pre-Independence period.

Independence & Partition

Following a lengthy freedom movement, India finally liberated itself from British domination in 1947. The road to Independence was an extraordinary one, influenced by Mohandas Karamchand Gandhi, later known as the Mahatma (Great Soul), who galvanised the peasants and villagers into a nonviolent resistance that was to spearhead the nationalist movement. A lawyer by qualification, he caused chaos by urging people to refuse to pay taxes and boycott British institutions and products. He campaigned for the Dalits (the lower classes of Hindu society, whom he called Harijans or the 'Children of God') and the rural poor, capturing the public imagination through his approach, example and rhetoric.

The freedom struggle gained momentum under him, so much so that the British Labour Party, which came to power in 1945, saw Indian independence as inevitable. The process of the handover of power was initiated, but Hindu–Muslim differences took their toll at this crucial moment and the country was divided along religious lines, with the formation of Pakistan to appease the Muslim League, which sought to distance itself from a Hindu-dominated country. Mahatma Gandhi was slain soon after Independence by a Hindu extremist who hated his inclusive philosophy.

> In an attempt to prevent partition, Mahatma Gandhi unsuccessfully argued that the leader of the Muslim League, Mohammed Ali Jinnah, should lead a united India.

Prior to the change of guard, the British had shifted their capital out of Calcutta (Kolkata) and built the imperial city of New Delhi through the early 1900s, work which was overseen by architect Edwin Lutyens. Meant to be an expression of British permanence, the city was speckled with grand structures such as the Rashtrapati Bhavan, the Central Vista and hundreds of residential buildings that came to be known as Lutyens Bungalows. After Independence, many of these colonial buildings were used to house the brand-new Indian government, as Delhi was

1885	1911	1940	1947
The Indian National Congress, India's first home-grown political organisation, is set up. It brings educated Indians together and plays a key role in India's freedom struggle.	Architect Edwin Lutyens begins work on New Delhi, the newest manifestation of Delhi, subsequently considered in architectural circles to be one of the finest garden cities ever built.	The Muslim League adopts the Lahore Resolution, which champions greater Muslim autonomy in India. Subsequent campaigns for a separate Islamic nation are spearheaded by Mohammed Ali Jinnah.	India gains independence on 15 August. Pakistan is formed a day earlier. Thousands of Hindus and Muslims brave communal riots to migrate to their respective nations.

MAHARAJA METAMORPHOSIS

The fate of the royal families of Rajasthan since Independence has been mixed. A handful of the region's maharajas have continued their wasteful ways, squandering their fortunes and reducing themselves to abject poverty. A few zealous ones, who hated to see their positions of power go, have switched to politics and become members of leading political parties in India. Some have skipped politics to climb the rungs of power in other well-known national institutions, such as sports administration bodies or charitable and non-profit organisations in the country. Only a few have chosen to lead civilian lives, earning a name for themselves as fashion designers, cricketers or entertainers.

The majority of kings, however, have refused to let bygones be bygones, and have cashed in on their heritage by opening ticketed museums for tourists and converting their palaces into lavish hotels. With passing time, the luxury hospitality business has begun to find more and more takers from around the world. The boom in this industry can be traced back to 1971, when Indira Gandhi, then India's prime minister, abolished the privileges granted to the Rajasthan royals at the time of accession. Coming as a massive shock to those at the top of the pile, the snipping of the cash cord forced many to reluctantly join the long list of heritage hotel owners.

In spite of the abolition, many kings choose to continue using their royal titles for social purposes. While these titles are little more than status symbols now, they still help garner enormous respect from the public. On the other hand, nothing these days quite evokes the essence of Rajput grandeur like a stay in palatial splendour surrounded by vestiges of the regal age, in places such as Rambagh Palace (p53) in Jaipur and Umaid Bhawan Palace (p120) in Jodhpur. Not all the royal palaces of Rajasthan are on the tourist circuit, though. Many of them continue to serve as residences for erstwhile royal families and some of the mansions left out of the tourism pie are crumbling away, ignored and neglected, their decaying interiors home to pigeons and bats.

reinstated to its former status as the administrative and political capital of the country.

Rajasthan Is Born

Ever since they swore allegiance to the British, the Rajput kingdoms subjugated themselves to absolute British rule. On the verge of redundancy, they also chose to trade in their real power for pomp and extravagance. Consumption took over from chivalry and, by the early 20th century, many of the kings were spending their time travelling the world with scores of retainers, playing polo and occupying entire floors of expensive Western hotels. Many maintained huge fleets of expensive cars, a fine collection of which can be seen in the automobile museum in Udaipur (p98).

1948	1948–56	1952	1971
Mahatma Gandhi is assassinated in New Delhi on 30 January by Nathuram Godse. Godse and his co-conspirator Narayan Apte are later tried, convicted and executed.	Rajasthan takes shape as the princely states form a beeline to sign the Instrument of Accession and give up their territories, which are incorporated into the newly formed Republic of India.	The first elections are held in Rajasthan and the state gets its first taste of democracy after centuries of monarchical rule. The Congress is the first party to be elected into office.	The Third Indo-Pakistan War spills into Rajasthan, with the Battle of Longewala fought in the Thar Desert. The conflict concludes with the independence of East Pakistan as Bangladesh.

While it suited the British to indulge them, the maharajas' profligacy was economically and socially detrimental to their subjects, with the exception of a few capable rulers such as Ganga Singh of Bikaner. Remnants of the Raj (the British government in India before 1947) can be spotted all over the region today, from the Mayo College in Ajmer to the colonial villas in Mt Abu, and in the black-and-white photographs, documenting chummy Anglo-Rajput hunting expeditions, which deck the walls of any self-respecting heritage hotel in the state.

After Independence, from a security point of view, it became crucial for the new Indian union to ensure that the princely states of Rajasthan were integrated into the new nation. Most of these states were located near the vulnerable India–Pakistan border and it made sense for the government to push for a merger that would minimise possibilities of rebellion in the region. Thus, when the boundaries of the new nation were being chalked out, the ruling Congress Party made a deal with the nominally independent Rajput states to cede power to the republic. To sweeten the deal, the rulers were offered lucrative monetary returns and government stipends, as well as being allowed to retain their titles and property holdings. Having fallen on hard times, the royals could only agree with the government, and their inclination to yield to the Indian dominion gradually brought about the formation of the state of Rajasthan.

To begin with, the state comprised only the southern and southeastern regions of Rajasthan. Mewar was one of the first kingdoms to join the union. Udaipur was initially the state capital, with the maharaja of Udaipur becoming rajpramukh (head of state). The Instrument of Accession was signed in 1949 and Jaipur, Bikaner, Jodhpur and Jaisalmer were then merged, with Jaipur as the state's new capital. Later that year, the United State of Matsya was incorporated into Rajasthan. The state finally burgeoned to its current dimensions in November 1956, with the additions of Ajmer-Merwara, Abu Rd and a tract of Dilwara, originally part of the princely state of Sirohi that had been divided between Gujarat and Rajasthan. Rajasthan is now India's largest state.

A Modern State

The long history of insurgency and unrest in India did not end with Independence. In 1962 India had a brief war with China over disputed border territories and went on to engage in three battles with Pakistan over similar issues. In 1974 in Pokaran, India detonated a nuclear device leading to Pakistan withdrawing from normalising relations talks and developing it's own nuclear bomb.

Political assassinations didn't recede into history either. Indira Gandhi, India's first female prime minister (and daughter of Jawaharlal

Discover the bygone days of Rajasthan's royalty in *A Princess Remembers*, the memoirs of Gayatri Devi, maharani of Jaipur. Cowritten by Santha Rama Rau, it's an enthralling read.

Plain Tales from the Raj by Charles Allen (ed) is a fascinating series of interviews with people who played a role in the fading days of British India.

HISTORY A MODERN STATE

1974	1984	2001	2013
India detonates its first nuclear bomb in Pokaran, Rajasthan, leading directly to Pakistan's development of a nuclear bomb.	Prime Minister Indira Gandhi is assassinated by her Sikh bodyguards. Her son Rajiv succeeds her as leader but is himself murdered in office in 1991.	A suicide attack on the Indian parliament in New Delhi nearly leads to war with Pakistan, with mass troop mobilisation along the border, including in Rajasthan.	The Bharatiya Janata Party (BJP) wins a staggering majority in the Rajasthan state assembly elections.

Nehru, India's prime minister at Independence), was gunned down by her Sikh bodyguards in retaliation for her ordering the storming of the Golden Temple, the holiest of Sikh shrines, in 1984. Her son, Rajiv, who succeeded her to the post of prime minister, was also assassinated, by Tamil terrorists protesting India's stance on Sri Lankan policies.

Rajiv's Italian-born widow, Sonia, was the next of the Gandhis to take up the dynastic mantle of power. She became president of the Congress Party and in 2004 anointed her son Rahul as her chosen successor. However, in Rajasthan, as seen elsewhere across India, the party that fed on the reputation and charisma of the Nehru-Gandhi dynasty since India's formative years was swept away in the 2013 state and the 2014 federal electoral tidal waves that brought the Bharatiya Janata Party (BJP) into power in both constituencies. The trend for Rajasthan state assembly elections to remove incumbent parties continued in the 2018 state elections when Congress took power with the aid of minor parties.

> The results of the 2011 census found India's population had increased by a staggering 181 million over 10 years.

2014	2015	2017	2018
Narendra Modi becomes prime minister as the BJP wins federal parliamentary elections in a landslide.	The anticorruption Aam Aadmi Party (AAP) unexpectedly wins state elections in Delhi, overturning the BJP ascendancy.	The much anticipated tax reform, the introduction of a goods and services tax (GST), is implemented across India, replacing 15 state and federal taxes.	Rajasthan tosses out the BJP in favour of Indian National Congress in the state elections, but it's not a landslide nor an outright majority and minor parties figure in the ruling coalition.

Rajasthani Way of Life

From the tribal villages of the Thar Desert to the modern hustle of Jaipur, there are few places in India where traditional and modern life jut up against each other as they do in Rajasthan, and in such an exciting and intriguing manner. Camel carts pass hi-tech solar farms and mobile phones are ubiquitous, yet conservative social mores underpin everyday life.

Contemporary Life

Indian society as a whole continues to grapple with competition between traditionalism and the effects of globalisation. Cities such as Jaipur may have acquired a liberal sheen on the outside and foreign influences are apparent in the public domain – satellite TV rules the airwaves, mobile phones are nothing short of a necessity and coffee shops are jam-packed on the weekends – but within the walls of a typical home, life often remains conservative at heart, with family affairs dominated by the man of the house. Gender politics are a touchstone issue, from sexual relationships outside marriage to the independence of women.

In the region's backyard, the scene is rather stark. Rural Rajasthan remains one of the poorest areas in the country. Being in close proximity to the Thar Desert, the climate here is harsh and people dwelling in the region's villages are locked in a day-to-day battle for survival, as they have been for ages. Unemployment is rife, which in turn has led to problems such as debt, drug abuse, alcoholism and prostitution. Indigenous tribes have been the worst affected and it isn't uncommon to see members from their communities begging or performing tricks at traffic signals in return for loose change.

Rajasthan also lags behind on the education front, its literacy rate being about 7% behind the national average of 74%. The nationwide 'education-for-all' program aims to impart elementary education to all Indian children. The project focuses on the education of girls, who have historically been deprived of quality schooling; a particular problem in Rajasthan, where the female literacy rate is just 52%, compared to 79% for men.

Marriage & Divorce

Indian marriages were always meant to unite families, not individuals. In rural Rajasthan, the case remains much the same today. Unlike in cities, where people now find love through online dating sites, marriages in villages and small towns are still arranged by parents. Those getting married have little say in the proceedings and cross-caste marriages are almost always forbidden. Few move out of their parents' homes after tying the knot; setting up an independent establishment postmarriage is often considered an insult to the elderly.

By and large, marriages in rural areas are initiated by professional matchmakers, who strike a suitable match based on family status, caste

Matchmaking has embraced the cyber age, with popular sites including www.shaadi.com, www.bharatmatrimony.com and, more progressively, www.secondshaadi.com – for those seeking a partner again.

and compatible horoscopes. Once a marriage is finalised, the bride's family often arranges for a dowry to be paid to the groom's parents, as an appreciation of their graciously accepting the bride as a member of their family. These dowries are officially illegal, but remain commonplace and can run into hundreds of thousands of rupees, ranging from hard cash to items such as TVs, motorcycles and household furniture.

Despite the exact amount of dowry being finalised at the time of betrothal, there have been sporadic cases reported where the groom's family later insists that the girl's parents cough up more, failing which the bride might be subjected to abuse and domestic violence. Stories of newly married girls dying in kitchen 'accidents' are not uncommon. In most cases, they leave the grooms free to remarry and claim another dowry.

Indian law sets the marriageable age of men and women at 21 and 18 respectively, yet child marriages continue to be practised in rural Rajasthan. It is estimated that one in every two girls in the state's villages are married off before they turn 15. Divorce and remarriage is becoming more common (primarily in bigger cities), but divorce is still not granted by courts as a matter of routine and is not looked upon very favourably by society. Even if a divorce is obtained, it is difficult for a woman to find another husband; as a divorcee, she is considered less chaste than a spinster.

Given the stigma associated with divorce, few people have the courage to walk out on each other, instead preferring to silently endure. Also facing frequent social stigma are widows. While the practice of *sati* (the ritual self-immolation of a wife on her husband's funeral pyre) has passed into history, many expect widows to remain in mourning for the rest of their lives, and face being ostracised from their families and communities.

Women in Rajasthan

According to the most recent census in 2011, India's population is comprised of 586 million women, with an estimated 68% of those working (mostly as labourers) in the agricultural sector. Women are seen primarily as mothers in Indian society and gender equality is a distant aspiration for the majority of Rajasthani women. Being socially disadvantaged,

FIRST IMPRESSIONS

It's not the turbaned maharajas or the call-centre graduates or even the stereotypical beggars, for that matter: the first people you run into upon your arrival in Rajasthan are a jostling bunch of overly attentive locals, who ambush travellers the moment they step out of the airport or the railway station and swamp new arrivals in a sea of unsolicited offers. Great hotels, taxi rides at half-price, above-the-rate currency exchange...the list goes on, interspersed with beaming smiles you would usually only expect from long-lost friends. Famed Indian hospitality at work? This is no reception party; the men are touts out on their daily rounds, trying to wheedle a few bucks off unsuspecting travellers. There's no way you can escape them, though a polite but firm 'no, thank you' often stands you in good stead under such circumstances. It's a welcome each and every newcomer is accorded in India.

It's hard not to get put off by the surprise mobbing, but don't let such incidents make you jump to the hasty conclusion that every local is out to hound a few rupees out of you. Walk out of the terminal and into the real India and things suddenly come across as strikingly different. With little stake in your activities, the people you now meet are genuinely warm (even if overtly curious), hospitable and sometimes helpful beyond what you'd call mere courtesy. For example, someone might volunteer to show you around a monument expecting absolutely nothing in return. And while it's advisable to always keep your wits about you, going with the flow often helps you understand the Indian psyche better, as well as making your trip to the region all the more memorable.

HIJRAS: THE THIRD SEX

India's most visible nonheterosexual group is the *hijras,* a caste of transvestites and eunuchs who dress in women's clothing. Some are gay, some are hermaphrodites and some were unfortunate enough to be kidnapped and castrated. Since it has long been traditionally frowned upon to live openly as a gay man in India, *hijras* get around this by becoming, in effect, a third sex of sorts. They work mainly as wandering entertainers at weddings and celebrations of the birth of male children and also as prostitutes.

Read more about *hijras* in *The Invisibles* by Zia Jaffrey, and *Ardhanarishvara the Androgyne* by Alka Pande.

women face many restrictions on their freedoms and, as keepers of a family's honour, they risk accusations of immorality if they mingle freely with strangers. For visitors to India, it can be quite disconcerting to walk through a rural village and see women beating a quick retreat into the privacy of their homes, their faces hidden behind the folds of their saris.

Screened from the outside world, most women in rural Rajasthan live a life that revolves around household tasks and raising children. Where women are permitted to work, this usually involves working in the family fields. Even in professional circles, women are generally paid less than their male counterparts. Besides all this, India's patriarchal society rarely recognises women as inheritors of family property, which almost always goes to male heirs. The birth of a girl child is often seen as unlucky, since it not only means an extra mouth to feed but also a dowry that needs to be given away at the time of marriage. Embryonic sex determination is practised, despite it being illegal, and local media occasionally blows the lid off surgical rackets where surgeons charge huge amounts of money to carry out female-foeticide operations.

Progress has been made, however, in the form of development programs run by the central and state governments, as well as nongovernmental organisations (NGOs) and voluntary outfits that have swung into action. Organisations such as the Barefoot College, URMAL Trust and Seva Mandir all run grass-roots programs in Rajasthan, with volunteering opportunities (p275), devoted to awareness, education, health issues and female empowerment. Women are entitled to vote and own property; however, they're still notably under-represented in the state and national parliaments, accounting for around 13% and 11%, respectively, of parliamentary members.

In the cities, the scene is much better. Urban women in Jaipur have worked their way to social and professional recognition and feminists are no longer dismissed as fringe extremists. Even so, some of India's first-generation female executives recall a time not very long ago when women encountered resistance when they put in a request for maternity leave, as motherhood had been precluded as an occasion that merited time off from work.

Opium was traditionally served to guests at social functions by several indigenous communities of Rajasthan. Though the sale of opium is now illegal, it continues behind law-enforcers' backs.

Peoples of Rajasthan

Much of Rajasthan's population still lives in rural villages, but the young are on the move. The cities attract people from all walks of life to create a high-density, multiethnic population. Religious ghettos can be found in places such as Ajmer and Jaipur, where a fair number of Christian families live; the Ganganagar district, home to a large number of Sikhs; and parts of Alwar and Bharatpur, where the populace is chiefly Muslim. Though most Muslims in Rajasthan belong to the Sunni sect, the state also has a small but affluent community of Shiite Muslims, called the Bohras, living in the southeast.

CRICKET

Cricket is a national obsession in India, and Rajasthan is no exception. Nearly everybody claims to understand the game down to its finer points and can comment on it with endless vigour. Shops down shutters and streets take on a deserted look every time India happens to be playing a test match or a crucial one-day game. The arrival of the Twenty-20 format and domestic leagues such as the Indian Premier League (IPL) has only taken the game's popularity a notch further.

Keep your finger on the cricketing pulse at www.espncricinfo.com and www.cricbuzz.com. Cricket tragics will be bowled over by *The Illustrated History of Indian Cricket* by Boria Majumdar, and *The States of Indian Cricket* by Ramachandra Guha.

Tribes & Indigenous Communities

Rajasthan has a large indigenous population, comprising communities that are native to the region and those that have lived there for centuries. Called Adivasis (ancient dwellers), most of these ethnic groups have been listed as Scheduled Tribes by the government. The majority of the Adivasis are pagan, though some have either taken to Hindu ways or converted to Christianity over time.

Bhils

The largest of Rajasthan's tribes, the Bhils live to the southeast, spilling over into Madhya Pradesh. They speak their own distinct native language and have a natural talent for archery and warfare. Witchcraft, magic and superstition are deeply rooted in their culture. Polygamy is still practised by those who can afford it and love marriages are the norm.

Originally a hunter-gatherer community, the Bhils have survived years of exploitation by higher castes to finally take up small-scale agriculture. Some have left their villages to head for the cities. Literacy is still below average and not too many Bhil families have many assets to speak of, but these trends are slowly being reversed. The Baneshwar Fair is a huge Bhil festival, where you can sample the essence of their culture firsthand.

Minas

For comprehensive information on India's native and tribal communities, check out www.tribal.nic.in, maintained by the Ministry of Tribal Affairs under the Government of India.

The Minas are the second-largest tribal group in Rajasthan and live around Shekhawati and eastern Rajasthan. The name Mina comes from *meen* (fish), and the tribe claims it evolved from the fish incarnation of Vishnu. Minas once ruled supreme in the Amber region, but their miseries began once they were routed by the Rajputs. To make matters worse, they were outlawed during the British Raj, after their guerrilla tactics earned them the 'criminal-tribe' label. Following Independence, the criminal status was lifted and the Minas subsequently took to agriculture.

Festivities, music and dance form a vital part of Mina culture; they excel in performances such as swordplay and acrobatics. Minas view marriage as a noble institution and their weddings are accompanied by enthusiastic celebrations. They are also known to be friendly with other tribes and don't mind sharing space with other communities.

Bishnois

The Bishnois are the most progressive of Rajasthan's indigenous communities. However, they can't be strictly classified as a tribe. The Bishnois owe their origin to a visionary named Jambho Ji, who in 1485 shunned the Hindu social order to form a casteless faith that took inspiration from nature. Credited as the oldest environmentalist community in India, the Bishnois are animal-lovers and take an active interest in preserving forests and wildlife. Felling of trees and hunting within Bishnoi territory are strictly prohibited.

Sacred India

Hindus comprise nearly 90% of Rajasthan's population. Much of the remaining 10% are Muslims, followed by decreasing numbers of Sikhs, Jains, Christians and Buddhists, respectively. Tolerance levels here are high, and while individual acts of religious-related violence regularly appear in the newspapers, orchestrated incidents of communal violence are rare.

Hinduism & the Caste System

Hinduism is among the world's oldest religious traditions, with its roots going back at least 3000 years. Theoretically, Hinduism is not a religion; it is a way of life, an elaborate convention that has evolved through the centuries, in contrast to many other religions, which can trace their origins to a single founder. Despite being founded on a solid religious base, Hinduism doesn't have a specific theology or even a central religious

Above Krishna depicted on a fresco. Mandawa (p116)

institution. It also has no provision for conversion; one is always born a Hindu.

Being an extremely diverse religion, Hinduism can't be summed up by a universal definition. Yet, there are a few principal tenets that most Hindu sects tend to go by. Hindus believe that all life originates from a supreme spirit called Brahman, a formless, timeless phenomenon manifested by Brahma, the Hindu lord of creation. Upon being born, all living beings are required to engage in dharma (worldly duties) and samsara (the endless cycle of birth, death and rebirth). It is said that the road to salvation lies through righteous karma (actions that evoke subsequent reactions), which leads to moksha (emancipation), when the soul eventually returns to unite with the supreme spirit.

If that's not complex enough, things are convoluted further by the caste system, which broadly divides Hindus into four distinct classes based on their mythical origins and their occupations. On top of the caste hierarchy are the Brahmins, priests who supposedly originated from Brahma's

HINDU GODS & GODDESSES

Brahman
The only active role that Brahma ever played was during the creation of the universe. Since then he has been immersed in eternal meditation and is therefore regarded as aloof. His vehicle is a swan and he is sometimes shown sitting on a lotus.

Vishnu & Krishna
Being the preserver and sustainer of the universe, Vishnu is associated with 'right action'. He is usually depicted with four arms, holding a lotus, conch shell, discus and mace, respectively. His consort is Lakshmi, the goddess of wealth, and his vehicle is Garuda, a creature that's half bird, half beast. Vishnu has 10 incarnations, including Rama, Krishna and Buddha. He is also referred to as Narayan.

Krishna, the hugely popular incarnation of Vishnu, was sent to earth to fight for good and combat evil, and his exploits are documented in the Mahabharata. A shrewd politician, his flirtatious alliances with *gopis* (milkmaids) and his love for Radha, his paramour, have inspired countless paintings and songs.

Shiva & Parvati
Although he plays the role of the destroyer, Shiva's creative role is symbolised by his representation as the frequently worshipped lingam (phallus). With snakes draped around his neck, he is sometimes shown holding a trident while riding Nandi the bull. With 1008 names, Shiva takes many forms, including Pashupati, champion of the animals, and Nataraja, performer of the *tandava* (cosmic dance of fury). He is also the lord of yoga.

Shiva's consort is the beautiful goddess Parvati, who in her dark side appears as Kali, the fiercest of the gods who demands sacrifices and wears a garland of skulls. Alternatively, she appears as the fair Durga, the demon slayer, who wields supreme power, holds weapons in her 10 hands and rides a tiger or a lion.

Ganesh
The pot-bellied, elephant-headed Ganesh is held in great affection by Indians. He is the god of good fortune, prosperity and the patron of scribes, being credited with writing sections of the Mahabharata. Ganesh is good at removing obstacles and he's frequently spotted above doorways and entrances of Indian homes.

Hanuman
Hanuman is the hero of the Ramayana and is one of Rajasthan's most popular gods. He is the loyal ally of Lord Rama, and the images of Rama and his wife Sita are emblazoned upon his heart. He is king of the monkeys and thus assures them refuge in temple complexes across the country.

mouth. Next come the Kshatriyas, the warriors who evolved from the deity's arms – this is the caste that the Rajputs fit into. Vaishyas, tradespeople born from the thighs, are third in the pecking order, below which stand the Shudras. Alternatively called Dalits or Scheduled Castes, the Shudras comprise menial workers such as peasants, janitors or cobblers and are known to stem from Brahma's feet. Caste, by the way, is not changeable.

Hindu Sacred Texts & Epics

Hindu sacred texts fall under two categories: those believed to be the word of God (*shruti,* meaning 'hearing') and those produced by people (*smriti,* meaning 'memory').

Introduced in the subcontinent (supposedly) by the Aryans, the Vedas are regarded as *shruti* knowledge and are considered to be the authoritative basis for Hinduism. The oldest works of Sanskrit literature, the Vedas contain mantras that are recited at prayers and religious ceremonies. The Vedas are divided into four Samhitas (compilations); the Rig-Veda, the oldest of the Samhitas, is believed to have been written more than 3000 years ago. Other Vedic works include the Brahmanas, touching on rituals; the Aranyakas, whose name means the 'wilderness texts', meant for ascetics who have renounced the material world; and the Upanishads, which discuss meditation, philosophy, mysticism and the fate of the soul.

The Puranas comprise a post-Vedic genre that chronicles the history of the universe, royal lineages, philosophy and cosmology. The Sutras, on the other hand, are essentially manuals, and contain useful information on different human activities. Some well-known Sutras are Griha Sutra, dealing with the nuances of domestic life; Nyaya Sutra, detailing the faculty of justice and debate; and Kamasutra, a compendium of love and sexual behaviour. The Shastras are also instructive in nature, but are more technical as they provide information pertaining to specific areas of practice. Vaastu Shastra, for example, is an architect's handbook that elaborates on the art of civic planning, while Artha Shastra focuses heavily on governance, economics and military policies of the state.

Shiva is sometimes characterised as the lord of yoga, a Himalaya-dwelling ascetic with matted hair, an ash-smeared body and a third eye symbolising wisdom.

The Mahabharata is a 2500-year-old, rip-roaring epic that centres on the conflict between two fraternal dynasties, the Pandavas and the Kauravas, overseen by Krishna. Locked in a struggle to inherit the throne of Hastinapura, the Kauravas win the first round of the feud, beating their adversaries in a game of dice and banishing them from the kingdom. The Pandavas return after 13 years and challenge the Kauravas to an epic battle, from which they emerge victorious. Being the longest epic in the world, unabridged versions of the Mahabharata incorporate the Bhagavad Gita, the holy book of the Hindus, which contains the worldly advice given by Krishna to Pandava prince Arjuna before the start of the battle.

Composed around the 2nd or 3rd century BC, the Ramayana tells of Rama, an incarnation of Vishnu, who assumed human form to facilitate the triumph of good over evil. Much like the Mahabharata, the Ramayana revolves around a great war, waged by Rama, his brother Lakshmana and an army of apes led by Hanuman against Ravana, the demon king who had kidnapped Rama's wife Sita and had held her hostage in his kingdom of Lanka (Sri Lanka). After slaying Ravana, Rama returned to his kingdom of Ayodhya, his homecoming forming the basis for the important Hindu festival of Dussehra.

Islam

Islam was founded in Arabia by the Prophet Mohammed in the 7th century AD. The Arabic term 'Islam' means 'surrender' and believers undertake to surrender to the will of Allah (God), which is revealed in the

RAJASTHANI FOLK GODS & GODDESSES

Folk deities and deified local heroes abound in Rajasthan. Apart from public gods, families are often known to pay homage to a *kuladevi* (family idol).

Pabuji is one of many local heroes to have attained divine status. Pabuji promised to protect the cows of a woman called Devalde, for which he would receive a mare. He was called upon during his own marriage and, in defending the herd against the villainous Jind Raj Khinchi, was killed, along with all his male relatives. To preserve the family line, Pabuji's sister-in-law cut open her own belly and produced Pabuji's nephew, Nandio, before throwing herself on her husband's funeral pyre.

Professional storytellers called Bhopas pay homage to Pabuji by performing *Pabuji-ka-phad* (reciting poetry alongside *phad,* or a cloth scroll, with paintings that chronicle the life of the hero). You can attend these performances at places such as Chokhi Dhani or Jaisalmer, if they happen at a time when you're around.

Gogaji was an 11th-century warrior and could cure snakebite; today, victims are brought to his shrines by both Hindu and Muslim devotees. Also believed to cure snakebite is Tejaji who, according to tradition, was blessed by a snake, which decreed that anyone honouring Tejaji by tying a thread on to a limb in his name would be cured of snakebite.

Goddesses revered by Rajasthanis include incarnations of Devi (the Mother Goddess), such as the fierce Chamunda Mata, an incarnation of Durga, and Karni Mata, worshipped at Deshnok near Bikaner. Women who have committed *sati* (ritual suicide) on their husband's funeral pyres are also frequently worshipped as goddesses, such as Rani Sati, who has an elaborate temple in her honour in Jhunjhunu, Shekhawati.

Barren women pay homage to the god Bhairon, an incarnation of Shiva, at his shrines, which are usually found under khejri trees. In order to be blessed with a child, a woman is required to leave a garment hanging from the branches of the tree. The deified folk hero Ramdev also has an important temple at Ramdevra, near Pokaran in western Rajasthan.

Quran, the holy book of Islam. A devout Muslim is required to pray five times a day, keep day-long fasts through the month of Ramadan and make a pilgrimage to the holy city of Mecca in Saudi Arabia, if possible.

Islam is monotheistic. God is held as unique, unlimited, self-sufficient and the supreme creator of all things. God never speaks to humans directly; his word is instead conveyed through messengers called prophets, who are never themselves divine. The religion has two prominent sects, the minority Shiites (originating from Mohammed's descendants) and the majority Sunnis, who split soon after the death of Mohammed owing to political differences and have since gone on to establish their own interpretations and rituals. The most important pilgrimage site for Muslims in Rajasthan is the extraordinary dargah (burial place) of the Sufi saint Khwaja Muin-ud-din Chishti at Ajmer.

> In Hinduism, the syllable 'Om' is believed to be a primordial sound from which the entire universe takes shape. It is also a sacred symbol, represented by an icon shaped like the number three.

Sikhism

Sikhism was founded on the sermons of 10 Sikh gurus, beginning with Guru Nanak Dev (1469–1539). The core values and ideology of Sikhism are embodied in the Guru Granth Sahib, the holy book of the Sikhs, which is also considered the eternal guru of Sikhism. The Sikhs evolved as an organised community over time and devoted themselves to the creation of a standing militia called the Khalsa, which carried out religious, political and martial duties and protected the Sikhs from foreign threats. The religion, on its part, grew around the central concept of Vaheguru, the universal lord, an eventual union with whom is believed to result in salvation. The Sikhs believe that salvation is achieved through rigorous discipline and meditation, which help them overcome the five evils – ego, greed, attachment, anger and lust.

Guru Nanak introduced five symbols, or articles of faith, to bind Sikhs together and display their religious devotion and they are the most obvious public elements of Sikhism that people encounter. These are: *kesh* (uncut hair, covered by a turban for men); *kangha* (a wooden comb, for cleanliness); *kara* (a steel bracelet, for the bonds of faith and community); *kaccha* (breeches, for self-control and chastity); and *kirpan* (a ceremonial sword, to defend against injustice).

Jainism

The Jain religion was founded around 500 BC by Mahavira, the 24th and last of the Jain *tirthankars* (path finders). Jainism originally evolved as a reformist movement against the dominance of priests in Hindu society. It steered clear of complicated rituals, rejected the caste system and believed in reincarnation and eventual moksha by following the example of the *tirthankars*.

Jains are strict vegetarians and revere all forms of life. The religion has two main sects. The Svetambaras (White Clad) wear unstitched white garments; the monks cover their mouths so as not to inhale insects and brush their path before they walk to avoid crushing small creatures. The monks belonging to the Digambaras (Sky Clad), in comparison, go naked. Jainism preaches nonviolence and its followers are markedly successful in banking and business, which they consider nonviolent professions.

Sufism is a mystic tradition derived from Islam that originated in medieval times. Being largely secular, it has attracted followers from other religions and is widely practised in North India.

Arts, Crafts & Architecture

If the Rajputs knew how to fight a battle, they also knew how to create an artistic legacy. Rajasthan's culture is a celebration of chivalry, hardship and beauty, manifested through its literature, poetry, music, dance, painting and architecture. The state also has a rich tradition of handicrafts, including gem cutting and jewellery, which are prized the world over, both for their intricate craftsmanship and ornamental appeal.

Arts

Dance

Ghungroos are anklets made of metallic bells strung together, worn by Indian classical dancers to accentuate their complex footwork during performances.

Folk dance forms in Rajasthan are generally associated with indigenous tribes and communities of nomadic gypsies. Each region has its own dance specialities. The *ghoomer* (pirouette) is performed by Bhil women at festivals or weddings and its form varies from one village to another. The Bhils are also known for *gair,* a men-only dance, that's performed at springtime festivities. Combine the two and you get *gair-ghoomer,* where women, in a small inner circle, are encompassed by men in a larger circle, who determine the rhythm by beating sticks and striking drums.

Among other popular forms, the *kachhi ghori* dance of eastern Rajasthan resembles a battle performance, where dancers ride cloth or paper horses and spar with swords and shields. To the south, the *neja* is danced by the Minas of Kherwara and Dungarpur just after Holi. A coconut is placed on a large pole, which the men try to dislodge, while the women strike the men with sticks and whips to foil their attempts. A nomadic community called the Kalbelias, traditionally associated with snake charming, performs swirling dances such as the *shankaria,* while the Siddha Jats of Bikaner are renowned for their spectacular fire dance, performed on a bed of hot coals, which supposedly leaves no burns.

Painting

Miniatures

Rajasthan is famed for its miniatures – small-scale paintings that are executed on small surfaces, but cram in a surprising amount of detail by way of delicate brushwork. Originating in the 16th and 17th centuries, they led to the emergence of eminent schools such as Marwar, Mewar, Bundi-Kota, Amber and Kishangarh, among others. Each school had its own stylistic identity; while paintings from the Mewar school depicted court life, festivals, ceremonies, elephant fights and hunts, those from the Marwar school featured vivid colours and heroic, whiskered men accompanied by dainty maidens. Miniatures gained immense value as souvenirs with the coming of the tourism boom.

Phad

Rajasthan is renowned for a kind of scroll painting called *phad,* which is done on cloth and portrays deities, mythology and legends of Rajput kings. *Phads* are used by nomadic Bhopas, who travel from village to village singing, dancing and performing and pointing to the scroll to assist the narrative. Bhilwara, near Udaipur, is one of the better-known centres for *phad* scrolls.

Fresco

Fresco painting, originally developed in Italy, arrived in Rajasthan with the Mughals, and its finest examples can be seen in the exquisitely muralled *havelis* (traditional ornately decorated residences) of Shekhawati. The region's *havelis* form an open-air art gallery, with work in a kaleidoscope of colours and styles.

Crafts
Jewellery, Gems & Enamelwork

Two jewellery-making styles particularly prevalent in Rajasthan are *kundan* and meenakari work. *Kundan* involves setting gemstones into silver or gold pieces; one symbolic variation is known as *navratan,* in which nine different gems are set into an item of jewellery, corresponding to the nine planets of Indian astrology. This way, it's an eternally lucky item to have about your person, since you will always be wearing, at any given time, the symbol of the ruling planetary body.

Meenakari, meanwhile, is a gorgeous type of enamelwork, usually applied to a base of silver or gold. Jaipur's pieces of meenakari are valued for their vibrant tones, especially the highly prized, rich ruby-red; a fantastic selection can be found on sale at the city's Johari Bazaar.

Leatherwork

Leatherworking has a long history in Rajasthan. Leather shoes known as jootis are produced in Jodhpur and Jaipur, often featuring *kashida* (ornate embroidery). Strange to Western eyes and feet, there is no 'right' or 'left': both shoes are identical but after a few wears they begin to conform to the wearer's feet.

Textiles

Rajasthan is renowned for the blazing colour of its textiles. Riotously woven, dyed, block- or resist-printed and embroidered, they are on sale almost everywhere you look throughout the state.

During the Mughal period, embroidery workshops known as *kaarkhanas* were established to train artisans so that the royal families were ensured an abundant supply of richly embroidered cloth. Finely stitched tapestries, inspired by miniature paintings, were also executed for the royal courts.

Get arty with *Indian Art* by Roy C Craven, *Contemporary Indian Art: Other Realities,* edited by Yashodhara Dalmia, and *Indian Miniature Painting* by Dr Daljeet and Professor PC Jain.

ARTS, CRAFTS & ARCHITECTURE CRAFTS

CINEMA IN INDIA

India has the world's biggest film industry. Films come in all languages, the majority pumped out by the Hindi tinsel town of Bollywood, in Mumbai, and Kollywood, its Tamil counterpart, in Chennai. Most productions, however, are formulaic flicks that seize mass attention with hackneyed motifs – unrequited love, action that verges on caricature, slapstick humour, wet saris and plenty of sexual innuendo. Nonetheless, the past 10 years have seen upscale productions aimed at a burgeoning multiplex audience. Check out the cricket extravaganza *Lagaan,* the patriotic *Rang De Basanti* or Shakespearean adaptations such as *Maqbool* (Macbeth) and *Omkara* (Othello).

India also has a critically acclaimed art-house movement. Pioneered by the likes of Satyajit Ray, Adoor Gopalakrishnan, Ritwik Ghatak and Shyam Benegal, the tradition now boasts directors such as Mira Nair *(Salaam Bombay, Monsoon Wedding, The Namesake)* and Deepa Mehta *(Fire, Earth, Water, Anatomy of Violence).*

PUPPETRY

Puppetry is one of Rajasthan's most acclaimed, yet endangered, performing arts. Puppeteers first emerged in the 19th century and would travel from village to village like wandering minstrels, relaying stories through narration, music and an animated performance that featured wooden puppets on strings called *kathputlis*. Puppetry is now a dying art; waning patronage and lack of paying audiences has forced many puppeteers to give up the art form and switch to agriculture or menial labour. Those that frequent tourist hotels in the evening usually have a 'day job' and are not paid by the hotel but, rather, hope for donations after the performance and maybe to sell a puppet or two. The colourful puppets have certainly retained their value as souvenirs.

Today, Bikaner specialises in embroidery with double stitching, which results in the pattern appearing on both sides of the cloth. In the Shekhawati district, the Jat people embroider motifs of animals and birds on their *odhnis* (headscarves) and *ghaghara* (long cotton skirts), while tiny mirrors are stitched into garments in Jaisalmer. Beautifully embroidered cloth is also produced for livestock and ornately bedecked camels are a common sight, especially at the Pushkar Camel Fair.

Paper Making

Paper making is centred in Sanganer, near Jaipur; its paper has traditionally been the most celebrated in India. The process makes use of discarded fabric rags, which are soaked, pulped, strained, beaten and then spread out to dry on frames. Though some of the town's factories nowadays use machines, there are places that still perform the process by hand – view the racks of paper spread out to dry along Sanganer's river or pop in for a visit at one of the town's paper-making factories.

Carpets & Weaving

Carpet weaving took off in the 16th century under the patronage of the great Mughal emperor Akbar, who commissioned the establishment of various carpet-weaving factories, including one in Jaipur. In the 19th century, Maharaja Ram Singh II of Jaipur established a carpet factory at the Jaipur jail and soon other jails introduced carpet-making units. Some of the most beautiful *dhurries* (flat-woven rugs) were produced by prisoners and Bikaner jail is still well known for the excellence of its *dhurries*. Recent government training initiatives have seen the revival of this craft and fine-quality carpets are once again being produced across Rajasthan.

Intricate *bandhani* (tie-dye) often carries symbolic meanings when used to make *odhnis* (headscarves). A yellow background indicates that the wearer has recently given birth, while red circles on that background means she's had a son.

Pottery

Of all the arts of Rajasthan, pottery has the longest lineage, with fragments recovered in Kalibangan dating from the Harappan era (around 3000 BC). Before the beginning of the 1st millennium, potters in the environs of present-day Bikaner were already decorating red pottery with black designs.

Today, different regions of Rajasthan produce different types of pottery and most villages in Rajasthan have their own resident potter. The most famous of Rajasthan's pottery is the blue pottery of Jaipur. The blue-glazed work was first evident in tiling on Mughal palaces and cenotaphs and later applied to pottery.

Architecture

The magnificence of Delhi, Agra and Rajasthan's architectural heritage is astounding and here you'll find some of India's best-known buildings. From temples and mosques to mansions and mausoleums, the region has it all. Most spectacular, however, are the fairy-tale forts and palaces built by Rajputs and Mughals, which still bear testimony to the celebrated history of North India.

Temples

Rajasthan's earliest surviving temples date from the Gupta period. Built between the 4th and 6th century, they are small and their architecture restrained – the Sheetaleshvara Temple at Jhalrapatan is a notable example. Temple architecture (both Hindu and Jain) developed through the 8th and 9th centuries and began to incorporate stunning sculptural work, which can be seen on temples at Osian and Chittorgarh. Structurally, the temples usually tapered into a single *sikhara* (spire) and had a *mandapa* (pillared pavilion before the inner sanctum). The Delwara temples (p109) at Mt Abu epitomises the architecture of this era. Built in the 11th century, it has marble carvings that reach unsurpassed heights of virtuosity.

The most famous marble quarries were located in Makrana, west of Jaipur, from where the marble used in the Taj Mahal and the Delwara temples was sourced.

Forts & Palaces

The fabulous citadels of Rajasthan were conceived and built for protection from invading armies, but gradually they became more extravagant to realise the lavish and profligate royal whims.

Most of Rajasthan's forts and palaces were built between the 15th and 18th centuries, which coincided with the Mughal reign in Delhi and saw the Rajputs borrowing a few architectural motifs from the Mughals, including the use of pillared arches and the *sheesh mahal* (hall of mirrors). Another ornamentation widely used across Rajasthan was the spired Bengal roof, shaped like an inverted boat. Magnificent examples of Rajput architecture across the state include the Amber Fort (p61), Jaipur's Hawa Mahal (p43) and the City Palace (p95) in Udaipur.

The most famous examples of Mughal architecture lie just beyond Rajasthan's borders in Delhi, with its famous Red Fort and Jama Masjid, and Agra, home to the legendary tomb, the Taj Mahal (p199).

Towards the end of the British era, a novel architectural style called the Indo-Saracenic school emerged in India, which blended Victorian and Islamic elements into a highly wrought, frilly whole. Some striking buildings were produced in this style, including Albert Hall in Jaipur and Lallgarh Palace in Bikaner.

Havelis

Rajasthani merchants built ornately decorated residences called *havelis* and commissioned masons and artists to ensure they were constructed and decorated in a manner befitting the owners' importance and prosperity. The Shekhawati district of northern Rajasthan is riddled with such mansions that are covered with extraordinarily vibrant murals. There are other beautiful *havelis* in Jaisalmer, constructed of sandstone, featuring the fine work of renowned local *silavats* (stone carvers).

The Kumbhalgarh Fort, a former Mewar stronghold in the Rajsamand district of Rajasthan, has the second-longest fortification in the world after the Great Wall of China.

Step-Wells & Chhatris

Given the importance of water in Rajasthan, it's unsurprising that the architecture of wells and reservoirs rivals other structures in the region. Impressive *baoris* (step-wells) worth seeking out include Raniji-ki-Baori (p83) in Bundi, Panna Meena Baori (p61) in Amber, and the extraordinary Chand Baori (p62) near Abhaneri.

Chhatris (cenotaphs) are a statewide architectural curiosity, built to commemorate maharajas, nobles and, as is the case in the Shekhawati district, wealthy merchants. In rare instances, *chhatris* also commemorate women, such as the Chhatri of Moosi Rani at Alwar. Literally translating to 'umbrella', a *chhatri* comprises a central dome, supported by a series of pillars on a raised platform, with a sequence of small pavilions on the corners and sides.

ARTS, CRAFTS & ARCHITECTURE ARCHITECTURE

CHRISTOPHE CAPPELLI / SHUTTERSTOCK ©

1. Colourful Rajasthani bangles, Jodhpur (p117) **2.** Detail of an elephant parade in a mural, Udaipur (p94) **3.** Market in Jodhpur (p117) **4.** Handmade carpets, Jodhpur (p117)

P.HPIX / SHUTTERSTOCK ©

2 Rajasthani Colour

The most vivid impression on visitors to Rajasthan is that of colour: brilliant, bright tribal dress, glittering gold jewellery and rainbow-coloured bangles adorn the locals and illuminate the bazaars. Inside the palaces, *havelis* (traditional residences) and even humble homes, this trend continues.

The people of Rajasthan have a passion for decoration, having taken advantage of their position on trade routes to acquire artistic skills from many lands. This passion is evident in the manifold variations of Rajasthani turbans and in the attire of the state's women, from their block-printed *odhnis* (headscarves) right down to their brilliantly embroidered jootis (leather shoes). Utilitarian items are transported into the world of art with ceramics such as the famous blue-glazed pottery from Jaipur.

Tie-dyed, block-printed and embroidered textiles and hand-woven carpets are functional yet decorative and colourful. Traditionally, all Rajasthan's textile colours were derived from natural sources such as vegetables, minerals and even insects. Yellow, for instance, came from turmeric and buttermilk; green from banana leaves; orange from saffron and jasmine; blue from the indigo plant; and purple from the kermes insect. Today, however, the majority are synthetically dyed; while they may not possess the subtlety of the traditional tones, they will, at least, stand a better chance in a 40°C machine wash.

BEST PLACES TO SEE...

Block-printed textiles Sanganer

Blue pottery Jaipur

Carpets Jaipur

Embroidery Jaisalmer

Jewellery Jaipur

Miniature Paintings Udaipur

1. Block printing
Traditional techniques are used to print on textiles (p245).

2. Palace walls
The hall room in Jaipur's City Palace (p42).

3. Bridal designs
A bride revealing her *mehndi* (henna designs).

4. Blue City
Sari-clad women in the blue streets of Jodhpur (p117).

Rajasthani Food

Rajasthan has a home-grown cuisine, both veg and nonveg, reflecting its desert surroundings and local produce. Nevertheless, you're more likely to find pizza or butter chicken than *govind ghatta* on a tourist hotel's menu. Most restaurants in tourist destinations attempt to cover all the options with popular North Indian curries, pizza and pasta and a few Chinese dishes. It's worth seeking out restaurants that specialise in Rajasthani cuisine.

Making a Meal of It

Spotlighting rice, *Finest Rice Recipes* by Sabina Sehgal Saikia shows just how versatile this humble grain is, with classy creations such as rice-crusted crab cakes.

Rajasthan's cuisine and staple ingredients are influenced by the region's harsh climate. Fresh fruit and vegetables are rare commodities in desert zones, but these parts of the state overcome the land's shortcomings by serving up an amazing and creative variety of regional dishes, utilising cereals, pulses, spices, milk products and unusual desert fruits in myriad ways. Regal feasts, meanwhile, are the stuff of legend. And modern Rajasthan ranks as one of the best restaurant destinations in the country, with scores of establishments serving up everything from butter chicken to international fusion cuisine.

Bread of Life

A meal is not complete in North India unless it comes with a bountiful supply of roti, little discs of unleavened bread (also known as chapati), made with fine wholemeal flour and cooked on a *tawa* (hotplate). In Rajasthan you'll also find *sogra,* a thick, heavy chapati made from millet; *makki ki* roti, a fat cornmeal chapati; and *dhokla,* yummy balls of steamed maize flour cooked with coriander, spinach and mint and eaten with chutney. Yet another kind of roti is a pastry-like *purat* roti, made by repeatedly coating the dough in oil, then folding it to produce a light and fluffy bread. *Cheelre,* meanwhile, is a chapati made with gram (chickpea) flour, while *bhakri* is a thick roti made from barley, millet or corn, eaten with pounded garlic, red chilli and raw onions by working-class Rajasthanis, and said to prevent sunstroke.

Alongside the world of roti come *puris, parathas* and naans. A *puri* is a delicious North Indian snack of deep-fried wholemeal dough that puffs up like a soft, crispy balloon. Kachori is similar, but here the dough is pepped up with potato, corn or dhal masala (a mixture of spices). Flaky *paratha* is a soft, circular bread, deliciously substantial and mildly elastic, which makes for a scrumptious early morning snack, and is often jazzed up with a small bowl of pickles and a stuffing of paneer (unfermented cheese), *aloo* (potato) or grated vegetables. Naan bread, made with leavened white flour, is distinguished from roti by being larger, thicker and doughier, cooked on the inner walls of a tandoor (oven) rather than on a *tawa*. Best plain, it is also delicious when laced with garlic and lashings of butter and filled with paneer, *aloo* or coconut and raisins.

Rice

Basmati rice is considered the cream of India's crop, its name stemming from the Hindi phrase for 'queen of fragrance'. Aside from the plain steamed rice variety, you'll find *jeera* (cumin) rice, and pilau (aka pilaf), a tasty, buttery rice dish, whose Rajasthani incarnations frequently include cinnamon, cardamom, cloves and a handful or two of almonds and pistachios.

Dhal & Cereals

India has around 60 different varieties of dhal. In Rajasthan, the dhal of choice is *urad,* black lentils boiled in water, then cooked with *garam masala,* red chillies, cumin seeds, salt, oil and fresh coriander.

The state's most popular dhal-based dish is *dhal-bati-choorma,* which mixes dhal with *bati,* buttery hard-baked balls of wholemeal flour, and *choorma,* sweet, fried wholemeal-flour balls mixed with sugar and nuts.

Gram-flour dumplings known as *gatta* are a delicious dish usually cooked in yoghurt or masala, and *mangodi* are lentil-flour dumplings served in an onion or potato gravy. A speciality of Jodhpur is *kabuli Jodhpuri,* a dish made with meat, vegetables and yet more fried gram-flour balls. *Govind gatta* offers a sweet alternative: lentil paste with dried fruit and nuts rolled into a sausage shape, then sliced and deep-fried. *Pakora* (fritters), *sev* (savoury nibbles) and other salted snacks generally known as *farsan* are all equally derived from chickpea gram.

Meat Matters

While Rajasthan's Brahmins and traders stuck to a vegetarian diet, the Rajputs have a far more carnivorous history. Goat (known as 'mutton' since the days of the British Raj), lamb and chicken are the mainstays; religious taboos make beef forbidden to Hindus and pork forbidden to Muslims.

In the deserts of Jaisalmer, Jodhpur and Bikaner, meats are often cooked without the addition of water, instead using milk, curd, buttermilk and plenty of ghee. Cooked this way, dishes keep for days without refrigeration, a practical advantage in the searing heat of the desert. *Murg ko khaato* (chicken cooked in a curd gravy), *achar murg* (pickled chicken), *kacher maas* (dry lamb cooked in spices), *lal maas* (a rich red dish, usually mutton) and *soor santh ro sohito* (pork with millet dumplings) are all classic desert dishes.

Maas ka sule, a Rajput favourite, is a dry dish that can be made from partridge, wild boar, chicken, mutton or fish. Marinated chunks of meat are cooked on skewers in a tandoor, then glazed with melted butter and a tangy masala spice mix. Mughlai meat dishes, meanwhile, include rich korma and rogan josh, the former mild, the latter cooked with tomatoes and saffron, and both generously spiked with thick, creamy curd.

Gorge yourself by reading about the extravagant royal recipes of Rajasthan in *Royal Indian Cookery* by Manju Shivraj Singh, the niece of the late Maharaja Bhawani Singh of Jaipur.

RAJASTHANI FOOD MAKING A MEAL OF IT

VEGETARIANS & VEGANS

Vegetarians will have no problem maintaining a varied and exciting diet in Rajasthan.

Vegetarian food is sometimes divided up in India into 'veg' and 'pure veg', a frequently blurred and confusing distinction. As a general rule of thumb, 'veg' usually means the same as it does in the West: without meat, fowl or seafood, but possibly containing butter (in India's case, ghee), dairy products, eggs or honey. 'Pure veg' often refers to what the West knows as vegan food: dishes containing no dairy products, eggs or honey. Other times, 'pure veg' might also mean no onions, garlic or mushrooms, which some Hare Krishna believe can have a negative effect on one's state of consciousness, or even no root vegetables or tubers since many Jains, according to the principles of ahimsa (non-violence), are loath to damage soil organisms.

Though it's extremely easy to be vegetarian in Rajasthan, finding vegan food – outside 'pure veg' restaurants – can be trickier. Many basic dishes include a small amount of ghee, so ask whether a dish is 'pure veg', even in a vegetarian restaurant.

Fruit & Vegetables

Rajasthan's delicious *sabji* (vegetable) dishes have to be admired for their inventiveness under frequently hostile growing conditions. Dishes you might come across include *papad ki sabzi,* a simple pappadam made with vegetables and masala, and *aloo mangori,* ground lentil paste sun-dried then added with potato to a curry. Traditionally rolled by hand, the paste is now often forced through a machine in a similar way to making macaroni. A common vegetarian snack is *aloo samosa,* triangular pastry cones stuffed with spicy potato, while another scrumptious local snack is *mirch bada,* a large chilli coated in a thick layer of deep-fried potato and wheatgerm.

There are a few vegetables specific to the deserts of Rajasthan. These include *mogri,* a type of desert bean, which is made into *mogri mangori* (similar to *aloo mangori*), or a sweeter version known as *methi mangori* – *methi* being the leaf fenugreek. Another use for *methi* leaves is in *dana methi,* where they are boiled with *dana* (small pea-shaped vegetables) and mixed with sugar, masala and dried fruit.

With developments in infrastructure, more vegetable dishes are now available in Rajasthan than during its barren, warrior-filled past. Heads of cauliflower are usually cooked dry on their own, with potatoes to make *aloo gobi.* Fresh green peas turn up stir-fried with other vegetables in pilaus and biryanis, in samosas along with potato, and in one of North India's signature dishes, *mattar paneer* (peas and fresh, firm white cheese). *Brinjal* (eggplant or aubergine), *bhindi* (okra or ladies' fingers) and *saag* (a generic term for leafy greens) are all popular choices.

The desert bears a handful of fruits, too. The small, round *kair* is a favourite of camels as well as people, to whom it is usually served with mango pickle; *kachri* is frequently made into chutney. If you order something that arrives looking like a plate of dry sticks, these are *sangri* (dried wild desert beans). The seeds and beans are soaked overnight in water, boiled and then fried in oil with masala, dried dates, red chillies, turmeric powder, shredded dried mango, salt, coriander and cumin seeds.

> There's really no such thing in India as a 'curry'. The term is thought to be an anglicisation of the Tamil word *kari* (black or blackened, ie cooked), coined by bewildered Brits for any dish that included tempered spices.

Pickles, Chutneys & Relishes

You're in a pickle without a pickle, or *achar:* no Indian meal is complete without one or two *chatnis* (chutneys) and relishes on the side. A relish can be anything from a sliced onion to a delicately crafted fusion of fruit, nuts and spices. The best known is raita (mildly spiced yoghurt or curd often containing cucumber, tomato or pineapple), which makes a refreshing counter to spicy meals.

Other regional variations include *goonde achar, goonde* being a green fruit that is boiled and mixed with mustard oil and masala. *Kair achar* is a pickle with desert fruit as its base, while *lahsun achar* is an onion pickle. *Lal mirch* is a garlic-stuffed red chilli and *kamrak ka achar* is a pickle made from *kamrak,* a type of desert vegetable with a pungent, sour taste.

TERRIFIC THALIS

Thalis are the traditional cheap and filling meals made up of a combination of curried dishes, served with relishes, pappadams, yoghurt, *puris* and rice. The term 'thali' also covers the characteristic metal tray-plate on which the meal is frequently served. If you're strapped for cash, thalis are a saviour, especially at local hole-in-the-wall restaurants and railway-station dining halls, since they're far heavier on the stomach than the wallet. In southern Rajasthan, many restaurants serve more sophisticated, sweet and lightly spiced Gujarati thalis – one of the best ways to sample a taste of Gujarati cuisine.

The most widely served are made of raw mango, mixed with spices and mustard oil, lime, shredded ginger or tiny whole shallots.

Dairy

Milk and milk products make a staggering contribution to Indian cuisine (despite the sanctity of the cow and the health condition of most cows!). In Rajasthan milk products are ubiquitous: *dahi* (curd) is served with most meals and is handy for countering heat in terms of both temperature and spiciness of dishes; firm, unmeltable paneer cheese is a godsend for the vegetarian majority and is used in apparently endless permutations; popular lassi (yoghurt-and-iced-water drink) is just one in a host of nourishing sweet or savoury drinks, often with fruit such as banana or mango added; ghee (clarified butter) is the traditional and pure cooking medium; and the best sweets are made with plenty of condensed, sweetened milk or cream.

Sweets & Desserts

Indians have a heady range of tooth-achingly sweet *mithai* (sweets), made from manifold concoctions of sugar, milk, ghee, nuts and yet more sugar. Rajasthani varieties include *badam ki barfi*, a type of fudge made from sugar, powdered milk, almonds and ghee, and *chakki*, a *barfi* made from gram flour, sugar and milk. Gram flour, sugar, cardamom, ghee and dried fruits combined make *churma*, while *ladoo* comes in ball form.

Ghewar is a paste based on *urad* (a mung-bean type pulse) that's crushed, deep-fried and dipped in sugar syrup flavoured with cardamom, cinnamon and cloves. It's served hot, topped with a thick layer of unsweetened cream and garnished with rose petals.

Kheer is perhaps India's favourite dessert, a delectable, fragrant rice pudding with a light flavour of cardamom, saffron, pistachios, flaked almonds and cashews or dried fruit. *Gulab jamun* are spongy deep-fried balls of milk dough soaked in rose-flavoured syrup. *Kulfi* is addictive once experienced; delicious, substantially firm-textured, made with reduced milk and flavoured with nuts, fruits and berries, and especially tasty in its pale-green pistachio incarnation, *pista kulfi*.

Alongside these more sophisticated offerings are food-stall sweets such as *jalebis* (orange-coloured whirls of fried batter dipped in syrup), which melt in the mouth and hang heavy on the conscience.

To find out more about veganism in India, and for recipe ideas, pick up a copy of *Spicy Vegan* by Sudha Raina.

Drinks
Tea & Coffee

India runs on chai (tea). It's a unique and addictive brew: more milk than water, stewed for a long time and frequently sugary enough to give you an energy boost. A glass of steaming, sweet chai is the perfect antidote to the heat and stress of Indian travel.

BEWARE OF THOSE BHANG LASSIS!

It's rarely printed in menus, but some restaurants in Rajasthan clandestinely whip up bhang lassi, a yoghurt-and-iced-water beverage laced with bhang, a derivative of marijuana. This 'special lassi' can be a potent concoction – some travellers have been stuck in bed for several miserable days after drinking it, others have become delirious and it's not unknown for sufferers to be robbed in such circumstances.

If you just crave a simple cuppa, many cafes and restaurants can serve up 'tray tea' or 'English tea'. Coffee used to be fairly unusual in the region, but Delhi and the well-travelled parts of Rajasthan have caught up with the double-mocha-latte ways of the West. At bus and train stations, coffee is still almost indistinguishable from chai: the same combination of water, boiled milk and sugar, but with a dash of instant-coffee powder.

Cooling Off

Aside from the usual gamut of Pepsis and 7Ups, India has a few of its own sugary bottled drinks: the vaguely lemonish Limca and orange Mirinda. Masala soda is the quintessential Indian soft drink, but it's an acquired taste. Freshly squeezed orange juice is also widely available, though the most popular street juices are made from *mosambi* (sweet lime) and sugar cane, pressed in front of you by a mechanised wheel complete with jingling bells.

Jal jeera is made with lime juice, cumin, mint and rock salt and is sold in large earthenware pots by street vendors as well as in restaurants. *Falooda* is a sweet rose-flavoured Muslim speciality made with milk, cream, nuts and strands of vermicelli.

By far the most popular of all Indian cold drinks, however, is a refreshing sweet or salty lassi (yoghurt drink). Jodhpur is famous for its sweet *makhania* lassis, flavoured with saffron and hearty enough to stand in for a meal. *Chach* is a thin, salted lassi and *kairi chach* is unripe mango juice with water and salt added, widely available in summer and allegedly a good remedy for sunstroke.

Cheers

Most travellers champion Kingfisher beer; other brands here include Royal Challenge, Foster's, Dansberg, London Pilsner and Sandpiper. Served ice-cold, all are equally refreshing. But if you can find draught beer, such as Kingfisher and Golden Peacock, you will certainly notice the better taste over the bottled beer, which has glycerine added as a preservative. So-called strong beer of higher alcoholic content has a strong local following, but most travellers find it difficult to stomach.

Though the Indian wine industry is still in its infancy, there are strong signs that Indian wines are being accepted into local markets. Two of the best-known Indian wine producers are Sula and Fratelli, which create a whole slew of different varieties with grapes grown in northern Maharashtra. Meanwhile, Grover Vineyards, established in 1988 near Bengaluru (Bangalore), also has a solid reputation, with a smaller range of wines.

Learn more about Sula Wines and its environmentally friendly sustainable agriculture programs at www.sulawines.com.

At the other end of the scale, *arak* is what the poor drink to get blotto, poignantly called *asha* (hope) in the north of India. The effects of this distilled rice liquor creep up on you quickly and without warning. Only ever drink this from a bottle produced in a government-controlled distillery. *Never* drink it otherwise – hundreds of people die or are blinded every year in India as a result of drinking *arak* produced in illicit stills.

Naturally Rajasthan

Rajasthan is the India of hot, dry plains. Dominated by desert and scrub, but punctuated by an ancient range and secluded jungles, it's home to a rich variety of flora and fauna. Some are easy to spot, such as the monkeys that remain ubiquitous even in the cities, while others require a little more tracking, such as the tiger, king of India's cats, whose vulnerable populations endure in two or three of the state's national parks.

The Lie of the Land

The rugged Aravalli Range splits Rajasthan like a bony spine, running from the northeast to the southwest. These irregular mountains form a boundary between the Thar Desert to the west and the relatively more lush vegetation to the east. With an average height of 600m, in places the range soars to over 1050m; the highest point, Guru Shikhar (1722m), is near Mt Abu. It's thought to be the oldest mountain range in the world. A second hilly spur, the Vindhya Range, splays around the southernmost regions of Rajasthan.

The Thar Desert is the most densely populated desert in the world, with an average of more than 60 people per square kilometre.

The state's sole perennial river is the wide, life-giving swell of the Chambal. Rising in Madhya Pradesh from the northern slopes of the Vindhyas, the river enters Rajasthan at Chaurasigarh and forms part of Rajasthan's eastern border with Madhya Pradesh.

The arid region in the west of the state is known as Marusthali or Marwar (the Land of Death), which gives some idea of the terrain. Sprawling from the Aravallis in the east to the Sulaiman Kirthar Range in the west is the Thar Desert, which covers almost three-quarters of the state.

It's hard to believe, but this desolate region was once covered by massive forests and populated by huge animals. In 1996 two amateur palaeontologists working in the Thar Desert discovered animal fossils, some 300 million years old, that included dinosaur fossils. Delhi lies on the vast flatlands of the Indo-Gangetic Plain, though the northernmost pimples of the Aravallis amount to the Ridge, which lies west of the city centre. The Yamuna River flows southward along the eastern edge of the city. To the south, Agra lies on the banks of the Yamuna, in the neighbouring state of Uttar Pradesh.

DESERT – JUST ADD WATER

It sounds too simple and it probably is. Irrigating India's vast arid lands has long been the dream of rulers and politicians. The Indira Gandhi Canal was initiated in 1957 and, though it is still incomplete, it includes an amazing 9709km of canals, with the main canal stretching 649km. Critics suggest that the massive project, connected with Bhakra Dam in Punjab, was concerned with short-term economics and politics to the detriment of the long-term ecology of the region.

The canal has opened up large tracts of the arid region for cash crops, but these tracts are managed by wealthy landowners rather than the rural poor. Environmentalists say that soil has been damaged through over-irrigation, and indigenous plants have suffered, adding to the degeneration of the arid zone.

Wild Rajasthan

For a place apparently so inhospitable, Rajasthan hosts an incredible array of animals and birds; the stars are of course the tigers, most easily seen at Ranthambhore National Park (p79), and the magnificent migratory bird show of Keoladeo National Park (p63).

Arid-zone mammals have adapted to the lack of water in various resourceful ways. For example, some top up their fluids with insects that are composed of between 65% and 80% water, and water-bearing plants, while others retain water for longer periods. Faced with the incredible heat, many creatures burrow in the sand or venture out only at night.

Deer, Antelopes & Gazelles

Spotted deer (chitals) can be seen in large herds in most reserves in Rajasthan. Often they are found browsing for discarded fruit under trees full of feeding langur monkeys. The deer and the monkey sharing lookout duties for predators. Sambar, the world's largest deer, are often seen when on safari, either in small family groups or alone. Their nervous disposition understandable as they are a favourite food of tigers.

Blackbuck antelopes, with their amazing long spiralling horns, are most common around Jodhpur, where they are protected by local Bishnoi tribes. Bishnoi conservation has also helped the chinkaras (Indian gazelles); these delicate, small creatures are extremely fast and agile and are seen in small family herds.

Also notable is the extraordinary nilgai (or blue bull), which is the largest of the antelope family – only the males attain the blue colour. It's a large, muscular animal whose front legs appear longer than its rear legs, giving it a rather ungainly stance.

Big Cats

Tigers were once found along the length of the Aravallis. However, royal hunting parties, poachers and, more recently, habitat destruction have decimated the population. The only viable tiger population in Rajasthan can be found in Ranthambhore National Park (p79). Some of Ranthambhore's tigers have been relocated to Sariska Tiger Reserve & National

Park (p69) after its population was wiped out by poaching in 2004. In late 2018, the two national parks contained populations of approximately 60 to 67 and 17 tigers, respectively.

The mainly nocturnal and rarely seen leopard inhabits rocky declivities in the Aravallis and parts of the Jaipur and Jodhpur districts. One of the best places to spot a leopard is the tiny Jhalana Forest Reserve (p49) on the edge of Jaipur.

Dogs

Jackals are renowned for their unearthly howling. Once common throughout Rajasthan, they would lurk around villages where they scavenged and preyed on livestock. Habitat encroachment and hunting (for their skins) have reduced their numbers, though they are still a very common sight in Keoladeo, Ranthambhore and Sariska parks. The dhole, or Indian wild dog, has also seen its numbers dwindle due to habitat loss, and today sightings are extremely rare.

Wolves used to roam in large numbers in the desert, but farmers hunted them almost to the point of extinction. They have begun to reappear over recent decades, due to concerted conservation efforts. The wildlife sanctuary at Kumbhalgarh (p106) is known for its wolves.

The sandy-coloured desert fox is a subspecies of the red fox and was once prolific in the Thar Desert. As with wolves, the fox population has shrunk due to human endeavours. Keep your eyes open for them scavenging roadkill on the highway near Jaisalmer.

The website of India's premier wildlife magazine, *Sanctuary* (www.sanctuaryasia.com), highlights the latest conservation issues and has numerous related links.

Monkeys

Monkeys seem to be everywhere in Rajasthan. There are two common types: the red-faced and red-rumped rhesus macaque and the shaggy grey, black-faced langur, with prominent eyebrows and long tail. Both types are keen on hanging around human settlements, where they can get easy pickings. Both will steal food from your grasp at temples, but the macaque is probably the more aggressive and the one to be particularly wary of.

Bears

In forested regions you might see a sloth bear – a large creature covered in long black hair with a prominent white V on its chest and a peculiar muzzle with an overhanging upper lip. That lip helps it feed on ants and termites dug out with those dangerous-looking claws on its front paws. Sloth bears feed mostly on vegetation and insects but aren't averse to a bit of carrion. The bears are reasonably common around Mt Abu and elsewhere on the western slopes of the Aravalli Range.

Birds

Keoladeo National Park (p63), a wetland in eastern Rajasthan, is internationally renowned for birdwatching. Resident and winter migrants put on an amazing feathery show. Migratory species include several varieties of storks, spoonbills, herons, cormorants, ibis and egrets. Wintering waterfowl include the common, marbled, falcated and Baikal teal; pintail, gadwall, shoveler, coot, wigeon, bar-headed and greylag geese; common and brahminy pochards; and the beautiful demoiselle crane. Waders include snipe, sandpipers and plovers. Species resident throughout the year include the monogamous sarus crane, moorhens, egrets, herons, storks and cormorants. Birds of prey include many types of eagles (greater spotted, steppe, imperial, Spanish imperial and fishing), vultures (white-backed and scavenger), owls (spotted, dusky horned and mottled wood), marsh harriers, sparrowhawks, kestrels and goshawks.

If you want to put names to feathers on your travels, pick up a copy of *Birds of Northern India* by Richard Grimmett and Tim Inskipp.

TOP NATIONAL PARKS & WILDLIFE SANCTUARIES

NAME	LOCATION	FEATURES	BEST TIME TO VISIT
Desert National Park	western Rajasthan	great Indian bustards, blackbuck, nilgai, wolves, desert foxes, crested porcupines	Oct-Mar
Jhalana Forest Reserve	eastern Rajasthan	leopards, hyenas, deer, nilgai, foxes, birds	Oct-Apr
Keoladeo National Park	eastern Rajasthan	400 bird species, including migratory birds & waterbirds (wetlands)	Oct-Mar, Jul & Aug
Kumbhalgarh Wildlife Sanctuary	southern Rajasthan	wolves in packs of up to 40, chowsinghas (four-horned antelopes), leopards	Oct-Jun
Mt Abu Wildlife Sanctuary	southern Rajasthan	forest birds, sloth bears, wild boar, sambars, leopards	Mar-Jun
Ranthambhore National Park	eastern Rajasthan	tigers, chitals, leopards, nilgai, chinkaras, birdlife, ancient fort	Oct-Apr
Sariska Tiger Reserve & National Park	eastern Rajasthan	leopards, chitals, chinkaras, birdlife, fort, deserted city, temples	Nov-Jun
Tal Chhapar Wildlife Sanctuary	northern Rajasthan	blackbuck, chinkaras, desert foxes, antelopes, harriers, eagles, sparrowhawks	Sep-Mar

The remaining forests and jungles that cling to the rugged Aravalli Ranges harbour orioles, hornbills, kingfishers, swallows, parakeets, warblers, mynahs, robins, flycatchers, quails, doves, peacocks, barbets, bee-eaters, woodpeckers and drongos, among others. Birds of prey include numerous species of owls (great horned, dusky, brown fishing and collared scops, and spotted owlets), eagles (spotted and tawny), white-eyed buzzards, black-winged kites and shikras.

Common birds of the open grasslands include various species of lark. Quails can also be seen, as can several types of shrike, mynahs, drongos and partridges. Migratory birds include the lesser florican, seen during the monsoon, and the Houbara bustard, which winters in the grasslands. Birds of prey include falcons, eagles, hawks, kites, kestrels and harriers.

The Thar Desert also has a prolific variety of birdlife. At the small village of Kichan, about 135km from Jodhpur, you can see vast flocks of demoiselle cranes descending on fields from the end of August to the end of March. Other winter visitors to the desert include Houbara bustards and common cranes. As water is scarce, waterholes attract large flocks of imperial, spotted, pintail and Indian sandgrouse in the early mornings. More desert dwellers include drongos, common and bush quail, blue-tailed and little green bee-eaters and grey partridges. Desert birds of prey include eagles (steppe and tawny), buzzards (honey and long-legged), goshawks, peregrine falcons and kestrels. The most notable of the desert and dry grassland dwellers is the impressive Indian bustard.

Survival Guide

Scams

India has an unfortunately deserved reputation for scams, both classic and new-fangled. Of course, most can be avoided with some common sense and an appropriate amount of caution. They tend to be more of a problem in the major gateway cities (such as Delhi or Mumbai), or very touristy spots (such as Rajasthan). Chat with fellow travellers and check the India branch of Lonely Planet's Thorn Tree forum (www.lonelyplanet.com/thorntree) to keep abreast of the latest cons.

Contaminated Food & Drink

➡ Most bottled water is legit, but ensure that the seal is intact and the bottom of the bottle hasn't been tampered with.

➡ While in transit, try to carry packed food if possible, and politely decline offers of food or drink from locals on buses or trains; hygiene can be an issue and people have been drugged in the past.

➡ Though there have been no recent reports, the late 1990s saw a scam where travellers died after consuming food laced with dangerous bacteria from restaurants linked to dodgy medical clinics. In unrelated incidents, some clinics have given more treatment than necessary to procure larger payments from insurance companies.

Credit-Card Cons

Be careful when paying for souvenirs with a credit card. While government shops are usually legitimate, private souvenir shops have been known to surreptitiously run off extra copies of the credit-card imprint slip and use them for phoney transactions later.

Ask the trader to process the transaction in front of you. Memorising the CVV/CVC2 number and scratching it off the card is also a good idea, to avoid misuse. If anyone asks for your PIN with the intention of taking your credit card to the machine, insist on using the machine in person.

Druggings

Be extremely wary of accepting food or drink from strangers, even if you feel you're being rude. Women should be particularly circumspect. Occasionally, tourists (especially those travelling solo) have been drugged and robbed or even attacked. A spiked drink is the most common method, but snacks and even homemade meals have also been used.

OTHER TOP SCAMS

➡ Gunk (dirt, paint, poo) suddenly appears on your shoes, only for a shoe cleaner to magically appear and offer to clean it off – for a price.

➡ Some shops are selling overpriced SIMs and not activating them; it's best to buy your SIM from an official outlet such as Airtel, Vodafone etc and check it works before leaving the area.

➡ Shops, restaurants or tour guides 'borrow' the name of their more successful and popular competitor.

➡ Touts claim to be 'government-approved' guides or agents, and sting you for large sums of cash. Enquire at the local tourist office about licensed guides and ask to see identification from guides themselves.

➡ 'Tourist offices' turn out to be dodgy travel agencies whose aim is to sell you overpriced tours, tickets and tourist services.

Gem Scams

Don't be fooled by smooth-talking con artists who promise foolproof 'get rich quick' schemes. In this scam, travellers are asked to carry or mail gems home and then sell them to the trader's (nonexistent) overseas representatives at a profit. Without exception, the goods – if they arrive at all – are worth a fraction of what you paid, and the 'representatives' never materialise.

Travellers have reported this con happening in Agra, Delhi and Jaisalmer, but it's particularly prevalent in Jaipur. Carpets, curios and *pashmina* woollens are other favourites for this con.

Overpricing

Always agree on prices beforehand while using services that don't have regulated tariffs. This particularly applies to friendly neighbourhood guides, snack bars at touristy places, and autorickshaws and taxis without meters.

Photography

Ask for permission where possible while photographing people. If you don't have permission, you may be asked to pay a fee.

Theft

➡ Theft is a risk in India, as anywhere else. Keep your eye on your luggage at all times on public transport, and consider locking it, or even chaining it on overnight buses and trains. Remember that snatchings often occur when a train is pulling out of the station, as it's too late for you to give chase.

➡ Take extra care in dormitories and never leave your valuables unattended. Use safe deposit boxes where possible.

KEEPING SAFE

➡ A good travel-insurance policy is essential.

➡ Email copies of your passport identity page, visa and airline tickets to yourself, and keep copies on you.

➡ Keep your money and passport in a concealed money belt or a secure place under your shirt.

➡ Store at least US$100 separately from your main stash.

➡ Don't publicly display large wads of cash when paying.

➡ Consider using your own padlock at cheaper hotels.

➡ If you can't lock your hotel room securely from inside, stay elsewhere.

➡ Remember to lock your door at night; it is not unknown for thieves to take things from hotel rooms while occupants are sleeping.

Touts & Commission Agents

➡ Cabbies and autorickshaw drivers will often try to coerce you into staying at a hotel of their choice, only to collect a commission (added to your room tariff) afterward. Where possible, prearrange hotel bookings and request a hotel pick-up.

➡ You'll often hear stories about hotels of your choice being 'full' or 'closed' – check things out yourself and reconfirm and double-check your booking the day before you arrive.

➡ Be very sceptical of phrases like 'my brother's shop' and 'special deal at my friend's place'. Many fraudsters operate in collusion with souvenir stalls.

➡ Avoid friendly people and 'officials' in train and bus stations who offer unsolicited help, only to guide you to a commission-paying travel agent. Look confident, and if anyone asks if this is your first trip to India, say you've been here several times and that your onward travel is already booked.

Transport Scams

➡ Upon arriving at train stations and airports, if you haven't prearranged a pick-up, use public transport, or call an Uber or equivalent, or go to the prepaid taxi or airport shuttle-bus counters. Never choose a loitering cabbie who offers you a cheap ride into town, especially at night.

➡ While booking multiday sightseeing tours, research your own itinerary, and be extremely wary of anyone in Delhi offering houseboat tours to Kashmir – we've received many complaints over the years about dodgy deals.

➡ When buying a bus, train or plane ticket anywhere other than the registered office of the transport company, make sure you're getting the ticket class you paid for. Use official online booking facilities where possible.

➡ Train-station touts (even in uniform or with 'official' badges) may tell you that your intended train is cancelled/flooded/broken down or that your ticket is invalid or that you must pay to have your e-ticket validated on the platform. Do not respond to any approaches at train stations.

Women & Solo Travellers

Women Travellers

Reports of sexual assaults against women and girls are on the increase in India, despite tougher punishments being introduced after the notorious gang rape and murder of a female intern in Delhi in 2012. There have been several instances of sexual attacks on tourists over the last few years, though it's worth bearing in mind that the vast majority of visits are trouble free.

Unwanted Attention

Unwanted attention from men is a common problem.

➡ Being stared at is something you'll simply have to live with, so don't let it get the better of you.

➡ Be aware that men may try to take surreptitious photos with their phones – objecting loudly may discourage offenders.

➡ Refrain from returning male stares; this will be considered encouragement.

➡ Dark glasses, phones, books or electronic tablets are useful props for averting unwanted conversations.

➡ Wearing a wedding ring and saying you're due to meet your husband shortly can ward off unwanted interest.

Sexual Harassment

➡ Many women travellers have experienced provocative gestures, jeering, getting 'accidentally' bumped into and being followed, as well as more serious intrusions.

➡ Incidents are particularly common at exuberant (and crowded) public events such as the Holi festival. If a crowd gathers, find a less busy spot.

➡ Women travelling with a male partner will receive less hassle, but still be cautious.

Clothing

In big cities, you'll see local women dressing as they might in New York or London. Elsewhere women dress conservatively, and it pays to follow their lead.

➡ Avoid sleeveless tops, shorts, short skirts (ankle-length is recommended) and anything skimpy, see-through, tight-fitting or which reveals too much skin.

➡ Wearing Indian-style clothes such as the popular *salwar kameez* (traditional dress-like tunic and trousers) is viewed favourably.

➡ Drape a dupatta (long scarf) over your T-shirt to avoid stares – it also doubles as a head-covering for temple visits.

➡ Avoid going out in public wearing a choli (sari blouse) or a sari petticoat; it's like being half-dressed.

➡ Indian women tend to wear long shorts and a T-shirt when swimming; it's wise to wear a sarong from the beach to your hotel.

Staying Safe

The following tips will help you avoid uncomfortable or dangerous situations during your journey:

➡ Maintain a healthy level of vigilance, even if you've been in the country for a while. If something feels wrong, trust your instincts.

➡ Women have been drugged in the past so don't accept any food or drinks, even bottled water, from strangers.

➡ Keep conversations with unknown men short – being willing to chat can be misinterpreted.

➡ If you feel that a guy is encroaching on your space, he probably is. Protesting loudly enough to draw the attention of passers-by can stop unwelcome advances.

➡ The silent treatment can also be effective.

➡ Instead of shaking hands say *namaste* – the traditional, respectful Hindu greeting.

➡ Avoid wearing expensive-looking jewellery and carrying flashy accessories.

➡ Only go for massage or other treatments with female therapists, and go to cinemas with a companion.

➡ At hotels, keep your door locked, particularly at night;

never let anyone you don't know well into your hotel room.

➡ Avoid wandering alone in isolated areas – gallis (narrow lanes), deserted roads, beaches, ruins and forests.

➡ Use your smartphone's GPS maps to keep track of where you are; this will also alert you if a taxi/rickshaw is taking the wrong road.

➡ Try to look confident about where you are going in public; consult maps at your hotel (or at a restaurant) rather than on the street.

Taxis & Public Transport

Being female has some advantages; women can usually queue-jump for buses and trains without consequence and on trains and metros there are special ladies-only carriages. There are also women-only waiting rooms at some stations.

➡ Prearrange an airport pick-up from your hotel, particularly if you will arrive after dark.

➡ If travelling after dark, use a recommended, registered taxi service; travel with a companion where possible.

➡ Never hail a taxi in the street or accept a lift from a stranger.

➡ Never agree to have more than one man (the driver) in the car – ignore claims that this is 'just my brother' etc.

➡ Uber (www.uber.com) and Ola Cabs (www.olacabs.com) are useful, as you get the driver's licence plate in advance; pass the details on to someone else as a precaution.

➡ When taking rickshaws alone, call/text someone, or pretend to, to indicate that someone knows where you are.

Sanitary Items

Sanitary pads are widely available, but tampons are usually restricted to pharmacies in some big cities and tourist towns.

Websites

Peruse personal experiences proffered by female travellers at www.journeywoman.com and www.wanderlustand lipstick.com. Blogs such as Breathe, Dream, Go (https://breathedreamgo.com) and Hippie in Heels (https://hippie-inheels.com) are also full of tips.

Solo Travellers

Travelling solo in India may be great, because local people are often so friendly, helpful and interested in meeting new people. You're more likely to be 'adopted' by families, especially if you're commuting together on a long rail journey. If you're keen to hook up with fellow travellers, try tourist hubs such as Delhi and Agra, or browse the messages on Lonely Planet's Thorn Tree

forum (www.lonelyplanet.com/thorntree).

Cost

The most significant issue facing solo travellers is cost.

➡ Single-room accommodation rates are sometimes not much lower than double rates.

➡ Some midrange and top-end places don't even offer a single tariff.

➡ It's always worth trying to negotiate a lower rate for single occupancy.

➡ Ordering a *thali* (set-meal platter) at restaurants is an affordable way to try out a number of different dishes.

Safety

Most solo travellers experience no major problems in India, but, as anywhere else, it's wise to stay on your toes in unfamiliar surroundings.

➡ Some less honourable souls (locals and travellers alike) view lone tourists as an easy target for theft and sexual assault.

➡ Single men wandering around isolated areas have been mugged, even during the day.

Transport

➡ You'll save money if you find others to share taxis, autorickshaws, or a hired car and driver.

➡ Solo bus travellers may be able to get the 'co-pilot' seat beside the driver, handy if you've got a big bag.

SAFETY ON BUSES & TRAINS

➡ Don't organise your travel in such a way that it means you're hanging out at bus/train stations late at night.

➡ Solo women have reported less hassle by opting for the more expensive classes on trains, but try to avoid empty carriages.

➡ If you're travelling overnight by train, book an upper outer berth in 2AC; you're out of the way of wandering hands and the presence of fellow passengers is a deterrent to dodgy behaviour.

➡ On public transport, don't hesitate to return any errant limbs, put an item of luggage between you and others, be vocal (attracting public attention) or simply find a new spot.

Directory A–Z

Accessible Travel

India's crowded public transport, hectic urban life and variable infrastructure can test even the hardiest able-bodied traveller. If you have a physical disability or you are vision impaired, these factors can pose even more of a challenge. If your mobility is considerably restricted, you may like to ease the stress by travelling with an able-bodied companion.

Accommodation Wheelchair-friendly hotels are almost exclusively top end. Make pre-trip enquiries and book ground-floor rooms at hotels that lack adequate facilities.

Accessibility Some restaurants and offices have ramps; most tend to have at least one step. Staircases are often steep and uneven.

Footpaths Where pavements exist, they can be riddled with holes, littered with debris and packed with pedestrians and parked motorcycles.

Transport Hiring a car with a driver will make moving around a lot easier; if you use a wheel-chair, make sure the car-hire company can provide an appropriate vehicle to carry it.

Further advice Consult your doctor about your specific requirements before heading to India.

Accommodation

Accommodation ranges from grungy backpacker hostels with concrete floors, plywood walls and cold 'bucket' showers to opulent palaces fit for a modern-era maharaja.

As a general rule, budget covers everything from basic hostels and railway retiring rooms to simple guesthouses in traditional village homes.

Midrange hotels tend to be modern-style concrete blocks that usually offer extras such as cable/satellite TV and air-conditioning.

Top-end places stretch from gorgeous heritage hotels to luxury five-star international chains.

Reservations

➡ It's a good idea to book ahead, online or by phone, especially when travelling to more popular destinations. Some hotels require a credit-card deposit at the time of booking.

➡ Some budget options won't take reservations as they don't know when people are going to check out. Call ahead to check.

➡ Other places may ask for a deposit at check-in – ask for a receipt and be wary of any request to sign a blank impression of your credit card. If the hotel insists, pay cash and get a receipt.

➡ Verify the check-out time when you check in – some hotels have a fixed check-out time, while others give you 24-hour checkout.

Seasons

➡ Rates given are full price in high season, which coincides with the best weather (October to mid-February). In areas popular with tourists there are additional peak periods over Diwali, Christmas and New Year – make reservations well in advance. At other times, you may find significant discounts; if the hotel seems quiet, ask for a discount.

➡ Temple towns (such as Pushkar) have additional peak seasons around major festivals and pilgrimages.

BOOK YOUR STAY ONLINE

For more accommodation reviews by Lonely Planet authors, check out http://lonelyplanet.com/hotels/. You'll find independent reviews, as well as recommendations on the best places to stay. Best of all, you can book online.

Taxes & Service Charges

➡ At midrange and top-end accommodation, you have to pay goods and services tax (GST) on room tariffs. The rates are 0% below ₹999, 12% for ₹1000 to ₹2499, 18% for ₹2500 to ₹7499, and 28% for rates of and greater than ₹7500.

➡ Rates quoted include taxes unless noted.

Accommodation Types

BUDGET & MIDRANGE HOTELS

➡ Room quality can vary considerably within hotels, so try to inspect a few rooms first.

➡ Shared bathrooms (sometimes with squat toilets) are usually only found at the cheapest lodgings.

➡ Most rooms have ceiling fans and better rooms have electric mosquito killers and/ or window screens, though cheaper rooms may lack windows altogether.

➡ If staying at the very cheapest of hotels, bring your own sheet or sleeping-bag liner, along with a towel.

➡ Traffic noise can be irksome; pack good-quality earplugs and request a room that doesn't face a busy road.

➡ It's wise to keep your door locked, as some staff (particularly in budget accommodation) may knock and walk in without first seeking your permission.

➡ Note that some hotels lock their doors at night. Members of staff may sleep in the lobby but waking them up can be a challenge. Let the hotel know in advance if you'll be arriving or returning to your room late in the evening.

➡ Away from tourist areas, cheaper hotels may not take foreigners because they don't have the necessary foreigner-registration forms.

DORMITORY ACCOMMODATION

There are a several private chains developing well-thought-out backpacker dorms and rooms for the burgeoning number of domestic student travellers. Also a number of hotels have dormitories, though these may be mixed. Dorms can be found at the handful of hostels run by the YMCA, YWCA and Salvation Army but these can be crowded and noisy.

PAYING GUEST HOUSE SCHEME (HOMESTAYS)

Rajasthan pioneered the Paying Guest House Scheme, so it's well developed in the state. Prices range from budget to upper midrange – contact the local Rajasthan Tourism Development Corporation (RTDC) tourist reception centres for details.

RAILWAY RETIRING ROOMS

Most large train stations have basic rooms for travellers holding an ongoing train ticket or Indrail Pass. Some are grim; others are surprisingly pleasant but suffer from the noise of passengers and trains.

They're useful for early-morning departures and there's usually a choice between dormitories and private rooms (with 24-hour checkout), depending on the rail class you're travelling in.

Some smaller stations may have only waiting rooms (again divided by class).

PALACES, FORTS & HAVELIS

Rajasthan is famous for its wonderful heritage hotels created from palaces, forts and *havelis* (traditional, ornately decorated residences). There are hundreds and it often doesn't cost a fortune to stay in one: some are the height of luxury and priced accordingly, but many are simpler, packed with character and set in stunning locations.

TOP-END HOTELS

As a major tourist destination, Rajasthan boasts many top-end hotels. If you're staying at a top-end hotel, it's often cheaper to book it online. Nevertheless, unless the hotel is busy, you can nearly always score a discount from the rack rates.

Customs Regulations

➡ Technically, you're supposed to declare any amount of cash over US$5000 or total amount of currency over US$10,000 on arrival. Indian rupees shouldn't be taken out of India.

➡ Officials very occasionally ask tourists to enter expensive items such as laptop computers in a 'Tourist Baggage Re-export' form to ensure they're taken out of India at the time of departure.

➡ Exporting antiques (defined as objects of historical interest not less than 100 years old) from India is explicitly prohibited. Reputable antique dealers know the laws and can make arrangements for an export-clearance certificate for old items that are OK to export, but it's best to look for quality reproductions instead.

Electricity

230V/50Hz. Plugs have two or three round pins.

Type C
230V/50Hz

Type D
230V/50Hz

Type M
230V/50Hz

Embassies & Consulates

The foreign diplomatic missions listed here are based in Delhi, but there are various consulates in other Indian cities. Many foreign diplomatic missions have certain timings for visa applications (usually mornings), so phone or check the website for details.

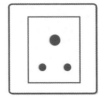

Australia (☑011-41399900; www.india.highcommission.gov.au; 1/50G Shantipath, Chanakyapuri; Ⓜ Lok Kalyan Marg)

Bangladesh (☑011-24121394; www.bdhcdelhi.org; EP39 Dr Radakrishnan Marg, Chanakyapuri; Ⓜ Chanakyapuri)

Bhutan (☑011-26889230; www.mfa.gov.bt/rbedelhi; Chandragupta Marg, Chanakyapuri; Ⓜ Chanakyapuri)

Canada (☑011-41782000; www.india.gc.ca; 7/8 Shantipath, Chanakyapuri; ⊙ consular services 9am-noon Mon-Fri; Ⓜ Chanakyapuri)

China (☑consular 011-24677525, visas 011-30013601; http://in.china-embassy.org; 50-D Shantipath, Chanakyapuri; ⊙9am-12.30pm & 3-5.30pm Mon-Fri; Ⓜ Chanakyapuri)

France (☑011-24196100; www.ambafrance-in.org; 2/50E Shantipath, Chanakyapuri; Ⓜ Chanakyapuri)

Germany (https://india.diplo.de; 6/50G Shantipath, Chanakyapuri; Ⓜ Chanakyapuri)

Ireland (☑011-24940 3200; www.dfa.ie/irish-embassy/india; C17 Malcha Marg, Chanakyapuri; ⊙9am-1.30pm & 2.30-5pm Mon-Fri; Ⓜ Chanakyapuri)

PRACTICALITIES

Newspapers Major English-language dailies include the *Hindustan Times, Times of India, Indian Express, Hindu, Statesman, Telegraph, Daily News & Analysis (DNA)* and *Economic Times*.

Current-affairs magazines Titles include *Frontline, India Today,* the *Week, Tehelka* and *Outlook*.

Radio Government-controlled All India Radio (AIR) is India's national broadcaster with more than 220 stations broadcasting local and international news. There are also private FM channels broadcasting music, current affairs, talkback and more.

TV & Video The national (government) TV broadcaster is Doordarshan. Most people watch satellite and cable TV; English-language channels include BBC, CNN, Star World, HBO and Discovery.

Weights & Measures Officially India is metric. Terms you're likely to hear are: lakhs (one lakh = 100,000) and crores (one crore = 10 million).

Israel (☎011-30414500, visas 011-30414538; www.embassies. gov.il/delhi; 3 Dr APJ Abdul Kalam Rd; ⊗9.30am-1pm Mon-Fri; ⊠Khan Market)

Japan (☎011-26876581; www.in.emb-japan.go.jp; 50G Shantipath, Chanakyapuri; ⊗9am-1pm & 2-5.30pm Mon-Fri; ⊠Chanakyapuri)

Malaysia (☎011-24159300; http://mw.kln.gov.my/web/ ind_new-delhi/home; 50M Satya Marg, Chanakyapuri; ⊗8.30am-4.30pm Mon-Fri; ⊠Chanakyapuri)

Maldives (☎011-41435701; www.maldivesembassy.in; C-3 Anand Niketan; ⊠Sir Vishveshwaraiah Moti Bagh)

Myanmar (☎011-24678822; www.myanmedelhi.com; 3/50F Nyaya Marg; ⊗9.30am-4.30pm Mon-Fri; ⊠Lok Kalyan Marg)

Nepal (☎011-23476200; http://in.nepalembassy.gov. np; Mandi House, Barakhamba Rd; ⊗visa services 9am-1pm Mon-Fri; ⊠Mandi House)

Netherlands (☎011-24197600; www.netherlandsworldwide.nl/ countries/india; 6/50F Shantipath, Chanakyapuri; ⊗9am-5pm Mon-Fri; ⊠Chanakyapuri)

New Zealand (☎011-46883170; www.nzembassy.com/india; Sir Edmund Hillary Marg, Chanakyapuri; ⊗8.30am-5pm Mon-Fri; ⊠Sir Vishveshwaraiah Moti Bagh)

Pakistan (☎011-26110601; www.mofa.gov.pk; 2/50G Shantipath, Chanakyapuri; ⊠Lok Kalyan Marg)

Singapore (☎011-46000915; www.mfa.gov.sg/newdelhi; E6 Chandragupta Marg, Chanakyapuri; ⊗9am-1pm & 1.30-5pm Mon-Fri; ⊠Chanakyapuri)

Sri Lanka (☎011-23010201; www.slhcindia.org; 27 Kautilya Marg, Chanakyapuri; ⊗8.45am-5pm Mon-Fri; ⊠Lok Kalyan Marg)

Thailand (☎011-49774100; http://newdelhi.thaiembassy. org; D-1/3 Vasant Vihar; ⊗9am-5pm Mon-Fri; ⊠Vasant Vihar)

UK (☎011-24192100; Shantipath, Chanakyapuri; ⊗9am-5pm Mon-Fri; ⊠Lok Kalyan Marg)

US (☎011-24198000; https:// in.usembassy.gov; Shantipath, Chanakyapuri; ⊠Lok Kalyan Marg)

Food & Drink

See Rajasthani Food (p252) for details on this region's cuisine.

Taxes & Service Charges

Most upscale or midrange restaurants add the goods and services tax (GST) of 5% to their restaurant bill. Star-rated hotels that charge over ₹7500 for rooms (hence attracting 28% GST on rooms) will charge 18% GST in their restaurants.

Insurance

➡ Comprehensive travel insurance to cover theft, loss and medical problems (as well as air evacuation) is strongly recommended.

➡ Some policies specifically exclude potentially dangerous activities such as scuba diving, skiing, motorcycling, paragliding and trekking – read the fine print.

➡ If you plan to hire a motorcycle in India make sure the rental policy includes at least third-party insurance.

➡ Check in advance if your insurance policy will pay doctors and hospitals directly or reimburse you later for overseas health expenditures (keep all documentation for your claim).

➡ It's crucial to get a police report in India if you've had anything stolen; insurance companies may refuse to reimburse you without one.

➡ Worldwide travel insurance is available at www.lonelyplanet.com/ travel-insurance. You can buy, extend and claim online anytime – even if you're already on the road.

Internet Access

Internet cafes are becoming less common as wi-fi and 3G and 4G phone services increase. Wi-fi access is widely available in hotels and restaurants and it's almost always free.

Security

➡ Be wary of sending sensitive financial information from internet cafes; some places can use keystroke-capturing technology to access passwords and emails.

➡ Avoid sending credit-card details or other personal data over a wireless connection; using online banking on any nonsecure system is generally unwise.

Legal Matters

If you're in a sticky legal situation, contact your embassy as quickly as possible. However, be aware that all your embassy may be able to do is monitor your treatment in custody and arrange a

EATING PRICE RANGES

Prices reflect the cost of a standard main meal (unless otherwise indicated). Reviews are listed by writer preference within the following price categories:

$ below ₹150

$$ ₹150–300

$$$ above ₹300

lawyer. In the Indian justice system, the burden of proof can often be on the accused and stints in prison before trial are not unheard of. Travellers should note that they can be prosecuted under the law of their home country regarding age of consent, even when abroad.

Antisocial Behaviour

Smoking in public places is illegal, but this is rarely enforced; if caught, you'll be fined ₹200. People can smoke inside their homes and in most open spaces such as streets (heed any signs stating otherwise). The status of e-cigarettes is in flux, but there are currently bans in several states and this could be expanded at any time.

A number of Indian cities have banned spitting and littering, but, as is obvious to everyone, this is hardly enforced.

Drugs

➡ Indian law doesn't distinguish between 'hard' and 'soft' drugs; possession of any illegal drug is regarded as a criminal offence, which will result in a custodial sentence.

➡ Sentences may be up to a year for possession of a small amount for personal use, and up to a minimum of 10 years if it's deemed the purpose was for sale or distribution.

➡ Cases can take months, even several years, to appear before a court while the accused may have to wait in prison. There's also usually a hefty monetary fine on top of any custodial sentence.

➡ Be aware that travellers have been targeted in sting operations in some backpacker enclaves.

➡ Marijuana grows wild in various parts of India, but consuming it is still an offence, except in towns where bhang is legally sold for religious rituals.

➡ Police are particularly tough on foreigners who use

drugs, so you should take this risk very seriously.

Police

➡ You should always carry your passport; police are entitled to ask you for identification at any time.

➡ If you're arrested for an alleged offence and asked for a bribe, note that it is illegal to pay a bribe in India. Many people deal with an on-the-spot fine by just paying it to avoid trumped-up charges.

➡ Corruption is rife, so the less you have to do with local police the better; avoid potentially risky situations.

LGBT+ Travellers

Homosexuality in India was decriminalised in 2009, made illegal in 2013, and decriminalised again in 2018. Trans rights have fared better: in 2014, there was a ruling that gave legal recognition of a third gender in India, a step towards increased acceptance of the large yet marginalised transgender (hijra) population. LGBT+ visitors should be discreet in this conservative country. Public displays of affection are frowned upon for both homosexual and heterosexual couples.

There are low-key gay scenes in many larger cities, including Delhi and Mumbai.

Gay Delhi (www.gaydelhi.org) LGBT+ support group, organising social events in Delhi.

Gaysi Zine (www.gaysifamily. com) A thoughtful monthly magazine and website featuring gay writing and issues.

Indian Dost (www.indiandost. com/gay.php) News and information, including contact groups in India.

Indja Pink (www.indjapink.co.in) India's first 'gay travel boutique', founded by a well-known Indian fashion designer.

Queer Ink (www.queer-ink.com) Online bookstore specialising in gay- and lesbian-interest books from the subcontinent.

Money

The Indian rupee (₹) is divided into 100 paise, but paise coins are rare. Coins come in denominations of ₹1, ₹2, ₹5 and ₹10; notes come in ₹5, ₹10, ₹20, ₹50, ₹100, ₹200, ₹500 and ₹2000. The Indian rupee is linked to a basket of currencies and has been subject to fluctuations in recent years.

ATMs & Eftpos

➡ ATMs are found in most urban centres. Visa, MasterCard, Cirrus, Maestro and Plus are the most commonly accepted cards.

➡ Some banks in India that accept foreign cards include Axis Bank, Citibank, HDFC, HSBC, ICICI, Standard Chartered, State Bank of India (SBI) and Bank of India (BOI).

➡ Before your trip, check whether your card can reliably access banking networks in India and ask for details of charges.

➡ Most ATMs have withdrawal limits of ₹10,000 to ₹15,000.

➡ Notify your bank that you'll be using your card in India (provide dates) to avoid having your card blocked; take along your bank's phone number just in case.

➡ Always keep the emergency lost-and-stolen numbers for your credit cards in a safe place, separate from your cards, and report any loss or theft immediately.

➡ Away from major towns, always carry cash as backup.

Cash

➡ Major currencies such as US dollars, British pounds and euros are easy to change throughout India. Many banks in Rajasthan also accept other currencies such as Australian and Canadian dollars, and Swiss francs.

→ Private moneychangers deal with a wider range of currencies.

→ When travelling off the beaten track, always carry an adequate stock of rupees.

→ Whenever changing money, check every note. Don't accept any filthy, ripped or disintegrating notes, as these may be difficult to use.

→ It can be tough getting change in India: jealously hoard your ₹10, ₹20 and ₹50 notes.

→ Officially, you cannot take rupees out of India, but this rule is laxly enforced. You can most easily change any leftover rupees back into foreign currency at the airport (some banks have a ₹1000 minimum). You may be required to present your encashment certificates or credit-card/ATM receipts and show your passport and airline ticket.

Credit Cards

→ Credit cards are accepted at a growing number of shops, upmarket restaurants and midrange and top-end hotels; they can usually be used to pay for flights and train tickets.

→ Cash advances on major credit cards are also possible at some banks.

→ MasterCard and Visa are the most widely accepted cards.

Encashment Certificates

→ Indian law states that all foreign currency must be changed at official money changers or banks.

→ For every (official) foreign-exchange transaction, you'll receive an encashment certificate (receipt), which will allow you to exchange rupees back into foreign currency when departing India.

→ Encashment certificates should be able to cover the amount of rupees you intend

to change back to foreign currency.

→ Printed receipts from ATMs are also accepted as evidence of an international transaction at most banks.

Money Changers

Private money changers are usually open for longer hours than banks and are found almost everywhere (many also double as travel agents). Upmarket hotels may also change money, but their rates are usually not as competitive.

Tipping

Restaurants A service fee is often already included your bill and tipping is optional. Elsewhere, a tip is appreciated.

Hotel Bellboys appreciate anything from around ₹20 to ₹100.

Train/airport Porters appreciate anything from around ₹20 to ₹100.

Taxi/rickshaw drivers A tip is not mandatory/expected.

Hire car with driver A tip is recommended (around ₹100 per day) for more than a couple of days of good service.

Opening Hours

Official business hours are 9.30am to 5.30pm Monday to Friday, with many offices closing for a lunch hour around 1pm. Many sights are open from dawn to dusk.

Banks 10am–2pm or 4pm Monday to Friday, to noon or 1pm Saturday

Post Offices 10am–4pm Monday to Friday, to noon Saturday

Restaurants 8am–10pm or lunch; noon–2.30pm or 3pm; 7–10pm or 11pm

Shops 9am–9pm, some closed Sunday

Photography

For useful tips and techniques on travel photography, read Lonely Planet's guide to *Travel Photography*.

Restrictions

→ Indian authorities are touchy about anyone taking photographs of military installations – this can include train stations, bridges, airports, military sites and sensitive border regions.

→ Photography from the air is officially prohibited, although airlines rarely enforce this.

→ Many places of worship, such as monasteries, temples and mosques, also prohibit photography. Taking photos inside a shrine, at a funeral, at a religious ceremony or of people publicly bathing (including rivers) can also be offensive – ask first.

→ Flash photography may be prohibited in certain areas of a shrine or may not be permitted at all.

→ Exercise sensitivity when taking photos of people, especially women, who may find it offensive – obtain permission in advance.

→ When photographing people use your instincts; some people may demand money afterwards.

Post

India has the biggest postal network on earth, with about 155,000 post offices. Mail and poste-restante services are generally good, although the speed of delivery will depend on the efficiency of any given office. Airmail is faster and more reliable than sea mail, although it's best to use courier services (such as DHL) to send and receive items of value – expect to pay around ₹1500 per kilogram to Europe, Australia or the USA. Private couriers are often cheaper, but goods may be repacked into large packages to cut costs and things sometimes go missing.

Letters

→ Posting letters to anywhere overseas costs ₹25.

→ International postcards cost around ₹15.

→ For postcards, stick on the stamps *before* writing on them, as post offices can give you as many as four stamps per card.

→ Sending a letter overseas by registered post adds ₹70 to the cost.

Parcels

→ Posting parcels can be relatively straightforward or involve multiple counters and a fair amount of queuing; get to the post office in the morning.

→ Prices vary depending on weight (including packing material).

→ An (unregistered) airmail package costs around ₹400 to ₹1000 (up to 250g) to any country and ₹50 to ₹150 per additional 250g (up to a maximum of 2kg; different charges apply for higher weights).

→ Parcel post has a maximum of 20kg to 30kg depending on the destination.

→ Choose either airmail (delivery in one to three weeks); sea mail (two to four months); or Surface Air-Lifted (SAL), a curious hybrid where parcels travel by both air and sea (around one month).

→ Another option is EMS (express mail service; delivery within three days) for around 30% more than the normal airmail price.

→ Parcels must be stitched up in white linen and the seams sealed with wax – agents at the post office offer this service for a fee. It's a joy to watch.

→ The post office can provide the necessary customs declaration forms and these must be stitched or pasted to the parcel. If the contents are a gift under the value of ₹1000, you won't be required to pay duty at the delivery end.

→ Carry a permanent marker to write on the parcel any information requested by the desk.

→ Books or printed matter can go by international book post for ₹350 (maximum 5kg): the parcel has to be packed with an opening so it can be checked by customs.

→ India Post (www.indiapost. gov.in) has an online calculator for domestic and international postal tariffs.

GOVERNMENT TRAVEL ADVICE

The following government websites offer travel advice and information on current hotspots.

Australian Department of Foreign Affairs (www. smartraveller.gov.au)

British Foreign Office (www.fco.gov.uk/en)

Canadian Department of Foreign Affairs (www. voyage.gc.ca)

German Foreign Office (www.auswaertiges-amt.de)

Japan Ministry of Foreign Affairs (www.mofa.go.jp)

Netherlands Ministry of Foreign Affairs (www.govern ment.nl)

Swiss Department of Foreign Affairs (www.eda. admin.ch)

US State Department (http://travel.state.gov)

Public Holidays

There are officially three national public holidays – Republic and Independence Days and Gandhi's birthday (Gandhi Jayanti). Every state celebrates its own official holidays, which cover bank holidays for government workers as well as major religious festivals. Most businesses (offices, shops etc) and tourist sites close on public holidays, but transport is usually unaffected. It's wise to make transport and hotel reservations well in advance if you intend visiting during major festivals.

Republic Day 26 January

Holi March

Ramanavani April

Dr BL Ambedkar's Birthday 14 April

Mahavir Jayanti April

Good Friday March/April

Buddha Purnima April/May

Eid al-Fitr May

Eid al-Adha July

Independence Day 15 August

Janmastani August

Dussehra October

Eid-Milad-un-Nabi October

Gandhi Jayanti 2 October

Diwali October/November

Guru Nanak Jayanti November

Eid-Milad-un-Nabi October

Christmas 25 December

Safe Travel

Travellers to India's major cities may fall prey to petty and opportunistic crime. Have a look at the India branch of Lonely Planet's Thorn Tree travel forum (www. lonelyplanet.com/thorntree), where travellers often post timely warnings about problems they've encountered on the road.

→ India's roads are lethal places and visitors should approach all road travel with care and definitely avoid any driving or riding at night.

➡ India has a bit of a reputation for scams (p262) and these are indeed common in the tourist hotspots in Rajasthan.

Telephone

Useful online resources include the Yellow Pages (www.indiayellowpages.com) and Justdial (www.justdial.com).

Mobile Phones

Roaming connections are excellent in urban areas, but poorer in the countryside. Local prepaid SIMs are widely available; the paperwork is fairly straightforward but you may have to wait two to four hours for activation.

INDIAN MOBILE PHONE SERVICES

➡ Indian mobile phone numbers usually have 10 digits typically beginning with 9 (sometimes also 7 or 8).

➡ There's roaming coverage for international GSM phones in most cities and large towns.

➡ To avoid expensive roaming costs (often highest for incoming calls), get hooked up to the local mobile-phone network. You'll need to have an unlocked phone to use an Indian SIM card or buy a local handset (from ₹2000).

➡ The leading service providers include Airtel, Vodafone and Jio. Coverage varies from region to region.

GETTING CONNECTED

➡ Getting connected is inexpensive and fairly straightforward in many areas. It's easiest to obtain a local SIM card when you arrive if you're flying into a large city.

➡ Foreigners need only supply their passport for obtaining photocopies of

SECURE IT OR LOSE IT

➡ The safest place for your money and your passport is next to your skin, in a concealed money belt or pouch. Never, ever carry these things in your luggage or a shoulder bag. Bum bags are not recommended either, as they advertise that you have a stash of goodies.

➡ Never leave valuable documents in your hotel room. If the hotel is a reputable one, you should be able to use the hotel safe.

➡ It's wise to peel off at least US$100 and keep it stashed away separately from your main horde, for emergencies.

➡ Separate your big notes from your small ones so you don't display large wads of cash when paying for things.

➡ Consider using your own padlock at cheaper hotels.

➡ If you can't lock your hotel room securely from the inside, stay somewhere else.

their passport identity and visa pages. Often mobile shops can arrange the photocopying for you, or you can ask your hotel to help you. It's best to try to do this in tourist centres, at the airport and in cities.

➡ You must also supply a residential address, which can be the address of your hotel. The phone company may call your hotel any time up to 24 hours after your application to verify that you are staying there.

➡ It's a good idea to obtain the SIM card somewhere where you're staying for a day or two so that you can return to the vendor if there's any problem. Only obtain your SIM card from a reputable branded phone store to avoid scams.

➡ Prepaid mobile-phone kits (SIM card and phone number, plus an allocation of calls) are available in most Indian towns from around ₹250 from a phone shop or grocery store.

➡ Credit must usually be used within a set time limit and costs vary with the amount of credit on the card.

➡ The amount you pay for a credit top-up is not the

amount you get on your phone – taxes and service charges come off first.

CHARGES

➡ Calls made within the state or city in which you bought the SIM card are cheap – ₹1 per minute – and you can call internationally for less than ₹10 per minute.

➡ SMS messaging is even cheaper. Usually, the more credit you have on your phone, the cheaper the call rate.

Phone Codes

Calling India from abroad Dial your country's international access code, then 91 (India's country code), then the area code (without the initial zero), then the local number.

Calling internationally from India Dial ⌨00 (the international access code), then the country code of the country you're calling, then the area code (without the initial zero if there is one) and the local number.

Toll-free numbers These begin with ⌨1800.

Time

India uses the 12-hour clock and the local standard time is

known as IST (Indian Standard Time). IST is 5½ hours ahead of GMT/UTC.

City	Noon in Delhi
Beijing	2.30pm
Dhaka	12.30pm
Islamabad	11.30am
London	6.30am
Kathmandu	12.15pm
New York	1.30am
San Francisco	10.30pm
Sydney	5.30pm
Tokyo	3.30pm

Toilets

Public toilets are most easily found in major cities and tourist sites and the cleanest ones (usually with sit-down toilets) are most reliably found at modern hotels, restaurants and shopping complexes. Beyond urban centres, toilets are of the squat variety and locals will use the 'hand-and-water' technique, which involves performing ablutions with a small jug of water and the left hand. It's always a good idea to carry your own toilet paper/wipes and hand sanitiser.

Tourist Information

Incredible India (www.in credibleindia.org) The tourism website of the Government of India.

Rajasthan Tourism Development Corporation (RTDC; www. rtdc.tourism.rajasthan.gov.in) Operates Tourist Reception Centres in most places of interest. These vary in their efficiency and usefulness, but most have free brochures and often a free town or city map.

Visas

Apart from citizens of Nepal, Bhutan and the Maldives, everyone needs to apply for a visa before arriving in India.

Visa on Arrival

Citizens from more than 100 countries, from Albania to Zimbabwe, can apply for a 60-day, double-entry e-Tourist visa online at http://indianvisaonline.gov.in a minimum of four and a maximum of 120 days before they are due to travel. The fee is US$80 for most nationalities and it's necessary to upload a photograph as well as a copy of your passport, and have at least six month's validity in your passport and at least two pages blank. The facility is available at 26 airports, including Delhi and Jaipur, though you can exit through any airport. You should also have a return or onward ticket, though proof of this is not usually requested. If your application is approved, you will receive an email with an attachment, which you'll need to print out and take with you to the airport. You'll then have the e-Tourist visa stamped into your passport at the airport, hence the term 'Visa on Arrival', though you need to apply for it beforehand. It is valid from the date of arrival.

Travellers have reported being asked for documentation showing their hotel confirmation at the airport, though this is not specified on the VOA website.

Other Visas

If you want to stay longer than 60 days, or are not covered by the VOA scheme, you must get a visa before arriving in India (apart from Nepali or Bhutanese citizens, but with the exception of Nepali citizens who are entering via China). Visas are available at Indian missions worldwide, though in many countries, applications are processed by a separate private company. In some countries, including the UK, you must apply in person at the designated office as well as file an application online.

Note that your passport needs to be valid for at least six months beyond your intended stay in India, with at least two blank pages. Most people are issued a standard six-month tourist visa, which for most nationalities permits multiple entries.

➡ Student, business and journalist visas have strict conditions (consult the Indian embassy for details).

➡ Tourist visas are valid from the date of issue, not the date you arrive in India.

➡ Five- and 10-year tourist visas are available to US citizens only under a bilateral arrangement; however, you can still only stay in the country for up to 180 days continuously.

➡ Currently, you are required to submit two passport photographs with your visa application; these must be in colour and must be 5.08cm by 5.08cm (2in by 2in; larger than regular passport photos).

➡ An onward travel ticket is a requirement for some visas, but this isn't always enforced (check in advance).

➡ Additional restrictions apply to travellers from Bangladesh and Pakistan, as well as certain Eastern European, African and Central Asian countries. Check any special conditions for your nationality with the Indian embassy in your country.

➡ Visas are priced in the local currency and may have an added service fee.

➡ Extended visas are possible for people of Indian origin (excluding those in Pakistan and Bangladesh) who hold a non-Indian passport and live abroad.

➡ For visas lasting more than six months, you're supposed to register at the **Foreigners' Regional Registration Office** (FRRO; ☎011-26711443; https://boi.gov.in; 2nd fl, East Block 8, Sector 1, Rama Krishna Puram, Swami Vivekananda Marg; ☺9.30am-3pm Mon-Fri;

Ⓜ Green Park) in Delhi within 14 days of arriving in India; enquire about these special conditions when you apply for your visa.

Visa Extensions

India is extremely stringent with visa extensions. At the time of writing, the only circumstances where this might conceivably happen are in *extreme* medical emergencies or if you were robbed of your passport just before you planned to leave the country (at the end of your visa).

In such cases, you should contact the FRRO in Delhi. This is also the place to come for a replacement visa if you need your lost/stolen passport replaced (required before you can leave the country). Note that regional FRROs are even less likely to grant an extension.

Assuming you meet the stringent criteria, the FRRO is permitted to issue an extension of 14 days (free for nationals of most countries; enquire on application). You must bring your confirmed air ticket, one passport photo (take two, just in case) and a photocopy of your passport identity and visa pages. Note that this system is designed to get you out of the country promptly with the correct official stamps, not to give you two extra weeks of travel.

Volunteering

Many charities and international aid agencies work in India and there are numerous opportunities for volunteers. It may be possible to find a placement after you arrive in India, but charities and NGOs normally prefer volunteers who have applied in advance and been approved for the kind of work involved.

Lonely Planet does not endorse any organisations that we do not work with directly, so it is essential that you do your own thorough research before agreeing to volunteer with any organisation.

The website www.ethicalvolunteering.org has useful tips on choosing an ethical volunteer organisation.

The **Concern India Foundation** (☎011-26210998; www.concernindiafoundation.org) may be able to link volunteers with current projects around the country; contact it well in advance for information.

Overseas Volunteer Placement Agencies

For long-term posts and information on volunteering, check out the following organisations:

AidCamps International (www.aidcamps.org)

Coordinating Committee for International Voluntary Service (www.ccivs.org)

Global Volunteers (www.globalvolunteers.org)

Idealist (www.idealist.org)

Indicorps (www.indicorps.org)

Voluntary Service Overseas (www.vso.org.uk)

Volunteer Abroad (www.goabroad.com/volunteer-abroad)

Working Abroad (www.workingabroad.com)

Aid Programs in Rajasthan

The following programs may have opportunities for volunteers with specific skills.

Animal Aid Unlimited (☎9784005989, 9829843726; www.animalaidunlimited.org; Badi Village) Volunteers can help rescue, treat and care for injured, abandoned or stray animals (mostly dogs, cows and donkeys) at its spacious premises a few kilometres outside Udaipur. Make an appointment before going to see it. There's no minimum period, but volunteers are encouraged to stay long enough to learn the routines and develop relationships with individual animals.

Help in Suffering (☎0141-2760012; www.his-india.in; Maharani Farm, Durgapura) Jaipur-based animal-welfare charity. Welcomes qualified voluntary vets (three-/six-/12-month commitments). Apply first in writing.

Marwar Medical & Relief Society (☎0291-2545210; www.mandore.com; Dadwari Lane, c/o Mandore Guesthouse) Runs educational, health, environmental and other projects in villages in the Jodhpur district. Guests at its guesthouse in Mandore and other short- or long-term volunteers are welcomed.

Sambhali Trust (Map p118; ☎0291-2512385; www.sambhali-trust.org; c/o Durag Niwas Guest House, 1st Old Public Park, Raika Bagh, Jodhpur) Organisation aiming to empower disadvantaged women and girls in Jodhpur city and Setrawa village, primarily through textile production, literacy and English-language learning. Volunteers can teach and help organise workshops on topics such as health, women's rights and nutrition.

Seva Mandir (☎0294-2451041; www.sevamandir.org; Old Fatehpura, Udaipur) A long-established NGO working with rural and tribal people in southern Rajasthan on a host of projects including afforestation, water resources, health, education and empowerment of women and village institutions. Volunteers and interns can get involved in a wide range of activities.

Urmul Trust (☎0151-2523093; www.urmul.org; Ganganagar Rd, Urmul Bhawan, Bikaner; ◷9am-5pm Mon-Fri) Provides primary healthcare and education to desert dwellers in arid western Rajasthan, as well as promoting their handicrafts and women's rights. Volunteer placements (minimum one month) are available in teaching English, healthcare, documentation and other work.

Transport

GETTING THERE & AWAY

Plenty of international airlines service India and overland routes are open to and from Nepal, Bangladesh, Bhutan and Pakistan. Flights, cars and tours can be booked online at www.lonelyplanet.com/bookings.

Entering the Country

Entering India by air or land is relatively straightforward, with standard immigration and customs procedures.

Passport

To enter India you need a valid passport and an onward/return ticket. You'll also need a visa (p274). Your passport should be valid for at least six months beyond your intended stay in India, with at least two blank pages. If your passport is lost or

stolen, immediately contact your country's representative. Keep photocopies of your airline ticket and the identity and visa pages of your passport in case of emergency. Better yet, scan and email copies to yourself. Check with the Indian embassy in your home country for any special conditions that may exist for your nationality.

Air

Airports & Airlines

India has six main gateways for international flights. Most Rajasthan-bound travellers fly into Delhi's **Indira Gandhi International Airport** (☑01243376000; www.newdelhiairport.in; ⓂIGI Airport). A growing number of international flights from the Middle East and Asia serve **Jaipur** (☑0141-2550623; www.jaipurairport.com) – for details,

enquire at travel agencies and see www.aai.aero.

India's national carrier is **Air India** (☑1860-2331407, 011-24667473; www.airindia.com), which also runs an extensive domestic service. Air India has had a relatively decent air safety record in recent years.

Land

It is possible to travel from Rajasthan to Pakistan on the train that links Jodhpur and Karachi. To reach Nepal overland, you'll have to transit through Delhi and take a bus or train to the border.

Rajasthan to Pakistan

Given the rocky relationship between India and Pakistan, crossing by land depends on the current state of relations between the two countries – check locally. If the crossings are open, you can travel

CLIMATE CHANGE & TRAVEL

Every form of transport that relies on carbon-based fuel generates CO_2, the main cause of human-induced climate change. Modern travel is dependent on aeroplanes, which might use less fuel per kilometre per person than most cars but travel much greater distances. The altitude at which aircraft emit gases (including CO_2) and particles also contributes to their climate change impact. Many websites offer 'carbon calculators' that allow people to estimate the carbon emissions generated by their journey and, for those who wish to do so, to offset the impact of the greenhouse gases emitted with contributions to portfolios of climate-friendly initiatives throughout the world. Lonely Planet offsets the carbon footprint of all staff and author travel.

from Rajasthan to Pakistan by train from Jodhpur, on a weekly train to Karachi.

You must have a visa to enter Pakistan. It's easiest to obtain this from the Pakistan mission in your home country. At the time of research, the **Pakistan embassy** (☏011-26110601; www.mofa. gov.pk; 2/50G Shantipath, Chanakyapuri; Ⓜ Lok Kalyan Marg) in Delhi was not issuing tourist visas for most nationalities, but this could change.

GETTING AROUND

Air

Within Rajasthan, there are airports in Bikaner, Jaipur, Jaisalmer, Jodhpur and Udaipur.

Security at airports is stringent. In smaller airports, all hold baggage must be x-rayed prior to check-in. Every item of cabin baggage needs a label, which must be stamped as part of the security check (don't forget to collect tags at the check-in counter). You may also have to allow for a spot-check of your cabin baggage on the tarmac before you board.

Keeping peak hour congestion in mind, the recommended check-in time for domestic flights is two hours before departure – the deadline is 45 minutes. The usual baggage allowance is 20kg (10kg for smaller aircraft) in economy class.

Airlines in India

With vast numbers of passengers travelling annually, India has a very competitive domestic airline industry. Major carriers include Air India, Jet Airways, IndiGo, GoAir, SpiceJet and Vistara.

Airline seats can be booked cheaply over the internet or through travel agencies. Apart from airline sites, bookings can be made through reliable ticketing portals such as Cleartrip

(www.cleartrip.com), Make My Trip (www.makemytrip. com) and Yatra (www.yatra. com). Keep in mind that fares fluctuate dramatically, affected by holidays, festivals and seasons.

Bicycle

Rajasthan offers an immense array of experiences for a long-distance cyclist. Nevertheless, long-distance cycling is not for the faint of heart or weak of knee. You'll need physical endurance to cope with the roads, traffic and climate.

There are no restrictions on bringing a bicycle into the country. However, bicycles sent by sea can take a few weeks to clear customs in India, so it's better to fly bikes in. It may actually be cheaper (and less hassle) to hire or buy a bicycle in India itself. Read up on bicycle touring before you travel – Rob Van Der Plas's *The Bicycle Touring Manual* and Stephen Lord's *Adventure Cycle-Touring Handbook* are good places to start.

Hire

➡ Tourist centres and traveller hang-outs are the easiest spots to find bicycles for hire.

➡ Prices vary between ₹40 and ₹200 per day for roadworthy, Indian-made bicycles. Mountain bikes are usually upwards of ₹600 per day.

➡ Hire places may require a cash security deposit (avoid leaving your airline ticket or passport).

Practicalities

➡ Roadside cycle mechanics abound but you should still bring spare tyres and brake cables, lubricating oil, a chain repair kit and plenty of puncture-repair patches.

➡ Bikes can often be carried for free, or for a small luggage fee, on the roof of

public buses – handy for uphill stretches.

➡ Contact your airline for information about transporting your bike and customs formalities in your home country.

Buying a Bike

➡ Indian mountain bikes such as Hero and Atlas start at around ₹7000.

➡ Reselling is easy: ask at local cycle or hire shops or put up an advert on travel noticeboards. If you purchased a new bike and it's still in reasonable condition, you should be able to recoup around 50% of what you originally paid.

On the Road

➡ Vehicles are supposed to drive on the left side in India, but in reality road rules are virtually nonexistent.

➡ Cities and national highways can be hazardous places to cycle, so, where possible, stick to the backroads.

➡ Be conservative about the distances you expect to cover – an experienced cyclist can manage around 60km to 100km a day on the plains and 40km or less on dirt roads.

Bus

➡ The Rajasthan state government bus service is Rajasthan State Road Transport Corporation (RSRTC; www.transport. rajasthan.gov.in/rsrtc), sometimes still known as Rajasthan Roadways.

➡ Often there are privately owned local bus services as well as luxury private coaches running between major cities – these can be booked through travel agencies.

➡ Avoid night buses unless there's no alternative, as driving conditions are more hazardous and drivers may be suffering from lack of sleep.

➡ All buses make snack and toilet stops (some more frequently than others), providing a break but possibly adding hours to journey times.

➡ Females enjoy a 30% discount on RSRTC buses in Rajasthan (often extended to some private buses).

Bus Types & Classes

➡ On the main routes in Rajasthan you have a choice of ordinary, express, deluxe and super-deluxe. Express and deluxe buses make fewer stops than ordinary buses – they're still usually crowded though. The fare is marginally higher than ordinary buses, but worth every rupee.

➡ On selected routes there are AG Sleeper buses – these have beds and make overnight trips more comfortable. Beds have a bunk-bed arrangement, with rows of single beds, each with a curtain for privacy.

➡ Air-conditioned super deluxe, Volvo or Volvo-Mercedes Line buses are the best bus options and serve the Jaipur–Delhi and Agra–Udaipur routes.

➡ Private buses also operate on most Rajasthani routes; apart from often being quicker and usually more comfortable, the booking procedure is much simpler than for state-run buses. However, private companies can often change schedules at the last minute to get as many bums on seats as possible.

Luggage

➡ Luggage is either stored in compartments underneath

the bus (sometimes for a small fee) or carried on the roof.

➡ Arrive at least an hour ahead of the scheduled departure time – some buses cover the roof-stored bags with a large canvas, making last-minute additions inconvenient/impossible.

➡ If your baggage is stored on the roof, make sure it is securely locked and tied/chained to the metal baggage rack.

➡ Theft is a risk – keep an eye on your bags at snack and toilet stops and *never* leave your daypack or valuables unattended inside the bus.

Reservations

➡ Most deluxe buses can be booked in advance – usually up to a month ahead for government buses – at bus stations or local travel agencies.

➡ Online bookings for many routes can be made through the portals Cleartrip (www.cleartrip.com) and Redbus (www.redbus.in).

➡ Reservations are rarely possible on 'ordinary' buses and travellers often get left behind in the mad rush for a seat.

➡ To maximise your chances of securing a spot, send a travelling companion ahead to grab some space.

➡ Many buses only depart when full – you may find your bus suddenly empties to join another bus that's ready to leave before yours.

➡ At many bus stations there's a separate women's queue, although this isn't always obvious because signs are often in Hindi and men frequently join the melee. Women travellers should sharpen their elbows and make their way to the front, where they will get almost immediate service (and a 30% discount on the bus fare).

Car

Few people bother with self-drive car rental – not only because of the hair-raising driving conditions, but also because hiring a car with a driver is wonderfully affordable in India, particularly if several people share the cost. Hertz (www.hertz.com) is one of the few international rental companies with representatives in India.

Hiring a Car & Driver

➡ Most towns have taxi stands or car-hire companies where you can arrange short or long tours.

➡ Use your hotel to find a car and driver – this achieves a good level of security and reliability and often a better rate.

➡ Not all hire cars are licensed to travel beyond their home state. Even those vehicles that are licensed to enter different states have to pay extra (often hefty) state taxes, which will add to the rental charge.

➡ Ask for a driver who speaks some English and knows the region you intend to visit, and try to see the car and meet the driver before paying any money.

➡ For multiday trips, the charge should cover the driver's meals and accommodation. Drivers should make their own sleeping and eating arrangements.

➡ It is *essential* to set the ground rules with the driver from day one, in order to avoid anguish later.

Costs

➡ The price depends on the distance and sometimes the terrain (driving on mountain roads uses more petrol, hence the 'hill charges').

➡ One-way trips usually cost the same as return trips (to cover the petrol and driver charges for getting back).

→ To avoid potential misunderstandings, ensure you get *in writing* what you've been promised (quotes should include fuel, tolls, sightseeing stops, all your chosen destinations, and meals and accommodation for the driver).

→ If a driver asks you for money to pay for fuel en route (reasonable on long trips), keep a record (he will do the same).

→ Operators usually charge from ₹9 to ₹12 per kilometre per day (depending on the size of the car), with a 250km minimum per day and an overnight charge of up to ₹300 (covering driver expenses).

→ For sightseeing day trips around a single city, expect to pay anywhere upwards of ₹1800 with an eight-hour, 80km limit per day (extra charges apply beyond this).

→ A tip is customary at the end of your journey; ₹150 to ₹200 per day is fair.

Motorcycle

→ Cruising solo around India by motorcycle offers the freedom to go when and where you desire. There are also some excellent motorcycle tours available, which take the hassle out of doing it alone.

→ Helmets, leathers, gloves, goggles, boots, waterproofs and other protective gear are best brought from your home country, as they're either unavailable in India or are of indeterminate quality.

Licence

→ To hire a motorcycle in India, technically you're required to have a valid international driver's permit in addition to your domestic licence.

→ In tourist areas, some places may rent out a motorcycle without asking for a driving permit/licence,

but you won't be covered by insurance in the event of an accident and may also face a fine.

Hire

→ The classic way to motorcycle round India is on a Royal Enfield Bullet, still built to many of the original 1940s specifications. As well as making a satisfying sound, these bikes are easy to repair (parts can be found almost everywhere in India). On the other hand, Enfields are less reliable than Japanese-designed bikes.

→ Plenty of places hire motorcycles for local trips and longer tours. Japanese- and Indian-made bikes in the 100cc to 150cc range are cheaper than the 350cc and 500cc Enfields.

→ As a deposit, you'll need to leave a large cash lump sum (ensure you get a receipt that also stipulates the refundable amount), and copies of your passport or your air ticket. It's strongly advisable to not leave your passport as a deposit; you'll need it to check in at hotels and the police can demand to see at any time.

→ For three weeks' hire, a 500cc Enfield costs from ₹25,000; a 350cc costs from ₹15,000. The price can include excellent advice and an invaluable crash course in Enfield mechanics and repairs.

Purchase

Secondhand bikes are widely available and the paperwork is a lot easier than buying a new machine.

Finding a secondhand motorcycle is a matter of asking around, checking travellers' noticeboards and approaching local motorcycle mechanics.

A looked-after, secondhand 350cc Enfield will cost anywhere from ₹50,000 to ₹120,000. The 500cc model costs anywhere from ₹85,000 to ₹140,000. You

will also have to pay for insurance. It's advisable to get any secondhand bike serviced before you set off.

When reselling your bike, expect to get between half and two-thirds of the price you paid if the bike is still in reasonable condition. Shipping an Indian bike overseas is complicated and expensive – and you may find it can't be registered in your home country owing to safety and pollution regulations.

Helmets are available for ₹800 to ₹2000 and extras such as panniers, luggage racks, protection bars, rear-view mirrors, lockable fuel caps, petrol filters and tools are easy to come by. One useful extra is a customised fuel tank, which will increase the range you can cover between fuel stops. An Enfield 500cc gives about 25km/L; the 350cc model gives slightly more. Check out www.royalenfield.com for more information.

The following dealers are recommended:

Delhi Run by the knowledgable Lalli Singh, **Lalli Motorbike Exports** (☏011-28750869, mobile 09811140161; www.lallisinghadventures.com; 1740-A/55 Hari Singh Nalwa St, Abdul Aziz Rd; ☺10am-7pm Tue-Sun; Ⓜ Karol Bagh) sells and hires out Enfields and parts, and buyers get a crash course in running and maintaining these lovable but temperamental machines. He can also recommend other reputable dealers in the area.

Jaipur For hiring, fixing or purchasing a motorcycle, visit Rajasthan Auto Centre (p59). To hire a 350cc Enfield Bullet costs ₹600 per day (including two helmets); if you take the bike outside Jaipur, it costs ₹800 per day. Ask for Saleem, the Bullet specialist.

Ownership Papers

There's plenty of paperwork associated with owning a motorcycle; the registration papers are signed by the local registration authority when the bike is first sold and you'll need these papers when you buy a secondhand bike.

Foreign nationals cannot simply change the name on the registration like locals. Instead, you must fill out the forms for a change of ownership and transfer of insurance. If you buy a new bike, the company selling it must register the machine for you, adding to the cost.

For any bike, the registration must be renewed every 15 years (for around ₹5000) and you must make absolutely sure that it states the 'fitness' of the vehicle, and that there are no outstanding debts or criminal proceedings associated with the bike.

The process is complicated and it makes sense to seek advice from the company selling the bike – allow two weeks to tackle the paperwork and get on the road.

Fuel, Spare Parts & Extras

➡ If you're going to remote regions it's also important to carry basic spares (valves, fuel lines, piston rings etc).

➡ Spare parts for Indian and Japanese machines are widely available in cities and larger towns; Delhi's Karol Bagh is a good place to find parts.

➡ Make sure you regularly check and tighten all nuts and bolts, as Indian roads and engine vibration tend to work things loose quite quickly.

➡ Check the engine and gearbox oil level regularly (at least every 500km) and clean the oil filter every few thousand kilometres.

➡ Given the road conditions, the chances are you'll make at least a couple of visits to a puncture-wallah – start your trip with new tyres and carry spanners to remove your own wheels.

Insurance

➡ The minimum level of cover is third-party

insurance – available for ₹600 to ₹800 per year. This will cover repair and medical costs for any other vehicles, people or property you might hit, but no cover for your own machine. Comprehensive insurance (recommended) costs upwards of ₹1500 per year.

➡ Only hire a bike with at least third-party insurance – if you hit someone without insurance, the consequences can be very costly. Reputable companies will include third-party cover in their policies; those that don't probably aren't trustworthy.

➡ You must also arrange insurance if you buy a motorcycle (usually you can organise this through the person selling the bike).

Road Conditions

➡ Given the varied road conditions, India can be challenging for novice riders.

➡ Hazards range from cows and chickens crossing the carriageway to broken-down trucks, pedestrians on the road and perpetual potholes and unmarked speed humps. Rural roads sometimes have grain crops strewn across them to be threshed by passing vehicles – a serious sliding hazard for bikers.

➡ Try not to cover too much territory in one day and avoid travelling after dark – many vehicles drive without lights and dynamo-powered motorcycle headlamps are useless at low revs while negotiating around potholes.

➡ On busy national highways expect to average 45km/h without stops; on winding backroads and dirt tracks this can drop to 10km/h.

Organised Motorcycle Tours

Dozens of companies offer organised motorcycle tours around India with a support vehicle, mechanic and guide.

Blazing Trails (www.blazingtrails tours.com)

Classic Bike Adventure (www. classic-bike-india.com)

H-C Travel (www.hctravel.com)

Indian Motorcycle Adventures (www.indianmotorcycleadven tures.com)

Lalli Mobike Adventures (☑09811 140161, 011-47652551; www.lallisingh adventures.com; 1266/4 Naiwala St, Payarelal Rd; ⊙10am-7pm Tue-Sun; Ⓜ Karol Bagh)

Moto Discovery (www.moto discovery.com)

World on Wheels (www.worldon wheels.tours)

Local Transport

➡ Buses, cycle-rickshaws, autorickshaws, taxis and urban trains provide transport around cities.

➡ Apps such as Uber and Ola Cabs have transformed local transport. If you have a smartphone, you can call a taxi and the fare is electronically calculated – no arguments and often cheaper than an autorickshaw.

➡ On any form of transport without a fixed fare, agree on the price before you start your journey and make sure that it covers your luggage and every passenger.

➡ Fares usually increase at night (by up to 100%) and some drivers charge a few rupees extra for luggage.

➡ Carry plenty of small bills for taxi and rickshaw fares as drivers rarely have change.

➡ Carry a business card of the hotel in which you are staying, as your pronunciation of streets, hotel names etc may be incomprehensible to drivers. Some hotel cards even have a sketch map clearly indicating their location.

➡ Some taxi/autorickshaw drivers are involved in the commission racket.

Autorickshaw & Tempo

➡ The Indian autorickshaw is basically a smog-belching three-wheeled contraption with a low tin or canvas roof and sides, providing room for two passengers and limited luggage.

➡ They are also referred to as autos, tuk-tuks, Indian helicopters or Ferraris.

➡ Jaipur has increasing numbers of quiet, comfortable, electric autorickshaws.

➡ Autorickshaws are mostly cheaper than taxis (except Uber and Ola Cabs) and while most have meters, getting the driver to turn on the meter can be a challenge.

➡ Tempos and *vikrams* (large tempos) are outsized autorickshaws with room for more than two passengers, running on fixed routes for fixed fares.

Bus

Urban buses, particularly in the big cities, are fume-belching, human-stuffed mechanical monsters that travel at breakneck speed (except during morning and evening rush hours, when they can be endlessly stuck in traffic). It's usually far more convenient and comfortable to opt for an autorickshaw or taxi.

Cycle-Rickshaw

➡ A cycle-rickshaw is a pedal cycle with two rear wheels, supporting a bench seat for passengers. Most have a canopy that can be raised in wet/sunny weather, or lowered to provide extra space for luggage.

➡ Many of the big cities have phased out (or reduced) the number of cycle-rickshaws, but you can still find them in Jaipur and they remain a means of local transport in many smaller towns.

➡ Fares must be agreed upon in advance – speak to locals to get an idea of what

is a fair price. Remember, this is extremely strenuous work and the wallahs are among India's poorest, so a tip is appreciated and haggling over a few rupees is unnecessary.

Metro

Metro systems have transformed urban transport in India's biggest cities and are expanding. Joining Delhi, Kolkata, Mumbai and Chennai is Jaipur's new **Metro** (☏0141-2385790; www.jaipurmetrorail.in; fare ₹6-17, 1-day tour card ₹50), which, when finished, will cut right under the Pink City.

Share Jeep

➡ Share 4WDs (often called 'share jeeps') supplement the bus service in many parts of Rajasthan, especially in areas off the main road routes, such as many of the towns in Shekhawati.

➡ 4WDs leave when (very) full, from well-established 'passenger stations' on the outskirts of towns and villages; locals should be able to point you in the right direction. They are usually dirt cheap and jam-packed and tend to be more dangerous than buses.

Taxi

Most Indian airports and many train stations have prepaid taxi and radio cab booths, normally just outside the terminal building. Here, you can book a taxi for a fixed price (which will include baggage) and thus avoid commission scams. However, officials advise holding on to the payment coupon until you reach your chosen destination, in case the driver has any other ideas. Smaller airports and train stations may have prepaid autorickshaw booths instead.

➡ Taxis are usually metered, but drivers often claim that the meter is broken and proceed to request a hugely elevated 'fixed' fare instead – threatening to get another

taxi will often miraculously fix the meter.

➡ Apps such as Uber and Ola Cabs are the most efficient option in larger cities.

➡ Analog meters are often outdated, so fares are calculated using a combination of the meter reading and a complicated 'fare adjustment card'. Predictably, this system is open to abuse.

➡ In tourist areas in particular, some taxis flatly refuse to use the meter and you have to negotiate a fare.

➡ To avoid fare-setting shenanigans, use prepaid taxis where possible.

Train

Travelling by train is a quintessential Indian experience. Trains offer a smoother ride than buses and are especially recommended for long journeys that include overnight travel. India's rail network is one of the largest and busiest in the world and Indian Railways is the largest utility employer on earth, with roughly 1.5 million workers. There are around 7000 train stations scattered across the country.

Although we list the most useful, there are hundreds of train services. The best way of sourcing updated railway information is to use relevant internet sites such as Indian Railways (www.indianrail.gov.in), India Rail Info (www.indiarailinfo.com), IRCTC enquiry (www.erail.in) and the useful www.seat61.com/India. There's also *Trains at a Glance* (₹70), available at many train station bookstands and good bookshops/news stands, but it's published annually so it's not as up to date as websites. Nevertheless, it offers comprehensive timetables covering all the main lines.

TRAIN CLASSES

Air-Conditioned 1st Class (1AC) The most expensive class of train travel; two- or four-berth compartments with locking doors.

Air-Conditioned 2-Tier (2AC) Two-tier berths arranged in groups of four and two in an open-plan carriage. The bunks convert to seats by day and there are curtains for some semblance of privacy.

Air-Conditioned 3-Tier (3AC) Three-tier berths arranged in groups of six in an open-plan carriage; no curtains.

AC Executive Chair (ECC) Comfortable, reclining chairs and plenty of space; usually found on Shatabdi express trains.

AC Chair (CC) Similar to the Executive Chair carriage but with less-fancy seating.

Sleeper Class (sl) Open-plan carriages with three-tier bunks and no air-con; the open windows afford fresh air and views.

Unreserved/reserved 2nd Class (II/SS) Wooden or plastic seats and *a lot* of people – but cheap!

Booking Tickets in India

You can either book tickets online, through a travel agency or hotel (for a commission) or in person at the train station. Larger stations often have English-speaking staff who can help with reservations. At smaller stations, the stationmaster and his deputy usually speak English.

At the station Get a reservation slip from the information window, fill in the name of the departure station, destination station, the class you want to travel and the name and number of the train. Join the long queue to the ticket window where your ticket will be printed. Women should use the separate women's queue – if there isn't one, go to the front of the regular queue. Larger stations often have a counter for foreigners.

Tourist Reservation Bureau Larger cities and major tourist centres have an International Tourist Bureau, which allows you to book certain tickets in relative peace – check www.indiarailinfo.com for a list of these stations.

BOOKING ONLINE

You can book online through IRCTC (www.irctc.co.in), the e-ticketing division of the government's Indian Railways, or portals such as Cleartrip (www.cleartrip.

com), Make My Trip (www.makemytrip.com) and Yatra (www.yatra.com). Remember, however, that online booking of train tickets has its share of glitches: travellers have reported problems with registering themselves on some portals and using certain overseas credit cards; you may also need an Indian phone number to register.

When booking online, it pays to know the details of your journey – particularly station names, train numbers, days of operation and available classes. Start by visiting www.erail.in – the search engine will bring up a list of all trains running between your chosen destinations, along with information on classes and fares.

Step two is to register online for an account with IRCTC. This is required even if you plan to use a private ticket agency. Registration is a complex process, involving passwords, emails, scans of your passport and texts to your mobile phone. The ever-helpful Man in Seat 61 (www.seat61.com/India) has a detailed guide to all the steps.

Once registered, you can use a credit card to book travel on specific trains, either directly with IRCTC or with private agencies.

You'll be issued with an e-ticket, which you should print out ready to present alongside your passport and booking reference once you board the train.

Reservations

Bookings open 120 days before departure and you must make a reservation for all chair-car, sleeper, and 1AC, 2AC and 3AC carriages. No reservations are required for general (2nd class) compartments. Trains are always busy in India so it's wise to book as far in advance as possible; advanced booking for overnight trains is *strongly recommended*. Train services to certain destinations are often increased during major festivals but it's still worth booking well in advance.

Reserved tickets show your seat/berth number and the carriage number. Before your train pulls up locate the intended position of your carriage on the platform from the overhead signs. When the train pulls in, keep an eye out for your carriage number written on the side of the train (station staff and porters can also point you in the right direction). A list of names and berths is also posted on the side of each reserved carriage.

Be aware that train trips can be delayed at any time of the journey, so, to avoid stress, factor some leeway into your travel plans.

If the train you want to travel on is sold out, be sure to enquire about the following:

Reservation Against Cancellation (RAC) Even when a train is fully booked, Indian Railways sells a handful of RAC seats in each class. This means that if you have an RAC ticket and someone cancels before the departure date, you will get that seat (or berth). You'll have to check the reservation list at the station on the day of travel to see where you've been allocated to sit. Even if no one cancels, as an RAC ticket holder you can still board the train and, even if you don't get a seat, you can still travel.

Taktal Tickets Indian Railways holds back a limited number of tickets on key trains and releases them at 8am two days before the train is due to depart. A charge of ₹10 to ₹500 is added to each ticket price. 1AC and Executive Chair tickets are excluded from the scheme.

Tourist Quota A special (albeit small) tourist quota is set aside for foreign tourists travelling between popular stations. These seats can only be booked at dedicated reservation offices in major cities, and you need to show your passport and visa as ID. Tickets can be paid for in rupees (some offices may ask to see foreign exchange certificates – ATM receipts will suffice).

Waitlist (WL) Trains are frequently overbooked, but many passengers cancel and there are regular no-shows. So if you buy a ticket on the waiting list you're still quite likely to get a seat, even if there are a number of people ahead of you on the list. Check your booking status at www.indianrail.gov.in/enquiry/PNR/PnrEnquiry.html by entering your tickets' PNR number. A refund is available if you fail to get a seat – ask the ticket office about your chances.

Refunds

Tickets are refundable but fees apply. If you present more than one day in advance, a fee of ₹30 to ₹240 applies. Steeper charges apply if you seek a refund less than four hours prior to departure, but you can get some sort of refund as late as 12 hours afterwards.

Classes & Fares

Shatabdi express trains are same-day services between major and regional cities. These are the fastest and most expensive trains, with only two classes; AC Executive Chair and AC Chair.

Shatabdis are comfortable, but the glass windows cut the views considerably compared to non-AC classes on slower trains, which have barred windows and fresh air.

Rajdhani express trains are long-distance express services running between Delhi and the state capitals, and offer 1AC, 2AC, 3AC and 2nd class. Two-tier means there are two levels of bunks in each compartment, which are a little wider and longer than their counterparts in three-tier. Costing, respectively, a half and a third as much as 1AC, the classes 2AC and 3AC are perfectly adequate for an overnight trip.

Fares are calculated by distance and class of travel; Rajdhani and Shatabdi trains are slightly more expensive, but the price includes meals. Most air-conditioned carriages have a catering service (meals are brought to your seat). In unreserved classes, it's a good idea to carry portable snacks. Male/female seniors (those over 60/58 years) get 40/50% off all fares in all classes on all types of trains. Children below the age of six travel for free; those aged between six and 12 years are charged half-price, up to 300km.

Health

There is huge geographical variation in India, so in different areas heat, cold and altitude can cause health problems. Hygiene is poor in most regions, so food- and water-borne illnesses are common. A number of insect-borne diseases are present, particularly in tropical areas. Medical care is basic in various areas (especially beyond the larger cities), so it's essential to be well prepared.

Pre-existing medical conditions and accidental injury (especially traffic accidents) account for most life-threatening problems. Becoming ill in some way, however, is common. Fortunately, most travellers' illnesses can be prevented with some common-sense behaviour or treated with a well-stocked travellers' medical kit. However, never hesitate to consult a doctor while on the road, as self-diagnosis can be hazardous.

BEFORE YOU GO

You can buy many medications over the counter in India without a doctor's prescription, but it can be difficult to find some of the newer drugs, particularly the latest antidepressant drugs, blood-pressure medications and contraceptive pills. Be circumspect about self-medicating, as travellers mixing the wrong drugs or overdosing have on occasion ended in tragedy. Bring the following:

➡ medications in their original, labelled containers

➡ a signed, dated letter from your physician describing your medical conditions and medications, including generic medication names

➡ a physician's letter documenting the medical necessity of any syringes you bring

➡ if you have a heart condition, a copy of your ECG taken just prior to travelling

➡ any regular medication (double your ordinary needs).

Insurance

Don't travel without health/travel insurance. Emergency evacuation is expensive. There are various factors to consider when choosing insurance. Read the small print.

➡ You may require extra cover for adventure activities such as rock climbing and scuba diving.

➡ In India, doctors usually require immediate payment in cash. Your insurance plan may make payments directly to providers or it will reimburse you later for overseas health expenditures. If you do have to claim later, make sure you keep all relevant documentation.

➡ Some policies ask that you telephone back (reverse charges) to a centre in your home country, where an immediate assessment of your problem will be made.

Vaccinations

Specialised travel-medicine clinics are your best source of up-to-date information; they stock all available vaccines and can give specific recommendations for your trip. Most vaccines don't give immunity until *at least* two weeks after they're given, so visit a doctor well before departure. Ask your doctor for an International Certificate of Vaccination (sometimes known as the 'yellow booklet'), which will list all the vaccinations you've received.

Required & Recommended Vaccinations

The only vaccine required by international regulations is that for yellow fever. Proof of vaccination will only be required if you have visited a country in the yellow-fever zone within the six days prior to entering India. If you are travelling to India from Africa or South America, you should check to see if you require proof of vaccination.

The World Health Organization (WHO) recommends

VACCINATIONS FOR LONG STAYS

The following immunisations are recommended for long-term travellers (more than one month) or those at special risk (seek further advice from your doctor):

Japanese B encephalitis Three injections in all. Booster recommended after two years. Sore arm and headache are the most common side effects. In rare cases an allergic reaction comprising hives and swelling can occur up to 10 days after any of the three doses.

Meningitis Single injection. There are two types of vaccination: the quadravalent vaccine gives two to three years' protection; the meningitis group C vaccine gives around 10 years' protection. Recommended for long-term backpackers aged under 25.

Rabies Three injections in all. A booster after one year will then provide 10 years' protection. Side effects are rare – occasionally headache and sore arm.

Tuberculosis (TB) A complex issue. Adult long-term travellers are usually advised to have a TB skin test before and after travel, rather than vaccination. Only one vaccine is given in a lifetime.

the following vaccinations for travellers going to India (as well as being up to date with measles, mumps and rubella vaccinations). Note that there is no vaccine for malaria (p286), so prophylaxis is used instead.

Adult diphtheria and tetanus Single booster recommended if none in the previous 10 years. Side effects include sore arm and fever.

Hepatitis A Provides almost 100% protection for up to a year; a booster after 12 months provides at least another 20 years' protection. Mild side effects such as headache and sore arm occur in 5% to 10% of people.

Hepatitis B Now considered routine for most travellers. Given as three shots over six months. A rapid schedule is also available, as is a combined vaccination with hepatitis A. Side effects are mild and uncommon, usually headache and a sore arm. In 95% of people lifetime protection results.

Polio Only one booster is required as an adult for lifetime protection. Inactivated polio vaccine is safe during pregnancy.

Typhoid Recommended for all travellers to India, even those only visiting urban areas. The vaccine offers around 70% protection, lasts for two to three years and comes as a single shot. Tablets are also available,

but the injection is usually recommended as it has fewer side effects. Sore arm and fever may occur.

Varicella If you haven't had chickenpox, discuss this vaccination with your doctor.

Medical Checklist

Recommended items for a personal medical kit include:

➧ Antibacterial cream, eg mupirocin

➧ Antibiotic for skin infections, eg amoxicillin/clavulanate or cephalexin

➧ Antifungal cream, eg clotrimazole

➧ Antihistamine – there are many options, eg cetirizine for daytime and promethazine for night

➧ Antiseptic, eg Betadine

➧ Antispasmodic for stomach cramps, eg Buscopam

➧ Contraceptive

➧ Decongestant, eg pseudoephedrine

➧ DEET-based insect repellent

➧ Diarrhoea medication – consider an oral rehydration solution (eg Gastrolyte), diarrhoea

'stopper' (eg loperamide) and antinausea medication (eg prochlorperazine); antibiotics for diarrhoea include ciprofloxacin; for bacterial diarrhoea azithromycin; for giardia or amoebic dysentery tinidazole

➧ First-aid items such as scissors, elastoplasts, bandages, gauze, thermometer (but not mercury), sterile needles and syringes, safety pins and tweezers

➧ Ibuprofen or another anti-inflammatory

➧ Iodine tablets (unless you are pregnant or have a thyroid problem) to purify water

➧ Migraine medication if you suffer from migraines

➧ Paracetamol

➧ Pyrethrin to impregnate clothing and mosquito nets

➧ Steroid cream for allergic or itchy rashes, eg 1% to 2% hydrocortisone

➧ Sunscreen (with a high SPF)

➧ Throat lozenges

➧ Thrush (vaginal yeast infection) treatment, eg clotrimazole pessaries or Diflucan tablet

➧ Ural or equivalent if prone to urinary-tract infections

Websites

There's a wealth of travel-health advice on the internet; www.lonelyplanet.com is a good place to start. It's a good idea to consult your government's travel-advisory website (p272) to see if there are any specific health risks to be aware of.

Further Reading

Recommended references include *Travellers' Health* by Dr Richard Dawood and *Travelling Well* by Dr Deborah Mills, which is now also available as an app; check out the website (www.travellingwell.com.au) too.

IN INDIA

Availability & Cost of Healthcare

Medical care is hugely variable in India. Some cities now have clinics catering specifically to travellers and expatriates; these clinics are usually more expensive than local medical facilities, and offer a higher standard of care. Additionally, the staff members know the local system, including reputable hospitals and specialists. They may also liaise with insurance companies should you require evacuation. It's usually difficult to find reliable medical care in rural areas.

Self-treatment may be appropriate if your problem is minor (eg traveller's diarrhoea), you are carrying the relevant medication, and you cannot attend a recommended clinic. If you suspect a serious disease, especially malaria, travel to the nearest quality facility.

Before buying medication over the counter, check the use-by date, and ensure that the packet is sealed and

properly stored (eg not exposed to the sunshine).

Infectious Diseases

Malaria

This is a serious and potentially deadly disease. Before you travel, seek expert advice according to your itinerary (rural areas are especially risky) and on medication and side effects.

Malaria is caused by a parasite transmitted by the bite of an infected mosquito. The most important symptom of malaria is fever, but general symptoms, such as headache, diarrhoea, cough or chills, may also occur. Diagnosis can only be properly made by taking a blood sample.

Two strategies should be combined to prevent malaria: mosquito avoidance and antimalarial medications. Most people who catch malaria are taking inadequate or no antimalarial medication.

Travellers are advised to prevent mosquito bites by taking these steps:

➡ Use a DEET-based insect repellent on exposed skin. Wash this off at night – as long as you are sleeping under a mosquito net. Natural repellents such as citronella can be effective but must be applied more frequently than products containing DEET.

➡ Sleep under a mosquito net impregnated with pyrethrin.

➡ Choose accommodation with proper screens and fans (if not air-conditioned).

➡ Impregnate clothing with pyrethrin in high-risk areas.

➡ Wear long sleeves and trousers in light colours.

➡ Use mosquito coils.

➡ Spray your room with insect repellent before going out for your evening meal. A variety of medications are available:

Chloroquine and Paludrine combination Limited effectiveness in many parts of South Asia. Common side effects include nausea (40% of people) and mouth ulcers.

Doxycycline (daily tablet) A broad-spectrum antibiotic that helps prevent a variety of tropical diseases, including leptospirosis, tick-borne disease and typhus. Potential side effects include photosensitivity (a tendency to sunburn), thrush (in women), indigestion, heartburn, nausea and interference with the contraceptive pill. More serious side effects include ulceration of the oesophagus – take your tablet with a meal and a large glass of water, and never lie down within half an hour of taking it. It must be taken for four weeks after leaving the risk area.

Lariam (mefloquine) This weekly tablet suits many people. Serious side effects can be an issue with this drug, though, and include depression, anxiety, psychosis and seizures. Unusually vivid nightmares that last months after use of the drug are not uncommon. Anyone with a history of depression, anxiety, other psychological disorders or epilepsy should not take Lariam. It is considered safe in the second and third trimesters of pregnancy. Tablets must be taken for four weeks after leaving the risk area.

Malarone A combination of atovaquone and proguanil. Side effects are uncommon and mild, most commonly nausea and headache. It is the best tablet for scuba divers and for those on short trips to high-risk areas. It must be taken for one week after leaving the risk area.

Traveller's Diarrhoea

This is by far the most common problem affecting travellers in India – between 30% and 70% of people will suffer from it within two weeks of starting their trip. It's usually caused by bacteria, and thus responds promptly to treatment with antibiotics.

Traveller's diarrhoea is defined as the passage of more than three watery

DRINKING WATER

➜ Never drink tap water.

➜ Bottled water is generally safe – check that the seal is intact at purchase.

➜ Avoid ice unless you know it has been made without tap water.

➜ Be careful of fresh juices served at street stalls in particular – they're likely to have been watered down with tap water or may be served in jugs/glasses that have been rinsed in tap water.

➜ Avoid fruit that you don't peel yourself, as it will likely have been rinsed in tap water. Alternatively, rinse fruit yourself in mineral water before you eat it.

➜ Boiling water is usually the most efficient method of purifying it.

➜ The best chemical purifier is iodine. It should not be used by pregnant women or those with thyroid problems.

➜ Water filters should also filter out most viruses. Ensure your filter has a chemical barrier such as iodine and a small pore size (less than four microns).

➜ In tourist areas, some guesthouses, cafes and restaurants use water filters; use your own judgment as to whether you think this water will be safe to drink.

bowel actions within 24 hours, plus at least one other symptom, such as fever, cramps, nausea, vomiting or feeling generally unwell.

Treatment consists of staying well hydrated; rehydration solutions like Gastrolyte are the best for this. Antibiotics such as ciprofloxacin or azithromycin should kill the bacteria quickly. Seek medical attention quickly if you do not respond to an appropriate antibiotic.

Loperamide is just a 'stopper' and doesn't get to the cause of the problem. It can be helpful, though (eg if you have to go on a long bus ride). Don't take loperamide if you have a fever or blood in your stools.

Amoebic dysentery Amoebic dysentery is very rare in travellers but is quite often misdiagnosed by poor-quality labs. Symptoms are similar to bacterial diarrhoea: fever, bloody diarrhoea and generally feeling unwell. You should always seek reliable medical care if you have blood in your diarrhoea. Treatment involves two drugs: tinidazole or metronidazole to kill the parasite in your gut and then a second drug to kill the cysts. If left untreated, complications such as liver or gut abscesses can occur.

Giardiasis Giardia is a parasite that is relatively common in travellers. Symptoms include nausea, bloating, excess gas, fatigue and intermittent diarrhoea. The parasite will eventually go away if left untreated, but this can take months; the best advice is to seek medical treatment. The treatment of choice is tinidazole, with metronidazole a second-line option.

Other Diseases

Avian flu 'Bird flu' or Influenza A (H5N1) is a subtype of the type A influenza virus. Contact with dead or sick birds is the principal source of infection and bird-to-human transmission does not easily occur. Symptoms include high fever and flu-like symptoms with rapid deterioration, leading to respiratory failure and death in many cases. Immediate medical care should be sought if bird flu is suspected. Check www.who.int/en.

Cholera There are occasional outbreaks of cholera in India. This acute gastrointestinal infection is transmitted through contaminated water and food, including raw or undercooked fish and shellfish. Cases are rare among travellers, but those who are travelling to an area of active transmission should consult with their health-care practitioner regarding vaccination.

Dengue fever This mosquito-borne disease is becomingly increasingly problematic, especially in the cities. As there is no vaccine available it can only be prevented by avoiding mosquito bites at all times. Symptoms include high fever, severe headache and body ache and sometimes a rash and diarrhoea. Treatment is rest and paracetamol – do not take aspirin or ibuprofen, as these increase the likelihood of haemorrhage. Make sure you see a doctor to be diagnosed and monitored.

Hepatitis A This food- and water-borne virus infects the liver, causing jaundice (yellow skin and eyes), nausea and lethargy. There is no specific treatment for hepatitis A; you just need to allow time for the liver to heal. All travellers to India should be vaccinated against hepatitis A.

Hepatitis B This sexually transmitted disease is spread by body fluids and can be prevented by vaccination. The long-term consequences can include liver cancer and cirrhosis.

Hepatitis E Transmitted through contaminated food and water, hepatitis E has similar symptoms to hepatitis A but is far less common. It is a severe problem in pregnant women and can result in the death of both mother and baby. There is no commercially available vaccine, and prevention is by following safe eating and drinking guidelines.

HIV Spread via contaminated body fluids. Avoid unprotected sex, unsterile needles (including in medical facilities) and procedures such as tattoos. The growth rate of HIV in India is one of the highest in the world.

Influenza Present year-round in the tropics, influenza (flu) symptoms include fever, muscle aches, a runny nose, cough and sore throat. It can be severe in people over the age of 65 or in those with medical conditions such as heart disease or diabetes – vaccination is recommended for these individuals. There is no specific treatment, just rest and paracetamol.

Japanese B encephalitis This viral disease is transmitted by mosquitoes and is rare in travellers. Most cases occur in rural areas and vaccination is recommended for travellers spending more than a month outside cities. There is no treatment, and the virus may result in permanent brain damage or death. Ask your doctor for further details.

Rabies This fatal disease is spread by the bite, scratch or, if you already have an open wound, possibly even the lick of an infected animal – most commonly a dog or monkey. Rabies is almost always fatal once symptoms appear, but treatment before this is very effective. You should seek medical advice immediately after any animal bite and commence postexposure treatment. Having pretravel vaccination means that postbite treatment is greatly simplified. If an animal bites you, immediately wash the wound with soap and water for several minutes, and apply iodine-based antiseptic. If you are not prevaccinated you will need to receive rabies immunoglobulin as soon as possible, ideally within a few hours. If travelling with a child, make sure they're aware of the dangers and that they know to tell you if they've been bitten, scratched or licked by an animal.

Tuberculosis While TB is rare in travellers, those who have significant contact with the local population (such as medical and aid workers and long-term travellers) should take precautions. Vaccination is usually only given to children under the age of five, but adults at risk are advised to have pre- and posttravel TB testing. The main symptoms are fever, cough, weight loss, night sweats and fatigue.

Typhoid This serious bacterial infection is also spread via food and water. It causes a high and slowly progressive fever and headache, and may be accompanied by a dry cough and stomach pain. It is diagnosed by blood tests and treated with antibiotics. Vaccination is recommended for all travellers who are spending more than a week in India. Be aware that vaccination is not 100% effective, so you must still be careful with what you eat and drink.

Zika At the time of writing, most of India had been categorised as having a moderate risk of Zika virus (except for Rajasthan, which had a high risk, especially Jaipur), though there have been recent cases in Tamil Nadu and Ahmedabad. Check online for current updates.

Environmental Hazards

Air Pollution

Air pollution is a huge problem in India. According to the World Health Organization (WHO), Delhi is the most polluted major city in the world. The next six most polluted cities are also in North India. If you have severe respiratory problems, speak with your doctor before travelling to India. All travellers are advised to listen to advisories on pollution levels from the Indian press or government officials. It's worth taking a properly fitted face mask if you are affected by air quality. In North India air pollution is at its worst during the cooler winter months (November and December particularly), partly due to the stubble-burning of crops in rural regions surrounding the big cities, and not helped by all the firecrackers let off during Diwali.

Short-term exposure can lead to a sore throat, sore eyes, itchy skin and a runny nose. As well as face masks, throat lozenges can help, as can frequently rinsing your face, hands and hair. Long-term exposure is, obviously, more serious.

Diving & Surfing

Divers and surfers should seek specialised advice before they travel to ensure that their medical kit contains treatment for coral cuts and tropical ear infections. Divers should ensure that their insurance covers them for decompression illness – get specialised diving insurance through an organisation such as Divers Alert Network (www.danasiapacific.org). Certain medical conditions are incompatible with diving; check with your doctor.

Food

Dining out brings with it the possibility of contracting diarrhoea. Ways to help avoid food-related illness:

➡ avoid tap water, and food rinsed in it

➡ eat only freshly cooked food

➡ avoid shellfish and buffets

➡ peel fruit

➡ cook vegetables

➡ soak salads in iodine water for at least 20 minutes

➡ eat in busy restaurants with a high turnover of customers.

Heat

Many parts of India are hot and humid throughout the year. For most visitors it takes around two weeks to comfortably adapt to the hot climate. Swelling of the feet and ankles is common, as are muscle cramps caused by excessive sweating. Prevent these by avoiding dehydration and excessive activity in the heat. Don't eat salt tablets (they aggravate the gut); drinking rehydration solution or eating salty food helps. Treat cramps by resting, rehydrating with double-strength rehydration solution and gently stretching.

Dehydration is the main contributor to heat exhaustion. Recovery is usually rapid and it is common to feel weak for some days afterwards. Symptoms include the following:

➡ feeling weak

➡ headache

➡ irritability

➡ nausea or vomiting

➡ sweaty skin

➡ a fast, weak pulse

➡ normal or slightly elevated body temperature.

Treatments include:

➡ getting out of the heat

➡ fanning the sufferer

➡ applying cool, wet cloths to the skin

➡ laying the sufferer flat with their legs raised

➡ rehydrating with water containing a quarter of a teaspoon of salt per litre.

Heatstroke is a serious medical emergency requiring urgent attention. Symptoms include the following:

➡ weakness

➡ nausea

➡ a hot, dry body

➡ temperature of over 41°C

➡ dizziness

➡ confusion

➡ loss of coordination

➡ seizures

➡ eventual collapse.

Treatment:

➡ get out of the heat

➡ fan the sufferer

➡ apply cool, wet cloths to the skin or ice to the body, especially to the groin and armpits.

Prickly heat is a common skin rash in the tropics, caused by sweat trapped under the skin. Treat it by moving out of the heat for a few hours and by having cool showers. Creams and ointments clog the skin so they should be avoided. Locally bought prickly-heat powder can be helpful.

Altitude Sickness

If you're going to altitudes above 3000m, acute mountain sickness (AMS) is an issue. The biggest risk factor is going too high too quickly – follow a conservative acclimatisation schedule found in good trekking guides, and *never* go to a higher altitude when you have any symptoms that could be altitude related. There is no way to predict who will get altitude sickness, and it is quite often the younger, fitter members of a group who succumb.

Symptoms usually develop during the first 24 hours at altitude but may be delayed up to three weeks. Mild symptoms include the following:

➡ headache

➡ lethargy

➡ dizziness

➡ difficulty sleeping

➡ loss of appetite.

AMS may become more severe without warning and can be fatal. Severe symptoms include the following:

➡ breathlessness

➡ a dry, irritative cough (which may progress to the production of pink, frothy sputum)

➡ severe headache

➡ lack of coordination and balance

➡ confusion

➡ irrational behaviour

➡ vomiting

➡ drowsiness

➡ loss of consciousness.

Treat mild symptoms by resting at the same altitude or lower until recovery, which usually takes a day or two. Paracetamol or aspirin can be taken for headaches. If symptoms persist or become worse, immediate descent is necessary; even 500m can help. Drug treatments should never be used to avoid descent or to enable further ascent.

The drugs acetazolamide (Diamox) and dexamethasone are recommended by some doctors for the prevention of AMS; however, their use is controversial. They can reduce the symptoms, but they may also mask warning signs; severe and fatal AMS has occurred in people taking these drugs.

To prevent AMS, carry out the following steps:

➡ ascend slowly – have frequent rest days, spending two to three nights at each rise of 1000m

➡ sleep at a lower altitude than the greatest height reached during the day, if possible. Above 3000m, don't increase sleeping altitude by more than 300m daily

➡ drink extra fluids

➡ eat light, high-carbohydrate meals

➡ avoid alcohol and sedatives.

Insect Bites & Stings

Bedbugs Don't carry disease, but their bites can be itchy. You can treat the itch with an antihistamine.

Lice Most commonly appear on the head and pubic areas. You may need numerous applications of an antilice shampoo such as pyrethrin.

Ticks Contracted while walking in rural areas. Ticks are commonly found behind the ears, on the belly and in armpits, and bites can lead to serious infections such as Kyasanur forest disease. If you have had a tick bite and have a rash at the site of the bite or elsewhere, fever or muscle aches, see a doctor.

CARBON MONOXIDE POISONING

Some mountain areas rely on charcoal burners for warmth, but these should be avoided due to the risk of fatal carbon-monoxide poisoning. The thick, mattress-like blankets used in many mountain areas are amazingly warm once you get beneath the covers. If you're still cold, improvise a hot-water bottle by filling your drinking-water bottle with boiled water and covering it with a sock.

Doxycycline prevents tick-borne diseases.

Leeches Found in humid rainforest areas. They don't transmit any disease, but their bites are often itchy for weeks and can easily become infected. Apply an iodine-based antiseptic to any leech bite to help prevent infection.

Bee and wasp stings Anyone with a serious bee or wasp allergy should carry an injection of adrenaline (eg an Epipen).

Skin Problems

Fungal rashes There are two common fungal rashes that affect travellers. The first occurs in moist areas of the body, such as the groin, the armpits and between the toes. It starts as a red patch that slowly spreads and is usually itchy. Treatment involves keeping the skin dry, avoiding chafing and using an antifungal cream such as clotrimazole or Lamisil. The second, *Tinea versicolor,* causes light-coloured patches, most commonly on the back, chest and shoulders. Consult a doctor.

Cuts and scratches These become easily infected in humid climates. Immediately wash all wounds in clean water and apply antiseptic. If you develop signs of infection (increasing pain and redness), see a doctor.

Sunburn

Even on a cloudy day sunburn can occur rapidly.

➡ Use a strong sunscreen (factor 30) and reapply after a swim.

➡ Wear a wide-brimmed hat and sunglasses.

➡ Avoid lying in the sun during the hottest part of the day (10am to 2pm).

➡ Be vigilant above 3000m – you can get burnt very easily at altitude.

If you become sunburnt, stay out of the sun until you have recovered, apply cool compresses and, if necessary, take painkillers for the discomfort. One per cent hydrocortisone cream applied twice daily is also helpful.

Women's Health

For gynaecological health issues, seek out a female doctor.

Birth control Bring adequate supplies of your own form of contraception.

Thrush Heat, humidity and antibiotics can all contribute to thrush. Treatment is with antifungal creams and pessaries such as clotrimazole. A practical alternative is a single tablet of fluconazole (Diflucan).

Urinary-tract infections These can be precipitated by dehydration or long bus journeys without toilet stops; bring suitable antibiotics.

Language

India's linguistic landscape is varied – 23 languages (including English) are recognised in the constitution, and more than 1600 minor languages are spoken. This large number of languages certainly helps explain why English is still widely spoken in India and why it's still in official use. Despite major efforts to promote Hindi as the national language of India, phasing out English, many educated Indians speak English as virtually their first language. For the large number of Indians who speak more than one language, it's often their second tongue. Although you'll find it very easy to get around India with English, it's always good to know a little of the local language.

While the locals in Rajasthan, Agra and Delhi may speak Punjabi, Urdu, Marwari, Jaipuri, Malvi or Mewati to each other, for you, Hindi will be the local language of choice. Hindi has about 600 million speakers worldwide, of which 180 million are in India. It developed from Classical Sanskrit, and is written in Devanagari script. In 1947 it was granted official status along with English.

Pronunciation

Most Hindi sounds are similar to their English counterparts. The main difference is that Hindi has both 'aspirated' consonants (pronounced with a puff of air, like saying 'h' after the sound) and unaspirated ones, as well as 'retroflex' (pronounced with the tongue bent backwards) and nonretroflex consonants.

WANT MORE?

For in-depth language information and handy phrases, check out Lonely Planet's *India Phrasebook*. You'll find them at **shop.lonelyplanet.com**, or you can buy Lonely Planet's iPhone phrasebooks at the Apple App Store.

Our simplified pronunciation guides don't include these distinctions – read them as if they were English and you'll be understood.

Pronouncing the vowels correctly is important, especially their length (eg a and aa). The consonant combination ng after a vowel indicates nasalisation (ie the vowel is pronounced 'through the nose'). Note also that au is pronounced as the 'ow' in 'how'. Word stress is very light – we've indicated the stressed syllables with italics.

Basics

Hindi verbs change form depending on the gender of the speaker (or the subject of the sentence in general), so it's the verbs, not the pronouns 'he' or 'she' (as in the case in English) which show whether the subject of the sentence is masculine or feminine. In these phrases we include the options for male and female speakers, marked 'm' and 'f' respectively.

Hello./Goodbye.	नमस्ते ।	na·ma·ste
Yes.	जी हाँ ।	jee haang
No.	जी नहीं ।	jee na·heeng
Excuse me.	सुनिये ।	su·ni·ye
Sorry.	माफ़ कीजिये ।	maaf kee·ji·ye
Please ...	कृपया ...	kri·pa·yaa ...
Thank you.	थैंक्यू ।	thayn·kyoo
You're welcome.	कोई बात नहीं ।	ko·ee baat na·heeng

How are you?
आप कैसे/कैसी हैं?   aap kay·se/kay·see hayng (m/f)

Fine. And you?
मैं ठीक हूँ ।   mayng teek hoong
आप सुनाइये ।   aap su·naa·i·ye

What's your name?
आप का नाम क्या है? · aap kaa naam kyaa hay

My name is ...
मेरा नाम ... है। · me·raa naam ... hay

Do you speak English?
क्या आपको अंग्रेज़ी · kyaa aap ko an·gre·zee
आती है? · aa·tee hay

I don't understand.
मैं नहीं समझा/ · mayng na·heeng sam·jaa/
समझी। · sam·jee (m/f)

Accommodation

Where's a ...?
... कहाँ है? · ... ka·haang hay

guesthouse	गेस्ट हाउस	gest haa·us
hotel	होटल	ho·tal
youth hostel	यूथ हास्टल	yoot haas·tal

Do you have a ... room?
क्या ... कमरा है? · kyaa ... kam·raa hay

single	सिंगल	sin·gal
double	डबल	da·bal

How much is it per ...?
... के लिये कितने पैसे लगते हैं? · ... ke li·ye kit·ne pay·se lag·te hayng

night	एक रात	ek raat
person	हर व्यक्ति	har vyak·ti

air-con	ए० सी०	e see
bathroom	बाथरूम	baat·room
hot water	गर्म पानी	garm paa·nee
mosquito net	मसहरी	mas·ha·ree
washerman	धोबी	do·bee
window	खिड़की	kir·kee

Directions

Where's ...?
... कहाँ है? · ... ka·haang hay

How far is it?
वह कितनी दूर है? · voh kit·nee door hay

What's the address?
पता क्या है? · pa·taa kyaa hay

Can you show me (on the map)?
(नक्शे में) दिखा सकते है? · (nak·she meng) di·kaa sak·te hayng

Turn left/right.
लेफ्ट/राइट मुड़िये। · left/raa·it mu·ri·ye

NUMBERS

1	१	एक	ek
2	२	दो	do
3	३	तीन	teen
4	४	चार	chaar
5	५	पाँच	paanch
6	६	छह	chay
7	७	सात	saat
8	८	आठ	aat
9	९	नौ	nau
10	१०	दस	das
20	२०	बीस	bees
30	३०	तीस	tees
40	४०	चालीस	chaa·lees
50	५०	पचास	pa·chaas
60	६०	साठ	saat
70	७०	सत्तर	sat·tar
80	८०	अस्सी	as·see
90	९०	नब्बे	nab·be
100	१००	सौ	sau
1000	१०००	एक हज़ार	ek ha·zaar

at the corner	कोने पर	ko·ne par
at the traffic lights	सिगनल पर	sig·nal par
behind ...	... के पीछे	... ke pee·che
in front of ...	... के सामन	... ke saam·ne
near ...	... के पास	... ke paas
opposite ...	... के सामने	... ke saam·ne
straight ahead	सीधे	see·de

Eating & Drinking

What would you recommend?
आपके ख्याल में क्या अच्छा होगा? · aap ke kyaal meng kyaa ach·chaa ho·gaa

Do you have vegetarian food?
क्या आप का खाना शाकाहारी है? · kyaa aap kaa kaa·naa shaa·kaa·haa·ree hay

I don't eat (meat).
मैं (गोश्त) नहीं खाता/खाती। · mayng (gosht) na·heeng kaa·taa/kaa·tee (m/f)

I'll have ...
मुझे ... दीजिये। · mu·je ... dee·ji·ye

That was delicious.
बहुत मज़ेदार हुआ। · ba·hut ma·ze·daar hu·aa

Please bring the menu/bill.
मेन्यू/बिल लाइये। · men·yoo/bil laa·i·ye

Key Words

bottle	बोतल	bo·tal
bowl	कटोरी	ka·to·ree
breakfast	नाश्ता	naash·taa
dessert	मीठा	mee·taa
dinner	रात का खाना	raat kaa kaa·naa
drinks	पीने की चीज़ें	pee·ne kee chee·zeng
food	खाना	kaa·naa
fork	काँटा	kaan·taa
glass	गिलास	glaas
knife	चाकू	chaa·koo
local eatery	ढाबा	daa·baa
lunch	दिन का खाना	din kaa kaa·naa
market	बाज़ार	baa·zaar
plate	प्लेट	plet
restaurant	रेस्टोरेंट	res·to·rent
set meal	थाली	taa·lee
snack	नाश्ता	naash·taa
spoon	चम्मच	cham·mach

Meat & Fish

beef	गाय का गोश्त	gaai kaa gosht
chicken	मुर्गी	mur·gee
duck	बतख़	ba·tak
fish	मछली	mach·lee
goat	बकरा	bak·raa
lobster	बड़ी झींगा	ba·ree jeeng·gaa
meat	गोश्त	gosht
meatballs	कोफ़्ता	kof·taa
pork	सुअर का गोश्त	su·ar kaa gosht
prawn	झींगी मछली	jeeng·gee mach·lee
seafood	मछली	mach·lee

Fruit & Vegetables

apple	सेब	seb
apricot	खुबानी	ku·baa·nee
banana	केला	ke·laa
capsicum	मिर्च	mirch

carrot	गाजर	gaa·jar
cauliflower	फूल गोभी	pool go·bee
corn	मक्का	mak·kaa
cucumber	ककड़ी	kak·ree
date	खजूर	ka·joor
eggplant	बैंगन	bayng·gan
fruit	फल	pal
garlic	लहसुन	leh·sun
grape	अंगूर	an·goor
grapefruit	चकोतरा	cha·kot·raa
lemon	निम्बू	nim·boo
lentils	दाल	daal
mandarin	संतरा	san·ta·raa
mango	आम	aam
mushroom	खुम्भी	kum·bee
nuts	मेवे	me·ve
orange	नारंगी	naa·ran·gee
papaya	पपीता	pa·pee·taa
peach	आड़ू	aa·roo
peas	मटर	ma·tar
pineapple	अनन्नास	a·nan·naas
potato	आलू	aa·loo
pumpkin	कद्दू	kad·doo
spinach	पालक	paa·lak
vegetables	सब्ज़ी	sab·zee
watermelon	तरबूज	tar·booz

Other

bread	चपाती/ नान/रोटी	cha·paa·tee/ naan/ro·tee
butter	मक्खन	mak·kan
chilli	मिर्च	mirch
chutney	चटनी	chat·nee
egg	अंडे	an·de
honey	मधु	ma·dhu
ice	बर्फ़	barf
ice cream	कुल्फी	kul·fee
pappadams	पपड़	pa·par
pepper	काली मिर्च	kaa·lee mirch
relish	अचार	a·chaar
rice	चावल	chaa·val
salt	नमक	na·mak
spices	मिर्च मसाला	mirch ma·saa·laa
sugar	चीनी	chee·nee
tofu	टोफू	to·foo

Drinks

beer	बियर	bi·yar
coffee	काईफ़ी	kaa·fee

milk	दूध	dood
red wine	लाल शराब	laal sha·raab
sweet fruit drink	शरबत	shar·bat
tea	चाय	chaai
water	पानी	paa·nee
white wine	सफ़ेद शराब	sa·fed sha·raab
yoghurt	लस्सी	las·see

Emergencies

Help!
मदद कीजिये! ma·dad kee·ji·ye

Go away!
जाओ! jaa·o

I'm lost.
मैं रास्ता भूल गया/गयी हूँ। mayng raas·taa bool ga·yaa/ga·yee hoong (m/f)

Call a doctor!
डॉक्टर को बुलाओ! daak·tar ko bu·laa·o

Call the police!
पुलिस को बुलाओ! pu·lis ko bu·laa·o

I'm ill.
मैं बीमार हूँ। mayng bee·maar hoong

Where is the toilet?
टॉइलेट कहाँ है? taa·i·let ka·haang hay

Shopping & Services

I'd like to buy ...
मुझे ... चाहिये। mu·je ... chaa·hi·ye

I'm just looking.
सिर्फ़ देखने आया/आयी हूँ। sirf dek·ne aa·yaa/aa·yee hoong (m/f)

Can I look at it?
दिखाइये। di·kaa·i·ye

How much is it?
कितने का है? kit·ne kaa hay

It's too expensive.
यह बहुत महँगा/महँगी है। yeh ba·hut ma·han·gaa/ma·han·gee hay (m/f)

There's a mistake in the bill.
बिल में गलती है। bil meng gal·tee hay

bank	बैंक	baynk
post office	डाक ख़ाना	daak kaa·naa
public phone	सार्वजनिक फ़ोन	saar·va·ja·nik fon
tourist office	पर्यटन ऑफ़िस	par·ya·tan aa·fis

Time & Dates

What time is it?
टाइम क्या है? taa·im kyaa hay

It's (10) o'clock.
(दस) बजे हैं। (das) ba·je hayng

Half past (10).
साढ़े (दस)। saa·re (das)

morning	सुबह	su·bah
afternoon	दोपहर	do·pa·har
evening	शाम	shaam

Monday	सोमवार	som·vaar
Tuesday	मंगलवार	man·gal·vaar
Wednesday	बुधवार	bud·vaar
Thursday	गुरुवार	gu·ru·vaar
Friday	शुक्रवार	shuk·ra·vaar
Saturday	शनिवार	sha·ni·vaar
Sunday	रविवार	ra·vi·vaar

TRANSPORT

Public Transport

When's the ... (bus)?	... (बस) कब जाती है?	... (bas) kab jaa·tee hay
first	पहली	peh·lee
last	आख़िरी	aa·ki·ree

bicycle rickshaw	साइकिल रिक्शा	saa·i·kil rik·shaa
boat	जहाज़	ja·haaz
bus	बस	bas
plane	हवाई जहाज़	ha·vaa·ee ja·haaz
train	ट्रेन	tren

At what time does it leave?
कितने बजे जाता/जाती है? kit·ne ba·je jaa·taa/jaa·tee hay (m/f)

How long does the trip take?
जाने में कितनी देर लगती है? jaa·ne meng kit·nee der lag·tee hay

How long will it be delayed?
उसे कितनी देर हुई है? u·se kit·nee der hu·ee hay

Does it stop at ...?
क्या ... में रुकती है? kyaa ... meng ruk·tee hay

Please tell me when we get to ...

जब ... आता है,	jab ... *aa*·taa hay
मुझे बताइये।	mu·*je* ba·*taa*·i·ye

Please go straight to this address.

इसी जगह को	is·ee ja·gah ko
फ़ौरन जाइए।	*fau*·ran *jaa*·i·ye

Please stop here.

यहाँ रुकिये।	ya·*haang* ru·ki·ye

A ... ticket (to ...).	(...) के लिये ... टिकट दीजिये।	(...) ke li·ye ... ti·*kat* *dee*·ji·ye
1st-class	फ़र्स्ट क्लास	farst klaas
2nd-class	सेकश्ड क्लास	se·*kand* klaas
one-way	एक तरफ़ा	ek ta·ra·*faa*
return	आने जाने का	*aa*·ne *jaa*·ne kaa

I'd like a/an ... seat.	मुझे ... सीट चाहिये।	mu·*je* ... seet *chaa*·hi·ye
aisle	किनारे	ki·*naa*·re
window	खिड़की के पास	*kir*·kee ke paas

bus stop	बस स्टॉप	bas *is*·taap
ticket office	टिकटघर	ti·*kat*·gar
timetable	समय सारणी	sa·*mai* *saa*·ra·nee
train station	स्टेशन	*ste*·shan

Driving & Cycling

I'd like to hire a ...	मुझे ... किराये पर लेना है।	mu·*je* ... ki·*raa*·ye par *le*·naa hay
4WD	फ़ोर व्हील ड्राइव	for vheel *draa*·iv
bicycle	साइकिल	*saa*·i·kil
car	कार	kaar
motorbike	मोटर साइकिल	*mo*·tar *saa*·i·kil

Is this the road to ...?

क्या यह ... का	kyaa yeh ... kaa
रास्ता है?	*raas*·taa hay

Can I park here?

यहाँ पार्क कर सकता/	ya·*haang* paark kar sak·taa/
सकती हूँ?	sak·tee hoong (m/f)

Where's a service station?

पेट्रोल पम्प कहाँ है?	*pet*·rol pamp ka·*haang* hay

I need a mechanic.

मुझे मरम्मत करने	mu·*je* ma·*ram*·mat
वाला चाहिये।	*kar*·ne vaa·laa *chaa*·hi·ye

The car/motorbike has broken down at ...

कार/मोटर साइकिल	kaar/*mo*·tar *saa*·i·kil
... मेश ख़राब	... meng ka·*raab*
हो गयी है।	ho ga·*yee* hay

I have a flat tyre.

टायर पष्कचर हो	*taa*·yar *pank*·char ho
गया है।	ga·*yaa* hay

I've run out of petrol.

पेट्रोल ख़त्म हो	*pet*·rol katm ho
गया है।	ga·*yaa* hay

GLOSSARY

ahimsa – nonviolence and reverence for all life

apsara – celestial maiden

Aryan – Sanskrit word for 'noble'; people who migrated from Persia and settled in northern India

ashram – spiritual community or retreat

autorickshaw – a noisy three-wheeled device that has a motorbike engine and seats for two passengers behind the driver

Ayurveda – the ancient and complex science of Indian herbal medicine and healing

bagh – garden

baithak – salon in a *haveli* where merchants received guests

baksheesh – tip, donation (alms) or bribe

bandhani – tie-dye

baori – well, particularly a stepwell with landings and galleries

betel – nut of the betel tree; chewed as a stimulant and digestive in a concoction know as *paan*

bhang – dried leaves and flowering shoots of the marijuana plant

Bhil – tribal people of southern Rajasthan

bindi – forehead mark

Bishnoi – tribe known for their reverence for the environment

Bodhi Tree – *Ficus religiosa*, under which Buddha attained enlightenment

Brahmin – member of the priest caste, the highest Hindu caste

Buddha – Awakened One; the originator of Buddhism, who is also regarded by Hindus as the ninth incarnation of Vishnu

bund – embankment, dyke

chajera – mason employed by Marwari businessmen of Shekhawati to build *havelis*

charpoy – simple bed made of ropes knotted together on a wooden frame

chaupar – town square formed by the intersection of major roads

chhatri – cenotaph (literally 'umbrella')

choli – sari blouse

chowk – town square, intersection or marketplace

chowkidar – caretaker; night watchman

crore – 10 million

cycle-rickshaw – three-wheeled bicycle with seats for two passengers behind the rider

dacoit – bandit

Dalit – preferred term for India's *Untouchable* caste

dalwar – sword

dargah – shrine or place of burial of a Muslim saint

dharamsala – pilgrims guest house

dhobi – laundry

dhurrie – cotton rug

Digambara – Sky Clad; a Jain sect whose monks show disdain for worldly goods by going naked

Diwan-i-Am – hall of public audience

Diwan-i-Khas – hall of private audience

dupatta – long scarf for women often worn with the *salwar kameez*

durbar – royal court; also a government

garh – fort

ghat – steps or landing on a river; range of hills or road up hills

ghazal – Urdu song derived from poetry; sad love theme

ghoomer – dance performed by women during festivals and weddings

gopis – milkmaids; Krishna was very fond of them

guru – teacher or holy person

Harijan – name (no longer considered acceptable) given by Gandhi to India's *Untouchables*, meaning 'children of god'

hathi – elephant

haveli – traditional, ornately decorated rseidence

hijra – eunuch

hookah – water pipe

howdah – seat for carrying people on an elephant's back

jali – carved marble lattice screen; also refers to the holes or spaces produced through carving timber

Jats – traditionally people who were engaged in agriculture; today the Jats play a strong role in administration and politics

jauhar – ritual mass suicide by immolation, traditionally performed by *Rajput* women after military defeat to avoid dishonour

jootis – traditional leather shoes of Rajasthan; men's *jootis* often have curled-up toes; also known as *mojaris*

kabas – the holy rats believed to be the incarnations of local families at Karni Mata Temple at Deshnok

Kalbelias – nomadic tribal group associated with snake charming

karma – Hindu, Buddhist and Sikh principle of retributive justice for past deeds

kashida – embroidery on *jootis*

kathputli – puppeteer

khadi – homespun cloth; Mahatma Gandhi encouraged people to spin *khadi* rather than buy English cloth

khadim – Muslim holy servant or mosque attendant

kotwali – police station

Kshatriya – warrior or administrator caste, second in the caste hierarchy; Rajputs claim lineage from the Kshatriyas

kundan – type of jewellery featuring *meenakari* on one side and precious stones on the other

kurta – long cotton shirt with either a short collar or no collar

lakh – 100,000

lingam – phallic symbol; symbol of Shiva

madrasa – Islamic college

Mahabharata – Vedic epic poem of the Bharata dynasty; describes the battle between the Pandavas and the Kauravas

mahal – house, palace

maharaja – literally 'great king'; princely ruler; also known as maharana, maharao and maharawal

maharani – wife of a princely ruler or a ruler in her own right

Mahavir – the 24th and last *tirthankar*

mahout – elephant driver/ keeper

mandapa – chamber before the inner sanctum of a temple

mandir – temple

mantra – sacred word or syllable used by Buddhists and Hindus to aid concentration; metric psalms of praise found in the *Vedas*

Marathas – warlike central Indians who controlled much of India at times and fought against the *Mughals* and *Rajputs*

marg – major road

masjid – mosque

Marwar – kingdom of the Rathore dynasty that ruled from Mandore, and later from Jodhpur

meenakari – type of enamelwork used on ornaments and jewellery

mehfilkhana – Islamic building in which religious songs are sung

mehndi – henna; intricate henna designs applied by women to their hands and feet

mela – fair, festival

Mewar – kingdom of the Sisodia dynasty; ruled Udaipur and Chittorgarh

moksha – release from the cycle of birth and death

monsoon – rainy season; June to October

mosar – death feast

Mughal – Muslim dynasty of Indian emperors from Babur to Aurangzeb (16th to 18th centuries)

nawab – Muslim ruling prince or powerful landowner

nilgai – antelope

niwas – house, building

NRI – nonresident Indian

odhni – headscarf

Om – sacred invocation that represents the essence of the divine principle

paan – chewable preparation made from betel leaves, nuts and lime

PCO – public call office

pol – gate

prasad – sacred food offered to the gods

puja – literally 'respect'; offering or prayer

purdah – custom among some conservative Muslims (also adopted by some Hindus, especially the Rajputs) of keeping women in seclusion; veiled

raga – any conventional pattern of melody and rhythm that forms the basis for free composition

raj – rule or sovereignty; British Raj (sometimes just Raj) refers to British rule before 1947

raja – king; also *rana*

Rajputs – Sons of Princes; Hindu warrior caste, former rulers of western India

rana – see *raja*

rani – female ruler; wife of a king

rawal – nobleman

Road – railway town that serves as a communication point to a larger town off the line, eg Mt Abu and Abu Road

RSRTC – Rajasthan State Road Transport Corporation

RTDC – Rajasthan Tourism Development Corporation

sadar – main

sadhu – ascetic, holy person, one who is trying to achieve enlightenment; usually addressed as 'swamiji' or 'babaji'

sagar – lake, reservoir

sahib – respectful title applied to a gentleman

sal – gallery in a palace

salwar kameez – traditional dresslike tunic and trouser combination for women

sambar – deer

sati – suicide by immolation; banned more than a century ago, it is still occasionally performed

Scheduled Tribes – government classification for tribal groups of Rajasthan; the tribes are grouped with the lowest casteless class, the Dalits

shikar – hunting expedition

Sikh – member of the monotheistic religion Sikhism, which separated from Hinduism in the 16th century and has a military tradition; Sikh men can be recognised by their beards and turbans

sikhara – temple-spire or temple

silavat – stone carvers

Singh – literally 'lion'; a surname adopted by Rajputs and Sikhs

Sufi – Muslim mystic

tabla – pair of drums

tempo – noisy three-wheeled public transport; bigger than an autorickshaw

thakur – Hindu caste; nobleman

tikka – a mark devout Hindus put on their foreheads with *tikka* powder; also known as a *bor* or *rakhadi*

tirthankars – the 24 great Jain teachers

tonga – two-wheeled passenger vehicle drawn by horse or pony

toran – shield-shaped device above a lintel, which a bridegroom pierces with his sword before claiming his bride

torana – elaborately sculpted gateway before temples

tripolia – triple gateway

Vaishya – merchant caste; the third caste in the hierarchy

Vedas – Hindu sacred books; collection of hymns composed during the 2nd millennium BC and divided into four books: Rig-Veda, Yajur-Veda, Sama-Veda and Atharva-Veda

wallah – man; added onto almost anything, eg *dhobi-wallah*, *chai-wallah*, *taxi-wallah*

yagna – self-mortification

zenana – women's quarters

Behind the Scenes

SEND US YOUR FEEDBACK

We love to hear from travellers – your comments keep us on our toes and help make our books better. Our well-travelled team reads every word on what you loved or loathed about this book. Although we cannot reply individually to your submissions, we always guarantee that your feedback goes straight to the appropriate authors, in time for the next edition. Each person who sends us information is thanked in the next edition – the most useful submissions are rewarded with a selection of digital PDF chapters.

Visit **lonelyplanet.com/contact** to submit your updates and suggestions or to ask for help. Our award-winning website also features inspirational travel stories, news and discussions.

Note: We may edit, reproduce and incorporate your comments in Lonely Planet products such as guidebooks, websites and digital products, so let us know if you don't want your comments reproduced or your name acknowledged. For a copy of our privacy policy visit lonelyplanet.com/privacy.

READER THANKS

Many thanks to the travellers who used the last edition and wrote to us with helpful hints, useful advice and interesting anecdotes:

Ian Gardner, John Eadington, Karen Chamberlain, Mark Adams, Maurice Catherall, Nigel Tully, Surekha Narain

AUTHOR THANKS

Lindsay Brown

Thanks to all the folks who assisted me throughout my travels in Rajasthan. I am very grateful to Satinder, Ritu, Raj, Dicky and Kavita in Jaipur, Anoop and Bunty in Pushkar, Nikhil and Atush in Jodhpur, Ravindra in Ranthambhore, Harsh in Bikaner, Vikram in Jaisalmer, and Keshav and Manish in Bundi. Special thanks to Jenny.

Bradley Mayhew

Thanks to Rouf in Rinagar; Anil and Ramesh Wadhwa in Agra; Zaheer Bagh in Kargil; Juma Malik and Tashi of Hidden North in Leh; Harish and Michael Schmid in Varanasi. Thanks to Carolyn for keeping me company in Varanasi.

Daniel McCrohan

Love, hugs and kisses to my amazingly patient wife, Taotao, and two incredible children, Dudu and Yoyo; and to mum for helping out so much. At LP, huge thanks to Joe for trusting in me, and to my fellow writers, especially Abi, Isabella, John, Bradley, Mark

and Kevin. In Delhi, a big thank you to Pradeep, Shahadutt, Pash, Catriona and Paula (amessing!), and of course to Nick, and to Dilip and his beautiful family, for being such wonderful hosts.

Sarina Singh

Gratitude to the many readers who wrote to us with their feedback and travel experiences. At Lonely Planet, thanks to Joe for being such a delightful editor; to my fellow co-writers; and to everyone involved in this book's production. Finally, warm thanks to my parents for always being so fantastic.

ACKNOWLEDGEMENTS

BL & McMahon TA (2007) 'Updated World Map of the Köppen-Geiger Climate Classification', Hydrology and Earth System Sciences, 11, 1633–44.

Cover photograph: Sari factory, Rajasthan, Tuul & Bruno Morandi/Getty Images ©

Ilustrations pp216–17 by Michael Weldon, pp154–5 and pp200–1 by Javier Zarracina.

THIS BOOK

This 6th edition of Lonely Planet's *Rajasthan, Delhi & Agra* guidebook was curated by Lindsay Brown. This guide was researched and written by Lindsay, Joe Bindloss, Bradley Mayhew, Daniel McCrohan and Sarina Singh. The previous edition was written by Lindsay Brown, Bradley Mayhew and Abigail Blasi. This guidebook was produced by the following:

Destination Editor
Joe Bindloss

Senior Product Editors Kate Chapman, Anne Mason

Product Editor Kate James

Senior Cartographer
Valentina Kremenchutskaya

Book Designer Mazzy Prinsep

Assisting Editors Sarah Bailey, James Bainbridge, Judith Bamber, Imogen Bannister, Katie Connolly, Andrea Dobbin, Samantha Forge, Emma Gibbs, Carly Hall, Helen Koehne, Kellie Langdon, Jodie Martire, Alison Morris, Lauren O'Connell, Kristin Odijk, Monique Perrin, Chris Pitts, Simon Williamson

Cover Researcher
Naomi Parker

Thanks to Jennifer Carey, Lauren Egan, Bailey Freeman, Evan Godt, Gemma Graham, Niamh O'Brien, Matt Phillips, Ross Taylor

Index

LONELY PLANET IN THE WILD

Send your 'Lonely Planet in the Wild' photos to social@lonelyplanet.com
We share the best on our Facebook page every week!

Map Legend

Sights
- Beach
- Bird Sanctuary
- Buddhist
- Castle/Palace
- Christian
- Confucian
- Hindu
- Islamic
- Jain
- Jewish
- Monument
- Museum/Gallery/Historic Building
- Ruin
- Shinto
- Sikh
- Taoist
- Winery/Vineyard
- Zoo/Wildlife Sanctuary
- Other Sight

Activities, Courses & Tours
- Bodysurfing
- Diving
- Canoeing/Kayaking
- Course/Tour
- Sento Hot Baths/Onsen
- Skiing
- Snorkelling
- Surfing
- Swimming/Pool
- Walking
- Windsurfing
- Other Activity

Sleeping
- Sleeping
- Camping
- Hut/Shelter

Eating
- Eating

Drinking & Nightlife
- Drinking & Nightlife
- Cafe

Entertainment
- Entertainment

Shopping
- Shopping

Information
- Bank
- Embassy/Consulate
- Hospital/Medical
- Internet
- Police
- Post Office
- Telephone
- Toilet
- Tourist Information
- Other Information

Geographic
- Beach
- Gate
- Hut/Shelter
- Lighthouse
- Lookout
- Mountain/Volcano
- Oasis
- Park
- Pass
- Picnic Area
- Waterfall

Population
- Capital (National)
- Capital (State/Province)
- City/Large Town
- Town/Village

Transport
- Airport
- Border crossing
- Bus
- Cable car/Funicular
- Cycling
- Ferry
- Metro/MTR/MRT station
- Monorail
- Parking
- Petrol station
- Skytrain/Subway station
- Taxi
- Train station/Railway
- Tram
- Underground station
- Other Transport

Routes
- Tollway
- Freeway
- Primary
- Secondary
- Tertiary
- Lane
- Unsealed road
- Road under construction
- Plaza/Mall
- Steps
- Tunnel
- Pedestrian overpass
- Walking Tour
- Walking Tour detour
- Path/Walking Trail

Boundaries
- International
- State/Province
- Disputed
- Regional/Suburb
- Marine Park
- Cliff
- Wall

Hydrography
- River, Creek
- Intermittent River
- Canal
- Water
- Dry/Salt/Intermittent Lake
- Reef

Areas
- Airport/Runway
- Beach/Desert
- Cemetery (Christian)
- Cemetery (Other)
- Glacier
- Mudflat
- Park/Forest
- Sight (Building)
- Sportsground
- Swamp/Mangrove

Note: Not all symbols displayed above appear on the maps in this book

Sarina Singh

After finishing her business degree Sarina bought a one-way ticket to India where she met an aspiring photographer who asked her to write a paragraph for one of his photos in the hope he could get it published. The magazine asked Singh to turn her 100-word 'caption' into a 3000-word feature, and so began her accidental writing career. After five years in India she returned to her home town of Melbourne to pursue postgraduate studies. Sarina has written on 50 Lonely Planet titles, including more than 10 editions of *India*; four editions of *Rajasthan, Delhi & Agra* and three editions of *South India*. She has also written for dozens of other international publications such as the UK's *Sunday Times* and the USA's *National Geographic Traveler*. Find her on Twitter @ sarina_singh and www.sarinasingh.com.

OUR STORY

A beat-up old car, a few dollars in the pocket and a sense of adventure. In 1972 that's all Tony and Maureen Wheeler needed for the trip of a lifetime – across Europe and Asia overland to Australia. It took several months, and at the end – broke but inspired – they sat at their kitchen table writing and stapling together their first travel guide, *Across Asia on the Cheap*. Within a week they'd sold 1500 copies. Lonely Planet was born.

Today, Lonely Planet has offices in Franklin, London, Melbourne, Oakland, Dublin, Beijing and Delhi, with more than 600 staff and writers. We share Tony's belief that 'a great guidebook should do three things: inform, educate and amuse'.

OUR WRITERS

Lindsay Brown

Rajasthan Lindsay started travelling as a young bushwalker exploring the Blue Mountains west of Sydney. Then as a marine biologist he dived the coastal and island waters of southeastern Australia. He continued travelling whenever he could while employed at Lonely Planet as an editor and publishing manager. Since becoming a freelance writer and photographer he has co-authored more than 45 Lonely Planet guides to Australia, Bhutan, India, Malaysia, Nepal, Pakistan and Papua New Guinea.

Joe Bindloss

Joe first got the travel bug on a grand tour of Asia in the early 1990s, and he's been roaming around its temples and paddy fields ever since on dozens of assignments for Lonely Planet and other publishers, covering everywhere from Myanmar and Thailand to India and Nepal. Joe was Lonely Planet's destination editor for the Indian subcontinent until 2019. See more of his work at www.bindloss.co.uk.

Bradley Mayhew

Agra & the Taj Mahal Bradley has been writing guidebooks for 20 years. He started travelling while studying Chinese at Oxford University, and has since focused his expertise on China, Tibet, the Himalaya and Central Asia. He is the co-writer of Lonely Planet guides to Tibet, Nepal, Trekking in the Nepal Himalaya, Bhutan, Central Asia and many others. Bradley has also fronted two TV series for Arte and SWR, one retracing the route of Marco Polo via Turkey, Iran, Afghanistan, Central Asia and China, and the other trekking Europe's ten most scenic long-distance trails. Bradley has also written for Rough Guides, has contributed chapters to *Silk Road: Monks, Warriors & Merchants* and is a co-writer of Insight Guide's *Silk Road*.

Daniel McCrohan

Delhi Daniel is a British travel writer who specialises in Asia and who has authored more than 40 guidebooks for Lonely Planet and Trailblazer. His expertise lies in China and India, but he has written guides to countries right across the continent, including Mongolia, Russia, Tibet, Thailand and Bangladesh. He also has written numerous British walking guides. Daniel has been a guest speaker at international travel shows, and was a co-host on the Lonely Planet television series *Best in China*. He speaks Chinese fluently and Hindi badly, owns three cycle rickshaws and never uses cars. Find him on Twitter (@danielmccrohan).

OVER PAGE MORE WRITERS

Published by Lonely Planet Global Limited
CRN 554153
6th edition – Oct 2019
ISBN 978 1 78701 368 1
© Lonely Planet 2019   Photographs © as indicated 2019
10 9 8 7 6 5 4 3 2 1
Printed in China